WHEN THE WHITE HOUSE CALLS

United States Ambassador John Price. (Official State Department photo, March 15, 2002)

WHEN *the* WHITE HOUSE CALLS

From Immigrant Entrepreneur to U.S. Ambassador

JOHN PRICE

THE UNIVERSITY OF UTAH PRESS
Salt Lake City

The opinions and characterizations in this book are those of the author, and do not necessarily represent official positions of the United States government.

 The Defiance House Man colophon is a registered trademark of the University of Utah Press. It is based upon a four-foot-tall, Ancient Puebloan pictograph (late PIII) near Glen Canyon, Utah.

15 14 13 12 11   1 2 3 4 5

Library of Congress Cataloging-in-Publication Data

Price, John, 1933–
   When the White House calls / John Price.
        p. cm.
   Includes bibliographical references and index.
   ISBN 978-1-60781-143-5 (cloth : alk. paper)   1. Price, John, 1933–   2. Ambassadors—United States—Biography.   3. Ambassadors—Mauritius—Biography.   4. Ambassadors—Seychelles—Biography.   5. Ambassadors—Comoros—Biography.   6. Businesspeople—Utah—Biography.   I. Title.
   E901.1.P75A3 2011
   327.2092—dc22
   [B]   2011011202

Photo Credits and Sources:

Official White House Photo: Figure 19.7, 19.8, 21.2
Official State Department Photo: Frontispiece, Figure 19.6
U.S. Navy: Figure 12.7, 18.8
U.S. Embassy Port Louis: 10.6, 11.1, 13.1, 16.2, 16.3, 16.4, 16.5, 16.6, 18.4, 19.1, 19.2, 19.3, 22.5, 22.6, 22.7, 24.10, 24.12, 24.13, 24.14
Union of the Comoros: 14.1, 14.2

Map Sources:

Base maps copyright Ng Maps/National Geographic Stock: Maps 3, 4, 5
Base map copyright 2007 by World Trade Press: Map 2
Base map U.S. Government: Maps 1, 6

Printed and bound by Sheridan Books, Inc., Ann Arbor, Michigan.

To the children, the future of sub–Saharan Africa

Contents

Maps

PREFACE

I have been an entrepreneur and businessman for most of my life. I have also been involved in local and national politics for many years. I was honored when President George W. Bush appointed me to serve as United States ambassador to the Republic of Mauritius, the Republic of Seychelles, and the Union of the Comoros. I served my country with distinction from February 8, 2002, to June 17, 2005. Wanting to make a difference by representing U.S. interests and enhancing our country's image abroad, I am grateful for the profoundly warm welcome I was given by the host countries.

I recall the words of Fred Fielding, a former counsel to President Ronald Reagan, who so aptly stated in 1983, "It is important to remember that our Nation has a tradition of citizen soldiers and citizen public servants—individuals who have been willing to put aside their private lives and notwithstanding the costs in money, personal privacy, and all the rest, put their talents and energies to work for the Country that has so richly blessed us all." So when the White House called, I responded affirmatively, as any citizen would do, to serve his country.

For me, serving as U.S. ambassador was a double honor. I was not born in this country, and was fortunate that President Franklin D. Roosevelt allowed my family to immigrate to the United States in September 1940, to escape the Holocaust in Germany. With a good education, hard work, and success beyond my wildest expectations, I achieved the American dream. Now it was time for me to give back by serving the country I love so much.

In this book, I want to share some insights into my formative years, anecdotes from along the way, stories of mentors who helped me to succeed, and an account of the midlife crisis I went through while seeking the fountain of youth. I want to explain my workaholic nature, which could not resist another deal, but which also took away from the precious years of seeing my children grow up. I am grateful for my wife, Marcia, who stood by my side through all our trials and tribulations, and for our children, who are the beneficiaries of her strength and wisdom. I will not make the same mistake with my grandchildren that I made with my children.

Early on in business, I learned the benefits of plain talk and a commonsense approach to solving problems. During my posting, I adapted this same methodology to better serve the three host countries, the Republic of Mauritius, the Republic of Seychelles, and the Union of the Comoros. These island nations are linked to the Horn of Africa and East Africa, which I believe face considerable risks today. Although I am no longer U.S. ambassador to those countries, the three-plus years I spent there provided me a wealth of experiences, challenges, successes, setbacks, and lessons about how to help the less fortunate. That time also exposed me to a number of challenges during my meetings and consultations in Washington, D.C.

Solving problems and thinking outside the box have long been my strong suit. I believed my background and expertise would provide a beneficial lens through which to view sub-Saharan Africa, U.S. policies, and our mutual interests in the region. Working in my host countries, I quickly learned that these nations sorely needed our assistance to integrate their economies into the global economy. I thought I could help them advance toward that goal.

However, as an employee of the State Department, I had limited say over many matters and actions affecting our bilateral relations and how we presented U.S. foreign policy to the host countries. I have always believed our word is what we are measured by in life, and when I gave mine, I expected the Bureau of African Affairs and other government agencies to support my actions—or at least to be clear in their dissent. Unfortunately, I was embarrassed more than once, which created a credibility gap for me. For reasons such as these, the United States has too often been perceived as a fair-weather friend.

The three Indian Ocean island nations I was accredited to are truly unique. While they are all places of great beauty, each has a different degree of democracy, prosperity, transparency, and political soundness in its government.

The ethnic mix in Mauritius comes from India, China, France, England, Madagascar, and the continent of Africa, bringing together rich cultures and traditions, languages and religions—more than eighty different religious denominations exist in Mauritius, and more than twenty languages are spoken, although English is the official language. Yet even with their different backgrounds, the population has enjoyed a long period of peaceful coexistence.

While embracing cultural diversity, Mauritius has worked hard to diversify its economic base of sugar plantations. The country now features beautiful resorts, high-quality textile and other product manufacturing operations, and a growing offshore banking and financial services sector.

The Seychelles, a picture-perfect chain of 115 beautiful, ecologically sensitive islands, has a cultural mix that stems from European, African, Indian, and Chinese origins. Creole is the predominant language spoken, although French and English are also considered official languages.

Seychelles has struggled since independence in 1976, and a subsequent Marxist coup to shed its burden of autocracy. Since that time, the government-controlled economy has held back the country. Economic growth has come mainly from the tourism and fishery sectors. In the past Seychelles depended upon the traditional plantation economy of cinnamon bark, copra, vanilla, and some coconut, but today this has virtually disappeared; in 1996, only three hundred tons of cinnamon bark were exported. There has been talk for several years of helping farmers establish new farming and livestock-rearing techniques on the outer islands. There is also considerable interest in implementing hydroponic farming.

Seychelles is now at a political and socioeconomic crossroads. Although international pressure helped bring about free and fair elections in the 1990s, corruption and government control of the economy continue to plague the country. Reportedly, millions of dollars have been siphoned off via parastatal entities and offshore banking accounts. It is time to move on with leadership that will stand up to the old regime. The Seychellois deserve better—as does their pristine archipelago.

Comoros is a Sunni Muslim nation, with its population spread over three islands. Its cultural mix can be traced back to early Persian and Arab traders, as well as African and Malagasy settlers. French and Arabic are the official languages, although the Comorian dialect is a blend of Swahili, Arabic, and words borrowed from a variety of other languages. Since Comoros became independent in 1975, there has been constant instability, with twenty coups and attempted coups. Democracy, however, took hold in 2002 with the nation's first free and fair elections for president of the Union of the Comoros.

The core of the Comoros economy is based on ylang-ylang, vanilla, and cloves, the country's main agricultural exports; however, fluctuations in the world commodity markets have caused a dramatic drop in the price of vanilla. Business operations, including perfume distillation, account for a small percentage of the country's gross domestic product, while the services and hospitality sectors contribute about half of GDP. With a potential for increased tourism, foreign direct investment will become a key ingredient.

Economic development remains the most important element in the process of continued democratization: there is a clear linkage between prosperity and political stability. Steps toward eradicating poverty, improving health care, creating a better public education system, implementing sustainable development programs, and mentoring small businesses would help abate concerns about Comoros's democracy, while strengthening hopes for counterterrorism cooperation.

Since 1970, I visited seventeen sub-Saharan African countries, some shortly after they received their independence. For most people, conditions are no better now than they were then. Their quality of life has not advanced in meaningful ways in areas such as nutrition, health care, secular and free education, human rights, freedom of speech, transparency, free and fair elections, sustainable development, and employment opportunities. All of these difficulties overshadow the beauty of the continent.

Only a few sub-Saharan African countries, such as Mauritius, South Africa, Botswana, Lesotho, Senegal, Uganda, Mozambique, and Ghana, have made significant strides economically. Today those nations have stable governance, leading to their growing prosperity. Other countries, including Rwanda, Gabon, Angola, Liberia, Seychelles, and Comoros, are becoming more transparent and making greater efforts toward good governance.

Sub-Saharan Africa has more than 800 million people, of which more than 275 million are of the Muslim faith. Estimates are that by the year 2035, the population in sub-Saharan Africa will double. Despite the rise in radical Islamist teachings in sub-Saharan Africa, many scholars of Islam downplay its potential spread and influence. They note that historically Islam spread to sub-Saharan Africa by largely peaceful means, and was overlaid on—rather than displacing—local tribal traditions and belief systems. The result has been a diverse and syncretic practice of Islam, characterized by tolerance and moderation. Yet in various pockets of sub-Saharan Africa, reality tells another story of rigid doctrines and unbridled militancy.

One can only theorize what life was like in sub-Saharan Africa before European colonization disrupted the multitudes of tribal cultures that had existed for centuries. Partitioning by the colonialists took place without regard to ethnicity, traditions, sacred homelands, or natural boundaries, instead creating artificial states and displacing many people. Most original tribal landowners saw their natural resources sent overseas, with little benefit for them, their families, or their quality of life. While they were eventually granted freedom from colonial rule, their independence came with a legacy of despair.

A 2004 United States Agency for International Development (USAID) study, referred to as "CBJ 2004 Sub-Saharan Africa," stressed, "Terrorist organizations find more fertile ground for the exploitation of vulnerable people where conflict or disasters disrupt normal life." Today, in many failed or failing states, lawlessness, violence, terrorism, clan conflicts, corrupt leadership, fragile alliances, hopelessness, and extreme poverty have become the norm. It is in these environments that radical Islam, which feeds on the problems of the impoverished, is far more likely to exacerbate the situation.

In this part of the world, few places are immune. The three island nations that I was accredited to as U.S. ambassador are in the Indian Ocean but generally grouped as part of the Horn of Africa and East Africa region. As a consequence, unstable conditions there have a direct impact on the economy and security of these archipelagos.

For radical jihadists such as Fazul Abdullah Mohammed, this region has become a sanctuary. Born in Comoros, Fazul has been identified as the mastermind responsible for U.S. embassy bombings, suicide attacks, and surface-to-air missile attacks. Fazul has also been implicated in efforts to smuggle and sell "blood diamonds" from the West African country of Sierra Leone, the proceeds of which are believed to have been a major source of funding for the 9/11 attacks. Currently, as a leader of al-Qaeda in East Africa, Fazul has been linked to the Somalia-based al-Shabaab extremist Islamist group.

How do we stem the tide of such violence? One of my main objectives was—and remains—to help prevent radical movements from penetrating more deeply into the fabric of sub-Saharan Africa. In order to do this, we have to witness and identify with a vast continent largely unfamiliar to most of us. To better understand the critical nature of the region, congressional delegations need to spend more quality time in sub-Saharan Africa, especially in its thousands of multicultural and multiethnic villages. In fact, I believe every elected member of Congress should be required to visit with the people in sub-Saharan Africa. Their constituents would be far safer for it.

Most important, the United States cannot afford to turn a blind eye. Many of our leaders in Congress, in my opinion, have a myopic view of this faraway continent and a limited understanding of its importance to our national security. We need a more consistent foreign policy in this part of the world, and we need to engage sub-Saharan Africa and its people in a more meaningful way. If matters are left unchecked, sub-Saharan Africa will continue to deteriorate, as will any remaining quality of life and hope for a brighter future.

During my assignment, I saw erosion of my efforts in one of the host countries regarding basic health care, primary education, and sustainable development. In all three countries, I witnessed an increase both in radical Islamist attitudes and in negative rhetoric about our country.

As we have learned, aid and loans given at the top levels in sub-Saharan countries over the past fifty years have not been the answer. Billions of our tax dollars have been deposited into private bank accounts around the world by corrupt leaders. This is another reason to engage with people directly and administer programs with proper oversight. Each village in sub-Saharan Africa must prosper and grow in a sustainable way for the United States to claim success.

This book is not intended to be an academic tome. It does, however, represent real experiences, historical accounts, practical views, and, I hope, offer solutions that will lead to more political engagement of sub-Saharan African countries. With the urging of my peers, I decided to write this book. My decision to do so has been fostered by the hope that we can better understand the complex issues facing us in this fragile region; that members of Congress will shake off their ennui and undertake meaningful measures to help create a way forward with sustainable development programs for otherwise vulnerable people; and that the State Department will carry this necessary course of action well into the future so that generations of young Africans can have a better life. Schools in America can help by emphasizing global geography and the lessons learned from our failures. The young leaders of tomorrow also need to understand world issues that will affect their own lives and the decisions they make on our shrinking global stage.

I believe the United States, the most powerful and richest country on earth, needs to take a greater leadership role in sub-Saharan Africa's future, so that the spreading radical Islamist tenets do not gain a stronger foothold. It is my hope that the United States would rather see sub-Saharan African countries export economic products instead of terrorism. I fear, however, that the Horn of Africa and East Africa region could become a new epicenter for terrorist organizations.

It is my further hope that this book will serve, in a small way, as a wake-up call to Congress and other policy makers about the dangers that lie ahead if we don't fully engage sub-Saharan Africa. And the bounty for Africa if we do.

Acknowledgments

Years ago friends and business associates urged me to write about my life and the challenges I experienced reaching the top. I resisted, and to my dismay many of these fine people are now gone. Some mentors were instrumental in my climbing above the fray to succeed in business; I remember them fondly and thank them for their encouragement.

Among early naggers were Dr. Newell Warr (while working on my teeth); General Gil Iker (while thrashing me on the handball court); banker Fred Stringham (deceased), while negotiating loans; Sam Souvall (deceased), a longtime business associate and former board member; Sam Sapitsky, the retired owner of a pawn shop where once I borrowed money to meet a payroll; Jim Anderson, my college classmate and former board member; and Blaine Huntsman, former Dean of the School of Business at the University of Utah, a banker, and a former board member.

It was on March 14, 2001, that Stuart Holliday, Special Assistant to the President and Associate Director of Presidential Personnel, called to say, "President Bush would like you to serve as United States Ambassador to Mauritius." Thus began a new chapter in my life. Well-wishers were fascinated, envisioning a romantic experience on drop-dead-beautiful, sun-soaked beaches. Being an ambassador turned out to be anything but a vacation in paradise, but it offered many opportunities that inspired the writing of this book.

Several months after my return, in April 2006, I met retired Air Force Colonel Mark Bean, working on his doctoral degree, and Howard Lehman, Associate Professor, Political Science Department and Asia Center, at the University of Utah. Both were intrigued with the idea of a book on my time in Africa and the challenges I faced as U.S ambassador, among which were poverty concerns, the need for sustainable economic development, and the growing threat of terrorism. With their ongoing interest in the project, an outline evolved. I spent more than three years reliving my experiences and putting them on paper. I owe thanks to Mark and Howard for guiding me in the right direction.

Planning the course of *When the White House Calls* through uncharted waters has been an incredible adventure for an amateur writer like me. I am grateful to the tenacious, multifaceted editor and author Eileen Hallet Stone. The challenges of refining my voluminous manuscript set the scene for many debates, numerous revisions, edits, and downsizing over the next two years, until the final version became reality. Eileen, bless you, and thank you for patiently guiding me through some of the difficult decisions we made.

I wish to thank my wife, Marcia, the glue in the family, and supportive matriarch; our loving children, Steven, Deirdra, and Jennifer, who constantly heard me say "I am on the computer"; my wonderful sons-in-law, Tony and Farhad; and our eight incredible grandchildren, Ashleigh, Chelsea, Garrett, Hannah, Alexandra, Savannah, Jackson, and Lucy Sophia. My family loves Africa as much as I do.

Sincere thanks go to my brother, Wolfgang (Bill to me), who for this book took the time to catalog our family history into two impeccable volumes, including memorabilia, passports, documents, letters, photos, and other information about our relatives. Especially important to the story are my tenacious father and mother (both deceased), who made the escape to this country possible. Further thanks go to my mother, who judiciously preserved the history of our early years.

I thank local historian Ron Fox, who through his contacts found lost articles and photos dating back to my arrival in Utah that helped bring back many memories. Also, I want to thank Katie Story, a mainstay at Price Realty Group, who compiled material and interfaced with translators about interviews and documents in various languages. And finally, thanks to Mike Washburn, who among his busy property management responsibilities helped shepherd the manuscript paper flow through its various phases.

The book would not have become a reality without the encouragement of President Michael Young and John Francis, Associate Vice President for Academic Affairs, at the University of Utah; the incredible staff at the University of Utah Press and its director, Glenda Cotter, and acquisitions editor Peter DeLafosse; the Preservation Department of the J. Willard Marriott Library; and Dean and University Librarian Joyce Ogburn.

I would be remiss if I did not thank the other people and resources I may have inadvertently left out; I apologize for any omissions.

WHEN THE WHITE HOUSE CALLS

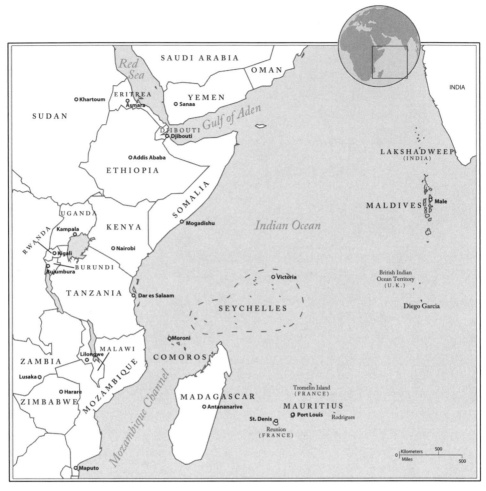

Map 1. Horn of Africa, East Africa, and Indian Ocean Region

(I)

THE CALL TO SERVICE

*It is important to remember that our Nation has a tradition of citizen soldiers
and citizen public servants—individuals who have been willing to put aside
their private lives and notwithstanding the costs in money, personal privacy,
and all the rest, put their talents and energies to work for the Country
that has so richly blessed us all.*

—FRED FIELDING,
FORMER COUNSEL TO PRESIDENT RONALD REAGAN,
IN *DIRECTORS AND BOARDS*, SPRING 1983

On February 8, 2002, at the Utah State Capitol, I was sworn in as Ambassador Extraordinary and Plenipotentiary of the United States of America accredited to the Republic of Mauritius, the Federal Islamic Republic of the Comoros, and the Republic of Seychelles, located in the Indian Ocean off the east coast of Africa. On that same day, President George W. Bush officially opened the 2002 Winter Olympic Games in Salt Lake City, Utah.

The coincidence of my swearing-in ceremony occurring within hours of the Olympic opening events was breathtaking. The idea that in between events President Bush and First Lady Laura Bush would pay a visit to our home, Fairfax House, in Salt Lake City, was nearly overwhelming. I had to pinch myself several times to believe that after so many months of paperwork, seminars, meetings, and interviews, this was indeed really happening. But now, standing in front of Secretary of State Colin Powell with Governor Michael Leavitt looking on, my wife, Marcia, by my side, and my left hand on the Declaration of Independence and the Constitution of the United States, I stood resolute to represent the country I love, to the best of my abilities.

I didn't yet know that the complexities of my assignment—including diplomatic relations with the host countries, our U.S. interests there including trade relations, the potential problems of terrorism, and the regional challenges created by pandemics and human poverty—would further strengthen my resolve.

Marcia and I had been friends with the Bush family since actively supporting President George H. W. Bush in the 1988 presidential campaign. In 1989, I was appointed to the Industry Sector Advisory Committee for Small and Minority Business, which coordinated with the Department of Commerce. I was also asked to serve on the Advisory Committee of the Small Business Administration. In 1990, the president appointed Marcia to the President's Advisory Committee for the Arts, which later, under President Clinton's administration, became the National Committee for the Performing Arts, "to support, enhance, and advocate national arts education." As of 2011, Marcia continues to serve as a member of the NCPA board, which functions at the Kennedy Center.

In 1999, I was asked by former President George H. W. Bush to serve on the National Finance Advisory Council for the George and Barbara Bush Endowment for Innovative Cancer Research, at the University of Texas M. D. Anderson Cancer Center. I remained on the council until I had to resign from all boards as part of the ambassador nomination process.

On two occasions, August 16, 1999, and July 30, 2001, Marcia and I attended council meetings and afternoon retreats at Walker's Point, the Bush family summer residence in Kennebunkport, Maine. At this seaside community, long considered the jewel of the southern Maine coast, President Bush and his wife, Barbara, hosted traditional Maine lobster and clambake feasts at the picturesque River Club.

During our last visit, I had the thrill of speeding through the shallow waters off the rocky coastline with the former president at the wheel of his sleek new 31-foot Fountain Tournament Edition fishing boat. Powered by twin 275-hp Mercury engines, the high-performance *Fidelity II* left the Secret Service in its wake. As the members of his security detail strained to keep up in their Zodiac inflatable boats, I asked the president, "Are you sure you know where the rocks are?" After a glance and a slight smile, he nodded—then gunned the engines! Only once did he slow down, to navigate around what appeared to be giant boulders beneath the surface of the clear blue ocean water. I held my breath and hung on as the boat was tossed by the chop. Offered another ride later that day, I opted instead to join Marcia on a tour of the beautiful grounds at Walker's Point.

Since the 1988 Bush campaign, I had also been following his son George W. Bush's rise to power as governor of the State of Texas, and I considered myself one of the early supporters in his presidential campaign. We held one of his first national presidential exploratory committee fund-raising events at Fairfax House on July 7, 1999. It was a successful occasion, attended by more than three hundred supporters and well-wishers. Since the president's birthday was the day before the event, we surprised him with a birthday cake.

Earlier, in March 1998, Utah Governor Michael Leavitt had invited me to go with him to Austin, Texas, to meet with Governor George W. Bush and have lunch together.

A handsome Renaissance Revival–style building, the Texas State Capitol was completed in 1888, and is second in size only to the Capitol in Washington, D.C. After our meeting, the governor led us to the State Senate chamber, where one of the legislators, a knowledgeable historian, concluded the tour with us. Then Governor Bush went off for his daily jog, saying he would meet us later for lunch.

While waiting for the governor at the historic Governor's Mansion, we met up with Michael Dell, founder of Dell Computer, who was also joining us. I admired how Michael had changed the way people bought computers. By simplifying the technology and selling directly to customers, Michael turned a fledgling garage start-up into a multibillion-dollar, worldwide enterprise.

After lunch, at which it was suggested that Governor Bush consider setting up a presidential exploratory committee, we ran into Karl Rove, a key advisor to the governor, who had lived and attended school in Salt Lake City. I told him about our lunch conversation and said I would be happy to help Governor Bush in his presidential campaign should he decide to run. Several weeks later, Karl came to Utah and spoke at my home to a group of business leaders I was trying to recruit. That night, Karl had dinner with Mike Leavitt and me. An interesting political conversation ensued in which Karl discussed his fondness for President William McKinley and the style of campaign McKinley had run in 1896, a realigning election that marked the beginning of the Progressive Era. President McKinley was pro-business, and many of his supporters were businessmen. He ran a successful, well-funded campaign, and would serve with Republicans having won control of both houses of Congress.

Later, in the fall of 1998, I was invited by Heinz Prechter to go quail hunting at his 10,000-acre ranch in Wheeler, Texas. Heinz, who emigrated from Germany after World War II, was an early pioneer in the automobile sunroof business and founded the American Sunroof Company, which employed several thousand people. Heinz, an early Bush supporter, was hosting the weekend retreat for George W. Bush and his wife, Laura. Among the twelve invited business leaders and active fund-raisers were businessmen Robert Wood ("Woody") Johnson IV, who later became the owner of the New York Jets football team, and Dave Checketts, who was president and chief executive officer of Madison Square Garden. I had met Dave when he was president and general manager of the Utah Jazz basketball team. (Several years later, Dave founded and became the chairman of SCP Worldwide, the owner of the Real Salt Lake soccer team.)

The main purpose of this retreat was for everyone to become better acquainted with George and Laura. Since bird hunting was not a sport I enjoyed, I opted to stay behind and talk with Laura and several other guests.

The weekend turned out to be a great time for bonding. After some pointed questions during a chat with the governor on the economy, his pro-business stance, lower taxes, and security matters, I was convinced he was the right candidate for the GOP, and I committed to fully support him. I wasn't alone. By the end of the weekend, Governor Bush emerged as the "GOP moneyed elite's candidate," as noted in a report by Texans for Public Justice. During the ensuing months, the presidential exploratory committee was formed under the leadership of Donald Evans, the governor's longtime friend and future U.S. Secretary of Commerce. The committee expanded nationally. I became Utah's chairman and also a member of the national finance committee. We met regularly in Austin, Texas, tracking the groundswell of support as it came from every corner of our great nation.

In the meantime, Utah was heavily involved with plans for the 2002 Winter Olympic Games. In June 1995, the International Olympic Committee (IOC) had met in Budapest, where they awarded the XIX Olympic Winter Games to Salt Lake City. On April 8, 1998, I was appointed by Governor Michael Leavitt and Salt Lake City Mayor Deedee Corradini to be a member of the Salt Lake Organizing Committee (SLOC) Board of Trustees. Later, on February 11, 1999, I was also selected to be on the Management Committee.

In early December 1998, Governor Leavitt asked if my Hawker 800 jet was available to take several SLOC members to Los Angeles. The trip would include Mitt Romney, whom the governor was trying to recruit as president of the Salt Lake Organizing Committee. I said yes, and a week later, on a snowy day, we met at the Million Air FBO, located at the Salt Lake City International Airport.

Mitt had previously expressed ambivalence about the prospect of becoming head of the SLOC, but we were determined to prevail upon him to accept. Frankly, we needed a new, squeaky-clean image. The scandal-plagued SLOC was in trouble, damaged by allegations of bribery involving top officials. Although he was an outsider to Utah, Mitt had strong family ties to the state. He also had great credentials as a business leader who in 1984, with two partners, had founded Bain Capital, the highly successful private equity investment firm. Mike believed he was the right person for the job. I looked forward to seeing Mitt and talking about the opportunities that lay ahead.

Unfortunately, just before our departure, I received an urgent phone call from my office, and suggested that Mike and the others go on to Los Angeles without me. I said goodbye to Mitt, and prematurely but wholeheartedly welcomed him on board. That evening, Mike phoned to say he was confident that Mitt would agree to serve as the president and chief executive officer of SLOC. When Mitt was unanimously hired by the SLOC Board of Trustees on February 11, 1999, it was great news for the committee, the State of Utah, and all the participating athletes and spectators from around the world.

Once at the helm, Mitt discovered the full extent of the financial trouble facing SLOC. A numbers of sponsors either had withdrawn or were on the fence. The prospect of budget cuts was looming, and Mitt was concerned that the Cultural Olympiad program would suffer from the cutback. One evening over dinner at Adolph's, one of Park City's favorite restaurants, we discussed the possibilities of raising money for this important component. We believed the cultural aspect of the Olympic Games was an integral part of its success. Without it, we would lose the people-to-people contact between countries and a substantial amount of cultural diversity. That evening I agreed to donate $1 million if Mitt would match it. He did, and we were encouraged that others would do the same.

Shortly after our meeting, Marcia and I received a letter from Mitt thanking us for our donation. "I could not have been more pleased by the powerful words and symbolic gesture which you made," he wrote. "The night will stand out in the history of the 'new' SLC and 2002 Winter Games. I will not forget your friendship and help."

Within days, a committee to support the Cultural Olympiad was formed, chaired by Mitt's friend Kem Gardner, a Utah businessman. Ultimately, more than $20 million was raised. According to Ray Grant, the director of the 2002 Cultural Olympiad, all these efforts ensured one of the best-attended Cultural Olympiad programs in recent Olympic history.

On January 25, 2002, fifteen days before the opening of the 2002 Winter Olympics, Paul Rademacher, the director of Senate Affairs at the State Department, called to say that I and seven other ambassadors had been confirmed by the Senate.

At the same time, the Secret Service was in the process of securing our home and grounds in preparation for President Bush's visit to Fairfax House during the upcoming Olympic Opening Ceremonies.

Our home, Fairfax House, was named after the adjacent street. Originally known as the Governor's Mansion, it was built in 1959 for two-term Utah Governor George Dewey Clyde. Governor Calvin O. Rampton and his family lived in the Governor's Mansion from 1965 to 1977. During Rampton's three terms, as Utah grew substantially, many notable dignitaries were wined and dined at the mansion, and many deals were struck there, or so I was told.

We purchased Fairfax House from the State of Utah in 1979 when the state decided to restore the original turn-of-the-century Thomas Kearns Mansion, on South Temple Street, which had been used from 1918 until the late 1950s as the official governor's residence. Marcia and I remodeled and expanded the house for our family of three children. We also continued to maintain the surrounding four acres of landscaped grounds and well-established woods. Periodically we used the lovely gardens for our children's weddings, festivities, community functions, and political hosting events.

After I received the exciting news from Paul Rademacher, the chief of the Presidential Appointments Staff at the State Department, Sharon Bisdee, phoned from Washington to confirm the date of March 7, 2002, for my swearing-in ceremony, which would be held in the Benjamin Franklin Room on the eighth floor of the State Department. She added that the March date was the earliest Secretary Colin Powell would be available because of his heavy travel schedule.

I was excited by the news—yet hesitant. I had spent nearly four years on the Salt Lake Organizing Committee and was committed to attend all the events of the 2002 Winter Olympic Games. We had plans to entertain visitors, friends, and guests from around the globe. We had also invited a number of Mauritians to be our guests, including the country's current IOC member, Rampaul Ruhee, his son Raj, and Janeeta Anderson and her family, who live in Utah. In a previous administration, Janeeta's father, Chitmansing Jesseramsing, served for fourteen years as the Mauritian ambassador to the United States. Because of all these events, planning for the Washington ceremony was going to be complicated.

Marcia and I went over the logistics of having family and friends travel to Washington, D.C., finding hotel rooms, and arranging for meals and transportation. Marcia was adamant that I take the oath on one of the original twenty-five copies of the Declaration of Independence produced by Philadelphia printer John Dunlap in 1776, instead of the Bible traditionally used for the ceremony. She said the Declaration of Independence was the most important and appropriate document representing our country's freedom and what it means to immigrants who come to this land.

"Great," I countered. "But where am I going to find one?"

"Try to borrow one," she responded.

I immediately put in a call to my friend Ron Fox, who not only knew sources for such rare literary items but also was politically connected in Washington. If a copy of the Declaration could be found for the occasion, this remarkable historian might well be able to do it.

Meanwhile, pre-Olympic activities were under way. Having crossed the country, the Olympic torch was traveling through Utah on its way to Salt Lake City and the Opening Ceremonies.

On Tuesday, February 5, I was working late at my office when the phone rang. Gary Doxey, from the governor's office, was on the line. He asked if I could meet the governor on the front lawn of the Capitol promptly at eight that night and accompany him in the state helicopter for a flight to Provo. The governor wanted to be there when the Olympic torch entered Brigham Young University's LaVell Edwards Stadium. We needed to be there on time, as a large crowd was expected, and entertainment and fireworks were scheduled.

I raced out of my office with just ten minutes to cover the twelve miles from my office to the Capitol. Luckily, there was no traffic in Salt Lake City's downtown district to impede my excessive speed.

That night the sky was slightly overcast; a chill was in the air. The only noise I could hear was that of the helicopter rotors spinning in a synchronized fashion. Mike was standing by the door of the helicopter, wearing a brightly colored Olympic jacket and surrounded by several Utah Highway Patrol troopers and his personal security detail.

The helicopter climbed into the misty winter sky. Flying low over the city, we saw several high-rise buildings brightly lit and encased in shrink-wrap plastic film displaying massive silk-screened images of American Olympic athletes. Strobes and searchlights were everywhere, aimed at the sky. As we gazed from the helicopter, it was like looking into the Milky Way. Within minutes, though, we had left the metropolitan area. Clouds hid the moon and stars, and only an occasional light from a home below peeked through the cloud layers as we headed toward Provo.

The governor sat quietly, deep in thought. Suddenly he turned to me and asked how the confirmation process was going. I brought him up to date about my pending swearing-in ceremony at the State Department on March 7.

"Why then?" he asked.

I explained that was the first day Secretary Powell would be available. I also mentioned Marcia's request that I use an original copy of the Declaration of Independence instead of a Bible. I added that Ray Grant had told me Norman Lear was bringing his original copy of the document to Utah for display in the Capitol Rotunda during the Olympics, and that I planned to have Ray ask him if we could borrow it for the Washington ceremony and return it within twenty-four hours. Lear's copy was the only one known to be in private hands and had been discovered only in 1989, concealed on the back of a painting. Lear had purchased it in 2001 for $8.1 million.

"Mike," I said, "I really want to make this once-in-a-lifetime event very special by having the Declaration of Independence."

The governor fell silent again. Then, grinning, he turned to me and said, "Let's do it here."

"Where?" I asked.

"Here, at the State Capitol on Friday."

"Mike, it can't be done."

"Why?" he asked.

"We need to have Colin Powell."

"Okay."

"What do you mean, okay?"

"He'll be here on Friday."

"Here in Salt Lake City? You're kidding. Mike, do you think this is really possible?"

"Yes, we'll do it here."

"Will Powell do it?"

"We'll find out in the morning," he quipped.

Just then the helicopter landed in the LaVell Edwards Stadium parking lot, and a large crowd gathered to greet Governor Leavitt. Mike moved through the crowd shaking hands, hugging children, laughing and talking. *What a great communicator he is,* I thought. *What energy he has.*

After the ceremony, as we flew back to Salt Lake, my mind was racing. Mike's suggestion of holding the swearing-in ceremony at the Utah State Capitol that coming Friday would eliminate a lot of the problems involved in planning for a larger, more complicated event in Washington. But Friday was only three days away—and the day of the 2002 Winter Olympics Opening Ceremonies. Could Mike really pull it off?

After we landed on the front lawn of the Capitol, I thanked him for the helicopter ride and walked back to my car, thinking that fate had put us together that evening.

When I told Marcia the news, she was delighted—and even more determined to get the copy of the Declaration of Independence. When I said it was in the works, she was pleased. However, I explained the document was in an airtight display case and I could only place my hand on the glass surface while taking the oath of office.

By this time it was late, and I was tired—the busy day and night had done me in. I needed to close my eyes for a few hours. After all, at four-thirty in the morning, the Olympic torch would be heading toward Orem, a town several miles north of Provo, Utah, and we had to be there on time. Earlier, I had asked our oldest granddaughter, Ashleigh, to take my segment as torchbearer in Orem. She was overjoyed with the idea, and with receiving the official Olympic torch relay outfit: blue and white running pants, parka, hat, and gloves. She was less than thrilled, though, about having to wake up at three in the morning in order to get to the starting line on time—and she wasn't the only one who felt that way. Nevertheless, at three o'clock Marcia and I were on the road, driving to meet Ashleigh and the rest of our family to cheer her on. Ashleigh was all smiles.

Just a few hours later I was back in my office and on the phone talking with Ron Fox. Governor Leavitt had given him the assignment of putting together the swearing-in ceremony. I then called Sharon Bisdee at the State Department to let her know what had transpired. I also alerted Blossom Perry, the country desk officer in the State Department's Office of East African Affairs, and Alayne Peterson, the governor's administrative assistant, who already had the ball rolling with the governor's staff. Now we just needed approval from Washington. Over the next several hours, phone calls were made back and forth between the White House and the governor's office. By nightfall there was still no answer. As nervous as I was, I reminded myself to have confidence in Mike's ability to put this together.

That evening was the James Beard Foundation dinner, one of the pre-Olympic sponsored events. When Marcia and I arrived, we were delighted to see Ray Grant and hear that Norman Lear was already convinced that loaning us the document was a good idea and had agreed to move the document from the Capital Rotunda into the Gold Room for the swearing-in ceremony. We were elated by Norman's kind gesture; to our knowledge, no other original copy of Declaration of Independence had been used for such a ceremony. But we still did not have final approval from the White House.

I spent most of Wednesday night making a list of all the things that needed to be done before the ceremony. For security reasons, Ron was told, only twenty-five people would be allowed in the Gold Room. We had sixteen family members; that left only nine invitations for close friends and well-wishers. It wasn't enough, and I was determined to press for more. I also worried we still hadn't heard from Washington.

At seven-thirty Thursday morning, my administrative assistant, Marlene Luke, and I waited at the office for Ron to arrive. We were to work on the details of the event and prepare the invitations. After an hour, I was concerned by Ron's absence and unable to reach him on his cell phone. When he finally did appear, he looked frazzled but satisfied.

"The White House cleared the way," he said.

"What a relief!" I exclaimed.

After scanning the invitation language and reluctantly adding an additional five names to the list, Ron raced off to the printers. I called Sharon, who already knew that the request had been sent to Secretary Powell for final clearance and White House approval. An hour later, Governor Leavitt's office called with final affirmation.

Shortly after, Ron confirmed that the fifteen-minute ceremony was set for 1:30 p.m. on Friday, February 8, 2002, in the State Capitol's Gold Room. He stressed that no more than thirty people could be in attendance. By late afternoon, the printed invitations were ready to be hand-carried to family and friends. Ron also said he had a copy of a 1976 edition of a book containing the Declaration of Independence and Constitution that we could have and use for the event, rather than Lear's glass-covered document.

During the dress rehearsal for the Olympic Opening Ceremonies at Rice-Eccles Stadium on Thursday evening, the governor pulled me aside to reassure me that everything was set. I embraced him and thanked him several times for making this dream come true.

By the time I returned to my suite and slumped down on the couch, I was limp. Tears came to my eyes as I reflected on what had transpired during the past forty-eight hours. This was a great honor. Thirty-four years earlier, in 1968, another Utahn, Congressman David King, had become the first U.S. ambassador to Mauritius. I was to become the second such diplomat. Now, back home, as it neared midnight, I practiced the oath of office and reviewed my acceptance speech.

Early Friday morning, I was fully awake watching several national news channels showing President Bush boarding Air Force One and heading west. After a short stopover in Denver, he would be arriving in Salt Lake City to participate in the Opening Ceremonies of the 2002 Winter Olympic Games.

At 12:35 p.m., when Air Force One landed, Governor Leavitt was there to greet President Bush and Secretary Powell. He accompanied the president on a courtesy call to the First Presidency of the Church of Jesus Christ of Latter-day Saints (LDS) before driving up State Street toward the Capitol for the two o'clock Olympic kickoff event.

We too were on our way. SLOC had assigned John Peterson as our driver to take us around to the different Olympic venues, and to get us to the swearing-in ceremony on time. Although the ceremony was slated for one-thirty, we had been cautioned to arrive early enough to avoid the crowd assembling in the Rotunda to see President Bush.

The first wave of family members was waiting in John Peterson's van, parked in our driveway, with the second wave ready to go. Nervously pacing outside the house, John worried we'd be late. Finally Marcia and I made it out the door and into the van for the three-mile ride to the State Capitol. John then returned to pick up the rest of the family.

Passing through the security magnetometers at the side entrance, we were escorted by several Utah Highway Patrol officers through a growing crowd of people waiting for the president. Located next to the governor's office in the west wing of the Capitol, the splendid State Reception Room is often called the Gold Room because of its elaborate polished bird's-eye marble, gold-leaf moldings, original paintings, and nineteenth-century furniture. The room was used primarily for official events, visiting dignitaries, and high-level functions; the ambassador swearing-in ceremony would be a first.

Inside this exquisite space, I immediately saw Norman Lear's precious copy of the Declaration of Independence. On the nearby wall was a painting of George Washington in prayer at Valley Forge, by American artist Arnold Friberg, a great American icon best known for his religious and patriotic interpretation of historical events. I couldn't help but think nothing else could have been more appropriate.

Marcia and I, our children—Steven with his former wife, Drue; Deirdra with her husband, Farhad; and Jennifer with her husband, Tony—and our six delightful grandchildren, Ashleigh, Chelsea, Garrett, Hannah, Alexandra, and Savannah, were chatting with guests when a number of dignitaries arrived, followed by press photographers. The cabinet members travelling with the President included Secretary of Housing and Urban Development Mel Martinez, Secretary of the Interior Gayle Norton, and EPA Director Christine Todd Whitman. Other luminaries included Justice Ted Stewart, Congressman Chris Cannon, as well as Lieutenant Governor Olene Walker and Utah Attorney General Mark Shurtleff. National Security Advisor Condoleezza Rice and White House Press Secretary Ari Fleischer also stepped into the room to see what was going on.

Because President Bush would be speaking at the 2002 Winter Olympics kickoff event, security was tight at the Capitol. Utah Highway Patrol officers and Secret Service were stationed everywhere. At exactly one-thirty, the doors to the Gold Room were closed. In the distance, you could hear the faint strains of the Mormon

Tabernacle Choir practicing "The Battle Hymn of the Republic." Ron, who was in charge of the event, stayed in contact with the Secret Service, and when he was told Secretary Powell was about to enter the Gold Room, he announced, "Ladies and gentlemen, the Secretary of State, Colin Powell, and Governor Michael Leavitt."

Secretary Powell walked toward me. We shook hands and warmly embraced. For a moment he admired the encased Declaration of Independence while I explained its presence in the Gold Room. Standing between Secretary Powell and Governor Leavitt, I suddenly began to tremble and feel weak. Luckily, an adrenaline rush kept me going.

In his introduction, the governor spoke about the 1997 visit he and I had made to New York and Ellis Island. We had attended a dinner at the restored monument, which for many decades had served as a portal for immigrants coming to America. The governor recalled asking if I had been there before, and I replied, "Only once"—when I came through Ellis Island with my parents and my brother, escaping the Holocaust. I was immediately flooded with memories.

In 1938, during what has become known as Kristallnacht, the Night of Broken Glass, in Germany and Austria, Nazi storm troopers, the SS, and Hitler Youth groups broke into and pillaged thousands of homes and businesses while the German police stood by and did nothing to stop the destruction. Window after window was broken and smashed. Nearly two hundred synagogues were vandalized and burned. Hundreds of sacred Torahs were desecrated; one hundred Jews were killed; and more than thirty thousand Jews were rounded up, arrested and sent to concentration camps. Among them were some of our relatives and close family friends. There was shock and outrage worldwide, but no one challenged Hitler.

Jews were singled out by being forced to wear a yellow Star of David. Out of fear we hid in our apartment. Then one night, mere weeks before the German borders were closed to all Jews leaving, we disappeared into the dark, heading toward freedom.

"Only in America could the son of immigrants fleeing the Nazi Holocaust rise to such prominence in the business world. Now he enters public service for his nation," Governor Leavitt said in his remarks. This brought tears to my eyes.

Secretary Powell then spoke about our similar immigrant backgrounds. He went on to say, "We both went to the best college, which was attended by many immigrants, City College of New York, where we both studied geology." Jokingly, he added, "I went into the Army, and John went on to make money."

When Secretary Powell asked if I was ready to be sworn in, I was shaking, but I said I was. Marcia held out the book containing the Declaration of Independence and Constitution, upon which I impulsively placed my right hand, when I should have used my left. Secretary Powell smiled and waited a beat before quipping, "Now, put your *right* hand on it," which gave everyone a good laugh.

1.1. The swearing-in ceremony conducted by Secretary of State Colin Powell, February 8, 2002. (Photo courtesy of Newman Photography)

Secretary Powell then asked me to repeat after him the oath of office:

I, John Price, do solemnly swear that I will support and defend the Constitution of the United States against all enemies foreign and domestic; that I will bear true faith and allegiance to the same; that I take this obligation freely and without any mental reservation or purpose of evasion; that I will well and faithfully discharge the duties of the Office on which I am about to enter, so help me God.

"Congratulations, Mr. Ambassador!" he concluded.

Thanking Secretary Powell, I stepped up to the podium and spoke about what I wanted to accomplish in the host countries and how I believed I could make a difference. I promised to make trade, business promotion, and economic development among

1.2. The Price family at the swearing-in ceremony, February 8, 2002. (Photo courtesy of Newman Photography)

the top priorities during my tenure in Mauritius. I pledged to protect and preserve the fragile Indian Ocean ecosystem, and confront the challenges of pollution and oil spills.

"I am deeply honored," I said. "I look forward to working with the citizens of all three countries—Mauritius, Seychelles, and Comoros—to build stronger relationships and understanding between our countries."

And I spoke of my family's support as I changed careers from being a businessman to serving the country I love so dearly.

After a few photographs were taken with Secretary Powell, Mike and Jackie Leavitt, and Marcia and our family, the ceremony was over. It was hard to believe, but I was now officially a United States ambassador.

When I heard the 23rd Army Band of the Utah National Guard play "Hail to the Chief," I knew President Bush was entering the Rotunda. Upon leaving the Gold Room, I stopped to talk with Condoleezza Rice, Ari Fleisher, and Chief of Staff Andy Card, who were waiting for President Bush to make his remarks. I was told the president had been standing nearby during parts of my swearing-in ceremony, which made me smile. But there was no time for reflection.

We were cautioned by the Secret Service that if we wanted to get back to Fairfax House in time to greet President Bush and the First Lady, who would be arriving in thirty minutes, we should leave immediately, because of the tight security. The plan was for the Bushes to relax and have some down time before dinner and the evening's Olympic Opening Ceremonies.

Because we would have the honor of hosting the President, our house had undergone weeks of preparation by White House advance teams and security personnel, with extra measures being taken specifically as a consequence of the September 11, 2001, terrorist attacks. The Secret Service and the White House advance team had worked in tandem with our security and property manager, Mike Washburn. Our house was wired for secure telephone communication service worldwide, and our property was protected by the more than twenty-five people stationed on the grounds. Military vehicles and personnel were positioned on nearby hills, sharpshooters were concealed on nearby rooftops, and several helicopters hovered above our home.

The invited media allowed onto our property were confined to a small section of the garage, where tables were set up with food and drinks. Two large-screen television sets were mounted for viewing the president's events during the day and at the evening's Olympic Opening Ceremonies. Since the president's entourage would have little time to shop for Olympic memorabilia, we set up a temporary Olympic gift shop in the garage as well.

Marcia and I anxiously waited at the front portico for the President and Mrs. Bush to arrive. But at the last minutes we were rushed by the Secret Service down the back hallway—for security reasons, the President would be using the rear entrance of the house. Several athletic-looking men wearing dark suits followed closely behind the President, one carrying what appeared to be a black box and an attaché case. Trailing after them were Roland and Lois Betts, the president's traveling companions.

It had been several years since the president's last visit. After warm greetings and a quick tour of our home, we offered the President and Mrs. Bush the privacy of the master bedroom suite and the adjacent family room to enjoy during their visit.

In the kitchen, two Secret Service agents watched our caterer, Mary Kraft, and a New York chef from the James Beard Foundation prepare special dishes for our guests.

While Laura and her friend Lois rested, the president removed his tie, unbuttoned the top button of his shirt, and relaxed with a cigar outside the garden room, chatting with Roland, his old Yale chum. The outside temperature was falling below freezing, and I suggested the president come in out of the cold. He considerately asked, "Do you mind if I smoke a cigar?"

I replied, "I like a good cigar once in a while myself."

Over a cup of coffee, we discussed the countries in Africa to which I was being posted. Roland asked if I had a map of Africa so he could see exactly where they were located. I quickly went to my office and brought back a full-size map of Africa, which included Mauritius, Comoros, and Seychelles, Indian Ocean island nations off the east coast of Africa. I gave Roland a brief overview, then thanked the President for the honor to serve our country. I also asked if he would inscribe the book containing the Declaration of Independence that I'd taken my oath on. On the inside front cover, the President wrote: "To my friends, John and Marcia. Thanks for serving our nation. Best always, George Bush, Feb. 8, 2002."

After a short discussion about Utah's hard work in hosting the 2002 Winter Olympic Games, and how special the Opening Ceremonies were going to be, the president put out his cigar and asked to be excused until dinner so that he could rest. Roland also retired, so I joined Andy Card, Condoleezza Rice, and Ari Fleischer at the makeshift gift shop, where they were buying Olympic memorabilia. Marcia was in the kitchen with Mary Kraft and the chef putting the final touches to the dinner menu for the president and his party. Several of the president's staff prepared the breakfast room for a quiet early dinner. And, of course, the Secret Service looked on.

Once everyone was seated for dinner, Laura told Marcia what a lovely experience the ambassador posting was going to be. "Enjoy it, since it's not forever," she said, and suggested, "You can always go back to whatever you are currently doing." We both agreed that was good advice from the First Lady. The dinner turned out to be a lovely experience, although Marcia and I were both nervous.

At exactly five o'clock, Brian Montgomery, the White House Director of Advance, entered the room with the President's evening schedule. The President jotted down some notes on a card and excused himself. Minutes later, after thanking us for dinner and our hospitality, the President and his entourage were gone.

Exhilarated and exhausted, Marcia and I reflected on the events that had taken place that day. It was almost like a fairy-tale afternoon, unforgettable and over much too quickly! Marcia particularly enjoyed the President's written notation in the book and later that night was delighted to find the note he left on the pillow in the master bedroom.

> Dear John and Marcia,
>
> Thank you so very much for your wonderful hospitality. Laura and I appreciate your friendship. You can judge a man by the quality of his shower. You are indeed a fine man. We send all our very best wishes for your new assignment.
>
> God speed, George Bush

John Peterson was at the door at six o'clock that evening to take us to Rice-Eccles Stadium, where we joined family and friends for the Opening Ceremonies.

It had been a long road traveled since Utah was awarded the XIX Olympic Winter Games in June 1995 by the International Olympic Committee. Now, on

February 8, 2002, the time had come to, in the words of IOC President Jacques Rogge, "let the Games begin!"

The Opening Ceremonies of the 2002 Winter Olympic Games were truly artistic and magical, beginning with the lighting of the Olympic flame, which inspired the theme, "Light the Fire Within." The entertainment included singer LeAnn Rimes and the Mormon Tabernacle Choir accompanied by the Utah Symphony Orchestra; cellist Yo-Yo Ma; the singer Sting; the Dixie Chicks; and Olympic skater Kristi Yamaguchi. As part of the cultural events, representatives of the five Native American tribes of Utah entered on five rotating platforms adorned with patterns from each tribe, signifying both their culture and the five symbolic rings of the Olympic movement. A sad moment was seeing the tattered American flag that had hung at the World Trade Center as a tribute was paid to the catastrophic events of September 11, 2001.

The next seventeen days of the 2002 Winter Olympics were hectic and fun-filled. They were also incredibly challenging logistically, since the competitive events and cultural programs were spread out along the Wasatch Mountains, a range nearly a hundred miles long. But there was no stopping us from attending as many events as we could. After all, this too was a once-in-a-lifetime experience for all of us.

On Saturday, February 23, as the ice skating competitions at the Delta Center were coming to a close, I hosted a party in our suite in honor of Mauritius. John Peterson had located several of the country's flags, which we proudly displayed on the walls. The evening was lively with congenial conversation among our family and guests, including IOC member Rampaul Ruhee and his son Raj; Jacques de Navacelle of Barclays Bank and his young son; and Janeeta Anderson and her family.

It was enjoyable getting acquainted and sharing mutual interests. Marcia and I said we looked forward to being in Mauritius and participating in everything this new assignment had in store for us.

Sunday, February 24, was the last day of the 2002 Winter Olympic Games. Our morning began with Governor Leavitt's reception at the State Capitol honoring New York Mayor Rudy Giuliani, whose popularity had soared after the 9/11 attacks. The Capitol was packed with people, and Mayor Giuliani's words were inspiring. Also, this was the first time I was considered a dignitary and included on the dais. The term "Mr. Ambassador" was slowly starting to sink in.

Later that evening, Vice President Dick Cheney and his wife, Lynne, were expected to be present for the Closing Ceremonies at Rice-Eccles Stadium. Flying into Salt Lake City with their daughter Mary and her partner, Heather Poe, they planned to watch the ice hockey championship match that afternoon between the United States and Canada. Then they would come to Fairfax House for a brief visit and dinner before attending the evening ceremonies. Our home was, of course, ready, still wired and very secure.

Marcia, our daughter Deirdra, and I were determined to attend this historic hockey event with the U.S. team in the finals. But here, too, timing was crucial. We had to be at Fairfax House to greet the vice president and his family. Fortunately, our seats were directly across from where the vice president and his wife were sitting, so we decided that when they got up to leave, we would as well. Immediately after the game—Canada won, 5 to 2, for the gold medal—we returned to our home in a helicopter provided by the State of Utah while the Cheneys traveled by motorcade. Even so, we got back only minutes before the vice president's motorcade pulled into our driveway.

Ron Fox, who also did advance work for the vice president, arrived with an Olympic medal that he presented to Vice President Cheney. We gave U.S. Olympic team hats to the women and an Olympic baseball cap to the vice president. Since the temperature was steadily dropping, we also had Olympic down coats, jackets, and gloves for everyone to wear while sitting outdoors in the president's box for the Closing Ceremonies.

After a few photographs were taken, followed by a brief tour of our home and art collection, the Cheneys went off to rest in the master bedroom suite. Security again was tight, with helicopters hovering above and military personnel stationed in the hills behind Fairfax House. The garage area was once more set up for the staff to have dinner and watch the events on television. Meanwhile, our caterer, Mary Kraft, and a chef from Halifax, Nova Scotia, were working in the kitchen under the watchful eyes of the Secret Service. They prepared a stunning dinner for seven that included fresh wild salmon flown in from Nova Scotia.

At five o'clock, we sat down at the dining room table, which had been superbly decorated with flowers. During dinner, the vice president offered insights on a number of global issues. Lynne spoke about her new children's book, *America: A Patriotic Primer,* which would be coming out in the spring of 2002. Our daughter Deirdra discussed her book, *Healing the Hungry Self,* which dealt with a diet-free solution to lifelong weight management. Deirdra and Lynne agreed to exchange copies of their books by mail.

Promptly at six o'clock, Cheney's staff jumped into action. Within minutes, our get-together was over, and after a warm exchange, everyone left to attend the 2002 Winter Olympics Closing Ceremonies at Rice-Eccles Stadium. We were hustled off to the stadium by a state trooper escort and arrived just as the ceremonies were beginning.

The extravaganza that followed is nearly impossible to describe. There were many participants dressed in brightly colored costumes, and a parade of competing athletes. On a large temporary ice sheet there were choreographed skaters, including Olympic skater Dorothy Hamill. Onstage were a number of performers, including Kiss; Earth, Wind, and Fire; Bon Jovi; Harry Connick Jr.; Christina Aguilera; and Gloria Estefan. For the finale, a fireworks display lit up the Utah sky.

As we were leaving the stadium, heavy snow started to fall and visibility became poor. As we drove toward the house, I received an urgent call from Mike Washburn telling us we had fifteen minutes to "hurry home, pick up a toothbrush, and leave."

1.3. At Fairfax House with Vice President Dick Cheney and Lynne Cheney, February 24, 2002. (Photo courtesy of Newman Photography)

The Cheneys' plans to go on to Jackson, Wyoming, that night had been cancelled, as the Jackson airport was socked in with terrible weather conditions, and they were all returning to Fairfax House.

As we neared our home, we saw that the police had already cordoned off the streets. Inside the house, the Secret Service was reinstalling equipment that had been removed just hours earlier.

Marcia and I quickly packed, and as we were pulling out of the driveway we glimpsed Cheneys' motorcade slowly coming up the street. Marcia decided to bunk with our daughter Jennifer, who lived nearby. Since I had to be in Park City early the next morning for meetings, I decided to drive to our home near the Deer Valley Ski Resort. Some thirty miles from Salt Lake City, it was close to where many of the Olympic events had been held. As it turned out, the heavy snowfall made it impossible for me to reach our ski chalet by car; I didn't have four-wheel drive and the snow was unrelenting. Wearing only a pair of loafers and a light fleece jacket, I left the car by the side of the road and walked the last half mile to our mountain retreat. At that moment, trudging through the snow and soaking wet, I didn't feel much like a U.S. ambassador.

Later, as I reflected over a cup of tea about the events that had begun with my swearing-in ceremony on February 8 and continued through seventeen days of an exhilarating Winter Olympics, reality sank in: I would soon begin a new chapter in serving my country.

(II)

The Early Years

Escape to Freedom

The boat had come to Bremerhaven to deliver bananas. We hid down in the hold; it smelled of stale bananas. There were four of us; then another four, a family. So there were eight on this boat—a boat that could have taken a hundred people or more. That was the last boat that left Bremerhaven for a foreign country and freedom.

I was born Hans Joachim Praiss on August 18, 1933. In Hebrew, Joachim means "for whom God exalts." My brother, Wolfgang Samuel Praiss, was three years older, and we lived in Germany with our parents, Selmann and Minna Margarete (Loser) Praiss. When we came to America, our point of entry was Ellis Island, where, after much paperwork, my father's brother William, our sponsor, came to rescue us. Family conjecture is that for expediency and to move us through the lines more quickly, the U.S. Immigration and Naturalization Service officers gave us a new, Americanized identity—like a tattoo that would stay with us forever. I became John Price. My brother, now called William (Bill), rebelled and never would let us refer to him by anything other than his proud Germanic name. Father became Simon Price, and our mother Margaret Price. Our naturalization papers confirmed these changes in 1946.

The earliest recollection I have of being in Germany was when I was five years old, living in a second-floor apartment over a retail clothing store my parents owned in Spandau, a small town ten miles from Berlin. My father and mother owned one-third of what must have been a five-acre block of buildings that surrounded a courtyard.

On the first level were retail stores—some owned and operated by my parents, including a clothing store, linen shop, dry goods store, and laundry. Other spaces, rented to relatives and longtime friends, included a kosher butcher shop and bakery.

20

2.1. Parents Selmann and Margarete Praiss (Price) with Wolfgang and Hans (John), circa 1938.

On the two levels above the stores, small offices and apartments overlooked the street: with access to the inner courtyard and garden area, where neighbors gathered and children played. The layout of this block was much like a predecessor of an early shopping center.

My parents worked together to build these businesses and expand their property investments. My father also owned and operated a movie theater on this block. There was a rear entrance to the movie theater with a stairway that led to the inner courtyard. Sometimes after school my friends and I, still wearing leather knapsacks on our backs, would sneak up that stairway to catch the end of a matinee before going home. Although sound movies of the mid-1930s were primitive, we thought the experience was great.

My father was born May 30, 1890, in Wislitza, Poland. He enlisted as a soldier in the German army during World War I and thus became a German citizen. On July 13, 1934, he was awarded the Iron Cross by Field Marshal Paul von Hindenburg for his courageous frontline service in the Battle of the Argonne Forest, the bloody hundred-day offensive by the Allies in which thousands died.

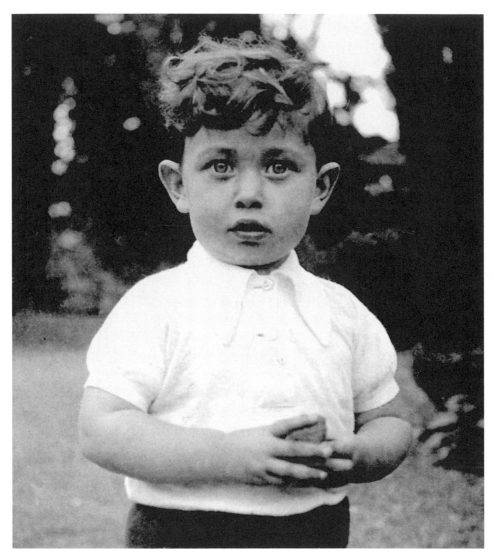

2.2. Hans (John) as a young boy in Spandau, Germany, September 1935.

He had already started his businesses when he met my mother through mutual friends. Born January 27, 1903, in Berlin, she was thirteen years younger than my father.

My parents received only basic schooling, and neither went on to higher education. But my father had the tenacity of his Teutonic personality, as well as brothers to help him start out. Three of the Praiss brothers were champion prize-fighters: Father was a middleweight, Willie a light heavyweight, and Herbert a heavyweight. Strong, hardworking, and driven, they wanted to improve their lot, and fisticuffs in the ring made them extra money. Herbert was the most highly ranked, having barely lost the German heavyweight title to his boxing club

2.3. The Praisses' store was vandalized during Kristallnacht, November 9, 1938.

teammate Max Schmeling—the same Schmeling who went on to beat Joe Louis in their first match on June 19, 1936, and become the world heavyweight champion. Herbert and Max were good friends; family photographs show them in a warm embrace.

I remember seeing pictures of my parents in cars when they were courting. My father had a penchant for automobiles—an interest I inherited. In the photos, my parents looked happy. When they married on June 19, 1928, I think everybody believed they would have a good life together, and for nearly a decade they did.

There were early signs that Jews were in danger, and talk of people leaving Germany. In 1935, Nazi Germany adopted the Nuremberg Laws on Citizenship and Race, which legally disenfranchised Jews and classified them as noncitizens. Jews could no longer vote, hold government jobs, or serve in the army. To segregate them from the rest of the community, yellow benches were set up in Berlin parks and labeled "only for Jews."

In Spandau, our parents tried to shield us from the rising anti-Semitism and from Nazi pressure to boycott Jewish businesses. Father insisted we continue with our Jewish traditions: we celebrated the High Holy Days at the neighborhood synagogue, went to religious services, and attended Hebrew school regularly. But suddenly we found ourselves always being escorted home by one parent or the other.

In 1937, the boycott on Jewish enterprises nearly ruined the family businesses. Years later, my mother told us, "We hardly sold anything and because of this we did not purchase new items. Our income went lower and lower."

2.4. Portrait of Selmann Praiss in the German army, World War I, 1917.

On April 26, 1938, all Jews were ordered to register their property. Three months later, a law was passed forbidding Jews to work in commercial services, including real estate brokerage, and in the civil service. On September 30, licenses held by Jewish physicians were revoked; soon after, Jewish lawyers were forbidden to practice law.

I had aunts, uncles, cousins, and grandparents who lived on the block and in nearby areas. In late 1938, some of them went on trips and never returned home. No one talked about it with us—why they left, where they went, and when, or even if, they were coming back. After all, we were children and they didn't want to frighten us. Years later, I learned many of them ended up in concentration camps. I also learned that after Hitler became chancellor on January 30, 1933, many of our relatives and friends tried to convince my father to leave Germany.

2.5. Grandparents Samuel and Florentina Prajs (Praiss), Wislitza, Poland, circa 1892–93.

At some level Father must have known what lay ahead. He had helped his two younger brothers leave Germany to begin a new life in America. Willie went to New York City; Herbert journeyed to Houston, Texas. Samuel, an older brother who years earlier had gone to Chicago, Illinois, stopped writing soon after his arrival; no one knows what fate befell him.

Only one other brother, Adolph, stayed behind in Germany. He owned two taxi-cabs. Prohibited by the Nazis from operating them, my uncle made a deal with an

Aryan friend, an aircraft mechanic, and was able to stay in business. This same friend was also very close to Nazi leader Hermann Goering, who interceded on my uncle's behalf, sparing him from deportation and death. But it was difficult to survive as a Jew in Germany, and my uncle Adolph died in 1947, just a few years after the war ended.

My father didn't want to leave Germany. He and others didn't—couldn't— believe that these hard times were going to last. They thought Hitler would not continue as chancellor for long, that he would be voted out. But it didn't work out that way. Few Jews could escape the reality of the November 9, 1938 pogrom: the merciless day in history commonly referred to as Kristallnacht, the Night of Broken Glass.

In an apparent retaliation for the assassination of a German diplomat by a young Polish Jew in Paris protesting the injustice done by Nazis to his parents, storm troopers and gangs of Nazi youth carrying bats and sticks went from one block to the next of Jewish-owned businesses and smashed all the windows in their storefronts. They broke into the shops, destroyed property, soiled items, and ransacked everything in sight. Whatever was left—walls, mirrors, shattered windows—they splattered with yellow paint, graffiti, and big Jewish stars. The Nazis demanded the liquidation of German Jewish businesses, and the mobs of soldiers and civilians destroyed everything in their way.

It was frightening. We were upstairs, above the shop, and all of a sudden we could hear the roar of big crowds coming. We closed our drapes, turned off the lights, and hid where we thought no one could find us.

These riots raged throughout Germany and in parts of Austria. Nazis broke into and looted more than 7,500 homes and stores. They set fire to nearly 200 synagogues and torched countless sacred Torahs. They beat up and killed Jews on the street, and arrested more than 30,000 Jews, forcing thousands into concentration camps. Dachau, the first concentration camp in Germany, was established in March 1933.

Outside our home, the noise seemed endless. Father covered our heads as he prayed over and over again in Hebrew. He sometimes even chanted, "Why us?"

The next day, a friend and advisor of my father, Herr Trautschold, came to our home and talked quietly with him in the kitchen. Then with my brother, Wolfgang, they swept up the glass and carefully gathered what was left of the linens, dry goods, kitchenwares, and clothing. Mother said she remembered sweaters, shirts, ties, and socks pulled off the shelves and thrown on the floor, dirty and torn.

My father and his friend salvaged some wood planks to cover the broken windows. The few items that were not soiled or damaged went in one box, while the rest of the merchandise, now worthless, went into another. Mother continued to operate out of one shop on a limited basis, hoping to sell the leftover goods at huge discounts. The losses were staggering. My father had insurance and applied for compensation, but the claim was never paid. Instead, a fine of a billion marks was imposed collectively upon all German Jews.

From then on, Jewish children were barred from attending German public schools, and all Jews were required to wear a yellow Star of David attached to their outer clothing. By 1939, my parents had to carry identity cards with a big *J* (for *Jude*, "Jew") emblazoned on the front; the *J* was also required on all passports. Soon we all were made to carry identification cards with the same generic middle name, Israel for males and Sara for females, added to our own names. We were an openly marked and targeted people.

Father recognized then that the situation was critical. Although he loved his country, he knew the plight of Jews would only get worse. After Kristallnacht we kept out of sight. Some of our relatives, friends, and neighbors were not so careful. One after another they disappeared, and Father was concerned we would be next.

He almost waited too long. Fortunately, with the help of Herr Trautschold, a non-Jew who had a few police connections, he managed to get passports and visas for us to leave the country. The authorities extracted almost everything we had in exchange for the exit documents, but Father was willing to give up the shops, the real estate, everything, to get us to safety.

The German passports were issued on February 2, 1939, and the visas from the consul general of Panama on February 20. Herr Trautschold found a ship leaving for Panama from Bremerhaven on April 8.

Until the morning of our departure, Wolfgang and I had no knowledge of this plan. My parents had never discussed leaving Germany; I guess they were fearful we would say something to one of our friends.

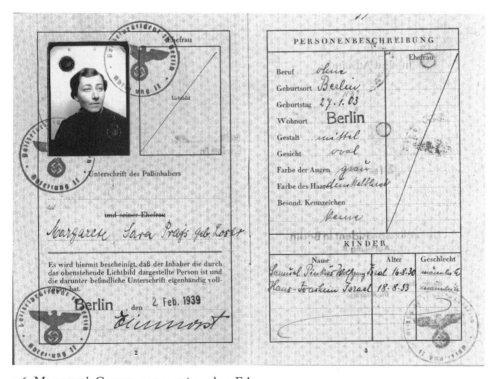

2.6. Margarete's German passport, issued on February 2, 1939.

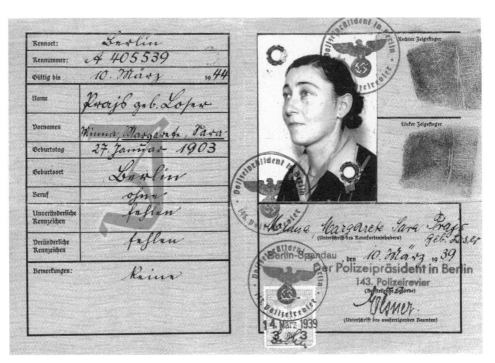

2.7. Margarete's Jewish identity card, issued on March 10, 1939. The middle name Sara was added to every Jewish woman's name.

2.8. Selmann's Jewish identity card, issued on March 10, 1939. The middle name Israel was added to every Jewish man's name.

Early on the foggy and overcast morning of April 8, Father woke us up, saying we were going on a short trip for the day. He wanted us to select one or two of our favorite possessions and a few warm clothes. Mother wrapped our best silverware and candlesticks in linen, along with several small Meissen porcelain figurines. Father carried several small artworks wrapped inside butcher paper and a few pieces of family jewelry, including three gold pocket watches. My brother told me later that Father also brought with him several Leica cameras, which he sold when he needed money. As I recall, my brother carried an old Bible and several books. We both packed extra clothes in a small suitcase. Finally, we removed the anti-Semitic symbol—the insidious yellow star—from our outer clothing.

We left early that morning by train for a five-hour journey to Bremen. Once in the city, we went by taxi to the small freighter waiting at the port. When the captain spotted my father, the crew quickly helped us aboard and concealed us in the cargo hold.

My brother recollects Herr Trautschold going with us to Bremerhaven to make sure there were no problems. I don't remember that, but I do recall that the cargo hold was dark and musty, with a smell of stale bananas.

When the engines started, the noise muffled our anxious breathing. It was only then that Father explained what was happening. He told us we would never return to Germany. Most likely we would never again see any of the relatives and friends who considered Germany their homeland and refused to leave—all the exits were closing. Looking around the spare, empty vessel, we realized there would have been enough room for them on this "freedom boat," and each day we prayed for their survival.

Once at sea, Wolfgang and I passed the time by playing tag and exploring the inner passageways of the freighter. Though the ship looked large enough to hold a hundred people, we thought at first we were the only ones escaping on it. It wasn't until sometime later that we discovered another family of four hiding on board. The fear of discovery was daunting for all of us, so we kept to ourselves. Sleeping in the cargo area was also frightening. We had heard stories about snakes, spiders, and rats hiding in the empty banana crates. But we were fortunate and saw none.

By the end of April 1939, the German borders were sealed, and no more Jews were allowed to leave. The difference between our escape to freedom and certain death in a Nazi concentration camp was a matter of weeks.

Later we discovered that Father had managed to send ahead to the ship some pieces of furniture, four large Persian rugs, three framed oil paintings—a small portrait of Rembrandt done by a student follower; a large, brightly colored pointillist pastoral scene; and a dark, somber painting of a man in prayer—four large *koffers* (suitcases), and one large blue steamer trunk filled with undamaged merchandise, brought along for resale.

On April 22, 1939, we arrived safely in Panama. We soon heard from acquaintances that some of our relatives had been rounded up and sent to concentration

2.9. Wolfgang and Hans (John) on the boat to Panama, April 1939.

camps. Not long after that, we received news about an uncle and aunt who had managed to escape to Bolivia and a cousin who had made it to Argentina, for which we were thankful. Then we learned that several other relatives had found their way to America.

Life in Panama was difficult for my parents. My brother and I were young, so we picked up languages easily and were excited about having new adventures, but our parents spoke only German and kept to themselves. Still, my father was resourceful and found refuge for us in a small apartment not too far from the Canal Zone, where he worked as a painter. Mother said he painted apartments for American families on a military base. He had never done that type of labor before, so it was difficult for him and he was extremely underpaid. Mother, who always had been active in the family business, found piecework as a seamstress. Both our parents performed other menial jobs as well, to make ends meet. My father faced inequity even in Panama because of his German heritage. Yet no matter how difficult the times were, he made it possible for us to have a new start in life.

Wolfgang and I were accepted into a nearby Catholic school. The teachers were strict, and I, being the more rambunctious of us two, often had my hands slapped with a ruler. One day, out of frustration, I placed a tack on a nun's chair. The effect was loud and clear. I immediately pled guilty and had to sit in the corner of the classroom for several days in a row.

Father had worked diligently to obtain the official *Deutsches Reich Reisepass* (German passport) that allowed us to leave Germany, as well as the entry visas that brought us into Panama. However, the Panamanian visas were valid only until March 1941, when we would have to leave the country. Fortunately, one of my father's brothers in the United States agreed to sponsor us—a condition required for immigration. My father went right to work and on September 13, 1940, received U.S. immigration visas for all four of us—two under the quota for Germans and two under the Polish quota. We were excited at the thought of going to America—as, I'm sure, were the Catholic nuns at our school!

We were grateful that Vice Consul John Goodyear, at the American consulate, aided us in obtaining funds from the National Refugee Service to pay for our passage. Sailing on the S.S. *American Legion*, we landed in the United States on September 22, 1940. Like most immigrants, we entered by way of Ellis Island, located at the mouth of New York Harbor and within sight of the Statue of Liberty. So began life in a new country, and with it the American dream.

Uncle Willie, who had a modestly successful business, was our main sponsor and guarantor, accountable for our welfare after our arrival. He and a friend my parents knew from Germany helped us find a small three-room apartment in Jackson Heights, Queens. Although the apartment was very cramped and offered little privacy, it represented freedom. We could come and go as we pleased, and we came to appreciate all the cultural opportunities that were available to us—from the numerous great museums and concert halls to the many smaller local art and music venues. In our tiny apartment, my parents hung their artwork with pride; the furniture, rugs, silverware, and ceramics stood as reminders of their once comfortable past, made possible by their hard work. Although my parents are now gone, the cherished paintings remain for future generations, a historical reminder of the family's past.

Right from the start, I worked at odd jobs when I wasn't in school, starting with washing windows and shoveling snow. When I was eight years old, I purchased a used American Flyer wagon and stood in front of the Bohack or Safeway grocery store on Fridays and Saturdays, offering to help people carry their groceries. I charged 25¢ for the first block and 10¢ for each additional block. If I had to walk upstairs in one of the apartment buildings, I would get an additional 5¢ per floor. In the first month, I earned enough money to pay for the wagon and even buy a second one, which I rented to a friend. That was my first experience as an employer. I did this for a couple of years, until business fell off. I thought we were offering a service, but in reality most of my customers were self-sufficient; most likely people paid us because they thought we were cute kids, and as we got older, we lost our marketing appeal. But I thirsted for pocket money, so, without missing a beat, I added other endeavors. Every night, for example, I picked up bundles of the *Daily News* from the subway station and dropped them off at a neighborhood corner sundries store.

Looking back, I would say my parents helped shape my work ethic. My father was a proud man, a quick-tempered one, yes, but a hard worker. He loved his homeland, was an active member of his community in Spandau, and worked diligently for financial independence and his family's future. But he was a Jew in Germany, so it was not meant to be. My father, who saved our lives and those of his brothers, never fully recovered. Arriving in America penniless, we had to depend upon his younger brother Willie, who seemed to act more out of a sense of duty than from compassion. Father now had to find the wherewithal to build himself up again.

The Japanese bombed Pearl Harbor on December 7, 1941, and America entered the war. Although we were victims who had escaped the Holocaust, most German Jewish immigrants to the United States had a hard time making friends in their new country. It was difficult to avoid the stigma attached to German brutality and Hitler; we were often characterized as German sympathizers. It was embarrassing at times to speak German in public with my parents, who struggled with the English language. Still, we felt compelled to communicate in German with them and carry on some of our cultural traditions while we helped them through the difficult times in this strange and new country.

As for employment, though my father felt distanced by his peers because he was German, he had no difficulty finding work in the machine shop at a Long Island City factory that made parts for submarines. My mother also found work making hair nets and later became a comptometer operator; together, they scrimped and saved. Then, during the latter part of the war, my mother noted the lack of ornaments for women's clothing and came up with the idea of making stylish animal-face brooches. Experimenting, she ordered die-cast molds, which we used to stamp out leather backs and a variety of fur fronts. The edges were glued together, leaving just enough room to stuff cotton inside before the opening was sealed up. Different styles of eyes, ears, and other details were added to the faces, and a pin attachment was glued onto the back.

The idea caught on, and before long my mother, Wolfgang, and I were producing vast numbers of these cute little creatures. Thanks to my father's natural tenacity, as well as help from a family friend who was a broker and spoke English fairly well, sales took off.

Father soon moved the business to a second-floor loft space in Long Island City. The building was adjacent to a subway station, which made it possible for us to deliver the brooches to stores throughout the city, and it was close enough to the post office so that we could ship the merchandise for out-of-state distribution. The business lasted until the war ended, when many new fashion products became available and sales of the animal brooches fell off. Though the demise of the business spelled the end of an era, the endeavor had made my parents proud.

My uncle Willie had a friend who had left Germany right after Hitler took power, and now lived in Rutherford, New Jersey. He owned an umbrella factory, which during the war supplied the military with water-repellant material. After the war ended, suburbia exploded with new families moving away from the city, and demand surged for consumer products. Plastic quickly became the rage, and Willie's friend converted his factory, Toscony Fabrics, to extrude translucent plastic into rolls of colorful print fabric. Father met with him and began experimenting with the fabric, making tablecloths and shower curtains. Satisfied with the results, he contracted out the sewing operations, and we kids did the packaging and labeling on the dining room table every day after school. Producing a large assortment of patterns, sizes, and styles, Father developed a good working relationship with J. C. Penney and Sears, and business boomed.

The products were heavy—the bundles we lugged to the post office or on the subway were almost half our weight. For three years we did this physically arduous work. Despite the emerging competition in a new and innovative industry, Father's business continued to thrive and even expand.

Father developed a cough that wouldn't go away, and eventually he went to see a doctor. The examination was not conclusive, so we all went back to work.

My parents worked as a team, and they labored day and night. Periodically they would get together for coffee klatches with other displaced friends; once in a while Willie and his wife, Ruth, would join them. Willie had carved out a different life for himself and his wife with a window display business; occasionally he would hire Wolfgang to work for them.

With my penchant for making a buck, I didn't fit in with the neighborhood kids who hung out at the corner soda fountain. I had several altercations with bullies who called me a "Nazi," which was humiliating, but I refused to let that bother me. I had plenty to do.

I attended P.S. 69, six blocks from our apartment, and excelled in my classes. I joined a Cub Scout den, and when I was twelve years old I became a Boy Scout in Troop 217. I enjoyed the challenges of achieving merit badges and going on field trips away from the city. I quickly became a Life Scout, the youngest in the troop to do so. I never did join the ranks of Eagle Scouts, even though I had more than the twenty-one merit badges needed to qualify; I couldn't find the time to complete the required bird study merit badge. I also wasn't into birds then, and sincerely believed the Boy Scouts would eventually give up that requirement.

Though my father worked hard, he still found time to reconnect with his Jewish faith. Judaism had become more important to him as a source of solace after he arrived in this country. He would attend Friday night services, and sometimes Saturday mornings as well, at the neighborhood synagogue, located several blocks from our apartment. On occasion he would rise early in the morning and join a minyan, a prayer quorum. After Wolfgang turned thirteen and had his bar mitzvah, he would often join my father. Donning the tefillin (two long thin straps of leather with a small box on each containing scrolls of parchment with verses from Exodus and Deuteronomy) for weekday morning prayers became a ritual for the two of them. As I approached my thirteenth birthday I too began to study segments of the Torah with the rabbi, in anticipation of my own bar mitzvah.

Classes, homework, and after-school activities left little spare time for me to study the necessary passages in Hebrew. Nevertheless, my father and the rabbi agreed I would perform the Haftarah— a passage from the Prophets of the Hebrew Bible—a week after my thirteenth birthday, in the latter part of August 1946. For three months prior to the ceremony, I practiced the passages over and over again, two afternoons a week.

On the appointed Saturday morning, I was joined at the synagogue by my father, mother, and brother; Uncle Willie and his wife, Ruth; Uncle Herbert and his wife, Charlotte, who came up from Houston, Texas; a few of my parents' friends from Germany; and several neighbors from our apartment building. Barely tall enough to be seen behind the lectern, I opted for a wooden step. Nervously, I melodically chanted readings that corresponded to that week's portion of the Torah, the scroll that contains the five books of Moses.

As I started to chant, I could see my aunt Charlotte waving a wristwatch back and forth. After the ceremony I would discover that the watch—a Bulova, popular at the time—was my gift from her and my uncle. But as I stood before the congregation I vowed not to be distracted, and looked away. I concluded my segment of the haftarah with only one mistake. I felt proud of this accomplishment, a testament to my new manhood. I continued going to services intermittently until school, Scouting, the newspaper route, and my other odd jobs overwhelmed me. Later, when my father died, I attended early morning services at the synagogue in his honor for the better part of a year.

2.10. Price Family Holocaust Memorial Garden, dedicated September 12, 2002.

Although Judaism stayed in my heart and I am proud to be Jewish, over the years I drifted away from attending formal services. I partake in observances of the High Holy Days on occasion, as well as family events such as Chanukah and Passover. I am never far from my roots: I support the U.S. Holocaust Memorial Museum in Washington, D.C., and in 2002 established the Price Family Holocaust Memorial Garden at the I. J. and Jeanné Wagner Jewish Community Center in Salt Lake City.

During the 1947–48 school year, I took on a paper route for the *Star,* a Long Island newspaper, and learned that delivering the paper on time meant bigger tips. Come Christmas, some of my customers would ask me to locate Christmas trees for them. I did so, and for a four-week period I enhanced my revenues by hanging around the tree lots to carry home trees for other people, and even finding new subscribers for the *Star.* On snowy days, shoveling out cars stuck in neighboring parking lots guaranteed exceptional tips.

I recall the big snowfall of December 1947. It was the worst blizzard since 1888 (and remained the record holder until 2006). I was at the parking lot of the Roosevelt Avenue/74th Street train station in Jackson Heights, Queens, shoveling out people's cars. Since there was more than two feet of snow on top of the cars and I was too short to reach much of the roof areas, I decided to climb up on top of a car and carefully remove snow from the roofs of several cars in that row. What I didn't realize was that the car I'd picked to stand on was a convertible; suddenly the cloth top gave way and I fell into the compartment below.

Just then a burly man appeared. Wearing a heavy overcoat and brimmed hat and smoking a cigar, he surveyed the situation, a frown on his face. But then he smiled, and there was even a hint of a chuckle. I began apologizing profusely, but he motioned me to clean out the snow from inside the car. Together we pushed the support crossbars back into place as best we could. Then he asked, "Do you know who I am?"

I didn't recognize him, so I said, "No."

"I'm Babe Ruth," he said with a smile.

I may not have recognized one of the most famous baseball players of all time, but I certainly knew who he was! Though I wanted to crawl under the car and die, he put his arm around me, thanked me for trying to extricate the cars from the disastrous snowstorm, and, for clearing—I assume—his convertible of snow, rewarded me with a crisp $5 bill.

In the summers of 1948 and 1949, I spent some of my savings on a two-week trip to a Scout camp located near Narrowsburg, New York—Camp Man at Ten Mile River. While I was at camp I worked on my merit badges. As one of the youngest patrol leaders, I was honored when I was "tapped out" both summers and inducted by my peers into the Order of the Arrow. Despite all the balls I was juggling, I continued with Scouting as I got older, finding time to be the assistant scoutmaster of Troop 217 in 1950, while still a student at Stuyvesant High School. After I graduated, I briefly continued in this leadership position while attending City College of New York (CCNY).

At Boy Scout camp I developed a fondness for woodworking and wood carving. At Stuyvesant High School I took woodworking classes. Soon I became the class's main supplier of dry old-growth maple. Each night I would go to a neighborhood bowling alley after it closed, collect all the damaged bowling pins, and haul them away free, which made the owner happy. On occasion, I would luck out and find some pins that were only slightly damaged. I would lug all of them on the subway to school in lower Manhattan and, depending upon their condition, sell them to the other students for 15¢ to 25¢ each. We shaped the pins on a lathe to make candy bowls, candlesticks, table lamps, and other imaginative forms. When they were finished, we kept some and sold others. Earning extra money while using the school shop equipment, I found a loyal clientele for some of my beautifully polished wood creations.

In 1949, when I was almost sixteen years old, my friend Joey Belin and I decided to go into the ice cream vending business. We each borrowed $60 from his father, purchased two used Good Humor tricycle ice cream wagons, coated them with fresh paint and decals, rebranded them as Eskimo Pie ice cream wagons, and bought ice cream products and dry ice from a supplier in Long Island City.

Joey, who was taller than I was, could easily pedal his bike. Unfortunately, I had to push mine, and I had to carry a footstool to step on when I needed to reach down into the bottom of the freezer box. When school was in session, we worked only on weekends and holidays. In the summer, we had a full-time, seven-day-a-week work schedule. We sold ice cream everywhere from local factories and tenements to public pools and parks. Sunday was our busiest day. After the first summer, which was a scorcher, Joey decided to quit. I purchased his ice cream wagon and hired my older brother.

I built up a good customer base, made more than $400 a month in profits, and saved every penny. Not even a flirting girl would get any product free. One day I came home to find my brother looking really sad and apologetic. He said he had stopped at a soda fountain to have a milkshake and parked the ice cream wagon at a right angle to the curb. A driver backing up his car didn't see the tricycle's narrow rear wheel sticking out and hit the wagon, damaging it substantially.

What does one say to a brother who has almost put you out of business? Worse, I couldn't understand why he, being in the ice cream business, would go to a competitor for a milkshake! After all, we were selling a much better product, one that cost only pennies to buy wholesale.

After the repairs were made using some of my savings, I sold the wagon my brother had been using, and decided to continue the business alone for another season. I believe Wolfgang was relieved not to be bossed around by his younger brother anymore.

While I was busy working, I put out feelers to find work the following summer as a busboy or possibly a waiter at the resort hotels in the Borscht Circuit of the Catskill Mountains. I thought that for the time required, the tips would be more than I was able to make selling ice cream. Besides, the ice cream business was very competitive, and I couldn't take any time off without losing customers to my competitors.

The year I was fourteen, my father purchased a new 1947 Plymouth Deluxe, a four-door sedan. He had been on a two-year waiting list, but when he opted to pay a little under the table, the car suddenly showed up earlier.

Mother later told me she was glad the Plymouth arrived when it did, so that my father had some time to enjoy it. I recall photos of him in Germany, in the 1920s and '30s, when he drove fast-looking sports cars. He never lost his love of cars and was proud of this new possession. It was his first and only car in America—he passed away from cancer on February 4, 1949, shortly after the disease spread to his lungs. My father was only fifty-nine years old when he died.

After his death, Mother kept the car sitting in a garage for the most part. She never learned to drive and preferred to use public transit. My brother, however, drove the Plymouth until his Air National Guard unit was activated in March 1951 and he was shipped off to Japan as part of the Korean War deployment. But before that, he would travel with Mother to distant points in New England to visit department stores to unload the leftover plastic inventory. As for the items that remained unsold, Mother used them for years as gifts.

I too got a chance to drive the Plymouth—but I'm sorry to say that I did not do well by Father's car. Not long after I started driving, I had the misfortune to go through a red light and hit an oncoming car. Although the car was repaired, it was never the same.

In my last year at Stuyvesant High School, I took a part-time afternoon job at a small enterprise called Nu-Art Display. The company built internally illuminated advertising display shadow boxes out of sheet metal. I learned to cut, shape, bend, and solder sheet metal into different sizes of enclosures. I then painted the units and installed electrical components and a glass front. In addition, flat sheet-metal wall advertising signs were cut, shaped, and painted, and advertising was silk-screened onto the face. It was an interesting learning experience, working as a two-man team with the owner, Harold Schwartz.

When I turned eighteen, I was required to register with the Selective Service System. Subsequently, while attending City College of New York, I joined the Reserve Officers' Training Corps (ROTC) program. I was subject to call-up to serve in the military, but students attending college full-time could request an exemption.

In my first year at CCNY, I joined the Police Athletic League program as a counselor on weekends. I was assigned to West 42nd Street, a neighborhood known as Hell's Kitchen. At the time, it was considered one of the more dangerous, high-crime sections of New York City. It was a challenge to become friends with at-risk and troubled young teenagers. One night, while I was supervising a dance, three known troublemakers attempted to crash the party. I objected, and found myself staring at a long, sharp ice pick that had been pulled out of an umbrella shaft. Luckily, I negotiated my way out of a potentially dangerous situation, but the following day I decided that this type of work was not my forte. Fortunately, I had other job opportunities in mind.

❴ III ❵

GO WEST, YOUNG MAN

Go West, young man, and grow up with the country.

—ATTRIBUTED TO HORACE GREELEY (1811–1872),
AMERICAN NEWSPAPER EDITOR

In retrospect, I feel fortunate to have attended Stuyvesant High School, but at the time I wanted to go to Bryant High School, located near our home in Long Island City, part of Queens Borough. The school was coeducational and close to where I had my odd jobs. Wolfgang was a junior attending the elite all-male Stuyvesant High School, located on the Lower East Side of Manhattan—a good forty-five-minute train ride from our apartment in Jackson Heights. He insisted I take the necessary test for admission, though only 10 percent of applicants were accepted. I resisted until my strong-willed mother intervened. The only way out was to fail the test, which I tried to do—but I passed anyway. Happily for me, within a few short weeks the advanced academic curriculum became addictive. I was hooked on education.

Founded in the early 1900s as a trade school for boys, Stuyvesant evolved into a specialized school offering a strong academic curriculum including science, mathematics, and technology. My experiences there prepared me for the engineering and geology curriculum I ultimately pursued at City College of New York (CCNY), the prestigious city-subsidized institution that catered to some of the brightest students in New York. At the time, admission to CCNY was based on academic merit alone. The coursework and the mentoring offered by the professors left an indelible mark that helped shape my thinking, my ability to solve problems, and my future success.

While attending classes at CCNY during the evenings and spending days working at different jobs to pay for my education, I continued to live with my mother in Jackson Heights and was able to help contribute to her support. My mother, never one to be idle, worked at Maidenform, Inc., a manufacturer of women's undergarments.

A cultured woman, she also found some time to enjoy the museums and theater productions with her friends—although only when she could get discounted tickets, as she was reluctant to part with any of her hard-earned money. Her favorite activity became rummaging through the racks at Saks Fifth Avenue for triple markdowns.

Wolfgang had graduated from Stuyvesant in June 1949 and attended CCNY in the evenings for three semesters while working in a metal fabricating shop during the day. He joined the Air National Guard in 1950 and left for active duty in the Korean War the following March. Long considered the "forgotten war," the Korean War took the lives of nearly thirty-seven thousand American servicemen. My brother was awarded three medals and returned home in late 1952. The following year he went to work as a sales engineer for E. F. Drew & Co., a chemical manufacturer. Shortly thereafter the company transferred him to Wisconsin, and he decided to attend the University of Wisconsin during the evenings, under the GI Bill.

My brother liked the engineering curriculum at Marquette University so he switched, graduating in 1959 with a degree in chemical engineering. He then went on to Cornell University in Ithaca, New York, where in 1960 he received a master's degree in labor economics and labor relations.

Offered a position with the Atomic Energy Commission, Wolfgang relocated to Albuquerque, New Mexico, and worked at Sandia National Laboratory. For the next seven years he was involved with the nuclear weapons production process, monitoring the government's main contractors.

In a career change, Wolfgang went to work as a management consultant for one of the large national accounting and consulting firms. He directed the reorganizing and restructuring of several U.S. government departments and was also instrumental in creating a new government agency. Another assignment included the restructuring of the Small Business Administration.

3.1. Wolfgang, Margaret, and John in front of their apartment building, circa 1951.

In late 1975, Wolfgang decided to open his own consulting firm, and over the years had numerous assignments that took him to Europe. Today, living in Vienna, Austria, my brother continues to consult with governments and businesses, and takes time to teach management classes and lecture on the subject.

One memorable job changed the direction of my life forever. I had first considered obtaining a degree in mechanical or electrical engineering because of the demand for engineers at the time. I applied at an international elevator manufacturing company with the hope of getting some drafting and junior engineering experience. Like others before me, I began in the company's mimeograph department. But after six months, I remained in this entry-level position, while others had moved on to the drafting department. I became friends with an engineer who, never promoted higher in the company, had held the same position for many years. During frank discussions, I learned not only was he Jewish, but also apparently he was the only Jewish person in the engineering department. He told me I should leave the company before I became as trapped as he was and too old to find suitable employment elsewhere. I heeded his advice.

For a brief time I worked at a local lumber company doing estimating and assembling inventory for home builders' projects. I then decided in the fall of 1952 to matriculate as a full-time student at CCNY and, having developed an interest in geology and paleontology, changed my major.

While I was looking for part-time work, a professor encouraged me to apply for a job at the CCNY seismograph and weather station. The station was located on campus in the basement of Army Hall, the building where I attended ROTC classes.

My job required changing the recording drum's continuous graph paper that documented all earth tremors, including major earthquakes around the world. I would then fold and file the drum recordings for future reference. I also sent aloft a weather balloon to check atmospheric pressure, temperature, wind velocity, and other weather-related data, which were called in to the weather bureau.

It was exciting to work at one of the foremost seismograph stations in the world. Many of New York City's skyscrapers are built directly on the Manhattan schist bedrock formation, and hence able to withstand major earthquakes. Structures built on natural soil or reclaimed land may not be so lucky.

Between classes, I earned meals by busing tables in the cafeteria and worked at a college bookstore to pay for my books; and delivered mail for the post office during Christmas break. Somehow I also found time to work for a city bicycle courier service, be on the CCNY wrestling team, and remain active in the ROTC program.

It seemed like all my spare time, apart from school activities, was dedicated to making a buck. Because of the money I could make from tips, I found work at several of the hotel resorts seventy-five miles away in the Catskill Mountains, known as the Borscht Belt. In its heyday, from the 1940s through the late 1960s, the Borscht Belt was a popular resort destination for working-class Jewish families who otherwise were discriminated against and restricted from other hotels and resorts on the East Coast.

Most of these resort hotels were located in and around the towns of Monticello, Fallsburg, Liberty, Narrowsburg, Ellenville, and Loch Sheldrake. In the early 1950s I worked at almost a dozen hotels: Grossinger's, Kutsher's, the Concord, Flagler's, the Nevele, Raleigh, Brown's Loch Sheldrake, the Sagamore Hotel (located in the Adirondacks on Lake George), and the Lake Spofford Hotel (in Spofford, New Hampshire).

The Borscht Belt hotels were well known for their kosher food and daily activities, and they kindled the careers of many star entertainers such as Jerry Lewis, Red Buttons, Milton Berle, Buddy Hackett, Lenny Bruce, Carl Reiner, Shecky Greene, Joey Adams, Morey Amsterdam, Mel Brooks, Sid Caesar, Myron Cohen, Rodney Dangerfield, Phyllis Diller, Alan King, Jackie Mason, Eddie Fisher, Tony Curtis, and Danny Kaye.

Working weekends, holidays, and during my summer breaks, I filled in wherever a job was available. I started out as a busboy and ultimately became a waiter; one summer I worked as a bellhop. For extra money, I worked as the editor of the hotel's daily newsletter, as a part-time lifeguard, and as a gardener. I easily engaged

3.2. Bellhops at the Lake Spofford Hotel, Spofford, New Hampshire, summer 1953; John is third from right.

people and generally talked about my college goals and future ambitions, which helped increase my tips. Soon I was able to afford my own car, a used 1950 Ford Victoria. Mother was happy to receive the money she got when I sold the family Plymouth. Offering rides to other college students working in the resort hotels helped pay for my new possession.

My career choice had changed once before, but in a 1954 geology class at CCNY a professor named Dr. O'Connell changed my life forever. Dr. O'Connell strongly urged me to go out west to fulfill my summer field geology course requirement. He suggested I work on an oil rig as a roustabout, a driller assistant laborer. Most important, he encouraged me to leave New York: he believed the real work opportunities for geologists were in the western part of the United States. That summer I decided to take his advice and head west to Tulsa, Oklahoma, where the Sun Oil Company was advertising available jobs working on drilling rigs as a roustabout.

Several years earlier, I had met fellow student Mel Papulak while we were both at Stuyvesant High School. I ran into Mel again at CCNY. Although he was graduating ahead of me, we attended some of the same geology classes and had become good friends. After I shared my plans with him, he asked if he could come along and agreed to pay his share of expenses. Mel, however, was apprehensive about traveling outside of New York City. He had never driven a car; like so many other students at CCNY, he depended upon subways, buses, or taxis for transportation. Years later, Mel told me that while he had been determined to escape New York because he felt trapped being in the city, he'd also hated the idea of working as a laborer on an oil rig.

We had no assurance of finding work in Tulsa. But if we were lucky enough to be hired by Sun Oil, I hoped they would put us on the same oil rig.

I had a vision that somewhere west of the Hudson River lay my future, and I was excited about the unknown that was ahead. My mother, on the other hand, was devastated. She would be living alone in the apartment and was concerned about paying the rent. Even under the existing rent control, it would be too expensive for her to manage. I reassured her that once I'd found work, I would send enough money home for her to continue to enjoy living in the apartment, close to her neighborhood friends. Besides, I told her, I was only planning to be gone for the summer. In her wisdom, however, my mother knew my adventuresome soul would get the better of me.

Mel and I began our journey in the early part of June and two days later arrived in Tulsa. We were told that "pro-rationing rules" were in effect, reducing drilling activities and the number of rigs operating in the area. I learned that with the oversupply, oil and gas production was scaled back, and so jobs were scarce. We had only the brief summer months to make some much-needed money, so we had to move on.

It was late in the day and we were exhausted. Unwilling to spend our meager savings on a motel room, we decided to drive to a neighborhood park and sleep in the car; in the morning, we would discuss our options. We were sound asleep when, shortly after midnight, a policeman tapped on the car window and told us to leave the park immediately or be hauled off to jail for vagrancy.

We left the park, then pulled over and flipped a coin to decide whether to go back to New York, as Mel wanted, or venture further west to Denver or Grand Junction, Colorado, as I wanted. We had heard there was a uranium boom going on and that people with geology knowledge were in great demand. I called heads and won. Mel grumbled, so I offered him the option of a Greyhound bus ride back to his parents' apartment in Manhattan. He agreed to continue on with me.

Job opportunities in Denver were no better than they had been in Tulsa, so once again we got back on the road. This time, though, as we pulled into Grand Junction we saw numerous drilling rigs and trucks filled with equipment. Every other vehicle seemed to be a vintage four-wheel-drive jeep hooked to the back of a pickup truck. Grand Junction was a wild frenzy of activity, similar to what California must have been like years earlier during the 1848 gold rush. Prospectors, geologists, and engineers were racing in and out of makeshift meeting rooms and assay offices. An array of cigar-smoking speculators wearing broad-brimmed cowboy hats filled hotel lobbies, restaurants were jam-packed, and living space was difficult to find.

The first company we visited immediately offered us jobs doing surveying and geology assessment work. They had set up a camp on claims staked out on the Colorado Plateau, some eighty miles southwest of Grand Junction. We were told food and supplies were provided along with a cook. With a map in hand, we were soon off the main highway following freshly cut jeep trails that headed south over some barely passable terrain. The camp had two sleeping tents, another one that housed the kitchen, and a latrine and shower a short distance behind. Joe the cook was a burly, tattooed soul who had lived a hard life and looked much older than his forty-five years.

On this rugged plateau, I taught Mel—the city boy who had never been behind the wheel of a car—how to drive a jeep. At first he had difficulty with his coordination, shifting and grinding through the gears. During our second session, his foot slipped off the clutch and he drove the jeep right through our tent and into the cook's refrigerator. Thirty feet or so more and he would have driven us into a steep ravine.

For the next four weeks, our assignment was to cut through the thick underbrush, establish survey lines for staking out additional claims, and record promising outcrops for future assessment work. We looked for signs of uranium mineralization in the vast Jurassic Morrison sandstone formation.

Cutting survey lines through the scrub oak and underbrush was difficult. We suffered massive numbers of insect bites over much of our bodies, causing severe swelling and fever. However, we believed the opportunity to put our geology knowledge to work—and our need for money—made it well worth the agony and pain. But after finishing our assignment, we realized we didn't like the boomtown atmosphere of Grand Junction. We decided to move on to Salt Lake City, known then as the Wall Street of uranium stocks, where numerous small exploration and mining companies sought to raise money.

Driving into Salt Lake City, I immediately fell in love with the beauty of the snow-capped Wasatch and Oquirrh mountain ranges and the high desert valley that nestled in between. The ever-present reflection from the sun on the expansive waters of the Great Salt Lake was breathtaking, as was the clear air. The temperature, although over 90°F, was bearable because of the area's low humidity. Most of the main streets in the downtown area were 132 feet wide, which in pioneer days provided a full turning radius for ox-drawn wagons. The streets were laid out in north-south and east-west grids; in ten-acre-square blocks, making it easy to get around.

With persecution and bigotry behind me, I felt I could have a new start here among strangers whose ancestors also had suffered from discrimination. Almost immediately I felt a certain comfort and knew this was the place where I would settle.

Mel decided to meet with the Utah Geological Survey and inquire about job openings. Their senior geologist, John Powers, eventually became our friend and advisor. I decided to visit the University of Utah campus and review their geology and mining curriculum. I enrolled in the autumn quarter at the university and, luckily, was able to transfer all my CCNY credits. I also changed my major from geology to the more specialized geological engineering. I had a burning desire to finish my education so that I could get on with the economic part of my life. Although this would require an additional two years to complete, I was certain I was making the right decision.

Back in New York, I had been on the CCNY wrestling team, in the 157-pound division. I reached the quarterfinals of the Amateur Athletic Union tournament before a wrestler from the U.S. Merchant Marine Academy used a double bar arm hold and pressed me into submission, fracturing my sternum. Joe Sapora, the CCNY coach from whom I'd learned the sport of many holds, was in his day a scrappy, nationally ranked 123-pound division champion. When I wrote to him about my intention to stay in Utah, he replied asking only two things of me: that I continue in wrestling and that I keep him informed of my success.

I met with Marv Hess, who had just taken over as the University of Utah wrestling coach. He was glad I could fill the open 157-pound slot. I hadn't wrestled or worked out since my sternum fracture. Now healed, though, I was anxious to get back into competition shape again, and at the same time find employment.

In the early 1950s, the uranium boom consumed the entire intermountain region, with Salt Lake City as its capital. Almost everyone I met wanted to strike it rich. They staked out claims in the hope of finding a uranium ore body and were enthralled by stories of people such as Charlie Steen, who'd found a multimillion-dollar deposit of high-grade uranium ore at his Mi Vida mine in the Lisbon Valley area, southeast of Moab, Utah. Many "would-be miners" let their work fall by the wayside as they chased the uranium rainbow.

Mel and I had no trouble finding work through the Bowman Brothers brokerage and investment firm. The Bowmans' brother-in-law, a geologist and engineer named Louis Reese, had just been in a serious automobile accident and would be laid up for several months. We visited him at the hospital and agreed to work on his current projects under a new entity we subsequently formed, called Geo-Consultants.

By 1954, more than eighty uranium companies were listed on the local Utah stock exchanges, all having raised money from the public to finance exploration and mining activities. Our assignments with some of these companies included geological research, ore sample analysis, field survey work, and writing reports on our findings. On occasion we engaged in some prospecting, staked claims, and did field assessments.

Uranium, a very dense metal, occurs abundantly around the world in different geologic formations, including igneous, hydrothermal, and sedimentary deposits. In sandstone formations, uranium deposits occur in the medium- to coarse-grained sediments laid down in a marine environment, with clay areas interbedded therein.

Lenses of uranium minerals result from the precipitation of oxidized groundwater that leaches uranium from surface rocks, then flows into the more permeable sandstone. These mineralized lenses tend also to be rich in organic and carbonaceous material from plants, trees, and even marine algae.

Sandstone deposits account for roughly 18 percent of the world's uranium sources. Depending upon the price of uranium, some ore bodies, with a grade as low as 0.05 to 0.4 percent, can be mined profitably. Individual ore bodies can be as small as 30,000–50,000 tons and still be profitable. The Colorado Plateau, where we were heading, remains one of three major sandstone formation regions in the United States where uranium occurs in abundance.

We spent much of our time in the La Sal Mountains, Lisbon Valley, White Canyon, Henry Mountains, and San Rafael Swell areas of the Colorado Plateau. We also ventured into some of the less accessible canyon areas along the Colorado River in southeast Utah.

The "muddy," as the river was fondly nicknamed, meandered through the high walls of canyons sculpted by millions of years of water and wind erosion. Here, the river spilled its muddy contents on the banks as it rippled (or, during runoff periods, rushed) over boulders and native flora—a breathtaking sight.

Exploring the uraniferous sandstone beds within the Morrison formation on the Colorado Plateau was a massive undertaking. This was the sandstone formation overlying the majestic vermilion Wingate cliffs that overlook the Colorado River in the Grand Canyon and its tributary canyons. We looked for radioactivity and mineralization within the exposed lower seams of impermeable shale and mudstone, interbedded between sedimentary deposits; this added to the challenge of exploration.

Many years later, I still have fond memories of the wildlife—the elk, deer, bighorn sheep, coyote, fox, and bobcat—that surprised us on several occasions. Along the river bends were log dams (which produced great swimming holes) and an occasional river otter that I mistook for a beaver. Once, on a nearby ridge, a black bear appeared.

I realize how fortunate I was to have been in the Grand Canyon mere years before the Glen Canyon Dam construction project got under way in 1956. The dam covered up much of the beauty seen by geologist and explorer John Wesley Powell, a U.S. Army major who mapped the region in 1869 and 1872, long before the thirst for uranium existed. I caught a glimpse of what now is submerged.

Much of the ecosystem has changed forever. Native plants have disappeared. Fish species unable to survive with the water temperature change are gone. Many birds have been lost from these breeding grounds. And contamination of the lake caused by recreational use will continue to further diminish the ecosystem. Geologically, many naturally eroded features such as bridges and arches are entombed below the water, as are numerous Native American archaeological sites and petroglyphs depicting early human history.

What I miss most is the notable Hite Ferry, operated by its originator, Arthur Chaffin. I remember taking this water crossing between the banks of a narrow part of the Colorado River on a number of occasions when I was traveling to Hanksville and Blanding, Utah. The rough, primitive dirt road (now Utah Highway 95) could be life-threatening during the rains because of the potential for flash floods. A great reprieve was the Chaffin house, on the lush shores of the river with its adjacent gardens, an oasis filled with fruit trees and a prolific melon patch.

The ferry, connected to a suspended steel cable, was powered by an old Ford car. In October 1956, the ferry was doomed when construction began on the Glen Canyon Dam. Its last crossing took place on June 5, 1964.

With a radiation detection scintillometer (or Geiger counter) in one hand and a pickaxe in the other, Mel and I explored the Jurassic Salt Wash member of the Morrison sandstone formation. We looked for radioactive uranium mineralization. We also trekked down to the river to explore the underlying Triassic Chinle and Shinarump coarse-grained sandstone sediments. We spent many days in the blistering heat looking for "hot spots" along these massive sedimentary formations.

With the uranium boom in full swing, it was difficult to find any Willys four-wheel-drive jeeps, Dodge 6×6 Power Wagons, or International 4×4 trucks, which were the primary off-road vehicles used at the time. Since his pickup truck had been destroyed in the accident, Louis Reese arranged to let us use a two-wheel-drive 1950 Ford coupe. We knew we could not venture too far off the more solid desert roads with this light vehicle for fear of being stuck in a sandy wash. To reach some of our exploration sites, we resorted to walking many miles carrying all our gear.

On one trip, we went to the San Rafael Swell, forty miles southwest of the town of Green River, Utah. The Swell is a huge oval-shaped formation uplifted on end, exposing millions of years' worth of compressed sediments, and it had some known radioactive mineralization. This area, isolated and difficult to reach, was where experienced geologist and prospector Vernon Pick developed the successful Delta Uranium mine.

With desert temperatures during the day reaching over 100°F in the blazing sun, it didn't take long to fry an egg on the hood of the car. Water was so scarce that we needed to bring several large canvas bags filled with this precious commodity. Usually people hung filled water bags over the front of their vehicle's radiator so that the air flowing around the bags would keep the car running cooler and prevent overheating.

Mel and I took enough equipment and supplies for each day's reconnaissance trip. Our plan was to gather some samples from each area of interest for an assay analysis; if our findings warranted it, we would return again for a longer period. One day we spread out the map and zeroed in on a location we wanted to explore, about five miles into the Swell. We didn't know how many samples we would need to gather, so to save time we decided to take a chance on driving the Ford up a dry wash that appeared solid.

Mel walked ahead of the car, checking for soft sandy areas for me to avoid. When we were halfway up the wash, the hardpan surface broke under a back wheel while I was shifting gears. Soon the Ford was buried up to its axles. For hours we tried but failed to dislodge the coupe. We then realized our focus needed to be on our survival rather than uranium samples.

We agreed to wait until nightfall and cooler temperatures before attempting to walk out to the main highway by following a one-lane dirt road called Highway 24. Farmers, ranchers, miners, and prospectors traveled on this road between Green River and the small town of Hanksville near the Henry Mountains, some thirty miles south of where we were. We were hoping we would meet one of these travelers.

We were down to two water-filled canvas bags, and our remaining food supply equaled a meager two candy bars apiece. With the moonlight to show us the way, we walked until about four in the morning, when our legs and our water supply gave out. Suddenly a strong desert wind came up, blowing sand in our direction. Speculating that we had covered fifteen to eighteen miles, a distance less than halfway to the main highway, we took refuge behind a rock and dozed until sunrise.

As the heat of the day started to beat on us again, panic set in. We were now without water or food, and becoming weak and disoriented. Talking to each other to stay awake and shore up our confidence, we went on for another four hours. The temperature rose to 100°F, and soon we were parched, our bodies so dry we didn't perspire anymore. Like Mel, I found that my tongue was stuck to the roof of my mouth and my lips were glued shut. We quit talking and just focused on putting one foot in front of the other.

Along the dirt road in front of us, the hot air rising from the desert floor made it look like there was a lake ahead of us, which we knew did not exist. It was a mirage. Eventually we saw what we first thought was another mirage, of something floating on the lake, but this one seemed to move closer toward us. As a cloud of dust cut through the lake, we realized it wasn't a mirage. As it drew closer I recognized the apparition as a Dodge 6×6 Power Wagon. We were so weak we could not get out of its path. Fortunately, the truck screeched to a halt in front of us and two hardy-looking farmers clad in overalls stepped out of the vehicle.

I could barely open my mouth to ask for water. When I finally did, they chuckled and said they only had beer. I murmured that any liquid would do. After two cans of the brew, Mel and I were loopy but alive, and explained our plight. The pair turned out to be prospectors from Wellington, Utah, who were heading to an area south of the Henry Mountains. They agreed to rescue the Ford coupe, and we agreed to help them with two days' worth of geology and survey work on their staked claims before returning to Salt Lake City.

We never did get back to this isolated area in the San Rafael Swell to explore the potentially radioactive hot spot, and we never did find out if the old-timers who saved our lives ever struck it rich. But after our harrowing experience, Mel decided to take a job with the Atomic Energy Commission in the small southern Utah town of St. George. He transferred to Spokane, Washington, several years later but eventually returned to Salt Lake City, where he built a successful oil and gas leasing business.

Over the next two years, I continued my studies at the University of Utah and participated in several wrestling events within the region. One day, while I was working out in the gym, located under the dance studio, two young, fit women wearing leotards ventured in and asked for my help: they wanted me to lift women in their modern-dance routines. I agreed, and after learning that some of their stretching exercises could help limber me up for wrestling matches, I began joining the class on a regular basis. Shirley Ririe and Joan Woodbury, the dance instructors, were always encouraging, and later formed the successful Ririe-Woodbury Dance Company; we became lifelong friends.

Along with my activities on campus, I also worked on a number of geology projects to earn money. In several of my geology classes was another student named Jim Anderson, who had grown up in the historic mining town of Eureka, Utah. Jim was the most organized student I knew: he made copious notes in class and typed them after school. We often studied together, and he would share his notes when I couldn't get back in time from a geology field trip and missed a class.

Jim went on to work for Bear Creek Exploration, a division of Kennecott Copper, and later became a close confidant of Armand Hammer of Occidental Minerals. Jim eventually moved into the post of vice president of exploration for the Homestake Mining Company. He too became a lifelong friend and, after his retirement from the mining business, joined JP Realty Inc. as a board member.

From 1955 through 1956, over long weekends, school breaks, and holidays, I worked for a Canadian company exploring for uranium and other precious metals in the vast expanses of the Lac La Ronge region in northern Saskatchewan. I spent time with the native Cree Indians, who in their motor-powered canoes guided me through the vast stretches of lakes. We would fly into these areas on a Cessna aircraft outfitted with pontoons in the summer; in the winter we'd change to metal skis to land on the frozen lakes and then use sleds to move around our equipment. John Bird and his fellow tribe members aided in the logistics and exploration since they knew the area well.

Although I discovered a number of radioactive outcrops and some signs of copper mineralization while exploring the surface of the landmasses, there was not enough evidence that mining in the area could be economically feasible. The short prospecting season on these low-lying islands surrounded by massive waterways made prospecting a difficult task, especially during the long, harsh winter months. Any mining operation also would be a challenge.

On three occasions flying around the region, we had close calls. Once the plane was overloaded; we took off downwind and barely missed the pine trees at the end of the runway. Another time, while flying in a snowstorm, the pilot got vertigo. Luckily, he was able to turn around, find a break in the cloud cover, and land safely back at Lac La Ronge.

The third incident occurred while taking off from the Winnipeg River in a new Cessna aircraft that just had its pontoons installed. Once we were airborne, the pilot discovered the torpedo tube was plugged with a bees' nest, which caused the airspeed indicator to malfunction. The pilot was forced to attempt a precarious landing on the river; he narrowly missed power lines and a bridge structure. Eventually it became too difficult to commute to northern Saskatchewan on a regular basis, so I had to give it up.

I was then asked to do exploration work on some claims the same Canadian company had acquired in the Henry Mountains in southeastern Utah. Several mineralized outcrops looked promising; the radioactivity was quite high. By early summer 1956, we'd started drilling and blasting into the mountainside. We followed a small vein of pitchblende with the hope of finding a larger uranium ore body. We employed six miners throughout the summer and each day went deeper into the mountain.

On one site trip, I invited a young woman I had been dating to come along with me. Marcia Poulsen was curious about my geology work and uranium exploration. On this occasion, I carried two boxes of dynamite in the trunk of the car and stowed a box of blasting caps in the glove box, next to the radio. As we drove, Marcia tried to turn on the radio, and I would immediately but politely turn it off. This went on throughout the entire trip, and she found it strange. When we finally arrived, I shared my fears with her: I thought that if the radio stayed on, it might overheat the dash area, detonate the caps in the glove compartment, and set off the dynamite in the trunk. That was the beginning of our romance.

I met Marcia in 1955 quite literally by accident at the local Spudnut coffee shop, located near the university. One day we both rushed into the crowded coffee shop and collided by a stool at the counter. Two days later, we ran into each other again at the same stool; this time she was knocked to the floor. As I pulled her up, a mutual friend, Barbara Finkelstein, introduced us.

Marcia and I were both attending the University of Utah at the time, and we dated for almost two years before marrying on August 17, 1957. I had graduated in June 1956 with a degree in geological engineering, and in 1957 Marcia graduated with a bachelor of arts degree. While Marcia was busy planning for the wedding, she continued to work at Universal Travel Agency, and I went on doing geology and exploration work for the Canadian company.

Marcia and I honeymooned in sunny Pismo Beach, California. On the second day, I became severely sunburned, and we decided to return home so I could

3.3. Marcia and John's wedding, held at the Art Barn in Salt Lake City, August 17, 1957.

recuperate. While loading up the car, Marcia accidentally left the car keys in the trunk of our 1956 Cadillac convertible. Thankfully, Marcia had a small frame and could slide into the dark trunk through the area behind the backseat. I held on to her toes while she rummaged through the luggage in search of the keys. Ten minutes later she emerged, almost faint for lack of air, but with keys in hand.

After we returned home, I began thinking about making a career change, so that I would not have to stay away for extended periods of time on geology exploration work. I had been talking to a local real estate agent about building some new homes in the Salt Lake City area, a job that would draw on my drafting skills and engineering background. I called my employer in Canada and told him of my plan to go into the construction business. He understood and wished me well as I ventured forward.

Since arriving in America in 1940, my mother had rarely left New York City except to travel occasionally to the resorts in the nearby Catskill Mountains. When she came to the wedding, that was the third time we had seen each other in three years—and it was a cultural shock for her. After all, back then New York City had a population of 7.8 million, while Salt Lake City's barely topped 200,000. My mother was definitely an East Coast person who enjoyed having coffee with her friends at the local café, walking to the neighborhood grocery store, and dining out at a variety of restaurants. She especially liked to ride the subway into Manhattan and visit museums, go to the theater, and shop for discounts. Like I said, she would never pay retail.

My mother had become a strong person, able to survive almost any situation. She was a sensible woman, and her resilience in the face of adversity had always been her defining feature. I knew she had a support network of close friends, but I also worried about her being alone without her children living near her. My worries eased when on October 21, 1960, she married Henry Kalb, a widower whom she'd met through friends. Henry, like our family, had escaped the Holocaust; he had initially settled in Argentina, then eventually moved to New York. Henry and my mother were married for seventeen years, until his death in November 1977.

As my business ventures became more successful, Marcia and I visited with my mother more often. Later, when I was into running and entered marathons in New York City and a triathlon in Hawaii, Mother would be found patiently waiting at the finish line regardless of the time or weather. As our children grew, each one had a chance to take in their grandmother's New York, including her kosher cooking—to this day, her recipes for matzo ball soup and cheesecake remain a hit. In the early 1980s, I purchased a condominium at the Essex House on Central Park South in New York so that we would be able to spend more time with her. Although she said she enjoyed the time spent with us in Utah, Salt Lake City was just too small for her, and oh, how she missed New York.

In late February 1983, only weeks after her surprise eightieth birthday party on January 27, while vacationing at our condominium in Coronado, California, my mother suffered a stroke. Though imprisoned in a weakened body, her mind was still alert at times, but she was not in charge anymore. It was a blessing for her when she died on March 12, 1989.

⟨ IV ⟩

A Half-Century of Endeavors

It is not the critic who counts: not the man who points out how the strong man stumbles
or where the doer of deeds could have done better. The credit belongs to the man who is
actually in the arena, whose face is marred by dust and sweat and blood, who strives
valiantly, who errs and comes up short again and again, because there is no effort without
error or shortcoming, but who knows the great enthusiasms, the great devotions, who
spends himself for a worthy cause: who at best knows in the end, the triumph of high
achievement, and who, at the worst, if he fails, at least he fails while daring greatly,
so that his place shall never be with those cold and timid souls who know neither
victory nor defeat.

—Theodore Roosevelt, twenty-sixth President of the United States

Reading the Tea Leaves

Reflecting on the early days of my forty-five-year business career, when I sometimes struggled to meet the payroll, I remember those challenges as most rewarding. Seeing buildings come to life was exhilarating; the many sleepless nights spent reviewing new projects were exciting. Even the various economic recessions that occurred along the way did not deter my enthusiasm. From the very first, my attitude in business was always that my cup was half full, not half empty. No matter how complicated the task, I never gave up. Business was—and is—my passion.

I began my business in the autumn of 1957. I rented a one-room office during the day. In the corner of the room stood an Addressograph machine—a steel frame with an integrated keyboard used for stamping out address plates for labeling. For a few hours at night, a local retailer named Mr. Freshman would use the machine to label his invoices. This was fine with me. I would return around midnight, long after he was gone, and work until late the next afternoon. To have an office—which included lights, heat, and a telephone—to hold meetings was well worth the $15 a month.

54

At the time, we lived in a remodeled house with four apartments at 368 University Street, adjacent to the University of Utah campus. I managed the building for a reduction in rent and became friends with Don Draper, a local real estate broker who represented the apartment house owner. On several occasions, Don and I talked about building some homes on the upper north bench of the Avenues area in Salt Lake City. Don convinced me there was a market for quality homes in the subdivision he was promoting and that he could arrange financing for the construction with the local Prudential Federal Savings and Loan Association. Agreeing to build homes in time for a grand opening the following Labor Day, I purchased three lots and thus began J. Price Construction Company. Marcia continued to work at the Universal Travel Agency and in the evenings helped me process payables, invoices, and statements and also typed correspondence for my fledgling business. What I did not realize was that I had picked a difficult time to get started in the construction business: the economy had begun to spiral into a major recession.

My three homes and several others built on speculation in the Avenues subdivision did not sell for more than a year after completion, causing a lot of stress. I reduced the prices of the homes just to get out from under the mortgage. Even then, I still owed Prudential Federal Savings and Loan Association money that the sales didn't cover, which I paid back over time. I was lucky. So was another contractor, Dale Dearden, who also built two homes in the subdivision and suffered a similar fate. This experience could have had a more disastrous ending—bankruptcy.

The same year, I decided to run for the Salt Lake City Commission. Ever since arriving in Salt Lake City just a few years earlier, I had believed the city needed more diversity—fresh blood, broader thinking—in its government. Although my finances were limited, several friends persuaded me to run for election. With their zealous support, they introduced me to other like-minded individuals who helped raise enough money for me to make it through the primary and into a runoff for the two city commission seats up for election. Unable to raise adequate funding for media advertising, posters, and literature to distribute door-to-door, I was defeated by Ted Guerts for one of the seats by less than three thousand votes. The incumbent, Joe Christensen, won the other seat. Running in the odd years is difficult: turnouts are low and generally dominated by city employees, vendors, and political allies committed to help incumbents. I believe disinterest and voter apathy added to my defeat.

Despite the defeat I had garnered some name recognition, and in the fall of 1958 I ran for the Utah House of Representatives as the Democratic challenger in my district against the Republican incumbent, Ralph Sheffield. Representatives work part-time and are in session for a forty-five-day period during January and February, and sometimes into March, which I felt would not conflict with other business ventures. I was not able to beat Sheffield, who recruited his beautiful daughter and her many friends to distribute literature in the neighborhood and help solicit votes on Election Day. My one-man campaign proved futile, but I lost by less than one hundred votes.

I considered next a run for Salt Lake County Surveyor, but decided it would be a full-time position, which would conflict with my construction business. By then I also had realized that politics was not really the direction I wanted to go in as a career path.

When I'd relocated to Utah in 1954, I'd forwarded my new address to the local Selective Service System board in New York. I heard nothing back until early 1958, at which time I was asked to report to the local military processing center. I was concerned about being newly wed, just starting a business, and involved in a political race. With all these balls in the air, my "nervous stomach"—a condition diagnosed when I was a child—acted up. In pain, I went to see my friend and doctor, Stanley Altman, whose diagnosis was a bleeding duodenal ulcer. Stan surmised it might be stress-related and immediately put me on a bland food diet and medication; he also recommended I cut back on my activities.

Within weeks, my official notice came for a military examination. A head-to-toe exam also concluded I was color-blind and had flat feet, so on December 5, 1958, I was classified 4-F (not meeting the standards for physical fitness), but kept on reserve status. When my children were born, I was thankful I was not called up to serve in the Vietnam War. I would serve my country in other ways.

Dale Dearden and I worked well together and had teamed up to form Dearden & Price Construction Company. Dale was an excellent craftsman who knew construction well. Our first commercial contract award was for a new Salt Lake County fire station; our second was to remodel a local mortuary; and our third was to build a retail grocery store for the small Valley Foods chain. Dale also had a burning passion for flying. Since we were a new business and didn't always have enough money to draw a salary, Dale supplemented his income by piloting aircraft for a local fixed base operator.

In the meantime, one day Dale laid out a business plan to charter a World War II–era C-47 and, several times a week, ferry baby calves from California to Utah for summer grazing in Heber Valley. A rancher had approached him with this idea. Traditional long-distance highway travel was problematic: many young calves were crushed or, at the very least, exhausted from enduring the extreme heat. Dale and the rancher believed transporting calves by air was safe and cost-effective, and somewhat reluctantly I agreed to lend a hand, since the extra money would be helpful to us.

On our maiden voyage, we carefully strapped in place fifty calves, standing them up sideways, alternating head to tail. It was a nice spring day. The winds were calm. As the plane lumbered toward Utah, though, we ran into blustery weather and the C-47 became unstable. The plane began to roll from side to side as the calves rocked back and forth in unison. One calf after the other got airsick. By the time we landed in Salt Lake City, they were all ill, crying profusely and throwing up. Sadly, several did not survive the trip.

Neither of us had the energy to clean up the mess on board after unloading the calves. Instead we decided to wait until the following day—which proved to be a big mistake. Twenty-four hours later, everything eliminated by the calves was solidly encrusted on the metal surfaces. Normal hosing down with hot water didn't budge the mess. It took us almost an entire day, on our hands and knees and using scrapers, before the plane was clean again, though the smell lingered on. That was my first and last time in the cattle shipping business, and my first attempt at diversification.

By now, we had also outgrown our small downtown office and purchased an office and construction yard on Haven Avenue in South Salt Lake. Two companies had failed there before, but we felt that as the third to occupy the space, we would be "charmed."

Although our construction business started to prosper, Dale's heart was in aviation. In 1960 we divided up our business assets and parted company, and I continued to operate the business, now known as John Price Associates, Inc. (JPA). I was fortunate that a key member of our staff, construction foreman Ken Hollingsworth, had decided to stay on with me; he would head up our field operations for the next twenty-five years. Ken's knowledge, tenacity, and ability to plan and lead made it easier to share field responsibilities, and allowed me the time to handle sales and other business matters. Ken grew up in a construction family. His father and brother were carpenters and cement finishers; they would come on board when we needed their help. Another key figure in the company was Carl Olson, who also would stay with us for twenty-five years; his construction and estimating ability helped keep projects within budget.

Right from the start, I never had a dull moment. On typical days, I would spend mornings reviewing the work with the crew at the construction sites; three times a week, though, armed with coffee and doughnuts, I would start at five o'clock in the morning and meet with architects and engineers to review project issues. Afternoons I spent with clients reviewing their project status; at times I would return to the construction sites late in the day to check on major events such as concrete placement or steel erection. Several days a week, I would also work on new proposals. On weekends, I revisited project sites to review the week's progress and the workmanship without any distractions; sometimes my son Steven would accompany me, because at five years old, he enjoyed the tractors and other four-wheeled equipment.

Superintendents, subcontractors, architects, and engineers soon knew who was calling them at all hours of the day and night. Even in the dead of winter, I would get up in the middle of the night to check that projects were protected against rain, snow, and frost, and that roofs and walls were properly braced to prevent wind damage.

In general, I took catnaps and never slept more than three hours a night and hence gained more than thirty-five hours a week of extra work time. Over my entire career, I am certain, I added more than ten years to my productive business life. And often the early bird got the worm.

It was a great learning experience for me to work directly with my clients, the innovators of their varied businesses. Along the way, I acquired several industry mentors who showed faith in the ability of this thirty-year-old to handle design-build projects. Vin Carver of Litton Industries gave me the first break when he hired me to build a state-of-the-art manufacturing plant for military navigational and guidance systems. Mac Duncan, a former Pepsi Cola Company executive and then franchisee, allowed me to be creative in building a soft drink bottling plant. Hard-charging taskmaster Tex Boynton walked me through the competitive business needs for an Avis car rental agency and his Yellow Cab operations center. Deseret Pharmaceutical Company's Dale Ballard and Vic Cartwright, two ingenious inventors and marketers of disposable medical devices, trusted me to build a "clean room" environment assembly plant for them.

Maury Yates, a friend and investor, offered me the opportunity to design a new-concept business park with multiple tenants. Paul Cox and his partners allowed me the freedom to design their book printing, binding, and distribution operation. Keith Knight, a fatherly type and successful local real estate broker, taught me the nuances of ownership and leasing of commercial buildings.

Herman Franks, a crusty individual whose bark was bigger than his bite, had a great heart and liked helping young entrepreneurs. He was a partner in the Valley Foods stores operation, for which I built several stores. Herman, a baseball legend, was ninety-five years old when he died on March 30, 2009. He had introduced me to other luminaries of the sport, including Pee Wee Reese, Alvin Dark, Stan Musial, Bob Kennedy, and Willie Mays, who became investors in some of my real estate projects.

In 1959, business acquaintance Sam Souvall introduced me to Warren McCain, the merchandising manager for Albertsons' food stores. Through him I met Joe Albertson in Boise, Idaho, which led to a telephone call from Clix Cannon, who handled site acquisition and property development for Albertsons in Utah—and to an opportunity to build a store at their new 3300 South location in Salt Lake City. Twelve years earlier, there had been six stores in the Albertsons chain; by 1962, the chain included one hundred stores in Idaho, Washington, Utah, Oregon, Montana and Wyoming. Over the years, we built a number of Albertsons stores in several states. My relationship with Albertsons continued for years under CEOs Warren McCain and Gary Michael.

In 1960, I met Maurice Warshaw, a remarkable man who influenced me greatly and in many ways reminded me of my father. After surviving the Kishinev pogrom of 1903, during the onset of the Russo-Japanese War (1904-1905), in which Jews suffered great persecution, the young Maurice, his stepmother, and siblings hid for seventeen days in a friend's basement before they made their escape from Kishinev to Poland and then Bremen, Germany, where they gained passage in steerage on the S.S. *Bremen* for the nineteen-day journey to America. As soon as Maurice's family was processed through Ellis Island, they boarded a train at Grand Central Station, where the size and bustle overwhelmed the young boy, and headed for Philadelphia to reunite with Maurice's father and a brother who had fled earlier.

When he was fourteen years old, Maurice headed west with family members to take part in a newly organized Jewish agricultural colony called Clarion, located near Gunnison, Utah. He quickly discovered farming was not his forte and relocated to Salt Lake City, where he and his father eked out a living during the Depression years by peddling merchandise and produce. When his stepmother died and his father moved to Cleveland, Maurice remained in Salt Lake City and soon opened a produce and variety stand on Ninth South and Main Street and named it Grand Central Market—a flashback to his first days in this country. Volume, variety, and low pricing gained him wide customer acceptance. Word spread quickly, and many traveled from distant areas to make their purchases. Mabel Poulsen, Marcia's mother, worked for Maurice in the early days and recalled how focused he was: a fair merchant always offering deals to capture more of the market. Our paths, though years apart, were parallel—the persecution of Jews continued unabated from his generation to mine.

Maurice gave me the opportunity to build a number of retail stores, two distribution centers, and their office and warehouse building. This growing mass merchandiser was a family affair that included son Keith Warshaw and sons-in-law Don Mackey and Tom Panos, who together headed up the merchandising team. Our nineteen-year friendship ended suddenly when Maurice died on January 5, 1979, which left me devastated. Grand Central was acquired in 1984 by the Fred Meyer chain.

In the early 1960s, I met Sam Skaggs, who at the time had three small family-run drugstores. Over the years I built a number of buildings for Sam, who exemplified family traditions and the early pioneer spirit in retail merchandising, and

4.1. Maurice and Inez Warshaw with Marcia and John, 1970.

subsequently built the Skaggs Drug Centers chain. We had become friends, and I wanted to continue our association as they expanded their operations. However, I made the mistake of placing a competitor on a property adjacent to a new Skaggs store I had recently built. To my dismay, I lost all future business with Sam. Eventually Skaggs became an industry giant and in 1979 took control of American Stores, which in 1999 was merged with Albertsons.

Dee Smith, the founder of Smith's Food and Drug, was another mentor. I first met Dee in his Brigham City, Utah, store. He was stocking the shelves with products at the time and could only spare a few minutes to listen to my pitch. I later built Dee's third retail store in the chain, followed by many more over the years. After Dee's untimely death in 1985, his sons Jeff, Richie, and Fred took over with the help of Allen Martindale, who had run the Arden-Mayfair food chain in California. Together, the Smith brothers and Martindale built a vast empire of stores that in 1997 merged with Fred Meyer and in 1999 the Kroger Company. Allen Martindale eventually became a board member of J.P. Realty Inc.

As my company's reputation for performance, workmanship, and competitive pricing spread, new doors opened and we moved into a larger office space. Most clients preferred to focus on their own business rather than the details of construction, so they liked our turnkey construction approach, which combined the engineering, architecture, and construction phases.

As companies and their suppliers in the region expanded, so did their need for office, warehouse, and manufacturing space. JPA broadened its operations into the commercial and industrial design-build area for them. I developed the concept-to-completion paradigm, which at first was not warmly received by the construction industry. We consistently beat the competition, which infuriated construction companies, architectural firms, and real estate brokers who had control over this industry for many years in Utah.

By the early 1970s, I was building retail shopping centers and industrial complexes throughout the intermountain region. Most competitors soon felt comfortable implementing this paradigm, which in the private sector changed how business was done.

When the country suffered another major recession, financing became difficult and I struggled for more than two years. Profits were slim, yet with tight controls JPA's net worth started slowly to grow. As the chain stores expanded, so did their need for cash infusion into their own operations. This opened the opportunity to develop, build, lease, and manage shopping centers with retail grocery and drugstore operators becoming the anchor tenants.

The concept-to-completion program caught on even with government agencies. Eventually I convinced the State of Utah to let me undertake the new Symphony Hall, Art Center, and Capitol Theater restoration projects under a model called construction management—an approach that was new at the time in the country for public works. I guaranteed the cost of construction and hence had control over the design, materials, and architect's concept. In addition to JPA handling the construction phases, I formed the development and ownership entity Price Rentals Inc. in 1972; by 1977, it had grown into Price Development Company (PDC). Development, design, construction, management, and ownership became our hallmark. One opportunity led to another until we became one of the dominant retail and industrial builders and developers in the intermountain and western regions, marketing the integrated building concept. Although I am proud of that achievement, the model was emulated by many competitors and created more competition for me.

In the early 1960s, when I seized upon the idea of vertical integration in the construction industry, my goal was to own an interest in some of the subcontractors and suppliers I employed so I could share in the profits generated from the construction opportunities I created. My first such venture was with John Yates, a successful electrical subcontractor. I helped finance his business and, in turn, took an ownership position. He introduced me to two electrical salesmen, Cal Maughn and Ron Holt, who worked with the Mine and Smelter Supply Company. In 1962, the four of us started Calron Electric Supply Company. The ensuing recession of the early 1970s and mounting competition severely affected these businesses. Many of their receivable accounts became delinquent, some turning into bankruptcies. In 1975, I decided to exit both electrical business investments and turned over my ownership to the others involved. I hoped they could survive the difficult times ahead. Unfortunately, Calron Electric Supply Company closed shortly thereafter.

At the time, I had not met Calron's young star sales performer, Dale Holt, who was the son of a partner. Striking out on his own that year, Dale formed a new entity called Codale Electrical Supply Inc. Within a few short months, the economy started to recover, and he began to make a profit. Thirty-five years later, Dale continues to have one of the largest and most successful electrical supply businesses in the western United States and has never had a "loss year," so he has told me.

Another foray into the construction supply business was the Utah Sand and Gravel Company, one of the early successful concrete ready-mix suppliers in the Utah Valley. I acquired a stock interest buying shares on the open market and amassed a sizable block. I considered a buyout plan and met with the company's management but could not get enough stock ownership to accomplish this goal at the time. Later, a San Francisco investment group purchased shares and made an offer to management they could not refuse. I sold my shares to this group at a nice profit and moved on to other prospective opportunities.

In 1967, the Salt Lake Hardware Company (SLH) received a tender offer from Anderson Hardware, a large wholesale distributor located in California. Since the late 1800s, Salt Lake Hardware had been a Utah wholesale landmark. It was well known throughout the intermountain region as the premier distributor of hardware, structural steel, non-ferrous metals, plumbing supplies, electrical supplies, lawn and garden equipment, and more.

SLH was also recognized for its vast inventory of some forty thousand items, each one listed in catalogs that weighed more than fifty pounds and were carried everywhere by company salesmen. But around this time, the wholesale supply business throughout the country was being changed by retailing visionaries, including Sam Walton, Fred Meyer, Maurice Warshaw, Sol Price and other discounters and mass merchandisers. Their mantra was to undo traditional shopping habits and offer everyday low prices to the consumer. They were rapidly altering the buying habits of customers by attracting them to their new low-cost, large-selection store operations. To stock their shelves, they bypassed the wholesaler-middleman and purchased their goods directly from the manufacturer. This put the squeeze on Salt Lake Hardware, whose shares were already languishing because of marginal earnings.

One snowy Sunday morning I was reading the *Salt Lake Tribune* and noticed the tender offer by Anderson Hardware to the Salt Lake Hardware shareholders for $24.50 a share, provided they could buy enough shares to take over control. Their newspaper solicitation intrigued me. I saw this as an opportunity to make a small profit, and offered $25 a share for any shares tendered to me by the shareholders. I believed I could sell the shares acquired to the successful buyer. I arranged for a small loan at Valley State Bank, thinking I might end up with as much as twenty thousand shares. After the deadline of the tender offer passed, I was shocked to learn that enough shares had come my way to give me control of Salt Lake Hardware and its wholly owned subsidiary Strevell-Patterson Hardware.

As the shares came into the bank for payment, I received an urgent phone call from the bank vice president, Fred Stringham. He wondered how I was going to pay for the large number of shares, since the amount was substantially above the modest line of credit the bank had given me.

I told Fred, "I suppose we have a problem." He replied, "We?" And I responded, "Yes, we!" That was the beginning of a long and successful business relationship with Valley State Bank, which did help fund the SLH stock purchase and, eventually, the takeover of this 100-year-old institution.

I joined hands with Ed Parsons, an investment banker from Cleveland, Ohio, who had purchased friendly shares on the open market as an investment, which together gave us absolute control. Ed later provided financing so I could pay off Valley State Bank. Once I did, I purchased Ed's shares, which increased my ownership stake. I then made a deal to trade the SLH shares owned by the company's president, Howard Price (no relation), for the subsidiary Turf Equipment Company, a distributor of the Toro line of industrial equipment. This solved a contentious issue in my plan for going forward as I took control of SLH.

I became president of the company in December 1969, and for a number of months I struggled with management, which was out of touch with the new business paradigm of discounters and mass merchandisers. They could not accept the fact that the distribution business had become a dinosaur. It was a shock for them to hear we needed to quickly change the way we did business or we would find ourselves liquidating the entire company in a few years.

In the building itself, half a floor was filled with bookkeepers, many of whom worked with comptometers and an archaic bookkeeping system. Management had given up on early efforts to modernize the company with the new IBM computer, which at the time used a punch card system. They didn't have faith in the mainframe's high-speed processing ability. Looking down the long row of accounting people wearing plastic shirt sleeve protectors held up with rubber bands and green visors, I was taken back to the Gatsby era of the 1920s. Yet this was 1969.

The Salt Lake Hardware building was five stories high, with nearly 40,000 square feet of inventory on each floor! I couldn't believe how much money was tied up in inventory just because management thought it had to carry everything listed in their catalogs. Some inventory items sold only one or two a year, such as the six heavy, bulky cement mixers stored out of the way on the fifth floor and covered with cobwebs.

Many nights I wondered what I had gotten myself into; however, the worst part of this acquisition still lay ahead. Shortly after I took over as president of the company, I received a phone call from Harold Steele, vice president of First Security Bank of Utah: SLH had an outstanding loan of almost $3 million due in ninety days. Not knowing me at the time, Steele thought I was going to raid the company's assets, and he suggested we pay off the loan immediately. I tried to convince him to extend the loan for six months, which would allow us time to liquidate some of the slow-moving inventory in an orderly way. He said he would talk with the bank's loan committee and get back to me.

I then set up an appointment to get acquainted with Udell Curry, the president of the Strevell-Patterson (SP) subsidiary. In our first meeting, he made it clear he wanted to separate SP from SLH. He was positioning himself to buy SP and made a lowball offer. He added because of the overlapping market, these companies might be investigated and an antitrust lawsuit filed against the parent, SLH, a suggestion that was most disturbing. Although both operations had been owned by the same shareholders for many years, they were independent and competed against each other in the marketplace. Because SLH was under new ownership, he was trying to buy the SP franchise on the cheap! When I didn't buckle, he used the company's resources to institute a lawsuit in federal court against Salt Lake Hardware Company, and convinced the presiding judge, Sherman Christensen, to hand down a ruling noting that the potential existed for monopolistic practices, and ordering Salt Lake Hardware to divest itself of Strevell-Patterson Hardware.

I met again with Curry to see if a fair purchase price could be reached, for the benefit of the shareholders. He returned with another lowball offer, which I rejected. If we had to sell this subsidiary, I was determined to maximize shareholder value and get the highest price, so that we could pay back the outstanding loan.

I immediately went to seek advice from a good friend, client, and mentor, Al Smith, the president of the Utah Wholesale Grocery Company. Al expressed an interest in the acquisition of Strevell-Patterson Hardware. He thought it might be a good fit for his wholesale foods and dry-goods operation. After several negotiating sessions, Al agreed to pay a fair price for the inventory and the company's goodwill, offering slightly more than the book value. The purchase price would help to substantially reduce the bank loan. I smiled, thinking how Harold would be surprised when I walked in with a check to pay down the loan after having just received an extension. Timing was important, I told Al, and he agreed to a quick closing.

Al and I scheduled the closing of the transaction for a Friday afternoon two weeks away. On that particular morning, though, I had already scheduled some minor outpatient surgery on my hand that turned out to be more invasive than I had thought. In the recovery room and still groggy, I suddenly realized my meeting with Al was in two hours, but the nurse would not discharge me without the doctor's permission.

I quickly called my assistant, Marlene Gibbs (now Luke), who reluctantly agreed to meet me at the side door of the hospital and whisk me away in her car. At exactly 2:00 p.m., I arrived at Al's office with my left hand bandaged and in a sling. Wobbly and light-headed, I negotiated the stairway up to Al's office in the old World War II–era arms plant now occupied by the Utah Wholesale Grocery Company operation. I must have looked strange standing there in my sweatpants instead of a business suit, but we signed the closing documents and Al handed me a cashier's check in the full amount, $2.5 million. I then headed back to the hospital to get my official release. No one knew I had been AWOL for several hours.

Sometime later, Al reminded me that while he was signing the purchase documents, I'd gone over to his chalkboard and with my good hand joyfully scribbled in large print the figure of $2,500,000—an action that must have been prompted by the lingering effects of the anesthesia.

The following Monday, Harold Steele was delighted when I showed up with a check for $2.5 million to pay down his loan—more than four months earlier than the bank-approved extension. It turned out to be a fortuitous event. The selling of overlapping inventory and the antitrust issue were behind us. Now all we had to do was tackle the five-story building, where cobwebs covered the labyrinth of slow-moving inventory.

Overwhelmed by the thought of the restructuring needed at SLH, I made a deal in 1970 to bring on board Sam Souvall and his brother George, both of whom had a vast business, marketing, and distribution background. Along with other family members, these brothers had perfected the retail merchandising art of rack jobbing and developed a full return policy program for unsold merchandise. Their customers included discounters and mass merchandisers, such as Wal-Mart and Grand Central, other grocery chains and drugstores, and traditional department stores such as JCPenney. The Souvall brothers' operation handled a variety of sundry and dry-goods items including health and beauty aids, textiles, and music (records, eight-track tapes, and cassettes). With their marketing expertise, they turned inventory quickly and kept returns low. As part of our agreement, we purchased their music rack-jobbing business and then later the Family Loom operation, which had a textile manufacturing and distribution operation headquartered in Charlotte, North Carolina.

With our business operations becoming more diversified and expanding beyond the intermountain region, I decided in 1971 to change the name of the company to Alta Industries Corporation. Under the new structure, I became chairman of the board, with Sam as president and George as president of our Arizona subsidiary focusing on music distribution. In our need for a chief financial officer, I remembered Warren (Pat) King, who was a numbers genius and whose forte was the ability to cut through a lot of detail very quickly and get to the bottom line. I had dealt with Pat years before when he was the contracting officer for Memcor, which became a division of E-Systems, an early technology company. I successfully built several buildings for the division. Pat agreed to come on board as CFO, and also committed to acquire some Alta shares.

We asked several people at Salt Lake Hardware to continue working under the new structure. One such person was Bob Marks, the company attorney, who had been there for nearly sixty years. When I first met Bob, he sat behind a turn of the-century rolltop desk that had been used before him by his father. He had an incredible mind for a person I guessed to be more than eighty-five years old. He looked like an Edwardian professor and in meetings took notes in shorthand, a trait lawyers of his era had been expected to master.

To streamline the behemoth hardware division, we discontinued the use of the massive catalogs and used the industry rule that 20 percent of inventory would satisfy 80 percent of our customers. We sold off at a discount all the slow-moving and specialty inventory items, focusing more on faster-moving industrial products. We then instituted a cash-and-carry program for all purchases made for less than $500. Within weeks, our inventory shrank to under sixteen thousand items, increasing our product turnover substantially and freeing up considerable cash. Now it was time to pay off the remaining bank loan. When we took Harold Steele to lunch and handed him a check for the balance of the loan, he was astonished.

Sam, Pat, and George slowly computerized all the business operations while briefly running a parallel manual bookkeeping system at each division. Within a short time, we substantially reduced our labor overhead. Soon most of the Alta Industries divisions became profitable and were growing steadily. As the earnings rose, the Alta shares reflected this in their market value: our quarterly dividends consistently increased over the next thirty years. During this time, Harold Steele became a shareholder, board member, and lifelong friend.

In 1970 I became acquainted with Bob Hinckley Jr., whose family owned the Hinckley Dodge dealerships in Salt Lake and Ogden. I also met his father, Robert

Hinckley Sr., a senior statesman who liked our business philosophy and entrepreneurial style. Bob junior agreed to become a board member, representing his family, who had become major shareholders.

I was honored also to have Robert Hinckley Sr. as an advisor to us. He served in the Franklin D. Roosevelt administration as Assistant Secretary of Commerce, administrator of the Federal Emergency Relief Administration, and chairman of the Civil Aeronautics Board. After World War II, Mr. Hinckley directed the Office of Contract Settlement in Harry Truman's administration. In 1946, he founded the American Broadcasting Company (ABC) with a close friend. Under his leadership over the next twenty years, ABC became a major national television network. Robert Hinckley Sr. was personally instrumental in Alta's acquisition of ABC's subsidiary music distribution business, which helped to increase our market share in the rack-jobbing and distribution division.

4.2. Pat King and John skiing at the Whistler Ski Resort, British Columbia, March 1997.

As part of our streamlining of low-margin businesses, and since we did not have a dominant position in the Boise market, we sold the subsidiary Idaho Plumbing and Heating Company to a competitor. We liquidated other low-margin hardware operations in Grand Junction, Colorado, and Boise, Idaho. The Boise hardware building would later become the downtown public library, adding to the economic resurgence of the industrial section of the city.

During 1976 and 1977, while attending high school, my son Steven expressed the desire to earn some money, so I found him a part-time job in the cash-and-carry and shipping departments of the hardware division. I asked Darrell Tilley, the manager, to take him under his tutelage so he could learn more about the operation of the business. Learning about business left a lasting impression on my son.

In the meantime, Sam, Pat, and George were doing a great job for Alta Industries shareholders. With more demands on my time now, with the expansion of the construction and real estate business and my recent acquisition of a television station and production studio in San Juan, Puerto Rico, I decided it was in the shareholders' best interests to turn over the position of chairman of the board to Sam, while continuing on as chairman of the executive committee. Pat assumed the role of president and CEO and strategically guided the company's future direction.

The role of the middleman in the product supply chain continued to lessen, so in 1979 we divested ourselves of the Salt Lake Hardware division and sold it to the division manager, Darrell Tilley, and a group of outside investors.

In the early 1970s, we decided to expand the Family Loom textile division's product line. We worked with Claude Sampson, the innovator of a manufacturing process that had brought the panty hose brand Little Prune to life. An early pioneer in this industry, Claude developed a technique to convert regular nylon stocking manufacturing equipment to the production of panty hose. He modified World War II–vintage stocking manufacturing machines to add a crotch and panty section. From this revolutionary process evolved Family Loom's version of the new panty hose craze.

Little Prune was the best product on the market. The demand was so great we contracted with Hampshire Designers to help manufacture our product. Little Prune used a four-strand, 20-denier nylon fiber that was twisted more than one hundred times per inch in each direction, giving the nylon fiber a permanent memory. The finished product compressed into a small odd-shape ball resembling a prune, which is how the name Little Prune originated.

This new miracle nylon fiber could be stretched for a better fit. It was stronger, lasted longer, and was almost indestructible. But the quality we put into the product meant that we had to sell the product for more than our competitors charged for theirs. While we sold Little Prune panty hose for $1.99, later reduced to $1.49, the competitor's product, called L'eggs, was sold for 89¢ and below. We found most women would rather pay less even if the product didn't last through numerous washings.

Although Little Prune was the rage for a long time, with its colorful shades, a nude heel for flattery, and a super fit on almost anybody, we could see the handwriting on the wall. We eventually sold the rights to the brand to Hampshire Designers.

Over the years, Sam and George cultivated strong relationships with the retailers, which created opportunities to expand our distribution operations. When Albertsons, who was a customer, divested itself of the Mountain States Wholesale Division in 1977, Alta acquired their record, eight-track tape, and cassette operations.

In 1977, George, a founding member of the National Association of Recording Merchandisers (NARM), was elected to a one-year term as president of this prestigious trade association, which serves music retailing business through lobbying and trade representation. Alta, considered a major innovative force in the music industry, continued to expand its wholesale music distribution operations throughout the intermountain region and the western states.

By the 1980s, increased competition from mass merchandisers, who bought directly from the manufacturers, was cutting out the distributors in the music business, too. We needed to preserve our market share, so we decided to start a retail chain of our own—and with our distribution network, we believed this vertical integration would allow us to compete in the marketplace. Thus in 1988 the Eli's Tapes and Records retail concept was born, named after a Souvall relative. Over the next several years, we opened fifteen such outlets. The concept, however, was only marginally successful, given the increased competition, so we eventually sold the retail music division to a competitor, Hastings Books and Records.

At the Steelco subsidiary, several value-added manufacturing components were introduced to make it more profitable. A mainstay of that division continued to be the "Mine-Safety" product line. One of the value-added products we developed included a cut-to-length roofing and siding metal panel line, manufactured from flat-roll-stock steel. Another was structural steel purlin building components. We also added machinery to bend, shape, and weld up to a three-inch-thick steel plate to make round vessels and pipes. A roll-stock slitter operation was set up to cut roll-stock coils down to the narrow banding sizes used in industrial and manufacturing applications.

For construction industry and manufacturing customers, the Steelco division stocked one of the largest inventories of steel plate, bars, coils, and other steel products, including steel processing capabilities, in the region. With the demand for steel in the 1970s, our Steelco division set up an automobile crusher and shredder operation to recycle these steel components and haul the compacted bales of metal on our trucks to steel mills, even exporting to Japan. After a number of years and fluctuations in market prices, we disbanded this operation.

Later, in our diversification expansion in the 1990s, Steelco purchased from one of our customers a waste disposal container manufacturing operation. Shortly thereafter, not reaching our profit objectives and losing money on each container sold, we closed down the operation.

Overall, Alta Industries continued to be a great financial success for more than three decades.

In the 1970s, I reached a major crossroads when I expanded our construction and development operation into the Las Vegas and Reno, Nevada, markets and built retail stores for Smith's, Albertsons, and Grand Central, among others. During these early years in Nevada, gambling and the underworld influence stymied much of the region's growth. Many national banks and insurance companies were not willing to make loans, as they did not want to be involved in this gambling mecca, long associated with organized crime. Most of the construction financing in Las Vegas had been provided by trade unions and several local banks, and was designated mostly for hotels and casinos. The recession of the early 1970s didn't help matters, either, since financing was scarce everywhere in the country.

By mid-1970, the economy had improved and the population of Las Vegas and Reno was growing. Retail stores were in demand, but reasonable lending sources were not available. We were among the first developers to convince some of the national insurance companies and regional savings and loan association lenders that the retail projects we were planning would be successful, and not gambling-related. After much groundwork, we finally convinced the Salt Lake City–based Prudential Federal Savings and Loan Association (which later became Washington Mutual) to finance a retail store for Grand Central and Smith's Food and Drug in Nevada. (We convinced Aetna Life Insurance to finance several retail projects for us as well.)

During that time, I was developing a retail shopping mall in Rock Springs, Wyoming, reputed to be a "Wild West" town with an occasional shooting on K Street. Concerned about a loan being considered for the retail mall project, Frank Kelly, the attorney for Aetna Life, compared the risks of investing in Rock Springs with those associated with Las Vegas. Frank was a buttoned-down easterner, and until I invited him to visit, he had never ventured out west. When I greeted Frank at the Wyoming site, I gave him cowboy hat, gun belt, a toy gun, and a T-shirt with his name emblazoned in green on the front and "Rock Springs, the Wild West" in red on the back. These items embarrassed Frank, but we both had a good laugh, which broke the ice. Driving around, he discovered the town was not at all what he had envisioned. After visiting the Nevada sites next, he recommended the loans be approved—a first in both states. The projects proved to be profitable; word spread, and other lenders offered to make loans in these markets as well.

Over the next few years in the Las Vegas and Reno markets, many retail shopping center opportunities were offered to me. However, I became disenchanted when some retailers discovered that slot machine income could cover their rent, and stationed six to ten slot machines in a store's vestibule. At first I didn't object to this use of space. But one day I watched a young mother with two toddlers putting quarter after quarter into a slot machine, hoping to win. After a while, I saw her leave the store with a carton of cigarettes, a gallon of milk, and a loaf of bread. That this woman would gamble away the nourishment of her children really bothered me. I saw similar scenes play out over and over again.

I finished the construction projects I had on the drawing boards for my clients, but decided not to build any more retail stores in Nevada. This decision probably cost me millions of dollars in business over the next twenty or so years, but I never regretted that decision for a moment. The money for food and basic necessities should be off-limits to gambling.

With the American automobile industry expanding and growing rapidly in the intermountain region in the late 1970s, I also found myself building automobile dealerships for Cadillac, Oldsmobile, Pontiac, Buick, Chevrolet, Lincoln, Mercury, Ford, Chrysler, and Dodge franchises. Some of the Utah pioneers in this industry became my mentors, including Ken Garff, Ray Stout, David Robinson, and Laury Miller.

Since many of the dealers were financed by Motors Holding, a division of General Motors Corporation, and Dealer Development, a division of the Ford Motor Company, I cultivated both of their representatives, and subsequently built more than twenty-five automobile dealerships throughout the Intermountain region.

At that time, none of the major U.S. automobile manufacturers would allow their dealers to represent foreign manufacturers under the same roof. This created additional building opportunities with foreign automobile dealerships: Volkswagen, Isuzu, and Mercedes-Benz.

Many dealers also could not afford to own their own facilities. It was easier for them to lease from a private investor, where they could have favorable buy-back provisions. I stepped in as landlord in a dozen dealership facilities, and when the automobile industry underwent a major consolidation, I sold off the facilities for a nice profit and moved on to other types of investment opportunities.

In 1974, as I mentioned briefly before, I ventured into broadcasting by acquiring the San Juan, Puerto Rico, ABC television affiliate, WAPA-TV, and a production studio, Televicentro. My partner in this venture, Dale Moore, was an experienced television station owner and operator from Missoula, Montana. We purchased the Puerto Rico assets for $8 million, on favorable terms, from Columbia Pictures Industries, Inc., which needed to reduce its outstanding debt. While the ongoing economic recession made financing difficult, we made a down payment of $500,000 and assumed $7.5 million of the debt Columbia owed to the banks.

Dale and I also became good friends, spending time at his Missoula ranch, where he raised Polled Herefords for breeding. My son Steven worked on the ranch one summer when he was a teenager. Being away from city life and living among ranch hands and cowboys served as another good learning experience for him.

The recession in the United States, which lasted through 1975, did not dramatically affect our Puerto Rico business; nor was my construction and development business materially affected, since we had financing commitments on our projects that would take us through this economic slowdown. Inflation had become a major concern and the Federal Reserve tightened the availability of funds, which in turn reduced bank lending. Interest rates increased to a point that it affected investment in real estate and other industries. Fortunately, during this period our need for additional financing was low. Government tax cuts generated more disposable income, which stimulated an economic recovery for most industries, thus ending the recession.

Meanwhile, with an aggressive marketing team, our sales at the television station increased, as did our bottom-line profits. We also tightened up all our operating costs, which further added to profits. Televicentro produced a number of successful *telenovelas*, game shows, and family entertainment programs. By 1980, we had paid off our obligation to the banks and were substantially in the black.

During the 1977–1981 Carter administration, the economy tanked into the worst recession since 1957. By 1980, short-term interest rates climbed to nearly 21 percent, while long-term rates hovered around 13 percent—if you could even get a loan.

When President Reagan came into office in 1981, one of the first issues he addressed was the stabilization of the economy, to ease credit and reduce interest rates. This soon made reasonable real estate financing available again.

Dale wanted to consolidate his other media holdings and involve his sons in the business, so he suggested buying me out. We agreed to a total value for the entire operation of $30 million, which after a seven-year investment left me with a sizable profit for my half. It also solved a critical problem in my core construction and development business: I had numerous short-term loans due at the banks and was paying exorbitant interest rates. The timing of this transaction was fortuitous.

Even with my involvement in Alta Industries and other businesses over the years, I never lost sight of JPA and PDC, the driving engines of my success, which helped finance these investment ventures. PDC continued its dominance in the intermountain and western regions, growing with the markets as they expanded.

In the intermountain region, businesses from across the country discovered expansion opportunities for their industrial, commercial, and retail operations. Our construction and development business was thriving. We employed several thousand craftsmen and more than one hundred people in the office. Our corporate headquarters had expanded into three buildings, totaling 50,000 square feet of space. In addition, we kept many subcontractors, suppliers, architects, and engineers busy. We had also shifted PDC's focus more to the enclosed retail mall paradigm, which had started with the Cache Valley Mall in Logan, Utah.

The year 1975 was a memorable one, as we ventured into our first enclosed retail mall project by buying forty acres of land in Logan from one of Utah's early pioneer developers, Sid Horman. Along with the deal came two leases with JCPenney and Zion Cooperative Mercantile Institution (ZCMI), a local Utah department store. Both retailers would anchor a number of other malls we developed throughout the intermountain region. Years later, the May Company purchased ZCMI; then

May subsequently merged with Federated Department Stores and was rebranded as Macy's.

Over the next twenty-seven years, we developed eighteen enclosed malls, more than forty-five retail community centers, and a number of office and industrial park complexes, totaling almost twenty million square feet of building space.

Early in the 1970s, seeing that department store anchor tenants for some of the smaller markets were scarce, I approached the Buttrey department store chain in Montana to locate a store in one of our developments in Idaho Falls. We then purchased their three store operations and renamed them Jonathan's. I wanted to use the concept as an anchor in our smaller market retail projects. These remerchandised department stores started off great but soon found it difficult to compete against the larger mass merchandisers and discounters that had moved into the region. After two years of weak sales, I closed the operation at a loss of more than $1 million.

In the following decade, Price Development Company experimented with a new concept: we introduced a food court in our malls as a way to keep customers shopping longer. Numerous food concepts were being developed, and we experimented

4.3. Grand opening event at East Ridge Mall, Casper, Wyoming, October 1982. From left to right: Steven, Marcia, Governor Ed Herschler, John, Margaret, Dean and Mabel Poulsen (Marcia's parents).

4.4. Grand opening, Spokane Valley Mall, August 1997.

with our own Mario's Pizza, which we combined with other tenants' fast-food operations.

In the food court, six to eight noncompeting yet compatible concepts were clustered next to one another with adequate seating areas. We found that any more than this specific number of tenants would dilute sales and make survival difficult for the vendors. In each new mall, different locations were tested for the best traffic draw. When we learned customers would seek out the food court wherever it was, we moved it to areas harder to lease, such as on the second level or near a theater location.

Under a franchise agreement, we also operated Orange Julius, Dairy Queen, Steak and Fry, and Karmel Korn, in addition to Mario's Pizza. As time went on, new brands joined the food courts in our malls, and the food court became a major component for any retail project. Soon our newly formed Western States Food Company had more than thirty fast-food operations located in various malls.

When I purchased a mall site from industry pioneer Ernie Hahn in Kelso, Washington, I faced an interesting challenge. I was never certain whether Hahn sold this site because he thought the market was too small or because the recent eruption of Mount St. Helens had filled part of the site with almost eighty feet of fine debris. From a geologic point of view, once the fine powder was in place, it became a solid base, which didn't concern me. So we built a successful mall development on the remnants of the Mount St. Helens eruption.

In 1975, the State of Utah was making preparations for the bicentennial celebration. As part of this momentous occasion, Salt Lake County residents passed a bond issue for the construction of the new Symphony Hall, the adjacent Art Center, and the restoration of the historic Capitol Theatre in Salt Lake City. The architects' design concept for the three projects together exceeded $30 million, while available funding was less than $20 million. Several other architecture firms competing in the selection process came up with interesting designs, but all were over budget.

The Utah Bicentennial Commission chairman, Obert C. Tanner, a successful businessman, educator, and community leader, named Jack Gallivan as chairman of the Planning and Construction Committee. The committee also included several community-minded individuals, but few had any construction or cost-control experience.

Having established a reputation in the construction industry as a quality builder with tight cost controls, John Price Associates Inc. could handle such a construction project from the earliest stages through completion, saving the owner substantial money and also providing earlier occupancy. In the fall of 1975, I received a call from Frank Nelson, president of United Bank, and George Nicolatus, a respected architect at First Security Bank who was in charge of their facilities planning and construction. I had worked with George on several projects over the years when he was in private practice, so we had developed a good working relationship. When I met with Frank and George, I agreed to help the committee as a consultant, since the arts complex was a community endeavor. Jack Gallivan, the publisher of the *Salt Lake Tribune*, was also an acquaintance as a result of my business dealings with a *Tribune* partner in the television and cable business, George Hatch, and so he too had confidence in JPA.

My engineering staff worked around the clock to come up with alternatives for materials on all three projects that would be cost-effective yet stay close to the preferred architectural designs and finish aspects. When the joint planning was done, the edifices were an outstanding collaboration by all the participating organizations. I told the committee I would be willing to guarantee completion of the three building projects within the $20 million budget, but I would require some control over architectural matters.

Several of the committee's members were friends with the architects and were reluctant to go along, but ultimately the committee agreed. To help keep costs within the budget, I decided to donate back a portion of my construction management fee and instead negotiated a sharing clause on savings below the budget as an incentive for the hardworking JPA staff, as well as an added insurance to avoid overruns.

4.5. Symphony Hall (now Abravanel Hall), 1979.

To my knowledge, this was the first civic project of this size in the country to be built under the construction management concept. Initially there were mixed feelings about this approach: as noted, the architects were not too happy under this arrangement, and neither were some of the arts groups, who wanted more embellishments than could be provided with the available funds.

In October 1978 the restored Capitol Theatre was reopened to the public; and the following year, Symphony Hall (renamed Abravanel Hall in 1993) and the Salt Lake Art Center greeted the public. The JPA team of contractors, subcontractors, suppliers, and finish artisans delivered these three magnificent structures in a first-class manner, on time, and more than $1 million under budget! The architects and engineers received accolades for the projects and ultimately became believers in the construction management approach. The arts groups were also happy to have been consulted, and provided valuable input; plus, because JPA donated back half of the savings-clause share that it earned, these groups were able to have some of the embellishments they had desired. Today these buildings are as magnificent as when they were first built—a tribute to this great community endeavor. All these years later, I still choke up with pride when I visit these edifices for a performance or show.

In part because of my exposure to the performing and visual arts, I had considered becoming a filmmaker as a hobby. My friend Mayor Ted Wilson introduced me to his close friend Robert Redford, the well-known actor and director and the founder of the Sundance Institute, located at his new Provo Canyon Sundance Village development and ski resort. After a meeting in 1981 with Sundance's executive director, Sterling Van Wagenen, who was also Redford's brother-in-law, I was asked to become one of the original members of the Friends of Sundance Institute, an advisory board. During the next four years, I attended numerous filmmaking workshops and met many actors, writers, musicians, directors, and producers.

In 1986, Redford asked me to serve as one of the founding board members of the Utah Committee for the Sundance Institute (see Appendix E). I was enthused about his great vision of developing a special niche in Utah's film industry, and accepted Bob's invitation. The Institute helped emerging filmmakers, directors, producers, film composers, screenwriters, playwrights, and performing artists to learn from successful industry resources. Eventually, the world-renowned Sundance Film Festival evolved in Park City, Utah, and provided a valuable outlet for independent filmmakers from around the world. After spending considerable time in their workshops, I realized filmmaking was not my forte—although I stayed on the advisory board for several years.

In 1976, I purchased First Security Savings and Loan Association, which had three branches in eastern Idaho, from First Security Bank Corporation (FSB), which had to divest the S&L under a Federal Reserve mandate. At the time, I was on the bank's local advisory board. When I heard about this divestiture, I approached George Eccles, the bank chairman, about purchasing the S&L. He agreed and, after negotiating a favorable deal, gave me a short time frame to close the transaction, since it had to take place before year's end. I headed to Chicago the next day to seek financing with the Continental Illinois National Bank, with whom I previously had done real estate and other financing deals. As luck would have it, seated next to me in the airplane was David Kennedy, the former chairman of Continental Illinois, who was heading to Chicago for a meeting.

David Kennedy was a well-respected banker, a current member of the FSB board, and familiar with the S&L transaction. He was also a true friend of business entrepreneurs. He had served as chairman of Continental Illinois until 1969, when he was asked by President Richard Nixon to serve as Secretary of the Treasury, a position he held until 1971, when Nixon appointed him to serve as ambassador at large with cabinet status.

David and I discussed the terms of the S&L purchase, and I expressed my concern over the short window for closing the transaction. The FSB board had approved the transaction at their meeting the day before, David told me, so he knew of my deadline. He then offered to go to the bank with me, explain the transaction, and help get approval of a loan on my behalf. We arranged to meet with Chuck Smith, whom I knew well from other transactions with the bank.

David was very helpful in asking Chuck to make the loan to me on terms that would allow its payback over time, using the earnings of the S&L as collateral. A loan of $7 million on these favorable terms was agreed to while we were still there—the quickest approval process ever!

To avoid any confusion from the name First Security Bank, I agreed to change the entity to Security Savings and Loan Association. During the next three years, our savings accounts went up substantially, and we aggressively expanded the loan portfolio, with plans to take the S&L statewide. However, I could also see the spreads tightening—the interest we paid on savings accounts versus the interest rate we were able charge on loans. This concerned me. I felt, as others did, that the economy could be heading for another recession. When I received an unsolicited offer from a Boise savings and loan association in 1980 to buy Security Savings and Loan at two times the book value, I seriously had to consider the offer. I decided to sell the S&L to them, but had to take some of the proceeds over a two-year period, secured by savings accounts. It was only a few years later that the whole savings and loan industry started to unravel, falling under the weight of bad loans. I was thankful I had read the tea leaves correctly—my timing was, again, fortuitous.

Not All Work, Some Play

I was a hands-on type of manager. As I continued to grow our business empire, its demands took me away from my family. I had limited time to spend with each of our children: Steven (born in 1959); Deidre (1961); and Jennifer (1966). But we did manage to take a number of trips together and kept a boat on the Flaming Gorge reservoir for summer outings. Once, in 1972, we took a motor home trip to Canada that turned out to be a memorable disaster—one that the family would rather forget.

It was early spring when I approached Bob Hinckley, a board member of Alta Industries, Ltd., about renting a motor home for a possible family trip to the Northwest that summer. He said he'd call back in a few days about one that was currently rented but might become available. That night I discussed the idea during dinner with Marcia and Steven, then twelve; Deidre, ten; and Jennifer, six. There were no immediate cheers, but only Marcia was truly apprehensive.

It was the beginning of July when I arranged to pick up the used 1971 Dodge Travco twenty-seven-foot motor home. At the time, we were living in the upper Avenues area on the bench several hundred feet above Salt Lake City, the location of my first construction venture. Driving there in our vacation home on wheels became my first experience navigating such a lumbering vehicle in and out of traffic. Even with its enormous sideview mirrors, visibility was limited. On the way, I stopped at the Automobile Club of Utah office, which I had built for a friend, Steve Zoumadakis, several years earlier. He was personally preparing our trip routing and arranged for some hotel stops to break up the time we would be spending in the tight quarters of this motel on wheels.

Maps in hand, I headed up the hill toward home. Even empty, the vehicle chugged and strained in low gear as it climbed the three-hundred-foot rise. When I arrived home, the radiator was spewing antifreeze onto the street. When I opened the door to step out and see what the problem was, the automatic platform did not engage, so I had a long step down to solid ground. Then, as I was leaving the vehicle, it started to roll. I quickly jumped back in to secure the hand brake, which would not take hold.

I made a quick call to Bob, who tried to reassure me. The antifreeze issue wasn't a concern; in fact, it was normal for this type of vehicle, he said. All I had to do was carry some extra fluid to top it off. As for the platform, Bob said, it did sometimes stick—nothing to worry about. And Bob assured me that the parking brake would work well on lesser inclines, so all I had to do was put it in gear—and carry a good-sized rock to place behind the rear wheels. I decided not to mention that when I'd tried to lock the door, the key got stuck halfway, and only with great difficulty was I finally able to dislodge it.

Since most of our time would be spent in the motor home, we decided to use the drawers and closets for our clothes and not bring suitcases to clutter up the tight space. I didn't think we had room for Steven's bright orange 1970 Rupp Roadster minibike, but for months he had been practicing in the nearby hills and open fields, and he insisted we take it along or else he wouldn't go. At midnight, I was still trying to figure out where to put it. The rack on the back was too narrow and not suited for this 125-pound machine. Finally I agreed we could strap it down inside, just in front of the built-in couch.

Marcia was concerned about this new kitchen experience, but I assured her it was safe to use the propane cooktop. The refrigerator, although small, would be adequate as long as we restocked it at our fuel stops.

Later that night, with the kids asleep, Marcia and I moved all our travel paraphernalia into what would be our home away from home. From clothes to towels and sheets, the list was long. We made it a point to assign each child his or her own storage space, so that loud disagreements inside the motor home could be held to a minimum. At three in the morning, I wrestled the heavy minibike up the narrow steps, then used a regular clothesline tied with Boy Scout knots to hold it in place.

At daybreak, when I wanted to leave, everyone was cranky and nervous. For me, anxiety overcame my excitement about this family adventure. Finally, everyone was on board by eight o'clock, each kid carrying his or her "security blankets"—a pillow, a doll, or the remnants of a ten-year-old blanket. As I crept down the steep street, hoping the low gear would help slow down the vehicle so I would not have to test the brakes, I announced that our next stop would be Boise, Idaho.

Sixteen miles north of Salt Lake City, as we reached the small Utah town of Farmington, I started wondering whether we needed our passports to enter Canada. This was 1972, before cell phones and computers, and I had no way to check with anyone. To be safe, I decided to turn back to retrieve them. Again, the motor home strained as it chugged up the long hill, and as we arrived, the radiator belched its discomfort.

At that point Steven decided that he wanted me to bring along a .25-caliber pistol I had, saying we could do some target shooting. In reality, he wanted to torment pot guts—marmots—along the way. And before we could leave again, Deidre and Jennifer also needed to make a bathroom stop.

By ten o'clock we were on the road again. I assured Marcia we had plenty of gas, as long as I didn't exceed 60 mph—the motor home would get 12 miles per gallon at 55 mph, but mileage would drop down to 7 to 8 mpg at 65 mph. Not thrilled about me doing math concerning fuel consumption, Marcia suggested we top off the tank. But being the tour leader on this venture, I quickly shot down that idea, and we headed for Boise.

The day was hot, and I feared using the rooftop air conditioners could strain the engine, so I shut them off. Even with the windows open, the heat almost consumed us. The little ones in back were flushed and looked like they might fold. Marcia was mum and unwilling to make eye contact. At the time, I weighed over 220 pounds, from years of working around-the-clock, little exercise, and smoking and drinking martinis daily.

Ten miles out of Boise, the motor home started to sputter and we soon came to a halt in the blazing hot afternoon sun. There was no shade anywhere, we were out of gas, and there wasn't a service station in sight. No one said anything like "I told you so" or "Gee, that's too bad." They just looked at me as if this were my problem to solve. Wrestling with Steven's unwieldy minibike, I managed to get it out by myself, while the family looked on in disbelief. It must have been a comical sight to see a large man, legs scrunched up to his belly, balancing himself on the tiny minibike going down freeway.

After finding a service station that would loan me two one-gallon gas cans, I was off again, holding the handle of each can with two fingers while steering with the other three fingers. Several times I came close to losing my balance, but when I arrived back at the motor home, no one was sympathetic, since I'd left them standing for over an hour in 100-degree heat. I also hadn't realized I needed a spigot, so some of the precious fuel landed on the hot pavement and immediately evaporated. I hoped we had enough gas to get us to Boise!

That night, no one wanted to sleep in the motor home—they were drained and just wanted the comfort of a shower and a nice bed. Plus, Marcia served notice she was not cooking that night. Luckily we found refuge at a Rodeway Inn owned by a client and friend. By morning, everyone had recovered and ribbed me about how I'd looked on the minibike, narrow-brimmed hat tied to my head with a segment of clothesline so it wouldn't blow off, and the bench seat so overloaded the tires were buckling.

We planned to be in Seattle by dinnertime, where we'd stay at a motel. On other days we planned to rough it in the motor home at a campground. As we worked our way through the picturesque mountain ranges west of Boise, we traveled on Highway 84—the route of the old Oregon Trail. Soon we came upon the Snake River, which we followed for a distance, winding our way down into the fertile Oregon farming and ranching valleys. As we approached the confluence of the Snake River and the Columbia River, a gust of wind lifted the motor home and moved it laterally, scaring everyone. Drawers and shelves opened and their contents bounced out into the aisle. The wind gusts continued for the next several miles, which was a frightful experience. When we stopped at a service station to refuel, everyone quickly pitched in to repack the clothing and reorganize the kitchen. We wouldn't realize until several hours later that the winds had also blown out the pilot light for the water heater, and the refrigerant line to the refrigerator had become kinked, cutting off power and spoiling all the fridge's contents. If that weren't enough, one of the rooftop air conditioners decided to fail in sympathy with the other appliances.

Finally taking Highway 5 up to Seattle, we arrived at the Red Lion motel late that night. Tired, we crashed with cereal and milk, which I picked up at a nearby service station. By now everyone was getting tired of the motor home experience. We had no food in the refrigerator and Marcia did not want to restock it. The pilot light for the water heater could not be restarted, so we couldn't take hot showers, and the propane no longer reached the cooktop. The roof air-conditioning unit circuit breaker could not be reset, and with only one unit working, the motor home was stifling by midday.

When the winds had tossed us around the day before, the minibike had become a missile, barely missing Marcia, who was sitting in front. When I reanchored it, I detected a gas smell, which after inspection turned out to be coming from a drip in the gas line. I could not fix it right away, so temporarily I used a towel to catch the gas drips. This also added to the intoxicating atmosphere.

When we left Seattle the next morning, I found out we didn't need our passports to enter Canada; we could have avoided the extra trip home, which had caused us to run out of gas on the way to Boise. The desk clerk also told us firearms were not allowed to be taken over the border, so I had to secure a safe-deposit box to stow the gun, which we would pick up on our return through Seattle. Steven was sad that he wouldn't get to use it.

After gassing up, we headed north to Vancouver, Canada. At the border we learned the gun could have been brought with us, so now Steven was doubly bummed out. Fortunately, we had no major mishap that day—except the toilet was starting to smell. We hadn't emptied the tank since we left Salt Lake City, and I avoided going to a dump station, since I'd forgotten to get the instructions from Bob.

Late in the day, we arrived at the Bayshore Hotel, located on the way to the waterfront dock where we would be catching the ferry the next morning to Victoria on Vancouver Island. As I recall, this was the most restful evening so far on the trip. However, everyone was embarrassed to be seen carrying all their clothes and toiletries into the hotel in their arms, since we had decided not to bring any suitcases. Several times we had to backtrack to pick up a fallen T-shirt or toothbrush.

Next morning, I roused everyone bright and early so that we could have a quick breakfast and beat the rush of cars and trucks, getting in the ferry queue early for a good position. There were three lanes and I decided to park in the inside one closest to the walkway leading to the passenger lounge area, so that we could grab a good seat for the hour-and-a-half trip. Several large trucks were already ahead of us. I was guided into position by a crew member, who kept motioning me to steer closer to the curb. I was now bumper to bumper with a giant semi- trailer in front of me and an equally large one behind. In the adjacent center lane was the metal wall of another semi-trailer. When I tried to get out, I discovered that the door of the motor home was blocked by the ferry's smokestack. I could barely open the door six inches. We were trapped! The only option was the window above the couch, which was over four feet from the ground. We had never totally opened it before nor removed the screen, which took a screwdriver to dislodge; we eventually discovered that the window was stuck and wouldn't open all the way.

The kids and Marcia, being smaller-framed, had no problem helping each other climb out the window. I was another story, however. Between the window and the smokestack there was less than two feet of space. I was admittedly rotund and feared getting wedged in, never to see daylight again. The family, staring at me from the walkway, eventually decided to give me a hand, and I made it out. As I dusted myself off, though, reality set in: how was I going to make it back through the window? I'd worry about it later, I thought, as I ordered a stiff Bloody Mary to calm me down. Finally, we decided that I would boost Marcia through the window. She would start the motor home and slowly move it forward past the smokestack. It worked, and we were on our way to Victoria.

Our plan was to visit the Qualicum Provincial Park, which we were told had a beautiful waterfall cascading over large rock outcroppings in a dense forest. The Qualicum Falls area was lush with vegetation because of the high annual rainfall and constant mist. We were all dressed in light summer clothing for the hike. I was wearing a white T-shirt and white cotton trousers. I had become a camera freak, always carrying a large Nikon camera with a variety of lenses. I didn't want to miss a shot, which irked the family, especially the kids, who had lost their camera smiles way back in Boise. As we walked on the damp path adjacent to the ravine, we could see the massive waterfall in the background. I suggested that Marcia, Deidre, and Jennifer stand in the center of the wooden footbridge that spanned the steep-sided ravine, so that we could use Qualicum Falls as a backdrop. Steven would come with me and carry the extra lenses.

To get a better angle, I wanted to get closer to the ledge. I noticed a sign saying to stay on the path, since the moss-covered ground was slippery and dangerous when wet. But I was determined to get a good shot; after all, we had come a long way and would probably not be back here again. As I started to position myself, my feet came out from under me, and soon I found myself clinging onto a small rock outcrop. The camera lens hit me in the face, then ricocheted off the rocky ledge and cascaded

4.6. Deidre, Marcia, Jennifer, and Steven at Little Qualicum Falls Provincial Park, summer 1972.

downward. One hand on a small rock lip and the friction of my clothes were all that was keeping me from tumbling down the hundred-foot abyss.

Steven, only twelve years old and slight, instinctively dropped the camera bag and reached out to grab my free hand while he braced himself up against a rock outcropping. With great effort, I slowly clawed my way back up the wet rock surface. Steven held on to me tightly as I searched for solid footing, saving my life!

Meanwhile, Marcia and the girls were on the footbridge watching, wondering what I was doing hanging over the side of the cliff. They hadn't seen me slip and fall—all they saw was me clinging to the sheer vertical wall with Steven's outstretched arms holding on to me. When they finally realized what was happening, they came running, but by then I was safe, though my face was bloody and my jaw swollen from hitting the rocky ledge as I fell. Based on my incoherent reaction, Marcia thought I had a concussion and didn't want me to drive, but I insisted. My white outfit was covered with mud and blood. And I never got my perfect shot of Qualicum Falls.

As we drove back to our hotel, I must have been delusional: several times I mentioned that I saw a lion or tiger in the woods in front of me. By the time we arrived at the regal Empress Hotel, everyone thought I would be going into shock from the injury to my head.

Parking the motor home next to some exquisite sports cars in front of the massive, elegant turn-of-the-century hotel, we immediately felt out of place. In our soiled clothes, rumpled hair, and muddy shoes, our arms filled with clothing, we looked like a strange group. As the five of us approached the front desk, tracking

4.7. Marcia outside our home away from home: the Dodge Travco motor home, summer 1972.

mud onto what appeared to be antique handwoven Persian rugs in the lobby, the neatly dressed clerk eyed us up and down. "How many more in your group?" he murmured. I dare say he was not eager to honor our reservation—and he did ask for payment in advance! On our way to the rooms, I noticed the sign about the hotel's strict dress code.

That night we had room service and did not venture out of our rooms again. The next morning, with our arms full of soggy, dirty clothes, we returned to the motor home and drove to the ferry at the dock for the three-hour trip back to Seattle. This time, I took the outside lane and had no problems. However, the smell from the toilet had become unbearable, so I decided to look for an RV dump station as soon as we disembarked.

Arriving in Seattle in midafternoon, we proceeded to hunt for a service station that had a sewage dump tank. We stumbled upon a brand-new Chevron station that hadn't officially opened yet, but the operator reluctantly agreed to let us dump the toilet's contents there. Workers from a construction company were at one end of the seamless sea of pure white concrete, mopping on a surface sealer to prevent the penetration of petroleum product spills. The dump station area had not yet received such a sealer, so I was cautioned to be extra careful.

Marcia and the girls went off to use the restroom, and since there were two valves to open, I asked Steven to open the one inside when I was ready. I carefully twisted the flex hose onto the exit pipe under the motor home and ensured that the coupling was secure. I then opened the dump tank lid. Steven asked me to help him with the inside valve, which appeared stuck. I thought he might be turning it in the wrong direction, so I went to help him after opening the valve under the motor home, and inserting the flex hose into the collar of the tank. While helping Steven open the inside valve, I looked out the window and saw the flex hose stiffen with the fluid mix. The sudden rush was too much for the opening in the ground to handle, and within seconds the contents were spewing all over the new concrete pavement. I quickly jumped out of the motor home and attempted to shut off the valve, but the pressure was too great. As best I could, I tried guiding the hose ending into the tank collar, but the damage was done. The station operator came running out yelling. Being in the construction business, I could sympathize with him, but I couldn't reverse the outcome. A full blast of water did not remove the mess; it only became diluted, spreading even further.

Topping off the gas tank made for only a $3 sale, so I gave the operator a hundred dollars, hoping he wouldn't be fired. At that moment Marcia and the girls returned from the rest room; when they saw what had happened, they just rolled their eyes. Embarrassed, I quickly drove away. Everyone was silent for the next fifty miles.

With a stop at the Red Lion to pick up the gun, we were running behind in trying to reach Coeur d'Alene, Idaho, by nightfall, so we decided to stop in Wenatchee, Washington, for the night. Driving down the main street, where the motels were located, we found one that had a sign indicating a vacancy. It had a steep gutter at the street, which concerned me, since I didn't want to high-center the motor home and get stuck. So I gunned the engine, scraping the rear end as I bounced over the gutter. Hearing the loud noise, the owner came out to see what was going on. He confirmed he had two rooms and guided me under the portico, which appeared low to me. As I crept through, he motioned for me to hurry up, so I hit the gas pedal. Instantly there came a shrill scraping noise, followed by a thud—like something falling behind the motor home. In my sideview mirror I could see two fluorescent fixtures smashing against the concrete slab. The air-conditioning unit on top was the culprit. I parked and walked to the office, stopping to pick up the light fixtures and clean up the broken glass. The owner stopped me, saying he would do it since it was his fault for guiding me through the portico. We all needed a good night's sleep.

The next day was Sunday and I believed we could easily get out of town without a lot of traffic. We decided to drive through Spokane, spend the night in Coeur d'Alene, and continue on to Missoula the next day. The drive was supposed to be spectacular, with majestic pine trees lining much of the way. I noticed the motel owner had repaired the portico ceiling scrapes and replaced the light fixtures. I asked the owner to guide me carefully back through the portico so that the air conditioner would miss the fixtures.

When he motioned me to move on through, I again stepped on the accelerator—and again heard the familiar shrill scraping noise. I bounced to a halt in the steep gutter, dragging two light fixtures behind me. Now I was stuck: high-centered in a gutter that looked more like a ravine, with the rear of the motor home, where the generator was located, wedged against the concrete. I rocked the motor home back and forth for a few moments, then felt a release as the motor home lurched forward. I also heard a loud thud and, looking back, saw the generator and its steel housing sitting on the ground.

As I stepped out of the motor home, the motel owner and I just looked at each other and threw our hands in the air. He again was apologetic, since he had guided me through the portico. But now we had a new, more serious problem: I was blocking his driveway, the generator was lying on the pavement, and it was Sunday. We needed a winch and hoist and a welder to put the motor home back together. After making several calls, the motel owner found a welder willing to come over—but not until after church.

Several hours and $200 later, we were under way again. No one was interested in the scenery; they all just wanted to get to the next destination intact.

Arriving in Coeur d'Alene, we passed a wooded campground, and I suggested spending the night there. The family unanimously voted me down. As a reprieve, we stayed at the new Coeur d'Alene Resort Hotel on the lake. Steven got to ride his minibike on the nearby bike trails, and even had a chance finally to harass some pot guts. Meanwhile, Deidre and Jennifer enjoyed the pool on the lake's edge. Marcia was stretched out in the room, not wanting to be disturbed. I worried about the next day's travel, since friends had told me about the long downhill stretches of the Bitterroot Valley trail, with its sharp curves, switchbacks, and narrow mountain passes.

Leaving early in the morning bothered everyone, but my anxiety got the better of me. The minibike once again was anchored down, although the fumes from the gas leak engulfed the motor home. The bathroom was starting to smell bad again, and the curvy roads were making the girls dizzy. Seat belts were not common then, so a white-knuckled Marcia was constantly bracing herself against the armrest.

We were soon surrounded by the Bitterroot National Forest and its two majestic mountain ranges that protruded skyward like giant bookends. As we approached the lower valley, following the Bitterroot River, the road narrowed. I used low gear, which did little, so I carefully pumped the brakes, fearing that I would burn them out and the motor home would become an out-of-control runaway missile. We turned off the air conditioner, too, since the engine was overheating. Several times we had to stop to let the engine cool down, and added some water to the radiator.

Much of the way was marked as a no-passing zone, which meant extra pumping of the brakes when we came up close behind other vehicles. The drafting effect of semi-trailers passing constantly pulled us sideways, and I feared hitting another vehicle. I do not recall seeing any scenery other than the continuous double yellow line that lay ahead of me, separating our motor home from potential disaster. Finally, by late afternoon, we passed through the rugged Lost Trail Pass near the Idaho border. The pass was very narrow and curvy, and everyone could hear my heavy breathing and see the sweat running down my cheeks. No one made a peep.

Eventually we came to Salmon, Idaho, but we couldn't find a motel with a vacancy, and even the campground was full. We kept driving, looking for a place to park the motor home overnight. In the light of a full moon, I spotted a gravel road leading to an open field with several shade trees sitting astride. In the dim headlights, I noticed the area was low and a little spongy, covered with vegetation. At last,

I thought, we would finally have a real camping experience, under the moon and the bright stars of the Milky Way. Marcia and I had a nice glass of wine, but before retiring I had to put the minibike outside again so we wouldn't be asphyxiated. The kids, no longer dizzy, played several games of hearts. It was a magical night.

At sunrise the air was crisp, the mist over the bog was eerie, and there wasn't a sound—not even a bird chirping. I noticed then I had parked near the marshy edge of a streambed. A few more feet and the motor home, with us inside, would have sunk in up to its axles.

Concerned about getting stuck, I suggested we quickly eat some cereal and be on our way, so that we would reach Salt Lake City by nightfall. When we finished our breakfast, I opened the window and tossed out the dregs from the cereal bowls. I dreaded the task of lifting the minibike back up the narrow steps. When I opened the door, I was shocked to see the minibike covered with the cereal and milk. As I cleaned it off, the flies and mosquitoes bit me from head to foot. I could hear chuckles from inside, although everyone was out of sight.

Itchy and miserable, I backed the motor home out, watching the water fill the vehicle's tracks as I retreated. I was glad to reach Highway 84, a major thoroughfare with service stations along the way. By that afternoon we were less than two hundred miles from home, and I was upbeat. As we passed Burley, Idaho, however, the engine began to sputter.

At first I thought it was a gas issue again, but the gauge still showed a quarter tank. Then I feared there was water in the gas from the local station where I'd filled up the previous day. The sputtering came and went. Finally, five miles out from Burley, the motor home came to a shaky halt. Several times I tried to restart the engine, but it only coughed.

Once again we were parked along the highway in the hot sun. And once again I pulled out the minibike. I headed back to Burley, hoping to find a pay phone so that I could call AAA for help. In the outskirts of town, near a small grocery store, I found a pay phone and called the first listing, which was in Rupert. By the time I returned to my stranded family, the wrecker truck had arrived, and the mechanic concluded that the fuel pump had failed. The best he could do was to pull the motor home to a local repair shop; if they couldn't fix the pump, we would have to wait a day until one could be brought in from Salt Lake City.

The five-mile trip to Rupert seemed longer as we were towed along the narrow two-lane road. It was evening when we arrived, and I did not feel comfortable staying in front of the repair shop, which was in a nonresidential area of town. The tow truck driver offered to haul the motor home to a park near the town square, which would give us much more comfort, and agreed to come back and get us at eight o'clock sharp so we could be at the repair shop when it opened. Luckily, we had enough food to hold us for the night, and by this point we were unfazed by the gasoline and bathroom smells mixed together.

However, a curious crowd was gathering and staring at this strange vehicle. Maybe they thought we were using their lovely park as a campground. In any event, they hung around, and when Marcia and the kids finally fell sleep, I stood guard. Sometime after one in the morning, the crowd lost interest in us and moved on.

Bright and early, the AAA truck arrived to haul us a few short blocks to the garage. Keeping my fingers crossed, we lucked out. The fuel pump was filled with gunk, probably sucked up from the bottom of an old service station fuel tank. The dirt and grit were easy to dislodge and wash away. Tips, repair charges, and gas added up to $150—not bad, I thought—and soon we were on our way to Salt Lake City, hoping we would not have any further mishaps. The last 180 miles were a countdown, and every mileage marker brought another smile from Marcia and the kids.

Finally we were back in Salt Lake City, and I was on South Temple Street heading toward I Street, the last hill leading up to our home. My heart raced until the massive concrete wall surrounding our house was in sight. Just a few hundred yards more and I could turn off the engine of this Dodge Travco motor home forever! Everyone yelled with cheers and hugged as we reached our destination.

The last thing we had to do was unload and clean the motor home before returning it to Hinckley Dodge. As I tried to open the door, the handle fell off, and the rest of the mechanism landed in my hand. We all stood in silence looking at the bolted door. Finally Marcia and the kids once again climbed out the window, and I heaved all our belongings out through the opening and into their hands. I made one last tour of the motor home to see if we'd left anything behind, and when I got back to the window, I noticed I was alone—everyone else had gone inside. I struggled out the window by myself.

Some time later, as I was flying to Denver on business, I was telling one of my executives this saga of survival when a voice from behind me bellowed out, "Next time, take a Winnebago." The gentlemen, an executive with that coach manufacturer, slipped me his card.

In the early 1970s, I became interested in collecting, restoring, and showing antique automobiles. At least one weekend a month, Marcia and I traveled to auctions around the country. I particularly liked open racers dating back to the early 1900s. When I went to Reno on business, I would stop to see Bill Harrah's incredible collection of more than twelve hundred automobiles, and soon Bill and I became friends. Bill enjoyed the company of serious collectors, and he taught me about the value and desirability of certain cars for my growing collection.

We attended many auctions and car shows, especially the annual Concourse d'Elegance, swap meet, and auction in Hershey, Pennsylvania, a highlight for car collectors from around the country. While we were in Pennsylvania, Marcia visited the nearby towns of Lancaster and Harrisburg, looking for turn-of-the-century shoes, hats, dresses, gloves, parasols, baby carriages, and many other collector's items she deemed ideal for a museum we were planning. The children stayed with me in Hershey to help clean and polish the brass on our show cars—a labor of love that they soon came to hate.

By 1975, our collection had grown to thirty-seven automobiles. We displayed many of these antique and vintage automobiles in our retail malls and at the annual International Council of Shopping Centers convention in Las Vegas. Eli Williams and his young son Jim, with the help of Orville Larsen, actively restored and maintained the collection. They were aided by incredible local craftsmen who understood the unique nature of these early machines: disassembling them, building parts for them, and bringing them back to their original factory condition. Marcia and the children and I would travel with the cars to shows across the country, winning trophies and ribbons at Hershey, Pebble Beach, Silverado (Napa Valley), and Reno. My favorite was the antique racer that got me hooked: a bright yellow 1913 Mercer Raceabout Type-35R.

On June 13, 1975, Bill Harrah and his wife, Verna Lee, came to Salt Lake City to dedicate the Price Automobile Museum, which was housed in a warehouse located in our Pioneer Square Industrial Park. We enjoyed having thousands of visitors, many of them students, over the next fourteen years, and participated in many public events with this rare car collection. But during the difficult economic times of the late 1980s, we sold the car collection, since bankers saw this as a frivolous endeavor.

My love of these fast, beautiful early racing machines never waned, however, and in late 1999 I began to amass a new collection of famous and rare race cars and other exquisite period automobiles, which today are displayed in the Price Museum of Speed. Ab Jenkins's record-setting race car, the Mormon Meteor III, is the capstone of the museum's collection.

The life of the Mormon Meteor III began in 1937 at Indianapolis, Indiana where the car was built and tested at the "Old Brickyard"—the Indianapolis Motor Speedway. On July 26, 1939, Ab Jenkins, fifty-six years old at the time, set out to recapture some of the distance records set the previous year by notable British drivers John Cobb, Malcolm Campbell, and George E. T. Eyston. In motorsports history, world land speed holder, Ab Jenkins, challenged time and distance—and his competitors—on the Bonneville Salt Flats in the western Utah desert to become the father of salt racing.

Ab Jenkins was born David Abbott Jenkins in 1883 in Spanish Fork, Utah. He began his racing career on a bicycle in the 1890s. With the invention of the internal combustion engine, Ab turned to racing motorcycles on dirt and wooden tracks. He was soon hooked by the challenge of speed and endurance and the high of winning.

Ab was an early pioneer in racing from Salt Lake City through the western Utah salt beds to the town of Wendover, 125 miles to the west. It wouldn't be until

4.8. Pebble Beach Concours d'Elegance, August 1975. John, Marcia, Deidre, and Jennifer are in the car, a 1916 Stutz Bearcat, while Steven is helping to push. Winner in its class, the Stutz ran out of gas at the podium.

almost ten years after World War I that this stretch of uncharted salt beds would become world renowned for the records Ab set there. Notoriety came to Ab in 1925 when he made a $250 bet that he could beat a Western Pacific train in a borrowed Studebaker off the showroom of a local car dealer, Naylor Auto. He reached the finish line in Wendover a full five minutes ahead of the train.

In his quest to prove himself, Ab began racing longer distances between western towns, on cross-country sojourns and on numerous board tracks. He was also

4.9. From the John Price Automobile Collection, vintage clothing modeled by the Price family, summer 1975.

enticed by hill climbs and other endurance challenges. In 1931, an illness prevented Ab from making his debut at the Indianapolis Speedway, but later he would return to participate in special race events. It was in April 1937 when Ab and co-driver Billy Winn, driving a Cord 812 around the two-and-a-half-mile track for twenty-four hours straight, won the Stephens Trophy race. Ab garnered sponsors and supporters such as Studebaker, Pierce-Arrow, Cord, and Firestone.

By now, however, salt was deeply ingrained in Ab Jenkins blood. In 1935, the Duesenberg Special, a converted speedster, was subsequently branded the Mormon Meteor I. Although sturdy and able to take Ab to some impressive new records, the Duesenberg engine needed continual engineering improvements to beat the competitors.

In 1936, a more powerful 1,570-cubic-inch, 750-horsepower Curtiss Conqueror V-12 aircraft engine was installed. With this new engine, the renamed Mormon Meteor II was set to take on the famed British drivers. That summer, endurance records on the Bonneville Salt Flats went back and forth between these fine competitors. However, Ab, averaging 164.47 mph for 500 kilometers, or 310 miles, broke Eyston's record. After some mechanical repairs, Ab later returned to the salt beds in September and set further milestones, averaging 153.823 mph for twenty-four hours and 148.641 mph for forty-eight hours, ending the 1936 season by winning back the records.

During the 1937 summer race season, weather conditions wreaked havoc and it wasn't until September that it was safe to get onto the salt. During one run, a piece of wire flew into the cockpit and hit Ab. He removed the metal lodged in his arm and soon was back at the wheel. When the race was over, Ab and his co-driver Louis Meyer had driven more than 3,700 miles at an average speed of 157.27 mph.

In late 1937 Ab approached his friend Augie Duesenberg to build a car from scratch, one that could be fitted with two Curtiss Conqueror engines in order to some-day compete in straight-line measured mile records against the British, who were using twin engines for their record-breaking straight-line cars. Augie agreed to design and build just such a car. It would not only become an endurance car but quite possibly evolve into the fastest straight-line racer in history.

At age fifty-six, the youthful-looking Ab Jenkins was setting endurance records that much younger racers could only shake their heads in astonishment. Even seasoned relief drivers, who admired Ab, constantly complained of burnout, sore backs, leg fatigue, and blistered hands. Ab's power of concentration and tenacity were legendary. During the 1939 race season on the salt flats, Ab set endurance records for distances up to 638 miles, averaging 171.3 mph in the Mormon Meteor III, outfitted with the Conqueror engine that had been in the Mormon Meteor II. Augie was on hand in the pit area to fine-tune the race machine's aerodynamics as needed.

Once during a pit stop, a support crew fueling error caused a gigantic fireball inside the locked cockpit. Thinking quickly, Ab's son Marvin rammed a screwdriver into the slot, loosening the bolt connection that held the cockpit enclosure, allowing his father to escape death, though Ab did incur second- and third-degree burns on his right leg and arm. After medical attention at the site, Ab still wanted to continue racing. Instead, he was taken to a Salt Lake City hospital, where they treated his burns, and less than three weeks later he returned to the track. Not yet healed but determined, Ab set the twelve-hour endurance record at 169.99 mph.

Unfortunately, he could not stave off infection and once again found himself in the hospital. While there, a movement began for him to run for mayor of Salt Lake City that fall. Ab agreed, and ran with automobile safety as part of his platform. Hailed as a "one-man public relations machine," Ab did almost no campaigning and spent not a dime of his money. He won the election on October 24, 1939, by a slim margin.

In 1940, as mayor, Ab took charge of the city's public safety, which included the police and fire departments. He also continued to be involved with his racing endeavors and traveled to different cities on behalf of car manufacturers and sponsors until World War II broke out. Then, in the November 1943 elections, Ab was defeated in his reelection bid.

In the meantime, his son Marvin was committed to his father's quest for setting records. Twenty years old, Marvin prepped the Mormon Meteor III and tested it at speeds reportedly approaching 200 mph. In 1940, with relief driver Cliff Bergere, Ab covered 3,868 miles during a twenty-four-hour run, averaging 161.18 mph. This remarkable record was not eclipsed until 1991, when a team of eight drivers drove three specially built Corvettes. I do not feel it was a comparable endurance challenge, so from my viewpoint Ab's record still stands today, in addition to twelve others yet to be broken.

After this challenging record run in 1940, Bergere, an experienced driver at the Indianapolis 500—a race that then took four and a half hours to complete—said,

"I'll take my hat off to Ab Jenkins. Any man who can drive that car for six hours at the speed Ab got out of the machine is a marvel. I've never seen anything like it." That same summer, Ab set a number of records, including one hour at 190.68 mph, six hours at 172.38 mph, and 12 hours at 170.21 mph.

Ab never installed the second Conqueror engine, which he had loaned to the Army Air Corps for training purposes; from what I was told, the engine went missing after the war. But even in the early 1950s, a still-fit Ab, now in his mid-sixties, set several more records in the Mormon Meteor III, though he depended more on relief drivers, which included his son Marvin. Ab's dream of setting another world record ended when he died of heart failure on August 9, 1956.

Ab had donated the Mormon Meteor III to the State of Utah in 1943 for public display and periodically borrowed it back to race. It sat in the State Capitol for years, and I became acquainted with its charm and sleek lines. More than once I pressed my nose against the glass enclosure with awe. Marvin repossessed his father's gift in the 1990s. Sad to say, one of the world's most important endurance race cars had deteriorated while in the state's possession.

Subsequently, Marvin and a team of restorers at Dixie College painstakingly undertook a ground-up restoration of the Mormon Meteor III.

In 2007, Marvin was pondering what was best for the Ab Jenkins legacy when we met and shared the vision of perpetuating and preserving the great racing machines of yesteryear for future generations to enjoy. Marvin believed our proposed museum was the best location for the Mormon Meteor III's new home as part of the Bonneville Salt Flats legacy.

4.10. The Mormon Meteor III, built in 1938 by Augie Duesenberg and Ab Jenkins, back on the Bonneville Salt Flats, Utah, September 2008.

In our possession, we dismantled and rebuilt the Curtiss Conqueror engine to its original racing condition. One of our goals was to return the Mormon Meteor III to the Salt Flats and Indianapolis, race-ready, with Marvin behind the wheel.

Nearing ninety years of age, Marvin guided us tirelessly from memory and drawings through the tedious engine rebuilding process. Stricken with cancer and relying on a walker, he worked with us until the task was completed. We planned to test the Mormon Meteor III on September 20 and 21, 2008, and had reserved two days of salt time and built a five-mile oval course for the event. On the Tuesday before the test drive was to take place, Marvin died. Determined to make the test runs as planned, to pay homage to this fine gentleman, I took the Mormon Meteor III flawlessly through its paces on the salt flats oval track in honor of Marvin. I was sure Ab was somewhere not too distant from his record-setting racing machine.

Part of our goal was to take the Mormon Meteor III back to its birthplace in Indianapolis once more. Fortuitously, in May 2009, Joie Chitwood, president of the Indianapolis Motor Speedway, invited us back to the racetrack. That year was their one-hundredth anniversary, and they wanted the Mormon Meteor III to participate in the celebration, especially since it had been built there and tested on the track. We were given unimpeded track time and made a number of historic laps over the ceremonial bricks. Feeling Ab and Marvin's presence close by, I chanced to look up in the stands and spotted Marvin's son Charlie and his son James watching, both with their engaging Jenkins smile.

Before leaving Indianapolis we visited the site of the original Duesenberg factory, a building that still stands proudly. We paused for a few minutes in reflection and thanked Augie Duesenberg for his automotive genius and Ab Jenkins for his untiring and tenacious racing soul.

{V}

Born-Again Athlete

Seeking the Fountain of Youth

In 1978, I became a born-again athlete with a mission to extend my life by improving my health. As I've said, over the years of working long hours I had been drinking martinis, smoking, and sleeping only three to four hours a night, and my weight started to rise. I did make it a point to meet my friends Gil Iker, Ross Thoresen, Grant Southwick, Larry Lunt, and John A. Price (no relation) at the Towne House Athletic Club in downtown Salt Lake City to play handball and racquetball on a regular basis. But what I needed was a complete overhaul.

One day over locker room talk, my friends bet me that I could not run in an upcoming marathon. Since I thrive on challenges and had several months to prepare, I immediately stopped smoking and drinking, and I even changed my eating habits.

I had never been a runner. A friend who was one told me about Phil Knight's new waffle-soled running trainers, and I promptly purchased a pair. Phil Knight was the co-founder and chairman of Nike. His trainers were lightweight, made of leather and nylon fabric stitched and glued to a thin rubber sole, which Knight's partner, former track coach Bill Bowerman, invented by pressing latex in a heated waffle maker that transferred a gridlike imprint. These early trainers had little arch support or cushioning, and initially I felt every bump in the road. Soon enough, though, they became so comfortable I wouldn't give them up. I repaired the worn soles with Shoe Goo and wore them during several marathons before graduating to the next generation of Nike running shoes, which had better arch support and cushioning.

The July 24, 1978, *Deseret News* Marathon was my first long-distance race—the one my friends had bet I couldn't finish. To everyone's surprise, I not only completed the 26.2 miles but did so in under five hours—4:39:52, to be precise. And there were my friends at the finish line, each one holding a $10 check. After a week's rest to let my muscles recover, I went back to running—I was hooked!

When I began training, I suffered injuries along the way and could only manage twenty-five miles a week. I didn't stop working out, though, and built up to running forty miles a week in preparation for the Hawaii Marathon on December 10, 1978, which I finished in 3:46:17.

It was during the 1977 Hawaii marathon that U.S. Navy Commander John Collins and several other athletes debated whether swimming, biking, or running was the most difficult. Ultimately they decided to combine all three sports back to back in an extreme endurance race. The winner would later be dubbed an "Ironman."

The first of what would become the Ironman triathlons was held on February 18, 1978, at the Waikiki Swim Club in Honolulu. Fifteen men showed up for a rough-water swim of 2.4 miles, a 112-mile bike race around the island of Oahu, and a 26.2-mile run. Prior to this triathlon, none of the contestants had ever competed in a bike race. They had to supply their own support crew for liquids, food, and verbal inspiration. At the end of a long day, twelve had finished; the winner completed the race in a little over 11:15.

I followed news of this with interest. In 1979, I trained again for the *Deseret News* Marathon, finishing in 3:45:34, and ran the October 21 New York City Marathon, finishing in 3:52:53. The next year, I competed in a series of shorter training races, followed by the *Deseret News* and New York City marathons, where my best time was 3:26:41. I thought this was an incredible accomplishment for a person who just three years earlier had been a nonrunner, and I felt I was now ready to take on the triathlon—the Fourth Annual Nautilus International Triathlon, scheduled for February 1981.

In the spring of 1980, I started to train eight to ten hours a day. I began with a run at three o'clock in the morning. I swam laps at the Deseret Gym in downtown Salt Lake City and took long bike rides as far away as Brigham City, Utah—a round-trip distance of more than one hundred miles. I would alternate my routine to avoid injury, which the longer I trained, became a real concern. I trained throughout the winter months by doing long runs and bike rides in rain, snow, and icy conditions. I'd then go to the office, work until eight in the evening, and finally head back home to quickly eat and pass out. I was soon back down to my college wrestling weight of 157 pounds—extremely fit for a forty-eight-year-old triathlete wannabe.

Salt Lake City physiotherapist, marathon runner, and triathlete Robin Beck—who finished the 1980 triathlon event in 11:21:24—became instrumental in my quest to finish the Nautilus International Triathlon set for February. She helped me set up my training schedule and nutritional guidelines, and took time to join me on some training runs. Swimming was difficult for me; my breaststroke style was inefficient. I hired a Brigham Young University (BYU) swimming coach to teach me the Australian crawl, a more efficient stroke, but it continued to be an impediment for me at my age. I went back to the breaststroke and built up my shoulder muscles and quads so I could pull my body through the water while thrusting with both legs. Knowing I would emerge from the water far behind the more accomplished swimmers, I focused on developing an efficient bike riding style and building up my stamina for the long marathon run. The combined time of the event was what counted: I could make up the lost time once I was out of the water.

In the meantime, training for the triathlon took its toll on everyone around me at home and at work. I was told I became a different person because of my new obsession.

Since this was only the fourth Ironman triathlon event, there were few sponsors other than Nautilus. But more than four hundred participants had signed up—so many more than anticipated that the venue had to be moved from Oahu to the Big Island, Hawaii, to alleviate concerns about traffic congestion. The route was planned so that all the stages would start and finish at the Kailua–Kona Bay pier, with water stops provided along the way and specified checkpoints where participants had to stop to have their physical condition assessed, mainly for signs of dehydration.

Nautilus provided T-shirts and trophies to the finishers, and these became prized possessions. No one in these early races was in it for the prize money—there was none! I entered this extreme endurance challenge with the Ironman mantra in mind: just finishing was a victory. Commander Collins put it more succinctly: "Swim 2.4 miles! Bike 112 miles! Run 26.2 miles! Brag for the rest of your life!"

I didn't want to come all the way to Hawaii and fail to finish because I didn't know the course or have proper support (spare bicycle parts, special food, liquid nutrients, basic medical supplies). For this reason, I went to Kailua–Kona Bay twice before the event to train on the actual course and make plans for the needed support.

Swimming continued to be my weakest event, and the out-and-back course in the open ocean made me seasick. I swallowed lots of salt water, and feared that high waves would impede my breaststroke. But I knew I could handle the bike race and marathon, even in the extreme heat—the temperature of the asphalt could climb to more than 100°F.

On the long hill halfway to the town of Hawi, I encountered strong crosswinds that played havoc with my specially built fifteen-pound titanium bike. This lightweight miracle, with nonstructural areas drilled out to reduce the amount of metal, had been custom-built by a professional bike builder referred to me by Ed La Grassa, a New York friend and cycling enthusiast.

Arriving a few days before the event, my son Steven was walking ahead of me carrying the bicycle components when a horde of reporters and photographers swarmed around him, calling out questions about his expected completion time and training particulars. He was speechless for a moment before finally responding he wasn't the contestant—his father was. They all looked past him to where I was walking, and I could see on their faces that they were skeptical whether this skinny middle-aged man with gray hair was really the triathlete.

At six in the morning on February 14, I joined the other competitors at the Kailua–Kona Bay pier to have our arms marked with a number in waterproof ink. One hour later, the starter's gun went off and, with a magnificent sunrise in the distance, more than four hundred entrants, already knee-deep in the water, started thrashing like sharks and kicking their way through the starting line into the surf. The day before had been stormy, but on this day the waters were calm and the swells manageable. I turned in my best time, a little more than two hours in the 2.4-mile swim segment.

Once back on terra firma, I was pumped up for the 112-mile bike race. It was crazy. All around us were support cars and vans operated by novices. They zigzagged on the highway between the participants. Sometimes they came dangerously close to colliding with each other and us. This bike race was anything but the Tour de France. As I approached the Hawi hill climb, I noticed some shiny objects on the asphalt. I quickly realized someone had thrown tacks into our paths. Luckily, I managed to avoid the hazard. Others were not so lucky.

Jim Anderson, a friend since college, cautiously drove my support vehicle, carrying several family members. Jim handed me replacement bottles filled with water and an electrolyte mixture along the bike segment. I survived the race on liquids and adrenaline.

By afternoon, most people were well into the 26.2-mile marathon stage. Some were spent and struggling as they trudged over the hot lava landscape. Along the route, I ran into a fellow runner from Salt Lake City. I had trained with him before and could see he was in bad shape and disoriented. To distract him from his

5.1. The Nautilus International Triathlon, 2.4-mile swim segment, February 14, 1981.

5.2. On the road and in traffic during the triathlon's 112-mile bicycle segment.

pain as we slowly jogged along the highway toward the next aid station, I encouraged him to count the power poles located every hundred feet. Once he had a mixture of water and electrolytes in his system, I talked him into continuing the run. We were only at the eight-mile mark, but I decided to stay with him until we finished the marathon.

Crossing the finish line together in 14:25:05.5, we finished 189th out of the 386 participants who completed all three stages. I was strong enough to have completed the triathlon in less time, but my time was not as important as helping another triathlete cross the line.

The winner that year was Olympic cyclist John Howard, who had a time of 9:38:29. But I have to admit, finishing the Ironman Triathlon, the culmination of a year's grueling training, was the highlight of all my athletic endeavors.

Although I continued running some eighty miles per week—admittedly, I was driven—I was also burned out and not motivated to return to Hawaii the following year as originally planned. My family, my friends, and those I worked with were relieved, since my obsession had taken a toll on them.

One evening I was watching a broadcast of the SCORE International Baja 1000 event, a thousand-mile off-road race from Ensenada to La Paz, Mexico. It looked

5.3. Making it to the triathlon finish line after completing the 26.2-mile marathon segment. Total elapsed time for all three segments: 14:25:05.5.

like an incredible endurance challenge event. The next day, I called Otto Therkelson, a great mechanic and well-known personality in local racing circles, and said I wanted in. He introduced me to Larry Olsen, the owner of an off-road supply business, who had competed in a number of off-road races, and we soon found a used off-road race truck for sale. The Ford F-150 was owned by Ivan Stewart, one of off-road racing's great pioneers, who had used it to win the Baja Class 8 division in 1980.

He sold it to me, and Otto helped me prepare it for our first race—June 6, 1981, just four months after my exhilarating triathlon event.

In 1981, the Baja 500 started and finished in Ensenada. Larry Olsen, who had experience racing in the Baja, was my co-driver for this event. He trained with me on a number of occasions in the open west Utah desert near Salt Lake City. In one training mishap, I missed a turn at high speed and rolled the vehicle several times, ending upright and shaken. Larry's response was a mild-mannered, "Now you got that out of the way."

On race day, we had difficulties right from the start: our engine failed two hundred miles out on the course, and we had to be towed back. It was thrilling, though, to hear the loud roar of all the engines as the vehicles zoomed past each other on narrow trails at high speeds. Among the different vehicle classes, I liked best the Class 8 division, with 550 hp engines under the hood.

When we returned to Salt Lake City, Otto rebuilt and fine-tuned the engine in time for the 1981 Fourth of July Fireworks 250 race at Barstow, California. Once again Larry joined me, and we came in second in the Class 8 division and third overall among the heavy metal race trucks.

After this confidence-building race, I decided to purchase a new Ford F-150 and use the other as a pre-runner and chase truck. In converting a street truck to a race version, Otto had to adhere to SCORE's specifications. He dismantled and rebuilt the entire truck from the frame up. This included a new solid lock-rear end (axle shafts), front spindles, splines, special alloy wheels fitted with quick knock-off hubs, heavy-duty all-terrain radial tires (and two mounted spares), sixteen special high-lift shock absorbers (ten in the front, six in the rear), special disc brakes, a special racing-type automatic transmission, a blueprinted 550 hp engine, new water and oil cooling systems, special carburetors, and a dust filtering system. He installed a smaller compact truck bed with external fenders, a specially built lightweight plastic hood with easy-release pins, eight powerful night driving lights, special roll bars, an automatic fire suppression system, a special gas tank bladder to hold forty-five gallons of jet fuel with two-point fueling access, a racing-style steering wheel, racing seat belts and shoulder harnesses, lightweight bucket seats, side window webbing (replacing glass), special frame-mounted race gauges, emergency high-lift jacks, a two-way radio and helmet intercom system, and a front brush guard.

In the process, we removed all the hardware, trim, dash, sun visors, seats, liners, and floor coverings. We painted the racing machine white with our Price Development Company logo in beige, brown, and orange on both doors. Finally, after the truck passed SCORE technical inspections on race day, we would plaster equipment supplier and sponsor decals all over the truck.

Running marathons was an individual endurance sport. Off-road racing was a team effort requiring a pit crew of fourteen to twenty racing enthusiasts, depending on the race distance. Small teams stationed along the route, leapfrogging one another, had to be prepared with fuel, extra tires, a mobile repair shop, time statistics, and route condition information. Steve Bogden, a loyal twenty-year company executive, helped train the pit crew to execute the tire change, fuel fill, window cleaning, and oil and water inspection in thirty seconds. As we raced through the rugged desolate terrain, my attorney—also a volunteer—tracked our position from his airplane for emergency purposes.

Our new racing-version F-150 was ready to go for the November 6-7, 1981, Baja 1000 race, which again began and ended in Ensenada. Although we completed the difficult course, we got stuck in deep sand along the coastline just long enough to put us out of contention. We then participated in the Parker 400 (February 6, 1982), the San Felipe 250 (March 27, 1982), the Mint 400 (May 2, 1982), the Baja 500 (June 5, 1982), and the Barstow 250 (September 25, 1982).

On November 5, 1982, we raced again in the long, grueling Baja 1000, this time from Ensenada to La Paz, and came in fourth in the Class 8 division. This race proved to be the most challenging of all. The route took us through many changes in terrain, some quite dangerous, such as the rugged mountain ranges with their steep climbs, and the sandy western shoreline, which could easily consume a vehicle. Night driving at high speeds was also dangerous, and at times the narrow roads or trails were confusing to follow. One could easily become disoriented and lost.

There were many tracks created by people taking shortcuts, which presented other problems. If you got off the marked route, you could easily lose time trying to find your way back onto the course. The orange ribbons placed periodically on trees, marking the route, were absent on some stretches—apparently the result of mischievous spectators or drivers trying to change the outcome of the race. Whichever the case, these problems added to an already challenging event.

5.4. Race day at the Baja 1000, 1981.

We finished two Baja 500 and two Baja 1000 races and came in among the top four in the Class 8 division twice, but we never won. My mantra from the Ironman Triathlon, that just to finish was winning, reinforced my off-road racing mind-set. But bouncing around at high speeds, sometimes exceeding 125 miles per hour, with only a helmet, race suit, kidney belt, and seat belt to hold me together and protect my vital organs, was not something I could do forever. In addition to all the challenges in the race, we almost lost our attorney, as well as our company president, Rex Frazier, and chief mechanic, Otto Therkelson, when the chase plane ran off the runway on landing at a small airstrip. Otto, Larry Olsen, Steve Bogden, and the rest of the volunteer support team were also getting burned out. Meeting at the conclusion of our last Baja 1000 race, we toasted the Baja, reminisced a little, enjoyed the moment, and never raced again.

In June 1987, Dick Bass, a friend and owner of the Snowbird Ski Resort, approached me about supporting the upcoming Snowbird Everest Expedition and their attempt to place the first American woman on top of Mt. Everest, the world's highest peak at 29,028 feet. He told me the organizers needed financial help and a support group to help set up the Everest base camp for the expedition team. After talking with Karen Fellerhoff, the team co-leader, I decided to go along with the group to the Himalayas. All I had to do now was prepare myself for this new extreme endurance adventure.

I enrolled in the mountaineering school at Snowbird and over the next few weeks took a series of rock-climbing and safety lessons. I then amassed the 250 items needed for this endeavor, ranging from special climbing boots and equipment to appropriate high-altitude clothing and medical supplies.

The Snowbird Everest Expedition members included co-leaders Pete Athans and Karen Fellerhoff along with team members Sally McCoy, Mary Kay Brewster, Kellie Rhoads, Pete Whittaker, Renny Jackson, Margie Lester, Robert Link, Steve Fossett, and Chris Noble. The team members were all experienced mountain climbers. The support group, which helped fund part of the expedition team costs, would accompany the members on the three-to-four-week acclimatization trek into the Himalayas to the Everest base camp located at the foot of the Great Khumbu Icefall at 17,575 feet.

Dick Bass, an experienced climber, had made it to the summit of the highest peak on each of the seven continents, reaching the summit of Mt. Everest in 1985. Since he was familiar with the area, he would help with the logistics and guide the support group trekkers.

The plan was that our group would leave first, while the expedition team stayed behind in Kathmandu, Nepal, to gather up their gear and additional supplies. On August 18, which was also my birthday, the government's large Puma helicopter was to transport the support group and their gear from Kathmandu, at 4,383 feet, up to the remote mountain village of Lukla, at 9,350 feet, where our trek would begin. Once there, we would acclimate to the high altitudes by trekking three to six hours each day at varying elevations. Along the way, we would attempt climbs on Chukkung Ri, a peak 18,231 feet high, then Kala Pattar, 18,450 feet, and Island Peak, 20,305 feet.

The expedition members would meet the support group trekkers near the village of Lobuche. Together we would make the six-hour trek across the glacial moraine to the Everest base camp. We would spend a week to ten days setting up the base camp. Then the Snowbird team would make a series of ascents to the higher camps and, weather permitting, ultimately ascend to the top of Mt. Everest sometime in September or early October.

We arrived by helicopter in Lukla under heavy cloud cover and rain. For the next three weeks, it rained on and off, keeping us constantly damp. To help us acclimate to high-altitude trekking, Dick showed us the art of rhythmic pressure breathing and utilizing a slow, measured pace for walking, making this new experience easier. Just above Namche Bazaar at 12,000 feet, two people on the support team developed serious high-altitude sickness and had to be quickly evacuated to lower altitudes.

Those of us who felt ready climbed to the top of Chukkung Ri, which was an incredible trek and offered great vistas of Ama Dablam (which resembled the Matterhorn), Island Peak, and Makalu. The group then ascended Kala Pattar, where

5.5. Visit with a lama at Pangboche Monastery, who gave his blessing for a safe expedition. Each participant received a white *khata* silk scarf and a cotton cord placed around the neck for good luck, August 1987. Sherpas will not guide anyone through the Khumbu Icefall without such a blessing, for fear of angering the gods.

we enjoyed grand views of the Himalayas, with the main attraction, Mt. Everest, and Lhotse as backdrops.

On August 28, nine members of the trekking group and several Sherpas attempted an ascent of Island Peak. After we reached the lower Island Peak base camp, at approximately 16,000 feet, it began to rain. Early the next day, we climbed to an upper base camp located at 18,300 feet. A very narrow area, it allowed only limited flat space for a campsite approximately 2,000 feet below the Island Peak summit. It rained and snowed intermittently throughout most of the night.

The next day, Ang Gyalzen, the Sherpas' climbing leader, agreed to try to install fixed ropes on the upper vertical icefall and develop a safe route for us to follow. Before leaving, the Sherpas held a religious ceremony, burning juniper and chanting mantras. Returning in midafternoon, they said that the snow at the upper elevations was very deep and could create serious avalanche danger. They had not been able to place the fixed ropes to the summit area. That evening, our group took a vote and decided to go up at least to the 19,500-foot level and proceed from there with caution.

On Monday, August 31, we began our climb at five o'clock in the morning. Four hours later, we still did not know whether we would make the ascent to the top of Island Peak. Thin air, slippery rocks, and heavy snow made the trek quite dangerous. Several snow bridges collapsed beneath us. Fortunately, no one was injured, as we were roped together in teams of three with a Sherpa leading each group. Along the way, I marveled at the beauty around us: the glacial lakes, icefalls and ice walls, exposed séracs, and seemingly bottomless crevasses.

When we reached an icy area, we put on crampons and continued to the higher elevations. At the ice wall where they planned to set ropes, visibility was poor:

5.6. Snowbird-Everest Expedition Sherpa guides, August 1987.

5.7. En route to Island Peak, August 31, 1987.

clouds had covered up most of the peak area. The weather was not cooperating, and it became apparent we would not make the ascent that day.

Since the Island Peak climb was one of the highlights of the trip, we were disappointed but safety was our first priority. Slowly winding our way down through the icy slopes, several times we had to scramble to keep from slipping into dangerous crevasses or over the edges, where drops exceeded a thousand feet. By late afternoon, we were back at the lower base camp.

That evening, I developed severe chills. I wrapped myself in whatever blankets and extra clothes I could find and curled up in my sleeping bag for warmth. The fear crossed my mind that I was developing hypothermia: I could feel my body temperature falling well below normal. I could not eat or stand up without feeling weak and disoriented. Even after sipping four cups of chicken broth, I still shook and felt totally exhausted. That night was the most miserable for me; I was not able to breathe regularly. Fortunately, by morning I felt somewhat better, and after several more cups of broth and two cups of local tea, I was ready to join the group for our descent.

Somewhere between Lobuche and Gorak Shep we were to meet up with the expedition team. They had spent extra time in Kathmandu gathering more gear and supplies. Arriving at Gorak Shep, word reached us that the team would not be meeting us. The helicopter was unable to get all the equipment to Lukla, and several expedition members would have to trek in by foot. This would require an additional nine days from Kathmandu and more than fifty porters to carry the balance of the gear. It also created a timing problem for the support group, as we were scheduled to fly from Lukla back to Kathmandu on September 6. A plan was then made for the support group to trek to the Everest base camp and then decide whether to wait for some of the expedition team to catch up or head back to Lukla.

Crossing over the glacial moraine, we encountered loose rocks, and I slipped and fell several times, once coming close to falling into a glacial lake. Crevasses were everywhere, interspersed with séracs standing nearly a hundred feet high. I could hear the glacier creaking and groaning as it moved beneath us; from the distance came the cracking sound of avalanches.

When we arrived at the Everest base camp, positioned on the northern edge of the Khumbu Glacier, I was surprised to see how austere it looked, with large glacial boulders and the residual glacial moraine. Several brightly colored tents belonging to other climbers were squeezed into semiflat, rock-laden areas. Colorful prayer flags, known as *lung ta* or wind horses, were strung everywhere. Made most often from rectangular cloths sewn onto a string, they conferred the blessings of good luck and a safe journey for Tibetans and foreigners while in the Himalayas.

For the next six to eight weeks, this windblown, rocky escarpment would be home to the Snowbird Everest Expedition team. The support group was needed to help clear the icy areas to set tent platforms and stack glacial rocks to create walls for the kitchen and dining tent used during their stay.

Unable to wait for the expedition team to arrive the following week, we headed back down to Pheriche and spent the night. In the morning, we retraced our footsteps on the long trek back down to Lukla, the starting point of our journey. Along the way, I wondered what it is that attracts climbers to the high peaks of the Himalayas and to the many other places where no one has yet been. Deep in thought, I was oblivious to the low clouds, the rainfall, and the slippery surfaces beneath me. All I could think about was that for years people had trekked up and down the Great Khumbu region, with trail markers indicating those who gave their lives trying.

Along the trail, Dick Bass stopped for a moment at a marker inscribed with the name Marty Hoey. Dick explained Hoey was one of the most skilled climbers of her time, but during the May 1982 expedition to summit Mt. Everest, she had a fatal accident. She had reached the 26,000-foot level on the Great Coulier on the north face and was waiting to ascend higher when her waist harness, attached to a fixed climbing rope, came unbuckled, and she plunged to her death. Dick's brief eulogy touched us all.

Just above Phakding, we ran into co-leaders Pete Athans and Karen Fellerhoff heading up to the base camp. Although we were disappointed at how the plan had worked out, we expressed how incredible the experience in the Himalayas had been. All of us wished them success in their attempt to place the first American woman on top of the world.

We had to wait an extra day in Lukla for the government's Puma helicopter to arrive and take us back down to Kathmandu. On the morning of September 7, a small four-seat French Alouette military helicopter arrived instead. I was among the first group to leave, and on the way out I could smell oil burning when we were at an altitude of about 7,000 feet. The pilot looked at his gauges and quickly made an emergency landing near an army outpost. After adding a few quarts of oil, we were off again and landed in Kathmandu—our hands white-knuckled from tensely clutching our seats.

Throughout the balance of September, the Snowbird Everest Expedition team set up staging areas at higher elevations. On October 4, however, a raging storm blew away tents and equipment and forced four members of the expedition team to retreat down from their camp at 24,000 feet. The climbers made several attempts to summit, but the bad weather continued. On October 17 and 18, several feet of snow fell at the 21,500-foot camp. As the blizzard raged around them, Pete Whittaker, Robert Link, and three Sherpas were trapped inside their tents for nearly two days, staying inside for fear of being blown away.

After another major storm on October 19, any further attempts by Karen Fellerhoff, Kellie Rhoads, Pete Athans, and Renny Jackson were called off. A telex sent by Karen from Kathmandu encapsulated their frustration: "Expedition called off November 1 due to jet stream winds from north above Camp 2 and extreme cold. Major collapse in the icefall taking out 300 meters of fixed rope. Storm 18th October destroyed camps 1, 2, 3, 4, and fixed ropes on Lhotse face were taken out in massive avalanche. Because of meter deep snow to base camp, yaks took four days to ferry loads out."

It would be one year later, on September 29, 1988, that Stacy Allison, with another expedition, would become the first American woman to reach the top of Mt. Everest.

On January 10, 1988, at the Mt. Everest Expedition reunion held at the Snowbird Resort, I discussed with Karen Fellerhoff my goal to make a major mountain climb. A few days later, she sent me a plan for summiting Mt. Aconcagua, the highest peak in the Western Hemisphere at 22,835 feet above sea level. She said it was doable given my limited experience and conditioning. Karen and Pete Athans would plan the logistics of the trip and guide me to the top.

With less than two weeks to plan the trip, I told Karen to go ahead and put it together. Since I had kept all my gear ready for just such a climb, packing was easy. We agreed to meet in Miami on Saturday, February 20, 1988, for our Pan Am flight to Buenos Aires, Argentina, the next day, and then take Aerolineas Argentinas to Mendoza, a city nestled in the foothills of the Andes at 6,000 feet. Once there, we would obtain our climbing permits and depart for Puente del Inca to begin our trek. We planned to make the ascent, weather permitting, on March 4 and then be back in Mendoza by Wednesday, March 9.

On Tuesday, February 23, we hired a driver with an older Dodge 1500 vehicle equipped with a rack on top for our gear. We were soon off to Puente del Inca, located at 9,400 feet at the foot of Aconcagua. Beautiful hues of red and deep crimson inter-laced the rock formations, which had been uplifted and twisted over eons. They towered now as pinnacles reaching toward the sky without a pattern or direction.

Halfway to Puente del Inca, we stopped at Uspallata and once again at Punta de Vacas to show the police our climbing permits. For a while we thought we would be walking rather than riding: as we reached the higher altitudes, the old Dodge sput-tered and vapor-locked several times along the way.

That night at the Hosteria Puente del Inca, Hernandez, the owner of the three mules we hired for the next day, showed slides of specific routes that could be taken. One trail lead to the Confluenza, up the Polish Glacier, while another route traversed the north ridge.

The following morning, Hernandez loaded up the mules for our trek to the Confluenza, where two glaciers—the Horcones Superior and Inferior—meet. Our trail followed the Superior segment at the Confluenza. Right from the beginning, I saw the awesome, isolated mountain towering to the skies with clouds interspersed around its peak. At every twist and turn in the trail, Mt. Aconcagua looked slightly different, gigantic and majestically alone.

On the first day, it took more than six long hours to reach the Confluenza camp, at 11,200 feet. It rained, the wind was gusting fiercely, and for two hours we strug-gled to anchor our tents and sort out our gear to dry. The wind continued to increase and the rain turned to snow. Facing almost two weeks of strenuous workouts and logistics to ensure a safe ascent to the top, I was not looking forward to the addi-tional problem of inclement weather.

The next morning, the weather improved, the mules were loaded up, and we were off to the Plaza de Mulas base camp at 13,500 feet. The trek up the Horcones Valley, also called the Horcones Superior, was reminiscent of the trek to the Island Peak base camp. It was a glacial moraine, and I remembered well the resting-step and pressure-breathing techniques I'd learned in Khumbu. After nearly seven hours of trekking, putting one foot in front of the other and taking several breaths of air with each step, we arrived at the Plaza de Mulas camp. I was exhausted and dehydrated, and had quite a headache from being at 13,500 feet.

At rest points, Karen encouraged me to remain standing and walk around to keep the blood and oxygen flowing through my system. Our plan was to stay at Plaza de Mulas for several days to acclimatize, trekking to the higher elevations with sup-plies and gear to set up staging areas and returning to the lower camp for the night.

On Friday, February 26, Karen was not feeling well and stayed behind while Pete and I accomplished a two-hour acclimatization trek to 16,000 feet. We carried some food, supplies, and high altitude snow gear to stash at some convenient place along the way. Just above camp, we traversed through séracs that looked like wor-shippers leaning in the same direction and praying.

The traverse up the mountain was slippery and dangerous. A loss of footing could send any one of us careening into one of the sharp-edged ice formations. When we came upon loose scree, we stepped carefully to keep from sliding down the steep slopes—including some that were almost vertical. When we were a thousand feet above the camp, I needed to take two breaths for each step. By the time I reached the 16,000-foot level, I had no choice but to take three breaths with every step. Slipping, sliding, and exhausted, we crested at a small, intermediate campsite located halfway up to our next camp. We immediately stowed all the items we'd carried up and placed rocks over them for protection against inclement weather and potential theft. Having gone from 13,500 feet to 16,000 feet in two hours, I really believed I'd accomplished something that day.

Pete and I sat for a few minutes before descending. He explained that the next day we would take most of our gear and supplies all the way up to the next camp and hike all the way back down to Plaza de Mulas for the night. The day after that, we would break camp and take the remainder of our supplies and gear to the next camp. We would continue this same process of working our way up until we reached Campo Berlin, the highest camp, from which we would summit.

For the next two days we trekked more than five hours a day, ascending and descending more than three thousand feet each time. After we reached the 17,200-foot level, where we would set up our tents the next day, I developed a headache, became light-headed, and nearly passed out. Hiking back to the lower camp that night, I was still unstable but, supporting myself with poles, managed to make my descent.

By Sunday, the long day's hike had taken its toll on me. I was physically spent and itching all over from an allergic reaction to my Capilene underwear. My face was swollen and sunburned, my lips were blistered and my throat raspy, and I had difficulty breathing. My body was swollen with edema. I drank tea, hoping it would act as a diuretic, and it did, all night. I spent a restless night dozing off only intermittently; the thought of aborting the climb here crossed my mind, since going higher would make that option more difficult.

By seven the next morning, when Pete brought me a cup of tea, I was feeling somewhat better. We packed, ate a quick cup of oatmeal, and were on our way to the Nido de Cóndores camp at 17,200 feet. The trek past Plaza Canada was my third time on this route, and traversing the scree and slippery rocks wasn't getting any easier. Several times I lost my footing and had to rely on my poles to save me from falling.

Reaching the Nido de Cóndores camp entailed almost seven hours of arduous trekking with a vertical rise of 3,700 feet. The last hour or so, we walked through deep snow, step-kicking to make a platform for the next step. This process took up so much added energy that by the time we arrived at our campsite I was exhausted and unable to help Pete and Karen set up our tents. Fortified again with a cup of tea, and seeing that our camp was situated on a saddle ridge, I helped Pete look for large rocks to hold down the tent corners in case a strong wind came up during the night.

Other climbers had already taken the only three outcropping rocks that provided shelter from the wind. We were stuck in the middle of the open saddle area.

The long vista, with the high peaks sitting overhead, was inspiring. From our vantage point, I could see down the valley and watch the storm clouds building up.

My upper back hurt tremendously from the pressure of carrying a sixty-pound backpack. I lost my appetite and consumed only tea and small amounts of soup. It was cold. Although I wore all my clothes, it never got warm enough inside my sleeping bag. I tried to go to sleep at nine o'clock but was awakened by the most intense storm I had experienced on this trip. The wind was howling through the saddle at fifty miles an hour, gusting up to eighty, and continued throughout the night. Several squalls almost sent my tent flying over the saddle ridge with me still inside it. Pete came to my rescue with an assortment of stuff bags filled with stones he'd managed to gather for ballast. I couldn't help him: I was the only ballast holding the tent from going over the ridge.

Although the tent was now somewhat secure, I spent the rest of the night with a headache, upset stomach, sore throat, chills, sunburn, and swollen and crusted lips; at times I was disorientated. By morning, the wind hadn't stopped; throughout the day, gusts of blinding snow ricocheted off the sides of the tent. Every time I stood up, the wind moved the tent, so I just stayed in one place, stretched out in solitude, staring at the small puncture holes overhead in the roof of the tent.

To reach Campo Berlin at 19,000 feet required a strenuous two-thousand-foot climb up from the Nido de Cóndores camp. I was already drained, and realized the upper reaches above Campo Berlin would only become more difficult if my condition worsened. I knew that in my weakened condition I would not be able to carry gear and needed rations to the higher elevations, especially walking in knee-deep snow. I made the decision then and there to abort my ascent to the top of Mt. Aconcagua and not hamper Pete and Karen's chance to summit. Over the howling wind, I called out to Pete. When my voice finally reached him, he struggled against the wind as he crawled over to my tent. I told Pete of my plan to return to Plaza de Mulas and find someone to trek out with to Puente del Inca, where I could catch a bus or taxi back to Mendoza.

Pete urged me to press on, saying I was stronger than most other people he had seen and would not hold either of them back. Karen also encouraged me to remain for at least another day, in hopes of seeing some improvement in the weather conditions. She said they would move the tents closer to a more protected area, sharing space with another American expedition. But during a brief break in the storm, Lyle, the other American group's trek leader, said the barometer was dropping and that he thought the wind and snow conditions would continue. This could mean delaying a final ascent, especially if we reached Campo Berlin with limited food and resources and had to wait for the weather to clear. If Pete and Karen saw a window for their ascent to the summit, they would have to complete the nearly four-thousand-foot climb in six to seven hours. I knew I could not manage that in my condition.

While I gathered my gear, Pete packed one tent and some supplies for our return trek to Plaza de Mulas. Storing some of the food items with the American group for their return to Nido de Cóndores the next day, Pete stashed everything else. The three-hour journey down the mountain told me I had made the right decision. My legs were weak, my muscles were cramping, and my back pain hadn't subsided. My breathing was irregular, hives still covered most of my body, my face and lips were swollen and sunburned, my stomach was still upset, and I had some chills.

At Plaza de Mulas I met a trekker, Francisco Arancibia, from Mendoza. He had plans to leave early the next morning, and he welcomed my joining him on the trek down to Puente del Inca and back to Mendoza.

The next morning, March 2, there was a certain amount of sadness as I prepared to leave. That was the day we had planned to carry equipment up to Campo Berlin in preparation for our summit of Aconcagua. Before departing, I told Pete and Karen to get to the top safely—Utah would be proud of them. I thanked them for all their efforts in putting together this adventurous undertaking, then lingered for one last look at the top of Mt. Aconcagua, shrouded in clouds.

Pete and Karen returned to Nido de Cóndores and spent the night on the wind-swept saddle. A Taiwanese team found a break in the weather to summit that day. The following day, the other American team made it to 20,000 feet, where they were turned back by severe winds. Pete and Karen spent another day at Nido de Cóndores before climbing to Campo Berlin at 19,000 feet. They were lucky enough to find room in one of the two small A-frame huts. The weather turned again, and for a day and a half they remained at Campo Berlin.

Finally the skies cleared, but the winds did not abate. Despite that, on March 7 they climbed for seven hours to summit Mt. Aconcagua. In his letter to me of March 28, Pete wrote, "I have to admit that it was one of the most marginal days I have ever spent in the mountains. Visibility from the summit was less than one hundred meters, but occasionally would open briefly for a stunning view down the south face. . . . I was wearing more that day than I wore on Everest last fall."

Over the years, Pete Athans had become one of the world's foremost high-altitude climbers. After five attempts, he summited Mt. Everest in 1990, and he would go on to summit Everest a total of seven times, the only non-Sherpa to complete the climb so many times. I often wondered whether I could have summited Mt. Aconcagua with Pete and Karen had I stayed!

{VI}

Back to Business

Diversification and JPR Merger

In early 1982, I received a call from my friend and mentor George Hatch, whom I considered one of the most astute businessmen in broadcasting, newspapers, and cable television. He was acquiring several television stations in Kansas and Arkansas and in order to get FCC approval needed to spin off one FM radio station in Wichita, Kansas, that had been part of the package but which, under FCC duopoly rules, would cause a media concentration in the market. He offered the radio station to me at a discount. With my trust in George, I agreed to purchase the station sight unseen, and without a review of the financial statements.

To help him move forward, I agreed to meet with him at his New York apartment on East 53rd Street. While there I was introduced to John Malone, president of Tele-Communications Inc., a cable television provider. Bob Magness founded TCI in 1968, and five years later, at age thirty-two, John took over the reins as president. Eight years my junior, he was already on his way to becoming a giant in the cable industry. A large, square-jawed individual, Malone looked like a football player. He had a dry wit and was quick with words.

Among other mutual business interests, George Hatch and his associate Jack Gallivan represented local Utah cable interests and were early shareholders in TCI. John sat in as George and I discussed the Wichita radio station transaction. George agreed to provide me short-term financing until I could find a permanent funding source. This was the beginning of Price Broadcasting Company.

The following year, I acquired two radio stations in Salt Lake City and two in Wheeling, West Virginia, from the Screen Gems division of Columbia Pictures Industries Inc. I also made a new friend in Karl Eller, with whom I negotiated the transaction. My media ownership ultimately grew to twenty radio stations, two television stations, and a country and western concert business.

The Jamboree USA concert business was part of the famous 50,000-watt, clear-channel WWVA-AM radio station in Wheeling, West Virginia. The associated Capitol Theater held live weekly performances, aired continuously since 1933, second only to the long-running Grand Ole Opry in Nashville, Tennessee. For these weekly shows, busloads of people came from as far away as Canada.

Each summer, in the third week of July, we held a four-day Jamboree in the Hills, a concert event that attracted some fifty thousand country and western music fans to the outdoor amphitheater in St. Clairsville, Ohio, twelve miles west of Wheeling. Over the years, the Jamboree had been home to many new and seasoned performers, including the Oak Ridge Boys, Alabama, Johnny Cash and June Carter, Barbara Mandrell, Tom T. Hall, Willie Nelson, Kris Kristofferson, Merle Haggard, Naomi and Wynonna Judd, Janie Frickie, the Charlie Daniels Band, Charley Pride, Buck Owens, Ray Price, Glen Campbell, Loretta Lynn, Lee Greenwood, the Bellamy Brothers, Crystal Gayle, Mel Tillis, Tammy Wynette, Ricky Skaggs, George Jones, Marie Osmond, Sawyer Brown, Reba McEntire, Ray Stevens, Tanya Tucker, Billy "Crash" Craddock, and Nicolette Larson.

The Jamboree in the Hills and Capitol Theater audiences were loyal listeners to WWVA-AM. Since the radio station could be heard in most of the eastern two-thirds of the United States at night and into Canada, it also drew a large truck driver following.

In 1989, Dave Fischer and Jim Ririe formed the Cypress Packaging Company in Rochester, New York, as the outgrowth of a small local plastic packaging manufacturer they had just purchased. I met Dave, an attorney in the Reagan administration, in Washington. His close friend Jim Ririe worked at the Mobil Plastics division of Mobil Chemical Company in Rochester. They found this small local operation, thought it had a substantial upside potential, and presented me with a business plan. After Pat King and I visited the operation in Rochester, we made a substantial investment and became major shareholders in the business.

The company extruded sheer film from polyethylene pellets and made packaging for a national bread baking company. We then added airtight bags for the produce industry. Other value-added plastic packaging items increased sales for the company, but encroaching competition in the industry for basic bags and packaging soon caused our margins to shrink. The company then developed a new film type of packaging that blended a variety of polyethylene pellets to create a mono and multi-layer structure. One of our first customers was Dole Food Company's new fresh-cut produce division. They were having problems with their current film, which had a narrow heat seal range, resulting in defective bags coming off their production line. Bags filled with produce were also breaking in shipment, causing spoilage. The new bag Cypress developed helped garner most of Dole's produce bag business.

The price of polyethylene pellets was somewhat unpredictable, and continuing competition meant that we had to keep lowering our bag prices. Adding to the mix was an unstable financial market, so we decided to find a buyer for Cypress. In 1995, the Cryovac division of W. R. Grace and Company purchased Cypress, making a nice profit for the shareholders. Under a management contract, Dave and Jim remained with Cryovac. For me, leaving this competitive industry at that point was good timing.

Over the years, each business I was involved with had its share of problems related to events in the economy: the recessions of the late 1960s and early 1970s, the high interest rates in the late 1970s that continued into the early 1980s, the Tax Reform Act of 1986, the collapse of the savings and loan industry in the late 1980s, and pressure on the entire banking system that finally led to a massive government bailout and a recession in the early 1990s.

The uncontrolled abuses in the real estate industry in the 1980s were exacerbated by lenders making highly leveraged loans that were fee- and rate-driven. The precipitous drop in the stock market in October 1987, shortly after the major tax revision, created economic uncertainties in the financial markets that spread in a domino fashion to the entire country, leaving few businesses unscathed.

Projects failed and many banks and savings and loans collapsed when federal regulations tightened liquidity requirements. Banks carried many illiquid developers on their books to minimize their immediate losses and write-downs, even giving haircuts—substantial reductions in the loans due to the lenders. By contrast, financially sound developers didn't have their loans reduced; rather, the loans were called in, even if the project was producing enough cash flow for the developer to continue making payments on the loan. Experienced developers had been encouraged for years to borrow more money, but now the banks were extracting every cent they could from them, which threatened to render these formerly healthy companies illiquid as well. Bankers' greed created this massive industry failure, and down with it went many good business entrepreneurs.

Being caught in this squeeze was devastating for me. For more than thirty years I had never missed a payroll or a loan payment—I had even paid off many loans early. All my business affairs were managed in the most professional manner. But now, bankers, who had made loans that exceeded the ability of some borrowers to ever pay them back, were giving credit-worthy borrowers an ultimatum—I had to repay all my short-term "bullet loans," since they would not be rolled over, as had been their standard lending practice before. To meet the bank's demands, I needed to quickly sell one of my investments, the broadcasting company assets, to repay the outstanding loan. Consequently, I lost my equity.

Hence, with $6 million in cash flow and assuming a market value of ten times that, the assets would have been worth roughly $60 million. Even a bargain sale for these same assets, if we'd had time to seek out potential buyers, could have brought at least $36 million. Considering that the bank loans amounted to $22 million, there would have been an adequate loan-to-value coverage protection for the bank if they wanted to extend the loan. Even a one-year extension would have made a big difference, since the banking crisis was beginning to subside. But the bank wouldn't wait.

By 1992, I had liquidated all the broadcast properties except for two stations in Salt Lake City, which I leased and later sold to a buyer. I made myself a promise to be more careful in the future when dealing with bankers. I was foolish to have believed that I would be dealt with fairly because I had a consistent track record.

Meanwhile, the banking industry's problems continued to affect the real estate industry. In the early 1990s, loans were coming due on some Price Development Company and partnership properties, and new financing was almost impossible to obtain on any terms. This problem particularly affected one partnership that had a nonperforming mall property and a past-due loan of $12 million, which I had personally guaranteed. Tom Matesitch, a Chemical Bank loan officer with whom I had had a banking relationship for more than ten years, prevailed on my behalf to extend the loan for six months. Tom was one of the few bankers I had met who honored relationships.

To ensure repayment, I told Tom that I was seriously considering going the real estate investment trust (REIT) route to eliminate all our real estate debt. This structure had a special tax provision for corporations investing in real estate, and basically eliminated corporate income taxes. REITs are required to distribute at least 90 percent of their income in the form of a dividend to the shareholders. As such, the income is taxed at the shareholder level instead of the corporate level, allowing for a pass-through of the property income subject to a single tax only. In essence, the REIT structure avoids double taxation. Kimco Realty, an owner of numerous shopping centers, had gone public as a REIT in 1993, and other real estate developers were following.

To explore the possibility of Price Development Company becoming a REIT, we met with several Wall Street investment firms. They encouraged us to go forward with the plan since we were, at the time, the dominant retail developer in the intermountain region. I was elated when a number of them made offers to do the underwriting. We made the decision then to use Merrill Lynch as the lead underwriter, and also brought in Dean Witter Reynolds, AG Edwards, and Piper Jaffray as part of the underwriting team. We incorporated the proposed entity, JP Realty, Inc. (JPR), as a Delaware corporation. The process was very tedious, time-consuming, and expensive, but other options for reducing our outstanding debt were limited.

Over an eight-week period we undertook countless road shows across the country, making presentations to institutional investors on JPR's operations, its properties, and projects in the pipeline. The fact that the intermountain region was one of the fastest-growing areas in the country created a lot of interest.

The most difficult part of the whole transaction was rolling up eighty-three real estate partnerships and merging them into JP Realty, Inc. Wall Street valued REIT properties based on the net operating income the properties were generating. No value was given for empty or unleased space or for undeveloped land. The shareholders in turn would receive the bulk of the cash flow generated by these properties in the form of dividends paid on a quarterly basis. Any future share value increase would be predicated on several factors, including income growth and the net cash flow or funds from operations (FFO), which ensured that shareholder dividends would be paid on a consistent quarterly basis, with periodic increases. The premise was that people who became shareholders would receive regular dividends on their investment.

We believed the nonperforming mall property mentioned above should be included in the REIT, since alternative financing for its debt repayment was not available and several loan extensions by Chemical Bank had come to an end. This property did dilute the overall income generated from the other partnership properties. In allocating property values in all of the eighty-three partnerships, everyone was treated fairly based upon the cash flow generated. To make this one particular property cash-flow positive, I diluted my personal equity value in some of my other properties to give value to this property.

On the day that JP Realty, Inc. went public, the outstanding real estate loans owed to banks, insurance companies, pension funds, and so on were paid off. The money raised from the sale of REIT shares to the public replaced the outstanding mortgage debt.

We were invited to have breakfast at the New York Stock Exchange with its president, Richard Grasso, on Friday, January 14, 1994, and ring the opening bell at nine-thirty. Watching the first trade of JPR shares coming across the ticker at $17.50 was a very exciting and tearful moment for me.

Over the course of my business career I was involved in a number of successful businesses and a few that were not so successful, but I never lost my focus on Price Development Company as the engine that drove these investment opportunities. When I decided to take PDC and the real estate partnerships public in a REIT, I also made a commitment to adhere to the highest level of public governance and enhance JPR shareholder value.

For the next seven years, JPR saw excellent dividend and shareholder value growth. Over twenty-eight quarters, JPR continued to pay a dividend to our shareholders, with modest increases each year. As the intermountain region became a popular place to live and grow a business, many real estate competitors came to chase the western rainbow. Good development sites became harder to find, discounters and mass merchandisers were appearing almost on top of each other, and many retail categories were duplicated, ultimately leading to some mergers, failures, and pockets of empty space. Trends in the malls were also changing. To stay competitive, massive cash infusions were needed for remodeling. The dot-com crash that began in 2000 also added to the financial market's uncertainties.

Our tenacious staff, however, endeavored to deliver one new major retail project each year, while we continued to upgrade our existing portfolio of properties. Since our cash flow was first and foremost dedicated to meeting the shareholder dividend and to keeping our company debt at no higher than 50 percent, we had limited cash available for expansion outside our core market area. Our share price continued to grow modestly, as REITs were becoming a very popular and secure way to participate in the ownership of income-producing real estate. We had been approached by several other REITs to combine our operations in a merger of equals, but each time we determined that our shareholders would fare better if we continued on our course independently.

Faced with another recession, 2001 was difficult for commercial real estate and the retail industry. In January 2002, when the economy had entered a slow recovery, I received a telephone call from John Bucksbaum, the CEO of General Growth Properties (GGP), a publicly traded REIT and one of the largest retail property developers in the United States. I had known the Bucksbaum family for more than twenty years through my association with the International Council of Shopping Centers (ICSC), of which we were both members. I had served on the board of the ICSC with his father, Matthew Bucksbaum, who was chairman of GGP. On several occasions in the past, we had competed for retail site locations in our region.

GGP knew that JPR was a dominant force in the intermountain region and that our portfolio complemented theirs. Although we were smaller, we were a regional developer and had properties in the middle-size and larger markets. John Bucksbaum called to explore the opportunity for a merger.

Since I had accepted the call to service from President George W. Bush, and as part of my preparation to begin my ambassadorial duties I had developed a JPR management team succession plan. JPR had several qualified officers, each with many years of experience with the company. Rex Frazier had been with the company for more than twenty-five years and had served as my right arm; he would become chief executive officer. In addition, we had an experienced board of seasoned business leaders, some of whom had served on the board since inception; Pat King was selected to be chairman. My son, Steven, who had been with the company almost twenty years, would become vice president and part of the management team. Other key officers included Paul Mendenhall, Martin Peterson, and Greg Curtis, each of whom had been with the company for more than a quarter century. We were also fortunate to be able to count on many key people in the leasing, development, finance, and property management departments.

GGP had raised substantial money for acquisitions and needed to put these funds to work by the end of the second quarter of 2002. John Bucksbaum and Bernie Freibaum, their chief financial officer, met with Pat King and me and over several weeks of negotiations came up with an attractive offer to present to our board for consideration.

We had an obligation to our shareholders to create value for them, so we needed to explore this avenue of opportunity. In the retail mall development business there is a constant need for capital to keep up with newer competing developments, which was always of concern to us. GGP, because of its size, could readily infuse the necessary capital for new projects we were planning, as well as expansion and redevelopment of some of the aging properties in our portfolio.

After hours of discussion in a special board meeting, it was agreed that Pat King and I should have another meeting with GGP management. We wanted them to improve their offer, and we needed to outline definitive aspects of a term sheet for the board's further consideration.

I asked Pat, as chairman of the finance committee, to head up the negotiation team going forward. He was astute and an excellent negotiator; I had not met anyone brighter or quicker in getting to the bottom line. When the company needed a sounding board, we always went to Pat. In my forty-year association with Pat, we never had a business disagreement. We both knew issues could always be resolved between two rational people, and Pat was the most rational person I had ever met. His philosophy was that two heads are better than one. He always shared information and welcomed input, so everyone was on the same page.

Following six weeks of negotiations, GGP's final offer was presented to the board, providing for a 10 percent premium over the current market price of the shares. The board then wanted a fairness opinion based on the offer. We considered several Wall Street investment banking firms that had experience with REIT valuations and selected the UBS Warburg organization. We also contacted another REIT that in the past had shown an interest in a merger discussion, but thought GGP's offer was higher than they would consider.

On Friday, March 1, 2002, the JPR board of directors, including Pat King, Rex Frazier, Sam Souvall, Jim Anderson, Blaine Huntsman, and I, went to Chicago to meet with the GGP executive committee to discuss the final terms and conditions of the proposed merger. By Sunday night, an agreement in principle had been reached. It was agreed that Pat and Rex would stay on in Chicago to finalize the documentation for the merger transaction. The other directors returned to Salt Lake City, while I went on to Washington.

On Monday, with all the issues resolved, a news release was sent out. At eight-thirty that morning there was a conference call between General Growth Properties and the Wall Street financial community, institutional investors, and analysts to describe the merger. By Tuesday morning, March 5, the business world knew about the proposed merger agreement.

The next step in the process was to receive regulatory approval, prepare proxy statements for shareholder approval, and produce other relevant documentation needed for the merger to be completed. The final closing of the transaction was tentatively scheduled for the end of the second quarter of 2002.

The Sunday night before the merger announcement, I sat alone in my hotel room in Washington reflecting on my business career, which had begun with just an idea in a \$15-a-month office back in 1957. I had survived numerous recessions over the years, a major tax reform in 1986, the savings and loan debacle, and the disastrous banking industry collapse of the late 1980s and early 1990s, and still I had prospered.

My son, Steven, would go on to form the Price Realty Group, LLC (PRG), to carry on the family business legacy. PRG would focus on the construction and development of commercial and industrial buildings in the intermountain region. Martin Peterson, who was vice president of administration at JP Realty, Inc., would join PRG as executive vice president and chief financial officer. Martin had come to our real estate business in 1975. Prior to that time, he served as senior auditor for Price Waterhouse & Co., one of the major national accounting firms. As a senior executive at JPR, Martin contributed to its growth and success as the premier retail mall developer in the intermountain region. His extensive background in real estate and financial matters would complement Steven's real estate operation as he acquired and developed new projects. Martin had devoted his energy to our family business endeavors for more than thirty years. During that time, we had also seen his children grow into wonderful adults with families of their own.

Ken Rudy would join Steven's business team as vice president of development and construction. Ken came to JP Realty's development division in 1997 and served as a senior project director. With Ken's extensive construction experience, two of JPR's newest state-of-the-art enclosed malls were completed on time and within budget. His talents included the remodeling of commercial projects as well. Prior to joining JPR, Ken oversaw the construction of several retail projects for other national real estate development companies. He brought a wealth of knowledge and expertise to the PRG team.

Angela (Smith) Eldridge, another talented JP Realty alumna, joined Steven as his executive assistant in the new operation. Her knowledge and expertise included preparation of leases and associated documents, negotiation of terms and conditions, and follow-through on other tenant-related matters. Several years later, Katie Story joined the company and became an important asset. Starting as a receptionist and assistant accountant, she quickly gained knowledge and became a lease administrator.

Mike Washburn, the family's personal property manager and security consultant, had been associated with us since 1981, when he was twenty years old. After leaving to pursue a business venture in the late 1980s, he returned in 1995. A very talented and multifaceted individual, he is always on top of the many balls in the air. Mike raised a talented family, all of whom worked on our properties in varying positions. Mike's charm and can-do attitude meant that no challenge was too big. His ability to find the right people to work on the various properties always amazed us. Mike also had smoothly handled the visits by President George W. Bush to Fairfax House.

Along the way I had employed thousands of people, providing work for many of them through both good and bad times. I took on many construction projects during the winter months, when we would just break even, so that people could eat.

I trained and mentored many people in various aspects of sales, marketing, construction, development, finance, and management. Some became entrepreneurs in their own ventures and enjoyed financially successful careers. I was proud that many alumni had achieved millionaire status. The mentoring of people was as important to me as was my own personal business success.

{ VII }

THE STATE DEPARTMENT CULTURE

He served from 1776 to 1778 on a three-man commission to France charged with the critical task of gaining French support for American Independence. . . . He convinced France to recognize American independence and conclude an alliance with the thirteen states in 1778. Franklin presented his credentials to the French court in 1779, becoming the first American Minister (the 18th century American equivalent of ambassador) to be received by a foreign government.

—U.S. STATE DEPARTMENT, OFFICE OF THE HISTORIAN,
"BENJAMIN FRANKLIN: FIRST AMERICAN DIPLOMAT, 1776–1785"

For more than two hundred years, American diplomats have conducted negotiations between sovereign nations, encouraged international cooperation, furthered communication, and achieved political and economic advantages for our country. Today the United States has bilateral relations with more than 192 nations around the globe, and the issues have only become more complex. The ability to reach an agreement or compromise is paramount; tools such as the use of sanctions, force, and trade controls may be required to gain leverage.

For a non-career ambassador imbued with a businessman's commonsense approach to diplomacy, dealing with diverse issues on an ongoing basis is part and parcel of the trade. Good business practices have always involved protocol—saying the right thing at the right time to avoid ill will. Achieving goals through dialogue and negotiation is an essential ingredient in business success. My personal skills in decision making, problem solving, strategy, and intensive negotiations were integral to the success of my business and were sought after by community and civic organizations and by national boards. I believed that being given a comprehensive set of goals outlining our foreign policy and having a solid handle on good business practices would help me be effective in my new role as a diplomat.

From the time President Bush announced his intention to nominate me as a U.S. ambassador to my official arrival at the U.S. Embassy in Port Louis, Mauritius, eleven months had passed. During this time, Sharon Bisdee, chief of the State Department's Presidential Appointments Staff, sent numerous forms that I had to fill out and which would be reviewed by, among many others, the Office of the White House Counsel, the Office of Government Ethics, the State Department's Senior Ethics Counsel, the Senate Foreign Relations Committee, the Internal Revenue Service, the Federal Bureau of Investigation, and the Office of Medical Services.

To comply with all their requests, I submitted copious amounts of paperwork, including meticulously detailed financial disclosures. To accommodate the FBI background check for security clearance, I provided lists of both personal and professional information, including the names of people acquainted with me for the past twenty-five years and international travel itineraries that went back more than fifteen years. On questions relating to my job roles and related matters, I had to relive nearly forty-five years to compile the necessary material.

In addition to the treadmill of paperwork, there were many months of interviews, numerous meetings and briefings, training seminars, legal and ethics-related reviews, security clearances, and *agréments* issued by the host country governments. From June 4 to 15, 2001, Marcia and I had our first taste of the unique State Department Foreign Service culture while attending the concentrated two-week Ambassadorial Seminar at the National Affairs Training Center of the Foreign Service Institute.

On several occasions, my predecessor, Ambassador Mark Erwin, who served in Mauritius from 1999 to 2001, shared his insights into the host countries and his experiences there. Having gone through the seminar process and understanding its demands, he offered us the use of his condominium at the Ritz-Carlton during our stay. The thought was appealing, so Marcia and I gladly accepted his hospitality. It was a welcome reprieve after each day's lengthy and mentally tiring agenda.

Participating in the Ambassadorial Seminar, often known as "charm school," were eleven individuals from the private sector and members of the Foreign Service. Among our group, two were career members, three of the non-career members had previous government service, and one had served in the military with eight years of active duty.

The Ambassadorial Seminar sessions were co-chaired by two career members of the Foreign Service, Ambassadors Sheldon Krys and Tony Motley. They were pleasant and tried to add some humor to their recitation. But after attending the lectures and workshops, I thought the seminar would have been more effective if consideration had been given to each of the participants' different business and professional backgrounds and some of the programs tailored to their strengths and experience levels. For example, breakout sessions concentrating on embassy operations would help coach those who were serving for the first time, while lessons on basic business and management issues would add to the portfolio of Foreign Service career members. To broaden the scope of the curriculum, former non-career ambassadors could have taken part in the seminar as instructors sharing their knowledge, perspectives, and experiences; learning about the challenges they faced may have provided us with more tools to work with once we were on our own.

With the State Department segmented as it is, with many departments, there was not one source to go to for a comprehensive overview of an embassy's in-country functions. The ambassador, as chief of mission, we learned, depends upon the deputy chief of mission (DCM), who controls the embassy's day-to-day operations. In *The Diplomat's Dictionary* by Chas. W. Freeman Jr., a career officer in the U.S. Foreign Service and a former ambassador to Saudi Arabia, the DCM's role is defined as "the senior-ranking officer below the ambassador in an embassy of the United States. The deputy chief of mission supervises the diplomatic and administrative staff of the embassy for the ambassador, serves as his *alter ego*, coordinates the work of mission elements outside the embassy for him, and assumes the ambassador's duties as *Chargé d'Affaires ad interim* in his absence." I interpreted this as meaning that more control was given to an embassy's deputy chief of mission than I later read about in the President's letter of instructions to me.

As a chief executive officer in the private sector, I would have been able to pick my chief operations officer, or deputy, to help run the business. In the State Department culture, such options are limited: everyone is generally in place when you arrive. The only time an ambassador may have influence is when a deputy chief of mission rotates out and another one is under consideration.

Of course, I also learned that in addition to the embassy's in-country operation, we had to depend upon numerous people from outside support agencies located at other U.S. embassies to accomplish our embassy's mission. I found consistency and team building difficult to achieve when key people were constantly rotated to other assignments. Each time such a person left, we would have to take time to bring the new person up to speed. If he or she was from another agency of government, it was even more difficult. In an embassy operation, such as a Special Embassy Program (SEP) post with limited people resources, I found this to hamper the effort to be consistent in our bilateral relations.

In retrospect, I highly recommend the ambassador be given the opportunity to select both his deputy chief of mission and his management officer. As each individual becomes a key member of the ambassador's team, this might alleviate potential anxieties and friction in the embassy, which can create morale issues.

All in all, a two-week program is too short a time in which to grasp embassy operations. I was thankful I had an extensive business and management background, which allowed me to feel comfortable with many of the embassy's "moving parts."

In preparation for my departure, I spent considerable time researching the history of Mauritius and the other host countries, their political and economic issues, security concerns, ethnic and cultural diversity, and our foreign policy for the region. I also visited with numerous people at the State Department, other government agencies, and private sector nongovernmental organizations (NGOs) to gain as much information and knowledge as possible about these countries. At times this became confusing, with conflicting data from different sources.

After September 19, 2001, when President Bush formally sent my nomination to the Senate, I went to Washington for more meetings. During the first week in November, Marcia and I attended a diversity class at the Foreign Service Institute, went to a Security Overseas Seminar, and, in between sessions, met with Virginia Shore and Hafiz Imtiaz of the Art in Embassies program to review some artist selections for the ambassador's residence.

My country desk officer, Blossom Perry, scheduled meetings for me with the Bureau of African Affairs and other State Department sections, Treasury Department, Office of the U.S. Trade Representative (USTR), U.S. Agency for International Development (USAID), Bureau of Overseas Buildings Operations (OBO), and Department of Defense (DOD).

Many of these meetings were set up as courtesy calls to get acquainted rather than discuss current or specific issues. Some people, encumbered with work, had little time to spend with me; others had little to say. So many people seemed to be in some stage of transition, I was reminded of a relay race in which everyone hands off the baton. Sometimes I felt more like a vendor making a sales call than a U.S. ambassador who was seeking knowledge. In the private sector the scenario would be different: mentoring new people is a very important part of succeeding in business.

Later in the month, I spent the day with staff from the State Department's Bureau of Legislative Affairs and went through a dry run of my confirmation hearing remarks before the Senate Foreign Relations Committee. We rehearsed questions, including some that might be pulled from the briefing material I had been given to study. This intense "murder board" session, as it was often referred to, was intended to prepare candidates for the Senate hearings. I also sat through the dry runs of Kenneth Moorefield, nominated as ambassador to Gabon, and James McGee, who would serve in Swaziland. The rigorous role play took on the realism of being in a courtroom with feisty attorneys attacking a witness.

Alerted that the Senate hearings might be scheduled for that week, on Tuesday, November 27, I made another trip to Washington. That afternoon, while I was meeting with Blossom Perry, a fax arrived from the Senate Foreign Relations Committee stating that the hearings were scheduled for Thursday at three-thirty. For a moment I was speechless, thinking, *Can this really be true?* After handing me the fax, Blossom turned back to her computer and went on with her work—for her, this matter was routine.

I quickly called my administrative assistant, Marlene Luke, in Salt Lake City, to make arrangements for Marcia, our children, their spouses, and our grandchildren to fly to Washington early the next day. That night, I was up past three in the morning practicing my opening remarks to the Senate subcommittee. I also went over the data relating to the three countries at least a half dozen times before dozing off.

On that momentous Thursday, Marcia and I arrived at the front entrance of the Dirksen Senate Office Building at three o'clock sharp, and were delighted to see the rest of our family there. Walking into Senate Hearing Room 419, we were greeted by some friends and well-wishers, including former ambassador Mark Erwin; Art Silverman, Bill Simmons, Al Madison, and Jason Maloni from the Dutko Group, a political consulting firm in Washington; and former business associate Dave Fischer.

Utah senators Orrin Hatch and Bob Bennett came to introduce me to the members of the Senate Foreign Relations Subcommittee, for which I was most grateful. At the hearing also were James McGee, Kenneth Moorefield, and their families. We three were the last ambassador nominees to sub-Saharan African countries to be confirmed by the Senate.

At three-thirty, Senate Foreign Relations Subcommittee chairman Russ Feingold entered the room. There were six senators on the subcommittee, which also included Senators Chris Dodd, Barbara Boxer, Bill Frist, Sam Brownback, and Gordon Smith, but he was the only one who was present. The Senator began his introductory remarks on behalf of the subcommittee. Senator Hatch and Senator Bennett made some very kind introductory remarks on my behalf.

For my part, I introduced my family, with a special recognition of our adopted Chinese granddaughter, Savannah, who was celebrating her second birthday—which I felt was a good omen for the day. Suppressing tears, I talked about escaping the Holocaust in Germany and coming to America. I discussed my intention to fully engage the three host countries to which I would be accredited if confirmed by the Senate, and to represent our U.S. interests.

Trade would be a primary focus in Mauritius. The African Growth and Opportunity Act (AGOA) trade program, established by the U.S. Congress on May 18, 2000, allowed developing nations in sub-Saharan Africa duty-free and quota-free access to the U.S. markets. Under the AGOA program, I would strive to find new trading partners for American suppliers, particularly in the textile sector.

In the Seychelles, I would encourage diversification of their weak economy into more of a manufacturing base. In the extremely poor country of Comoros, which had suffered numerous coups, I stressed the need to support their efforts toward national unity and reconciliation between the three islands, and overcoming the weak governance that crippled their economy.

Since the terrorist Fazul Abdullah Mohammed came from Comoros and there were security concerns in the region, I pointed out all three countries supported the U.S.-led coalition in the fight against international terrorism, and I would make it a priority to have them continue their support. My responsibility would also include fostering and strengthening our relationship while helping them achieve economic progress and greater prosperity. My primary task, however, would be the continued protection of American citizens and promotion of U.S. interests.

Senator Feingold asked questions about environmental concerns, trade issues, democracy and human rights, and fund-raising issues. He was concerned about

Comoros's abuse record under the newly formed Human Rights Commission of 1998 and the country's ban of all religions other than Islam. I assured the senator I would work toward helping Comoros become more tolerant. Another pressing issue was the destruction of the coral reefs in Mauritius; I agreed to research the matter and respond in writing.

The senator spent considerable time talking about personal matters, including my campaign fund-raising activities. In conclusion, he said that other questions would be submitted for my written response. I had already answered questions previously submitted by Senators Feingold and Joseph Biden, which had delayed the scheduled Senate hearing until now. With this new addition, I was concerned about being confirmed before the Senate recessed for the year. We agreed to go over the questions the following day with Feingold's staff so the committee could take timely action on my confirmation.

On Friday I met with the staff as planned and answered additional questions posed by the senators. The following Tuesday, after more revisions were requested by Senator Biden's office, a final version was accepted for the record—but not so with Senator Feingold, who intended to review them over the weekend. I knew that time was of the essence—the next business meeting of the Senate Foreign Relations Committee was scheduled for Wednesday, December 12, after which there was only a slim chance for approval before the end of 2001.

Returning to Washington on Monday, December 10, I learned that Senator Feingold's staff had not received the package of written responses, which were sent on December 6 and for which Blossom Perry had the transmittal receipt. Hence, the Senate Foreign Relations Committee list for the Wednesday meeting did not include my name. Another package was quickly assembled and hand-delivered.

Fortunately, late Tuesday, Feingold's staff called and said the senator would not hold up my name from going to the full Senate Foreign Relations Committee the next day. However, he would reserve the right to request a roll-call vote.

Although I was anxious about the day's vote, Blossom made appointments for me to meet Wednesday with Molly Williamson, deputy assistant secretary of commerce for the Middle East, South Asia, Oceania, and Africa; Gerald Feldman, director, Office for Africa, International Trade Administration; Jed Diemond, an economist at the Department of Commerce who focused on African trade issues; Finn Holm-Olsen, a trade specialist on Africa; and Doug Rohn, division chief for West and Southern Africa, Bureau of Intelligence and Research. They would share their insights on the region.

Finally, at five o'clock, word reached us that my confirmation had been approved, along with several others. No roll-call vote was requested, and all senators present voted for approval. What a relief.

We were then told that on Thursday, December 20, the entire Senate would vote in executive session on the confirmations—the last step in the approval process. That night, however, I received a phone call from Paul Rademacher, the director of

Senate Affairs at the State Department, saying that several senators, including Senator John Kerry, had held up the confirmation of thirty nominations, among which were nine ambassadors, the director of the Peace Corps, several assistant secretaries, and administrators of government agencies, and then the session had adjourned. It was quite a disappointment.

Leaving the nine nominated ambassadors and the other government agency leaders suspended that way was a major blow to our foreign relations image. Nine U.S. embassies around the world would now have to function without a chief of mission. The Senate Foreign Relations Committee needed to move nominees through the confirmation process in a more timely manner, to help protect U.S. interests around the world. The Senate should set an example to the world for fairness and transparency in the confirmation process, to show how our great democracy works to develop our foreign affairs agenda, and above all to let the host countries know we care about them.

The incident that involved my confirmation was not the only one in which confirmations were delayed. We have left posts open without ambassadors for extended periods of time, sometimes even more than a year. This is problematic when we must press these governments for their support of U.S. interests and issues at the United Nations. The Senate needs to wake up before we lose the few remaining friends we have around the world, who are not just loyal to us for the money we send.

On January 25, Paul Rademacher called to say that the Senate, in executive session, had finally confirmed eight of the nine previously held-up ambassadorial appointments, without fanfare. One senator had put a hold on the confirmation of the ambassador to the Philippines.

From the time I'd first received the call from the White House on March 14, 2001, it had taken almost eleven months for me to be confirmed by the Senate. I think ambassadors should be vetted and ready to represent the President and our U.S. interests in the host countries as soon as their predecessors are scheduled to leave, in order to seamlessly carry on the work at the embassy.

It was on January 30 that I received from the White House President Bush's letter of instructions as his personal representative to Mauritius, Comoros, and Seychelles. My charge was to protect America's interests, "promote the growth of freedom and democratic institutions and help set loose the creative energies of millions of people through the spread of the free-market system." As the chief of mission for the three sovereign island nations, reporting directly to the President through the Secretary of State, I was given responsibility for the "direction, coordination, and supervision" of embassy employees and Department of Defense personnel on official duty. And I was instructed to "combat the proliferation of harmful technologies or weapons of mass destruction."

A copy of the President's letter was sent to the government agencies with whom I would be interfacing. This would support the teamwork necessary to advance U.S. foreign policy and strengthen our bilateral relations with the host countries. (See Appendix A.)

During the Senate confirmation process, I stayed in touch with Bisa Williams, my deputy chief of mission, and was kept abreast of the issues affecting the host countries and the region. Bisa had arrived at the U.S. Embassy in Port Louis on September 12, 2001, just one day after the horrific terrorist attacks of September 11. While serving as the deputy chief of mission and the chargé d'affaires at the embassy, Bisa worked twelve to fourteen hours a day writing reports, handling cable traffic, dealing with démarches (requests made of foreign officials), and overseeing the embassy operation. As a Special Embassy Program post with a limited staff, the chargé d'affaires was confronted with numerous issues in the three host countries.

In reality, the U.S. needed to have a full-time diplomatic presence in Seychelles as well as Comoros, which became evident during my three and a half years as U.S. ambassador, and continues to be true today. One particular episode clearly reveals this. On February 19, 2002, shortly after I was sworn in but before I arrived in Mauritius, Bisa shared an email sent by Ms. Ayinde Wagner-Simpson, the Africa desk officer for the Financial Crimes Enforcement Network (FinCEN), asking about the feasibility of a visit to Seychelles. FinCEN, which serves as the financial intelligence unit for the United States, is based at the Treasury Department. Much of their effort, Ms. Wagner-Simpson wrote, is focused on terrorist financing and money laundering around the world. These activities take many forms, from alternative remittance systems to commodity-based trade, and are an ongoing problem particularly in small and underdeveloped countries.

Seychelles could become susceptible to such activities, and Ms. Wagner-Simpson wanted to visit the country to determine the extent of money laundering, the laws and regulations that were in place, and how well the government's anti-money-laundering programs were working. She was planning to attend a March anti-money-laundering conference in Dar es Salaam, Tanzania, and pending approval to continue on to Seychelles, she asked about the likelihood of arranging such a trip.

Responding the following day, Bisa invited her to visit Seychelles as soon as possible. She affirmed Seychelles' commitment to countering such illegal activities, even though the United States had no permanent presence on the island nation. Bisa added that while such an investigation was a sensitive issue, the Seychelles government would respond favorably to a Washington representative. She also stressed the importance of a stopover at the U.S. Embassy in Mauritius, which would signal that the visit was a coordinated U.S. government effort. "Embassy affiliation has a more serious ring to it than happens-to-be-in-the-area does," explained Bisa. "I would like to let the government of Seychelles know that the left hand is aware of the right." This episode makes clear that the lack of a permanent presence in host countries is shortsighted.

In preparation for my departure to Mauritius, my country desk officer set up meetings for the week of March 4 at the State Department, a courtesy call on the Mauritian ambassador to the United States, and with several private sector nongovernmental organizations. Marcia joined me on this trip to Washington so that we could obtain our diplomatic passports, review the art for the ambassador's residence, and attend several official functions.

After we arrived at the International Passport Office, filled out the necessary forms, and had our pictures taken, we paid a courtesy call on Ambassador Usha Jeetah. The Mauritian ambassador shared her concern regarding U.S. policy toward Mauritius on interpreting the AGOA "third-country" fabric rule, which affected many of their apparel manufacturers. The requirement that raw materials be sourced only from the United States or Africa made many of the local textile manufacturers uncompetitive. I told her I would look into the matter.

During the next three days, I attended meetings at the Bureau of African Affairs with Charlie Snyder, deputy assistant secretary; John Sheely, deputy executive director; and Lauren Moriarty, director of the Office of East African Affairs. I also met with the State Department post management officer, the payroll and insurance officer, and the Army's political-military affairs advisor.

On an afternoon break Marcia and I viewed the final selections of art for the embassy residence. Marcia, who has always been very involved with the arts, selected a glass piece by Dale Chihuly. We are both taken by his work and have several of his pieces in our own collection, and in Salt Lake City we helped fund a heroic-sized piece that was installed in the lobby of Abravanel Hall in time for the 2002 Winter Olympics.

Continuing to make the rounds, I visited private sector trade advisors and NGOs actively involved in sub-Saharan Africa. I was warmly received by Peter Craig, who was the commercial trade advisor at the Mauritian Embassy, and Paul Ryberg, the president of the Mauritius-U.S. Business Association. I had an informative meeting with Stephen Hayes, the president of the Corporate Council on Africa, and Allen Terhaar, executive director of the Cotton Council, whose members were actively involved in business operations in sub-Saharan Africa.

I quickly became swamped with information regarding sub-Saharan Africa. It was a bit overwhelming, and my notes from the various meetings soon added up to an unwieldy amount. However, all this information would prove useful in representing U.S. business interests in the host countries.

I thanked Sharon Bisdee for being my coach during the confirmation process. Her dedication and wisdom had made this otherwise arduous, often humbling, and occasionally demeaning process more manageable. She was responsible for more than fifty ambassadors getting through the confirmation process during this cycle, and all were confirmed.

After the Winter Olympics ended, my life had become very hectic with the numerous courtesy calls and meetings with government agencies and private sector groups in Washington. A highlight of our last days in Salt Lake was the afternoon farewell reception on March 14 given in our honor by Governor Mike Leavitt and Jackie Leavitt. More than three hundred friends from all over the country showed up, many of whom we hadn't seen in years. We were also elated and surprised when President Gordon B. Hinckley of the Church of Jesus Christ of Latter-day Saints arrived in the Gold Room at the Capitol accompanied by President Thomas Monson and President James Faust (members of the First Presidency) to wish us well. The setting in the Gold Room brought back memories of my swearing-in ceremony.

Later that evening, needing to unwind, I arranged for a private room at the New Yorker, one of Salt Lake's finest restaurants, and I invited several longtime friends and business associates. These friends—successful entrepreneurs, bankers, and legal advisors—all had helped make JP Realty a great success story. I also included my son, Steven, who would be entering a new business phase in his life.

When I arrived, Pat King, my closest advisor and a board member, was enjoying a cocktail with my son and Jim Anderson, another board member, who was a retired executive of Homestake Mining Company and a former college classmate. Tom

7.1. Farewell reception, March 14, 2002. From left to right: John and Marcia Price, President Gordon B. Hinckley, President Thomas Monson, President James Faust, Church of Jesus Christ of Latter-day Saints. (Photo courtesy of Newman Photography)

7.2. From left to right: Attorney General Mark Shurtleff, his wife M'Lissa, Katie Dixon, longtime Salt Lake County Recorder and advocate for women and children, Marcia Price, and Ambassador John Price in the Gold Room at the Utah State Capitol, 2002. (Photo courtesy of Newman Photography)

Matesitch from Chemical Bank arrived, followed by Ted Buchanan who had been on the Dean Witter Reynolds team when we went public. Then came Jay Bernstein, a bright lawyer with the firm Rogers and Wells, who had been involved in JPR going public and now our merger. Finally, there was Chuck May, the vice president of leasing at Sears, one of our major mall anchors. They all had a hand in our rise to becoming the dominant shopping mall developer in the intermountain region. They toasted me that evening, and I heartily reciprocated. My life would not have been the same without such friends.

March and April seemed to leap by very quickly. Before leaving the country, I made my last trip to Washington for the April 15–18, 2002, Bureau of African Affairs, Chiefs of Mission Conference. I was at a disadvantage since I had not yet spent time in my three host countries. I believed that as a presidential ambassador nominee, I should have been allowed to visit these countries during the confirmation process. I also would have been better informed when dealing with the Senate Foreign Relations Committee. However, the rules prohibited this until after the formal confirmation and swearing in. Career ambassador nominees have an advantage in this regard, since they may have previously served in their host countries in some capacity, in the region, or in the State Department.

Members of the Senate Foreign Relations Committee would be well served to regularly visit the countries they oversee. News reports indicated that one senator visited Egypt and Libya in February 2004 and the Chad-Sudan border area in May and June 2005. Another senator on the Africa Subcommittee reportedly visited one country in sub-Saharan Africa shortly after he was elected to the Senate, visited Kenya, Tanzania, and Mozambique in February 2002, and attempted to visit Zimbabwe. Reportedly, to his credit, this senator visited twenty countries on the continent over a twelve-year period.

It should be noted that there are fifty-three African countries (forty-eight are in sub-Saharan Africa) with a total of one billion people, representing 14 percent of the world population, and that more than half the population lives on $1 a day or less. During the three-plus years I was posted, no senators serving on the Foreign Relations Committee visited my region. There was only one visit by a Senate congressional delegation, and neither of the senators involved, Senator Arlen Specter and Senator Richard Shelby, served on the Senate Foreign Relations Committee.

On my last trip to Washington before leaving the country, I asked Blossom to schedule additional meetings for me during the Chiefs of Mission Conference, and I revisited several people in the Bureau of East African Affairs.

On Tuesday morning, at the Chiefs of Mission Conference, Assistant Secretary of State for African Affairs Walter Kansteiner welcomed forty-two ambassadors and spoke about democratization, rule of law, human rights, economic development, and health-related concerns in sub-Saharan Africa. He said it was the department's intent to increase spending in sub-Saharan Africa by between 10 and 20 percent, with administration approval; this would make a significant difference in areas critical to their survival.

Deputy Assistant Secretary Charlie Snyder followed by saying that good project management in the countries we oversaw could lead to more money for other programs.

Deputy Assistant Secretary Bob Perry, Blossom's husband and former ambassador to the Central African Republic, stressed the importance of our diplomacy and public policy in rebuilding confidence in the sub-Saharan African countries and, since a large part of sub-Saharan Africa was Muslim, in conveying our message of friendship.

Under Secretary Grant Green addressed an entire range of management issues, from budget and performance, leadership training, outsourcing, and financial performance to right-sizing of embassies. He added that in the current environment, our management objectives needed to expand to encompass better security and safety at all embassies; some were not secure, and others were without even glass protection. He also addressed the need of much-deferred maintenance and overall embassy modernization. Lastly, he suggested rewarding people who do their best, a philosophy that came from his private sector business background. I, of course, couldn't have agreed more.

Deputy Secretary of State Richard Armitage said an ambassador's "mark of success is leaving a post a better place." He reinforced the need to build sound relationships. With a strong, thick neck and a raspy voice, the deputy secretary appeared more like an aging football player turned coach than a diplomat. His straightforward "give 'em hell" attitude was refreshing.

Frank Taylor, director of the State Department's Counterterrorism Bureau, discussed security concerns worldwide since 9/11 and said that a comprehensive counterterrorism program had been established for each embassy. He added that we should work with the host country governments to prevent money from moving to and from al-Qaeda through sub-Saharan Africa, and that better passport controls were needed in these countries.

His talk strengthened my belief that Congress needs to understand the extensive and growing presence of radical Islamic extremists and the al-Qaeda network in sub-Saharan Africa. The history of terrorist attacks against Western interests on the continent includes the bombing of the Norfolk Hotel in Nairobi, Kenya, on December 31, 1980; the attacks against U.S. military troops in Mogadishu, Somalia, on October 3–4, 1993; the bombing of the U.S. Embassy in Nairobi and the U.S. Embassy in Dar es Salaam on August 7, 1998; the bombing of the USS *Cole*, a guided missile destroyer, in the harbor of Aden, Yemen, on October 12, 2000; and the bombing of the Paradise Hotel in Mombasa, Kenya, on November 28, 2002.

Assistant Secretary of State for Diplomatic Security David Carpenter cautioned us to be vigilant. We needed to make our embassies more secure, he advised, and to always be alert to the possibility of kidnappings.

Under Secretary Charlotte Beers spoke on public diplomacy and the need to "network and communicate our American values." She noted how the country team needed to participate in outreach programs in the host country and work closely with the local media to get out our message.

Secretary of the Treasury Paul O'Neill said, "In your part of the world, we could make a difference in less than ten years, not with loans converted to grants, but with developments to create real economic growth and income growth." He added that we need to do better for the poorest people—going from $1 subsistence a day to $2 a day was not adequate. He further noted that many of these countries lack an established or functioning banking system and that there were "too many transactions off-balance-sheet, such as street transfers to other countries, with money potentially being sent to dubious receivers."

Secretary O'Neill favored the Millennium Challenge Account (MCA) program as a tool to help democratize countries, and stressed the importance of creating employment opportunities and teaching young children computer skills.

USAID Administrator Andrew Natsios reported that increased funding was available for sub-Saharan Africa projects dealing with HIV/AIDS, agriculture, and corruption. He added it was a huge mistake for USAID to have gotten out of the educational scholarship program. According to Natsios, the MCA program would change that by allowing students from Africa to attend smaller schools in the United States. He said the Treasury Department would have oversight of the MCA money used for these purposes, and that fifteen to twenty countries had already been selected to participate in the program. He believed that while they had shown that their leadership can make progress up to a certain point, they would need additional help in moving toward good governance, open economic policies, macroeconomic reforms, a focus on education and health issues, and making a good business climate available for entrepreneurs to flourish. All of these steps, he concluded, would enhance people's quality of life.

Under Secretary of State Alan Larson discussed the $500 million available for programs combatting AIDS and infectious diseases. He alluded also to an agricultural initiative for sub-Saharan Africa that would be rolled out in the near future.

Lastly, the Peace Corps' chief of operations, Lloyd Pierson, and regional director for sub-Saharan Africa, Henry McCoy, gave an overview of their operations. It was interesting to hear that they had a number of new programs under way in sub-Saharan Africa, since they were on my list to contact. I had become acquainted with the Peace Corps in the 1970s, when I spent time in East Africa. Many excellent Foreign Service officers that I met had begun with the Peace Corps in sub-Saharan Africa. In fact, I would have several such outstanding officers serving at the U.S. Embassy in Port Louis.

Lloyd Pierson said the Peace Corps had seven thousand volunteers in the field, a figure that would double by 2003. He stated their appropriation for 2002, $275 million, would be increased in 2003 to $325 million. Thirty-two countries had put in requests for Peace Corps volunteers, reinforcing that the "Peace Corps is a great U.S. tool to build bridges."

Henry McCoy, who was new to his position, was going to sub-Saharan Africa in May 2002 to acquaint himself with the situation. Director Gadi Vasquez would also be traveling there in mid-2002. I later asked if I could meet with them while on their trip in May. I was excited about the opportunity of meeting the two of them soon after my arrival in Mauritius and discussing the possibility of sending an assessment team to the host countries, where the Peace Corps once had been active. Since the Peace Corps had a regional office in nearby Madagascar, with more than fifty Peace Corps workers, I thought I could draw from these resources. Unfortunately, this did not happen, even after I built a compelling case in future meetings.

All the speakers sounded sincere, but as I discovered during my posting, when it came time to deliver on financial assistance programs to my host countries, very few came through. Time and time again, the United States came up short, which served as an embarrassment to me in our bilateral relations with these host country governments. I continually pushed and fought for funding. It just didn't happen.

Later that afternoon, all the ambassadors went to the White House to meet with President Bush. We were ushered into the Oval Office for a photo op with the President. I knew President Bush enjoyed a relaxed attitude, so I wasn't surprised when he greeted me with, "Price, how are you?" He again thanked me for inviting him and Vice President Cheney the use of our home during the Winter Olympics.

On April 18, we spent the morning at the Foreign Service Institute with Joseph Huggins, the executive director of the Bureau of African Affairs. He led a panel discussion on embassy personnel and resource issues. Rear Admiral Richard Jaskot and Brigadier General Leslie Fuller, of the European Command (EUCOM), also spoke. Much later, I would realize the Africa Bureau was remiss in not including Central Command (CENTCOM) and the Pacific Command (PACOM), since both had an area of responsibility in the Horn of Africa and East Africa region, where security concerns ran high. These were incredibly important areas for our national security, since many Islamic extremists and al-Qaeda terrorists come from this region, others use it for transiting purposes, and al-Qaeda had the ability to move around freely in sub-Saharan Africa, operating under the radar.

Further, having separate military operations (CENTCOM, PACOM, and EUCOM) with responsibility over the sub-Saharan African countries and the Indian Ocean region sometimes could create confusion. When the U.S. embassies in Comoros and Seychelles closed, all direct in-country reporting ceased. Thereafter, information was generated on an intermittent basis by the U.S. Embassy in Port Louis and other sources in the region.

As part of the military command briefing, I believe there also should have been an extensive discussion of Diego Garcia, the United States' most important and strategic military base in the Indian Ocean. Without Diego Garcia, we could not defend or support any military operation in the Middle East or the Indian Ocean region.

On the whole, I enjoyed the three-day Chiefs of Mission Conference with the other ambassadors serving in sub-Saharan Africa. All had spent their careers in the Foreign Service except Bob Royall, a successful banker and community leader from South Carolina serving in Tanzania. As his state's secretary of commerce and chairman of the State Ports Authority, Royall had reorganized both to create more efficient organizations, adding dramatically to the state's economic success.

Nearing the end of the conference at the Foreign Service Institute, the ambassadors headed over to the State Department for a meeting and group photo with Secretary Colin Powell. While there, I picked up our diplomatic passports and the packet of credentials for my presentation to the host country governments. With these documents in hand, I was set to leave the country.

{ VIII }

The End of an Era

When the Chiefs of Mission Conference ended, I was tired and mentally drained, but nonetheless raced to Reagan National Airport for my return to Salt Lake City to make last-minute preparations before leaving the country.

Early the next morning, I went to my office for one last meeting and a conference call with the JPR merger team. Since the transaction was almost complete, I felt the final closing issues could be left in the capable hands of Pat King, the vice chairman, representing the board, assisted by Rex Frazier, the president, and our strong team of legal and financial advisors.

I spent what seemed like hours staring out the window at the beautiful Wasatch Mountains, a view I had enjoyed from my office window since 1968. I was grateful for the many loyal company officers and staff members who had worked hand in hand, some for twenty-five years or more, to help build this business empire—they were like family. Many would have a new start with the GGP organization. I was proud to be part of this great business accomplishment.

Marlene (Gibbs) Luke, my administrative assistant, had planned a farewell luncheon for me. I knew that this occasion would mark the end of an era for Marlene as well. My unflappable assistant had been at my side for almost thirty-five years. I remember when I first met her in 1968. I was building our new office headquarters, and Marlene had been working for a friend and soon-to-be client. Poised and with great personality, Marlene wanted a job change, and real estate and construction sounded like an exciting career opportunity. Though he was loath to let her go, her boss agreed that Marlene's talents were well aligned with my business endeavors.

Marlene typed one hundred words a minute, took shorthand at a rapid clip, and kept up with a fast talker like me. Back in the days before computers and high-speed copy machines, her ability not only to type fast but to do it with six sheets of carbon paper without making erasures was a distinct art. The IBM Selectric typewriter was her machine of choice. As the computer age dawned, Marlene was one of the last in our office to embrace the technology. After all, the Selectric typewriter was her security blanket and she didn't want to give it up. Eventually she warmed up to the change and excelled.

Over the years, Marlene saw many changes in our businesses, the ups and downs of the stock market, and the way we clawed through the maze of banking chaos and economic declines. She had faith, and often told me that we would survive; for her, a single parent raising three children, this was an important belief. Over the years, she also saw our family grow up, took part in our activities, and saw me go through my personal evolution with its many sports endeavors and endurance challenges.

Not wanting to retire, she had decided to join Steven in his new real estate development business for a time. Later, when she graciously retired, she took on community endeavors. We continue to stay in touch to this day.

As her last assignment before I left, Marlene focused on the plans for my children, their spouses, and our six grandchildren to visit Marcia and me in Mauritius the following summer and continue on to an African safari experience that would include camps in the Masai Mara region of Kenya and the Serengeti plains in Tanzania to see the annual migration of the enormous herds of wildebeest.

As night fell, I did not have the heart to stay any longer in this office. It was time to say goodbye—there was much to do.

In the weeks before my departure, I spent many hours combing through a massive amount of business and personal paraphernalia, letters, and newspaper articles going back to the 1960s. I scanned almost every letter and newspaper article, all of which brought back many memories. It seemed like only yesterday that I'd built my first building, run my first marathon, competed in the triathlon, trekked my way through awe-inspiring mountain regions, and participated in body-jolting off-road races. I realized that in undertaking some of these extreme sports and endurance endeavors, I must have been looking for the fountain of youth.

I sorted through numerous family, travel, and business-related photos and slides dating back to the 1960s, reliving the journey. The physical transitions I'd gone through were quite funny: there were many hairstyle changes, beards and mustaches, brightly colored clothes and drab banker suits, and dozens of styles of eyeglasses. There were many photos and memories of my sports endeavors, antique automobiles, early wrestling days in college, and afternoons spent with friends playing squash, racquetball, and handball. These brought up many fond memories, a few sad ones, and a lot of laughs.

The night of April 19, I was up late finishing the last of my packing. I'd discovered three pinecones packed away from the time Steven was twelve, Deidre was ten, and Jennifer almost five, and I remembered well the once-in-a-lifetime experience of gathering these cones for their contents—savory little nuts.

It was a beautiful, crisp Sunday morning in September 1971. I loaded up our Chevy Blazer with a cooler brimming with drinks and sandwiches and strapped a six-foot ladder to the top and mounted Steven's minibike onto the back. Inside the car I stowed a long pole with prongs to shake tree branches, some empty cardboard boxes, and heavy-duty gloves for each of us. I had suggested we all wear old clothes, shoes, and hats for the event. No one seemed keen on the idea, but they were all good sports, and climbed on board.

I drove to an area east of Wells, Nevada, about 170 miles from Salt Lake City, in the high desert near the Humboldt Mountains. We turned off the main highway and ventured several more miles into the wilderness. The air was still, the temperature was in the fifties, and the pine trees interspersed among the sagebrush gave off a delightfully pungent aroma.

We had been advised by friends to spread the boxes underneath a tree and, standing on a ladder leaning against the tree, vigorously shake the branches until the pine nuts dislodged from the cones and tumbled down.

In theory, it sounded good. But we were there early in the season, and the pinecones had not yet opened enough to release the nuts inside. Our only option was to gather the unopened cones from the tree branches and let them dry out at home.

At each tree, Marcia, Deidre, and Jennifer worked among the lower branches and with the pole device pulled the limbs down to pick the cones. Steven held the ladder in place while I climbed the rungs to reach for the highest cones. Within two hours, I was covered from head to toe in sticky pitch. The sap even penetrated through the heavy cotton gloves I wore. My fingers and feet were practically glued to the ladder; I could barely move up and down. Everyone had to pitch in to lower me and the ladder to the ground.

Although Marcia and the children avoided diving into the innermost areas of the pine trees, we were all in various stages of stickiness and no one was smiling. Having had enough of this "wonderful adventure," we shoved the full boxes of cones into the back of the Blazer and headed home, sticking to the seats, steering wheel, pedals, and everything else we touched.

That evening, scrubbing off the sap from our skin with rubbing alcohol, we were left with traces of pitch that would not come off, welts, and red skin. It would take days before the cones were dry and open enough to release their precious contents. The clothes, shoes, ladder, and now-empty boxes were pitched into the Dumpster, the Blazer was never the same, and Deidre and Jennifer swore they would never go on another outdoor adventure. Steven was a little more liberal and forgiving of my choices—of course, he got to ride his minibike.

Growing up, Steven was the Pied Piper, and he still is. The little girls used to follow him around, and the boys chose him as their leader—even though he sometimes took them into uncharted waters. To this day, Steven has more friends than one can imagine. His personality has always been very engaging. During his formative

8.1. Pine nut hunting, September 1971. From left to right: Deidre on the Rupp minibike, Jennifer, Steven resting on the pine nut box, Marcia.

years at JP Realty Inc. this was a great asset in making deals. His honesty, patience, and engaging personality are his trademarks.

Steven is well balanced and loves children of all ages. This shows in the way he deals with his own children, all of whom have different combinations of his good traits. As a soccer coach for his children, Steven has shown fairness, patience, and an ability to build teamwork, which has attracted many parents who want their children to play on his team. As a result, he has turned out many good players who have confidence and a winning spirit. His sincerity in dealing individually with his five wonderful children has enriched their lives. He is truly a renaissance man.

Before and after graduating from California State University, Stanislaus, in Turlock, California, Steven worked in sales at the Modesto radio station owned at the time by Price Broadcasting Company. He then moved on to Boise, Idaho, where he worked as assistant manager at our newest and largest retail mall operation in the state, Boise Towne Square. Today, as the busy principal owner of the Price Realty Group LLC, Steven is also dedicated to raising his two younger adopted children, Savannah and Jackson. His oldest daughter, Ashleigh, is a recent University of Utah graduate, his second oldest, Chelsea, is attending the same university, and his oldest son, Garrett, is serving a two-year mission for his church.

In many ways, Jennifer has a personality similar to Steven's. She was always happy to go along on family outings as long as Steven was there. Even skiing on bitterly cold days, she would never complain as long as Steven went with her. A leader in her own right, Jennifer's trademark is her perpetual and photogenic smile. She has an engaging personality and many friends.

It was in an EMT class at the University of Utah that she met her husband, Tony Wallin. While he attended St. Louis University School of Medicine, Jennifer, whose family real estate genes took hold, managed a large apartment complex where they lived. She was never bashful about collecting the rent and worked hard to keep the complex full of tenants. After Tony graduated, the owner tried to convince them to stay; Jennifer had become one of their best managers, and she had such good people skills that they wanted her to come on board as an executive in their organization.

In her teenage years, Jennifer was a free spirit. An early bout with peritonitis from a ruptured appendix on March 12, 1980, almost cost her her life and quickly showed us what kind of delicate treasure she was. With the arrival of twin girls Hannah and Alexandra in 1995 and, a decade later, another lovely daughter, Lucy Sophia, Jennifer has become a wonderfully supportive mother. Today, Tony, a busy medical doctor, is the director of the Salt Lake Valley Intermountain Healthcare Urgent Care Centers. He judiciously coaches his teenage twins, who are competitive high school tennis players. Between attending to their three daughters' active daily calendar, Jennifer has taken on a leadership role at their youngest daughter's school and serves on other community boards. With her engaging smile and tenacity, she never receives a no when approaching potential donors for any one of her worthwhile organizations. As for Tony, he patiently takes our family calls for medical advice day or night.

As parents, we were probably too nervous with our firstborn, too easygoing with our last, and too strict with our middle child, sweet Deidre. Steven loved teasing her, and Jennifer wanted what she had. Of the three children, Deidre most demonstrates my strong-willed Teutonic traits. I must admit, I was tough on her at times—maybe because she was a lot like me. But Deidre's strengths have made her an exceptional woman.

Because she never liked her given name, Janet, or her middle name, which we spelled Deidre, when she went away to graduate school in California, she changed her name to Deirdra. Bright, introspective, studious, and fiercely loyal to her friends, Deirdra made a good decision to go to graduate school. Now, as a practicing psychologist, she is a leading expert in weight-control issues and the treatment of eating disorders, having helped hundreds of women and men overcome these problems. She has written an excellent book, *Healing the Hungry Self*, which offers a diet-free solution to deal with lifelong weight management, and she often lectures to groups on the subject. Her trademark is tenacity—it has led to her professional career success.

Deirdra developed Marcia's fondness for and knowledge of the arts, is involved with arts groups, and serves on several boards. She has taken an active role on a number of community initiatives. When injustice looms, she acts to right the wrong. Deirdra and her husband, Farhad Kamani, a businessman and real estate investor, enjoy traveling, and Deirdra especially likes exploring new horizons with Marcia. Farhad is an avid bird-watcher and trains pigeons as a hobby.

As I looked through some of the children's early artwork, notes, handmade cards, and school papers, many memories of my three children arose. Each one has a different personality and a unique outlook on life. Incredible human beings, spirited in causes they pursue, they work for the betterment of our planet, are loyal to the family, and understand the need for a strong legacy to pass on to the next generation.

I read articles about Marcia and her art endeavors and the evolution of the Marcia and John Price Museum Building. From Marcia's writings, I lingered on her poignant thought: "Our best endeavors as human beings are our creations."

In October 1995, Frank Sanguinetti, the director of the Utah Museum of Fine Arts, made a presentation to Marcia and me for a new museum building to be built on the University of Utah campus. While I was serving on the Board of Trustees at the university, President Arthur K. Smith and I held several meetings to discuss the idea of replacing the existing 35,000-square-foot building with a much-needed new building of approximately 61,000 square feet. Frank had spent more than three decades as the museum's director, starting on the third level of the Administration Building with eight hundred pieces of art, and growing the collection to more than fifteen thousand pieces housed in a cramped museum facility, with little chance for the public to enjoy them.

At first Marcia and I agreed to provide only a certain amount of capital to help get the project started. Financial enthusiasm for a $15 million brick-and-mortar museum project was lacking at the time, Frank told us, and only $5 million had been pledged for such construction. We decided that this project was important, so on June 20, 1996, our family foundation agreed to make the new museum become a reality, committing $7 million. The construction budget was set at $12.5 million, with added miscellaneous costs of $1 million, we still had a shortfall of $1.5 million. It was a workable budget, though, and with the University, the State of Utah, and additional donors that Frank had in mind, we could cover the shortfall. However, it was important that we not sacrifice the space requirements or the aesthetics for this arts facility. Drawing on my experience with the construction management approach, I agreed to meet regularly with the design and construction committee, which included the design-build team of architects Machado and Silvetti from Boston and Layton Construction of Salt Lake; Prescott Muir, the Salt Lake architect selected to deal with the conceptual programming and ongoing liaison activities; the

University of Utah Campus Facilities Planning representatives; the State of Utah Division of Facilities; and Frank Sanguinetti, representing the museum. With a cost savings agreement with Layton, a constant review of costs using different materials, and input from subcontractors and vendors, we were able to cut the cost down to close to $12 million. Although the 61,000-square-foot main museum building was to be completed by June 2000, an additional $2 million wing of 10,000 square feet—the Eccles/Sanguinetti wing—was added after the initial construction. The move-in, which had also started, would take several months to complete, since the vast art collection had grown to almost seventeen thousand pieces and needed to be carefully accounted for and properly stored.

Meanwhile, President Smith had left in 1998 and the new president, Bernie Machen, would officiate at the dedication of the Marcia and John Price Museum Building on June 2, 2001. When it was my turn to speak, I told the story of a little boy who with his father, mother, and brother escaped the Holocaust in Europe with only the clothes on their backs and a few possessions, leaving everything else behind as they fled for freedom. Yet clutched under the father's arms were three rolled-up paintings. It was not for the monetary value that he risked saving these paintings, but for their cultural value. I was that little boy, and I have never forgotten the importance of art. And as Marcia, with her love of art, has often remarked, "Art is the visual history of the past."

Having achieved financial success and been appointed to serve the United States as an ambassador, I was reminded of a famous saying: "The first third of life should be spent learning, the second third earning, and the last third giving back." The museum project had become important to both of us. I have often viewed Utah as part of a magnificent, vast desert, but without culture, it would just be another desert.

Marcia had spent much of her time over the years serving on arts boards, and she was a close friend and advisor to Frank Sanguinetti. She often said, "Our best endeavors as human beings are our creations of music, dance, theater, and the visual arts. A museum is a repository of our dreams, beliefs, and aspirations made visible as paintings, drawings, and sculpture. They tell our human story. A museum educates, enlightens, inspires, and entertains us. In ancient Greece, a city's success was measured by its cultural vitality. It is as true today as it was then. A museum is proof of that vitality."

We both shared the vision that the Utah Museum of Fine Arts would add to the visual experience for all future generations and open many young eyes to art for the first time. It was our hope that people from all walks of life would enjoy this exposure to the arts, and that this museum building would be home to many more great works of art and exhibits.

Finally, before dawn, I filed the last series of photographs representing our trip to the Horn of Africa and East Africa in February 1970, when Marcia and I

8.2. Marcia and John Price Museum Building, dedicated June 2002.

accompanied our good friends Maurice Warshaw and his wife, Inez, on a fact-finding mission for the CARE and UNICEF operations and the United Nations World Food Programme.

Over the years Maurice involved me in several Utah-based charities in which he was a major supporter and contributor. This would be our first trip to Africa to visit Ethiopia, Kenya, Tanzania, and Uganda, countries in which these organizations were active in supporting education programs, health assistance programs, and humanitarian food aid distribution to famine-stricken village regions; we were also going to review infrastructure projects they funded.

Our trip to Africa began with a stopover in Rome on February 12, 1970, where we met with the United Nations World Food Programme leadership for a briefing on their work. Later that afternoon, at the Hotel Excelsior, Maurice fell ill. Weak and pale, he collapsed in my arms, and I feared the worst as I eased him into a chair in the lobby. Within moments, though, the color returned to his face and he managed a smile. We surmised the problem was more than jet lag, and considered canceling the strenuous trip that lay ahead. But he would have none of it, and after twenty-four hours of bed rest he was determined to go on.

In Ethiopia, we visited several village projects in Afewerk, Tekle, and Lideta, and stopped by medical clinics, schools, and aid centers. Wherever we went, we witnessed extreme poverty. In the smaller towns, impoverished women and children congregated along the route, many sitting in dirt along the roadside, as if they had

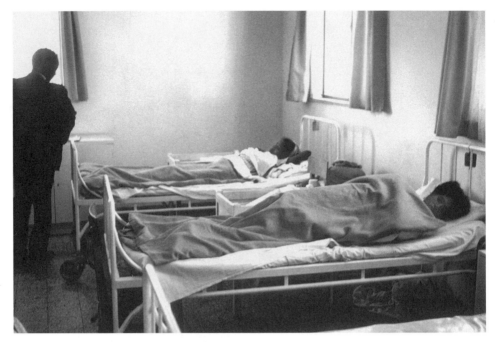

8.3. Lideta Women's Clinic, Ethiopia, February 1970.

nowhere else to go. In the background, men gathered in groups, seemingly oblivious to and apart from the pleading mothers and begging children. Older siblings nurtured younger ones. Flies were everywhere—even in infants' eyes.

At the Lideta Mother and Child Health and Community Center, mothers and their children waited for hours—and in some cases, days—for treatment. Medical supplies were sorely limited and the clinic painfully understaffed. They were unable to deal with the long lines of people in need. At schools, teachers too were overwhelmed; again, there was little educational material and few supplies. Students shared desks and books. Surprisingly, although many walked several miles each day to attend school, their uniforms were clean and they looked hopeful.

The village people were destitute but engaging and friendly and, despite limited sanitary conditions, clean. Some expressed the desire for their children to be educated, but hunger remained an overriding factor and survival foremost on their minds.

In Addis Ababa, we met many highly educated people, which was a hallmark of Haile Selassie's administration. Emperor Haile Selassie, often known as the "Lion of Judah," had come to power in 1930; he was forced into exile in 1936 but returned to the throne in 1941. We were impressed with the quality of educators and students we met while touring Haile Selassie University. Haile Selassie wanted to advance his people through education and modernization of the country but didn't have the support of the military. During one of our visits, we became acquainted with the charismatic Lion of Judah at the Royal Palace. The nickname came from Haile Selassie's belief that he was a direct descendant of King Solomon and the Queen of Sheba. On the grounds, he kept several of his famous black-maned lions and some other felines. Marcia had a chance to pet a cheetah he had in a cage.

Haile Selassie continued to rule Ethiopia through a period of civil unrest until September 12, 1974. With sentiment running against Haile Selassie and his administration, he was deposed in a military coup at the Royal Palace, and imprisoned; he was killed several months later. The military junta known as the Derg also killed members of Haile Selassie's family, his ministers, and generals loyal to him. Lieutenant Colonel Mengistu Haile Mariam, chairman of the Derg, ran a totalitarian Communist-style government backed by the Soviet Union. The Soviets signed a military assistance agreement with Mengistu in December 1976. Thereafter, the Ethiopian government took no further assistance from the United States and expelled our military from an established base in their country.

Our next stop was Nairobi, Kenya, which shares a border with Ethiopia, Somalia, Tanzania, and Uganda. The British had been in Kenya since the late 1800s, and the British East India Company arrived in 1888. Two years later, in 1890, Kenya became part of the British Empire. In 1895, the British established the East African Protectorate, controlling Kenya until the mid-1940s, when local discontentment began manifesting itself almost daily. In 1944, the Kenya African Union was formed as a political organization to express Kenyan grievances against British colonial rule.

In 1947, the KAU selected Jomo Kenyatta as its president. A group called the Mau Mau society was also formed, which started a rebellion against British colonial rule that began in October 1952 and lasted almost seven years. Jomo Kenyatta was linked to this group as its leader, for which he was tried and convicted. During the Mau Mau rebellion, the British forces killed many rebels and placed others—including Jomo Kenyatta—in detention camps. By October 1956, most of the Mau Mau rebels had been defeated, but general unrest continued in Kenya, as Kenyatta and other rebels remained confined.

In 1957, the British finally allowed Kenyans to participate in their first election for a seat on the Legislative Council. The British hoped a moderate African would be elected, someone to whom they could eventually hand over power while still retaining some influence. Then in May 1960, the Kenya African Union merged with the newly formed Kenya African National Union, controlled by Kenyatta's Kikuyu tribe. While still in jail, Kenyatta was elected president, and when released a year later he took over a seat on the Legislative Council.

In the May 1963 elections, the Kenya African National Union party gained control of the council with a majority of the seats. At that point, Kenyatta was selected as prime minister of the autonomous Kenyan government which, on December 12, 1963, declared independence. Exactly one year later, Jomo Kenyatta became the first president of the Republic of Kenya. Almost immediately, a four-year war began between the Kenyan army and ethnic Somali rebels wanting to unite their region in Kenya with Somalia. The Kenyan forces, with the help of British troops, defeated this dissident Somali faction in 1967. Kenyatta, fearing retaliation from the stronger Somalia, signed a defense cooperation agreement with Ethiopia in 1969.

The six-year-old pro-Western democracy under Kenyatta suffered from high unemployment. A weak economy and escalating poverty and health issues in many of the villages were all reaching a critical point. At that stage of Kenya's development, aid from humanitarian organizations was meaningful. Maurice planned to meet with government leaders, health providers, and educators to evaluate their need for aid and to visit programs under way in the region.

We toured several village medical clinics and schools under construction. Visiting local schools and clinics that were already in operation, we noticed they had minimal supplies to work with and great basic needs. The CARE and UNICEF organizations, active in the villages, were understaffed. However, they did commendable work with their available resources. Their staff gave us a briefing and an overview of their activities in the region.

Wanting to see some of these funded projects in outlying areas, we traveled to Nyeri, a village some ninety miles north of Nairobi. Along the way, we also stopped to inspect several wood bridge projects that were under construction. In Nyeri, we had arranged to meet local leaders to take us to a community water project, which we learned had cost $60,000 to complete. On our arrival, we were met by several villagers carrying machetes. This, of course, gave us concern. Our first thought was for our

8.4. CARE meeting and school construction. From left to right: John Price, CARE supervisors, and Maurice Warshaw, February 1970.

safety, since we were not sure if this meeting would become confrontational. (Later, Marcia would say that I slowly inched backward until I was standing behind her, so that she was closer to the machetes! In reality, I don't recall where I was standing, but I remember being nervous and sweating.)

As it turned out, the machetes were for cutting a pathway through the heavy underbrush, leading up a steep hillside to a concrete dam with a spillway that was supposed to be connected to a four-inch supply pipe that would bring water down to a central distribution area below.

For almost two hours, Marcia, Inez, Maurice, and I struggled over rocks and loose gravel and through heavy vegetation as the machete-toting villagers blazed a trail for us. When we did reach the designated spot, we found a small concrete catch basin that held only a few gallons of water and a one-inch pipe that we could trace down the hillside. This installation delivered a quantity of water to the villagers.

During a visit to one of the staging and distribution centers near Nairobi, boxes of CARE supplies and sacks of flour were being loaded. We were proud to see "CARE USA" stamped on them. In looking more closely at the sacks, though, we observed that some had markings, including a hammer and sickle, which had been stamped over in red. We were shocked to see that this humanitarian aid from CARE USA had apparently been hijacked by others, who were taking credit for our efforts. It didn't seem to make a difference to the CARE workers, though; they were more interested in getting the food and supplies distributed to the destitute villagers.

8.5. Bridge under construction (a funded program) on road to Nyeri, Tanzania. Marcia in foreground, Inez Warshaw in background, February 1970.

We then traveled on to Tanzania, which had been called Tanganyika when it was part of the British Commonwealth. Tanganyika received its independence on December 9, 1961, and merged with Zanzibar in 1964, forming the United Republic of Tanzania. Julius Nyerere, its first president, was a highly educated idealist who wanted to institute a "communal tribal village concept" throughout the country. He held that governance and social issues could all be solved at the tribal level. He introduced a collective farming program and in the process displaced many people from lands they had lived on for many years.

The failure of Nyerere's collective farming program combined with disastrous floods resulted in critical food shortages and disease in many villages. While his people were suffering from starvation, Nyerere supported a number of militant groups in neighboring sub-Saharan African countries wanting to overthrow the governments in power. Seychelles was one of those countries: in June 1977 President James Mancham was deposed in a military coup by Colonel France-Albert René, and Tanzanian troops also protected him in later coup attempts.

By the late 1960s, Tanzania had gone from being the largest exporter of agricultural products in Africa to becoming a large importer and, in the process, one of the poorest countries in sub-Saharan Africa. Nyerere continued to feel that the socialist model was the way forward for his people, rather than a capitalist free market approach.

China had had diplomatic and economic relations since the 1950s with a number of sub-Saharan African countries. Destabilization in some of these countries after independence in the early 1960s provided an opening for China and eventually the Soviet Union in the region. Both China and the Soviet Union became military advisors and suppliers of arms and weapons, and gained access to the vast commodities and mineral resources there. Nyerere was particularly influenced by Communist China and established a close relationship with the Beijing government; over the next several years Tanzania became China's most important African base of operations. China trained Tanzania's military and supplied it with arms, trucks, tanks, antiaircraft guns, and patrol boats. As a result, the Chinese were allowed to construct a major naval base in the Dar es Salaam harbor area, which gave them unfettered access to the Indian Ocean region.

We observed a large military presence, which included several vessels anchored in the harbor. China had developed a large economic interest in Tanzania in addition to becoming the country's major military supplier. For us, the presence of this unpredictable rising world power in East Africa was an interesting eye-opener.

While in Dar es Salaam, we visited several village medical clinics and schools. Here, too, employment for men was scarce, and poverty paramount. Some farmers were lucky enough to eke out a living on a few acres of arable land and sold their products at local markets. Others traveled miles carrying wares on their heads and backs for trading and bartering. Not all city dwellers had a roof over their head, but in the villages, no matter how simple their small huts, most people had shelter.

One town we visited was Bagamoyo, some forty miles north of Dar es Salaam. While in Bagamoyo, we decided to visit the historical dock area, from which a large number of African slaves were shipped by Arab slave traders who came from Zanzibar. This barbaric trade lasted until the 1870s. Just the sight of stone and cement blocks with remnants of chains and ankle bracelets used in this inhumane slave trade gave us some inkling of the anguish they must have suffered. It was a staggering reminder of an ugly and shameful period in history.

On our way again, we made a short stop in Entebbe, Uganda, before continuing on to the capital city, Kampala, to visit several village schools and medical clinics. Again, we discovered people were in desperate need of food and supplies. In addition, political instability had resulted from an attempted assassination the year before of President Milton Obote. (Obote would be toppled the next year by General Idi Amin, who accused the president of corruption and seized power in a coup while Obote was in Singapore at a Commonwealth conference.) Given the unrest, we were cautioned not to travel to the outlying villages.

Since we had twenty-four hours to spare before departing for Israel, it was suggested we take a side trip to see the White Nile and Murchison Falls, a short distance from Kampala. Marcia, Maurice, Inez, and I flew on a small twelve-seat commuter plane from Kampala to a picturesque tented camp staffed with a private butler, an assistant, and two chefs—surely a legacy from British colonial times.

Imagine having afternoon tea brought to you in a polished silver tea service and fine china while you are sitting outdoors in the wild, hippos and crocodiles all around you. Add to this a glorious red sunset, and you have a most memorable experience!

After a nice barbeque and some good South African wine, we went to our tents, carrying kerosene lanterns. A few hours later we heard rustling noises in the brush followed by loud snorts echoing through the silence of the night. Inez cried out in concern; we told her everything was going to be fine, and that she should just keep the tent zipped up. As I was dozing off again, I felt something heavy brush against the side of the tent, making the structure sway, and heard several more loud snorts. Soon it felt as if the earth under us were shaking. It dawned on me that a herd of hippos must have come out of the water and were moving around on land at night to graze. The sound of these huge mammals moving around continued for most of the night. I hoped their eyesight was good enough that they wouldn't stumble into the tents.

Between the hippos' activity and Inez's outbursts, few slept that night. Aware there were also crocodiles on the nearby riverbank, I was happy they found their meal somewhere else that night.

At five o'clock in the morning, our butler greeted us with tea and biscuits. The incredible yellow sunrise and crisp cool air made up for my lack of sleep. After a short guided tour on the White Nile, we returned to gather our belongings and head back to

8.6. At Murchison Falls with Maurice and Inez Warshaw and Marcia, February 1970.

the nearby airstrip. Arriving at the small frame structure, we saw several people already waiting. The small aircraft landed on time at noon. The pilot and co-pilot unloaded their passengers and cargo, and prepared to check us in for the return flight to Kampala.

Within minutes, the captain announced the plane could not carry all of us with our baggage. After a bit of negotiating by Maurice, it was agreed that the baggage would stay behind, as well as any outgoing mail and packages. This seemed like a good solution—until the co-pilot decided to calculate the total of everyone's weight. He found a rusty scale on which all of us were weighed as accurately as possible, right down to the last kilo. Maurice hovered over the scale with paper and pencil in hand, keeping track of the weights as they were added up. The higher the number went, the more concerned Maurice looked. Luckily, the four of us were smaller and appeared underfed by comparison to the other tourists.

Finally the pilot announced that one person would have to stay behind, and soon a big argument ensued. I had about forty hours of total flying experience, so I suggested that the co-pilot stay behind, and I would fly in his seat. I thought the captain could handle all of the major issues of this small plane with little help from me. He agreed reluctantly.

A half hour later, we were sitting at the end of the runway, burning off fuel to further lighten our load. We needed every inch of the runway before finally getting airborne, barely clearing the nearby treetops. Once at altitude, I began to worry: what if the captain suffered a heart attack? The hour's flight back to Kampala felt like it lasted a thousand years! Landing safely in Kampala, we all profusely thanked the captain and hoped he would not get in trouble for leaving the co-pilot behind.

As we left Africa, we all realized what an eye-opening experience it had been. The plight of its poorest people was of great concern. Seeing humanitarian aid programs succeed in sub-Saharan Africa was important, since the region had suffered through a difficult transition period after colonialism, with conflicts between ethnic groups creating a chaotic struggle for power. Out of this the African style of democracy was born, though tribal conflicts continue today.

As the sun came up on this final morning in Salt Lake City, the last of the pictures had been sorted and put away. I quickly got ready for our long-awaited journey to the Indian Ocean host countries of Mauritius, Seychelles, and Comoros. I felt prepared for the challenges that lay ahead, the dangers I might encounter, and the new friends I would make in sub-Saharan Africa.

Marcia and I headed to the airport for our Delta Airlines flight to London via Boston, taking off on time at 9:55 that morning. It was a glorious, sunny, and crisp spring morning—one of many we would surely miss.

(IX)

DIEGO GARCIA

The Chagos Archipelago

In London, meetings had been set up for me with Foreign Service officers at the U.S. Embassy there and with representatives of the British Foreign Office to discuss Indian Ocean region issues and the U.S. military base on Diego Garcia. Since 1966, Diego Garcia has been the most important piece of real estate the United States has access to in the Indian Ocean. Often referred to as "Camp Justice," Diego Garcia is a British territory mostly populated now by U.S. military and British personnel. Diego Garcia serves as a U.S. Naval Support Facility and as a regional base for U.S. Air Force B-2 and B-52 bombers and Navy P-3 patrol planes; USAF KC-135 tankers based there are used for refueling and other logistical support activities.

In 1965, the British Indian Ocean Territory was established. A formal agreement was signed in 1966 between the United Kingdom and the United States making Diego Garcia available for defense purposes for both countries for the next fifty years, running through 2016, with an option to extend the agreement until 2036.

In 1976, the British Indian Ocean Territory became a self-administered commission, with oversight of the Chagos Archipelago by the East Africa Desk of the British Foreign Office. Until 1971, the indigenous inhabitants of the archipelago—Chagossians or Ilois, as they are commonly referred to—made a profitable living working on copra and coconut plantations. Their ancestors were African slaves and Indian contract workers brought to the Chagos Archipelago by the French in the eighteenth and nineteenth centuries. Between 1967 and 1973, the British government forced 1,500 to 2,000 Chagossians to relocate so that the island could be turned into a military base. Today, approximately 4,500 Chagossian descendants live in Mauritius and Seychelles, while some who have British citizenship live in the United Kingdom.

During the Cold War era, the strategic atoll became an important tracking station from which to monitor the Soviet Union's activities in the region. Beginning in the late

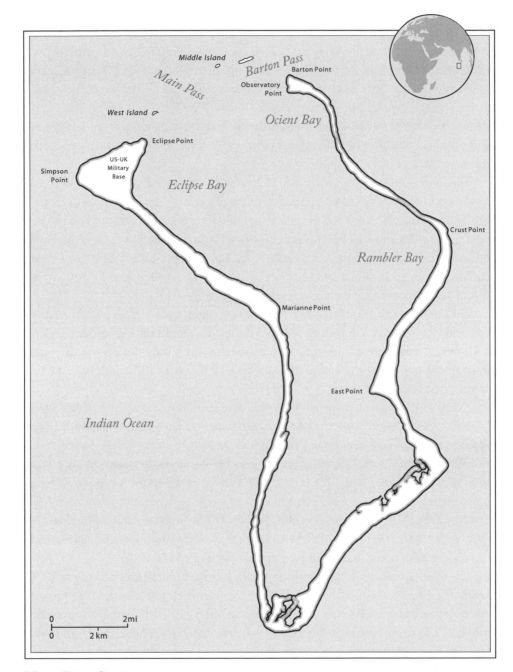

Map 2. Diego Garcia

1960s, Soviet warships were regularly deployed to Indian Ocean and East African ports, and over the next few years the Soviets escalated their intelligence gathering.

The 1979 overthrow of the Shah of Iran dramatically impacted Diego Garcia's significance for the protection of U.S. interests in the Persian Gulf region. The island's location in the vast Indian Ocean made it a critical security and supply link 2,000 miles east of Africa, 1,000 miles south of India, and 2,500 miles south of the Persian Gulf and Red Sea. The island is also located 1,100 miles southeast of the Seychelles and 1,200 miles northeast of Mauritius.

The 1990 Iraqi invasion of Kuwait, followed by the 1991 Persian Gulf War and Operation Desert Fox in 1998, underscored Diego Garcia's importance as a strategic base from which to carry out midair refueling of aircraft for attacks inside Iraq, some 3,000 miles away. In 2001, Diego Garcia was crucial again as the United States launched B-2 and B-52 bombers to attack Taliban strongholds inside Afghanistan. On March 20, 2003, when the invasion of Iraq began as Operation Freedom, air strikes were continuously launched from the Diego Garcia base.

One needs to think of this air base as no bigger than ten aircraft carriers—connected end-to-end. According to U.S Admiral Robert Hanks, every small island in the ocean could be considered like an unsinkable aircraft carrier, so one can readily grasp the importance of preserving unimpeded access to this small but strategically located atoll.

Diego Garcia was discovered by Portuguese explorers in the early 1500s and is the largest of the fifty-two islands in the archipelago. A long ribbon of land, Diego Garcia is shaped like a horseshoe and is approximately 40 miles from tip to tip, with an opening at the north allowing access to a 60–100-foot-deep lagoon that is 6.5 miles wide by 13 miles long. The land is tropically vegetated and covers 6,720 acres, approximately 10.5 square miles. Sandy stretches rise 22–24 feet in some places but generally are no more than 2–4 feet above sea level. The air base itself is less than two miles wide, with the 12,000-foot runway located on a landmass less than a mile wide. Most parts of the island, in fact, are less than one mile wide.

The Chagossians have been seeking the right, through the British courts, to return to the Chagos Archipelago, which they consider their homeland, to tend family cemeteries and reestablish their communities. In 2000, the British High Court ruled that the Chagossians could go back to the islands. Three years later, the High Court ruled their compensation claims were unfounded; in 2004, the British government successfully overruled the 2000 court decision by an order-in-council.

In a 2006 appeal to the High Court, the Chagossians again won the right to return to the islands; in 2007, the British government lost another appeal. However, under their lease agreement with the United States, the British continued to pursue this cause. In 2008, the House of Lords agreed in favor of the British government—once more eclipsing the islanders' hopes of returning.

Most Chagossians, I believe, know they cannot return to Diego Garcia, but some press to return to the outer islands of the archipelago—namely, the Salomon and Peros Banhos Islands, which are between fifty and a hundred miles from Diego Garcia. For security reasons, the United States is opposed to any access.

Meanwhile, Olivier Bancoult, a Chagossian descendant living in Mauritius, is a leading activist in the continuing pursuit to allow the Chagossians to return to the outer islands and seek compensation for the descendants.

I looked forward to learning more about the Chagossian dilemma at the U.S. Embassy in London. When we landed at Gatwick Airport, a Lincoln Town Car was waiting to take us to the Dorchester Hotel on Hyde Park, where we rested for most of the afternoon. On Monday morning, I called Charles Gurney, the first secretary at the U.S. Embassy, who was handling my calendar, and on Tuesday I made my way to the heavily barricaded and fenced embassy compound. Since the embassy was located in the center of one of the busiest business districts in London, security was extremely tight. I was surprised there was not more of a setback from the four surrounding streets that abut the embassy complex. I thought, *What a security nightmare—and a terrorist's dream.*

After passing through the Marine checkpoint at the front of the building, I was met by Charles Gurney. Stationed previously in South Africa for several years, Gurney had spent time during the Cold War in Mauritius and Seychelles. He appeared knowledgeable about sub-Saharan Africa matters, which helped in our discussions about the host countries.

We went to a meeting room where U.S. Air Force Colonel Michael Mahar, the air attaché, was waiting. It quickly became apparent that the Department of Defense wanted to protect the status quo on Diego Garcia, as provided in the lease agreement with the United Kingdom. Colonel Mahar stressed we needed to keep the entire archipelago, as far out as one hundred miles, "sanitized," or clear of any other occupants. Further, he explained, the United States did not want to get drawn into any discussion about paying reparations or claims to the Chagossians; that was an issue solely between the United Kingdom and the Chagossians.

Having reviewed the lease agreement, I asked them to show me where in the document the provision about the one-hundred-mile distance issue was. They said they would seek an interpretation to be sure, and let me know. In a separate meeting, Deputy Chief of Mission Glyn Davies agreed to keep me posted on the outcome of a meeting about Diego Garcia that was to be held the following month between American and British representatives.

Charles Gurney then took me to the British Foreign and Commonwealth Office for a meeting with British Indian Ocean Territory representatives. The British representatives gave a brief overview of the history of the Chagos archipelago going back to the eighteenth century.

Reportedly, reparations on behalf of the Chagossians had been made previously to settle any claims regarding their relocation: the British government had paid £3 million to Mauritius in 1968 for the resettlement of the Chagossians, and then an additional £650,000 in 1973 in conjunction with a full release agreement regarding any claims against the British government. In October 1982 another £4 million was paid to establish a trust fund to support the Chagossians. Most of this money was reportedly disbursed in 1983–84 to the Chagossians, with a balance of £250,000 distributed in 1987. The Chagossians claimed that most of this money had never reached them, that some of these funds had been eroded by high administrative costs in the Mauritian government, and that they still lacked a full accounting.

During this meeting, I was given more insight on Olivier Bancoult, whose family had left Diego Garcia for medical reasons but not been allowed to return—a predicament that must have been experienced by other Chagossians as well. There were discussions of the decision to give British passports to Chagossians in 2002 while allowing them to keep their Mauritius passports—in essence giving them dual citizenship status.

I understood that when Diego Garcia was no longer needed for military purposes, the United Kingdom would cede the islands to Mauritius. However, the government of Mauritius contended that the archipelago should have been ceded to them with their independence in 1968.

Even though the United Kingdom took responsibility regarding the Chagossians' claims, I was asked to work with the British High Commissioner in Mauritius on this issue, since it was in the best interest of the United States to do so. I was glad to have some background on Diego Garcia before arriving in Mauritius, to be able to deal diplomatically with this important issue. Diego Garcia would become the focus of countless bilateral discussions with the Mauritian government; it was always on the agenda. Mauritius continued to press for total sovereignty over the archipelago. Another suggestion was that I work with the British High Commissioner to push for more usage of the English language in Mauritius. Although English is the official language, French and Creole are the languages of choice for everyday use. It was noted that education funds were available for projects involving the English language.

After the meetings concluded at the British Foreign Office, I returned to our hotel to dine with Marcia and pack for our departure to Mauritius.

{ X }

THE REPUBLIC OF MAURITIUS

The Star and Key of the Indian Ocean

You get all sorts of information. From one citizen you gather the idea that Mauritius was made first, and then heaven; and that heaven was copied after Mauritius. Another one tells you this is an exaggeration; that the two chief villages, Port Louis and Curepipe, fall short of heavenly perfection . . .

—MARK TWAIN (SAMUEL CLEMENS), 1896, *FOLLOWING THE EQUATOR: A JOURNEY AROUND THE WORLD*

On Wednesday afternoon, April 24, Marcia and I left London for Paris, where we boarded an Air Mauritius Airbus A-340 for the twelve-hour direct flight to Port Louis, the capital of the island nation of Mauritius. The service was excellent in the business-class cabin, but anxiety and anticipation kept me up most of the night; Marcia, on the other hand, had no problem sleeping. We were heading south toward the Indian Ocean, halfway around the world. On arrival, we would be ten hours ahead of Salt Lake City, which was on Daylight Saving Time, so nighttime in Mauritius was morning in Salt Lake City. I would need to adjust my telephone calling habits.

Mauritius is part of the Mascarene Ridge, a chain of volcanic islands. These islands are located in the vast Indian Ocean, 500 miles east of Madagascar, 1,200 miles south of the Seychelles, and 2,400 miles southwest of India. Some nineteen million years ago, hot lava was thrust out of the bowels of the earth, forming a series of islands that includes Mauritius. The jagged outcrops around Mauritius are the weathered remains

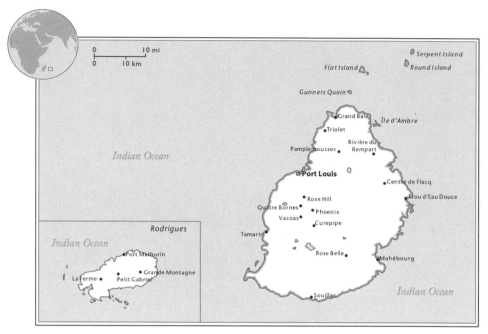

Map 3. Mauritius

of volcanic cones millions of years old—none of which are active today. Such weathering by nature's forces sculpted irregular peaks and created rich red fertile valleys.

The history of Mauritius is complex. The island nation has control over Rodrigues Island, 300 miles to the east, named for the Portuguese explorer Diogo Rodrigues, who visited the island in 1528. It also has control of the smaller and uninhabited St. Brandon Island, 250 miles north, as well as Agalega Island, 600 miles north. Réunion Island, 125 miles southwest of Mauritius, and Tromelin Island, 400 miles northwest, are both administered by Réunion, a department of France. Why were Réunion and Tromelin not taken over by the British when the French were defeated in the sea battles of 1810? Many speculate that the British did not want the burden of these additional islands, which, I am certain, they have realized on many occasions since was a big mistake. All the Mascarene Islands should have been ceded together to Mauritius at independence in 1968. Mauritius still claims title to Tromelin to this day, though they know France will never give up this island.

Mauritius is the largest of these islands, measuring thirty-eight miles north to south, twenty-nine miles east to west. With its undulating shoreline of ninety miles of sandy beaches and lava outcrops, the island measures less than eight hundred square miles, roughly half the size of the state of Delaware. The beaches and bright blue lagoons are protected from the open sea by the third-largest coral reef in the world, which almost entirely rings the island. Mauritius is located just above the Tropic of Capricorn, and year-round temperatures average 75°F during the day and 62°F at night. The central plateau area, approximately 1,250 feet above sea level, is cooler and

10.1. View of Mauritius from an Air Mauritius helicopter, 2003.

subject to more rain and microburst activity. Cyclones are prevalent from December through April.

Before the Portuguese discovered Mauritius in the early 1500s, there were no indigenous inhabitants on these islands. However, records and maps indicate that Arab and Malaysian sailors may have visited there as early as the tenth century, and in 1598 Dutch ships carrying spices from India and Indonesia stopped at the island to resupply. The Dutch named the island Mauritius after Prince Maurice of Nassau, but it wasn't until 1638 that their first permanent settlement took hold and they introduced sugarcane and Java deer to the island. Several decades later, citing severe weather patterns and substandard living conditions, the Dutch settlers abandoned Mauritius, saying there was nothing left that was worthwhile.

I understand their concern over the destruction caused by the seasonal cyclones each year but not the damage they did by denuding the island of its ebony trees and killing off rare fauna, including the flightless dodo bird, known only to have existed in Mauritius. A member of the pigeon family, the dodo weighed fifty pounds when fully grown. By 1710, when the Dutch left, hundreds of thousands of defenseless birds had been killed and the species driven to extinction. Of the forty-five species of birds that were on the island, all but twenty-one were wiped out. The Dutch also slaughtered hundreds of thousands of Aldabra tortoises, which weighed up to 550 pounds each, and hauled their shells off to Europe to be sold. The island of Rodrigues suffered similar consequences, including the devastation of its giant saddleback tortoise population.

With all the destruction, it was no wonder that the Dutch wrote that there was nothing left of value in Mauritius. Before their arrival, the island had a balanced ecosystem, undisturbed for millions of years. It was devastated by the Dutch in less than a century.

When the French settled Mauritius in 1715, they established a naval base and brought with them thousands of slaves from Madagascar, Senegal, Mozambique, and other parts of Africa to work the sugarcane fields. Today, most of the sugarcane plantations are still owned by descendants of those French settlers. The French renamed the island Ile de France. Under the capable leadership of French governor Mahé de Labourdonnais, the island enjoyed robust development, including roads, buildings, and a harbor in the capital city, Port Louis, named after King Louis X. Under the French, Mauritius was administered as a colony.

Trade flourished, with the island supplying sugar and rum to visiting ships and for export to the outside world. However, the French were not content with these enterprises. They sheltered pirates, called corsairs, and began intercepting British ships for their goods on board as they traveled to and from India. In 1810, a British fleet retaliated in battle against the French fleet on the open sea and won, ending the constant attacks on British ships by the corsairs, protecting the British trade routes to India, and effectively transferring control of the island to the British. In 1814, Mauritius was formally turned over to the British in the Treaty of Paris. The British administration of Mauritius thereafter followed English parliamentary law; however, they agreed to leave in place the French culture, tradition, language, and economy as well as laws pertaining to male-dominated real estate ownership. Since the British did not enforce the wide use of English as the official language then, today French is spoken everywhere on the island as the first language of choice, followed by Creole and, last, English. Generally, Mauritians speak English for government activities, bilateral relations, and education in the schools but out of comfort often resort to Creole and French under other circumstances. Cultural centers in Mauritius, called L'Alliance Française, work diligently to preserve the remnants of French culture.

In 1833, the British officially abolished slavery and soon began bringing in thousands of indentured Indian laborers to work the sugarcane fields. Today, these workers' descendants account for almost 70 percent of the population in Mauritius.

Mauritius gained its independence from the British on March 12, 1968. Adopting a constitution based on the British parliamentary system, the island remained within the British Commonwealth until 1992, when Mauritius officially became the Republic of Mauritius. Mauritius has been a stable democracy and in general shows respect for human rights, rule of law, and transparency in free and fair elections, which have been held every five years since 1992.

Mauritius's rich tapestry of cultures, traditions, languages, and religions can be traced to India, China, France, England, Madagascar, and the continent of Africa. Reportedly, more than eighty different religious denominations are established in

Mauritius, and more than twenty languages are spoken. Yet despite their varied backgrounds, the country's population has enjoyed a peaceful coexistence. Currently the Indo-Mauritian community comprises more than 68 percent of the population; Creoles, 27 percent; Sino-Mauritian, 3 percent; and Franco-Mauritian and Anglo-Mauritian, 2 percent. Muslims represent 16 percent of the population; most are Indian, and some are Creole.

Mauritius has one of the highest per capita incomes in sub-Saharan Africa. When I arrived in April 2002, the State Department's figures indicated a gross domestic product (GDP) of $4,000 per capita. By the time I departed in June 2005, the GDP was approaching $5,000 per capita; the State Department reported the GDP to be $5,214 per capita in 2006. In a March 12, 2008, interview for a *Financial Times* article on Mauritius, Minister of Finance Rama Sithanen cited the GDP as $6,300 per capita in 2007. In the same article, Prime Minister Navin Ramgoolam concurred, adding that GDP per capita would exceed $7,000 in 2008. GDP is based on the value of all goods and services produced within the nation in a given year, divided by the average population for that same year. Such figures bode well for this small island nation of 1.25 million people. (The International Monetary Fund's GDP for 2006 was $13,500 per capita, while the CIA reported the GDP for 2006 as $13,700 per capita; I believe these figures to be unduly inflated.) Mauritius is in an enviable position considering that the island has no energy resources—only people resources.

Coming from a nineteenth-century monocrop background, in the 1970s and 1980s Mauritius developed a diversified economy largely based on sugar plantations, tourism, and high-quality textiles. Expanding its potential over the next few decades, the island also has a growing industrial manufacturing base, a healthy financial services sector, offshore banking, computer and communications technologies, and a new cyber-city concept. With the planned establishment of a major hub for fishing fleets, Mauritius will introduce an enlarged fish-processing zone. And plans are in place for a duty-free island concept.

Under the European Union's 1975 Sugar Protocol, certain African, Caribbean, and Pacific sugar-producing countries gave Mauritius a subsidy that boosted the price of sugar to almost double what could be obtained on the open market. In 2005, 600,000 tons of high-quality sugar were sent to Europe; in 2007, sugar shipments were down to 475,000 tons. The European Union's subsidy will be phased out by 2015. Prices paid to sugar producers were cut by 19 percent in 2008, followed by a further price cut of 36 percent in 2009. This could impact their mainstay industry, one of the pillars of their economic success.

The offshore banking sector creates a very lucrative business for Mauritius, which has more than sixteen international banks and more than two hundred legal and accounting firms present on the island. Numerous international operating companies are doing business through Mauritius's network of thirty-three tax treaties—and several more are awaiting ratification.

In 1983, Mauritius became a tax haven for businesses under an Indo-Mauritian bilateral agreement. Domestic offshore companies registering in Mauritius benefit from the pass-through tax treaty arrangement by avoiding income taxes in India (which are set at more than 35 percent): in Mauritius, domestic offshore companies are subject to a withholding tax of 5 percent. Applying country income source rules, the tax effect could be reduced to 3 percent or lower, since regulations allow companies registered in Mauritius with incomes in other countries to obtain foreign tax credits equal to 80 percent of the Mauritian tax chargeable on foreign-source income. Estimates are that billions of dollars each year are invested in India and elsewhere through Mauritius, with investment and operating profit returns almost tax free to the domestic offshore companies.

In addition, there is no capital gains tax in Mauritius for tax residents on capital gains income from the sale of shares in an Indian company. Also, there is no withholding tax on the distribution of dividends to a parent company. Legislators in India are pressing to eliminate this pass-through tax treaty, which would have a drastic effect on the Mauritius offshore banking sector.

The cyber-island technology transformation, with the cyber-city commercial development under way, features a number of state-of-the-art buildings for the information technology and communications technology sectors. These are attracting both local firms and international companies from Europe, the United States, Canada, and India. Mauritius has a bright future, and is truly the "Star and Key of the Indian Ocean."

Mauritius has become a remarkable success story. Its economy is growing at a composite annual rate exceeding 5 percent. According to the 2008 Heritage Foundation Index on Economic Freedom, Mauritius is assessed as having the second-most improved economy over the past year. It is ranked the eighteenth freest in the world, and first among the forty-eight countries in sub-Saharan Africa.

Smaller than Mauritius, the dependent island of Rodrigues has a population of 37,000, mostly Creoles—descendants of African slaves. Ever since the island was annexed to Mauritius by the British, its inhabitants have never been satisfied with being a "stepchild," and they believe they have not been dealt with fairly. They have always wanted full autonomy and to be free of domination by Mauritius, which, however, does allow administrative autonomy through an elected island assembly.

Of volcanic origin and with limited arable land, Rodrigues hosts small cottage industries in wood and linen crafts, microfarming with dairy cows and sheep, offshore fishing and squid trapping, honey production, canned condiments, and destination tourism. Most visitors come from nearby Mauritius and Réunion Island. In emphasizing its rustic setting, this small island has become a popular ecotourism getaway for the rich and famous, including Princes William and Harry of the United Kingdom.

The United States has had an ambassador accredited to Mauritius since 1968. The ambassador's duties, in addition to consular and citizen issues, are to protect and advance American business interests and trade. Yet U.S. relations with Mauritius go back even further: in 1794, shortly after the birth of our nation, then Secretary of State Thomas Jefferson appointed William Macarty as the first consul general to be posted in Mauritius. Embassy reports indicate the United States was actively engaged in trade throughout the region even earlier.

As the plane descended, Marcia and I awoke to a glorious sunrise coming up over the island of Mauritius. Mauritius appeared smaller than I had envisioned but breathtaking. We saw craggy volcanic peaks protruding above the acres of green sugarcane fields that covered most of the island, and a sandy coastline surrounded by blue lagoons nestled inside an almost continuous barrier reef.

Humidity quickly fogged over our windows as the wheels of the plane touched down on the runway. The stalks of sugarcane in the surrounding fields were taller and greener than any I had ever before seen. The Airbus 340 came to a halt adjacent to a connecting jetway at Sir Seewoosagur Ramgoolam International Airport, named after the father of the country. My heart started pounding in my chest, and I experienced an incredible adrenaline rush. I looked at Marcia, and we both wondered what lay ahead for us over the next three-plus years on this small island.

"Mr. Ambassador," the chief steward called out as we deplaned. The chief of protocol in the foreign ministry greeted us warmly, as did the Foreign Service officers from the U.S. Embassy, including Deputy Chief of Mission Bisa Williams; Charlie Slater, the embassy administrative officer; Dan Claffey, the embassy public affairs officer; and Eric Needler, the consular-economic-political officer.

Marcia and I presented our diplomatic passports to the immigration officer, and within minutes, luggage in hand, we were off in a caravan of cars. According to protocol for an arriving diplomat, the government of Mauritius sent a driver and a shiny new black BMW sedan for our use until I presented my credentials to the President of Mauritius. Afterward, we would switch over to the U.S. ambassador's official vehicle.

The press had already been alerted of my arrival and had run several stories using my embassy-provided biography, though they had chosen to spice up their stories by including mention of a prior lawsuit that my company had been involved in.

With the American flag flying on the BMW's fender mast, we headed straight toward the ambassador's residence, some forty-five minutes away in the town of Vacoas. The name comes from a beautiful plant whose leaves and stems have been used for years in making baskets, hats, and other woven items.

Greeting us at Macarty House, named after the first U.S. consul general, was the gracious house manager and personal butler, Cassam Edoo. Of Indian heritage, Cassam was white-haired, trim, and a polite, fatherly sort of man. We felt comfortable with each other immediately. He offered us some great local vanilla tea, for which Mauritius is famous, and briefly explained that during his twenty-five years of

10.2. Macarty House, the U.S. ambassador's residence in Vacoas.

service he had worked for six prior ambassadors. He then introduced us to the other house staff, including the chef, Luc Ramtohul; the housekeeper, Danie Babet; and Fifi Seebaluck, who handled the laundry and cleaning duties at the residence.

The property was five acres surrounded by a ten-foot-high wall made of volcanic rocks cemented together. At the front and side entry gates were guardhouses. Security guards were on the premises twenty-four hours a day and continuously patrolled the perimeter of the property.

On this warm and humid morning, we sat on the patio, sipping our tea and looking at the lush tropical vegetation surrounding us. Adjacent to the patio was a clay tennis court; farther out was a two-bedroom guest cottage. Soon Tigar, the calico cat who had outlasted five ambassadors, came by to get acquainted. Charlie Slater also joined us and suggested we take a quick tour of the residence and make a punch list of items we desired to have changed, since they had barely completed painting and refurbishing the residence. The house was spacious, with a large living room, a formal dining room that could seat twenty people, and a covered veranda where we could have a sit-down dinner for sixty to seventy people. The kitchen too was large and well appointed, able to handle the many functions given by the ambassador. There were seven bedrooms, though we eventually turned four of them into sitting areas and an office each for Marcia and me. One other upstairs room, we decided, would house exercise equipment.

Some of our personal effects and supplies that had arrived were neatly stacked in the hallway. We had been led to believe that many necessary items might not be

10.3. Macarty House staff. From left to right: Fifi, Danie, Luc, and Cassam.

readily available in Mauritius, so we had prepared ourselves for almost any event that we foresaw might occur while we lived on the island, including a variety of staple goods and an assortment of medical supplies. We'd also brought china, only to find displayed in the dining room's two china closets several sets of dishes and glassware with the Great Seal of the United States etched in gold. Later we discovered several newer, well-stocked *hypermarchés* (giant markets) that carried almost every item we had brought from home. Many of the boxes we'd shipped, including those containing mattresses, sheets, pillowcases, comforters, and towels, were never unpacked. We did add more shelving and closet space for our clothing and set up the gym equipment. But we gave away some other items, including several bookcases.

We noticed that the house's dehumidifiers were straining in the high humidity. Cassam said he was constantly emptying them all day long. We had lived in the desert for so long that it was hard for us to imagine the air being filled with nearly 100 percent humidity for most of the year, which gave rise to concerns about mildew and mold. Charlie suggested adding more dehumidifiers in all the rooms, and I asked him to look for units that would drain directly to the outside with through-the-wall flex tubing.

After Charlie left, we rested for a short time before getting ready to go to Port Louis to visit the embassy for the first time. Cassam told us that living in Vacoas would be like being in a rain forest and that we should expect daily rains—no wonder everything around us was so lush and green. Charlie had said the changing weather made playing tennis difficult, what with constantly running on and off the court several times per set because of rain showers. I now understood my predecessor's recommendation to rent a beach house in the northern part of the island, where the weather was sunnier.

At noon we headed down the crowded M-1, the only four-lane highway, for the forty-five-minute drive to Port Louis. The ambassador's residence was on the slope of an extinct volcano, and the road to the capital had a constant downhill gradient, following the path of ancient lava flows to the ocean. Most of the cultivated land we passed was dedicated to sugarcane, which rustled in the sea breezes. Small villages and homes were hidden from view behind these fields, making the countryside look uninhabited. Along the way, we passed a newer shopping center and, nearing town, the new cyber-city development and the University of Mauritius. As we came closer to Port Louis, the area became more densely populated. Many people were riding on motorcycles, scooters, and bicycles, and many more walked along the side of the road. New buildings were interspersed with older ones. Many residential structures were unpainted and appeared unfinished, with rebar protruding from the roof structures as if in wait for another level to be built. I was told that for tax assessment purposes, these houses were considered to be under construction. Each year, a slight advance was made—often paid for from local family income and remittances received from relatives abroad.

The U.S. Embassy occupied the entire fourth floor of Rogers House, a five-story office building located on President John Kennedy Street, one of the busiest streets in the downtown area, with other medium- to high-rise office buildings. Rogers House also housed the Australian High Commission, on the second floor. With two embassies in the building, extra security had been added in and around the premises.

Everywhere you looked were street vendors selling colorful clothing and fabric in makeshift booths, along with a proliferation of counterfeit products brought in from outside the country. Office workers, families, schoolchildren, and tourists swarmed the busy area, spending their precious rupees. The humidity and heat were stifling; the newly constructed buildings walled off the breezes from the Indian Ocean, just a block away.

Upon our arrival, we were immediately welcomed by the country team—the embassy's Foreign Service officers—and escorted to the embassy offices.

In the lobby area on the fourth floor, two police officers were stationed along with the embassy's Foreign Service national (FSN) security guards, one directly behind the reception desk and one inside a secure control booth to prevent any breach of the embassy. The police and security officers saluted me on our arrival; Karl Rouxelin and Suresh Hurdowarsing, the two FSN guards, had a pleasant demeanor and, I thought, well represented the United States as the face of the embassy.

Inside, thirty-six FSNs were waiting to meet Marcia and me. Although jet-lagged and slightly fading, I was recharged with a sudden burst of energy as I was

10.4. Street scene in Port Louis, 2002.

10.5. U.S. Embassy Port Louis, on the fourth floor of Rogers House, 2002.

introduced to each person. Several times on the airplane, I had read the "Welcome to Mauritius" information manual, so I knew everyone by their picture and job description.

The staff had prepared a welcome luncheon with carefully prepared local dishes—Creole, Indian, and French—arrayed on a lovely table setting that stretched down a long hallway. Charlie Slater's wife, Lizzie, had baked a giant cake with American and Mauritian flags popping through the frosting. Thanking everyone, Marcia and I expressed our joy at being here.

We then took a tour of the embassy offices with the country team. My corner office had a commanding view of the port area and the adjacent Caudan commercial development, which included several office buildings, a shopping mall, restaurants, a casino, and the Labourdonnais Waterfront Hotel. The Caudan was a gathering place for visitors and locals, day and night. Subsequently, a sister hotel, Le Suffren, was built nearby on the wharf.

Deputy Chief of Mission Bisa Williams asked us to join the staff in the library for an awards ceremony honoring several outstanding employees for their achievements during the year. I felt this event was a good team builder, and I would press for such award ceremonies on a regular basis.

On the way home, I dozed off until we arrived at Macarty House, where Cassam was waiting with a cup of delicious and aromatic vanilla tea in hand. Marcia and I rested for a couple of hours before again leaving: this time we were attending the farewell reception at the Maritim Hotel in honor of the Chinese ambassador, Xia Shouan, hosted by Minister of Foreign Affairs Anil Gayan. Because this was our first official function, we decided to use the ambassador's official vehicle, a Mazda 929 that had been used by several of my predecessors. A second vehicle assigned to me was a heavily armored Toyota Land Cruiser. I wondered why we didn't promote U.S. interests more by making the ambassador's vehicle a Ford, Chrysler, or GM product, some of which were made in nearby South Africa. My driver, Ahmed Boodhooa, had been the ambassador's driver for twenty-two years. He knew all the back roads, even the rough, narrow ones that at times made me a little nauseated. I would have to get used to sitting in the backseat, I feared.

During the evening's cocktail hour, nearly everyone communicated with each other in French and Creole. The toasts that followed were in French. Only the greetings as we arrived were in English, as well as some small talk that followed as people welcomed us to Mauritius. The Chinese ambassador also spoke mostly in French, interspersed with a few words of English. I told Marcia we were going to have to accelerate our French lessons if we were going to survive these social gatherings.

Cocktails and toasts were followed by a sumptuous dinner. The evening's menu included some of the island's favorite Indian, Creole, and Chinese dishes: yogurt with cucumbers, hearts of palm, different types of curry dishes, and stir-fries. I sampled almost every delicious dish. Finally we had dessert and after-dinner drinks.

Our first day, and we were out until after midnight—I wondered how we would last for the next three years.

Friday morning came all too soon. I had only a few hours' sleep and still suffered from jet lag and anxiety. Luc was in the kitchen at six-thirty preparing bacon and eggs, while Cassam readied the breakfast room table for Marcia and me. He brought us a pot of hot tea, which was a nice touch and helped settle some jitters.

After breakfast we went to a briefing with Krishna Ponnusamy, the supervising officer in the Ministry of Foreign Affairs. And then we were off to Clarisse House—President Karl Offmann's official residence—to present my credentials.

Several military personnel were stationed at the front gate, and inside the gated area was an honor guard of twenty soldiers dressed in neatly pressed uniforms with brass buttons shining brightly in the morning sun. As we pulled up to the portico, the honor guard swung to attention, and the commanding officer saluted me. We were first escorted to a waiting room, and within moments we were led into another room where President Offmann was waiting. In his sixties, over six feet tall and with a full crop of white hair that contrasted with his smooth bronzed skin, the President looked like a former athlete.

I presented my credentials with these words:

> I have the honor to present to you the letters accrediting me as Ambassador Extraordinary and Plenipotentiary of the United States of America to the Republic of Mauritius. I also have the honor of conveying best wishes and warmest greetings from the President of the United States, George W. Bush, and the American people. I also want to present to you the letters of recall of my predecessor, Ambassador Mark Erwin.

I then handed the President the official letter of accreditation and we warmly shook hands. For a moment I just stood there relieved. When the President asked if I would like a cup of tea, I accepted gratefully, and for some forty-five minutes we began to get acquainted.

We discussed Mauritius's business success as a model for other sub-Saharan African countries. I commended him on their high literacy rate, stand on democracy, respect for human rights, transparency, and free and fair elections. I also thanked him for his and the Mauritian parliament's support for the global war on terror under UN Resolution 1373. His predecessor Cassam Uteem, who served as President from June 1992 to February 2002, had chosen to resign rather than support the global war on terror.

It was a nice first meeting. The President and I discovered that we shared many areas of mutual interest. Above all, he was a friend of the United States.

Next we headed to the embassy. I asked Ahmed to remove the U.S. flag from the car's fender post, thinking it better to be low-key as we traveled around the island. We agreed on its use for official events only.

At the embassy, I held my first country team meeting with the six Foreign Service officers, during which time I was given a brief update and overview of their issues relating to the host countries. The country team refers to the American direct hire State Department Foreign Service officers at the embassy as well as agencies located outside the region, including: the defense attaché, Commerce Department, Drug Enforcement Agency, and Customs officers based in other countries.

Bisa, Charles, Dan, Lizzie, Eric, and I then met in a private dining room at La Bonne Marmite restaurant, a favorite for locals and diplomats. We were joined by several visiting representatives from U.S. Government agencies with responsibilities in the region.

After lunch, Bisa hustled me out to our waiting car for a two o'clock meeting with the Minister of Foreign Affairs, Anil Gayan. I had met him previously at Mauritius's UN Mission in New York, and again at the farewell dinner for Ambassador Xia the previous evening, where he'd mentioned he wanted to discuss an important matter with me: the Diego Garcia and Chagos Archipelago sovereignty issue.

In our meeting that day, he got right to the point. Knowing the United States had the right to be in Diego Garcia until 2016, I pointed out that the lease with the United Kingdom stipulated that the United States potentially could control the island until 2036. He frowned, saying that U.S. control shouldn't even continue until 2016, and then reported that his government was going to submit a letter to President Bush in regard to sovereignty over the islands. He also mentioned that the Prime Minister, Sir Anerood Jugnauth, was planning to go to Washington in May with the hope of meeting with Secretary Powell for a discussion on this matter.

Gayan would have gone on, but I felt this adversarial situation was about to reach an uncompromising level of discourse, so I changed the subject and talked about my first impressions of this beautiful island and the warmth of the people. I did get a small smile from him at this.

I took several deep breaths before walking down the hall to meet with the Prime Minister. I expected another frontal attack like Gayan's. Instead, the Prime Minister, a seasoned politician in his seventies, was charming and greeted me warmly. He briefly mentioned Diego Garcia and his planned trip to the United States before asking if it was possible for me to set up a meeting with Secretary Powell as well as President Bush.

Prime Minister Jugnauth was referred to by many as "the father of the education initiative," and in the 1980s had been responsible for weaning Mauritius from its longtime dependency on sugar as a monocrop. Prime Minister Jugnauth had determined the country could not survive, grow, or prosper unless it became diversified. He focused on the island nation's growing population of young children as their main resource and strength for its future, and he pressed to expand quality education. This alone accounts for much of Mauritius's current economic success; today the country boasts a literacy rate of 90 percent. I commended him on the country's accomplishments and its respected position on the global stage, and I agreed to call Washington about his upcoming trip.

We next met with Deputy Prime Minister and Minister of Finance Paul Bérenger. With most of the government run by Indo-Mauritians, it was unusual for a Franco-Mauritian to be found at such a high level in the government. His power had come about as the result of a marriage of necessity between two rival political parties, the Mauritian Militant Movement (MMM) and the Militant Socialist Movement (MSM), which combined their efforts in 2000 to defeat Navin Ramgoolam's Mauritius Labour Party (MLP). In a power-sharing arrangement, Bérenger was to become Prime Minister after the midterm in August 2003, and Sir Jugnauth then would become President of Mauritius.

I found Bérenger to be a proud, handsome, slender, and charming individual with an engaging smile, a full head of shining white hair, and a mustache that made him look regal. He was dressed to perfection in a custom-fitted suit, shirt, and tie, and shoes to match. With his heavy French accent, one could have mistaken him for a top leader in the French government and never imagine that in the 1960s he had been a Marxist and a member of the Communist Party, creating havoc with his leftist ideology.

The Deputy Prime Minister talked about budget and finance matters under his jurisdiction, and touched very lightly on some bilateral issues. To my surprise, he did not bring up Diego Garcia.

10.6. With Mauritian government leaders, 2002. From left to right: Trade Minister Cuttaree, Prime Minister Jugnauth, Ambassador Price, and Deputy Prime Minister Bérenger.

On the drive home, I reflected on these three distinctively different personalities and what I could do to help strengthen the relationship between our two countries.

Mauritius has had a long history of democracy, which I believe stems from its not-too-distant past of slavery and indentured servitude. To Mauritians, freedom is a precious commodity to be fostered and preserved. As a result, its leadership has been chosen consistently on a transparent basis, without political upheaval. Political rallies and opposition marches have also been generally peaceful in the past.

From the country's independence in 1968 until 1982, Sir Seewoosagur Ramgoolam served as Prime Minister of the Independent State of Mauritius within the British Commonwealth. Sir Anerood Jugnauth served in the same post from 1982 until 1992, when the Republic of Mauritius was established, and as Prime Minister thereafter until 1995. Navin Ramgoolam, Seewoosagur's son, was then elected Prime Minister and served until 2000, when, as noted previously, the MMM and MSM agreed to work together to reelect Sir Anerood Jugnauth and then ensure the transition to Bérenger in 2003.

That evening Bisa hosted a reception for Marcia and me at Macarty House, where more than two hundred of the island nation's who's who came to meet us. Our country team formed a reception line at the front entrance of the residence. Prime Minister Sir Anerood Jugnauth and Lady Sarojini Jugnauth arrived in their new black Mercedes 600 sedan, surrounded by a roar of motorcycles and flashing red and blue lights, the likes of which I had not seen since Washington. Once Sir Anerood Jugnauth had moved through the crowd, Bisa introduced us to the enthusiastic gathering. It turned out to be a successful event, with everyone, including the Prime Minister, staying for quite some time.

On Saturday afternoon, April 27, Marcia, Bisa, and I went to the Caudan to attend a Rotary Club–sponsored Reading Day exhibit. Several exhibitors offered a nice selection of children's storybooks written in English. From there, we went to the South African National Day celebration, held in conjunction with an African trade fair, with hundreds of products on display and for sale. African dancers in native costume entertained the attendees. Many of the people I had met over the last two days were here as well, and I looked forward to seeing them often. We then traveled over an hour to the resort Le Saint Géran, where we were joined by Charlie and Lizzie Slater for dinner at Spoons restaurant, created by famous French chef Alain Ducasse. The food and wine were delicious—a delightful surprise on this small island.

On Sunday, Ahmed drove Marcia, Bisa, and me around much of the island so that we could become acquainted with some of its highlights. The island is comparatively small, but once you get off the fast-paced M-1 highway, travel on the narrow roads slows down significantly. There are no shoulders or sidewalks along these roads, which can become dangerous as one travels through the numerous small villages. The roads follow the natural contour of the ancient lava flows, now covered with sugarcane fields, and at higher speeds can lift the car up and down like a roller coaster. I quickly learned it takes a lot of patience and good driving skills to navigate safely around the island. Although the British system is followed, with traffic on the left side of the road, many European visitors initially forget and drive on the right side, which creates havoc, and most Mauritians tend to drive in the middle of the road. Buses, trucks, cars, motorcycles, scooters, bicycles, and pedestrians were everywhere. To make matters worse, people living in these villages often stopped their cars to chat with friends; honking just seemed to make them linger. Through it all, though, I felt congeniality among the people, who appeared to have strong family values and were bonded with each other. I was just glad I wasn't driving, I told Ahmed, who chuckled.

We traveled through the beautiful Black River Gorges National Forest in the southern part of the island. Since the guava plant, which bears fruit, was in season, we stopped to pick some. Marcia disappeared into the thick brush, and for a moment I thought she was lost. She returned a few minutes later carrying an armful of the tart fruit and beaming.

We headed next to the southwestern part of the island and stopped at a mountaintop restaurant, Varangue sur Morne, some two thousand feet above sea level. From there, the views of the surrounding forest and the clear blue ocean off in the distance were breathtaking. Several rain showers moving in and out left behind spectacular double rainbows. Afterward, we went on to the west coast and then north, and stopped in some of the villages to see several ornately decorated Hindu temples. We could also hear the echoes of the call to prayer from a nearby mosque.

For dinner, we stopped at Le Pescatore, a restaurant located on the water in the northwest village of Trou aux Biches. The lobsters we ordered were among the biggest and tastiest we had ever had.

That day turned out to be a long one, and we covered a good portion of the island. However, it was very informative, inspiring even, especially seeing the cultural and religious mix in the communities and people of different faiths and backgrounds living alongside one another in peace.

On Tuesday morning, I paid a courtesy call at the nearby residence of Ambassador Paul André Tsilanizara of Madagascar. He was a slightly built man, impeccably dressed, and looked troubled. He indicated he was unsure about his future in Mauritius. After his country's recent presidential election, both candidates had claimed victory, and the entire country was embroiled in a political struggle. He did not know the present status of the dispute between the contenders, Marc Ravalomanana and Didier Ratsiraka. Ravalomanana occupied the capital city, Antananarivo, and Ratsiraka had set up barricades surrounding the city. Both men had military troops loyal to them, but neither had proven he had enough votes to claim a true victory. The ambassador was worried a civil war was about to erupt. As it was, the country was under siege. Ratsiraka's supporters had blown up bridges to the capital, several people had died in the fighting, and a Canadian newsman had been caught in the crossfire.

10.7. Chamarel Waterfall, in the Black River Gorges National Park, 2002.

The government of Mauritius was very concerned. A number of textile companies had invested millions of dollars in Madagascar, where production had ceased because of the chaos.

In the following weeks, France, India, and South Africa accepted an outcome in favor of Ravalomanana. The U.S. position at first was to wait on the sidelines rather than accept the apparently flawed result. The French ambassador, Henri Vignal, met with me to press his government's wish for U.S. support of Ravalomanana. Foreign Minister Gayan and Deputy Prime Minister Bérenger also asked me to prevail on President Bush to show support for the Ravalomanana government. Their great fear was that a civil war would break out and severely affect the economic stability of the region. Finally, after a number of cables were sent back and forth to Washington, the United States released a statement supporting the Ravalomanana government. Ratsiraka conceded and left the country. However, the country remained volatile, and disruptive activity in Madagascar continued for some time thereafter—which later made me question why Madagascar received aid from the U.S. Millennium Challenge Account.

The Millennium Challenge Act of 2003, announced by President Bush in 2002, was approved in 2004 and funded by Congress in 2005 as the way of the future for properly administering financial aid. This represented a fundamental change in U.S. foreign assistance policy. Intended to provide new foreign assistance to low-income countries that were "governing justly, investing in their people, and encouraging economic freedom," the Millennium Challenge program had sixteen benchmarks that recipient governments needed to meet.

Over the years, the United States had set a precedent of giving financial aid, with few strings attached, to autocratic and corrupt rulers in sub-Saharan African countries. In the case of some fledgling democracies where the United States didn't have any economic interest, we weren't so generous. I believe a provision in the program is needed for those countries that are not able to meet all sixteen of the MCA requirements to qualify for assistance but are young democracies that risk becoming failed states susceptible to the influence of al-Qaeda and other Islamic extremists. There should have been a requirement to meet perhaps twelve out of the sixteen criteria, with ten mandatory requirements. Simply stated, let's make the requirements more like a Boy Scout merit badge program. While regular Scouts have 122 merit badge options from which to choose, of the twenty-one required for the level of Eagle Scout, twelve are mandatory. Adopting a similar plan could spark an incentive for fledgling democracies in sub-Saharan Africa to gain a higher level of financial assistance by attaining achievable performance standards.

Madagascar was the first recipient of funds from the MCA grant program, awarded $110 million under a compact signed on April 18, 2005. The deal was negotiated and approved by the Millennium Challenge Corporation board in under six months, which was a great surprise to me, since during my tenure as ambassador I had not even been able to get a response to my request for an assessment in one of my host countries. So how and why did the MCC board act so fast on behalf of Madagascar when the country's government did not govern justly, invest in its citizens, or encourage economic freedom?

The MCA program should be one of the United States' premier "kick-start" programs for sub-Saharan African democracies. Any country that has gone through at least one election deemed fair and transparent should qualify—if we don't want the country to slip backward again. Political candidates must have a fair and equal chance to compete unimpeded. Fair business competition practices must exist without government leaders having conflicts of interest. Unjust taxing of competitive businesses is an immediate red flag. Encouraging the creation and maintenance of education and health care facilities in every village is the only way a country can grow and prosper. Supplying building materials to villages for the construction of schools and clinics is not costly to the government and should be a priority.

Observing the rule of law, respecting human rights, maintaining transparency, and ensuring free and fair elections are basic tenets for any Millennium Challenge Corporation funding. Yet I wondered about the transparency of the MCC's interview and selection process. People I met with while I was ambassador were fearful of reprisals and talked only under assurances of confidentiality. Comparing other worthwhile country candidates in the region, I felt the MCC had jumped too quickly in approving Madagascar.

According to a former executive of a large international diversified food corporation that competes with Ravalomanana's dairy business in Madagascar, Ravalomanana had imposed economic stumbling blocks for the competition. Also, a regional oil company suffered a tanker embargo leading to extortive acts and threats of shutdown and confiscation of assets. If that weren't enough, there was the issue of Pierrot Rajaonarivelo, who had announced that he would run against Ravalomanana in the 2006 election but who had been prohibited, under threat of imprisonment, from returning to Madagascar to register as a presidential candidate.

On two occasions, in May and July 2003, Marcia and I visited villages in Madagascar that had not had a basic schoolroom or clinic for medical care until the Madagascar Ankizy Fund, an American-based organization I became acquainted with, built two schoolrooms and a clinic for about $10,000. The village elders were most thankful, and on one visit had an American flag-raising ceremony in which I participated. It was sobering to see all the eager young children, who had only basic school supplies but a will to learn. They were very happy when this American organization gave them building materials so they could build another needed schoolroom themselves.

I often wondered what Ravalomanana did with the money he extracted from businesses in Madagascar. Some of those funds could have been budgeted for building materials to be offered to villages to build schools and clinics. But were they? I believe Ravalomanana failed on all counts.

At my initial meeting in London, I had agreed to work closely in Mauritius with British High Commissioner David Snoxell, particularly in regard to issues involving Diego Garcia. When I visited him at his office, just above a plumbing supply house, he complained about the representative of Her Majesty's Government being above the sign "Toilets for Sale"!

We quickly got into the subject of Diego Garcia, including an overview of its history from his perspective. While the United Kingdom felt an obligation to the residents and their descendants it relocated, it wanted to keep full sovereignty over the Chagos Archipelago. However, the United Kingdom did promise Mauritius they would cede the islands to them when Diego Garcia was no longer needed for military purposes. Snoxell said the United Kingdom had also promised to charter a boat to take 125 Chagossian descendants for a visit to the outer islands in early July 2002. I offered the opinion that it was not a good decision, especially now that a number of them had been given British citizenship. We agreed to get together again as the planned boat trip to the outer Chagos Islands evolved.

I continued making the rounds to meet other diplomatic corps members to discuss issues of mutual concern in the region. I also met with business leaders to listen to their issues and improve trade relations with the United States. A growing area of interest was the textile manufacturing sector, in which Mauritius had become a leader.

The following week, on April 30, I received a phone call from the deputy assistant secretary of state in the Bureau of African Affairs, Ambassador Bob Perry. During the latest National Security Council meeting, Secretary of State Powell had approved holding the second annual AGOA Forum in Mauritius December 2–7, 2002. The ambassador said Secretary Powell would personally attend.

This was great news. The African Growth and Opportunity Act (AGOA) was established by Congress in 2000. The AGOA program provided for an increase in trade with the United States by qualifying sub-Saharan African countries able to export products from a list of more than 6,400 items approved for duty-free access. To qualify under the program, countries need to show improvements in democracy, rule of law, human rights, transparency and a commitment to work standards that excluded the use of child labor. The Second AGOA Forum would include delegates from the thirty-seven sub-Saharan African countries that qualified for duty-free access to U.S. markets. It was an honor to host the event in Mauritius. I immediately shared the information with Bisa and, subsequently, the rest of the country team. However, I wondered if our embassy, in conjunction with the government of Mauritius, could pull this off logistically and make it a success.

Bob Perry also said that Secretary Powell had agreed to meet with Prime Minister Jugnauth when the latter visited Washington in May. I mentioned to Bob that the Prime Minister's agenda would probably include the sovereignty issue over Diego Garcia and the prospect of extending the textile multifiber agreement for a minimum of three years. Bob agreed to alert everyone concerned.

On May 3, we held a country team meeting and attended a security presentation regarding recent tapes of the al-Qaeda terrorist threat that was exposed against U.S. interests in Singapore. Similar threats had been made against U.S. interests elsewhere, including sub-Saharan Africa.

Early Saturday morning, I was wakened by a call from Lauren Moriarty, the director of the Office of East African Affairs. Apparently at the UN Security Council meeting held on Friday, the Mauritian government circulated a position paper on behalf of the Organization of African Unity (now known as the African Union) to suspend sanctions that were in place against Liberia. This country had a reprehensible human rights record against its own people and in neighboring Sierra Leone. Its leaders were pillaging the diamond mines and other resources, supplying arms to rebels, and destabilizing the region. Lauren said a demarche was on its way by e-mail for delivery to the government of Mauritius. I was to meet with Mauritian government officials immediately to discuss this demarche and reiterate the issues at the highest level, so that Mauritius would not continue to push for the lifting of the sanctions but instead support at least a six-month extension of the current sanctions.

Liberia had previously agreed to the Mano River Union Accord with Sierra Leone and Guinea. However, Liberia was not honoring the peace agreement. The region was so unstable that 17,500 peacekeeping troops were active in Sierra Leone.

After downloading the proposed demarche, I discussed our approach with Bisa, and within the hour called Deputy Prime Minister Paul Bérenger at his home to deliver the State Department's message. I stressed the importance to the United States of Mauritius voting for continuing the sanctions on weapon imports, diamond exports, and senior government officials' travel, and informed him that the vote by the UN Security Council was set for Monday, May 6. We agreed to meet that morning so I could personally deliver the demarche. He promised to work on the matter beforehand and contact his mission in New York.

At our meeting, Bérenger said that their permanent representative to the United Nations, Jagdish Koonjul, had informed him in a phone call that the language in a resolution the United States and United Kingdom supported—that would provide for an audit and use of the proceeds language for oversight of Liberian revenue from the timber trade—was not acceptable, and that Mauritius might abstain from voting, along with France and Russia. That afternoon, Bérenger phoned to say that he had now seen the full report from the Mauritian mission regarding the proposed UN Security Council resolution on the Liberia sanctions, and that only the Russian delegation had expressed opposition to the audit language. In light of this, Mauritius was inclined to go along with the resolution for sanctions, despite the inclusion of the questionable audit language. Later in the day, we delivered a videotape entitled *Crimes of the Mano River* for the Deputy Prime Minister's review. We hoped it would help to convince the government of Mauritius of the destabilizing role Liberia continued to play in the region.

The next morning, Foreign Minister Anil Gayan confirmed that Mauritius would vote for the sanctions on Monday. The UN Security Council subsequently voted 15–0 to keep the sanctions in place.

The Liberia sanction resolution was my first demarche to the host country government, with many more to follow during the next three years asking for support of U.S. positions at the UN. On numerous occasions I was told by host country leaders that the United States expected support on all their issues but offered little back without conditions. As an example, the AGOA program was presented with many strings attached and was under constant review by the Congress. U.S. Customs officers' interpretations of the rules regarding textile products had become a genuine issue for Mauritian textile manufacturers, as Customs officers halted access to the United States for any textile product where sourcing of the fabric or yarn used was in question. Instead of simplifying the interpretation of the rules and the review process, it appeared that Customs was in no hurry to release the tied-up goods, which were now sitting in quarantine in containers offshore, and had little desire to create goodwill with the sub-Saharan African countries. I brought this to the attention of Washington on several occasions, but the situation was slow to change.

Just four days later, a second demarche was sent for immediate delivery at the highest level of the government. The United States had decided not to ratify the Rome Statute of the International Criminal Court. I informed Deputy Prime Minister Bérenger there were potential conflicts within the UN charter and that claims for jurisdiction over U.S. nationals could affect our peacekeeping forces around the world. The United States wanted Mauritius to concur with our position at the United Nations and not ratify the accord either.

Since my arrival in Mauritius, my calendar had been packed solid with meetings and visits to textile factories and other product manufacturing operations, many of which qualified for access to U.S. markets under the AGOA program. I also paid courtesy calls on most Mauritian government officials and business and community leaders. The numerous official and social functions kept me going day and night, and my weight was increasing dramatically from eating delicious deep-fried samosas and other Indian and Creole specialties served as hors d'oeuvres. There was little time left for normal dinners and quiet evenings spent at home.

Marcia and I continued with our French lessons. My linguistic skills did not improve enough for me to become fully conversant, which was somewhat frustrating for me at times when only French and Creole were spoken. I did understand parts of conversations, but not their entirety. Most people were considerate, but I knew I had to keep up with my lessons. To our delight, when Marcia and I were invited to a government event held at Clarisse House and hosted by Vice President Raouf Bundhun, more English was spoken—and we were served a delicious meal consisting of chicken curry, vegetables in a curry sauce, and rice.

On Thursday morning, May 23, I met with Charlie Slater and a regional political officer for a briefing on terrorism-related concerns. I wanted to know more about the Islamists who were coming to Comoros and their activities in the mosques and madrassas. I also wanted to know more about the large Comorian community in the isolated northwest seacoast town of Mahajanga in Madagascar. I had heard that Fazul Abdullah Mohammed, the most wanted Comorian terrorist, had relatives there and visited them from time to time. My concerns were that access to Mahajanga by boat from Comoros and neighboring Mayotte was easy, the seacoast town was isolated, and Mahajanga could provide a safe haven.

I then shared a cable concerning two informants who claimed that many new Muslims were appearing in the Comoros Islands. Questions were raised whether this was just coincidental or was linked to al-Qaeda activity. I felt the response was lacking direct answers. I asked if Mauritius was safe, and the political officer quickly replied that only a small number of vocal fundamentalist Muslim clerics lived there, and they were of no concern.

I mentioned my intention to travel to Comoros in the near future to present my credentials. I knew some people in Washington thought of Comoros as a country of limited importance, but I made it clear I fully intended to engage Comoros to improve our bilateral relations, image, and security interests. He listened attentively, but his responses were carefully measured. I finally asked him if he had concerns about my safety in going there to present my credentials. He had none, and we agreed to talk again after my visit.

The next day at noon, I met with the Deputy Prime Minister to deliver another demarche. This one detailed the United States' new position regarding Cuba, and again I had been asked to deliver it in person. It seemed I met constantly with the Deputy Prime Minister because of the Prime Minister's travel schedule.

As usual, Deputy Prime Minister Bérenger was punctual, well dressed and all smiles. I promptly said I guess we were getting together again for another geography lesson, and he broke out laughing. I then handed him the eight-page outline of President Bush's Initiative for a New Cuba, sent by the State Department. In summary, I said, the initiative sought to promote a rapid and peaceful transition to democracy and to help reinsert Cuba back into the democratic family of nations. It further called on the Cuban government to conduct a free, fair, and transparent election for the National Assembly in 2003.

The prime minister had never heard about the initiative, and asked when it had occurred. I replied that it had been four days earlier, on May 20, 2002, and added that it had received substantial news coverage. Bérenger replied that he could not press his colleagues from Cuba on this matter when he saw them. I told him I understood his position and would pass on his thoughts to Washington.

I then decided to bring up another cable that had been handed to me just as I was leaving the embassy. This one addressed the upcoming World Summit on Sustainable Development Partnership, a conference to be held in Bali on May 27, 2002, and we were asking Mauritius to participate. The cable outlined the basic concept and identified several key sectors for discussion, including health care, water, energy, sustainable agriculture, rural development, education, oceans, and forests.

In my haste, I did not read the cable's full text until later that afternoon, and I was shocked to see a major typo in the text I had delivered. Instead of "reducing poverty," it read "reducing prosperity." This document had gone around the globe to every embassy. Even now, Bérenger could be reading it. I quickly called his office to verbally clarify the embarrassing error. Back at the embassy, I had Bisa alert Washington about the error as well.

On May 30, the country team held a meeting to discuss concerns about local threats from radical elements targeted toward individuals at the upcoming AGOA Forum. I had been disturbed for some time by certain Islamic leaders' radical statements in the press and word-of-mouth comments regarding the U.S.-led global war on terror. Former President Cassam Uteem, who had resigned rather than support the global war on terror, had many Muslim followers who were outspoken about the issue as well. Could jihadist supporters really be here in Mauritius?

On Sunday, June 2, four Sri Lankan citizens tried to board an Air Mauritius flight bound for Paris and then on to New York. The alert counter agents, seeing they had no luggage to check and noting that they had arrived on Colombo–Port Louis tickets and had purchased one-way tickets to New York from a local travel agency in Port Louis and paid cash, became suspicious. In checking their visas, they were found to be counterfeit. After being rejected at the counter, the four disappeared before the police could question them, but they were subsequently apprehended in the town of Rose Hill at a small bed-and-breakfast.

Interestingly, a fifth Sri Lankan, who we assumed was the leader of the group, held all their travel money—and he had a ticket to Paris. He had a Norwegian passport and listed an Oslo address. He too was jailed with the other four men. It was discovered that the leader had received two Western Union transfers from France, for €5,300 and $1,000.

Their passport stamps left a trail that concerned us. One of them had been in Qatar for two years, returning only recently to Sri Lanka, and then spent two days in Singapore. In Sri Lanka, they all had listed a similar street address, yet were not from the same family. On the following Thursday, the police placed them all on a plane bound back to Sri Lanka without their passports. Similar situations happened often, with similar patterns. This time, had we stopped a terrorist event from happening in Paris or New York—or were they merely seeking jobs and their motives were purely economic?

The modus operandi of radical Islamists in the region was well known to the United States. However, these recent attempts by people trying to gain access to the United States through "soft" areas such as island tourist destinations added to the concern.

The influence of radical Islamists was on the rise, while friendship with the United States was declining, I observed. This is why I believe it is important for the United States to engage the predominantly Muslim countries in sub-Saharan Africa, where most of the population is poor, destitute, and easily indoctrinated by extremist imams. I had also become alarmed about the number of educated Muslim professionals and successful business leaders who were anti-American. In Mauritius, several government leaders, community leaders, and businessmen had taken trips to meet with Palestinian groups and had one-on-one meetings with Yasser Arafat and others with known terrorist backgrounds. Many of these Muslim leaders in the community were openly critical of U.S. support of Israel and wrote op-eds defaming the United States.

May 2002 initiated the beginning of what would be many AGOA Forum strategy meetings with our embassy team, Trade Minister Jayen Cuttaree and his staff, the American Chamber of Commerce, many private sector business leaders, and numerous people from Washington representing African interests. These planning sessions would only intensify.

Since the United States was bringing a large delegation from Washington, I wanted to make this a successful, world-class event. I was also concerned about the embassy's small staff burning out from the work involved in such a large undertaking. Our embassy country team, now comprising eight Foreign Service officers and thirty-eight Foreign Service nationals, were dealing with the logistics for public and private sector venues, a trade show, and separate breakout sessions. We were working in conjunction with the Mauritian government, the State Department, the Commerce Department, the U.S. Trade Representative, members of Congress, and the National Security Council, representing the White House.

Tight security was needed for the Forum event, given all the world leaders planning to attend. We received approval from the State Department for additional temporary duty officers to come from nearby countries for periods ranging from two to twelve weeks prior to the Forum. This took some pressure off our limited staff.

While we were in the midst of the AGOA planning on June 10, the Diego Garcia issue came to the forefront when a headline in the local news media announced that the 125 Chagossian descendants who had been promised by the U.K. government that they could visit two islands in the Chagos Archipelago were adamant that they visit gravesites on Diego Garcia. When I read this headline, I recalled telling High Commissioner Snoxell at our first meeting this would happen. The concern was that the Chagossian descendants who had British citizenship would jump ship and try to stay on the islands they were scheduled to visit, even though they could not sustain themselves there. The British would have to deal with an ugly removal situation, and housing and feeding them during the evacuation process. The news media worldwide would have a field day with it.

I had been summoned to Government House to meet with Deputy Prime Minister Bérenger, who immediately raised the matter of the proposed visit. He acknowledged that the policies of both Her Majesty's government and the United States government mandated that no visitors should be allowed onto the island of Diego Garcia. He also noted that the Ilois's visit to their ancestors' gravesites would be totally disassociated from the question of sovereignty over the archipelago; on previous occasions, he had said he considered the sovereignty claim to be a government-to-government issue.

Although I considered this to be a difficult request, I promised to relay the appeal to Washington. I also cautioned Bérenger that the extreme importance of the ongoing war against terrorism dictated keeping the entire island of Diego Garcia off-limits to visitors. I could tell he was not happy, but he did not openly show his displeasure.

During the ensuing months, the Diego Garcia issue would recur in most of the bilateral discussions.

On Wednesday, June 12, I had the opportunity to step back into the Cold War era with a visit to Russian Ambassador Valeri Nesterushkin, at his residence, a huge embassy complex with living quarters for more than one hundred people. In the Cold War period of the 1970s and 1980s, under the watchful eye of the Mauritian government, the United States and other country missions, the Soviet Union used this compound as a major tracking station and for intelligence gathering. That was an interesting time in history, since the United States also had a tracking station on the island. But that was yesterday, and now we enjoyed our time together as friends, with Russian vodka and caviar.

⟨ XI ⟩

An Active Embassy

The AGOA Forum planning was going well. Although December was the heavy tourist season, Charlie Slater reserved the number of hotel rooms needed for the event's visiting dignitaries and their delegations. Forum venues for the delegate conference, trade fair, and business sessions were also falling into place.

In fact, we were well into the final stages of preparation when on Friday, June 14, I received a cable from Bob Perry, who said President Bush wanted to move the Forum dates a month later since he was seriously considering coming to Mauritius in January 2003. That night I received a phone call from Bob to discuss the date change. He said there was almost a 70 percent chance that President Bush would be coming to Mauritius in January, and he wanted me to discuss the date change with the government of Mauritius. I told him that until we were absolutely certain of the date, I did not feel comfortable approaching the Prime Minister to discuss this change. Mauritius had an active press, I explained. If the information leaked out and the President then decided not to come, it would cause huge credibility problems for us. As it was, we had had a difficult time lining up nine hundred hotel rooms for the Forum participants for the December dates. To change the date and start all over again with these hotels after they had turned down numerous tourists for December would create insurmountable problems. Even if the government of Mauritius agreed, we would have to contact each of the thirty-six other sub-Saharan African countries to see if their delegations could accommodate this date change. We were both getting frustrated, so we agreed to wait until the next week for further input from the White House.

On Monday it was reported that four to six individuals had been spotted at different times around the embassy observing our activities. Some had attempted to blend in with the street hawkers; three of them, spotted on telephone poles near our embassy residences, appeared to be doing repair work. The concern was whether they were plotting an attack against the embassy or particular individuals. My regional security officer agreed to meet immediately with the police and discuss the actions of these suspicious individuals; pictures had been taken of them for further police review. The embassy was located on a busy thoroughfare, and without protection or a setback from the surrounding streets, it could become an easy target for a terrorist attack.

On Thursday, June 20, Bob Perry called late in the day saying that President Bush was going to announce at the Third Biennial Leon H. Sullivan Summit Dinner that he was coming to Africa for the AGOA Forum. I was asked to immediately feel out the Prime Minister about changing the Forum dates from early December 2002 to mid-January 2003. The following morning, I called Dan Claffey, our public affairs officer and acting deputy chief of mission (since Bisa was traveling). I asked him to set up an afternoon appointment with the Prime Minister that same day.

On arriving at the embassy, I was handed a cable asking me to meet with the foreign minister regarding the UN Security Council's consideration of the International Criminal Court (ICC) issue. Mauritius was over halfway through its term as one of ten rotating members of the fifteen-member UN Security Council. The Security Council seat was a great and well-deserved honor for a country as small as Mauritius. For U.S. interests, Mauritius's vote was very important.

My meeting with the foreign minister was scheduled just an hour before the meeting with the prime minister. On my way out of the embassy, I was handed a copy of President Bush's speech and the news release from the White House about the Leon H. Sullivan Summit Dinner. In the speech, the President noted that he wanted to continue building on America's partnership with Africa, and announced his intention to go to Africa the next year. He remarked on Africa's beauty, resources, and opportunities, and emphasized it is a continent where promise and progress were important but "sit alongside disease, war and desperate poverty." While democracy was taking hold in many nations, there were a few where terrorism was finding safe havens. The President emphasized that the people in the room shared a common vision of an Africa where people were healthy, literate, prosperous, and free of war and terror. Stressing that Africans would build this new Africa, the President added that America would stand with the African countries that were putting into place policies for success through such important new efforts as the Millennium Challenge Fund. The President committed $500 million to prevent mother-to-child transmission of HIV and $200 million to fund an initiative to improve basic education and teacher training, "to give Africa's children the advantages of literacy and learning so they can build Africa's future."

The President said obstacles to Africa's development included trade barriers in rich nations that impeded the sale of Africa's products. His administration strongly supported congressional efforts to enhance the benefits of AGOA and to encourage more U.S. companies to take advantage of opportunities in Africa.

Arriving early at Foreign Minister Gayan's office, I gave him my prepared talking points regarding the International Criminal Court [ICC] Article 98 non-surrender issue, which included the following:

1. The United States had a commitment to peace around the world, with 8,000 troops and 600 civilian police in the Balkans, South Korea, and elsewhere. I noted that in East Timor it would be easier for us to pull out because we were the only ones involved in peacekeeping there; elsewhere, we served jointly with other nations.

2. The United States was considering vetoing a resolution on the UN Mission in Bosnia and Herzegovina/Stabilization Force (UNMIBH/SFOR) because of the lack of protection for our people from the ICC jurisdiction. One solution to this problem was for the UN Security Council to act under the UN Charter's Chapter VII to create immunity for those involved with UN-authorized or -approved peacekeeping operations.

3. U.S. government lawyers had studied the proposed language and felt we were on firm ground, consistent with the Rome Statute. Our need to push for a decision, I emphasized, was the looming July 1, 2002, deadline for entry-into-force of the ICC statute. Also, there was concern over the upcoming deadline to renew the authorization for UNMIBH/SFOR troops that were committed in the region, leaving us no choice but to contemplate that action.

4. We therefore ask that the Mauritian delegation in New York work with the United States' UN delegation on the resolution regarding immunity under Chapter VII.

The foreign minister responded that he could not support our request, and questioned instead whether the Chapter VII provisions could be undertaken on a case-by-case basis. That was an impractical proposition in times of emergencies, I explained, as it would delay timely action. We needed the resolution based on the use of Chapter VII protection on a blanket basis.

The foreign minister still could not go along with this. I was disappointed, as I had fully expected the support of the government of Mauritius for the U.S. position regarding the International Criminal Court issue. As we sat in silence for a few moments, I thought he might not really understand the risks taken by peacekeepers. I decided to move on to the Madagascar issue.

The Organization of African Unity's Central Committee was meeting that very day in Addis Ababa to urge support for Marc Ravalomanana as President, who agreed to accept the Dakar II provisions for forming a government of national reconciliation and holding parliamentary elections by the end of 2002. The United States wanted to see the outcome of the OAU meeting but intended to accept Ravalomanana as President. The foreign minister's face brightened and a small smile crossed his lips, since this was the answer he had wanted from us all along.

He brought up Diego Garcia and the issue of sovereignty. When I reminded him of our lease agreement with the United Kingdom, he quickly lost his smile. This was not a comfortable meeting.

At two o'clock we walked down the hall to Prime Minister Jugnauth's office, where we were greeted with a pleasant smile and warm handshake. The Prime Minister was pleased about President Bush's plans to arrive in Mauritius in conjunction with the planned AGOA Forum. But he did not welcome changing the date. He had had to turn down hosting a UNESCO conference in Mauritius that was set for December, and January was the beginning of cyclone season. He reiterated that he would rather have the AGOA Forum in December with Secretary Powell leading the delegation and take the risk of not having it at all rather than move it to January. I didn't want to tell him that President Bush was also considering holding the AGOA Forum in South Africa or Botswana. I said only that I would relay his concerns to Washington.

I immediately called Bob Perry from my cell phone to relay the outcome of the meeting with the Prime Minister. Shortly thereafter, Assistant Secretary Walter Kansteiner called asking for an update, having not yet talked to Bob Perry. The upshot of the situation was very clear: either we change the date to January 2003 or the AGOA Forum would probably go to South Africa as a trading chip for the South African Customs Union Free Trade Agreement.

Later that afternoon, Harry Ganoo from the trade minister's office called to say their embassy in Washington had also discussed President Bush's plans with Prime Minister Jugnauth. Not wanting Mauritius to lose the AGOA Forum, Harry wished to set aside some time for us to speak with the Prime Minister during that night's Chinese Embassy reception. *Good*, I thought. I called Bob Perry to say the Prime Minister would go along with the January 2003 date. "Do all you can so we do not lose the Forum," I said. He assured me he would pass the message on to the National Security Council for their meeting and recommendation later in the day.

After greeting a few friends at the Chinese Embassy, I headed off to a corner sitting area, far from everyone else. Soon Harry Ganoo steered the Prime Minister away from a crowd of well-wishers, and toward the corner where I was. The Prime Minister was very apologetic for not having agreed immediately to the change. He wanted the Forum to take place in Mauritius and would support the January dates. I thanked him for his generosity in making the right decision so we could proceed. The National Security Council was going to make a recommendation at this afternoon's meeting.

I suggested to Harry that the Prime Minister call Secretary Powell in the morning and reconfirm his decision. I also suggested having Usha Jeetah, their ambassador in Washington, call Rosa Whitaker at the Office of the U.S. Trade Representative, and then have Peter Craig call his contacts as well. Harry agreed, embraced me, and moved on into the crowd.

Off in another corner, Foreign Minister Anil Gayan stood waiting to catch my eye. When he did, he asked, "Why didn't you tell me about the AGOA Forum problem?" I told him I hadn't had the liberty to do so; I had been instructed to discuss it only with the Prime Minister.

A moment later, the French ambassador, Henri Vignal, and British High Commissioner David Snoxell came over to discuss Madagascar and the Organization of African Unity vote. We agreed to talk again on Monday and decide if we would go public with support for Ravalomanana. Foreign Minister Gayan also wanted India on board. I quickly found High Commissioner Vijay Kumar and brought him into the conversation, then excused myself and departed for the Crystal Jubilee Concert, featuring the visiting Yale Glee Club choir.

On the way, I read a disturbing cable sent by a contact in Moroni, the capital of Comoros. Abdou El Bak, the President of Grande Comore, had just replaced several people in his government who appeared to be loyal to Union of the Comoros President Azali Assoumani. In retaliation, Azali sent in military forces to secure key government buildings and prevent them from being occupied by El Bak supporters. The tension between these two individuals had been ongoing for some time, since both the island and federal governments were located on Grand Comore. I needed to get over there as soon as possible.

On Tuesday morning, June 25, Harry Ganoo's boss, Trade Minister Jayen Cuttaree, called saying his Washington embassy commercial officer, Peter Craig, had been told the Forum would be held in Mauritius, with President Bush and Secretary Powell leading the delegation on January 12–13, 2003. President Bush would travel to several countries in Africa between January 8 and 16, 2003, before and after the AGOA Forum, beginning with visits to Senegal, Nigeria, and South Africa before coming to Mauritius, then ending his trip with a stop in Kenya.

This was certainly good news, but hearing this type of important information from third parties and not directly from the State Department or the National Security Council was troublesome. Washington called me at all hours of the day and night with demarches to deliver and problems to solve. Now, being intimately involved with the AGOA Forum planning from its inception, I had to hear circuitously about the final approval and the President's travel plans, which was disturbing.

On Wednesday morning, June 26, a cable arrived regarding a letter President Bush had sent to Marc Ravalomanana recognizing Ravalomanana's government in spite of the Organization of African Unity decision the previous weekend that neither candidate had been duly elected. The French had in the end done a turnabout and decided in favor of the OAU position. This was expected, as for twenty-five years they had been supporters of Didier Ratsiraka.

A cable followed from Blossom Perry stating that Secretary Powell had approved recognition of Ravalomanana and that chiefs of mission would be permitted to attend the Malagasy National Day celebration that day.

Another cable from Bob Perry reaffirmed the President's trip to Africa, January 8–16, 2003, based on information from the National Security Council. I was anxious to let the Prime Minister know, so I decided to stay for tea after the 42nd Regimental Parade review of the five hundred or so Special Mobile Forces at the Gymkhana Grounds that morning. The Prime Minister was pleased with the news.

That evening, I attended the Malagasy National Day reception at Curepipe Municipal Hall. As surmised earlier, only a few of the diplomatic corps were there and Ambassador Tsilanizara did not look happy. He said he was certain to be recalled; what fate awaited him, he did not know. He really did not want to leave, and hoped the Mauritian government would allow him stay as a private citizen.

The AGOA Forum had consumed the embassy in preparation for the December event. Now that the date had been moved to January, I worried again about our limited staff and potential burnout. Charlie Slater had stuck his neck out a mile with the hotel groups, guaranteeing nine hundred rooms and making deposits to hold these bookings.

Desperate, we called Trade Minister Jayen Cuttaree and Forum liaison director Harry Ganoo for help. We needed to cancel all the December hotel rooms without penalty or loss of our deposits and arrange instead for the event in January. That meant reserving another nine hundred rooms, the delegate conference and meeting areas, the trade show venue, and the business breakout session rooms.

An AGOA Forum strategy meeting was held the next morning, Thursday, at the Ministry of Trade offices with Trade Minister Cuttaree and Ganoo leading the charge. Nearly eighty people were assembled, representing the public and private sectors. I was surprised that the hospitality community and others responded so positively to this new date.

That evening I attended a reception held at Vicky and Van Lanza's beach house in Tamarin. Vicky was from Seychelles and had met Van while he was serving there at the U.S. Air Force tracking station. The Indian Ocean representative for British Airways, she was hosting a dinner for Robert Webb, a director of the airline.

While I was at the event, Charlie Slater called to say he had received a cable at the embassy from Blossom Perry and that I needed to immediately deliver a demarche to Foreign Minister Gayan regarding the U.S. position on the International Criminal Court issue. Charlie suggested we meet halfway, at a closed Shell station on the Flic en Flac road. I thanked my hosts and immediately went off with my driver, Ahmed, racing through a heavy rainstorm. Once at the Shell station, Charlie pulled alongside and jumped into my car, while Ahmed sat in Charlie's. The rain pounded hard on the windows and nearly drowned out our voices as we sat under the dim interior lights reviewing the demarche. After a short discussion, I decided to call Gayan at home from my cell phone. Even though it was now after ten o'clock and I might awaken him, it was important that we speak. We had started the day talking about issues, and now we were ending the day talking again.

"Anil," I said, "I received a cable from my government. I need to ask Mauritius to support the UN initiative regarding the ICC. We will not leave peacekeeping troops in such places as Bosnia unless we have an amendment to prevent prosecution of our military. This could affect all of our peacekeeping operations."

The foreign minister was steadfast in his previous position that each situation should stand on its own merits. No amount of discussion would sway him. After I ended the call, Charlie and I sat in the car in silence looking at the rain pounding against the windows. We agreed it was futile to try to change Gayan's mind. Now the United States government might need to veto any resolution that did not include protection for U.S. peacekeepers. Disconcerted, I said goodbye to Charlie and left for home.

It was almost midnight when I got in, just in time for a conference call with the JPR merger committee, headed by Pat King. I needed to sign a number of documents regarding the merger of JPR with GGP and return them to Salt Lake City prior to a July 8 deadline. The necessary documents, sent to my computer, arrived at 1:00 a.m. Mauritius time. I spent the next three hours downloading these documents and by morning had reviewed and signed them and arranged for a DHL pickup at the house.

Meanwhile, I had to be at the airport by six in the morning to meet my family, who were coming for a week's visit. It was great to see them all. By the time their luggage was gathered up and the passports cleared, I had only thirty minutes to get back to Macarty House and meet the DHL courier.

The residence was abuzz with activity, with workers preparing for our Independence Day celebration. Rarely held on July 4 on the island, this year's celebration was being held on June 30, a Sunday, since most people had the day off. Setting up the tented seating area, sponsors' booths, game areas, American-style food stands, ice cream freezers, popcorn makers, and coolers for soft drinks, beer, and wine was all quite an undertaking. Everything was covered with red, white, and blue bunting, and hundreds of balloons added to the decor. Loudspeakers were being installed and tested to ensure sound would reach the large landscaped areas, and the microphone and podium were put in place on the patio while Cassam and Luc worked on other last-minute details. How exciting, I thought, to have the entire family here for the Fourth of July event along with more than six hundred Mauritian and American guests.

Sunday morning I was awakened by the smell of meat cooking. Looking out the window, I saw five full-size lambs roasting on spits, with aromatic smoke filling the air. The embassy staff was busy with last-minute details, since guests would start arriving by midmorning. The Mauritius Police Band, with its twenty-plus musicians, was to perform. As I worked out in the upstairs gym, I could hear them practicing some favorite American songs out on the patio.

Joined by our three children, Steven, Deirdra, and Jennifer, Marcia and I stood in the garden under a canopy draped with red, white, and blue decorations to greet government leaders and other invited guests. At 11:15 a.m. sharp, Deputy Prime Minister Paul Bérenger arrived, followed by Foreign Minister Anil Gayan. The diplomatic corps and other guests with their family members arrived about the same time, keeping us busy shaking hands and nodding welcome.

At 11:45 a.m., the official program began, with champagne toasts to each other's country while the band played our national anthems. At noon, I gave some welcoming remarks, including a message from President Bush reflecting on 9/11 and our 226-year history since gaining independence in 1776. Deputy Prime Minister Bérenger followed with remarks about our countries' mutuality and friendship.

Afterward, Marcia and Mrs. Gayan cut the beautiful two-by-four-foot strawberry shortcake, shaped like an American flag and decorated with blueberries for stars, whipped cream for the white background, and strawberries lined up as the red stripes. The array of food at the different stations included spare ribs, fried chicken, lamb, hot dogs, coleslaw, potato salad, baked beans, corn on the cob, apple pie, and of course the strawberry shortcake. Children's games were under way, with sack races, relay races, face-painting activities, piñatas filled with candies, and more. The event was just a good old-fashioned American-style Fourth of July spent with our Mauritian friends and expatriates living on the island. Marcia and I circulated around the garden area and chatted with our invited guests. By three o'clock most of the people had left, and by late that night the staff had restored the area to a peaceful garden again. The next day we went back to work.

On top of the AGOA Forum, which was on everyone's mind, I was concerned about the additional workload we would have after I presented my credentials to the President of the Republic of Seychelles and the Union of the Comoros. With only seven Foreign Service officers now at the U.S. Embassy in Port Louis to cover

11.1. Fourth of July event, with a toast to our respective countries, 2002. From left to right: Foreign Minister Anil Gayan, President Karl Offmann, Ambassador Price, and Deputy Prime Minister Paul Bérenger.

11.2. Mrs. Gayan and Marcia cutting the cake at the Fourth of July event, with our family looking on, 2002.

11.3. Embassy Foreign Service national staff member Angela Henry enjoying the Fourth of July event with her family and friends, 2002.

three countries in this strategic Indian Ocean region, the workload was almost too much.

Since we were considered a Special Embassy Program (SEP) post, additional resources were limited to us. The Congress, under the Clinton administration in the 1990s, cut the foreign affairs budget, and nearly one-third of U.S. embassies worldwide, or fifty-five embassies, became SEP posts. The State Department's goal was to minimize staffing and still have an official U.S. presence in virtually every country with which we maintain diplomatic relations.

The Special Embassy Program was supposed to reflect the reduced communication and reporting capabilities of the smallest Foreign Service posts, exempting those posts from a number of reporting requirements. Yet the U.S. Embassy in Port Louis had the same reporting requirements as a full-sized embassy in other sub-Saharan African countries—with responsibilities multiplied by three.

In reality, the workload increased at a number of embassies, security at a number of overseas operations became suspect, reporting and intelligence gathering were impacted, and embassies were shuttered in Muslim-controlled countries, places where al-Qaeda and other Islamic extremists were gaining a strong foothold. A number of terrorists who attacked U.S. interests around the world came from these sub-Saharan African countries.

These ill-conceived, drastic budget cuts meant that U.S. political influence, which was already waning in the region, was further reduced, impacting America's safety around the world. Our start-and-stop, wait-and-see U.S. foreign policy did not sit well with governments already suspicious of our agenda in the region. When we needed these host countries to support our issues, we twisted their arm. Otherwise, we were not always proactively engaging them, and at times we resorted to using threats of aid cuts and sanctions to get our way.

In the early 1990s, the Port Louis embassy had more than twice as many Foreign Service officers as it did in the early 2000s, as well as a full Marine Guard detachment, not including the personnel at the U.S embassies in Seychelles and Comoros. But Congress had taken an axe to our foreign affairs programs, and the State Department succumbed to the mandated budget cuts without building a compelling case for a diplomatic presence in every country, with special attention to countries where radical Islam was on the rise.

As most American voters know, members of Congress observe few budget restraints when it comes to their own pork barrel projects, such as bridges that go nowhere, ferry operations with few users, five-star bus stops, and the multitude of wasteful research projects that take money away from America's pressing security interests at our overseas diplomatic missions and programs critical to the people in sub-Saharan Africa, particularly in the Horn of Africa and East Africa, where Somalia has become a failed state, Sudan is a failing state, and several others are weak and bordering on becoming failed states as well.

At every Chiefs of Mission Conference and during my consultations in Washington, I raised the issue of our post being overloaded, with a small staff required to do the same amount of reporting normally done at larger embassies. I emphasized we were constantly at risk of having our people burn out. Tensions were high and morale was low.

The answer was always "Yes, we understand," but I believe my message fell on deaf ears. Most people I met and spoke with were not concerned about the issues of the Special Embassy Program. It was just too daunting for them to deal with the matter or take it to their superiors. Privately, several career ambassadors discussed this issue with me, since it also affected them. But I recall, other than myself, only one or two who brought up this issue at a Chiefs of Mission Conference. A study was under way, though I didn't believe it would lead to ending the Special Embassy Program status.

Some time later, on May 10, 2005, the review of the program was completed, and a report entitled "SEP Review—Final Report" was sent to Secretary of State Condoleezza Rice. Sixteen days later, Secretary Rice approved the termination at forty-eight posts of this twenty-year Special Embassy Program. I believe that during the years of its existence, the SEP post category hampered our diplomatic relations worldwide and was another of the United States' penny-wise-pound-foolish foreign affairs decisions. I was glad Washington finally listened to everyone's input.

In "Overseas Rightsizing: A Quarterly Report by the Office of Rightsizing the U.S. Government Overseas Presence," issued in 2005 by the State Department, regarding Special Embassy Program posts, I noted:

> The program's original purpose was to maintain representation in countries where U.S. interests are limited. Posts in the program were to have very lean staffing and the Department would relieve them of a great deal of required reporting and otherwise reduce demands placed on staff. The Special Embassy Program did not work as well as originally intended. Workload demands proved hard to modulate and other agencies had no comparable program. In practice, SEP posts functioned the same as larger posts. The decision was made to preserve the limited benefits of SEP status for smaller posts but to use the parallel Overseas Staffing Model (OSM) to determine eligibility. The Special Embassy Program was terminated at the end of May, 2005.

Now, what was really said? Plain and simple, our government impaired our foreign relations. Had the originators of the program and those who approved it come from the private sector, such an incomplete operating paradigm would not have been put in place so widely or even been an option in dealing with our interests overseas. It was the result of bureaucrats who were unaware of a region's importance and the role an embassy serves in carrying out our bilateral relations. It took me only a few days at the post to figure that out, but more than three years of pushing buttons to see this change.

Observing the amount of daily cable traffic and the long hours (including weekends and holidays) the staff was spending at the embassy, I had concerns about the quantity of information that was expected by Washington. Since there were constant rotations and transfers, I was certain much of the data was not being read by the intended recipients. A lot of pressure was placed on the embassy's well-meaning Foreign Service officers. The embassy itself was also shorthanded, as staff periodically attended ongoing training seminars and conferences and took annual home leaves. We were constantly bringing in temporary duty officers from outside the region, which was a very costly process. When we were working with temporary duty officers, getting them caught up on issues took time, although most quickly got up to speed. In addition to their normal duties, our limited staff had to serve as control officers for high-level visitors, participate in numerous community events, and rotate on weekends to serve as the twenty-four-hour on-call duty officer for the embassy.

Prior to my arrival, we didn't have a regional security officer: Port Louis was a Special Embassy Program post, and it wasn't in the budget. However, given the embassy bombings in 1998 and the attacks against the United States on September 11, 2001, there should be at least one regional security officer stationed at every embassy to be our eyes and ears in the host country and the region. There is also a need to establish security and safety programs for the embassy and staff residences and to interface with the local police, military, and intelligence agencies. It didn't take me long to get a regional security officer on the way to Port Louis.

The regional security officer's first project was to install a layer of blast protection film on all exterior windows, to avoid the damaging effects of shattered glass in the event of a terrorist attack. Mauritius is also prone to serious cyclones between December and March each year that sometimes cause severe damage around the island. In fact, during my first cyclone season, many hours were spent covering the windows at the embassy to prevent damage. The RSO also set up a number of safety measures at the embassy and installed security upgrades at the embassy residences. All this housekeeping needed to be done before he could spend time on host country security issues.

I requested an information management specialist to assist Lizzie Slater, our information programs officer, whose workload was almost 24/7 when I arrived. After this position was filled in short order, I pressed to have the consular, economic, and political (CEP) role split between two positions, with both officers sharing consular duties. I thought the embassy should have had a full-time consular officer, considering that we had responsibility for three island nations in addition to the French islands of Mayotte and Réunion, which lay hundreds of miles apart in the Indian Ocean. Even with two people covering these regional responsibilities, it meant many long hours for each of them. The one CEP officer had spent almost 40 percent of his time on consular duties, with the busy political affairs officer serving as the primary alternative consular officer.

Finally, we had only one office management specialist (OMS), who handled the ambassador's schedule, helped with embassy and community events, prepared documents and letters for both the ambassador and the deputy chief of mission, answered the phones, and dealt with ambassador-hosted events and other projects. The workload caused tension and exhaustion. The State Department had promised to send an additional OMS for 2003–2004, but instead they sent a temporary duty officer from the Washington pool.

We were a busy embassy, and I was pleased that the country team would soon consist of ten Foreign Service officers. In addition, we would receive regional support from the State Department and other government agencies operating from several other embassies in nearby countries. Human resources issues and facilities maintenance were handled out of the U.S. Embassy in Nairobi; financial management and security support were done out of Antananarivo; medical, communications, and security engineering came from Pretoria; and our commerce department advisor was located in Johannesburg. Other agency advisors and support were located in Frankfurt, Paris, London, Djibouti, Manama, Honolulu, Tampa, and Washington. But in the 1990s, all such critical support resources had been located at U.S. Embassy Port Louis, so responses were immediate and not on a requisition-first basis. In a Special Embassy Program post, response time is not expected to be immediate because the support resources are not located in the embassy or the immediate vicinity. On an island, resources are hundreds of miles away over vast stretches of ocean. Sometimes our requests seemed to fall on deaf ears. Further complicating matters, the embassies at which some of these resources were located had their own priorities; although our embassy was charged a pro-rata share of the resource costs, we received less attention. From a territorial standpoint, we covered a larger geographic area than many of the other embassies in sub-Saharan Africa.

The pressure of the upcoming AGOA Forum, constant daily demarches, expanding the country team, solving morale issues, and preparing to visit the host country governments of Seychelles and Comoros was almost overwhelming. Then, on top of all that, we received notice that an Office of the Inspector General (OIG) assessment team would be visiting Mauritius to undertake a review of the embassy operation, as the last report had been done in 1994. Arriving on May 31, 2002, they would stay until June 10, 2002.

Ambassador Fernando (Fred) Rondon led the assessment team. A career member of the Foreign Service, he had been the U.S. ambassador to Madagascar in 1980 and was accredited to Comoros in 1982. Before then, Fred had worked at the U.S. Embassy in Port Louis and knew this region well. He and his staff interviewed everyone at the embassy and conducted a thorough review of the embassy's current operations. At our review session, Fred complimented us on the embassy's overall operation, saying it was one of the best they had inspected, and rated us very highly.

In Fred Rondon's 2002 report, he echoed some of the observations I'd made upon arriving in Mauritius only six weeks earlier. The embassy was not rightsized, he noted, and people were working unusually long hours. In addition, economic reporting was not getting done, and morale had suffered. The burden at the embassy would ease with the assignment of a new regional security officer and an information management specialist, "but work will continue to suffer at this busy embassy."

With the embassy's emphasis on Mauritius, he noted, Seychelles and Comoros were being ignored. "Regional analysts believe the United States needs to learn more about the desperately poor Comoros and the islands' ties to both conservative and radical Islamic influences," he wrote. "It remains to be seen whether Embassy Port Louis can contribute significantly to the knowledge deficit and articulate a strategy for modest engagement."

About Diego Garcia, the United States' most important military base in the Indian Ocean, Rondon noted, "which is essential to the deployment of U.S. power in the Middle East and Indian subcontinent." Even though the United States has control of Diego Garcia until 2036, Mauritius's claims of sovereignty are an issue between their government and the United Kingdom. The United States is "vitally interested in any developments affecting Diego Garcia's future [use]," Rondon wrote, and added, "[Currently] the embassy provides thorough coverage of this issue."

The OIG report did not address that the post had been without a chief of mission for almost eight months. No doubt, ambassador vacancies impede advancement of U.S. foreign policy and daily bilateral interface with the host countries, all of which have a vote at the United Nations. Some of these host country governments feel that they are not important to the United States, so in turn they are not always inclined to support our interests at the UN.

The engagement of Comoros would become a priority and a personal challenge for me over the next three years. My hope was to try to help eradicate poverty, make friends within the Muslim clerical hierarchy and the government, improve our public image, and be consistent in our bilateral relations, rather than continue the start-and-stop approach that we were constantly accused of. Comoros had more than its share of problems, but my greatest fear was that radical Islamists would ultimately overrun the country.

As President Bush's personal representative accredited to Comoros, I was determined to make a difference in this small island nation of 600,000—and the homeland of Fazul Abdullah Mohammed, one of the top ten most wanted terrorists. He reportedly masterminded the bombings of the American embassies in Nairobi and Dar es Salaam in 1998 and Israeli-owned Paradise Hotel in Mombasa in 2002. Because the Comoros had a history of twenty coups or attempted coups since independence in 1975, it was important we take an active interest in Comoros as the country moved toward developing into a democratic state. A U.S. embassy opened there in April 1985. Eight years later, in September 1993, it was closed because Congress wanted to save money in our overseas mission operations.

In addition to the embassies and consulates that were shuttered in the early 1990s, we cut 1,634 positions worldwide. In so doing, we combined in some missions the separate important economic and political functions, gave up reliable intelligence reporting, eliminated some consular services (which affected our ability to monitor suspicious travel), eliminated direct bilateral relations (which affected our interests at the UN), and could no longer directly protect our interests and American citizens in these countries.

These cutbacks affected many qualified people in the Foreign Service who had given up a lot to serve in hardship posts in sub-Saharan Africa, including many with excellent language skills who were stationed in poverty-stricken and densely populated Muslim countries.

The decision to shut U.S. embassies left a void in Comoros and Seychelles, and valuable in-country information ceased to flow directly to Washington. Thought was not given to being alert to the danger signals of al-Qaeda activity in the Horn of Africa and East Africa and the growing terrorist presence in a number of the region's countries.

During my consultations at the State Department and discussions with a former ranking member of Congress, the impression I got was that the U.S. government felt we did not need embassies in countries we considered benign. To me, this signaled that radical Islam could move in while we were moving out.

When the U.S. embassies in Comoros and Seychelles were closed, an American Presence Post (APP), with three or four Foreign Service officers reporting to the embassy in Mauritius, should have been established so we could still maintain political and economic reporting, continue consular services, and protect U.S. security interests in the region. Such a post would operate at minimal cost yet provide current and reliable reporting information.

In the Horn of Africa, the United States also closed its embassy in Mogadishu, Somalia, in 1991 and in Khartoum, Sudan, in 1996. These countries had significant Muslim populations, internal strife, interclan fighting, terrorist training activities, civil instability, and genocide—which have become the norm ever since. When we shuttered the embassies in Somalia and Sudan, the absence of intelligence made both countries a mystery to U.S. policy makers and antiterrorism experts. In a *Telegraph* article, it was reported that British intelligence, asked to look into Islamic groups in Somalia, "discovered some pretty big intelligence gaps." I believe the United States must take responsibility for the terrorist attacks that resulted from the shutoff of direct in-country intelligence and information gathering, a result of not having a permanent U.S. presence in these countries. Without our boots on the ground, al-Qaeda operatives were able to move around freely under the radar.

I did not want Comoros to go in this direction. I firmly believed that the United States should have kept a permanent presence in Comoros, with at least a smaller APP mission.

Comoros, which held its first national presidential election in April 2002, an election that was deemed mostly fair, was on the path to democracy. I believe we needed to support the newly elected President Azali Assoumani. We needed to demonstrate that America cared about Comoros now that they were becoming a democratic state. I wanted to start engaging this Muslim island nation, in the hope it would not end up in chaos with problems similar to those occurring in the countries in the Horn of Africa and East Africa. Concerned, I moved up plans for my visit to Comoros.

In the meantime, I worked up an outline to make the case to the State Department for considering an APP in Comoros and Seychelles that would consist of three Foreign Service officers reporting to the ambassador. I wanted also to present the idea at the next Chiefs of Mission Conference, as at least one other ambassador serving in sub-Saharan Africa was affected by similar multicountry accreditation issues. The basic plan for the APP was to have one CEP officer, one regional security officer, one OMS, and an FSN hire. They would cover consular issues, government interface, security matters, economic issues, and political reporting, and could engage the villages with extensive Ambassador's Special Self-Help and Democracy and Human Rights programs. Such an APP would be very cost-effective, yet give us an in-country presence for specific reporting and information gathering and for dealing with issues of poverty, education, health care, and sustainable development. Above all, with an active presence, we would make friends and better implement our foreign policy. It would show these countries that the United States takes its commitment seriously.

I continued to make courtesy calls on Mauritian government ministers, community leaders, religious leaders, and the movers and shakers in the business community. My activities in Mauritius were demanding. Still, I made it a point to visit many of the manufacturing plants in Mauritius that were exporting products to the United States under AGOA, which provided an incredible opportunity for businesses to gain almost unlimited duty-free access to U.S. markets. I thought this was a significant piece of legislation that would help sub-Saharan African countries increase their citizens' standard of living and eventually help move them out of the poverty trap.

The textile industry, one of the main pillars of the Mauritian economy, began in the early 1970s and had become very successful manufacturing products for worldwide consumption, from T-shirts and jeans to higher-quality knitwear, shirts, children's wear, linens, uniforms, and many other cotton and wool items. Since Mauritius was far from raw material sources, many of these manufacturers had developed their own cotton and wool spinning and weaving operations. Some of the larger textile manufacturers had become totally vertically integrated, beginning with the raw material and finishing with a shelf-ready packaged product.

Mauritian manufacturers had long had a diversified customer base in Europe and elsewhere. It wasn't until after the AGOA program was enacted in October 2000 that the U.S. market became a practical option for some of them, although Europe was still considered their core market.

A number of Hong Kong and mainland Chinese textile manufacturers, however, moved some of their operations to Mauritius to take advantage of the AGOA program, which was intended for qualifying sub-Saharan African countries. I saw the Chinese invasion as a circumvention of the rules to gain access to U.S. markets on a quota- and duty-free basis, in direct competition with Mauritian textile manufacturers (including local Sino-Mauritians) as well as other textile manufacturers in sub-Saharan Africa.

The Chinese operations also largely used imported Chinese contract workers, who continually complained of being forced to work long hours and being denied fair and adequate compensation. Because of the number of new manufacturers in Mauritius, other operators also turned to Chinese contract workers to fill the void in the existing labor pool.

In a conversation with the U.S. Trade Representative, Bob Zoellick, it became clear to me that he didn't consider this back-door access to the U.S. market by government-backed Chinese textile manufacturers a circumvention of the AGOA provisions. I told him I did, since these Chinese operators took their profits offshore and it was Chinese contract workers instead of poorer Africans who were benefiting from the AGOA program.

On September 17, 2001, China successfully concluded its negotiations for entry into the World Trade Organization (WTO), effective December 11, 2001, though their quotas on textiles would not be eliminated until December 31, 2004. As a result, China aggressively backed several major textile operations in Mauritius that over the next three years would manufacture a lot of products for the U.S. markets under the AGOA program. Their aggressive pricing concerned some of the local Mauritian textile manufacturers, who said the Chinese government was giving these manufacturers hidden subsidies and benefits. When the December 31, 2004, deadline passed, a number of Chinese manufacturers withdrew, while several stayed and continued to expand.

The Chinese-government-supported textile operations having access to the U.S. markets under the WTO and AGOA gave China more control over the United States and the worldwide textile industry. But discussing my concerns about China's circuitous access to AGOA benefits only fell on deaf ears in Washington.

Sugar has long been the main commercial agricultural product in Mauritius. Sugarcane was first introduced in 1638 by the Dutch, and after their arrival in 1715, French immigrants cultivated the land and became the plantation owners. I visited a number of the plantations, processing mills, and bagasse (cane pulp) burning operations that generated power to run their mills, with surplus capacity put into the power grid for resale. The Mauritian sugar industry accounted for 600,000 tons of refined sugar a year, most of it going to Europe. Much of the industry's success was attributable to the European Commission Sugar Protocol (subsidy) under which Mauritius benefited from export quotas and preferential guaranteed prices. The quotas were fixed at 500,000 tons. These subsidies gave Mauritius producers almost double the price that sugar was going for in the open markets. In the mid-1980s, the Mauritian government introduced the Sugar Action Plan, which reduced export duties as a form of tax relief for the producers.

As an efficiency measure, sugar producers were allowed to combine milling operations, closing older, inefficient mills. The increased earnings resulting from the protocol subsidy, duty reduction, and streamlining of their operations provided substantial cash which was deployed into diversified sectors, including textile manufacturing, tourism, hospitality, information technology, financial services, and other business activities in Mauritius and other sub-Saharan African countries.

With the phasing out of the Sugar Protocol subsidy program, profits decreased, but the sugar industry would survive because of efficiencies introduced over the preceding years. Some sugar operators who held large land parcels diversified by developing some of the land into destination beach resorts.

According to the Mauritian government's 2002 Integrated Resort Scheme, the program provided for the development of prestige resort hotels and luxury villas targeted for direct investment by foreigners. Under the resort scheme rules, anyone who invested at least $500,000 in such a luxury villa would also be granted resident status. To date, a number of such developments have been started, mostly on the sugar estate properties, since they own the bulk of the land in Mauritius.

On weekends, Marcia and I would visit some of the more than thirty resorts popular among both luxury and budget-minded travelers. By 2005, the tourism industry was welcoming almost 800,000 Europeans, South Africans, and Asians annually, along with 1,000 to 3,000 Americans. That aggregate number was expected to grow to 1 million by 2008 and to double by 2020.

During my posting, the embassy never really knew the exact number of American tourists. Most didn't contact us on arrival, and many came by private jet looking for seclusion. However, all of them enjoyed the incredible state-of-the-art hotels and spas, with their beautiful white sand beaches, azure lagoons surrounded by coral reefs, and the signature golf courses.

To diversify further from their dependency on sugar and textiles, Mauritius became an offshore financial banking center and a favorable country in which to register company domiciles doing business in India. Because of the pass-through tax treaty between both countries, there were savings of more than 30 percent in taxes. Mauritius also developed a diversified IT and communications sector, with numerous international call centers locating there. With the time differential of three hours to Europe and nine hours to the East Coast of the United States (eight hours during Daylight Saving Time), Mauritian backroom support operations could prepare financial data while other parts of the world slept, and the call centers would operate throughout the Mauritian night, while other parts of the world were awake.

Mauritius also has a Thoroughbred racetrack, and the turf club is the third-oldest in the world and the oldest in the Southern Hemisphere. Their season usually starts in the beginning of April and runs through the first week of December. On June 25, 1812, the Champ de Mars track was established by the British to serve as a common gathering place for everyone on the island and to help defuse tension between the different ethnic groups. The racetrack operation was of as high a quality as anywhere in the United States. It typically drew around 20,000 people on race day, but it was not unusual to draw up to 30,000 for special race events.

One major area of concern was overfishing in the Indian Ocean waters, a subject that had come up during my Senate confirmation hearings. Large Taiwanese fishing fleets operated in and around Mauritian waters, as did fleets from Japan, Korea, and European Union countries. There were also reports that there was illegal over-fishing in the Southern Arctic waters, and many long line fishing violations by fishing trawlers. I was told that illegally fished Patagonian toothfish (similar to the Chilean Sea bass) were transshipped through Mauritius in the past, though the practice had stopped in 2000. However, claims persisted about overfishing of tuna by these fleets. On one occasion I visited a large tuna canning operation for the Princes brand, owned by the Japanese giant Mitsubishi Industries. Their Canadian manager, Rick Heroux, had been in the canning industry for more than twenty-five years. The operation was clean and well run, processing 150 tons of tuna per day. Heroux assured me only legally fished yellowtail and skipjack tuna, brought in by Japanese trawlers, were being processed. He was sensitive to the overfishing issue and advised me that, ultimately, limits would need to be established so as not to deplete the fish in the targeted zones.

Another area of interest was the diamond cutting and polishing industry. My concern was that blood diamonds (also known as conflict diamonds) from areas such as Sierra Leone, Liberia, and Angola were being used in the manufacture of jewelry. The United States had been the leader in insisting on certificates of origin to accompany all raw diamonds exported from the diamond-producing countries, a standard that had been implemented in the Kimberley Process Certification Scheme (KPCS). I met with Steve Denton, the owner of Adamas Diamonds, who showed me the typical KPCS certificates that accompanied the diamonds he was processing for customers around the world. He too was concerned about the illegal sale of blood diamonds in sub-Saharan Africa, the proceeds of which had been used to finance civil wars, genocide, and terrorist activities. In fact, it was reported that al-Qaeda used blood diamonds to finance the 1998 U.S. embassy attacks in Kenya and Tanzania. Adamas employed more than 150 Mauritians who were trained as diamond cutters and did an excellent job of cutting and polishing raw diamonds.

During my posting in Mauritius, I made it a point to seek out business operations that might be linked to U.S.-based companies, either through ownership or by franchising their products. Mauritians are hardworking and very resourceful. I enjoyed visiting a number of office products distributors, technology companies, accounting firms, soft drink and water bottling plants, a plastic bottle extrusion operation, cellular telephone operations, name-brand food canning operations, and fast-food chain operations among others.

Some of the more adventuresome business people Marcia and I met were Owen and Marianne Griffiths. He was an Australian zoologist; she, a Mauritian, was educated as a biologist. In 1985, they opened a tourist attraction known as La Vanille Crocodile Park. It is located on what was once a vanilla farm in a wooded area on the south of the island, at Rivière des Anguilles. There they breed Nile crocodiles, which originally were brought over from nearby Madagascar, and the rare giant Aldabra tortoise.

La Vanille features palm trees, tropical flowers, and streams. In addition to the thousands of crocodiles and tortoises being bred, there is also a mini-zoo with deer, tenrecs, rabbits, bats, wild pigs, and skinks. Owen and Marianne also realized that the existence of feral macaque colonies on the island that were free of the B-virus (a virus that infects the majority of captive populations) and other simian viruses offered an opportunity to breed these monkeys for export to biomedical research and testing facilities in North America, Japan, and other countries. Their Bioculture (Mauritius) Ltd. monkey breeding operation has created employment for more than two hundred Mauritians. They and several other breeding operations combined export more than seven thousand monkeys each year. The Griffiths' monkey breeding operation was very clean, considering that there were thousands of monkeys running around in various enclosed fenced areas; the monkeys were separated by age, gender, and those being readied for shipment around the world. Marianne ran this operation to the highest sanitary and veterinary standards and paid particular attention to nutritious food allotments.

Over lunch during our visit, Owen shared his dream of being able to repopulate the nearby island of Rodrigues with the giant Aldabra tortoises, which had freely roamed the island before their extinction in 1794 by the early French traders.

In October 2006, I was informed that Owen had reintroduced almost three hundred tortoises, with an additional two hundred planned for release in 2007. I am sure the project to reestablish a flourishing tortoise population on Rodrigues will prove to be a success because of his drive and dedication.

During my three years in these islands, I had the opportunity to spend time with many innovative and creative entrepreneurs and businessmen—too many to name individually here. Their success lies partly in the fact that Mauritius has no natural resources to fall back on, so the people have become their own ultimate resource.

As I've noted, Marcia and I had traveled throughout Africa since the 1970s and enjoyed numerous safari trips in several sub-Saharan African countries. In later years, we included our three children, Steven, Deirdra, and Jennifer, and their spouses. When grandchildren came along, we helped inspire almost from birth their love of adventure in the amazing wild animal habitats. With our family visiting us in Mauritius for the Fourth of July celebration, we also planned a trip to several safari camps in Kenya.

On the morning of July 5, 2002, we left Mauritius and spent the night in Nairobi. John Bennett, the counselor for Regional Affairs at the U.S. Embassy in Nairobi, met us at the airport and escorted us to the Norfolk Hotel. The next morning, he accompanied Marcia and me on a courtesy call to Ambassador Johnnie Carson and his wife, Anne, at the ambassador's residence. We had a meaningful discussion on security issues and reviewed several cables and documents on terrorist concerns in the region. Walking through their spacious gardens, we spent several minutes of silence at the fountain memorial honoring the twelve Americans who lost their lives in the 1998 Nairobi embassy bombing. The five of us then had an enjoyable conversation about our longtime interest in sub-Saharan Africa. On our way back to the hotel, Bennett drove us by the new U.S. embassy compound under construction.

That afternoon, we took a small charter aircraft to Kichwa Tembo for our stay at the Bateleur Camp. Our family were the only guests at this five-star camp nestled in a wooded area on the edge of the Oloololo Escarpment, which is on the western border of the Masai Mara National Reserve in southwestern Kenya, along the Great Rift Valley. Overlooking the plains of the Masai Mara, we were in the direct path of

11.4. Masai tribesmen with Marcia, Masai Mara, Kenya, July 2002.

the annual migration of wildebeest and zebras traveling from as far away as the Serengeti Plains in Tanzania.

Early Wednesday morning, July 10, 2002, I received a fax that the merger of JPR and GGP was effective as of that day. It was five o'clock, and we were just leaving for a sunrise hot air balloon ride over the Masai Mara to view the animals as they started moving around. In the stillness of the morning, gliding over the Masai Mara, I became lost in thought, reflecting on the finality of the words in the fax. Suddenly the balloon dropped, snapping me back to reality. We barely missed a tree as we approached the landing area, and upon landing, our wicker basket was dragged along the ground for fifty yards, with all of us ending up tumbled on top of each other. At the champagne breakfast that followed, we made a toast to "the Mara and the merger," making this exciting morning adventure complete.

The next day, the family visited a Masai village near the Bateleur Camp, which employed many of the villagers. We gave the village chief some seed money to build a thatched-roof classroom building, and we resolved to stay only at camps that employed local villagers. Conservation Corporation Africa (CC Africa) owned more than twenty premier safari camps, such as Bateleur, throughout sub-Saharan Africa. The company plows 10 percent of its earnings back into neighboring villages for education and health care facilities.

In subsequent years, when staying at CC Africa camps, we would also visit the neighboring villages. On several occasions, family members brought suitcases filled

11.5. Family visit to Kawai village, Kenya, July 2002.

11.6. Emurutoto Primary School students, Kawai, Kenya, July 2002.

with fifty or so school kits packed in shoulder bags made out of surplus airplane seat fabrics, donated by the LDS Church in Utah. Each bag contained several pencils, a sharpener, writing paper, a small chalkboard, chalk, a twelve-inch ruler, and some hand tissues. Our son Steven, who is a soccer coach, brought a number of soccer balls and with his son Garrett, an excellent player, gave the young villagers some lessons, leaving behind the balls for them to enjoy. We would always leave some seed money for the village building fund.

The village leaders and schoolteachers were always very thankful. They also asked for help from the United States for sustainable development programs, infrastructure improvements, and medical and school supplies. The CC Africa people told us they built the classrooms and clinics for less than $10,000 each; if the villagers contributed their labor, they could be built for substantially less.

On July 13, our safari experience came to an end. Marcia and I sadly bid farewell to our family as we left Nairobi on an Air Kenya flight bound for Mahe, the capital island of Seychelles, to present my credentials to President France-Albert René and spend a week meeting with government and community leaders.

{ XII }

THE REPUBLIC OF SEYCHELLES

While the war in Iraq continues to preoccupy Americans, [and] while the U.S superpower moral authority is being questioned in many parts of the world . . . [t]he American people are understandably conflicted and in an introspective mood, engaged in a national debate on the next step forward—but this is no time for the U.S. to withdraw from a policy of global engagement.

—SIR JAMES MANCHAM,
FOUNDING PRESIDENT OF THE REPUBLIC OF SEYCHELLES, MAY 16, 2007

The Seychelles Islands run along the northerly edge of the Mascarene Ridge of the Indian Ocean and are part of a giant granite tectonic plate that once connected Africa to India. More than 200 million years ago, these were part of a single supercontinent. Subsequently, they slid apart and formed two landmasses, one north, the other south. The southern land mass also split, and later India and Madagascar separated from Africa. Where these last three landmasses had once been joined, a fragment of islands referred to as "Eden" was cast adrift 65 million years ago. These islands became the Seychelles, the oldest islands in any ocean, and the only ones composed of granite that is more than 700 million years old. By contrast, other islands in the Indian Ocean, such as Mauritius, Rodrigues, Réunion, and Comoros, are much more recent in origin, formed from giant volcanic flows of lava spewing from the earth's core onto the ocean floor.

The outer Seychelles are low-lying coralline islands. Most of the islands in the chain are surrounded by stretches of white sand beaches and clear azure ocean water sheltered by coral reefs. The live coral that grows on the offshore shelf protects the pristine shorelines from erosion.

The history of this archipelago goes back to 1502, when the Portuguese explorer Vasco da Gama discovered the uninhabited islands. A century later, in 1609, an

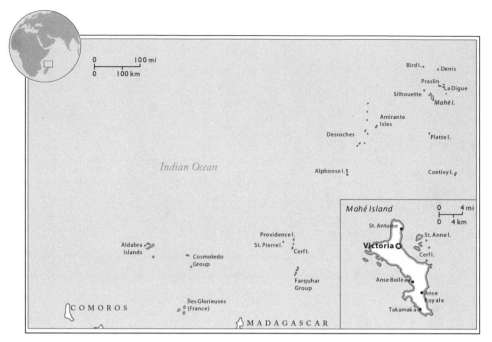

Map 4. Seychelles

English expedition briefly visited the islands but, like the Portuguese explorers, did not then create settlements.

It wasn't until after a series of reconnaissance voyages that a French expedition arrived in 1756 and named the islands after Louis XV's Minister of Finance, Jean Moreau de Séchelles. Ten years later, the French established a settlement. As trade with India and Asia increased, Seychelles became an important port of call for ships to replenish their larder with fresh provisions and water.

Early in the 1800s, the British battled the French for control of these islands, which were along the East Indies spice route. In 1813 they finally defeated the French, who under the 1814 Treaty of Paris ceded the Seychelles islands as well as the island of Mauritius to the British. These islands were thereafter administered from Mauritius as a British dependent territory.

Although arable land was limited in the Seychelles, some French-owned plantations existed, for which slave labor was imported. After the British banned slavery in 1835, laborers from India and China were brought in to work the plantations.

On August 31, 1903, Seychelles became a crown colony, no longer administered by Mauritius. A new constitution in 1967 vested authority in a governor, and further amendments in 1970 gave Seychelles even greater autonomy. On June 29, 1976, Seychelles gained independence from the British as a Republic within the Commonwealth. This included the transfer of the outer islands of Aldabra, Farquhar, and Desroches from the British Indian Ocean Territory.

The entire archipelago now consists of 115 islands, most of which are unoccupied and undeveloped. Aldabra, the outermost island, is located almost 800 miles southwest of Mahé, and 400 miles off the coast of Africa. Together, the islands of the Seychelles comprise an area of approximately 175 square miles—slightly more than two and a half times the size of Washington, D.C. Mahé, the largest island, encompasses 56 square miles and is located 1,000 miles east of the coast of Africa, 800 miles northeast of Madagascar, 1,000 miles northeast of the Comoros islands, 1,200 miles north of Mauritius, and 1,100 miles northwest of the Chagos Archipelago.

Over millions of years of isolation, the Seychelles developed unique fauna and flora that have remained for the most part undisturbed. Many species of birds and plants that flourish here can be found nowhere else but on these islands. Among its eighty-one endemic plants is the famous coco de mer, the world's largest coconut. This twin-sided oval seed of the coconut palm matures into the suggestive shape of a woman's lower torso and has been nicknamed the "love nut." Once coveted by European princes and Chinese emperors as an aphrodisiac, the coco de mer is designated an endangered species and prohibited from being removed from the islands. Vallée de Mai, a World Heritage site located on the island of Praslin, is so beautiful that some think it to be the original site of the Garden of Eden. Another World Heritage site, designated in 1982, is the island of Aldabra—home to more than 100,000 rare giant tortoises and several species of booby. These UNESCO World Heritage sites are operated by the Seychelles Island Foundation.

The reefs around these islands shelter more than a thousand species of fish, coral, and other forms of marine life. Since most of the islands are only a few feet above the surface of the ocean, the soil tends to be shallow but is generally suited for coconut palm trees.

Unique land birds found on these islands include the flightless Aldabra rail and the enigmatic Seychelles scops-owl. Other rare species include the Seychelles magpie robin, Seychelles warbler, Seychelles black paradise flycatcher, Seychelles blue pigeon, Seychelles kestrel, and Seychelles sunbird. Seabirds include the sooty tern, fairy tern, white-tailed tropicbird, noddy, and frigate.

The population of Seychelles in 2002 was approximately 80,000, with 29 percent of the population being under the age of fifteen; adult literacy is over 90 percent. Since there are no higher education facilities in the Seychelles, many students go abroad, primarily to the United Kingdom, to study for a university degree; some students go on to pursue advanced degrees.

The cultural mix of most Seychellois includes European, African, Indian, and Chinese origins. Creole is the predominant language spoken in the Seychelles, although French and English are also considered official languages. Roman Catholics make up 88 percent of the population, Anglicans another 8 percent; Baptists, Seventh-Day Adventists, Assembly of God, Pentecostal, Nazarites, and Jehovah's Witnesses make up 2 percent; and Hindus, Baha'is, and Muslims account for the remaining 2 percent.

In 2002 the Muslim Qur'aan and Sunnah Society of Seychelles in Victoria had approximately three hundred members and had been part of Seychelles society for many years. During my posting, from 2002 to 2005, the Muslim population almost doubled, with many of the new younger Muslim men who had relocated from abroad. These new arrivals tended to be more fundamentalist in their beliefs and, because of their ideological differences with Seychelles' traditional Muslim community, decided to move to the north of the island. There was concern expressed that some of them might be using Seychelles as a safe haven—they seemed to have ready cash but no visible means of support. The government of Seychelles, having signed on to the global war on terror, was very watchful of their activities.

Any radical or disruptive activities gaining a foothold on any of the islands would have a long-lasting, disastrous effect. The government of Seychelles agreed to tighten up controls at the airport and harbor and closely check people transiting through these areas. The country's policies for issuance of passports to noncitizens would also be reined in to prevent questionable individuals from gaining access worldwide using a Seychelles passport.

In 1976, shortly after the Republic of Seychelles became independent, Sir James Mancham, the leader of the Seychelles Democratic Party, became the founding president of Seychelles. He headed a coalition government that included the Seychelles People's United Party, whose leader, France-Albert René, became Prime Minister. On June 5, 1977, while attending a Commonwealth Conference in the United Kingdom, Mancham was deposed in a coup d'état led by his disloyal ally René, aided by a small group of armed rebels flown in from Tanzania. Subsequently, Mancham went into exile for almost fifteen years.

Taking over the presidency, René became a dictator, immediately suspending the constitution, dismissing the legislature, and ruling by decree. In 1979, the People's United Party was absorbed into the newly formed Seychelles People's Progressive Front, which today remains the controlling party. By referendum in 1979, René established a one-party state and a Marxist-style political system and further centralized his power.

In November 1981 there was a coup attempt. Disguised as rugby players, Colonel "Mad Mike" Hoare and forty-three mercenaries flew into Mahé. An observant customs agent saw a submachine gun in one of the pieces of luggage, and a struggle ensued, followed by the hijacking of an Air India plane that had been sitting on the tarmac. All but six of the mercenaries escaped back to South Africa, which René accused of helping Mancham try to return to power. The mercenaries who were caught were sent to prison for two years in Seychelles. Loyal Seychellois troops helped to restore order, aided by Tanzanian troops who were brought in. Other attempted coups took place in 1985, 1986, and 1987. At least one or two of these coups were blamed on Western countries, particularly France. However, René continued to rule the country with an iron fist until 1991, when international pressure brought reform to the electoral process, allowing opposition candidates to fairly participate in multiparty elections.

In an attempt to revive the Seychelles Democratic Party, Sir James Mancham returned from exile in April 1992. The first multiparty presidential and legislative elections were held thereafter under a new constitution. Leading his party ticket in the July 1993 presidential election, Mancham received only 36 percent of the vote, while René won the election handily with 59 percent. However, there were a number of reports of voting irregularities. Controlling the People's Progressive Front party, René won again in March 1998 with 66 percent of the vote against the opposition leader, the Reverend Wavel Ramkalawan, who had replaced Mancham. By then, the Seychelles Democratic Party had evolved into the Seychelles National Party. In this election, again there were a number of claims of irregularities. In the August 2001 election, René and his People's Progressive Front Party won by a smaller margin, with 54 percent of the vote, while Ramkalawan and the Seychelles National Party surprised everyone with 46 percent.

Stories circulated that René would deliberately hold back many containers of goods scheduled for delivery to the Seychelles Marketing Board until a week or so before the elections. Then the containers would arrive for distribution to the store shelves—a political move to gain votes.

I also heard from several government sources that René did not want to run again in the next election. He was concerned his party would face a much closer election. René had been less visible as well, and there were rumors about his health. At some point before the end of his term, René made the decision to step aside yet continue to be chairman of the Seychelles People's Progressive Front—in effect, he would still maintain control of the government.

President René had been spending some time in Australia, where I was told he had a large ranch. Sources divulged that he was trying without success to obtain a residency permit that would allow him to stay for longer periods of time.

During the past thirty years, Seychelles' economic growth has come mainly from the tourism and fishery sectors, while the rest of the economy has suffered. Reportedly, there has been a long history of cronyism and insider dealings, to the exclusion of the Seychellois business community. Government monopolies have been blamed as the main cause of the high cost of living and virtual collapse of the economy. The Seychelles Marketing Board, set up in 1984, was controlled by Mukesh Valabhji—the handpicked economic advisor to René—until 2006. Valabhji's fingerprints were on just about every aspect of the Seychelles' economy.

Environmental impact concerns arose when René's administration undertook a massive multiyear dredging operation on Mahé to create more usable real estate. By dredging ocean sand and coral, they added more than 1,600 acres of land.

In the process, they destroyed precious coral reefs, which has impacted the coastal ecosystems. Several other large-scale reclamation projects are planned, which will escalate degradation of Mahé's ecosystem. In addition to these larger projects, the government of Seychelles has allowed a number of smaller private reclamation projects that have adversely affected the ecosystem.

Although the cost of the government reclamation projects was never disclosed, several knowledgeable sources estimate that up to $100 million has been spent, further adding to Seychelles' already bloated debt. The cash outlays to dredging contractors and other vendors merely added to the foreign exchange problem. I couldn't find a marketing plan or price list for these real estate parcels, either, so it is not clear if they will generate any revenue for the government of Seychelles; if they do, I hope some of the revenue is used to fund lasting conservation projects.

From the start, the Seychelles Marketing Board did not operate in a transparent manner. Media and community sources have continually reported on insider deals with Compagnie Seychelloise de Promotion Hotelière, a water bottling company, a tea company, the local beer company, and a London-based rice trading company. There were undisclosed transactions with Gulf States royal families and deals involving undeveloped outer islands that had been controlled by René's son.

On several trips to Seychelles, I stayed at the Wharf Hotel and Marina on Mahé. This boutique facility was built on reclaimed land, which was reportedly purchased by an insider without going through a bidding process. The hotel property was sold in 2006 to an undisclosed offshore investor, and I understand that the seller retired to South Africa to enjoy his profits.

On my first visit to Seychelles, Marcia and I arrived at the airport in Victoria, the capital, located on the island of Mahé, on July 13, 2002. We were warmly greeted by Bisa Williams, my deputy chief of mission; Susanne Rose, our part-time Foreign Service national consular agent; and Selby Pillay, the first secretary in the Ministry of Foreign Affairs. The government of Seychelles kindly provided us with a Mercedes sedan for our visit, and with the American flag mounted on the fender mast, we headed to Victoria for a quick tour of the capital. This picturesque town has quaint buildings dating back to the nineteenth century and influenced by French-style architecture.

We then drove to the Fisherman's Cove Hotel, approximately two miles from Victoria. Mahé has many stretches of sandy beaches nestled between giant outcroppings of granite boulders. The hotel is located near the lovely beach town of Beau Vallon, which has several fine hotels and restaurants. To get there, however, we had to travel on a narrow road over numerous mountainside switchbacks that took us up through a densely forested area and then back down to the beach area.

Traveling around the island on these narrow roads was a challenge, especially when buses and construction trucks passed one another with little room to spare.

But each hairpin turn allowed for incredible vistas of the ocean below and gorgeous tropical islands in the distance.

The Seychelles are located on the equator. The temperatures are generally above 80°F and the humidity is high. Frequent rainfall provides for an abundance of lush vegetation around the island. The large island of Mahé is hilly, with peaks that can reach almost three thousand feet. Many huge weather-worn granite outcrops can be seen throughout Mahé as well as the nearby islands of St. Anne, Praslin, and La Digue, and with the pure white sand beaches and clear turquoise water create a backdrop of incredible beauty. At sunset, the light on the speckled boulders reflects shades of red.

That evening over dinner at the nearby Corsair Restaurant, we became acquainted with Air Force Colonel William Rasmussen, who represented the Kenya U.S. Liaison Office (KUSLO), a CENTCOM field office. This office coordinates U.S. security assistance, such as the International Military Education and Training (IMET) program and CENTCOM operations and training exercises. Colonel Rasmussen briefed us on security matters in the region and available program funding.

On Monday, I had a full schedule. In the morning, I watched the U.S. Navy and Seychelles Coast Guard conduct combined underwater training exercises. I also visited a women's craft nongovernmental organization.

During a luncheon I hosted at the Plantation Club resort for members of the Seychelles diplomatic corps, I listened to their impressions of a number of issues involving

12.1. The scenic view from Fisherman's Cove Hotel, Mahé, Seychelles, July 2002.

12.2. Marcia looks at the lovely handiwork made at a women's craft center, Seychelles, July 2002.

the Seychelles, some of which I had already been briefed on. I carefully measured what was being said, knowing that each diplomat had his or her own agenda on economic and military issues in the Indian Ocean region. China and France had the largest embassies; surprisingly, Cuba was also represented.

Later in the day, I visited the Indian Ocean Tuna plant, a 60/40 partnership between the global H. J. Heinz Company and the Seychelles Marketing Board. The plant employed 2,500 people and had the capacity to process 500 tons of tuna a day.

On Tuesday I woke early and took a walk along the beach while practicing my remarks for the morning's formal presentation of credentials to President France-Albert René. I was told the President dressed in "island casual" attire and that there was no need for me to wear a tie. Opting for the "island ambassador" look, I wore a plain short-sleeved white silk and linen Tommy Bahama shirt, black Tommy Bahama slacks, and a comfortable pair of black loafers.

State House is a magnificent turn-of-the-century wooden structure located on a hilltop overlooking the city of Victoria. At exactly ten o'clock I was ushered into President René's large office. The President had a soft smile. Pale and fairly overweight, he wore a light green flowered shirt. After some small talk, I gave my prepared remarks and handed him the resignation letter of my predecessor followed by the letters of accreditation from President George W. Bush. After shaking hands for the waiting photographers, we walked to a corner sitting area, where hot tea and éclairs were waiting.

I thanked the President for his support of the global war on terror and for allowing U.S. military overflights that we sometimes requested on short notice.

We discussed two U.S. ships from Bahrain that were scheduled to visit the islands before departing for Norfolk, Virginia, and San Diego, California. The President asked that we set up a bank on board the ships to exchange U.S. dollars for their Seychelles rupees. He did not want our troops to go into Victoria and get 10–14 rupees for each dollar in the black market, versus the official (artificial) bank rate of slightly over 5 rupees. He talked at length about how the lack of hard currency was affecting the Seychelles economy.

I told René that later that day I would be announcing awards totaling $35,000 for seven Ambassador's Special Self-Help (SSH) Program and two Democracy and Human Rights Fund projects. Two of the more successful programs undertaken by the U.S. Embassy at the grassroots community level, SSH aided struggling non-governmental organizations, local civic groups, and charity organizations while the Democracy and Human Rights fund aided democratic institutions and supported human rights.

One of the award recipients was the weekly newspaper *Regar*, which I knew was a sensitive topic for René. The financially strapped *Regar* supported the opposition party and had been known to print stories critical of the René administration. When the paper published the results of investigative reporting, it often incurred threats of libel lawsuits. To a lesser extent, *Le Nouveau Seychelles Weekly*, a voice for Mancham, also received threats from time to time, since it supported the opposition and took on the government. On the other hand, the government controlled the well-funded daily *Seychelles Nation* as well as the ruling party's newspaper, *The People*.

Some of the country's parastatals were led by individuals who did not always operate in a transparent manner and often were sensitive to criticism. Other media, including SBC TV and SBC radio, were also government-controlled and hence did not allow equal access for the opposition candidates.

President René was visibly shaken and not at all happy when he heard about the award to *Regar*; almost immediately I felt a chill in the room. He did not want to talk about the upcoming parliamentary elections, which had been scheduled to take place sometime before March 2003. The President needed only to give three weeks' notice prior to setting a voting date. Any opposition party candidate would have a difficult time putting together an effective campaign for the election in that amount of time.

As René sat quietly, I became uncomfortable and knew the meeting was over. After the *Seychelles Nation* photographers took a few more photos, an aide ushered us out of the office. Once on the veranda at the front of State House, I gave some prepared remarks to the waiting media—only representatives of the state-owned radio and television stations and the *Seychelles Nation*. Later, I learned that *Regar* had not been invited.

At midafternoon, I met Colonel Léopold Payet, commander of the Seychelles People's Defense Forces. He was a stern-faced individual who kept his distance and spoke in measured words. I tried to warm him up by discussing the opportunity of having some of his staff travel to the United States under a funded program for military training. Instead, Colonel Payet wanted U.S. instructors to come to Seychelles to do the training there.

I explained the benefits of the IMET program for his forces, but to no avail. I then suggested he send two officers to attend the next Golden Spear training exercise in Nairobi, Kenya, headed by U.S. Army General Tommy Franks and scheduled for the following week. He reluctantly agreed, and I surmised he was simply cool toward any engagement with the United States. I decided to make an effort to become his friend and try to develop some trust between us. I made it a point to visit with him whenever I came to Seychelles.

At my next appointment, the Coast Guard headquarters, Lieutenant Colonel André Ciseau took me for a cruise around the port area in one of six Coast Guard boats donated to Seychelles by the United States. Ciseau was a warm and friendly man, and I immediately felt I could trust him; we quickly became good friends and met often during my visits to Seychelles. As a military officer, Ciseau appreciated what the United States did for Seychelles, including military training and surplus equipment, as well as the numerous annual ship visits. On their way back from duty in the Persian Gulf region, thousands of military personnel arrived on the islands each year for rest and recuperation. These visits infused badly needed hard currency into the Seychelles economy.

The following day, I met Vivekanand Alleear, the chief justice of the Supreme Court, who was open and easy to talk with on a number of issues. He had a son and a married sister who lived in Mauritius. Since he traveled often to visit his family, we discussed the foreign exchange issue, in particular the limits on the amount of hard currency Seychellois can take out of the country. He was concerned about how difficult it was to travel with only $400 of hard currency, as mandated by the government of Seychelles.

After that visit, I paid a courtesy call on Police Commissioner André Kilindo. A nervous chain smoker, he—like Payet—was distant in his demeanor. He explained he was the coordinator for counterterrorism, which is the equivalent to the American director of Homeland Security. But I did not get the impression he was thoroughly trained to deal with the magnitude of current terrorism issues, or for that matter wanted our help.

At noon, I spoke with the Reverend Wavel Ramkalawan, the leader of the opposition. His office was located directly over the *Regar* newspaper office and printing plant. Prior to entering politics, Ramkalawan was an Anglican priest. During our visit, he talked about the political and economic issues surrounding the René government, and the skimming and self-dealing activities that he acknowledged took place. He explained that a number of insiders had vested interests in offshore entities that control the cost of products in the Seychelles, and that all products go through the Seychelles Marketing Board and are significantly marked up. Without readily available hard currency, a wide variety of goods are in short supply.

Discussing his campaign, he said he was pleased at having garnered 46 percent of the vote in the last election, and he felt prepared for the upcoming elections. I asked if he feared for his safety, since he had been roughed up in previous campaigns; he said he didn't. After concluding our meeting, we toured the *Regar* operation with Roger Mancienne, the paper's managing editor.

I later met with a member of the Seychelles International Business Authority, a quasi-public entity that licensed, regulated, and promoted offshore business. This gentleman was anxious about the economy, and I empathized: a free market economy rather than a controlled one was the only way to solve the foreign exchange issue. Without it, Seychelles would have serious monetary problems in the next five to ten years. His concern was that it might happen sooner.

Attending a Chamber of Commerce board meeting, I learned that the Seychelles economy was so sluggish that some business owners had had to make major staff layoffs. Basil Soundy, a board member who owned the supply company Bodco Ltd., lamented that in the last year his labor force had dropped from 180 employees to 18. The other business leaders at the meeting reiterated that few goods were able to be had on a regular basis because of the government's lack of hard currency and the requirement to deal through the Seychelles Marketing Board. In their business operations, they could keep only 15 percent of the hard-currency generated on sales, with the government forcing them to take the balance in Seychelles rupees. Despair marked the atmosphere; they asked what the United States could do to help.

That evening, Marcia and I met with more than a dozen Americans living in the Seychelles, including Peter Pomeroy (whose family owned La Reserve, a hotel on Praslin Island, and was part of a well-known San Francisco construction empire) and Sandra Hanks Benoiton (sister of Hollywood movie star Tom Hanks). Joined by several Seychellois invited by Susanne Rose, we all went for cocktails on board the USS *Trenton*. The ship's officers and personnel had not seen outsiders for 107 days while at sea and were thrilled to have company.

The Stars and Stripes were flying everywhere, and several officers made speeches. I was proud when they presented me with a plaque to commemorate the occasion.

Ship visits by the ambassador are important ways to bond with our military on duty. It was an honor for me to come together with these brave sailors and soldiers who serve our nation with distinction. I decided to make it a policy to be present for every such ship visit; if I had a conflict, I would send an embassy representative in my place.

Early Thursday morning, Marcia and I went to Praslin Island, a twenty-minute plane ride from Mahé. Our plan was to stay overnight at the Lemuria Resort and then visit several environmentally sensitive projects. The hotel was uniquely integrated into the landscape. Elevated walkways protected the forest and marshes; giant granite boulders had been left in place and the resort built around them, showing a great sensitivity to the natural environment.

Our guide, Michael Jean-Louis, then picked us up for a motorboat trip over to nearby Cousin Island. He had arranged for James Millett of BirdLife International (a nongovernmental organization that had received funds from the Ambassador's Special Self-Help Program) to accompany us. James arrived in bare feet, a T-shirt, and bathing shorts—he said he felt comfortable traveling this way—and had planned a personal tour to familiarize us with the ongoing Special Reserve project.

The rented boat was small, with barely enough room to hold the four of us. At times the choppy water was only inches below the gunwale.

On Cousin Island, we were met by several Nature Seychelles guides familiar with the island's environmental and preservation programs. (Nature Seychelles is a partner with BirdLife International.) The island is pristine. No food or drinks are allowed, and there are no rest rooms. It reminded us of our earlier visits to the Galapagos Islands, which were also pristine sanctuaries for endangered fauna and flora.

Cousin is a small granitic island that has been transformed from an ecologically impoverished coconut plantation into a thriving indigenous forest and habitat restoration project. In 1969 it became the first sea and island reserve in the Indian Ocean.

12.3. Going by motorboat from Praslin to Cousin Island, July 2002.

12.4. James Millet and Marcia greet an Aldabra tortoise on Cousin Island, July 2002.

In addition to its magnificent and rare birds, the reserve is also home to hawksbill sea turtles, Wright's skinks, giant Aldabra tortoises, and hermit crabs. Thousands of birds nest everywhere, even safely on the ground, since there are no rats, rodents, cats, or other predators on the serene island.

Early Friday morning, while it was still cool, Michael picked us up again, this time for a visit to the nearby Vallée de Mai, the World Heritage site famous for the uniquely beautiful coco de mer. These incredibly tall palm trees with huge fan-shaped leaves shade the ground so completely that little grows underneath them, making for unobstructed vistas. Some of these palms are more than four hundred years old. More than sixty thousand people from around the world annually visit this picturesque and well-protected forest.

We then went by boat to La Digue, a small island with a limited road system. Although vehicles are used to transport guests between the dock and the hotels, most people either walk or ride bicycles. We quickly rented bikes and headed out to explore the nearby beach areas. We meandered around giant granite boulders on our way to a long and wide expanse of blindingly white sand with turquoise waves lapping at the shoreline. Exquisite and timeless, this area has served as a location for many magazine photo shoots.

The next day, after further exploring the island, we took the ferry back to Praslin in time for our five o'clock flight to Mahé. Although this had been a whirlwind three-day adventure, it gave us a chance to see and understand more about these beautiful islands.

12.5. Michael Jean-Louis and Marcia examine a coco de mer at the Vallée de Mai Nature Reserve, July 2002.

On Sunday Marcia and I got up early, having promised Commander Robert Irelan that we would breakfast aboard the USS *Trenton* before it departed. Joining us on this visit was the assigned special agent of the Naval Criminal Investigative Service, stationed in Manama, Bahrain, who was in charge of protecting U.S. naval assets. Special agents would arrive several days before a ship's visit to "sanitize" the dock area, and they would remain involved during the ship's stay to handle security and personnel problems. A Seahawk helicopter was waiting to take us out to the

12.6. The incredible weather-sculpted granite outcrops on La Digue Island, July 2002.

USS *Trenton*. On deck, officers and personnel stood at attention as the loudspeakers announced my arrival.

After breakfast, the commander gave us a personal tour of the ship. The *Trenton* was an Austin-class amphibious transport dock, transporting and landing troops. In addition to Navy personnel, it had a full Marine unit on board. At ten o'clock sharp, the ship weighed anchor and pilot boats moved the *Trenton* through the channel. On behalf of President Bush, I thanked Commander Irelan and the military

12.7. Ambassador Price onboard the USS *Trenton* with the crew, July 21, 2002.

personnel on board for their service to the country. At eleven-thirty, the Seahawk ferried us to our next stop, the USS *Oak Hill*.

A large amphibious warfare ship, the *Oak Hill* had several giant hovercrafts on board—each one capable of carrying large numbers of Marines and gear and able to travel over water or terrain at speeds up to fifty knots. After a quick tour by Commander Ulysses Oca Zalamea, we had lunch in his private quarters with all his senior officers. Zalamea had come from the Philippines as a young man and enlisted in the U.S. Navy. Later he went to officer training school and worked his way up to the rank of commander. Discussing our immigrant backgrounds, we both agreed we had achieved the American dream.

By one-fifteen, Marcia and I were back on the Seahawk and airborne for the short flight back to Mahé. When we landed, our assigned driver, Patrick, was waiting to take Marcia and me to the Fisherman's Cove for a rest before we flew back to Mauritius. Our flight that night put us back in Port Louis after eleven; Ahmed was waiting to take us to Macarty House.

Having presented my credentials to President René, I was ready now to fully engage the Republic of Seychelles, and to represent and protect our U.S. interests as well as the American citizens visiting and living there. Most important, I understood better why the United States needed to take more of an interest in the Seychelles, in light of concerns over suspect individuals using the Seychelles to access the Indian Ocean and East Africa region looking for soft spots or safe havens. As I said, employing only a part-time Foreign Service national consular agent instead of establishing an American Presence Post makes no sense to me—especially if the United States is intent on knowing what is going on inside the country and within the region. Seychelles is a voting member at the UN; thus, we need their support continually on important issues, such as the global war on terror and the International Criminal Court Article 98 nonsurrender issue. We constantly had to do business long distance, by telephone or e-mail, or else lose four days' worth of precious time by flying in and out of Seychelles on limited flight schedules.

China, the United Kingdom, France, Russia, India, and Cuba have active embassies and consulates in Seychelles looking out for their interests. I strongly believe the United States must maintain an American presence in the Seychelles. Let us not forget that Diego Garcia, our most important military base, is located only 1,100 miles from Mahé.

{ XIII }

Embassy Business

On August 11–12, 2002, our first two-day congressional delegation (CODEL) came through Mauritius after having visited other sub-Saharan African countries. Its head was Senator Richard Shelby, the ranking member of the Senate Banking Committee, who arrived with his wife, Dr. Annette Shelby. Also in the delegation were Senator Arlen Specter, chairman of the Senate Appropriations Committee, his wife, Joan Specter, and several staffers. In our discussion with the CODEL team, we focused on the challenges facing the intelligence community in the region, overseas bilateral assistance programs, terrorism, economic issues, democracy initiatives, and American citizen issues. We held a country team meeting at the embassy to show the delegation what it was we did there. We gave a brief overview of the work undertaken by the Foreign Service officers and Foreign Service national staff at this Special Embassy Program post and explained how understaffed we were for what was expected of us, especially in the commercial and consular areas.

We highlighted the normally peaceful Muslim community, and explained that there was little concern about terrorism in Mauritius—although a minor issue had cropped up with the presence of a small group affiliated with the local Hizbullah Party. The CODEL was troubled by examples of visa and passport violations we had seen, and Senator Shelby inquired about banking oversight to stem the flow of funds to rogue organizations. Intellectual property rights violations were another issue of concern that we were pursuing vigorously, since they affected American companies whose trademarks were being violated. We then talked about the upcoming AGOA Forum in Mauritius. I was happy to report that Mauritian manufacturers were pleased about a recent change in the AGOA that allowed merino wool and knit-to-shape products to have duty- and quota-free access to the United States. Taking a quick tour of the Shibani textile plant, the delegation saw firsthand how a well-run integrated operation spun yarn and machine-knitted products.

Afterward, we went to Government House to meet with Prime Minister Sir Anerood Jugnauth and Deputy Prime Minister Paul Bérenger. I had already mentioned to the delegation that the Diego Garcia issue would come up in conversation;

13.1. Senators Richard Shelby and Arlen Specter, Dr. Annette Shelby, and Joan Specter with Ambassador Price, Bisa Williams, Dan Claffey, and several congressional staff members, August 11, 2002.

indeed, after the government leaders thanked the United States for the AGOA Act changes and the pending AGOA Forum in Mauritius, the topic of Diego Garcia and sovereignty was brought up. Also included was talk about Iraq and Saddam Hussein. Both Jugnauth and Bérenger encouraged the United States to not invade Iraq but rather try to negotiate on the issue of inspections. Both Senators Shelby and Specter stated that a war with Saddam Hussein was unavoidable; only the timing of the invasion had not been set. About Diego Garcia, they responded it was not a congressional issue but an executive one, which forestalled any further debate. As we left, a lively press was waiting to interview both senators.

That evening I hosted a dinner in honor of the CODEL at Macarty House, and invited as special guest Vice President Raouf Bundhun, who was accompanied by the director of national security, Narain Krishna Peerun. I also invited several U.S. citizens who were active in business in Mauritius. It was a small group, and I placed each senator at a separate table so that they could get better acquainted with the guests. Bundhun, a Muslim, talked about community concerns, which turned into a lively discussion about U.S. policy.

The next morning, Bisa Williams called to say that the delegation had boarded their Air Force Gulfstream jet and were on their way to Dar es Salaam. She also mentioned that Senator Shelby, as head of the delegation, had been a little bit hurt at not sitting with Bundhun and me the evening before. I had made the mistake of assuming Senator Specter was the more senior.

Even though both senators were respected members of the Senate and served on a number of important committees, neither was on the Senate Foreign Relations Committee. In the three years that followed, we would see no other senators passing through to acquaint themselves with the issues in the region.

Thursday, August 15, was a national holiday, the Feast of the Assumption, and the embassy was closed. I was working at home when someone from the Seychelles newspaper the *Nation* called, thinking I was with the opposition leader Wavel Ramkalawan, or that he was on his way to meet with me. This person asked if I had knowledge of alleged attempts or threats on Ramkalawan's life. I had no clue about Ramkalawan's whereabouts, nor had I had any contact with him, and I thought this was a strange probing call. It sounded as though President René somehow thought I was supporting the opposition, and possibly sheltering Ramkalawan somewhere. I truly hoped that Ramkalawan had not gone into hiding. I decided to meet with the regional security officer early the next morning at the embassy to research the matter.

On Monday, August 19, Roger Mancienne of the *Regar* newspaper in Seychelles, a beneficiary of the Ambassador's Democracy and Human Rights funding, came to see me regarding the threat on Ramkalawan's life. Ramkalawan was very proactive and sometimes outspoken to the point of stirring up mass rallies around the island, at which his supporters occasionally got caught up in altercations that required police intervention. Mancienne said the plot was real and being orchestrated by a military officer.

Eric Kneedler, as note taker, recorded the conversation and prepared a cable to be sent to Washington. I requested to be allowed to send a strong demarche to President René asking for his assurance of protection for Ramkalawan and a guarantee of transparency in the election process.

In early August, we held the annual signing ceremony for the twenty-two Mauritian groups receiving funding under the Ambassador's Special Self-Help Program and the three entities getting monies from the Democracy and Human Rights Program. The funds went for many tangible needs, such as video projectors, construction work, playgrounds, water tanks, office furniture, reference books and reading material, health care equipment, sewing machines, kitchen appliances, ceramics-making equipment, desktop computers, publication of books, seminars, restoration of damaged caves, and environmental education programs. In all cases, the participating organizations committed their own money and human resources to their programs, as required. In addition, we set performance targets for them to meet before they could receive the full balance of the committed funds. I believed that we should reduce funding of projects administered by the host country governments and instead give more money to community-based organizations under programs such as these so that we could monitor results in the villages.

The $70,000 budget was hardly enough for the United States to gain much mileage, and the amount allocated for each grant was not big. Since arriving at my post, I had pressed for an increase in our limited budget, which was allocated by the State Department. Still, the grants were certainly meaningful to these struggling organizations, and they were thankful for this seed money. While the people whose lives we made better through these programs might never know the source, at least *we* knew we were helping people less fortunate than most Americans. If we were given a budget ten times greater, the multiplier effect would mean that the United States could have a measurable impact in such a small country.

It would be a year later, in 2003, while we were preparing to hold the second annual awards ceremony of my tenure, that I would receive a demarche for delivery at the highest level—regarding unpaid parking tickets in New York City by the three host countries' UN mission delegations. Being a collection agency for New York City was now part of U.S. foreign policy, it seemed. I subsequently met with the Prime Minister of Mauritius, the President of Seychelles, and the President of Comoros to collect for the City of New York parking tickets that went back several years. Any money that we were unable to collect was to be deducted from the Ambassador's Special Self-Help and Democracy and Human Rights funds. As a consequence, we had to call several recipient groups, inform them that we did not have enough funding for their programs, and tell them not to show up for the awards ceremony. For me and everyone else at the embassy, this was one of our lowest and most embarrassing moments.

Presenting a demarche to the host country governments on a parking issue was foolish and affected bilateral relations. A rich country like ours that has doled out money to the most corrupt governments and forgiven billions of dollars of their debts has the ambassador trying to collect parking fines for the City of New York. And if that weren't bad enough, the funds for overseas programs that we had to use to make up the uncollected fines had come from taxpayer dollars allocated by Congress. The wasteful UN should have provided adequate off-street parking for their member states' diplomatic missions or instead pay for these parking tickets.

The small country of Mauritius had become one of the early and most successful beneficiaries under the AGOA program. As a reward, and as an inspiration to others, the United States had agreed to hold the second AGOA Forum, the first outside the United States, in Mauritius. With my business background, I could see the long-lasting benefit for the region of hosting the Forum, and because of my experience with logistics and promotion in the retail shopping center industry, I was certain we could pull off a successful event. I would have to press Washington for some additional temporary duty staff resources, but one way or another I was determined to make the Forum a great success.

This massive undertaking could not have succeeded without Trade Minister Jayen Cuttaree, who mobilized his staff and numerous community leaders to serve on our combined planning team. We met weekly in small and large groups as well as one-on-one. Cuttaree and I also talked almost daily by telephone, and had many an aside at almost every function where we ran into each other. The trade minister diligently worked personally to make the Forum a success. (In fact, Cuttaree would later go on to become a candidate for director-general of the WTO, a position for which he was most qualified. Unfortunately, the French power base in Europe got its way with the selection of Pascal Lamy.)

By now, the AGOA Forum was only five months away, and we still had not formally approved a site for all the program venues, including the large hall necessary for the opening and closing ministerial sessions and meeting rooms for the numerous breakout sessions and different country delegations.

Thinking that the University of Mauritius might be a potential site, I toured the campus with Pro-Vice-Chancellor Vinesh Hookoomsing. Bisa Williams accompanied me to help prepare our report, with venue pictures, which I would discuss in my upcoming meeting in Washington.

I was impressed that we could hold both the ministerial and private sector events in the university's facilities. It was ideally located, with access from three routes; Charlie Slater checked the drive times from the different hotel sites, downtown Port Louis, and the Mer Rouge Exhibition Center, where the Forum's International Trade Exhibition would be held. A helicopter pad was located nearby, at the President of Mauritius's official office and residence. There also were a post office, a clinic, two banks, and a service station close by—all of which could be secured. The university boasted a seven-hundred-seat auditorium, and right next door were two education buildings with multiple classrooms and two 140-seat auditoriums. In addition, the university's 400-seat cafeteria and an open reception area for food kiosks offered ample hosting opportunities. One building had underground parking for up to seventy-five cars—a great VIP amenity.

Looking over the construction and refurbishment items needed, I found them to be minimal: some roof repairs, upgrades to the air-conditioning system, wall painting, new carpeting, new drapes, and a good general cleaning. The lighting upgrades and the temporary raising and leveling of the floor in the large auditorium would be the biggest construction aspects. "It will work," I told the chancellor.

After our visit to the University of Mauritius, we met with Trade Minister Cuttaree and the Technical Committee to discuss our findings and the outcome of our walk-through. I briefed them on the upcoming meetings in Washington with the AGOA planning committee. I also made mention of the proposed Forum advance team meeting in Mauritius between October 8 and 20, 2002, to review the venues and discuss preparations. Finally, we agreed that all events except the Trade Exhibition would be held on the university campus.

The AGOA program had ongoing qualifying conditions that we used as a sledgehammer to press for parity of our business interests in the host country. On August 20, Robert Frank of the Nebraska-based Reinke Manufacturing Company, accompanied by Pierre Ah-Sue, the managing director of the engineering company Sotravic, came to see me. Apparently they were the low bidder for two irrigation system projects, but the government of Mauritius was negotiating around them with another bidder. Wanting full transparency in the bidding process, I immediately sent a note to Pravind Jugnauth, the minister of agriculture, asking for fairness regarding the low bidder. Later that day, I reinforced our position when I met with Jayen Cuttaree and Harry Ganoo in the Ministry of Trade. I impressed upon them the concern their bidding process posed under the AGOA program, and urged them not to lose eligibility and access to the United States for their products over such an issue. I did not want this to be a topic of debate with any of the agencies when I met with them in Washington.

That afternoon, speaking at the American Chamber of Commerce meeting, I gave the members a short update on the AGOA Forum. What followed was a discussion regarding the 1995 Intellectual Property Rights and the 1997 Copyright Act, both of which the government of Mauritius was updating. I expressed my concern about its implementation and enforcement. A heated discussion ensued over the Polo Ralph Lauren issue, which dated back some twenty-five years to when a local manufacturer had registered the Polo trademark in Mauritius after ceasing to work for the United States company. They continued to produce logo products for a network of retail shops on the island and export to other countries. Because the name was so popular, such merchandise was now produced by several local manufacturers and found in well over 150 shops on the island. All told, these businesses employed more than ten thousand people, and the government really did not want to shut them down. I place much of the blame on Ralph Lauren for not protecting their product trademark early on; most likely they couldn't imagine that the knockoff business would ever grow this big, or perhaps stopping the counterfeiting firms was not cost-effective. I expressed concern about the example this set for AGOA conformity and future offshore companies investing in Mauritius.

It wasn't until the following year, when a *Women's Wear Daily* article by local writer Bambina Wise focused on the Lauren issue and how much the counterfeiting business had grown, that the Ralph Lauren company sent someone to Mauritius to assess the problem. Pushing for closure, Ralph Lauren's senior director of international trademark administration came to see me on May 22, 2003. He seemed ill prepared for the magnitude of the situation: at every meeting, he showed up as if on a beach vacation, wearing a T-shirt, shorts, thong footwear or cowboy boots, and wraparound sunglasses. His long ponytail and earrings stood out amid the sedate suits and ties everyone in business and government wore to meetings. You can imagine the impression it left with the Prime Minister and other government leaders, who may well have thought that Ralph Lauren was not serious in trying to resolve the issue.

Ultimately, Ralph Lauren filed an action to stop manufacturing and distribution under the Polo brand name in Mauritius. However, the driving force was the embassy, which moved the ball forward for them, and I was concerned that we would become the legal enforcement arm for the company, which was not our role. The company's casual approach and the distance might have been contributing factors, as in the end we became more involved, to the point of pressing for immediate action to shut down the manufacturing operations and all of the retail outlets. From reports, I learned the counterfeit textile business accounted for $50 million to $100 million in sales, which were lost to Ralph Lauren. My mission was to protect U.S. business interests, and I could not let go of the matter. We worked directly with the legal system and the police commissioner, and over a period of months the retail stores were raided and shut down. The embassy was not very popular with the Mauritian business community for being so aggressive and involved in this issue.

I suggested the Ralph Lauren attorney work with the local people, since many of the retailers did not know the product was being manufactured illegally and had invested much money in their stores—especially since Ralph Lauren had been lax in not protecting the trademark for so many years. I proposed that Ralph Lauren allow them to phase out their inventory, rather than insist on it being confiscated and destroyed. I also advocated making a donation of the products to poor families in the surrounding villages, which the company ignored but which would have gained them some positive mileage.

Although manufacturing of the Polo line at the time was unauthorized, the quality was exceptionally high. Ralph Lauren could have structured a business plan to produce its product legally in Mauritius for the sub-Saharan Africa market, or worked out a franchise agreement with payment of royalties to Ralph Lauren, either of which would have saved the manufacturing base and small retail shop owners, but I was told the company refused. That was too bad. Winning did not help our image or retain friendships; it merely made the United States look greedy.

Once all the outlet operations were shut down, the Ralph Lauren attorney left Mauritius and the embassy never heard back from the company.

Throughout my service, I found other counterfeit products in Mauritius. Most of these came via South Africa but were manufactured predominantly in China. This is a worldwide problem, so the reader should not come away believing the Mauritians invented this aspect of the underground economy.

Later, I was encouraged by a cable I was able to send to Washington entitled, "Mauritian Retailers Gearing Up to Combat Counterfeiters." Their efforts could help avoid future problems like the Ralph Lauren issue. The Registered Trademark Holders and Retailers Association was newly formed to crack down on counterfeiters; more than twenty members signed up. Their goal was to have three hundred members by late 2003, with potential members carefully scrutinized, and begin their efforts with a consumer awareness program. One of the biggest challenges was convincing taxi drivers, who received 10–20 percent commissions from knockoff retailers for purchases made by customers the drivers delivered to the shops. To combat these problems, hotels were encouraging taxi drivers to turn in others so they could be barred from serving the hotels altogether.

On the evening of August 20, 2002, I attended a reception in honor of the United States having passed the AGOA II provisions on August 6. These provisions resolved the knit-to-shape preferential access issue, affecting millions of dollars of sales for Mauritian textile manufacturers and the other qualifying sub-Saharan African manufacturers. Present that evening were the Prime Minister, Deputy Prime Minister,

Foreign Minister, and Trade Minister as well as other dignitaries, community business leaders, and textile manufacturers. I was surprised when Jayen Cuttaree, the trade minister, credited the embassy for the AGOA II approval. He made mention of the close House vote, 215 to 212, and the telephone calls we had made to Washington on this issue. It is true that one of those calls was to Senator Orrin Hatch, who was from my home state of Utah and also served as the AGOA conference chairman. Orrin promised he would help get votes and support for the bill, since he believed in its importance to sub-Saharan Africa. We both agreed the stumbling block had been Senator Jesse Helms, from North Carolina, who was representing the textile interests in his state.

On August 26, in Washington, I met with Assistant Secretary Walter Kansteiner, Deputy Assistant Secretaries Charlie Snyder and Bob Perry, Director of the Office of East African Affairs Lauren Moriarty, and Desk Officer Blossom Perry to discuss the preparations for the AGOA Forum—and the need for a high-level U.S. delegation, including Secretary of State Colin Powell, U.S. Trade Representative Robert Zoellick, USAID Administrator Andrew Natsios, Agriculture Secretary Ann Veneman, Commerce Secretary Donald Evans, Treasury Secretary Paul O'Neill, National Security Advisor Condoleezza Rice, and a congressional delegation consisting of Trade, Foreign Affairs, Foreign Relations, and Ways and Means committee members.

Since I had the Africa Bureau decision makers together in one room, I used the opportunity to press for more post resources to adequately cover Comoros and Seychelles plus economic matters in Mauritius. What I really wanted was an American Presence Post for both Comoros and Seychelles, but that was quickly shot down. No matter how I pitched it, I felt the request fell on deaf ears; even voicing concern about the influx of terrorists who might use both Comoros and Seychelles as potential safe havens made no difference.

I explained the case of Susanne Rose, our part-time Foreign Service national hire in the Seychelles. She was overworked with all the consular duties as well as overseeing a number of U.S. military ship visits each month. Concerned about her safety, we had authorized a remodel of her offices, putting in more security and special door locks. If we had an American temporary duty officer on duty there with her until the upcoming elections in March 2003, it would have given our embassy valuable information on the country's political situation and the government's attempts to interfere with the opposition candidate's campaign. That suggestion was also shot down.

I mentioned my discussion with U.S. Ambassador Wanda Nesbitt, who had relayed concerns from a meeting she had with Souef El-Amine, the minister of foreign affairs of Comoros, while on a visit to Antananarivo, Madagascar. El-Amine told her about the large number of strange people coming and going in Comoros, attempting to recruit students to go to places such as Iran, Saudi Arabia, and Pakistan. Even with these concerns, the idea of establishing an American Presence Post to have eyes and ears in the host countries went nowhere.

I expressed to Kansteiner my concerns about the sovereignty issue involving Diego Garcia, a subject that came up constantly. I also stressed that the U.S. Embassy in Port Louis should not be categorized as a Special Embassy Program post. Mauritius was one of the few countries in sub-Saharan Africa that was working well, and we needed to do whatever we could to keep it moving forward. In building my case for more people resources, I mentioned that we should not ignore the growing Muslim population in Mauritius, which exceeded 16 percent. Comoros, by contrast, was 99 percent Muslim and was having an influx of Muslim clerics, mostly from Pakistan, whose movements were almost completely unmonitored. I made it clear that the United States needed to commit more human resources to actively engage these countries.

With President Bush planning to head the delegation to the AGOA Forum, I again stressed the need for more temporary duty officer assistance. We also needed to lock in the dates, which we had been telling everyone would be January 13 through 17, 2003. I was assured by Kansteiner's planning team they would press the White House for a firm commitment. I assured everyone that the University of Mauritius was the best site to hold the Forum activities.

In a meeting with Marc Wall, the new director of the Economic Policy Staff at the Africa Bureau, I highlighted the need to send cables to the U.S. embassies in sub-Saharan Africa directing them to work with their commercial section and request that their host country governments send high-level delegations for the ministerial and private sector segments of the Forum.

On Tuesday I met with Jendayi Frazer, special assistant to the president and senior director for African affairs at the National Security Council, and her deputy, Bobby Pittman, to review the AGOA Forum issues and reinforce the need to lock in the Forum dates. Bobby and I then went to the White House Conference Center, where he chaired an interagency meeting and I gave an overview of the current status of the AGOA Forum to representatives of four departments (the Treasury Department missed the meeting). Everyone present assured me that the U.S. agencies would be well represented, and at the highest level. I was also told we would need to supply housing and buses for the two hundred members of the press corps who would be traveling with the President, as well as another thirteen White House press people. Even though we would be reimbursed, I knew this would create another headache for Charlie Slater.

I then spoke with Gloria Cabe of the Corporate Council on Africa, Paul Ryberg, and Peter Craig to discuss getting quality speakers for the private sector part of the Forum. We discussed the Youth Forum, which I felt was a very important component of the activities and which needed leadership to make it successful.

Later that day, I had a meeting with Director Gaddi Vasquez and Chief of Staff Lloyd Pierson of the Peace Corps to ask for their support in Rodrigues, Comoros, and Seychelles. I was told money and people were in short supply and that there was more need in areas such as Madagascar. However, I pressed hard for an assessment team to visit these areas.

That night I flew to New York for a morning meeting with Claude Morel, the Seychelles ambassador to the United States and UN. I reiterated my concerns about possible democracy and human rights violations surrounding threats on the life of the opposition leader, Wavel Ramkalawan. I told Morel that the government needed to provide protection for Ramkalawan. We then discussed the widespread perception that having Mukesh Valabhji at the helm of the Seychelles Marketing Board was responsible for a significant part of the country's hard currency shortage and poor economic policies. I said Seychelles could see severe financial problems and overall stability issues in the next five years. Morel nodded, and it was clear he understood.

A few days later, Morel called to say that he had discussed my concerns with his government and that Foreign Minister Jeremie Bonnelame would like to meet with me in November when I next planned to be in Seychelles.

On my return to Mauritius, I was told Ramkalawan would be protected. I also received a cable regarding the attempted hijacking of an Air Seychelles flight from Mumbai, India. An Indian national had smuggled a knife on board the airplane and wanted the pilot to fly the airplane to eastern Europe. He was subdued by crew members and fellow passengers, and was detained when the airplane landed in the Maldives.

In early September, I learned the Ilois' planned visit to the Chagos Islands had been pushed back, news that relieved me. However, Diego Garcia issues never waned, and I finally decided that since Diego Garcia was under my jurisdiction, with Mauritius making ongoing claims for sovereignty over the Chagos Archipelago, I needed to become more familiar with the area.

On September 12, Eric Kneedler, the embassy CEP officer, sent an e-mail to Charles Gurney in London and Darryll Baker in Manama alerting them of my travel plans, which included Bahrain, Diego Garcia, and Singapore. Charles Gurney knew Diego Garcia was a major issue for our embassy, and in his email to Gurney, Eric brought attention to our tentative plans to visit Diego Garcia. We wanted to arrive in Bahrain on November 4, as that night there would be a military flight going to Diego Garcia. Marcia, Eric, and I would spend two full days there, then fly to Singapore on a military aircraft. During my visit to Bahrain I wanted to have a productive consultation with the Navy's Fifth Fleet on security matters and ship visits to Seychelles and Mauritius. I also wanted to pay a courtesy call on Ambassador Ronald Neumann at the U.S. Embassy in Manama to discuss regional security issues.

Charles Gurney forwarded the email to Damian Leader, a Foreign Service officer at the U.S. Embassy in London who had lead responsibility for the British Indian Ocean Territory. Damian Leader quickly responded, saying that for "the ambassador to visit DGAR or any other bit of the UK, all he has to do is request country clearance, which we will immediately grant."

Therefore, on October 16, Eric sent a cable to all concerned parties, asking for country clearance to visit Bahrain, Diego Garcia, and Singapore. The cable made reference to my top-secret clearance, indicated travel dates, and mentioned the meetings planned in Manama, the orientation visit to Diego Garcia, the security consultations at the U.S. Embassy in Singapore, and a courtesy call on Ambassador Franklin Lavin, an Ambassadorial Seminar classmate.

On October 22 I received a phone call from Lauren Moriarty, director of the Office of East African Affairs, suggesting I consider not going to Diego Garcia. I found this a bit strange, but explained all the weeks of planning and scheduling that had gone into this trip, and that I had received approvals from the United Kingdom and the U.S. Embassy in London. In conclusion, the door was left open.

Since Damian Leader was out of the country, Eric sent another email to Gurney on October 23 requesting the status of our country clearance. Later that day, an email came back from Gurney saying, "I understand this has been cancelled. Correct?" Eric immediately responded that it was not correct, and asked where Charles had heard that information. Several hours later, Gurney replied saying that he had received information that the country clearance request would be withdrawn from the U.K. desk at State.

Here I was, a U.S. ambassador, serving as President Bush's personal representative, coordinating my efforts through Secretary Powell, accredited to three countries and with oversight for Diego Garcia—and now I had been marginalized, presumably by a desk officer. I had already spent countless hours with the government of Mauritius, the U.K. High Commissioner in Mauritius, Foreign Service officers at the U.S. Embassy in London, and the British Foreign Office in briefings on how to deal with the Diego Garcia issues—just to find out that someone at the State Department had unilaterally cut me off at the knees.

Further review with Charles Gurney indicated that someone in the East Africa Bureau had started the cancellation process even before Lauren Moriarty had talked with me on October 22. So in essence we had been spinning our wheels for some time. This was a part of the State Department culture that was of concern to me. In talking with Assistant Secretary Walter Kansteiner on the night of October 23, I discovered that he thought it had been my idea to cancel the trip; yet as Moriarty's boss, he must have known of her phone call to me the previous evening. Now I began wondering whether there was some activity going on at Diego Garcia that an ambassador, even one with a top-secret security clearance, should not see.

I continued dealing with Diego Garcia issues almost daily in my bilateral meetings with the host government. I always said the same thing: that this was strictly an issue between Mauritius and the United Kingdom; the United States used Diego Garcia only as a military base and had a lease there until 2016, with an option to extend until 2036.

Of interest was a report on September 21, 2002, in which the United States requested permission from Britain to base a number of B-2 Stealth bombers on Diego Garcia. I wondered why we had to ask for such permission, since I didn't recall seeing that as a requirement in the lease document.

On September 25, in a meeting with Captain David Savy, the chairman of Air Seychelles, we talked about the hijacking of the flight from Mumbai. Passengers and crew members had subdued the hijacker, a Tamil from India who apparently was a computer programmer. During the fray, his knife injured a stewardess. He was removed in the Maldives and held for interrogation. Questioning did not lead to any connection to al-Qaeda or other terrorist group. We surmised media coverage was his intended goal.

Then Savy brought up the subject of Comoros. An executive of Air Austral, which is based in Réunion and serves Comoros, had told Savy about vocal al-Qaeda sympathizers working on the ramps at the airport. Savy said the government had been informed but had done nothing about investigating these claims, and asked if his Air Seychelles flights should continue serving Comoros under such circumstances. I didn't feel comfortable advising him, but suggested he needed to ascertain how important the route was to his bottom line. Most of the airline's five thousand annual passengers came into Comoros through Paris, France.

I knew Savy was a stepson of President René and had two other brothers who also were involved at high levels in government-controlled entities. He spoke about René, from his humble and very poor childhood to his fight to the top. He also discussed Colonel Payet as a long-standing loyalist going back to René's takeover in 1977. Mukesh Valabhji, the head of the Seychelles Marketing Board, was a relative through marriage and was well connected, coming from a wealthy Indian family involved in the oil business. Savy believed Valabhji's policies could hurt the country, but he noted that René did not like confrontation, and so rarely interferes with him. Also, René's health was currently not good, with problems from years of chain-smoking.

Regarding Wavel Ramkalawan, the opposition leader, Savy said he was volatile and had even been known to get into physical fights with legislators. He felt the threats on Ramkalawan's life were fabricated, and said Vice President Michel would be a better choice to succeed René. Michel and Mukesh did not get along, since Michel's role as finance minister had been handed over to Mukesh. Savy was very open, and I believed at the time that he was sincere. We agreed to talk again after my return from Comoros in September.

{ XIV }

THE UNION OF THE COMOROS

The name Comoros is derived from the Arabic word *kamar* or *kumr*, which means "moon." The "islands of the moon" are a country that the world needs to know better.

In the Comoran language, the title of the country's national anthem, "Udzima ya wa Masiwa," means "The Union of Great Islands." Up until the end of 2002, the three islands of the Union of the Comoros were referred to as the Federal Islamic Republic of the Comoros. This name had been used since independence on July 6, 1975, and was the name of the country throughout the years of political upheaval, anticolonialism, mercenary-abetted coups, and civil unrest as its people struggled toward becoming a democratic society.

The geologic history of the islands of the Comoros Archipelago—including Grande Comore (Njazidja), Anjouan (Nzwani), and Mohéli (Mwali), the three that make up Comoros, and Mayotte (Maori), which is a French overseas collectivity—dates back tens of thousands of years. The islands are primarily basalt from volcanic activity that occurred after the island of Madagascar drifted away from the African continent.

The youngest island in the chain, Grande Comore, is the least vegetated and most rocky because of more recent lava flows. Grand Comore's two volcanoes are the gently rounded, domelike Mt. Karthala, rising 7,748 feet above sea level on the southern end of the island, and the 3,280-foot La Grille.

On April 5, 1977, a massive eruption from Karthala covered the entire village of Singani, sparing only a small school; in the April 17–19, 2005, eruptions, approximately forty thousand Comorians had to be evacuated from the surrounding villages. Eruptions in 2005 and 2006 destroyed a two-mile-long crater lake in the volcano's caldera. Because of the ongoing volcanic activity, less than 45 percent of the island's area is available for agriculture—and much of the arable land is farmed on slopes as steep as 60 degrees.

Anjouan, triangular in shape, has peaks reaching more than 5,000 feet. Anjouan features dense tropical vegetation, dramatic black sand beaches, and beautiful waterfalls and springs; the island's sculpted peaks are often enveloped in clouds.

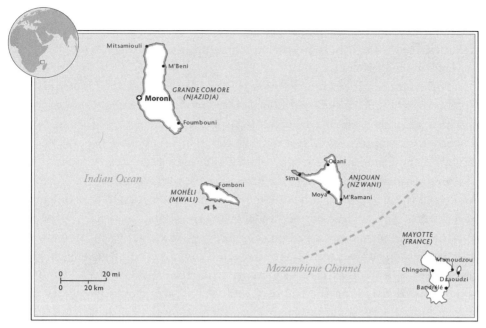

Map 5. Comoros

The smallest of the islands, Mohéli has many rivers, fertile land, and an abundance of coconuts and "perfume trees," or ylang-ylang. The least developed island of the archipelago, its northern coastal plains are home to nearly 85 percent of the island's population.

The French overseas collectivity of Mayotte, shaped like a seahorse, is geologically the oldest island. Surrounded by coral reefs, it offers the richest volcanic soil, the best natural harbors, and an excellent fish population.

The three islands of the Comoros—Grande Comore, Anjouan, and Mohéli—encompass 838 square miles, about half the size of Delaware, and are located in the Indian Ocean 200 miles southeast of Tanzania, separated from the mainland by the Mozambique Channel. The island of Grande Comore lies 300 miles northwest of Madagascar; the Seychelles are 1,000 miles to the northeast, and Mauritius is 1,100 miles to the southeast. Mayotte is 144 square miles, 40 miles southeast of Anjouan.

These islands were thought to have been inhabited as early as the sixth century by Polynesian, Malaysian, and Indonesian traders, who encountered the islands as they extended their empires. Between the ninth and tenth centuries, Swahili settlers found their way to the islands from the east coast of Africa. From the eleventh through the fifteenth centuries, the Comoros Islands were an important stop along early Islamic maritime spice and trade routes. Persian and Shirazi Arab traders founded small towns, introduced Islam to the islands, and, as more people embraced the religion, eventually built mosques. In the sixteenth century, the Portuguese, wanting to establish a trade monopoly in the Indian Ocean, regularly visited the Comoros for food supplies and trade goods. In 1527, Portuguese cartographer Diego Ribero added the islands to European maps of the known world. In the seventeenth and eighteenth centuries, Dutch, English, and French trading ships visited Comoros and the islands of Mauritius and Seychelles.

By the nineteenth century, Sunni Arabs from Iran had a strong foothold in the Comoros, and the Arab influence quickly increased due to nearby Zanzibar, which was then under the Omani Sultanate. In April 1841, French colonialists landing on Mayotte took control from Mayotte's king, Andrian Tsouli. Mayotte was the early capital of the Comoros in French colonial times. In June 1886, Queen Salimba Machimba turned over Mohéli to the French for the island's protection. Sultan Said Ali agreed to French protection of Grande Comore in 1886, and in 1909 Sultan Said Muhamed of Anjouan also stepped aside, giving the French control.

The islands were made a French colony in July 1912; starting in February 1914, the islands were administered by the French colonial governor-general of Madagascar. From September 1942 to October 1946, the islands were under British occupation. Shortly after the end of World War II, the islands went back under French control, with some autonomy given them in 1961.

On July 6, 1975, the Federal Islamic Republic of the Comoros declared its independence from France. However, France did not cede Mayotte with the other islands. The Comoros government continues to press France, directly and through the UN, for sovereignty over Mayotte.

In 1975, Ahmed Abdallah Abderemane became the first President of the Federal Islamic Republic of the Comoros. Abdallah ran a profitable family business exporting sugar, rice, cloves, vanilla, and ylang-ylang. He held numerous political positions and established the Comoros Democratic Union. Abdallah also had social reforms in mind, as well as ideas for modernizing the islands. However, diplomatic relations with France deteriorated. In a coup abetted by the French mercenary soldier of fortune Gilbert Bourgeaud, otherwise known as Colonel Bob Denard, Comorian socialist leader Ali Soilih deposed Abdallah in 1975.

President of the Comoros from 1976 to 1978, Soilih declared the islands to be a democratic, secular, socialist republic. He replaced Arabic script with Swahili writing, reallocated land, closed the civil service, and burned government records. After four attempted coups over thirty months, he was finally taken down in a May 13, 1978, coup led by the notorious Denard. Two months later, Soilih was killed, and Ahmed Abdallah Abderemane was reestablished in the presidency. Once restored to power, Abdallah abolished all existing political parties, including his own, and established the Comorian Union for Progress.

Colonel Bob Denard remained in Comoros as commander of the Presidential Guard and de facto ruler of the country; he eventually married a local woman. Although the mercenary leader lost the support of the French intelligence service in 1981, he managed to remain in charge of the influential Presidential Guard for six more years. Most Comorians wanted Denard to leave, as did France. President Abdallah, reelected in 1987 amid allegations of intimidation and fraud, withdrew his support of Denard and wanted him expelled. Two years later, Abdallah was killed in yet another coup led by the infamous Denard.

In 1989, France again pressured Denard and his men to leave Comoros, and Mohamed Djohar became President. But turbulent times lay ahead, including impeachment proceedings in 1991 and another coup attempt in 1992. Somehow regaining the good graces of France, Denard returned to Comoros in September 1995 and toppled Djohar in still another coup. Djohar fled the country and Denard took control of the islands. But when President Jacques Chirac of France ordered his Special Forces to retake the Comoros Islands, Denard was determined to hold his ground. This time he organized the local military along with his mercenaries for a standoff with the French forces. On October 3, 1995, when faced with battle, Denard realized he was greatly outnumbered. Rather than fight, he surrendered and was taken back to France and jailed.

Returning from exile in January 1996, Djohar resumed his presidency until March 1996, when Mohamed Taki Abdoulkarim was elected president. During his short term—Taki died in November 1998—the islands of Anjouan and Mohéli declared independence from Comoros. On April 30, 1999, five months after Taki's death, Colonel Azali Assoumani overthrew interim President Tadjidine Ben Said Massounde. Aided by the military, Azali took over as president in the islands' eighteenth coup and dissolved the constitution and all state institutions.

On February 17, 2001, representatives of the three islands met in Mohéli and signed the Fomboni Accord, which served as the framework for the Agreement for Reconciliation. A draft constitution, published in September 2001 and agreed on December 23, 2001, provided for the election of a Union president, island presidents, and national and island assemblies; each island had semi-autonomy. The constitution was then ratified and accepted by majority vote in a referendum by all three islands.

The constitution provides that the presidency of the Union of the Comoros will rotate between the three islands every four years. The Union controls foreign affairs, collects taxes and distributes funds, provides for defense, establishes the judicial system, and oversees religious issues. However, implementing a system of government with a clear separation of power between the three island governments and the Union government proved difficult. Concerns included the sharing of customs revenues, budget oversight, and island police forces, with a separate army defense force controlled by the Union. (After many months of negotiations and with the help of several members of the African Union, an agreement was signed in December 2003 between all the island parties agreeing to the separation of powers, although these issues continued to fester for some time thereafter.)

The Union presidential election was held in March and April 2002. On April 14, 2002, Colonel Azali Assoumani, supported by his political party, the Convention pour la Renaissance des Comores (CRC), was declared the winner of the election, with 75 percent of the votes in what was deemed a fair election by independent observers. He became President of the Union of the Comoros on May 26, 2002.

Elections for the presidencies of the Union of the Comoros and the islands took place from March to May 2002, at about the time I arrived in Mauritius. During my first visit to Comoros, for the presentation of my credentials to Union President Azali, I had planned to meet with the three island presidents, which included President El Bak of Grande Comore, President Bacar of Anjouan, and President Fazul of Mohéli. Bacar clearly wanted to establish his own identity outside the Union framework, and it was he who had led a separatist movement before the three islands were reunified in 2002 under the newly adopted constitution. Unfortunately, he was attending meetings in Paris at the time I arrived on the islands.

On September 28, Marcia, Bisa Williams, and I flew to Moroni, the capital of Grande Comore. Since there were no direct flights from Mauritius, we made two brief stops, one in Réunion and a second at Mayotte, before arriving at Prince Said Ibrahim International Airport. We were greeted by Ismail Chanfi, the secretary general in the Ministry of Foreign Affairs, who provided us with cars and drivers during our official visit. While waiting for our bags in the small VIP lounge, I was introduced to the French and Chinese ambassadors, who were just returning from trips abroad.

Soon we were off to the Itsandra Hotel, located halfway around the island on the west coast. The American flag anchored to the fender mast of the ambassador's car was straining as we sped along. It was a terrifying ride—we traveled at speeds exceeding 80 mph on the narrow two-lane road, which had not seen asphalt repairs in years. We barely missed gaping chuckholes and head-on traffic, let alone the people and animals crossing everywhere. We passed through several small but heavily populated villages where such speeds were not appreciated. There I was, the U.S. ambassador on my first visit to the country, scaring the villagers with our reckless driving. I tried to communicate with the driver and ask him to slow down, but the few words I could understand led me to believe his superiors had given him orders to get us to the hotel as quickly as possible. With our seatbelts tightened snugly, Marcia looked at me with dismay. Bouncing back and forth, I became dizzy; I had to close my eyes periodically to keep from getting nauseated.

Most of the way, the shoreline was rocky, with volcanic outcrops and signs of recent lava flows interspersed with short stretches of sandy beach. Few tracts of arable land were visible from the road, although coconut palms were abundant. The humid atmosphere encouraged sporadic patches of vegetation that clung to the volcanic landscape. Mangrove stands lined the sandy areas along the coast. I later learned that the island and its waters are home to more than five hundred species of plants, twenty-one species of bird, twelve species of mammals (including three species of fruit bats), more than ten species of reptiles, and "Old Four Legs," the endangered prehistoric fish called the coelacanth. The Comoros and neighboring Madagascar shared similar flora and fauna, including the famous Indri lemurs, which live in the Andasibe National Forest in Madagascar and have a small number of cousins in the Comoros.

On our drive from the airport, signs of poverty were visible everywhere. Most of the existing housing consisted of partially completed concrete and metal structures with small walled-off living areas. Reinforcing bars protruded from many of the unfinished structures. The houses appeared as if they had been under construction for years. In time, I discovered that more than eighty thousand Comorians resided in France, and that Comorians back home were often dependent upon remittances received from their relatives living and working abroad. They would use some of the money for the construction of homes that overseas family members planned to live in when they came back to the islands.

I was pleasantly surprised to see that most Comorians did have shelter, even if it meant these unfinished structures. Some of the more fortunate Comorians lived on main roads and had a small retail shop attached to their living quarters from which they could make a living.

The Comoros's population is nearly 99 percent Sunni Muslim, and most men wore neatly pressed white or beige cotton *gallabiya* robes, pants, and matching embroidered hats called *kofia*. The women wore brightly colored sari-style *shiromani* dresses with matching head wraps. Many women applied *msinzano*, a paste of ground sandalwood and coral mixed with water, to their faces. This cosmetic not only was considered to enhance beauty but tended to keep their skin soft and protected from the sun's harmful rays.

Finally, our driver slowed down and delivered us safely to our destination. The Itsandra Hotel with its fifty rooms was one of the few on Grande Comore that had access to the beach. The hotel manager, who was from Mauritius, greeted us upon our arrival. We could see at once that this grand hotel, once operated by the Sofitel chain, showed signs of age, lacking proper maintenance and repairs. Adjacent to the lobby, foundations had been poured for the construction of additional rooms, but it appeared that work had stopped some time ago. Tourism should have been the hallmark of the Comoros economy, as was the case in Mauritius and Seychelles. However, most of the better sandy beaches on Grande Comore, Anjouan, and Mohéli are found in undeveloped areas and are not readily accessible without some infrastructure improvements being made.

With the country's unstable economy and lack of tourists and destination resorts, hard currency was in short supply. The Comorian franc (KMF) was weak, valued at 500 KMF to $1 in 2002 (and currently still around 400 KMF to $1).

Until recently, another hotel, the 180-room Le Galawa beach resort on Grande Comore, had been successfully operated by Sun International Hotels in partnership with its sister company, Sun Resorts of Mauritius. But in November 2000 it was sold to a South African hotel operator. When these new owners became embroiled in a dispute with the government shortly after, the hotel was shut down. The long period of dormancy had taken its toll on the buildings, and a major infusion of capital for renovations would be necessary. Le Galawa and the Itsandra Hotel were now owned by the government, and under the difficult financial conditions, the Itsandra struggled just to stay open. Although there were several small bed-and-breakfast accommodations converted from family residences, at the time of our visit the Itsandra Hotel and Hotel Le Moroni in the capital were the only two full-service hotels with some resort amenities and beach access.

Volatile politics, an unsteady economy, and the country's inaccessibility have meant that tourism faces many challenges in Comoros. And on November 24, 1996, an Ethiopian Airlines jet carrying 175 people was hijacked over East Africa and ran out of fuel while flying over Grande Comore; the jet crashed into the ocean some 200 yards from Le Galawa, killing fifty-eight. That event sent shock waves through the hotel industry and severely affected the island's tourism. In 2003 there were fewer than nineteen thousand visitors to Comoros.

Later, on September 12, 2007, I would see an article in *EconNews* reporting that Dubai World, wholly owned by the government of Dubai, intended to invest $70 million to redevelop Le Galawa into a first-class 150-room beach resort, with spa, restaurants, water sports, and other amenities. One hundred residential villas were to be built adjacent to the resort. This partnership between Comoros and Dubai offered significant opportunities, and I was most happy for the Comorians. I was also pleased for the current President, Ahmed Abdallah Mohamed Sambi, and former President Azali Assoumani, who both had worked hard to get foreign direct investment (FDI) into this fledging democracy. The U.S. government, I felt, could have done more to help find similar investors for Comoros, since the potential was there. However, Comoros carried the stigma of being linked to al-Qaeda terrorists, which served as an impediment. Now that Comoros was gaining major FDIs from a Middle East country such as the powerful Dubai, the United States should consider establishing a presence in Comoros beginning with an American Presence Post and in years to come a permanent diplomatic mission.

The United States had had many warnings from the Comoros government that large numbers of foreigners and radical Islamic clerics were traveling to and from the Comoros in the 1990s. Knowing this, I wanted to meet with various government, business, and Muslim leaders as well as people associated with local nongovernmental organizations, to acquaint myself with the potential threats from this influx. I also wanted to know more about Fazul Abdullah Mohammed, one of the most hunted al-Qaeda terrorists, who was raised on Grande Comore.

Like many other young children, Fazul attended madrassas, or Koranic schools, which I was told receive no oversight from the government. Fazul was recruited by Islamic imams (preachers) in his hometown, Moroni, to study in Pakistan. Ostensibly, his family had sent him to study computer science, but ultimately he made his way instead to Afghanistan to train in terrorism with Osama bin Laden and al-Qaeda. Fazul then went to Kenya, with occasional trips to Tanzania and Somalia to help train and establish terrorist cells. Fazul planned the 1998 bombings of the U.S. Embassy in Nairobi, Kenya, and the U.S. Embassy in Dar es Salaam, Tanzania.

This terrorist (sometimes referred to as Haroun Fazul) became a top aide of bin Laden. He was also reported to be responsible for the November 28, 2002, bombing of the Israeli-owned Paradise Hotel in Kikambala, a beach resort fifteen miles north of Mombasa in southeastern Kenya, and the attempted surface-to-air missile attack on a Boeing 757 operated by the Israeli-owned charter company Arkia as it was leaving Mombasa.

I was told Fazul had returned to Comoros on August 14, 1998, a week after the embassy bombings, to hide out with his family. He could have been easily captured, since the government of Comoros invited the FBI to come to the island to apprehend him. By the time the FBI finally responded—three weeks later—Fazul had already fled the country. A slightly built man trained as an explosives expert, Fazul was said to have eluded capture by being a disguise expert, sometimes masquerading as a woman. He is on the list of the ten most wanted terrorists.

Between 2000 and 2001, a local judge in Moroni assigned to the Fazul case gleaned information that Fazul was periodically speaking to his wife on a neighbor's telephone. With no structure put in place by the United States for intelligence gathering, this critical information did not reach the right ears. If we had had an active diplomatic presence in Comoros at the time, the FBI and other agencies could have taken effective action, possibly leading to the capture of Fazul.

During scheduled meetings with the Comoros government leaders, I wanted to inquire about Fazul's whereabouts. But I felt uncomfortable asking questions at the time: I had been told that Comorians are a very close-knit, loyal group. Because I did not know how Fazul's family—his wife, children, parents, and other relatives still living in Grande Comore—was woven into Comorian society, I decided not to probe into his whereabouts. It was important, however, to find Fazul before he had a chance to do more damage.

On March 20, 2003, a cable arrived from the regional security officer at the U.S. Embassy in Antananarivo alleging, among other things, that al-Qaeda operatives were moving through Comoros and Seychelles. As many as two hundred foreigners were in Comoros, including a large number in Mohoro, a small village on Grande Comore. They were reported to be staying at the mosques and madrassas recently established in Mohoro.

I had known about the reported activities at the mosques and madrassas from my visits to Comoros. Now, this cable from another embassy validated some of the reports. I wondered whether Fazul Abdullah Mohammed might be one of the infiltrators.

Information about Fazul's whereabouts reached me on several occasions during my ambassadorship. We passed along to Washington information about Fazul's

plans to travel to Comoros for a family visit, to come to the country for a family funeral, and to visit Mahajanga, a town of ninety thousand Comorians located on the
northwest coast of Madagascar, a few hours by boat from the Comoros Islands.
From various other sources we learned Fazul had another wife in this town (and as
recently as February 2007, the local newspaper *Midi Madagasikara* reported that
Fazul had been seen there.)

On yet another occasion we reported that a watch salesman was coming from
Pakistan to Moroni to deliver a message from Fazul to his family, and we included
an itinerary and the flights he would be taking. Some of this information might have
presented an opportunity to capture Fazul.

When we forwarded any of this information on to Washington, it was not considered credible. The people we informed did not believe Fazul traveled to Comoros
to visit his family. Thus they did not follow up on any of our leads. I felt these contacts
considered me an alarmist. My predecessor told me he had had a similar experience.

I believed differently, and pressed the embassy's regional security officer to
obtain funding from the Bureau of Diplomatic Security for instituting a Rewards
for Justice program. The bureau also agreed to pay for the printing of large posters
with Fazul's picture and a photo taken of the bombed embassies set against a bright
red background to draw attention. We attached a large number of these posters to
telephone poles and placed many inside shop windows around Grand Comore. We
also distributed thousands of matchbooks with Fazul's picture on the cover. Boldly
printed in black letters was the information that a $5 million reward would be given
for information leading to his capture. Candidly, I would have offered twice that
amount if I thought we would get the Comorians' attention; I knew they were a
close-knit Arab Muslim society, and for them to consider turning in Fazul, it might
take a higher amount as an inducement. Also, Comorians expressed skepticism that
the United States would actually pay this amount to anyone. The United States really needed to maintain a constant presence in the Comoros and work with the
Comorians to build a relationship of trust, as this was the only answer in the long
run. Dealing long distance by telephone would lead to a less than desirable result.

Also, there were many Comorians living along the east coast of Africa and on
the islands of Zanzibar and Pemba. Some of these people could possibly have been
recruited to track Fazul and lead us to him. It would have been a smart idea to have
some money ready in exchange for information, as a good-faith gesture. The bottom
line was that we needed to have an active presence throughout the region if we were
going to develop friends and build lasting trust. But this did not seem to be a priority for the United States.

I suppose I should not have been surprised. The United States was unprepared
for the embassy bombings in 1998 and the attacks of September 11, 2001. Despite cables from Ambassador Prudence Bushnell to the State Department in 1996 regarding
the security of the U.S. Embassy in Nairobi and an assessment by General Anthony C.

Zinni in early 1998 noting that the embassy would be an easy target for terrorists, the State Department did not consider either Nairobi or Dar es Salaam high-risk areas and took no action. And I believe the FBI, CIA, and other U.S. agencies had ample evidence that al-Qaeda had training operations inside the United States, with operatives moving in and out of the country freely. Even long before the attacks, in the early 1990s, we had numerous opportunities to capture Fazul's mentor, Osama bin Laden, in Sudan, but did not. Then bin Laden began issuing communiqués declaring jihad against the United States. We cannot say we were not forewarned.

The United States recognized Comoros as a sovereign state in 1977 and opened a U.S. embassy there in 1983. A decade later, however, the embassy was closed. The State Department then developed an out-of-country accreditation program, whereby the ambassador would make periodic visits while residing in another country.

With such a cutback, U.S. bilateral relations with Comoros became almost nonexistent, as did in-country reporting and intelligence gathering. The establishment of the U.S. Virtual Embassy (VE) program precluded Comorians from having direct contact with the U.S. Embassy in Mauritius, which was located more than a thousand miles away. Phone calls were expensive, and a call often was answered by a time-consuming automated message. Information about visas and travel to the United States was posted on a VE Internet site, but it was often impractical to find a computer in a village with an unpredictable electricity supply.

To make matters worse, since 9/11 traveling to the United States had become significantly more complicated. Each person traveling to the States first had to visit the U.S. Embassy in Port Louis for a personal interview and fingerprinting. (Eventually the Comoros portfolio was moved to the embassy in Madagascar, but that was still a distance of almost 600 miles to travel for an interview. As of November 2006, all visa applicants had to complete the application form and schedule a visa appointment online. And then on January 1, 2008, the application fees went up 30 percent, to $131—a huge amount for Comorians who lived on less than $2 a day.)

After 1993, when the embassy in Comoros was shuttered, several U.S. government agencies did continue with some positive aid programs until the 1999 short-lived coup rattled the stability of the island. The United States then mandated sanctions against Comoros under Section 508 of the Foreign Operations Appropriations Act, which banned all aid to any state whose duly elected head of government was overthrown; aid could be restored only after a democratically elected government had taken office. Only minor humanitarian assistance was provided while the sanctions were in effect, in addition to any provided by private charitable organizations.

A larger issue was the budget cuts that short-circuited our ability to monitor terrorist activity. By closing diplomatic missions and cutting the positions of experienced multilingual officers just to save money, we lost intelligence-gathering capability in the Horn of Africa and East Africa, where the United States had been attacked by terrorists and the risk of radical Islam spreading was real.

Furthermore, USAID, the U.S. Information Agency, and the Peace Corps suffered severe budget cuts as well. All these agencies had programs that were success stories in sub-Saharan Africa. In Comoros, Peace Corps volunteers were making a difference in the impoverished country. They had helped some people find ways to put food on their table and work themselves out of their poverty trap and onto the road of economic progress. The volunteers had seen progress and did not want to leave, but had to when the Peace Corps program was ended in the Comoros.

U.S. funding for secular education, books, and libraries provided an important alternative for many young people yearning for an education they could use to find a decent job, make a living, and ultimately raise a family. But when this funding was cut, many turned to another option: receiving the religious teachings of radical imams in madrassas, which would keep them uninformed, impoverished, and in need.

The United States cannot expect democracy to take hold unless we offer our assistance and become part of the democratic process. For Comoros to succeed, mentors are needed to establish a sound educational system, deal with health care issues, and become involved in the development of sustainable economic programs. Most important, I believe the United States, which abounds in ingenuity and resources, should have pursued a more active role in helping this country prosper. Such aid gives people hope and combats radical imams' indoctrination of susceptible Muslims.

On several occasions during my diplomatic service, I told people in Washington that the closing of the U.S. Embassy in Comoros had served only to open the door to radical Islam. One need only look at Somalia: in 1991, the U.S. Embassy closed its doors in Mogadishu, allowing al-Qaeda operatives to move in and operate unimpeded. Or Sudan: we closed the U.S. embassy in Khartoum out of fear in 1996, and thenceforth terrorist groups operated freely there. A former Foreign Service officer who was the Somalia country-watcher in the mid-1990s and a former diplomat who was the Sudan country-watcher agreed that information gathering was difficult under the best of circumstances but would have been more accurate had the United States kept a presence in these countries.

I believe the United States erred in not having a diplomatic presence in the Comoros, with a population of 600,000 Muslims in 2003. Although Comoros is much smaller than Somalia, with its 9 million Muslims, and Sudan, with its 29 million Muslims, we need to remember it takes only one terrorist to inflict enormous damage on the United States.

Several hours after settling in at the Itsandra Hotel, I met with Vice President Ben Said Massoudi, who was also minister of home affairs and minister of religion, and

Ismail Chanfi, the secretary general in the Ministry of Foreign Affairs, who at times helped out as our interpreter. Bisa Williams and Mohamed Elhad, our part-time Foreign Service national embassy representative who dealt with consular matters and also owned a local accounting firm, were present as well. This would be my first interface with government leaders where I would be depending upon language translation—and it was at this meeting that I began to learn the importance of communicating through eye contact and body language. Fortunately, both Bisa and Elhad spoke fluent French.

I opened the conversation with a discussion of stability, good governance, democracy, transparency, and the rule of law, though I refrained from addressing religious freedom issues. I then became more specific and asked about the numerous strangers who were coming from Yemen, Saudi Arabia, Iran, and Pakistan. Living in mosques in the villages and teaching in the madrassas, these extreme fundamentalists were offering scholarships to a generation of young students to travel to other countries for further education—the kind of training that could lead to a radical form of fundamentalist Islamic indoctrination and activity.

I immediately sensed that Chanfi was uncomfortable relaying my remarks to Massoudi, who quickly retorted by saying that if we had specific information, they would check it out. I explained that the information had come from within their government. Massoudi hesitated briefly and then told me that they had heard such people were in the country, but they could not discern what their purpose was other than teaching the Koran and educational subjects.

I spoke of our concerns about questionable people using the islands as a safe haven and their involvement in possible money laundering through the banking system. As Massoudi was about to respond, the power went out and the air conditioner shut down. We sat for several minutes in the dark as the room quickly became stale and humid. I decided that we could not say much more, so in conclusion I told Massoudi that their upcoming elections for the National Assembly would send an important message to the United States regarding the country's democratic process.

Back at the Itsandra Hotel, we discussed the meeting, feeling uncertain whether anything would change. I was determined to work with the government of Comoros on these issues. My mission as U.S. ambassador was fourfold: (1) to help fully engage the Union of the Comoros and aid this fledgling democracy; (2) to strive to find meaningful funding for economic development and mentoring programs that could reduce poverty in Comoros; (3) to lessen the influence of radical Islamists who had taken over the teaching of so many of the islands' youth; and (4) to find Fazul Abdullah Mohammed.

That night I hosted a dinner for several American citizens and their children living in the Comoros Islands. They were all part of the Africa Inland Mission of Pearl River, New York, a Christian faith-based organization known for its humanitarian aid around the world. They had signed up to serve in Comoros for a minimum of three years (some had been there for ten), living among the villagers, working

with young people in the areas of education and sports, and giving free medical assistance to the villagers. Several were doctors who regularly helped out at the local
hospitals and clinics; one was a physiotherapist who worked with injured and handicapped individuals in rehabilitation programs. They were all well-educated, decent,
caring, and loving family people. *What a great experience for these children to be here
with them,* I thought.

During dinner, they reinforced the concerns voiced by many Comorian parents about the number of strangers coming to Grande Comore and indoctrinating their children in radical fundamentalist Islamic doctrine. They told me that
while these clerics could easily blend in among the Muslim communities, they
instead kept mostly to themselves, living in madrassas and mosques around the
island and seeking out impressionable children from the surrounding areas. With
so many coming and going, it was difficult to figure out who they were and what
was their intent.

On Sunday morning, September 29, Marcia and I took a stroll on the beach
adjacent to the Itsandra Hotel and ran again into the Mauritian hotel manager. We
talked about how, over the years, large numbers of people had migrated to Comoros
from the east coast of Africa and subsequently converted to Islam. These new residents by and large came from an easygoing tribal society, and only a few were fundamentalist in their Islamic beliefs. However, he believed that African Arabs had
deep Islamic roots and were particularly susceptible to fundamentalist doctrines,
especially the poorer ones, who had little hope for prospects to achieve an economic
future.

The hotel manager had been on the island for almost fourteen years and appeared to have a good grasp of the country's economy. He warned that if a solid
economic base was not established in the next five years, the Islamic fundamentalist
movement could become a very strong and dangerous influence. He offered little
hope of a future for the young people, since many were getting advanced indoctrination in Arab countries, and those in Comoros were aided by several Arab charities,
such as the Saudi-based al-Haramain Islamic Foundation, that were constructing
and financially supporting a number of madrassas and mosques.

Opportunities for secular education in France and the United States had ceased
for students coming from Comoros, presumably due to terrorism concerns. The
hotel manager and his wife, who was from South Africa, had helped send several
students to South Africa and Kenya for a university education. I hoped others would
follow—and that they would return to their home country afterward, since staying
abroad would adversely affect the country's economic growth and deprive the islands
of educated people.

On September 30, we went to the Presidential Palace for the formal presentation of
my credentials to President Azali Assoumani. With our assigned police escort, we

again raced through the villages at high speeds. Marcia and Bisa, in another vehicle behind me, later said they were frightened by the thought that if my driver braked suddenly, their car would run into mine.

But we arrived safely at the President's gated compound. The grounds were surrounded by a ten-foot-high wall with architectural metal spears on top to deter unwelcome visitors. Inside the complex, the buildings were surrounded by modest landscaping and decently maintained.

We were ushered to a long covered walkway with a red carpet runner, lined on both sides with a military honor guard standing at full attention. At the entrance to the building were two giant, intricately carved wooden doors. The chief of protocol led us into the reception area, where we waited for ten minutes, which seemed like an eternity. I did not know what to expect, and the suspense gave me a cold chill.

Suddenly a second set of heavy doors swung open, and I peered into a sixty-foot-long gold-carpeted ballroom with walls covered in brightly colored fabric and the ceiling adorned with crystal chandeliers. Standing at the far end of the room, near a microphone, was President Azali. He was a well-dressed, slightly built, balding man in his mid-forties. Near him were several other well-dressed men—some attired in Western-style suits, others in *gallabiya* robes—who were cabinet ministers and government officials. I took a place on one side of the microphone, a short distance from the President, and Marcia and Bisa were asked to stand by my side. The chief of protocol then motioned for me to present my credentials to President Azali.

14.1. Military honor guard on the way to present ambassadorial credentials to President Azali Assoumani, September 2002.

By now, having gone through similar ceremonies in Mauritius and Seychelles, I had the words memorized.

Bisa was asked to repeat my remarks in French for President Azali. He responded with a five-minute speech in French, Bisa whispering the English translation in my ear. Gazing around the room, I studied the people. It was difficult to comprehend the upheaval that many of them must have gone through with the numerous coups since 1975. They all looked like gentle, peaceful men, including Azali. And as I was introduced to the twenty or so leaders, I firmly grasped the hand of each one and wondered who came from Swahili Africa, which one had an Arab lineage, and who was of Asian or European ancestry. The President then asked everyone in the entourage to leave except Fakridine Mahamoud, his chief of staff and head of the army; Msaidie Houmed, the minister of budgets; and Ben Massoundi, with whom I had already met.

After some light conversation, I thanked Azali for his remarks about wanting to have more of a relationship with the United States. We sat for a while in the ornate room and touched upon a number of subjects, from stability to security concerns and ways of expanding the Comorian economy. I broached the issues of terrorism, border control, visa and passport control, the increased transiting of foreigners, and the radical teachings and the recruitment of young students. I was careful not to bring up Fazul's name, as I wasn't certain where Azali or some of the other government leaders stood on the issue—or even if they personally knew Fazul or his whereabouts.

Since our conversation was going well, I brought up the constitution and the proposed amendments that covered the reconciliation issues between the island presidents. We discussed the assembly elections, scheduled to be held before the end of the year, and I expressed the hope they would have wide participation. I encouraged him to work closely with the island presidents on good governance and cooperation, with the hope that everyone would stick to their agreement to maintain the Union.

Under the Union Constitution, each of the three islands would elect a president, but overall allegiance would be to the elected Union President, who would serve one four-year term, while the island presidents would serve one five-year term. Successive Union presidents would rotate during each election cycle, representing the other two islands respectively.

In reality, however, each island president wanted powers equal to those of the President of the Union. Each one wanted his own *gendarmerie*, or police force, and a standing army. Each wanted control of his island's budget and to collect customs duties and taxes assessed on income. And each wanted the right to engage in direct bilateral discussions with other country governments. A particular source of frustration for Azali was that Anjouan President Mohamed Bacar was having direct bilateral discussions regularly with France.

In the meeting, I mentioned the recent hijacking of an Air Seychelles flight in the Maldives. I also talked about the loading ramp personnel at the airport who were possibly al-Qaeda sympathizers, and the effect on airline companies, who were considering curtailing flights if they didn't feel safe landing in Comoros. I had already expressed such concerns to Ahmed Mohamed, the director of ground handling, at the international airport. Even though Mohamed was an independent operator, the Comoros government held part ownership and was responsible also for safety. The President indicated that he did not want any interruption in airline service; he understood what such drastic steps would mean for access to the island. He agreed to review the validity of the airlines' claims.

As our conversation was drawing to an end, I brought up the talking points regarding the Article 98 nonsurrender agreement, which would shield U.S. military personnel operating in foreign countries from prosecution by the International Criminal Court. Undersecretary for Arms Control and International Security John Bolton had been pressing to obtain at least ninety countries as signatories to this agreement before the deadline of July 1, 2003, and had been personally calling ambassadors to urge them to press their host countries to sign the Article 98 Agreement. We also were to urge them not to sign the Rome Statute of the International Criminal Court, or if they had already signed—as Comoros had—not to ratify the treaty. Each of the three small sovereign states I covered had a vote at the UN General Assembly, equal to the vote of any of the larger members.

I did not like having to convey to the host countries the veiled threat that failure to go along with the United States on this matter would result in loss of International Military Education and Training (IMET) funding and other military program funding to the host countries. However, IMET funding had already been withheld for several years from Comoros under the imposed Section 508 sanctions, so this poor country had nothing to begin with. What we were recklessly withholding was simply our friendship—so where was the bargaining chip?

I already thought that since Comoros was moving forward as a democracy, with the island presidents and the Union President working out their power-sharing arrangements, cutting off IMET funds (which were only $100,000 to $150,000) was foolish. Even this small amount, along with other reinstated programs, would have helped the country to build upon its recent successes, ensure the long-term stability of the country, and strengthen our efforts in the global war on terror. The April 2002 elections had been deemed fair by international observers, and any further "punishment" by the United States would do more harm than good. It was critical that Comoros not end up as another failed state in sub-Saharan Africa.

(In June 29, 2007, I noted on the website of the State Department's Bureau of Political-Military Affairs how the United States perceived our engagement of the impoverished country of Comoros, and why China and other countries were making friends there and other areas in sub-Saharan Africa. According to the Bureau, the primary U.S. national interests in the Union of the Comoros were promoting democracy and strengthening international counterterrorism cooperation. They emphasized "re-educating military factions that have grown accustomed to participating in recurring cycles of armed insurrection is one of the greatest challenges in Comoros." They stressed that the IMET programs would continue to "help build a professional military that respects civilian rule," and the courses listed included "professional military education and training on civil-military relations, military justice, and defense resources management." What the State Department website failed to mention was the key issue of promoting economic development in Comoros, important because of the linkage between prosperity and political stability. Obviously, any progress in eradicating poverty, improving health care, bettering educational opportunities, implementing sustainable development, and offering small business mentoring would help resolve some of our concerns in Comoros.)

Ultimately, the Article 98 agreement would be signed by Comoros on June 30, 2004. Seychelles signed on June 4, 2003, and Mauritius on June 25, 2003. John Bolton personally thanked me for helping him to meet and then exceed his goal—a total of ninety-five countries signed the Article 98 agreement after the deadline was extended.

I could see Azali was becoming uncomfortable. Since this was our first meeting, I did not want to wear out my welcome.

As we concluded, President Azali asked if I could set up a meeting with President Bush and Secretary Powell. I told him I would pass on the message to Washington. Then we moved out to the portico, where newspaper photographers snapped several photos of us that appeared the following day on the front page of the

14.2. Group photo after presentation of credentials: President Azali Assoumani, Vice President Ben Said Massoudi, cabinet ministers, Ambassador Price, Marcia, and Bisa Williams, among others, September 30, 2002.

state-owned newspapers, *Al-Watwan* and *La Gazette de Comores*. Undoubtedly these gave Azali some political mileage, which he needed.

As we shook hands and said goodbye, I assured him we would work closely together, and that the embassy staff would visit Comoros on a regular basis. My goal was to build a close relationship with Comoros. I knew it was important to have the sanctions lifted as soon as possible, but I needed the full support of the State Department. As the personal representative of President Bush, I felt I had the ability to open some doors in Washington.

Our convoy left the Presidential Palace compound to head back to Moroni, sirens blaring. Many people came out of their houses to see what was going on, and stood dangerously close to the passing vehicles. I was uncomfortable with this—and could just see the headlines if we had hit someone.

As we passed through one village after another, I was pleasantly surprised to see several older Muslim men and young boys saluting the American flag as we drove by.

We arrived back at the hotel, and since our afternoon was open, I decided to visit some of the nearby village agricultural operations and some local business enterprises. Observing these narrow roads, some barely passable and most in need of repair, I realized they were certainly not conducive for transportation of perishable agricultural products. The services and infrastructure in the villages were marginal at best, with 80 percent of the population living without indoor running water, toilets, or electricity. As more people became unable to make a living in the rural villages, they crowded into the already congested urban areas of Grande Comore, which presented another host of issues.

At the time, 600,000 Muslims were living on the three islands. Less than 50 percent were educated, and then only to the ninth grade. Unemployment was a major factor, and 15–20 percent of the adult population did not have a job. In rural parts of the three islands, unemployment ranged between 30 and 50 percent. While 80 percent of the Comorians were involved in agriculture, the sector accounted for 40 percent of GDP. Hence infrastructure, such as good road access to arable land, was very important. Yet in this poor country, Comorians first had to grow enough food to satisfy their own basic needs before they could focus on cash crops for export.

As we drove around Grande Comore, visiting some of the arable land areas located in the higher valleys, we saw land rich with volcanic soil where farming was done on slopes as steep as 60 degrees. Passing through a forest, we saw trees up to twelve inches in diameter that appeared to have been randomly cut down. It was apparent that excessive logging was destroying this beautiful, pollution-free, semi-rain-forest area. Reforestation of the logged-out areas was not taking place; in 2002, less than 30 percent of the original forest areas still remained. If trees continue to be cut down at that rate, the remaining forest areas will disappear within twenty years. Mentoring by U.S. timber experts could help the government of Comoros establish a conservation and reforestation program and develop a sustainable logging program, to the benefit of current and future generations.

In addition to the poor roads, there was no public transportation system linking the villages. Local taxis were the main mode of transportation. People would share them—sometimes squeezing six to eight people into each taxi. Again, American transportation know-how could make a difference in helping to solve that problem.

Our tour, which lasted several hours, was enlightening. Back at the hotel, I spent an hour alone reflecting on the day's events.

A majority of Comorians are subsistence farmers, and only a few are able to export their products for hard currency. Based upon a 2006 Thompson Corporation report, the U.S. CIA reported that Comoros GDP in 2001 was $424 million or a GDP per capita of $710 based on the population of 600,000. For the same period, the U.S. Embassy in Port Louis reported the GDP per capita as $360, based on a population of 660,000. The Comoros government indicated the population in 2003 to be closer to 576,000. The *CIA World Factbook* listed a GDP per capita of $600 for 2005. The World Bank pegged it at $660 for 2006, while the State Department reported a 2006 GDP per capita of $720, based on a population of 690,000.

The poor living conditions that I saw suggest that the embassy's lower GDP figure of $360 was much closer to reality. To make my case in Washington, I would use this figure, rounding it up to $400, which equated to slightly more than $1.00 per day.

The fluctuations in the GDP figures are the result of not knowing the exact amount of cash remittances from relatives living overseas, and of differences in population figures. According to the United Nations, 2001 remittances from the 150,000 Comorians living abroad amounted to $26 million or $43 per capita, while foreign assistance, mainly from France, China, and the United Arab Emirates, amounted to $48 per capita. The World Bank reported that 2001 household per capita consumption was $394, slightly more than $1 per day. At the time, approximately 60 percent of Comorians had incomes below the poverty level.

I would be encouraged to see a slight improvement by 2004, when the poverty level numbers fell to 50 percent. When you start at the level of $1 per day to live on, any improvement makes a significant difference. It is this poverty that makes it attractive for imams to preach their radical Islamic ideology and have great influence over the younger segment of the population on these islands.

During this first trip to Comoros, we decided to take the opportunity to present the cash awards for the 2002 Ambassador's Special Self-Help and Human Rights and Democracy programs, and visit several of the village projects funded by these programs. The small amount of money infused into village-based groups was very meaningful, helping people develop craft skills and creating jobs. Several of the Ambassador's Special Self-Help projects involved the processing of ylang-ylang, vanilla, and cloves, which were the country's main hard currency agricultural exports.

The archipelago is the world's leading producer of ylang-ylang, used in the manufacture of perfume, and the world's second-largest producer of high-quality vanilla. The islands also export cinnamon, copra, bananas, cassava, and coconuts.

During my time there, these products accounted for 40 percent of GDP, while business operations (including perfume distillation) represented 4 percent and the services and hospitality sectors totaled 56 percent.

Ylang-ylang exports accounted for 70 percent of world market supplies in the 1990s, but by 2004 output had declined by half, to thirty-five tons. Fluctuations in demand in the world commodity markets caused a drop in the price of vanilla from over $300 per kilogram in 2003 to under $50 in 2005. This decrease in demand was due to increased use of artificial flavors.

One problem facing Comorian agriculture producers is their traditional dependence on independent agents or brokers, who control the prices paid for these products. In a free market economy, the producers would probably get a better price by setting up cooperatives to help grade their products, establish quality control measures, handle sales and marketing (for example, explaining the benefits of using natural vanilla instead of artificial flavors), and increase the range of products offered.

American agricultural technology was desperately needed to show producers how to enhance production on the limited arable land, help set up cooperatives for marketing, and develop a new sustainable cash crop program. For example, livestock was raised for subsistence and local consumption, and considerable amounts of arable land were being used for grazing. With proper industry mentoring, a livestock feedlot operation could be established to free up more arable land for export production. Most important, the United States needs to bring back USAID, the Peace Corps, and private sector organizations willing to send in teams of volunteers as advisors. For instance, mentoring from companies such as Coca-Cola, one of the world's largest users of vanilla, would benefit the Comorian vanilla industry—and also build more loyalty for their drinks throughout the region.

Much of this mentoring is similar to what Starbucks Coffee did for coffee growers in Rwanda. Starbucks helped farmers in certain parts of sub-Saharan Africa enhance their coffee production, improve sales, and tighten quality control. In addition, they set up a Farmer Support Center with experts in soil management and field crop production in order to develop high-quality sustainable coffee production. They helped make affordable credit available to the farmers and provided adult literacy programs. In Rwanda, they committed to support women coffee growers with training in production, quality control, and commercialization.

In conjunction, USAID (working with the U.S. African Development Foundation, a small government-funded organization dedicated to connecting businesses in the United States with ones in Africa) has been a catalyst, working with the Rwandan farmers to upgrade their coffee farming and processing operations. USAID helped renovate and build coffee-washing stations, develop quality techniques, organize cooperatives, and introduce the coffee growers to U.S. coffee retailers, such as Starbucks. Growers were able to establish quality standards for their coffee beans, which led to higher prices for their coffee beans. As a result of this public-private partnership, poverty in Rwanda has been substantially reduced, with employment increasing considerably.

Later, in a February 18, 2008, *Washington Times* article, I would read that the U.S. African Development Foundation was responsible for General Mills investing in a grain-processing plant in Tanzania, which would help grain farmers prosper and eventually help in developing a middle class. Another excellent program in Tanzania helped established a cottage industry in woven baskets, using the Target Corporation's vast retail network to sell their products. According to the same article, successful entrepreneur Bill Gates, through the Bill and Melinda Gates Foundation, committed extensive funding to help African farmers improve production methods. And a September 28, 2009, State Department release noted that USAID and General Mills were introducing a program to improve the capacity of small and medium-sized food businesses in sub-Saharan Africa to produce healthful fortified food products. Such projects succeed because they are being done at the grassroots level and not at the government level, where money generally tends to be squandered and stolen. But the United States has not yet managed to bring these programs to Comoros.

As we continued with our tour of embassy-funded self-help projects, we visited a Comite des Pilotage Mt. Sambou school project in Oichili village, where we were greeted by the village elders all dressed in their neatly pressed *gallabiyas*. They were all appreciative of the U.S.-donated desks and chairs for their small one-room classroom, in which more than two hundred students attended school in shifts. Our next visit was in a village where we had donated sewing machines, books, and classroom material at the Federation des Associations pour le Development. We also gave aid for programs to counsel young people on drug prevention. I was proud to see what we had been able to do in terms of improving health care, educational opportunities, and trade skills with the small budget the embassy had available.

After the village visits, Elhad arranged for a tour of the Comoros Vanille et Plantes facility, where they dry and bundle vanilla beans and cloves and distill ylang-ylang essence for export. It was a small, well-organized, family-run operation, with an adjacent gift shop for tourists. Most of the products from this factory were sent to France except for the vanilla, the bulk of which went to the United States.

The Comoros, Madagascar, and Réunion all produce the Indian Ocean Bourbon variety of vanilla, which is considered the best in the world. The product quality was exceptional, but by Western standards the operations were primitive. I couldn't help but think the U.S. agriculture industry has experts who could advise the producers on how to set up a modern cooperative—bypassing the exclusive agents who control

14.3. Visit to a ylang-ylang distilling operation, September 2002.

the pricing of vanilla, to the farmers' disadvantage. With guidance, Comorian farmers could better market their products worldwide.

It was late in 2004 that I received a call from Robert Lindsey of the Coca-Cola regional office in South Africa, and we spoke candidly about the vanilla they were purchasing. I suggested they deal directly with local growers, so the fledgling industry could be expanded without working through offshore brokers. I asked Lindsey to help teach these local farmers business skills and better agricultural methods. He seemed to believe that the use of global brokers was the best approach, but I kept coming back to the importance of helping third-world countries grow out of their poverty, and stressed that the global business community has this obligation.

Lindsey said he would check into what he could do in that regard and get back to me. Subsequently, I had the embassy send correspondence to Coca-Cola's South Africa office asking for a meeting. I never heard back.

On Monday, September 30, 2002, I returned to President Azali's compound to talk with Hamada Madi Bolero, a close advisor to the President. Named Prime Minister by Azali in 2000, Bolero became the interim President on January 21, 2002, when Azali stepped down to run in the presidential election on April 14, 2002, which he won. When Azali took office as President on May 26, 2002, Bolero was appointed to a cabinet position as the minister of external defense and territorial security.

Bolero and I spoke frankly on a number of topics, including the timing for finishing the amendments to the constitution and the election dates for the national and island assemblies, slated to take place before year's end. Bolero suggested I bring up these issues when meeting with the three island presidents. He then spoke about regional security issues, alluding to the foreigners coming from outside the region and taking advantage of the Comorian people. These foreigners offered scholarships to Comorian children to attend schools in Egypt, Libya, Pakistan, and Afghanistan, and one could not tell their poor parents to not let their children go to these countries for what they believed would be a college education. Bolero told me that they had noticed many students returning with radical ideas; some students also came back with money to rent apartments and travel in and out of the country.

Bolero mentioned an incident that had happened the day prior to our meeting. A maritime agent in Beirut had called to tell him that a boat with arms and uniforms was headed for the Comoros Islands. The Union government had never purchased such items, and his concern was who had done so. Bolero said he had ordered the ship to be held in Beirut. One thought was that this shipment might have been headed to one of the island presidents who wanted control of his own military force.

As we were talking, the army's chief master sergeant, Taoufik Housseine, joined us. He was the army base's English instructor and also an advisor on security matters.

At 11:00 a.m., I paid a courtesy call on President El Bak of Grande Comore. He appeared nervous and spoke hurriedly, flanked by several advisors and stern-faced bodyguards. Our conversation turned out to be very lively. It was obvious he and President Azali did not get along. El Bak said he was marked by Azali for "assassination," and he believed he needed to maintain his own military force. He said Azali would not allow the assembly elections to happen that year, and he wanted our help in providing election observers and with the election process in general. He also wanted input with the amendments to the constitution, and handed me a copy of the current edition. I found him to be open and straightforward; although others told me they thought he was masking the truth. Only time would tell.

We agreed to stay in touch and keep our lines of communication open on these matters. On the way out, I wondered if he was the one attempting to bring in the boatload of military equipment and uniforms.

In the afternoon, I hosted a luncheon for the diplomatic corps at the Itsandra Hotel. Of interest were the remarks made by Oumarou Sanda of the African Union, who said they had been involved in observing the presidential election and did not think there were any problems. In fact, they considered the elections 80 percent free and fair. Having visited eight polling areas, Chinese ambassador Zhao Shunsheng concurred that the elections seemed to be fair. The European Union's Gilles

14.4. Meeting with President Abdou Soule El Bak of Grande Comore, September 30, 2002.

Desesquelles also said the election process was fair; he added that the opposition had known Azali would win and were trying to destabilize the elections. With voter boycotts and other irregularities reported, I hadn't had a clear picture of how the process went until now, so this input was invaluable.

That evening, along with government ministers and members of the diplomatic corps, Marcia and I were invited to the Chinese embassy for their National Day celebration. Ambassador Zhao Shunsheng greeted us warmly. The Chinese embassy was quite large, which didn't surprise me—their embassies in Mauritius and Seychelles were also disproportionately large for the size of those countries. Despite the strife associated with the staggering number of coups, China has had an embassy presence in Comoros since 1976. China also has been actively engaged in many sub-Saharan African countries with diplomatic missions and major commercial interests since the mid-1950s. It has had a military presence in Dar as Salaam, Tanzania, and the Horn of Africa region since the 1960s—which I had witnessed when I was there in 1970—and continues with a strong and growing presence throughout sub-Saharan Africa.

Over the years, China has been tenacious in undertaking numerous public works and development projects in sub-Saharan African countries. Now they are reaping the benefits, using these improvements to extract oil, gas, and minerals and to foster their business enterprises there. At the time of our visit, the Chinese had already constructed a state-of-the-art three-story building on Grande Comore for the Comoros government's television and radio broadcasting facilities. They had donated public works projects and several other public buildings, as well as private residences for government leaders on the three islands. More recently, the Chinese government had also started to make cash awards directly to the countries for self-administered projects, but did not get actively involved in humanitarian aid programs.

On Tuesday morning, Bisa and I met Captain Fakridine Mahamoud at his house for a breakfast working session. Fakridine was the director of the cabinet and headed up political, intelligence, and security matters for Azali and was his chief of staff. Houmed Msaidie, who served as deputy minister of finance, budget, and economy also attended. When we started talking about the sensitive subject of foreigners coming to Comoros to recruit young students, Fakridine ushered away the bodyguards who had been standing nearby. Then he and Msaidie expressed concern about the influx of foreigners and their extremist teachings.

We also discussed the upcoming assembly elections, the revisions to the constitution, and the goal of encouraging cooperation among the three island presidents to eliminate overlapping functions. Msaidie wanted to know what they could do to get U.S. aid programs, since they were trying hard to become a democracy. He

14.5. Meeting with Captain Fakridine Mahamoud, director of the cabinet, and Houmed Msaidie, minister of finance, budget, and economy, October 1, 2002. From left to right: Bisa Williams, Mahamoud, Ambassador Price, and Msaidie.

particularly referenced the Peace Corps and USAID. I was comfortable with Fakridine and Houmed's responses and felt they were straight shooters, sincere and concerned about moving Comoros forward.

Next we went to the army base, where the gendarmerie was also headquartered, to meet with Joint Chief of Staff Lieutenant Colonel Soilihi Mohamed. He introduced us to several of his officers, and we noticed they were outfitted in old boots with missing shoelaces and shirts with missing buttons—not the crisp look one would expect from a military organization.

As we talked over a cup of tea, I expressed concern about the lack of visa and passport controls at the airport and seaport. When I added that the airport also lacked computers and functioning metal detectors, the colonel became agitated and snapped that they didn't even have enough money to buy shoes, much less computers. I agreed to contact several U.S. government sources to see how we could help to upgrade the security at the airport and seaport.

One bright spot at the army base was a classroom outfitted with an old television set for visual education and vintage headsets for up to twenty military personnel

14.6. Visit to the Comoros army base, October 1, 2002. From left to right: Lieutenant Colonel Soilihi Mohamed, Ambassador Price, and Sergeant Taoufik Housseine.

to participate in English lessons. There had been plans for two more classroom additions; unfortunately, the lack of funding from the United States put the project on hold. An adjacent library was filled with older versions of U.S. training and testing manuals, while next door a mobile communications laboratory and repair shop contained mostly World War II–era equipment. Hardly any modern testing equipment existed, though I am certain our military could have spared some. Their engineer, however, was incredible. He could piece together anything, even with their limited spare parts. Over his shirt pocket he wore an award pin given to him when he completed his studies in China. I was proud to see the Comorians' persistence and efforts to improve their lot even under such limited circumstances.

During the tour of the army base, given by Taoufik, I was told the Union of the Comoros law enforcement and military had a decentralized structure based on the French concept, with approximately five hundred national police and approximately the same number of army personnel. The three island governments had their own forces as well—and sometimes they did not communicate well with one another. The Union forces were ill-equipped and marginally trained; it had taken only a small force of well-equipped mercenaries under Colonel Bob Denard to take control during the successful coups. The army's fleet of vehicles was small and antiquated; for national defense, their equipment was even more lacking.

In the afternoon, I paid a courtesy call on the French Ambassador, Jean-Pierre Lajaunie. He had been here for almost two years, so I assumed he had some insights on current security matters. I had Bisa carefully interpret his remarks, since I wanted his viewpoint and input on what was happening in Comoros, but he skirted many sensitive issues and talked in generalities. I brought up the need for France and the United States to work together on intelligence sharing. I was not sure that the French, who had substantial influence in sub-Saharan Africa dating back to colonial times, wanted any U.S. influence in the region—France wasn't about to do anything that would diminish its political and economic dominance, which it had enjoyed for more than a hundred years. The French still use all their former colonies as markets for their products and to perpetuate their language and culture. In fact, President Chirac held a meeting every year in Paris for the Francophone African countries, which gave him a chance to continue to exert control over them and their economies with programs and subsidies.

The ambassador did say security was not an issue in the Comoros, and I couldn't help but ask why, then, he was installing razor wire on top of the high walls that already surrounded the embassy. He offered no comment—just a long stare. Later that evening, Marcia and I had dinner at Ambassador Lajaunie's house, and I decided to keep the conversation light, steering clear of any political issues. Lajaunie did broach the subject of security and mentioned that he had concerns over passport and visa controls at the airport. I agreed these were critical issues that immediately needed better controls.

Earlier in the day, I had paid a courtesy call on Heywote Haile Meskal, the resident UN Development Programme representative, who had recently arrived in Comoros with her eleven-month-old adopted baby. We discussed precautions about child malaria and other medical concerns while living in Comoros. Anxious about the proposed amendments to the constitution, she asked if the United States could provide an expert to advise on such matters. She thought that with our country's vast experience, we could offer meaningful input and help bring the process to a quicker resolution. The next scheduled negotiation and draft review meeting was set for October 20—less than a month away. I asked Bisa to start the process that night with a phone call to Washington requesting help from the highest level she could reach.

Later, after we had returned to Mauritius, we made additional phone calls and sent cables from the embassy requesting an expert in constitutional law to attend the upcoming October 20 meeting. Indications came back that the United States would send such an expert to the conference, and I conveyed this news to Meskal. As I was leaving the embassy one evening, I read in an e-mail that Louis Aucion, a Washington attorney who was with the Institute for Peace and qualified in constitutional law, was willing to attend the conference. This was good news for Comoros, since the country wanted to distance itself somewhat from continued French control over its internal affairs. Just a few days before the Paris meeting was to be held, however, Washington sent a generic cable stating that the attorney could not attend the conference. I was disappointed that the United States could not spare one attorney for such an important milestone, and in so doing abdicated the process of drafting the constitution to the French, who Meskal later told me had sent two experts who actively participated in the process. I was frustrated that the United States constantly spoke of democracy, rule of law, and transparency, yet did nothing to help steer this fledgling democracy in the right direction.

After dining with the French ambassador, the next day, we took a charter flight to Anjouan for meetings in Mutsamudu, the island's capital. President Mohamed Bacar had left the day before to attend meetings in Paris, so we met with Doulclin Mahamoud, the minister of finance and acting president. Several other ministers were present, including Lieutenant Colonel Abdoul Bacar, commander of the military, gendarmerie, and overseas foreign relations. Anjouan's military force paralleled the Union of the Comoros military forces, which I thought was a duplication of effort and cost.

Our working session was held at Government House, a fairly new structure built by the Chinese in 1987. Our discussions were frank regarding democratic principles, the upcoming assembly elections, and the importance of resolving the constitutional issues. Abdoul said they felt the constitution was complete and not open to revision by Azali's government. This was concerning in light of the hard work and

14.7. Meeting with Anjouan Minister of Finance Doulclin Mahamoud, Lieutenant Colonel Abdoul Bacar, other ministers, and local consular agent Mohamed Elhad, October 2, 2002.

effort to date by all of the participating parties; I had thought they were close to reaching a resolution on the amendments for power sharing between the three island presidents. Without these amendments in the constitution, the Union of the Comoros could not go forward.

I restated the U.S. position that we would work only with one unified federal government. For that to become a reality, the three islands needed to work together. They needed to agree that the federal government would control their foreign affairs and deal with external defense; they had to have one country flag and one national anthem. Above all, they had to operate globally as one country: the Union of the Comoros.

Abdoul countered they did not want to allow financial matters or education to be controlled by the federal government. His reaction made me wonder whether they trusted Azali and his government. Reading between the lines, I gathered that the Anjouan leadership wanted to have full autonomy. At the same time, Abdoul complained about their island's poverty and the lack of necessary finances to go it alone, and acknowledged that they were willing to continue to be "connected" to the Union for the time being. He asserted they did not have a positive outlook on staying combined in the future, though, since they interpreted their rights differently under the constitution.

I knew then that I needed to continue to nudge the island presidents to cooperate and try to hold the Union together, without which there could not be any help coming from the United States or a lifting of the Section 508 sanctions.

14.8. Village children, Anjouan, Comoros, October 2, 2002.

After our meeting ended, we took a tour of the Cholera Center at Hombo Hospital, which was very poorly equipped and lacked sanitary conditions. We then visited a successful women's craft, knitting, and embroidery school and retail store. This organization had received funding from the Ambassador's Special Self-Help program.

During lunch at Government House, I was pleased to hear some of the ministers expressing great respect for the United States, commenting they were truly sorry about the tragic events of 9/11. Showing support of the global war on terror, they were open to discussing security matters, explaining they had no border control experience to monitor the movement of people but were eager for some input from us. Each one expressed a need for scholarships to Western countries for young students.

Next on our agenda was the island of Mohéli. Flying to its capital, Fomboni, we were met by Mohamed Elarif Hamadi, the minister of justice and internal affairs; Ahoumani Ahamada, the minister of finance; M. Said Ali, the commissioner for women's affairs and the only woman in the administration; and several other ministers.

Our visit in Mohéli began with a tour of the seaport area, where I asked about the design and purpose of the long pier. Unprotected by the harbor and exposed to the open ocean, it was unusable during inclement weather. I was told it had been a project undertaken by the European Union to provide access for large ships. The

14.9. Visit to the Women's Craft Center, Anjouan, Comoros, a recipient of the Ambassador's Special Self-Help Program funding, October 2, 2002.

14.10. Anjouan village elders, students, and teachers, October 2, 2002.

engineers, however, did not take into account the deep hulls on many ships, so quite a few still had to have their cargo off-loaded onto smaller dhow-like boats and then brought ashore, an inefficient process at best. I had seen the same problem with seaport access on Grande Comore.

Stopping at the small shack on the dock used by customs officials for passport and visa control, I observed that people were tracked coming and going simply by having them sign the log book; there were no security controls.

The dilapidated conditions at the island's Fomboni Hospital also disturbed me. All I could see were meager medical supplies, poorly functioning equipment, and unpurified tap water. Several years earlier, under the Ambassador's Special Self-Help Program, the United States had supplied a utensil sterilization unit and some operating room equipment, but we never made any electrical provisions to set up or install this medical equipment. The items were still sitting in their original boxes, with parts now missing, in the corner of an operating room where they were sorely needed. I was shocked at our lack of oversight and follow-through.

It was apparent Mohéli was the poorest of the three islands. During a lunch meeting with the government leaders, I discussed ways in which the United States could help. I would request more equipment and supplies, and help in installing the previously donated items. (Although I often discussed this issue with Washington, stressing what I had witnessed and what was needed, when I departed in June 2005, nothing had happened: no funding had been committed and no equipment had been delivered.)

Touring next a women's textile training center, where sewing machines had been donated the year before through the Ambassador's Special Self-Help Program, was uplifting. Seeing the success they had achieved by creating products for sale in their retail shop, I was encouraged, and included them in the next program cycle so they could obtain several more sewing machines. I also would investigate what Comoros needed to do to qualify for the AGOA program, since I felt a commercial textile manufacturing operation could be quite successful.

I talked with the Mohéli leaders about security training, border protection, and improving their legal system by instructing lawyers on matters such as rule of law and administration of justice. We were told they needed technical assistance to train doctors, computer technology training programs, school equipment, and books. They also wanted help with teacher training in subjects such as physics and chemistry, vocational training, and agricultural methods. Looking toward the future, they needed assistance with dependable power generation, communication systems, road improvements, sanitary sewers, and potable water systems. It was obvious Mohéli had in place little basic infrastructure; most of these issues also applied to the villages on Grande Comore and Anjouan.

The Mohéli ministers expressed their friendship for the United States. They were troubled, however, that their people could easily be influenced by radical foreigners. It was of concern to the government leaders on all three islands that the

United States had not had a diplomatic mission in Comoros since the 1993 embassy closing. Most of the influx of strange foreigners had taken place subsequent to that time. An American presence on the islands might have prevented these radical imams from entering the country and curbed their recruiting in the mosques and madrassas. We would have also been more familiar with some of the activities of the Comoros branch of the Saudi-based al-Haramain Islamic Foundation long before its 2004 designation by the U.S. Treasury Department and the UN 1267 Sanctions Committee as a rogue organization that financially supports terrorists and has links to al-Qaeda. (Other branches of this rogue charity in Somalia, Kenya, Tanzania, and Ethiopia were also designated by the United States and the UN between 2002–2004.)

Later that day, I met with the island president, Mohamed Said Fazul, a slightly built, humble man who appeared to be a moderate Muslim. He was most apologetic in asking for our help; foremost in his mind was the need to educate the island's youth. He wanted young people to be able to study in the United States, an issue I planned to press hard during my next Washington consultations.

When we arrived back on Grande Comore late in the day, I met with a government official regarding a previous discussion of offshore educational opportunities offered to young Comorians. As I've noted, many of the young men who were offered scholarships to study overseas had come back with radical Islamic beliefs and in some cases had become quite militant; others had simply not returned at all. To indicate how out of control the situation was becoming, the official provided me with a list of some nine hundred students who recently had gone abroad under these programs.

14.11. Mohéli President Mohamed Said Fazul presenting Ambassador Price with a handmade linen map of Comoros, October 2, 2002.

On October 2, we went to Le Moroni Hotel in town to have dinner with Souef Mohamed El-Amine, the minister of state, cooperation, and foreign affairs. We discussed the importance of concluding the amendments to the constitution (an issue I was especially concerned about after hearing Abdoul's comments earlier that day), scheduling the assembly election dates, signing the ICC Article 98 nonsurrender agreement, good governance, and—in light of Bolero's remarks—interception of vessels suspected to be carrying arms.

Since Souef had been part of the UN Mission in New York, his English was quite good, which made our direct discussions more meaningful—although he referred to Bisa Williams several times for translation of specific words. The hour was late, so we agreed to meet the next morning to cover a few remaining items before our departure to Mayotte.

The following morning at his office, I again encouraged cooperation, compromise, and consolidation of the three islands into the Union of the Comoros federal structure. I mentioned our report to Washington of his discussion with Ambassador Wanda Nesbitt while visiting Madagascar concerning the strangers currently in Moroni and others who had come in the past; I expressed the need for more research on this matter and promised to send our regional security officer to Comoros to review this and other security concerns. In turn, Souef would alert me to any further developments.

14.12. Meeting with the Comoros Foreign Minister Souef El-Amine, October 3, 2002.

On our way to the airport for our flight to Mayotte, I stopped at a small fishing village where several men who appeared to be in their seventies and eighties were hewing out a fishing boat from a tree trunk, to which they would attach outriggers for stability. Most of the local fishing by Comorians was done using these hand-crafted boats—a custom going back many centuries.

At the airport VIP room, we ran into Mahmoud Mdradabi, the opposition leader who ran against Azali. Angrily, he told me President Azali was a dictator and his government corrupt. Mdradabi said that every time gatherings, protests, or rallies took place, they were routinely broken up by Azali's military. Thus, Mdradabi would not accept the constitution and amendments or support the upcoming elections, which his party would boycott. They would do whatever it took to stop the process. Attempting to reason with him did not help. Even when I told him such actions would set the country back and not allow for any help or aid from the United States, he did not move off his position. I was resolved to talk with him again on one of our next trips, to help him see the sense of getting his political party to be part of the reconciliation process. Again, I wished we had some permanent U.S. representation in the Comoros so that we could be more engaged in resolving such areas of discord.

Soon we were on our way for the short flight to the nearby island of Mayotte, a French overseas collectivity that Comoros still claimed. We were met at Pamandzi Airport by island prefect Jean-Jacques Brot. Walking through the airport, I noticed that several direct flights per week to France were listed, giving Mahorians and French expatriates direct access to the outside world.

14.13. Handcrafted fishing canoes made from tree trunks, with attached outriggers for stability.

As we headed toward town, I could immediately see the difference between Mayotte and the sister islands of Grande Comore, Anjouan, and Mohéli. It was like night and day. Under French control, Mayotte had money allocated to it as would any other district in France. With such infusion of capital, Mayotte had developed into a modern island paradise. Investments in Mayotte had helped develop an agriculture sector, a fishing sector, and a tourism sector. The island had well-designed and -constructed roads and other infrastructure, landscaped public areas, modern street lighting, and many well-maintained historical buildings. In contrast, the three Comoros Islands not administered by France had a pre-1970s feel. It was obvious why the people of Mayotte had continued voting to stay under French control. Health care, education, employment, lifestyle, and amenities were worth their loyalty.

Mayotte consists of two islands—the larger Grande-Terre (Mahore) and the smaller Petite-Terre (Pamazi)—with a daily water ferry service between them. The population in 2002 was 160,000 and 25,000 on the respective islands. Sixty-five percent of the population was native-born, 28 percent were immigrants from the three islands of the Comoros, 4 percent were French, and 3 percent were from Madagascar. The majority of the population on Mayotte was Sunni Muslim, though there was also an active European Christian community.

Mayotte's GDP in 2003 was $2,600 per capita, substantially higher than that of the Comoros. Mayotte was obviously a better place to live and find work. Mahorians also had French passports, which gave them benefits similar to those enjoyed by other French citizens.

Jean took us to a government-owned French-style guesthouse overlooking the bay, where we had tea. Afterward, we went to his office, located in a beautifully maintained 1868 structure. We were told the steel construction was patterned after the design of the Eiffel Tower, in vogue at that time. The reception area had polished wood floors and wood paneling, as did the adjacent dining room. This building was a charming place for both work and entertainment.

Over lunch, we discussed security matters. In an attempt to stop illegal transiting of strangers through Mayotte, Jean proposed tightening up security at the airport and using computers to interface with international intelligence agencies. A bigger concern, he noted, was controlling the numerous small boats arriving without notice day and night from the Comoros.

While driving around the island I observed a set of large satellite dishes, which reportedly were manned by the French intelligence service and used to track activities as well as suspicious people using cell phones in the region. Several hundred people worked at this tracking station—some well trained to handle emergency situations in the region. With all the intelligence resources they had present, though, even they seemed unable to find the terrorist Fazul Abdullah Mohammed.

After seeing the main part of the town, we drove to the port, where Jean took us out in his boat for a tour around the island. The water was crystal clear; the reefs protected the two pristine islands. The dolphins and whales added to the experience that visiting tourists enjoy. All too soon we had to head back to the airport. We agreed to stay in touch on security matters and other issues of mutual interest in the region.

Our next stop was at Réunion, a French overseas department some 450 miles east of Madagascar, with more than 700,000 inhabitants, the majority of whom were French citizens. Landing in St. Denis, the capital, we took a taxi to the St. Denis Hotel, located in the center of the city and fronting a major highway running along the ocean shore. We dined on the terrace, looking around at the hotels and sidewalk cafes lining the streets; the feeling was of being on the Mediterranean in the south of France.

Réunion, as a department of France, receives considerable infusions of capital, which showed in its wide streets, long stretches of four-lane highways, and modern infrastructure everywhere. We saw numerous well-designed housing subdivisions, quality shopping centers, and a diversity of restaurants. Many of the French expatriates living there were retired, enjoying the same benefits offered to other French citizens—but at a fraction of the cost.

On Friday, Réunion Island prefect Gonthier Friederici was kind enough to send a car to pick us up at the hotel and bring us to his beautiful French-style gated complex, which was built in 1868. While having coffee in his office, we immediately began our discussion of security matters. He said since Réunion was being used by strangers transiting to France and other parts of Europe, they were currently beefing up their passport and visa controls at the airport. We agreed we needed to work closely on security matters and other issues of mutual interest in the region.

Gonthier also discussed their plans to establish a four-year engineering curriculum for university-level studies with the goal to bring in students from other countries in the Indian Ocean region. I agreed the need was great. Finally, since we did not have an active diplomatic presence in Réunion, I thanked him for being the U.S. Embassy's "first responder" in case any Americans needed assistance.

Marcia, Bisa, and I had decided to explore the island and arranged for a private car that afternoon to take us to the top of the ancient volcanic crater where the town of Cilaos was located. This charming town of 6,500 people, nestled on the crater floor at 6,000 feet above sea level, was surrounded by steep volcanic rock outcrops and densely covered with vegetation. It was a dizzying journey to get there, however, with more than two hundred tight hairpin turns, traffic congestion, and sheer drop-offs of several hundred feet making us a bit uneasy at times. Once we arrived in Cilaos, we were engulfed in low-hanging clouds, which gave the town an eerie, mystical feeling. The style of architecture, with flower-filled window planters, gave the flavor of a charming Swiss village. For the next day and a half, we explored the town and hiked in the surrounding foothills.

On the afternoon of October 6, we arranged for a van to take us back to a regional airport an hour from Cilaos. The forty-minute flight back to Mauritius went by quickly. It felt good to be going back to Mauritius after our whirlwind nine-day, five-island visit, which included meetings with more than one hundred people.

During my posting I reflected on the many meetings I had with Comorian government leaders and the leaders on the three islands, who all seemed to share the same concerns about regional security, terrorism, radical Islamic teachings, and passport and visa control. There were differing opinions on the federal unity issue, and these needed to be resolved. But most of these fine, dedicated people made it a point to express their disappointment about the 1993 closing of the U.S. embassy. They felt that diplomatic relations between the countries had all but ceased. Comorians hold Americans in high esteem and appreciate past aid by U.S. agencies, which included the Peace Corps, USAID, and the IMET program. The Section 508 sanctions had been imposed by the United States as a result of Azali's military coup in 1999, but most Comorians had not been involved in the event and did not understand why they were being punished with these sanctions. Neither did I.

Over the years, our embassy worked closely with the Union and the three island authorities. I believe we made substantial progress in their ongoing reconciliation process to bridge the mistrust that existed between Azali's Union government and the island presidents, El Bak, Bacar and Fazul. I spent considerable time working with Azali, which made a big difference in his embracing democracy and developing a friendship with the United States. I was sorry I did not have a similar chance with the other presidents while serving there. However, I believe that if we had had a U.S. presence there, such as an American Presence Post, it would have made a big difference in our relationship with the country. Thus I was elated to receive a letter on October 9, 2002, from the Peace Corps director, Gaddi Vasquez, as a follow-up to our Washington meeting in early September, noting that he was considering reestablishing a volunteer presence back in Comoros.

During my first visit to Comoros, as well as the others that followed, it became clear that the list of sustainable economic business models that would work in Comoros was nearly endless. But to accomplish any of these, the United States needs to set up mentoring programs through the embassy, bring back USAID and Peace Corps programs, and encourage nongovernmental organizations and the private sector, to assist Comorians in gaining vocational trade training; and basic business and marketing expertise by applying American ingenuity.

It became clear that deepwater ports needed to be developed on the islands of Grande Comore, Anjouan, and Mohéli to allow for year-round ship access and avoid the transshipping that was sometimes required when cargo ships had to bypass the Comoros during cyclone season. With a proper deepwater port, direct dock access to overhead cranes would allow the unloading process to be reduced to only a

14.14. View of the Moroni harbor area with the Friday Mosque in the background.

few hours, instead of the much longer period that was required to offload the cargo onto smaller boats.

An effective working port would also allow a commercial fishing and canning industry to develop in Comoros—an excellent opportunity, since none exists. Most fishing done currently by Comorians is for personal consumption and local sale. Yet there are large Asian and European trawlers using the surrounding deep waters, which are rich in tuna and other varieties of fish. Since many of these fleets operate without having been granted fishing permits, proper licensing and monitoring would provide the Comoros government with substantial added revenue and the ability to control the amount of fishing in their coastal and offshore waters.

Comoros does not have a coast guard or any other way to undertake offshore patrols. The United States could help set up a coast guard program, offer training on ship interdiction, and donate some of our surplus coast guard boats (including plenty of spare parts), as we did in the Seychelles. I had discussed this issue with the U.S. Pacific Command and brought it up on several occasions in Washington consultations. Such a program would also help us track ship traffic in this region and contribute to the global war on terror.

American companies with tuna processing experience, such as the H. J. Heinz Company, could become mentors to help establish a fish canning industry—similar to the one they set up on the island of Mahé in the Seychelles, which had been operating successfully for many years. A competitive fishing industry and other business operations created along the way could become part of a free trade zone program, which would attract some direct foreign investment dollars, spurring much-needed economic growth.

I observed many stretches of sandy beach areas that would be ideal for destination hotels and resorts. The tourism industry potential on the three Comoros Islands had not even been touched. As I became more familiar with the islands, I saw numerous opportunities for world-class scuba diving and snorkeling, ecotourism, and backcountry hiking and camping in the scenic high mountain volcano areas. A knowledgeable tour operator could package trips to include, for example, a safari in East Africa, diving in Comoros, several days of adventure and relaxation in Mauritius or Seychelles, lemur watching in Madagascar's rain forests, a visit to the volcanic crater in Réunion, and a final stop in Dubai for shopping on the way home. Such unique adventure packages could be marketed as the "Africa–Indian Ocean Experience." I am certain most airlines serving the region would be more than happy to expand their flight schedules between Europe, Africa, and the Indian Ocean islands to share in these new tourist revenues.

The traditional arts and crafts of the region, which include basketry, woodcarving, painting, embroidery, jewelry making, and colorful textile products, could be undertaken in cottage industry enterprises within the villages. The products could be marketed through a cooperative network to wholesalers and retailers around the world using the "Made in Comoros" label. Most of these products could also qualify under AGOA for duty-free status, giving them preferential access to U.S. markets. I had pressed for Comoros to become an AGOA qualifying country, but the 1999 coup was a problem under the strictly interpreted rules. Comoros had come a long way since holding its first free and fair presidential election, and I believed the country had met the spirit and intent of the rules, but my opinion did not seem to sway anyone in Washington.

After my term as ambassador ended, I was pleased to learn that on July 1, 2008, Comoros finally received the recognition it deserved by obtaining eligibility status as an AGOA beneficiary. Now they faced the hard work of helping turn these cottage industries into viable larger-scale operations, helping them locate the foreign direct investment necessary to be globally competitive. I hope the United States will provide the needed mentoring so they can quickly set up shop and gain access to American markets.

⟨XV⟩

Host Country Engagement

In a lengthy meeting on the afternoon of October 9, 2002, with Jayen Cuttaree, we discussed the upcoming meetings with the Washington advance team, at which we would work on the ministry and private sector meetings and the plenary and breakout sessions. We wanted the co-chairs of the sessions to be from AGOA-qualified countries notable for their diversity and their success in the program. Even though there were thirty-seven qualifying countries in sub-Saharan Africa, very few had proven to be model democracies, with good records on human rights, rule of law, health care, and transparency. After much debate, we settled on asking Kenya, Cameroon, Ghana, Mali, Cape Verde, Ethiopia, and possibly Nigeria to participate. We had considered Ivory Coast but decided to take it off the list because of its ongoing internal conflict. Since we were getting mixed signals about which high-level cabinet members would be attending, we decided to ask U.S. Trade Representative Robert Zoellick to be the keynote speaker at the public sector session at 6:00 p.m. Mauritius time, which would be 9:00 a.m. EST in Washington and New York—good for media coverage.

The following Thursday morning, I was awakened by the news of an explosion on a French oil tanker. Reports indicated the possible involvement of al-Qaeda terrorists in a small craft approaching the tanker. Al-Qaeda also had released tapes disclosing upcoming attacks on U.S. commercial interests. New York had tightened security around its landmarks and on Wall Street. When I arrived at the embassy, a secret file was centered on my desk, and the country team convened in the conference room to discuss the contents. Apparently a heightened alert was out worldwide. We discussed informing our wardens (American citizen volunteers) and the governments of the host countries. We believed that the threat was real and that we needed to be very observant and protective.

We talked openly of our concerns about radical Muslim influence in each of the host countries: in Comoros, the radical influence of foreign clerics, the continuing recruitment of young people to study in the Middle East and South Asia, and the possibility of the country becoming a safe haven for terrorists; in Seychelles, the influx of young foreign Muslims; in Mauritius, a small but radical group called Lalit, a vocal Muslim opposition party referred to as Hizbullah (although not connected with the Lebanese or Iranian terrorist groups by the same name), and an outspoken Muslim activist and Hizbullah leader named Cehl Meeah. Meeah had been arrested in 2000 for his reported role in the killing of three supporters of the Mauritian Militant Movement and Labour Party alliance during the 1996 general elections. Although Meeah won a seat in parliament, he was not allowed to serve while in prison. Meeah had also been accused of planning the assassination of former Prime Minister Navin Ramgoolam.

After our country team meeting, an email came in from the U.S. Embassy in Dakar indicating that all leaves scheduled between November 15, 2002, and the end of January 2003 might need to be canceled. The demarche that followed from Secretary Powell stated that chiefs of mission around the world needed to alert the highest-ranking official in each host country that a credible terrorist threat had been made against U.S. interests. I immediately called Prime Minister Anerood Jugnauth and, referring to the cable, told him that the targets might be oil and fuel storage areas, electrical generating plants, port operations, or other major facilities. Much of the information was based on the Arab media disclosing tapes from al-Qaeda leaders, but details also had been supplied by the FBI and CIA. We alerted the Australian, British, and French embassies as well. In the private sector, we called Shell Oil and Caltex (one of the Chevron brands).

In between calls, I had a quick lunch with a banker acquaintance who had been promoted and would soon be leaving the country. He had been helpful and insightful about the complex intertwining of various families' business operations in Mauritius, saving me months of finding out on my own. One of the powerful Indo-Mauritian families who had business interests throughout the Indian Ocean region and East Africa were the Currimjees, who had been very effective in taking on the other powerful Franco-Mauritian and Sino-Mauritian family businesses. Of political interest was the rice monopoly the Currimjees held in Seychelles. The Seychelles Marketing Board was controlled at the time by Mukesh Valabhji, and it seemed that the Currimjee family interests had an offshore partnership in London with Valabhji, who was representing President René. Evidently there was a huge markup before the rice entered the Seychelles, with the profits split with René and Valabhji. I told my banker friend this was no surprise, since I had heard this rumor from other people.

On Sunday, October 13, CNN carried a live broadcast from Bali, where several terrorist bombings had taken place the day before. Two nightclubs on a beach where young vacationers gathered were hit by car bombs. More than 180 people had been killed and 300 seriously injured. The known dead included several Americans and many Australians, some of whom were members of a national football team on vacation. A car bomb also had gone off in front of the U.S. Consulate, but no major damage was incurred. We knew this was connected to the warning we had received the prior week.

On Tuesday morning, October 15, Charlie Slater relayed a message from Washington that a universal embassy alert had been issued. Evidently an email on the State Department system indicated that a bomb would go off at an embassy somewhere in the world at 10:15 that morning. Precautions were set in motion: Charlie called the police to sweep the office building where our embassy is located, and to check the surrounding areas for strangers, vehicles, or packages left unattended.

Earlier that morning, Deputy Chief of Mission Bisa Williams had gone to the airport to meet the AGOA advance team from Washington. When I arrived at the embassy, fifty police officers had just finished their inspections and were starting to let people back into the building; the advance team also arrived at that moment. There was much confusion and worry among the other building tenants and their employees about the presence of the U.S. and Australian embassies in the building.

We held our country team meeting at 9:00 a.m., followed by a meeting with the advance team members. At some point I looked at my watch and suddenly realized that it was 10:30—no bomb had gone off. We were all relieved.

Several afternoons each week, I scheduled visits to local business and manufacturing operations. During the afternoon of October 15, I toured a totally integrated textile plant that employed more than five hundred people. More than 40 percent of their production went to the United States under the AGOA program. I was told again the major concern was competition from China and India, whose governments underwrote and subsidized some of their nationals' textile operations. From there, I went to one of the major Franco-Mauritian sugar estates, operated by the Harel family since 1838. To run their milling operation, they had built a new $100 million power plant, using Duke Engineering, a division of Duke Power Company of North Carolina. As I have previously noted, the power plant burned bagasse, the pulpy residue of sugar cane left over from the mill extraction process. The bagasse provided 25 percent of their fuel needs; the balance of their fuel was coal from South Africa.

Later that day, I returned to the embassy for an AGOA planning meeting with members of the advance team: Ambassador Robert Perry, deputy assistant secretary, Bureau of African Affairs; Bobby Pittman, director for African affairs, National Security Council; Wendell Albright, international economist, African Economic Policy staff; Colleen Hyland, trade officer, Economic Bureau; Holly Vineyard, senior policy advisor to the undersecretary, Commerce; Constance Hamilton, senior director for African affairs, Office of the U.S. Trade Representative; Madeleine Gauthier, USAID; Richard Helm, agriculture counselor, Foreign Agricultural Service; Blossom Perry, desk officer, Bureau of East African Affairs; Tony Sariti, of the Africa Bureau, Office of Public Diplomacy; and the embassy country team.

Before I left the embassy, Bisa Williams told me about three individuals who had been detained at the airport the previous weekend. Carrying Turkish passports when they were stopped, they were suspected of having forged documents. In their baggage, they had Iranian passports under a different name with entry visas from the Mauritian Embassy in Tehran. The visas looked real—except Mauritius does not have an embassy in Iran. They spent four days in jail before being sent back without any passports. Why they had been coming to Mauritius was a concern, since this was the same weekend that the bombings had taken place in Bali.

The next day, Bob Perry and I, accompanied by Blossom Perry, met with Deputy Prime Minister Paul Bérenger. The main issue of discussion was the stand the Mauritian representative to the United Nations, Jagdish Koonjul, had taken on the U.S.-sponsored revised Resolution 1441 on Iraq, which was before the Security Council. The British, French, Russian, and Chinese had agreed on the changes they wanted to see in the resolution. Koonjul was representing Mauritius, which was in the second year of its two-year term on the United Nations Security Council, and was *not* supportive. Bérenger said he was aware of this and was upset; he had already talked to Koonjul on this issue and promised me that Mauritius would support our resolution.

While the advance team took a tour of the University of Mauritius, Bob Perry and I met with Trade Minister Jayen Cuttaree and Harry Ganoo. We reviewed the plenary and breakout session country chairs, and the plans for the entire event, which now was not far away.

On Thursday morning, October 17, I awakened to a report of a bombing in the Philippines that had killed seven people; it sounded similar to the explosion by terrorists in Bali. That evening, I hosted a dinner and working session for the advance team at Macarty House. The following day, I met with Bob Perry and Bobby Pittman, who said the AGOA Forum meetings had gone very well and that the team was tying up some loose ends. Then we held a "postmortem" meeting with the advance team before their departure to review all the matters covered during their visit.

Several days later, after receiving a phone call from a top leader in the Hizbullah movement, the embassy's regional security officer alerted me to a possible threat of attack. There was a question about the credibility of the source and whether this was an immediate threat or simply a vague future plot. After clearing it with regional security sources, he was instructed to meet and debrief this individual. The plot turned out to be destabilizing activities planned for the AGOA Forum and the visit of President Bush.

The next day, the RSO showed me a cable he wanted to send to Washington. This cable would be a worldwide alert about Hizbullah threats against Christian churches and government buildings in Mauritius—actions we surmised were for domestic political reasons. We were rather surprised that a local Muslim businessman was behind this threat. We decided to immediately call all the members of the diplomatic corps, Police Chief Ramanooj Gopalsingh, and Secretary for Home Affairs Suresh Seeballuck. A warden's message was also issued to all American citizens living in Mauritius.

An hour later, the RSO returned concerned, saying we had another immediate problem. A man on a motorcycle had been observed sitting one block from the ambassador's residence, waiting there a few minutes, and then driving to the rear gate and parking across the street for fifteen minutes before driving back to his first location. This had been going on since the beginning of October. When challenged by the embassy residence guard, he claimed to be waiting for his girlfriend. The ambassador's residence was in a residential area of large walled estates; it seemed an unlikely place to pick up someone. In checking his license plate number, the Mauritian police discovered that this individual was tied to the Hizbullah party. Now I had one more issue to be concerned about.

I had lunch scheduled that day with British High Commissioner David Snoxell. Suggesting an open space where we would not be overheard, David took me to a garden restaurant near his office. I gave him a heads-up on the worldwide alert and asked him to see what he could find out about the local Hizbullah group from his intelligence sources. Concerned, David—who lived just a few blocks from me— mentioned the lax security at his residence, which had only one guard and a loose gate allowing easy access. After I told him about the individual on the motorcycle, he became tense.

Earlier that morning, I had been given instructions by Washington to deliver a demarche on the Iraq resolution. Prior to meeting with Deputy Prime Minister Paul Bérenger, I went to Government House to hear the National Millennium Development Goals report. One of the speakers was Foreign Minister Anil Gayan. His reference to Iraq included the phrase "support for a full and unconditional review and access" and the words "compliance" and "comprehensive"—just the words I was seeking for my talk with Bérenger.

When we met, I brought up Gayan's comments and told Bérenger we needed "teeth"—severe consequences—in the resolution in case of a material breach. We did not want the resolution watered down such that further meetings would need to take place before we could engage in unilateral action, as the French, Russians, and Chinese wanted, and we hoped Mauritius would support the U.S. position on the Security Council. Bérenger basically agreed on all points in support of our position.

Since Bérenger was on board with UN Resolution 1441, I decided to mention a second demarche, on the International Code of Conduct Against Ballistic Missile Proliferation. The United States was looking for universal acceptance of the code. We needed countries to show support on this issue by November 18, in time for a meeting scheduled to be held in the Netherlands on November 25–26, 2002. Bérenger quickly responded, "On this one, it is easy for us, since I totally agree." Leaving Bérenger's office, I felt relieved, having gone two for two.

As Ahmed rounded the corner to Macarty House, we saw a man sitting on a red motorcycle and fitting the description of the individual the regional security officer had mentioned. However, before we could alert the guards, he disappeared.

I wasn't home long before the State Department operator called me on my cell phone with Assistant Secretary Kansteiner on the other end. He did not know I had delivered the demarches to Bérenger, and was pleased with the results. He mentioned Secretary Powell was so concerned about passage of UN Resolution 1441 that he had asked Kansteiner to call Prime Minister Jugnauth and Deputy Prime Minister Bérenger directly. I of course told him that would not be a problem.

On October 25, negotiations were still going on behind the scenes on the acceptable wording for Resolution 1441. The French ambassador had met with Bérenger in an attempt to convince Mauritius to accept a watered-down version. Among other changes, France, Russia, and China wanted to take out the phrases "material breach" and "serious consequences." However, Bérenger agreed that without performance standards and a hammer, the resolution would be weakened. He also told me that he and Gayan had both talked with their UN representative, Koonjul, who was finally on board.

On October 31, I was given an email about Koonjul being recalled to Port Louis for "consultations." I had known this was coming because of his outspoken attitude against the United States on the Iraq resolution. The government of Mauritius was upset with Koonjul, especially because the press had reported early on that Mauritius and Syria would vote together against the resolution. Since then, of course, I had received assurances that Mauritius would support the resolution.

Amidst all these tensions, all of us at the embassy needed a break from the constant anxiety and long hours. So we decided that on October 31, we would hold a Halloween party at the embassy—the first ever, I was told. Almost everyone got caught up in the spirit. I arrived as a typical American tourist wearing sandals, rumpled jeans, a washed-out Hawaiian print shirt, a sweat-stained brimmed hat, sunglasses, an earring, and a camera slung around my neck. Marcia wore a *shiromani* dress she had purchased at a craft shop in Comoros. Bisa Williams dressed as a skeleton, Charlie Slater was James Bond in a tuxedo, and Lizzie Slater looked like Gravel Gertie from the *Dick Tracy* comic strip. Many other costumed staff paraded around as we tried to pick a winner. One of our Foreign Service national drivers, Jeanson Bathilde, who was dressed like a Native American and said he was Pocahontas's brother, won. Lizzie again had prepared many delicious cakes and pies for the embassy staff.

Before leaving the embassy that day, Bob Perry called confirming the plans for President Bush to arrive in Mauritius on Tuesday, January 14, 2003, to attend the Forum and depart a day or two later. The ministerial session would begin on January 15 with the President giving the opening speech. The next morning over coffee, I told Trade Minister Cuttaree the good news, drawing a big smile from him.

On November 1, Marcia and I boarded an Emirates Air flight to Dubai. We had meetings set up there as well as in Bahrain and Singapore. Because of the State Department mandate, I aborted my fact-finding mission to Diego Garcia.

Dubai was definitely becoming the center of business and commerce in the Middle East. Wanting to discuss the possibility of some U.S. businesses that were already in Dubai developing satellite operations in Mauritius, I arranged to meet with U.S. Consul General Richard Olson. Joining him was Commercial Attaché John Lancia of the U.S. Commercial Service. Their knowledge was most insightful and I came away thinking that the ruler, Sheikh Mohammed bin Rashid Al Maktoum, would not like to see any commercial opportunities slip away from Dubai, least of all to Mauritius, which was in competition with Dubai as a tourist destination.

I then met with the Dubai Development and Investment Authority. Tariq bin Belaila, a development director, showed me around town and through a number of new projects. Everything I saw was impressive and, in some cases, over the top. Even with the speed at which they were building—on a 24/7 basis—I was impressed with the quality of the work and the materials used. Knowing their workload, I was most impressed that Deputy Manager Salem bin Dasmal of the Dubai Development Authority took the time to have lunch with me. Salem had been born in England, did his university studies in the United States, wore local attire, and spoke English better than anyone else I met in Dubai. I realized he was not keen on my desire to attract money and U.S. investments to Mauritius, since he kept focusing only on Dubai. We talked about a number of business ideas and agreed to stay in touch.

On the morning of November 4, we left Dubai for the short flight to Bahrain. Our first meeting, set up by Jim Kenworthy, a Naval Criminal Investigative Service agent, was with Mark Clookie, special agent in charge, and James Macfarlane, assistant special agent in charge. We talked primarily about ship visits to Seychelles and Mauritius. This gave me another chance to lobby on behalf of our local hire in Seychelles, Susanne Rose, the embassy's consular agent, who dealt with the ship visits. My requests for an increase in pay for her had fallen on deaf ears at the State Department and at the Department of Defense. The NCIS, which was familiar with her hard work, was my last hope for obtaining additional funding, which fortunately came through several months later.

In meeting with Admiral Mark Milliken, U.S. Naval Forces, Central Command, who reported to Admiral Timothy Keating, commander of the U.S. Fifth Fleet, we talked about the ship visit issues and security in the region, including the possibility of the Navy increasing its presence in East Africa. I noted that we had received permission to board suspicious ships in international waters surrounding Seychelles, Mauritius, and Comoros.

Later that day, I met with Ambassador Ronald Neumann at the U.S. Embassy in Manama. A career member of the Foreign Service, as his father had been, he had served as ambassador to Algeria. In our discussion of the President's visit to Mauritius, he suggested we get a number of temporary duty officers well in advance, since there might be confusion and wrong signals if we waited too long. Talk turned to the government in Bahrain, and he told me that the king, Sheikh Hamad bin Isa Al Khalifa, had allowed elections for parliamentary seats, a democratic step forward.

When Marcia and I arrived in Singapore the next evening, we discovered one of the cleanest and most progressive countries in Asia. Singapore residents have the highest per capita income in the region. The country serves as a major seaport and hub for shipping around the world and is a tourist destination and jumping-off spot for many island resorts in Southeast Asia. It had been home to icons such as Somerset Maugham and Rudyard Kipling.

On Thursday morning at the U.S. Embassy in Singapore, I met with the regional security officer to discuss regional concerns, including the recent bombings in nearby Bali. I then spoke with Ambassador Frank Lavin, whom I had met in Washington while attending the Ambassadorial Seminar, and was taken on a tour. The impressive, high-security embassy structure was built in 1997 and had more than 250 people stationed there, of which almost 150 were Americans. A few months earlier, this embassy had received several terrorist threats.

After the tour, Frank offered valuable input on how he managed and measured his Mission Performance Plan by keeping it in focus with his country team. He also shed light on dealing with government officials and local media on sensitive issues. I had great respect for Frank, a political appointee who had served in several administrations before entering the private sector as an investment banker.

That evening, Marcia and I were invited to dinner at the ambassador's residence, where we met several interesting people, including the guest of honor, Fareed Zakaria, editor of *Newsweek International*. We also met Gregory Osberg, executive vice president and worldwide publisher of *Newsweek*; Shih Choon Fong, president and vice chancellor of the National University of Singapore; James Bush, president, Asia Pacific Region, American Express; and Albert Lam, managing director of Apple Computer, South Asia. It was an incredible evening of lively conversation on U.S. politics, regional issues, and Iraq and the upcoming resolution at the United Nations.

The next day we were invited to a formal function honoring the 227th anniversary of the U.S. Marine Corps. The Marine ceremony featured a full color guard consisting of the embassy Marine detachment's six members and culminated with the traditional cutting of a giant cake with a sword. I was told similar Marine balls were going on around the world.

While there, I was told that Bisa Williams was trying to get in touch with me: she had been asked by the press to get a statement from me on Ramadan, which was that month. President Bush had already issued a statement worldwide. However, with 16 percent of the Mauritian population being Muslim, this would be a good opportunity to reach out and do some bridge building. We carefully reviewed a prepared statement to be released to the press that evening.

When we returned to Mauritius on Saturday, I was happy to read a cable indicating that the UN Security Council had voted 15–0 in favor of Resolution 1441 regarding Iraq. The resolution that was adopted included a provision that Iraq would be considered to be in "material breach" if it did not disclose all weapons of mass destruction, and would face "serious consequences" if it did not abandon its prohibited missiles and other restricted weapons.

On Monday, November 11, the embassy was closed because of Veterans Day in the United States—though in Mauritius it was business as usual. Jayen Cuttaree hosted a function in honor of the visiting Ghana delegation, led by Deputy Minister of Trade Akwasi Osei-Adjei. They had come to Mauritius to learn more about the AGOA program. During this event, Cuttaree gave some great accolades to the United States for instituting this program in sub-Saharan Africa.

We had been told Ghana planned to attend the AGOA Forum with a large delegation, and on Tuesday the visiting delegation arrived at the embassy for a briefing on AGOA. Among them were several private sector clothing designers and manufacturers. Ghana at the time was one of the more stable, democratic countries, even though it was next door to the unstable Côte d'Ivoire.

I had received copies of the speeches made at the AGOA Business Roundtable in Washington by Secretary Powell, Secretary Evans, Secretary O'Neill, and U.S. Trade Representative Zoellick, all praising Mauritius's success under the AGOA program. I was delighted to learn that by all indications these high-ranking cabinet officials would be attending the forum.

On November 14 I met with Trade Minister Cuttaree and his staff for an AGOA Forum logistics planning session and to discuss the nongovernmental organization agenda for the Forum. The nongovernmental organization component was scheduled to run January 13–15, the private sector component would be January 14–16, and the ministerial component, with President Bush, Secretary Powell, and other speakers, would be January 15–17.

I also held a meeting at the embassy with Bisa Williams, Charlie Slater, and Jeff Burke. It appeared the U.S. government wanted to change the current rules for Foreign Service national background checks. Many of our local hires had worked at the embassy for years—some for even more than twenty years. They had shown their loyalty to the United States many times over, and worked hard for what they got paid. Now the rules would be extended beyond the current five-year police checks, which would mean reopening their files and subjecting many to new reviews. I thought this would cause a potentially serious morale issue. To ask neighbors and other sources about them created opportunities for people to take verbal potshots at them. We would eventually have to explain the proposed rule changes in an all-hands meeting, which I thought would create tension and feelings of mistrust.

I was then handed another cable from the Jeddah embassy reporting that Sheikh Usama Abdullah Khayat had delivered a sermon in Mecca, Saudi Arabia, preaching violence and attacks against Israel: "O God, give wisdom to the Muslim leaders.

O God, support our leader and promote Islam through him. O God, help the mujahidin elevate your religion and your word. O God, support them in Palestine. O God, destroy the tyrant Jews, for they are within your power. O God, defeat these tyrant Jews." Sermons similar to this had emanated from Riyadh and Medina before, but had fallen short of explicitly mentioning the Jews.

As part of our Muslim outreach program during Ramadan, the month of fasting, we planned to host an *iftaar* dinner, the evening meal with which Muslims broke their daytime fast. The November 20 event turned out to be very successful and was attended by thirty-two community and business leaders, as well as High Commissioner Athar Mahmood of Pakistan and his wife, Nafisa. We set up a temporary minaret for the call to prayer and provided separate carpeted prayer areas for men and women. Luc, our chef, prepared a complete Muslim-style dinner. At the moment of sundown, all the guests broke their fast with fruit, appetizers, and soft drinks. Immediately after, everyone left for their Maghrib prayers—on the patio for the men and in a back bedroom for the women. Then, with everyone in good spirits, we enjoyed Luc's Mauritian-style meal of rice, beef, chicken, vegetables, beans, numerous spices, and sauces.

15.1. An Iftaar dinner at Macarty House, November 20, 2002.

Later, discussions turned toward the concerns throughout the Muslim community about U.S. use of the words *extremist, terrorist, radical,* and *fundamentalist.* Some believed that these words targeted all of Islam, not just the few who misuse their faith. So after the meal, I made some bridge-building remarks, including some quotations from the speech President Bush had given at the *iftaar* dinner held at the White House. I stressed that our nation was waging a war only on radical networks of terrorists, *not* on Islam and *not* on an entire civilization. High Commissioner Mahmood rose to say a few words about the personal friendship between the two of us and that of the peoples of the United States and Pakistan.

The following day, I met with Sharon Nichols, our regional human resources liaison out of Nairobi. She had spent time with our embassy staff and was impressed with the staff's high morale; by the number of roles taken on by each person, such as Eric, who served as our consular officer, economic officer, and political officer; and with the quality of our multitasking. I told Sharon that I had requested additional personnel, including a full-time consular officer, a commercial officer, a second information technology officer, and one additional office management specialist to work with the deputy chief of mission. In addition, I wanted one full-time Foreign Service national local hire for Comoros and one for Seychelles. She listened to what I said but responded that because we were a Special Embassy Program post, my request would be difficult to accommodate. However, she could see that the officers were at burnout level, since their tasks were significantly greater than those expected in a typical SEP post.

Later in the week, Patrick Zahnd of the International Red Cross in Pretoria, South Africa, and Patrice Pellegrin from the Mauritius Red Cross came by to see me. I felt it was important to support their efforts in the region, not least because they had sent blood supplies to the United States in the aftermath of 9/11. It soothed me to think that some of the victims may have received blood from Mauritius's multicultural, multiethnic, and multireligious people.

At times, Foreign Minister Anil Gayan was tense about issues involving the United States. Since my arrival in Mauritius, he certainly had been quite vocal about the Diego Garcia and Chagos Archipelago sovereignty issues. But he had been supportive of the U.S. position on UN Resolution 1441, and expressed concern that the actions of their permanent representative might have diminished our friendship or country relations. I assured him they had not.

On November 21, when Gayan invited me for lunch, we discussed the ICC Article 98 agreement, and the need to conclude this document, the contents of which he finally agreed to in principle. I wanted it in hand before the AGOA Forum opened in January, and he asked if they were tied together. I replied it was a housekeeping matter to be resolved, and then gave him an overview of the AGOA Forum status and the confirmed dates.

Finally we discussed the Israeli-Palestinian issue. He did not agree with the extent of U.S. support for Israel, and on previous occasions he had commented that the United States was not doing enough to settle the issue and that we had a double standard. This time he expressed more defensiveness. I finally said, "When you feel like railing on the United States on any issue, call me and I will let you rail on me directly." I felt we both left lunch with a better understanding of how we could work together going forward, and we parted warmly. Over time we developed trust and a good friendship, one in which we could express our feelings to each other without the situation becoming stressful.

As I was leaving the embassy on November 22, I was handed a very disturbing cable regarding the upcoming AGOA Forum. Apparently U.S. Ambassador Martin Brennan in Zambia had written a cable to Washington about the lack of access that country's farmers had to U.S. markets, even though their products would qualify under the AGOA program. This evidently had been going on since 1998, because the U.S. Agriculture Department feared contamination by pests and had instituted pest control measures, and the farmers were all very frustrated. Ambassador Brennan thought the Zambian delegation that would be coming to Mauritius might cause embarrassment to President Bush. Since Secretary of Agriculture Veneman was planning to attend the Forum, a call was placed to Cuttaree asking him to include a plenary session on the topic of agriculture.

After a long day, I went back to Macarty House to rest for a few minutes before departing for New York and then on to Washington for consultations. The Air Mauritius flight to Paris and the Delta flight to New York gave me a chance to unwind, relax, and be rested for my upcoming meetings. Tuesday morning, November 26, I met for breakfast with Mauritius's UN representative, Jagdish Koonjul, to develop a better working relationship. I came right to the point: friendships are two-sided, and the AGOA program was just one area where the United States was helping Mauritius. We also created training, education, and exchange programs, and we were providing security for many countries around the world, including Mauritius. He said defensively that the government of Mauritius clearly was aware of how he was dealing with issues at the UN, which was certainly contrary to what Gayan had said.

Jagdish Koonjul added he was pro-American and did not regard his actions at the UN as anti-American. He reiterated he was a friend of the United States and that his intention in spurring a debate was to build consensus. He had wanted a unanimous vote from all fifteen members of the Security Council, he said, and believed his action had helped bring around France, Russia, and China, which had wanted changes in the wording of the resolution. However, he could not clearly explain the media reports that had stated Mauritius and Syria would team up to vote against Resolution 1441.

On the ICC Article 98 issue, Koonjul said that peacekeeping deployments should be considered on a case-by-case basis. This of course was contrary to the blanket nonsurrender language the United States wanted in a separate Article 98 agreement. I repeated that the United States would not allow local governments to hold any U.S. citizen as a result of actions taken during a peacekeeping mission. He was hesitant, so I cited the position of Deputy Prime Minister Bérenger and Foreign Minister Gayan, who had promised me the Article 98 nonsurrender agreement would be signed. He made no further comment.

Koonjul next brought up the extension of the "oil for food" agreement with Iraq. The issue was due for review on December 4, and while Iraq wanted a 180-day extension, as it had received on previous occasions, the United States wanted to give only 90 days. Koonjul thought this might be perceived as a sign that the United States was getting ready for war. I told him that at the end of the extension the issue could be reviewed again. He disagreed with me, and proudly stated he had been instrumental in giving a seven-day extension to the existing term so that further discussion could be undertaken. Again he seemed to be jumping into the middle of issues important to the United States. As he kept talking I sensed that a desire for self-promotion was responsible for his constantly being out front on these issues. Nevertheless, we ended the meeting amicably and agreed to stay in touch.

I was surprised when less than two hours later I received a copy of a speech Koonjul had given at the UN, with a note saying he wanted to dispel any "erroneous perceptions" and pointing out that there was nothing in his speech to suggest any pro-Saddam sentiment. "We consider the United States one of our major allies and trade partners," he wrote, "and you can rest assured that we will do everything to further strengthen our relations."

On Thursday, December 5, I went to Washington for my State Department consultations and the final interagency update meeting before the AGOA Forum. At our morning meeting the next day, Bobby Pittman of the National Security Council gave an overview of the status of U.S. government participation in the Forum. President Bush had yet to confirm his attendance, although we all assumed he intended to attend.

We were only five weeks out and needed a large number of temporary duty officers to help out. The call had been issued, I was told, and so far fifty people had responded. We also had to verify the number of press, which had been estimated to be between 150 and 200. Charlie Slater suggested thanking Chuck Greco and Janis Cook in the budget shop at the Bureau of African Affairs for the work they had done in getting us the $500,000 hotel deposit money, since Charlie had been about to lose the rooms—and face as well. The NGO programs and speakers were reviewed and blessed, with no changes requested at that time. A loose end remained the number of congressional delegations attending, since rooms were scarce.

In my meeting with Deputy Assistant Secretary Charlie Snyder of the Bureau of African Affairs, I pressed him to help get the Peace Corps, USAID, and IMET programs back in Comoros. With Elizabeth "Jamie" Agnew, executive director of the Bureau of African Affairs, I again asked for a full-time consular officer position and a new commercial officer position. She suggested I set out a strong case for these positions and take it up with Walter Kansteiner in January when he came to Mauritius. I then met with Wendell Albright, who added two plenary sessions to the Forum—"Mobilizing Capital for Development" and "Governance"—and a breakout session, "Building the New Economy."

That afternoon, I met with Jendayi Frazer, special assistant to the President and senior director for African affairs at the National Security Council. I also met her new assistant, Matt McLean. In preparation for our afternoon meeting with Condoleezza Rice, I mentioned to Frazer that the Mauritian government continually pressed for sovereignty over the Chagos Archipelago and was under the illusion that the United States supported its sovereignty claim. The main concern of the United States, of course, was to protect U.S. interests and our continued unimpeded use of Diego Garcia as a military base. We reviewed some talking points on U.S. use of Diego Garcia and security issues in the region:

1. Diego Garcia is an important military base.
2. We recognize British ownership of Diego Garcia.
3. We are comfortable with the lease arrangement.
4. We are not interested in changing our use of Diego Garcia.
5. We do not want to leave the door open by using the global war on terror as a reason for U.S. use of the island, since the global situation could change and we would still need Diego Garcia as a military base to protect U.S. interests around the world.

When we met in Rice's office in the White House, we discussed the subject of Diego Garcia. Jendayi explained that Rice's letter in response to Prime Minister Jugnauth's letter on the sovereignty issue was straightforward. But apparently, its tone had indicated to the government of Mauritius that the United States encouraged the next round of negotiation about sovereignty over Chagos. We then presented the five talking points on the Diego Garcia issue and noted that the National Security Council staff believed they were appropriate. Rice was totally attentive and focused the whole time, and after we had laid out the matter, she said we could have the President clear up the United States' position to Mauritius, as he had no problem being direct. We agreed that I would meet with Bérenger and Jugnauth and ask them not to bring up the sovereignty issue at the AGOA Forum.

I briefed them on the AGOA Forum plans, which were on track, and noted that while there were a few concerns about protesters, the event would be safe. Next I explained that with Mauritius still on the Security Council for the next few weeks its vote on Resolution 1441 was most important. I mentioned that the government of Mauritius had recalled its permanent representative because he had acted independently, with the intent of not supporting the resolution's passage.

I next met with Director Lauren Moriarty of the Office of East African Affairs to give an update on the Forum, and explain the need for more temporary duty officers.

On the evening of December 10, an event to celebrate Eid ul-Fitr, which marked the end of Ramadan, took place at the Golden Crest Hotel, located in the heart of Quatre Bornes, an older established Muslim community in Mauritius. I was happy to be able to participate before leaving for a late-night briefing with the Washington advance team leaders, who were arriving that day.

There was much to do. Bradley Blakeman, deputy assistant to the President for scheduling and advance, and Mary Haines, deputy executive secretary for scheduling and advance for Condoleezza Rice and the National Security Council, came by the residence with Bisa Williams for a review of their agenda while in Mauritius. We discussed how to deal with the bilateral meetings planned for the President and Secretary of State. They agreed neither one should meet separately with Bérenger or Jugnauth. I felt comfortable with the advance leaders, especially Blakeman, who had been involved in White House matters since the Reagan administration; in addition, we had a number of mutual friends in Washington.

Both left at midnight to work on revised schedules for President Bush and Secretary Powell during the AGOA Forum, and faxed me a copy at 1:40 a.m. The delegation would arrive on Air Force One at 4:40 p.m. on January 14, 2003, and depart at 7:30 a.m. on January 16, 2003. In addition to attending the Forum, there would be a short courtesy call on President Offmann and a thirty-minute bilateral meeting with Prime Minister Jugnauth, Deputy Prime Minister Bérenger, and Foreign Minister Gayan. In the meeting with the President would be Colin Powell, Condoleezza Rice, Jendayi Frazer, Walter Kansteiner, Andy Card, Ari Fleischer, and myself.

Early Wednesday morning I called Prime Minister Jugnauth to brief him on our intended schedule for a bilateral meeting, which would not allow for a breakout meeting with the President or Secretary of State. I further suggested that we keep the bilateral meeting on a positive note, in light of the November 28 terrorist bombing of a hotel in Mombasa, and minimize the Diego Garcia discussion. I might have overstepped my authority, but I felt it was important to protect the President and avoid an uncomfortable situation.

That day I was given a copy of a Reuters story from earlier that morning indicating that a North Korean ship carrying Scud missiles and chemicals and bound for the Middle East had been intercepted in the Arabian Sea by Spanish warships. The Spanish had turned the vessel over to the U.S. Navy, which had escorted it to Diego Garcia. This was further reason for limiting bilateral discussions on Diego Garcia at the AGOA Forum.

We then held an all-hands briefing with the advance team. First Bradley outlined for the group the logistics of the U.S. participants' travels. Beginning on January 14, 2003, three airplanes would arrive: one 747 carrying the two hundred members of the press corps, a 757 backup plane for the President, and Air Force One. There would be arrival ceremonies, followed by a forty-car motorcade. Bradley and Mary then gave the embassy staff a rundown of the Forum agenda.

After the briefing, we held a joint AGOA Forum planning committee meeting with the advance team and the government of Mauritius team, headed by Deputy Prime Minister Bérenger. He was accompanied by Suresh Seeballuck, Home Affairs; Krish Ponnusamy, Foreign Affairs; Clency Rosalie, Trade; Subash Gobin, press advisor; and Police Commissioner Ramanooj Gopalsingh. Afterward, the Advance Team took a tour of the University of Mauritius. Almost all the retrofitting had been completed for the Forum areas and everyone was impressed with the venue. At another meeting, Maurice Vigier de Latour, president of the Mauritius Freeport Development Ltd. and chairman of the AGOA private sector coordinating committee, updated us on the private sector component and noted that Microsoft, as part of the local team, would be providing a number of computers for Internet access during the Forum.

On Thursday morning, I headed to the Hilton for a wrap-up session with the embassy staff and the advance team before their midday departure for Nairobi. Just as the advance team's C-17 aircraft was preparing to depart, we received notice of a credible threat that an aircraft might attempt to fly into the U.S. Embassy in Nairobi. The advance team debated whether they should continue on to Nairobi. The C-17 was equipped with a mechanism to deflect a missile attack, and so they decided to leave as scheduled. But this new embassy threat was another serious issue we had to handle.

On Saturday, December 14, Dan Claffey, my public affairs officer, called about a recent news release regarding the President's upcoming trip to Africa. The White House press secretary was quoted as saying, "President Bush will travel to Africa, January 10–17, 2003, to continue to build America's partnership with the continent. This visit highlights the Bush administration's commitment to working toward a free and prosperous Africa. The President also looks forward to opening the second U.S.–Sub-Saharan Africa Trade and Economic Cooperation Forum (AGOA Forum) in Mauritius."

This was great news—the press secretary's statement made the visit official, after months of uncertainty. Charlie Slater, my administrative officer, came by Macarty House later in the day to tell me that the advance team had made it safely to Nairobi and that the embassy there had not been attacked. I let him know about the press release, and he too was relieved.

On Monday morning at our nine o'clock country team meeting, I was introduced to Daniel Norman, the embassy's new information management specialist, a position I had pressed for since arriving in 2002. Daniel would help Lizzie Slater, the embassy's information programs officer, who had been working fourteen-hour days and weekends. *One down and two to go,* I thought. And in a postmortem on the AGOA advance team's visit, everyone agreed that all aspects of the planning were moving forward nicely.

During the meeting, I was handed several cables, including some about potential al-Qaeda attacks. Such cables had become routine lately, but nonetheless caused anxiety among the embassy staff. I felt that was part of the al-Qaeda methodology—the messages ended up putting the world on constant alert, and they didn't have to fight any battles to scare us to death. One of the cables indicated that al-Qaeda plans included attacks on U.S. ships in northern Europe, plus ten additional maritime attacks elsewhere. Another indicated possible attacks by al-Qaeda in Djibouti, where U.S. and German forces were stationed. A third indicated that satellite images showed Iraq moving armed forces to its east border, to complement the troop buildup on its western border.

In another cable from the State Department, we were asked to prepare a report on Chinese investments in sub-Saharan Africa. I had been in Mauritius eight months and had already noted this as a major issue, though no one else in the U.S. government had seemed concerned. But Walter Kansteiner had recently made a visit to sub-Saharan Africa, and I supposed that what he had seen there had raised concerns about China's rapid growth and influence. I decided to bring up the matter with U.S. officials during the Forum. (As I would discover in later discussions with U.S. Trade Representative Bob Zoellick and Congressman Bill Thomas, chairman of the powerful House Ways and Means Committee, those officials were not nearly as concerned about China as I was. Thomas, in fact, would attack Mauritius—not the Chinese—for abusing AGOA and taking jobs away from Americans.)

On December 18, Maurice de Latour came to see me. Nervously wringing his hands, he said that his sponsors, which were paying from $5,000 to $50,000 for the private sector event, needed to have access to the U.S. delegation leaders, and preferably one-on-one sessions. I told him that would not be possible, and that buying access was against U.S. policy. He understood, yet told me he needed something for them. I suggested that his sponsors' group cohost the U.S. government reception. Other nonsponsors would also need to be invited, but at the reception the business interests could single out the people they wished to talk with. I felt this was a cleaner and more transparent approach, and he agreed.

The next day was a momentous one for the schoolchildren of Mauritius. Early on, when I became acquainted with Vice President Raouf Bundhun, he had expressed the desire that every child own a book. Not able to excite anyone in Washington about supplying thousands of books, I turned to the Church of Jesus Christ of Latter-day Saints. I was aware that they had a book distribution program, and so after the Vice President made his request, I worked for several months with the Church's attorney, Jamie Dester, and with Elder Russell Nelson to see whether they would participate. They came through, and two shipping containers filled with twenty-five thousand books arrived. The book donation ceremony was scheduled to take place at a port warehouse.

In addition to children's books, there were a number of reference books that would be given to the National Library. Minister of Culture Motee Ramdass and National Library Director Yves Chan Kam Lon were delighted to receive these books. There were also several thousand school kits for children filled with basic supplies. We thought many of the primary and secondary school children would be happy with the wide range of subjects, which included fiction, nonfiction, and some books on American history and world geography. Vice President Bundhun would select the schools to receive these gifts at a future date.

On December 20, Secretary Powell made a major speech about Iraq not having complied with the requirement to fully disclose its weapons programs. On this occasion he sounded more like a hawk than he had previously, which meant there was some real concern about Saddam Hussein. Then a report reached me indicating that B-1 bombers would soon be heading from Missouri to Diego Garcia. I suspected this might be the beginning of another Gulf War, this time with the intention of taking out Saddam Hussein.

Bisa handed me a demarche cable from Washington saying the United States would continue its ongoing consultations with UN Security Council members. It noted that Iraq's declaration indicated that it was not being forthcoming, and that inspectors had amassed findings that contradicted some of the information Iraq had provided.

Examples of omissions in Iraq's declarations were given to us as talking points. I carefully reviewed the long list in preparation for discussion with the government of Mauritius. The items included incomplete information, outright omission, or false denials about biological agents (including anthrax, botulinum toxin, and *Clostridium perfringens*), ballistic missiles, fuels for missiles, nuclear weapons, the nerve agent VX, destruction of chemical and biological weapons, empty munitions (which could be filled with chemical agents), their unmanned aerial vehicle program, and mobile biological weapon agent facilities.

The demarche concluded that these omissions in Iraq's declaration were no mere accident, oversight, or technical mistake. And Secretary Powell said that we were getting closer to the day when "Iraq will have to face serious consequences."

While reviewing emails later that night, I learned that Susanne Rose had stopped transiting of several suspicious-looking individuals in the Seychelles from getting U.S. visas. They seemed to have more than $4,000 each in cash, and though they claimed to barely speak English while communicating with her, the taxi driver who had taken them to a hotel told Susanne that they spoke English very well and said they were visiting fifty-two countries. They claimed to be in the perfume business—but had no samples. "We are running an international check," the message concluded.

"President Bush's trip to Africa is off." That was the shocking message I received at six o'clock in the morning on December 21, 2002, from Bisa Williams, who had been awakened some four hours earlier by Bob Perry with the news.

How could this be? Only a few days before, all the plans for the visit had been completed with the White House advance team. Bisa thought it had to do with Iraq, and also with the resignation of Senator Trent Lott, the Senate majority leader. However, she added, Bob did say that otherwise the AGOA Forum was still on as planned.

I thought, *This is not going to be a good day for any of us.* In addition to telling the Prime Minister—who I knew was counting on President Bush's visit—that the President had canceled his trip, I would also have to sit down with Jugnauth to review the demarche I had received about Iraq.

I called the Prime Minister's home and upon reaching him learned that he already knew: at five-thirty that morning he had received a call from Krish Ponnusamy in the foreign minister's office, followed by a call from Peter Craig at their Washington embassy with the same information. I was irritated that, once again, the State Department had preempted us.

I then placed a call to Deputy Prime Minister Bérenger, who also had heard the news. He, like the Prime Minister, queried me about what this meant for the Forum and the delegation. I assured him, as I had Jugnauth, as best as I could that Secretary Powell and U.S. Trade Representative Zoellick were still planning on coming.

When I arrived at the embassy, Charlie Slater had already heard the news on the radio. Since Washington was nine hours earlier, information reached Mauritius in time for the early news reports—sometimes even before we heard about it.

The White House press release was almost as short as the one announcing it a week earlier: "President Bush will reschedule his January 2003 trip to Africa until later in the year due to a combination of domestic and international considerations. The President looks forward to visiting Africa in 2003 to continue building America's partnership with the continent and to sharing firsthand with African leaders his commitment to working on issues ranging from the war on terrorism to economic development."

What had really changed in one week? I could not be sure. My intent, however, was still to make the AGOA Forum a great success, with a stellar attendance of sub-Saharan Africa finance ministers and dignitaries, business leaders from Africa and the United States, and a high-level Washington delegation.

During the week, I met with Dan Claffey to discuss putting out widespread AGOA Forum publicity to enhance attendance. A local business magazine was intending to run a generic article in their January edition, and I suggested that perhaps the story could take a more interesting slant, highlighting why American businesses should invest in Mauritius and in sub-Saharan Africa. The article would include my impressions from having been in Mauritius for eight months, and I outlined the numerous opportunities available here: niche opportunities in the textile sector, information technology, offshore banking, call center operations, high-quality retail shops aimed at the tourist trade, expansion of the fisheries sector, and the duty-free island concept. I mentioned some of the pitfalls as well, and suggested that Dan weave in mention of the rest of sub-Saharan Africa.

Dan wrote as quickly as he could, with a great big smile on his face, so I knew he was happy with the direction in which I was heading. Then he went off to write the story.

❨XVI❩

Rebuilding Support

Walter Kansteiner called saying he was coming for the Forum and would see me in Mauritius. He added that Secretary Powell would be able to come for one day only. I certainly hoped the Secretary would come, since the government of Mauritius had been disappointed when the President cancelled his trip. I asked Walter if there was a 60 percent chance that we would see Powell. He retorted that it was more like 70 percent but that he would get back with me within the next few hours to verify. By the following morning, I hadn't heard from Walter. When I finally did reach him in the afternoon, the news was disappointing: Secretary Powell was not coming.

I asked Walter to have Secretary Powell immediately write a personal note to Prime Minister Jugnauth for me to hand-deliver in order to keep up the enthusiasm for the Forum. Then I asked my deputy chief of mission to set up an appointment with the Prime Minister for Monday so I could personally rebuild confidence about U.S. support of the AGOA Forum.

On Monday, January 6, I held a joint country team meeting including the temporary duty officers who had arrived for the Forum. The letter from Powell had not arrived as promised. Since the Prime Minister was out of the country, I decided to meet with Trade Minister Jayen Cuttaree, the Mauritian coordinator for the AGOA Forum. Knowing things were heating up in the Middle East, he understood about Powell's change of plans and agreed that the Forum was still going forward. He asked for one last wrap-up meeting with his staff and our extended country team before the event.

Cuttaree was concerned that some of the sub-Saharan African ministers planning to attend the Forum might be less interested in lauding U.S. efforts in the region, minimize the benefits of the AGOA program, and demand greater U.S. government support for their problematic New Partnership for Africa's Development (NEPAD) plan. Furthermore, they would certainly notice that their delegations, which would include several ministers, might outrank the level of the U.S. delegation at the Forum, and Cuttaree cautioned that this could be a problem. At that point, I didn't have the heart to also tell him that Secretary Veneman had called in sick and that USAID Administrator Natsios had also cancelled. In addition, the Treasury Department would not have secretary-level representation.

I discussed the possibility of President Bush doing a digital video conference call or a live satellite feed for the opening of the Forum and saw a gleam of excitement in Cuttaree's eyes. After promising Cuttaree I would immediately go to work on such a plan, I met with Bisa and began to strategize on the wording of a strong cable—to go out that night.

Just then I was handed a copy of a notice from a group called the Mouvement Republicain that had been sent to Police Commissioner Gopalsingh. The group was intending to hold a nonstop demonstration in front of the embassy during the AGOA Forum. The law provided that demonstrations of fewer than ten people at a time required a notice only and were not subject to the approval of the police. The movement's purpose was to sensitize the public on the issue of the looming war with Iraq. With more than nine hundred visitors to Mauritius expected for the AGOA Forum and a local press that loved theatrics, this was an added problem I didn't need.

The cable we were working on would be going to the White House and Condoleezza Rice at the National Security Council with a copy to Andy Card, the President's chief of staff, so it had to be both strongly worded and carefully phrased, as I had great concern about overstepping my bounds. But I also didn't want the sub-Saharan African countries to be let down, or to reinforce their belief that the United States has a double standard: what suits us, when it suits us.

In the cable, I urged the President to consider a live video presentation addressing the thirty-seven African ministers, their delegations, and other international observers who would be attending the AGOA Forum on opening day. I stressed the gesture would symbolize sustained, top-level Bush administration commitment to African economic, trade, and strategic partnership goals. It would also stem the criticism that had resulted from the news that both President Bush and Secretary Powell were unable to attend the Forum. That night, while I was attending President Offmann's hosted dinner for members of the diplomatic corps, I received word that Bobby Pittman, responding to my cable, had also put in a request for a live address by the President that could take place during the U.S.-hosted reception that week. I was pleased, and later that night, after the dinner was over and I had the chance to reply, I told him to keep pressing. Almost immediately he answered, saying that the senior press people had already approved the idea. I kept my fingers crossed, but it looked as though we might get what we were hoping for.

Athar Mahmood, the Pakistani high commissioner to Mauritius, and I had become good friends—as had Marcia and his wife, Nafisa. In early January, he came to see me to discuss how my presentation of credentials and other formalities had been handled on my Comoros visit, since he was going there at the end of the month for the formal presentation of his credentials. I reviewed with him Comoros's years of turmoil and said that, with Azali having been fairly elected in April 2002, the country was moving in the direction of a fledgling democracy. I expressed concerns about the reported French destabilization efforts over the years in Comoros and France's possible involvement in several of the coups and attempted coups. But the main issue of concern was the influx in Comoros of fundamentalist clerics and their radical teachings, and their encouragement to students to study in other countries including Pakistan. I noted that Fazul Abdullah Mohammed, the Comorian terrorist, had been lured as a student to go to Pakistan and train with Osama bin Laden in Afghanistan.

Athar had told me on many occasions that most Pakistanis are moderate in their thinking. He himself was a moderate practicing Muslim, and he was against these fundamentalist teachings. He also said President Pervez Musharraf was moderate in his beliefs.

Later that night, I received a phone call from Ambassador Pamela Bridgewater to let me know that Bob Perry, deputy assistant secretary of the Bureau of African Affairs, was retiring, and that she would be his replacement.

This was another case of changing personnel in midstream, as it was only seven days before the Forum opening ceremonies. I was relieved to hear that she mentioned having seen my cable requesting a broadcast by President Bush and that she was supportive of the request. She did want to confirm that we could provide the technical hookups needed. Even though Dan Claffey and others at the embassy had

16.1. From left to right: The Ambassador, Nafisa Mahmood, Marcia Price, and Pakistani High Commissioner Athar Mahmood, January 2003.

researched this topic on a number of occasions for Washington, I quickly summoned Dan and Bisa into my office and then called her back to reconfirm our ability to supply the necessary hookup. "Just give us the nod to go ahead and we will make it happen," I said, emphasizing that the venue would be the January 15 evening USG Reception.

Jendayi Frazer from the National Security Council called saying she was sensitive to our request for President Bush to do a live or taped broadcast. She preferred a live speech, however, and in this she was supported by Rice. She said that Anna Perez, a deputy, or Deborah Loewer, the senior director of communications, would call for details on available technical equipment. I told Dan Claffey he could expect more phone calls on whether we could provide the necessary technology.

As we moved into the final stages of preparation for the Forum, more temporary duty officers were buzzing around the embassy, more equipment had arrived, and the air was filled with energy and excitement. As I headed for my office, I took a call from Jayen Cuttaree. "Now that the President is not coming," he asked, "do we still play the American national anthem at the opening session?"

I thought for a moment, then responded, "You know, we play it at the start of football games, at basketball games, at baseball games, and at hockey games—so why wouldn't we play it at the AGOA Forum event?"

On the morning of January 9 I received an email from Bobby Pittman stating the President's speech would be taped and sent via satellite. Another email indicated the First Lady was not going to do a live broadcast program with a girls' school, as previously planned; instead, Dr. Sarah Moten was going to bring a videotape done by Laura Bush.

Late that afternoon, we had an all-hands meeting at the Hilton Hotel, which included forty people from our embassy and forty-five temporary duty officers. We reviewed assignments of the control officers for the Washington delegations and CODELS. We also covered interface with the media, transportation issues, room assignments, and venue coverage. Our preparations had a backup plan for all aspects. The main snafus, I thought, would come from the delegations changing their minds or schedules. I stressed that we all needed to be tolerant and flexible. In the end, we were serving one country, one President, and in this case one objective: the success of the second AGOA Forum to improve U.S.-African trade relations and thereby help these poor third-world countries.

On January 10, it was confirmed that the U.S. delegation would include U.S. Trade Representative Bob Zoellick, Ambassador Jon Huntsman Jr., and Ambassador Andrew Young. The Treasury delegation would now include Undersecretary John Taylor. In yet another switch, USAID Administrator Andrew Natsios, who previously had said he would not be attending, had changed his mind, but Commerce Undersecretary Grant Aldonas would not. I was concerned that the U.S. delegation would not include many cabinet members, as originally contemplated. We needed to showcase the importance of each member of the U.S. delegation, so that the African ministers and other government leaders attending wouldn't feel that the United States placed less importance on the Forum.

At noon on Saturday, we met to discuss the private sector opening ceremony, the speakers, and the plenary sessions. The team was well prepared, having handled the private sector component for the first AGOA Forum in Washington.

I asked Gloria Cabe, who represented the Corporate Council on Africa, to compare our planning for this year's Forum with the previous year's event. The previous year was not a good example, she said, because of the 9/11 attacks: the Forum had been shortened and was not well attended. However, Cabe said we were quantum leaps ahead of other events she had worked on in the past, in terms of projected attendance and preparation. We had 930 registrations already, including 170 from the United States, 200 from Mauritius, 513 from sub-Saharan Africa, 8 from the Middle East, 12 from the European Union, and 16 from Asia. I felt proud of the U.S. Embassy Port Louis team for their efforts in putting together this Forum event.

On Monday afternoon, Marcia and I, Bisa, Jayen Cuttaree, his wife, Swatee, and several other Mauritius government ministers went to the airport to greet the CODEL that would be arriving. This would be only the second CODEL to come through Mauritius since I arrived. The group included Congressman Bill Thomas, chairman of the House Ways and Means Committee, and his wife, Sharon; Congressman Ed Royce, a ranking member of the House Foreign Affairs Committee; Congressman Jim McDermott, a ranking member of the House Ways and Means Committee; Congressman Phil English, a ranking member of the House Ways and Means Committee, and his wife, Chris; Congressman Jim Nussle and his wife, Karen; and several staff and a military escort. I was pleased that members of Congress came as part of the Washington delegation to participate in the AGOA Forum.

After the CODEL press conference, we joined them on the bus ride to the Sofitel Hotel. This gave us an hour to get acquainted and brief them on Mauritius and its culture, government structure, and business environment; the planned activities for the Forum; and the bilateral meetings set up with the government of Mauritius. When Congressman Thomas raised the question of transparency, I offered the example of the Mauritian government's closed bid practices, which favored EU countries. Hence, American companies generally declined to bid. I had been told this several times in the past by different sources that did not trust the bid process.

That evening at the Freeport Center, where we were holding the private sector opening reception, Bobby Pittman and Dan Claffey accompanied me through the exhibits. Approximately 180 booths were set up displaying products from more than twenty-two countries. The business representatives were eager to network and discuss these products. It had taken great effort to put together this major exhibition, and the credit went to Maurice de Latour, Didier de Senneville, and the others on their team. As I continued walking through the exhibits, I ran into many of the friends and acquaintances I had made over the past nine months.

At 7:30 p.m., the official opening of the trade show began and included remarks by Maurice de Latour, the coordinating committee chairman; Paul Ryberg, president of the African Coalition for Trade; Stephen Hayes, president of the Corporate Council on Africa; Jean-Raymond Boulle, chairman of Boulle Corporation; and myself, representing the U.S. government and filling in for Grant Aldonas. Representing the host country, Prime Minister Anerood Jugnauth and Deputy Prime Minister Paul Bérenger also offered kind words of welcome.

The assembled audience had grown to twelve hundred people. I was delighted and in my welcome said, "It is finally here. The second AGOA Forum is a reality. Businesses and governments are seeing firsthand the advantages that can be obtained by working together to create a favorable business environment in Mauritius."

Early Tuesday morning, Walter Kansteiner's plane landed and he headed to Macarty House to freshen up and join me for breakfast. By 8:00 a.m. we were on our way to the Radisson Hotel on the island's west coast for the private sector opening session. On the way, we reviewed issues that might be brought up in our bilateral meetings later that day, including Diego Garcia, Iraq, sourcing of materials under the AGOA program, and the importance of extending the program beyond 2008.

More than 350 participants attended the opening session. As we welcomed everyone, I was pleased to be able to cite the number of participants registered for the private sector sessions—more than 930. Most important, I said, the Forum demonstrated that America was ready to trade with Africa and that African countries were ready and able to produce the merchandise that American companies wanted to buy. Between 100,000 and 200,000 new jobs had been created in the apparel sector alone during the previous two years, and in the three years since the AGOA program was enacted there had been a remarkable 118 percent growth in African country exports to the United States. No doubt it was a great benefit for these countries to access U.S. markets.

I accompanied the CODEL to Government House for a bilateral meeting with Deputy Prime Minister Bérenger and Foreign Minister Gayan. The subjects brought up included the disarming of Iraq, the UN Security Council vote in support of the U.S.-sponsored resolution, and the long-lasting relationship between the United States and Mauritius going back to 1794. There was a tense discussion relating to the Southern Africa Customs Union free trade agreements that the United States was negotiating, which greatly concerned the government of Mauritius. Established in 1910, the SACU consists of Botswana, Lesotho, Namibia, South Africa, and Swaziland.

Foreign Minister Gayan noted that he was concerned about U.S. policy as it relates to small countries' needs for more access to the U.S. markets, and that the AGOA program provided an opportunity to help Africa get out of poverty. He also stressed that the World Health Organization had to do more regarding the HIV/AIDS issue. He then said the United States needed to engage Zimbabwe in dialogue instead of putting it in the corner because of the way its government had confiscated private farmland, most of it owned by whites; this had affected the United States' relations with the Southern African Development Community countries (SADC), which could not ignore the treatment of one of its members.

In response to Gayan's comment, Jim McDermott noted he had just been in Namibia, where farms owned by German descendants were being confiscated, and the problems were getting more drastic; he believed action was necessary to reverse the trend.

Focusing on the AGOA, Gayan agreed we needed to monitor eligible countries to see they were doing what they had said they would do on issues such as rule of law, transparency, and human rights. He was also firm in having indefinite access to U.S. markets, with no termination date to the AGOA program.

At that point, I could see Bill Thomas getting uncomfortable. He finally remarked that the program needed a "hammer" and that potential termination dates, extensions, and a review process served that purpose. He also pointed out the United States had opened its markets further than any other world power had. Jim McDermott chimed in, saying he didn't think Thomas's committee would let the program lapse, but rather would extend it beyond the expiration date.

Deputy Prime Minister Bérenger commented on the Zimbabwe, Ivory Coast, and Namibia land reform issues, saying it was necessary to establish a respect for rule of law and human rights before land reform is implemented, rather than just taking away people's rights. I thought that was a bold statement for him to make openly. He then voiced some thoughts on neighboring Comoros. The issue was that the three island presidents and Union President Azali were to have signed agreements regarding power sharing, revenue sharing, and security forces by mid-December 2002, which had not occurred. Tension was building up and there was talk of the Union collapsing. Bérenger remarked: "Other than Mauritius and the U.S. Embassy Port Louis, no one seems to care or is paying attention to the Comoros."

Bérenger briefly mentioned that Madagascar was on the right track and moving forward. Switching the focus to Mauritius, he acknowledged a new thrust into the IT sector to diversify the country's economy, and an emphasis on the education of their people to meet tomorrow's expanding challenges.

Jim McDermott suggested the government of Mauritius be more proactive on Capitol Hill by lobbying Congress for some help with these issues. He suggested the government of Mauritius give their ambassador a free hand to do so, as Ambassador Jesseramsing had done for the fourteen years he served there.

After the meeting Walter Kansteiner, Bob Perry, and Jim Dunlop (an economic advisor), and I went to Government House to meet with Jugnauth and Bérenger. With us was Secretary Powell's letter to the Prime Minister apologizing for not being able to attend the Forum.

Jugnauth expressed concern over the possible war with Iraq, which they hoped could be avoided. He said that Mauritius would support the United States in the event of such a war. Then, as usual, he brought up the Diego Garcia sovereignty issue, but he did not press it due to the pending Iraq issue.

Addressing terrorism, Bérenger brought up his concern about transshipping containers without fully knowing what was inside. Currently, the procedure was to check containers only from ports shipping directly to a U.S. port. He wanted the United States to help Mauritius acquire scanners to examine incoming cargo containers, especially those passing through Mauritius to other destinations, ultimately reaching U.S. ports. He used the example of a cargo container ship coming from Cape Town, South Africa, and stopping in Mauritius to off-load containers and then take on others destined for different ports, including U.S. ports. He wanted our help to purchase scanners to check all containers as a security measure. I too would express these concerns to top officials of the Transportation Security Administration (TSA) in Washington. The TSA didn't share the concerns Bérenger and I had; I thought that was shortsighted. (It wasn't until much later, on January 9, 2007, that all cargo containers coming into the United States would be checked.)

Driving back to Macarty House afterward, I shared with Walter the transcript of the President's videotape for the Wednesday night U.S. government reception. The AGOA participants would be pleasantly surprised: the President was going to ask Congress to extend the AGOA beyond 2008. He also was going to add money to the Millennium Fund and earmark more funds for education, teachers, books, and supplies, all of which would benefit the sub-Saharan African countries.

That evening, Marcia and I hosted a dinner in honor of the CODEL and representatives of the other U.S. agencies.

16.2. Ambassador Andrew Young with Marcia Price and Ambassador Price at the AGOA Forum dinner at Macarty House, January 14, 2003.

16.3. Ambassador Bob Berry, Assistant Secretary Walter Kansteiner, and Congressman Bill Thomas at the AGOA Forum dinner at Macarty House, January 14, 2003.

I gave some background information and statistics on Mauritius, where they were heading, and their leadership role in the region. Most didn't know Mauritian companies had numerous business ventures in other sub-Saharan African countries. I also wanted everyone to appreciate all the work that had been done by our embassy's limited staff. I had invited the country team for everyone to meet, and was sorry we could not have included the Foreign Service national staff, who contributed significantly to the Forum's success.

At the end of the evening, Thomas presented me with a gift of congressional tumblers in appreciation. However, in his remarks he thanked "Ambassador Rogers," and we all had a good laugh.

On Wednesday, morning January 15, Andrew Natsios arrived at Macarty House while I was working out. He rested in the guesthouse until we departed two hours later for the University of Mauritius, where the second AGOA Forum's opening ceremonies were being held.

When the dignitaries headed to their assigned seats, I sat in the front row with the U.S. delegation. The stage looked very colorful, with the flags of the thirty-seven AGOA nations surrounded by Mauritius's famous giant red antheriums. Many of the delegates were dressed in formal attire from their native countries.

Next to us sat the Seychellois delegation, including Selby Pillay and Foreign Minister Jérémie Bonnelame. We talked about their hard currency crisis, brought

16.4. Welcoming Ambassador Jon Huntsman Jr., Deputy U.S. Trade Representative, to the AGOA Forum dinner at Macarty House, January 14, 2003.

16.5. The United States delegation at the AGOA Forum ministerial session, January 15, 2003.

16.6. Address by Ambassador Robert Zoellick, U.S. Trade Representative, at the second AGOA U.S.-Sub-Saharan Africa Trade and Economic Cooperation Forum, January 15, 2003.

about partially by the control Mukesh Valabhji had over the Seychelles Marketing Board, and the concern that this would weaken the middle class. As I've noted, part of the foreign exchange problem had come about from their land reclamation program, which both required large hard currency payments and, at the same time, created ecological imbalances and destroyed precious coral reefs.

In talking with Bonnelame, I realized there was a lingering unresolved issue regarding an extradition treaty that was a vestige from colonial times but still recognized by the United Kingdom and the United States. We wanted Seychelles to acknowledge this treaty, with certain agreed-upon modifications. The treaty was important since there was an individual living in Seychelles whom the United States had asked to have extradited, without success. Foreign Minister Bonnelame said the embassy had been told they could come get him, and a letter had been sent to the embassy to that effect. I was not surprised, since with the embassy officer turnover, such issues tended to fall between the cracks.

Since Jendayi Frazer was here for the AGOA Forum, I felt it would be good for her to personally clarify the U.S. position on Diego Garcia, since she was at the National Security Council and reported directly to Condoleezza Rice. On Wednesday, January 15, at a meeting set up for Jugnauth with Jendayi Frazer, Bobby Pittman, and myself, Jendayi was pretty direct with the Prime Minister. She clarified our intention to keep all of our rights and options to Diego Garcia. She referred to the global war on terror, the recent Mombasa hotel bombing, and the potential for a war with Iraq. She emphasized that the Chagos Archipelago had to remain sanitized of visitors. I added that we all felt for the Chagossians, but we had to keep our eye on the ball and stay focused. Jendayi agreed, and the Prime Minister shook his head, understanding the seriousness of our concerns.

I looked at my watch and quickly excused myself so that I could run next door to catch up with the Zoellick delegation and their bilateral meeting with Deputy Prime Minister Bérenger and Trade Minister Cuttaree. Zoellick listened patiently while they asked for an extension of the AGOA benefits beyond the planned 2008 sunset of the program. Both Zoellick and I knew that President Bush had agreed to support the extension, as he would state in that night's taped video address, but we could not tell them—the President's remarks were embargoed until the presentation. The Mauritians also expressed their concern about the Southern African Customs Union negotiations; competition was their main concern.

Afterward, I took the Zoellick delegation next door to meet the Prime Minister, who also voiced concern about competition given the expansion of the AGOA benefits to thirty-seven countries. He feared that wages in many of these countries would be very low and that this might erode Mauritius's standard of living, which had taken many years to build up. Zoellick tried to calm him by discussing the overall benefits of the AGOA to Mauritius. As our meeting came to an end, Jugnauth finally shook his head, smiled a little, and said, "I look forward to working with you."

As we were leaving, we heard a distant noise. Soon the sound of drums could be heard coming closer, and a marching group of protesters appeared. The demonstration, part of the "People's Forum" in which the Mouvement Solidarité National was participating, marched on Government House and the U.S. Embassy to protest U.S. policies in Africa and in support of the Chagossians' plight.

As they passed, the marchers shouted something in Creole that we could not understand, adding, "Jugnauth, Jugnauth, Jugnauth." With a wry smile, Zoellick turned to Jugnauth and asked, "Are these your supporters?" Everyone had a good laugh, including the Prime Minister.

On the evening of January 15, the U.S. Embassy in conjunction with the U.S. government hosted the key reception event for the dignitaries, delegates, and invited guests attending the AGOA Forum. It was held at Domaine Anna, a restaurant uniquely situated in the midst of a sugarcane plantation. To reach the picturesque restaurant, one traveled on a dirt road surrounded by six-foot-high sugar cane on both sides until one reached a small clearing at the end of the road. The building that housed the restaurant was a beautiful structure made from indigenous lava rock. The local Chinese family who owned it had other well-known restaurants in Mauritius as well.

We had scheduled to start the speeches and video presentation at 8:45 p.m., but when the appointed hour arrived, Bob Zoellick, the U.S. delegation leader, was still in the midst of a private meeting with a textile group—and Jayen Cuttaree was waiting to meet with him privately for a few minutes. As the minutes ticked by, I was getting more and more anxious, feeling almost like a child with a secret I could scarcely keep to myself.

The moment Zoellick arrived, I went up to the podium. I could sense the excitement among the attendees and hoped they all were enjoying themselves. I then announced the presentation, the lights went out and the video players displayed an image of President Bush on three large screens mounted on the walls. I walked over to Prime Minister Jugnauth and Deputy Prime Minister Bérenger and stood between them with my hands momentarily on their shoulders as they watched President Bush's message.

When President Bush announced the AGOA extension beyond 2008, the crowd broke out in loud cheers and applause, which continued with his announcement of increased Millennium program and education funding. The President proposed a 50 percent increase in development assistance over the next three years and an additional $200 million over five years. He also announced a $30 million book and school supply program. The excitement dropped slightly when he announced the United States was working toward a free trade agreement with the Southern African Customs Union.

16.7. Taped address by President George W. Bush at the AGOA Forum reception for dignitaries, delegates, and invited guests, hosted by the U.S. Embassy Port Louis and the U.S. government, January 15, 2003.

Overall, the speech was extremely well received, so much so I had difficulty quieting down the crowd long enough to introduce Ambassador Zoellick, head of the U.S. delegation to the Forum and our guest of honor that evening. The ambassador's speech was smooth and well informed, with everyone listening intently.

The night was unusually warm and humid, and inside the crowded room there was not a breath of fresh air. With the excitement of the evening and my adrenaline rush, I was sweating profusely, as were most of the guests. By the time the event ended, I was soaked to the skin—my suit was totally drenched and my shirt clung to my back.

Once home, I took a long shower, and later that night I sat with a cup of tea reflecting on the events of the evening and the President's words. I also glanced again at my copy of Secretary Powell's January 7 letter to Prime Minister Jugnauth, which said that he was disappointed he was unable to attend the AGOA Forum but was pleased to send an enthusiastic and supportive U.S. delegation. He acknowledged the Prime Minister's efforts in hosting the Forum and noted that only "matters of the highest importance to world peace" had prevented his attendance. *What a profound week this has been so far,* I thought as I dozed off.

I went to the Radisson Hotel the next day to hear Ambassador Jon Huntsman Jr. speak at the private sector plenary session, "The Impact of AGOA on U.S.-Africa Trade." The ambassador stressed the importance of NGOs and the private sector, in partnership with the government, in the implementation of AGOA. He emphasized that the AGOA program had a humanitarian component, as countries and their people struggled to advance, even though its objectives might be misunderstood by small and medium-sized enterprises.

At the Maritim Hotel, where Trade Minister Cuttaree was hosting a luncheon for the private sector attendees, I met with Johnny Brown, the Commerce Department's commercial officer from Johannesburg, who introduced me to the Boeing executives active in the region: Walt Braithwaite, Laurette Koellner, and Miguel Santos. Their business perspectives on the region were insightful: there was room to grow the Boeing aircraft fleet from where it was then in sub-Saharan Africa, although the tough competitor Airbus used some of the European Union countries to put pressure on their African trading partners.

I was determined to help Boeing make inroads in replacing the older fleet of Air Mauritius, the national carrier, which had plans to replace one and perhaps two of its long-range fleet. The consensus was they could be a candidate for two of the new Boeing 777 models. To beat out Airbus became an important challenge for the embassy—I was told it would help Boeing sustain about ten thousand jobs at its Everett, Washington, plant. Santos was committed to making numerous trips to Mauritius for presentations to the government and Air Mauritius officials.

I thought about the earlier comments made by U.S. Trade Representative Bob Zoellick in our meeting with Deputy Prime Minister Bérenger and in our meeting at the Octave Wiehe Auditorium on the University of Mauritius Campus. In my opinion, the purpose of AGOA was to help create a steady local workforce, with fair wages and benefits. My interpretation of the rules would allow only permanently locally based operations in sub-Saharan African countries to qualify for the benefits of AGOA. But Zoellick was not concerned where the investment came from as long as it created employment, which implied that all potential employers were eligible to take advantage of the AGOA benefits. I found that troublesome since local reports indicated China underwrote some businesses in Mauritius and other parts of sub-Saharan Africa through either favorable loans or outright subsidies.

Again, what bothered me was that I believed these Chinese textile manufacturers were opportunists wanting access to the U.S. market under the AGOA program. Reportedly, their profits with few exceptions went back to companies domiciled in mainland China. In some cases, when wages got too high, they moved production to less costly AGOA-qualified countries. Instead of investing to enhance sub-Saharan Africans' lives through higher wages and better living conditions, the Chinese took advantage of lower wages in these countries. And not all of these jobs went to locals, either. China brought thousands of Chinese workers to these African countries, including Mauritius; in some cases these workers had to pay a hefty broker fee, guarantee that they would stay for at least three years, and rotate out as other Chinese workers came to take their place. Many were subjected to substandard living conditions. (By contrast, several successful homegrown Sino-Mauritian companies dealt fairly under AGOA, had a better track record than their mainland China peers, and hired thousands of Mauritian workers.)

In addition, it was reported to the embassy that textiles and clothing from China and other countries were being transshipped through sub-Saharan African ports, where these products were commingled with locally produced textiles and clothing and ultimately reached U.S. markets. This commingling of textiles and clothing to qualify under AGOA was a concern to our embassy and Mauritian customs officials.

While in December 2001 China had formally joined the World Trade Organization, it would not gain favorable quota access to the U.S. markets until becoming signatory to the Agreement on Textiles and Clothing, effective December 31, 2004. As of that date, China would have the unfettered access to the U.S. markets it always wanted. Subsequently, a number of Chinese textile and clothing manufacturers moved their overseas operations back to Hong Kong and mainland China. I believe with China's population growth its need for jobs will be insatiable. Hence, China will press hard to grow its access to all world markets, and by the year 2030, they will control the WTO and account for most of the manufactured goods worldwide.

Since our arrival to Mauritius, Marcia had looked forward to becoming involved with local charities and arts organizations, which was her forte in the United States.

She became particularly interested in an NGO that specialized in training students who were musically inclined but lacked the necessary funding to acquire musical instruments, and another that educated young women in crafts and cooking. But we quickly discovered that, as the ambassador's spouse, she was not allowed to be actively involved in embassy activities or serve on the advisory boards of local non-governmental organizations. Even our family foundation was prohibited from making financial contributions for worthwhile causes in communities in these countries. And I was not allowed to give up my salary and use it for community activities and programs, as I had wished. While we could give donations and my salary directly to the State Department, we could not earmark them for these Mauritian nongovernmental organizations.

Sadly, Marcia gave up trying to help these deserving organizations, and joined the diplomatic corps spouses' book club and several other social clubs. Yes, Marcia did enjoy hosting events and the numerous social functions, but these activities were no substitute for her desire to participate in community service. The United States lost in Marcia a highly motivated goodwill ambassador—she would have been a great one-woman Peace Corps.

One time when she was able to actively participate was during the AGOA Forum, when she was asked to take part in a panel discussion at a local girls' school, representing First Lady Laura Bush. That evening, Marcia and I went over to the Renganaden Seeneevassen State Secondary Girls' School for the inauguration of the International Studies Partnership with Fayette-Ware Comprehensive High School in Somerville, Tennessee. In a videotaped message seen by both schools, Laura Bush would launch the partnership, and a split screen would allow both groups of students to observe each other at their respective locations.

USAID had put together this partnership under its Education for Development and Democracy Initiative, and it was to be directed by Dr. Sarah Moten, who also served as moderator. Halfway around the world, these young girls began by shyly asking questions but quickly became engaged in lively discussion. Listed on the program were Sarojini Jugnauth, the wife of Prime Minister Jugnauth; Usha Jeetah, the Mauritian ambassador to the United States; Jendayi Frazer; and Marcia, representing the U.S. Embassy. As the program evolved, many people were asked to speak, but the moderator failed to call upon Marcia, the only one on the panel from the private sector with forty years of experience in the arts and education. Her insights would have added dramatically to this event and would have been a great inspiration to these young girls.

On Friday morning, January 17, sessions were held on HIV/AIDS issues in sub-Saharan Africa and on the Millennium Challenge program, followed by a wrap-up in the ministerial closing session. At noon, I went to a reception given by the Bank of Mauritius in honor of Undersecretary of the Treasury John Taylor. From there, I raced over to Fuxiao, a Chinese restaurant in the Domaine Les Pailles business and entertainment park, where Foreign Minister Gayan was hosting a luncheon for Tang Jiaxuan, Minister of Foreign Affairs of the People's Republic of China. I was told it was just a coincidence that he was here during the U.S.-trade-related AGOA Forum. On my arrival, they ushered me to a seat directly across from Tang; I felt they had been waiting for the U.S. ambassador to arrive before getting into some of the international issues. Foreign Minister Gayan spoke about the Iraq situation and about wanting to avoid a war with that country. He talked about going back to the United Nations Security Council before using force against Iraq, although he did say that Iraq needed to disarm. Speaking next, Tang said the Iraq issue had to be resolved within the framework of the Security Council. Referring to Africa, he asserted that with international assistance peace could be achieved on the continent. To me, it sounded like rhetoric for the attentive media: China's assistance in Africa over the years has been coupled with the extraction of resources from these countries, and also the influence it could buy with the leaders there for such unfettered access.

At 2:45 p.m., before closing the book on the second AGOA Forum, my last meeting was with Bob Zoellick. Bob began the conversation by asking about my background, including my multifaceted business career. We discussed JP Realty, Inc., the NYSE-listed REIT that I oversaw. Our largest shareholder was Alliance Capital, whose chairman, Dave Williams, was a mutual friend. At one time, Zoellick had been on the board of Alliance. We also discussed many of our mutual Wall Street connections and my long-standing friendship with Ambassador Jon Huntsman Jr., Zoellick's deputy. I thanked Bob for his leadership at the Forum and the targeted speeches he had given. He mentioned that before leaving Mauritius he wanted to meet and thank the embassy staff and temporary duty officers.

I later found out that it was Rosa Whitaker, from Bob Zoellick's office, who had persuaded Ambassador Zoellick to attend the Forum. I also found out that early in 2002 opinion had been three to one against holding the Forum in Mauritius, but that Jendayi Frazer helped reverse that decision in the White House and at the State Department.

Certainly Mauritius had deserved the honor of hosting the Forum. A small country compared to most of its peers, it had succeeded in establishing employment opportunities for its populace. I hoped the visiting ministers and other delegates would take notice, visit some of the manufacturing operations, and take back with them the knowledge that they could succeed if their countries espoused a free and open market environment.

{ XVII }

CONFLICTS AND DEMARCHES

On January 27, 2003, I delivered a demarche to the Mauritian government on the Anti-Terrorism Assistance (ATA) program and met with Foreign Minister Gayan. The United States wanted as many countries as possible to sign a proposed memorandum of intent allowing for a needs assessment within each of the signatory countries. The program would include specialized training for law enforcement entities to aid in their capabilities to counter the terrorist threat and assist in the international war on terrorism. The memorandum agreement was nonbinding; it did not provide for any rise in rights or obligations under international law. Gayan said he would review the document, but he generally seemed agreeable and thought the elements could be beneficial to Mauritius. The government of Mauritius subsequently agreed to have an assessment team visit Mauritius for the ATA program.

Turning to the subject of Iraq, Gayan cautioned us to go easy in our preliminary response to the UN inspectors' report. He also said that he felt a recent incident in which a representative of the United States had referred to France's opinion as the voice of "old Europe" had been a mistake. He added that he hoped the U.S. government and I would not take his criticisms of U.S. foreign policy as a personal affront.

I explained that the lack of documentation in Iraq's inventory reports from 1998 to the present was a problem—the inspectors were there not to create an inventory for Saddam but to validate a submitted list. Gayan and I did not agree on this issue, and he referred to the United States as being "trigger-happy." He capped off the dialogue by saying, "When we say what we think, you say that we are against you. But we are not." I believe Gayan's personal view was that it might be myopic for the United States to push for decided action against Iraq even after it had been determined that there had been a material breach of Security Council Resolution 1441. Gayan and I agreed to meet again after the UN inspectors made their report and President Bush gave a national address.

That evening, Bisa informed me of another demarche for Gayan: this one was on U.S. concerns about the upcoming African Union meeting in Addis Ababa, where discussion of and possible voting for a new North African–Middle East representative to the UN Security Council would take place. Libya's name had been mentioned to fill this opening in 2004. Our stand at the time was that we did not support the candidacy of Libya, a country then known for terrorist acts, human rights abuses, a lack of democracy, and support for rogue armies to undermine and overthrow regimes in some of the smaller African countries. Sub-Saharan African countries do not vote on North African candidates, but we were to encourage the government of Mauritius to proffer another choice, perhaps Algeria or Egypt—though this was not to say that either was without problems.

I reviewed all these points with Foreign Minister Gayan on his cell phone. He concluded that it would be difficult for him to tell them whom to pick if Libya was the only proposed candidate. I asked him to at least express the Mauritian government's concern; we hoped other sub-Saharan African countries would feel the same, and that the collective pressure would persuade the African Union to seek an alternative representative. He agreed to try. The next day, however, I read a report indicating the African Union did wind up supporting Libya's bid for the Security Council seat.

The next time I met with Prime Minister Jugnauth, he told me how happy he was to have received a telephone call from President Bush after the AGOA Forum to personally thank the Prime Minister for hosting the event and to say that everyone in the White House was talking about how successful it had been. President Bush also had thanked Mauritius for its support at the UN. I took the opportunity to mention the U.S. position opposing Libya for the rotating nonvoting slot on the Security Council and asked that the Mauritian government encourage its friends in North Africa to oppose Libya and propose instead an alternative candidate, despite the African Union statement that it would endorse Libya.

That afternoon I met with representatives from the State Department's Bureau of Diplomatic Security and the Office of Anti-Terrorism Assistance. They were here to present the ATA program to the government of Mauritius. In attendance from the government of Mauritius was Police Commissioner Gopalsingh, representing the military authorities participating in the ATA program. Also invited were the respective Seychelles and Comoros representatives who would participate in the program. I was pleased that Taoufik Housseine had been selected as the Comorian army's representative, as Taoufik truly loved his country and thoroughly liked everything about America. During side conversations I learned that he was quite a Harley-Davidson motorcycle fan, so I promised to bring him some logo decals and an American flag sticker for his motorcycle on my next trip to Comoros.

On Wednesday, February 5, we met again with Commissioner Gopalsingh, this time at the Line Barracks Police Headquarters, to review the proposed ATA program over the next sixteen- to eighteen-month period. Training was offered for twenty-four officers for the first round, adding other candidates as the program evolved. We talked about needing more police oversight, including airport security and port security, and discussed ways of dealing with human rights abuses, hostage taking, drug interdiction, corruption, visa and passport violations, and procedures for apprehensions.

The commissioner was anxious to cooperate, wanting ATA's input in all these critical areas.

One of the more important guidelines to measure performance and establish goals and priorities at the U.S. Embassy in Port Louis was the annual Mission Performance Plan. The MPP was used by the State Department as a tool to justify budgets for the foreign mission operations. As it was, U.S. Embassy Port Louis was underfunded compared to some of the other foreign missions doing similar work.

The annual MPP report was due by the end of February 2003. The goals and strategy sections, with embassy staff input, would be most important for the State Department to understand the work we did at this post and the need for additional staff. I decided to strengthen the chief of mission's statement in several other areas, including the need to properly cover Diego Garcia. Two members of the country team believed this should not be included, but I disagreed, since the Diego Garcia issue came up at almost every bilateral meeting with the government of Mauritius.

As it turned out, the State Department was concerned about the MPP's mention of Diego Garcia oversight, assuming it had been inserted to justify my ongoing requests for additional resources at the embassy. Nothing could have been further from the truth, but I didn't try to explain it past my desk officer: from the beginning, the Diego Garcia issues had been well documented in our cables to Washington.

On the evening of February 6, Marcia and I went to the Maritim Hotel, where Foreign Minister Anil Gayan was hosting a farewell dinner in honor of Athar Mahmood, the high commissioner of Pakistan, and Louis Mnguni, the high commissioner of South Africa, both of whom had become good friends of mine. Athar was going to a civil service training center in Lahore to prepare for a new high commissioner assignment. Marcia had become good friends with Athar's wife, Nafisa, who was a talented artist. The two women had a lot in common, so it was sad that their friendship would be short-lived.

After having served in Mauritius for over four years, Louis was returning to South Africa. A fun-loving person who enjoyed all the good things freedom had to offer, Louis was a member of the African National Congress (ANC) and a close friend of Nelson Mandela. Under the apartheid government, Louis had spent five years in prison on Robben Island with Mandela and other ANC members. I was surprised he was not bitter from that terrible experience.

The flow of demarche cables always represented demands from the United States that the host country's government support our position at the UN. I wished that at times we could have fulfilled some of the host country requests. I didn't like being referred to as a "fair-weather friend," although occasionally it felt like an appropriate moniker.

On February 7, I received several cables that needed immediate action. One was a request for the government of Mauritius to review Secretary Powell's speech at the UN and support the disarming of Iraq, including the request for increased funding of the International Atomic Energy Agency (IAEA) for the on-site inspectors. Another was to get the Article 98 nonsurrender agreement signed by the government of Mauritius, which John Bolton thought was long overdue. I was to press for support, since funding for military assistance and other programs could possibly be halted if they did not agree. I had to couch my words well to avoid having my approach be perceived as heavy-handed.

Earlier that morning, I had received a call from Alain Butler-Payette, the principal secretary for foreign affairs in the Seychelles, concerning the U.S. request for extradition of the wanted individual. As I noted earlier, this matter had been dragging on for months. I was asked to send a letter to the government of Seychelles recapping our position in the hope of reaching a solution on the extradition request.

With Eric Kneedler joining me as note taker, I then met with Foreign Minister Gayan and gave a synopsis of Secretary Powell's February 5 presentation to the UN Security Council. I highlighted some excerpts from his speech, such as the lengths to which Iraq had gone to deceive and frustrate the mission of the inspectors, its failure to meet its obligations under Resolution 1441, and its failure to cooperate and disarm. Powell was encouraging other governments to make public statements in support of our position since the issue would come to a head in a matter of weeks rather than months. Our hope for a peaceful solution was founded in showing international determination to disarm Iraq peacefully, if possible, and if necessary by force.

I then asked for the Foreign Minister's support for the additional funding needed by the IAEA. The amount budgeted was $21.5 million. However, I told Gayan it was my personal opinion that it would take substantially more than that.

Saving the most sensitive issue—the Article 98 agreement—for last, I reiterated the need to have it signed. I reminded him, as gently as I could, of the American Servicemembers' Protection Act enacted by Congress on August 2, 2002. Unless a country had signed and ratified the Article 98 agreement to protect against the surrender of covered persons, the act would put restrictions on U.S. military assistance programs for that country effective July 1, 2003. This could affect Mauritius, which was receiving International Military Education and Training funding amounting to $100,000. The Foreign Minister said the government of Mauritius was working on the letter and would get back to us in a week. He wanted to include safeguards that any accused person would be brought to trial in the United States and not just let off. I pointed out that such measures were in place already with our military court system, which seemed to satisfy him.

A few days later, Deputy Prime Minister Bérenger and I went over the outcome of his discussion with the Comorian President, Azali Assoumani, who was transiting through Mauritius from the African Union meeting in Addis Ababa. Bérenger said while the African Union had pressed Comoros to hold the new assembly elections, the island presidents had held out for firmer decisions over finances and security controls, which Azali insisted could not be addressed until the constitutional assembly was established after the proposed elections. Growing frustrated with the islands' lack of progress, Bérenger blamed the island presidents El Bak and Bacar, who resisted proceeding with National Assembly elections because they feared losing. Meanwhile, Bacar had left for France again and El Bak was headed for Mecca, Saudi Arabia.

I told Bérenger our embassy was willing to send observers to the elections, since it was in the United States' interests to see Comoros through the next phase of its democratization process.

Within hours, Taoufik Housseine called on behalf of the Comorian government asking me to come to Comoros as quickly as possible to meet with Azali. I surmised Bérenger had had a conversation with him, which prompted the call. I asked Taoufik to have this request put in writing, and he did—later that afternoon an email arrived signed by Foreign Minister Souef Mohamed El Amine on behalf of President Azali.

I was preparing to go to Comoros when I was told President Azali had left the country to attend the France-Africa Summit in Paris, so I cancelled my plans. However, on that particular day another cable crossed my desk regarding Comoros. In it were excerpts from the French news service Agence France-Presse with headlines blaring, "Coup Plot Foiled in Comoros Islands, Gendarmes Arrested," followed by "President Azali Reshuffles Cabinet, Appoints Ministers from Anjouan Island" and "Ministers Arrested Amid Comoros Alleged Coup."

According to the news report, four ministers—of finance, education, interior, and justice—and a dozen gendarmes had been arrested for allegedly plotting to overthrow President Azali. "We know that El Bak's government was preparing something, perhaps an uprising," an anonymous source was quoted as saying. Apparently the group had been infiltrated and a recording made of a meeting held by Minister of Interior Ali Bacar Kassim. Other tapes of meetings and a diary containing details of the coup plan were also found. If all this was true, it was yet another dark chapter in the Comoros's long history of coup attempts and instability. The report indicated Azali's decision to change the structure of his cabinet from six to nine members—his third cabinet reorganization since his election on April 14, 2002. Azali's chief of staff called me late in the day to let me know that everything was under control and reiterated I did not need to come to Comoros at this juncture.

On February 10, a cable arrived from the State Department asking me again to press Seychelles to sign the Article 98 agreement. Just then, Andy Frost, the embassy security coordinator, came to my door with three Coast Guard officers. The *Praslin*, a ship flying a Seychelles flag, had fired two sailors who, in retaliation, turned over to a French naval vessel in the harbor pictures that they claimed showed boxes of dynamite being transferred to another ship at sea. Our sniffers, however, had detected no explosives on the *Praslin*, Andy stated. The other ship, the one that the sailors claimed had received these boxes, had yet to show up in any port, though I was told that some ships stay out for several months. I was pleased they all reacted so quickly to this potential threat.

Information had also reached the embassy about potential attacks against Americans in Mauritius. On the following Wednesday morning, as I was preparing to leave the ambassador's residence, Andy Frost appeared next to the two ambassador's vehicles. For security reasons, he said, we would start using both vehicles everywhere we went, with one being for diversion. The vehicles would take different routes and go in different directions to reach the same destination. We were to continue this procedure until the threat level had subsided.

That morning, CNN aired a sixteen-minute taped message sent to Al-Jazeera (the English version of the Arabic-language news network) from Osama bin Laden condemning Washington for plotting a "Crusader war" against Islam to benefit Israel and to control Arab oil.

Osama bin Laden called on Muslims, especially in Iraq, to wage a jihad against the "invaders." He promised pain and suffering for the United States and made clear his support for the Iraqi people—exempting Saddam Hussein, whom he described as a socialist infidel. This tape probably had been developed in the previous weeks as tensions with Iraq escalated.

After weeks of countless revisions and hard work by the embassy staff, the Mission Performance Plan report was almost ready to be sent out. In our last review, on Friday, February 14, I decided there needed to be additional wording on engaging Comoros more aggressively to help the country get to the next level on its path of democratization. The final MPP turned out to be a great report, one of which the embassy staff could be proud. I just hoped some people at the top in the State Department would read it, because accomplishing the goals depended upon financial support and added people resources: not a high priority at the State Department, since we were a Special Embassy Program post.

At six o'clock Sunday evening, I received a demarche from Secretary Powell that needed to be discussed with Foreign Minister Gayan no later than the following day. I was to ask the Foreign Minister to instruct the Mauritian delegation at the UN in New York to speak at the open session of the UN, February 18, regarding the Iraq issue and reinforce the following points: Iraq continued to fail to meet the two key tests of Resolution 1441 (namely, the full, accurate, and complete declaration of all weapons and full, voluntary, unconditional cooperation with the UN's Monitoring, Verification and Inspection Commission and the IAEA inspectors), and Iraq's possession of weapons of mass destruction continues to be a threat to international peace and security. The Security Council needed to meet its responsibilities and take effective action to compel immediate Iraqi compliance.

Speaking to Anil Gayan on his home phone, I reviewed the bullet points and suggested we needed as many friendly countries as possible to speak up at the UN open session the next day. I was expecting a possible negative response and was relieved to hear him say he had just given an interview to the Mauritian radio station Radio One in which he had reinforced the same points. He assured me he would call his mission at the UN and review these issues.

Pleased with our conversation, I had the embassy quickly send a cable to Washington notifying them to expect some positive remarks from the Mauritian permanent representative to the United Nations.

❴XVIII❵

AMERICAN TRADE AND AMERICA AT WAR

The U.S. Embassy in Port Louis was planning to host an American trade show in August 2003 with the support of the government of Mauritius. We were focusing on the technology sector: one goal was to see Mauritius become a Wi-Fi-friendly island, and another objective was to provide ten thousand laptop computers to young students at manufacturer's cost. The catchy theme proposed was "Connecting the World." Looking to gain support, I met with Minister of Information Technology and Telecommunications Deelchand Jeeha. He was cold to the idea at first, opposed to the free use of broadband without licensing or controls. But we talked further about wireless access around the island, and he thoroughly liked the idea of reasonably priced laptops with Wi-Fi access getting into many students' hands, especially in the smaller villages.

That day, we sent another cable to Washington regarding Deputy Prime Minister Bérenger's request for X-ray scanners for the port and airport. The government of Mauritius wanted assistance to equip its Customs Division to help stop the smuggling of weapons and armaments, illegal drugs, and chemicals and paraphernalia intended for terrorists, yet not interfere with the free flow of legitimate goods to worldwide markets. Bérenger wished to purchase American-made scanners from American Science and Engineering and from Science Applications International, as they were of the highest quality, but he needed some financial help in purchasing them. Receiving a negative response from the United States, Mauritius went ahead and purchased Chinese-made scanners, which were of lower quality and cost, but financed and subsidized by China.

To put the scanner issue in perspective, the units cost approximately $3 million each. Assuming there were a hundred similarly sized ports around the world that could benefit from using this type of scanner, the total cost for scanners would have been approximately $300 million—a small price to pay for added security in the global war on terror.

Later in the afternoon, Bisa came into my office to speak about a cable we had received from Minister-Counselor for Political Affairs Josiah Rosenblatt in the U.S.

Embassy in Paris regarding the recently held UN Security Council open debate on Iraq. In the second day of the debate, thirty-five speakers took the floor, including representatives from Mauritius, who made statements very much in line with U.S. thinking on the matter (even though in some cases they reflected tactical differences over timing of the next steps).

The Mauritian representative, Jagdish Koonjul, surprised everyone with his positive remarks. He noted that although there had been measured cooperation with the inspectors, there was still a real deficit on substance, which under Resolution 1441 required full compliance. Koonjul noted that if there was no tangible progress by the time of the next report to the Security Council, the council would have to take the required response. He also pointed out that if Iraq chose not to comply, it would not be able to avoid the steps taken that would otherwise heighten the suffering of the Iraqi people. Basically, he was appealing to Iraq for full disclosure and cooperation. I thought Koonjul's remarks were worthy of a personal thank-you call to Foreign Minister Gayan.

On February 22, I was asked by Washington to convey a demarche to the Foreign Minister about the United States' current stand on Iraq. Since he would be attending the Non-Aligned Movement Summit in Kuala Lumpur, it was absolutely essential that the core point of the statement issued at the conclusion of the summit reaffirm unconditionally Iraq's obligation to comply with Resolution 1441, which was adopted unanimously by the Security Council. Anything less would be a dangerous and counterproductive signal that international pressure on Iraq to comply was lessening.

My call to Foreign Minister Gayan was timely: the sessions had not yet started. He said he understood the situation and would work on this issue, reiterating his position that Iraq must fully comply with Resolution 1441. He added that more than one hundred countries were represented there, including Korea, Egypt, and India. I thanked him again for having made a call to Koonjul and for the permanent representative's subsequent favorable remarks at the UN open session.

The pressure on Iraq, under the UNSC Resolution, was intensifying—this meant war was inevitable and only a matter of timing. Early on February 26, it was reported that the UN weapons inspector Hans Blix was making headway with more disclosures. He was emphatic Iraq start destructing their Al Samoud 2 missiles by the weekend. Having a range that exceeded ninety-three miles, these were to have been destroyed in 1991. In addition, they found several 500-pound bombs that could be used to deliver chemicals. It seemed like each day a little more data was uncovered.

Continuing with our day-to-day activities, I participated in an embassy program that held great promise for young Mauritians not only to pursue education in the United States but also to be exposed to the American way of life. Linda Henry, an

American citizen who was married to a Franco-Mauritian businessman and had lived in Mauritius for more than thirty years, was gracious enough to head up the Embassy Educational Advising Center.

At any given time, at least three hundred Mauritian students are continuing their education in the United States. In 2002, $750,000 in grant money was awarded by colleges and universities across America to Mauritian students, many of whom are sought after because of their excellent training.

During this time, Dan Claffey and I also discussed the upcoming Leamon R. Hunt Award for Administrative Excellence. We believed that with the number of hats Charlie Slater wore at the embassy, he exemplified the qualities for which the award was given. By the meeting's end, we had set the nomination process in motion.

Charlie and Lizzie Slater had endured much trauma resulting from the U.S. embassy bombings in 1998. Lizzie had been assigned to U.S. Embassy Dar es Salaam as an information management specialist two days before the August 7 attack by al-Qaeda terrorists, and she almost lost her life. Charlie, assigned as the senior financial management officer to the U.S. Embassy in Nairobi in 1998, was en route from Paris when the embassy was destroyed.

Charlie spent the next two years restoring the Financial Management Center and was part of the team that rebuilt the entire embassy from the ground up. Lizzie came to Nairobi shortly thereafter and became part of the team involved in the design, installation, and training of personnel on the use of the state-of-the-art equipment. In August 2000, Charlie was assigned as administrative officer to the U.S. Embassy in Port Louis, with Lizzie as the embassy's information programs officer. Being posted to the same embassy helped the couple put their lives back together with their young son, Forbes. I liked them both because of their can-do attitude, which I was familiar with from the private sector. And I had communicated with Charlie during the confirmation process on a number of logistical issues, which made our move to Mauritius almost seamless.

Unfortunately, security threats were on the rise as it became more evident the United States was heading for war with Iraq. On February 28, Andy Frost, our security coordinator, decided to ride with me in the ambassador's vehicle to discuss residence security. As we neared Port Louis, the phone rang: there had been a bomb scare at the embassy. An anonymous caller said that three bombs had been placed in Rogers House, the building where the embassy was located. Andy immediately verified that the police had been called; they were on the way and already had begun tracing the call. In a coincidence, the radical ZamZam Islamic Movement was planning a march with demonstrators from their Port Louis mosque to the embassy to deliver a letter to the ambassador in opposition to the Iraqi war. By the time we reached the embassy, the police had searched the building for suspicious packages and fortunately found nothing.

When the ZamZam demonstrators from the mosque in the Plaine Verte section of the city converged on the embassy to meet with me, Andy, who was concerned about my safety, instead sent Eric Kneedler, who was handed two letters from their leaders. One letter, from the Mouvement Solidarité National (MSN), stated the group's opposition to war with Iraq, saying there was still time to disarm Saddam through discussions, and that they believed blood should not be the price for the conquest of oil fields. The other letter, from the ZamZam Islamic Movement, began: "In the name of Allah, the Most Beneficent, the Most Merciful." This group not only was outspoken at times but also was headed by the extremist A. B. Bahemia Ariff. Excerpts from that letter, which I thought represented a more radical ideology, stated their belief that Saddam Hussein had neither the technology nor the desire to attack his neighbors. The letter said, "It is no secret the difference between Iraq and North Korea is oil. What you aspire to achieve is world economic dictatorship. As is crystal clear, attacking Iraq only benefits the U.S.A., not Europe, not Africa, not Asia, and not the Americas. Your government is evil. Your ideology is evil. And when your leaders speak they represent you perfectly [as] arrogant, proud, full of hatred, full of greed and one-eyed." The letter concluded, "How sad a vision of your great country that allows so many freedoms." Under the watchful eye of the Mauritian police, their march was peaceful, although vocal in opposition to the U.S. position on Iraq.

On March 3, I was invited to have lunch with Premnath "Dev" Ramnah, speaker of the National Assembly. Previously, I recommended Dev for a U.S. visitors program called Legal Governance. I thought the three-week program would give him a better understanding of American values, and I wanted to capture his observations of the experience.

Having never visited America, Dev said he was left with a very positive image of the United States. He told me that the program not only enriched his life but also encouraged him to have his children study in the States. Because of this experience, Dev was more open with me than he had been when we first met. It validated my belief that exposure to our country is an important way for the United States to engage host country leaders.

The next day, our plans for the American trade fair scheduled for August 27–31, 2003, were well enough along that we decided to hold a news conference. Dan Claffey invited MBC-TV and several newspapers and radio stations to the briefing. The "Connecting the World" event would feature a three-day seminar with demonstrations and networking opportunities, followed by two days of product sales, focusing on information and communication technology by showcasing U.S. technology and products.

One of the press asked if this trade fair was going to be used as an opportunity to sell U.S. products to reduce the negative trade balance the United States had with

Mauritius. I thought this was absurd, considering that sales would amount to only a few million dollars, while the U.S. trade imbalance with Mauritius was $200 million.

Later, as I was thumbing through some cables on my desk, I found intermingled among them a handwritten letter. Our regional security officer had instructed everyone that all letters received through the mail should be opened outside the embassy, as a result of the Washington anthrax scare in 2001. But somehow this letter, from the ZamZam organization, had slipped through and ended up on my desk. Its piercing radical warning of biological attacks using anthrax and ricin in retaliation for our involvement with Iraq gave me cold shivers. Having had several scares that week, the RSO was concerned both about the source of this threat and also about how the letter had found its way to my office.

On the morning of March 6, Eric Kneedler spoke about four planned ship visits in the Seychelles during March and April: the USS *Fletcher*, the *Briscoe*, the *O'Kane*, and the *Austin*. Two of the ships were destroyers. Because of these visits, I believed that if war with Iraq was inevitable, it would not start until sometime in the early part of April—shore leave for these troops at this time would indicate a more relaxed situation, especially with these ships being far away from the Persian Gulf.

At a social function, Trade Minister Jayen Cuttaree referenced a telephone conversation he had had with Ambassador Zoellick. We had arranged for the call to discuss the upcoming Financing and Investment Seminar to be held in Washington in June 2003. We were seeking to have the seminar held in conjunction with the meeting of the Corporate Council on Africa. The Trade Minister said Zoellick liked the idea and would see if it could be dovetailed with the seminar. We also wanted to press for having the third annual AGOA Forum in one of the other eligible sub-Saharan African countries. From my perspective, I still believed that the U.S. government leadership, including members of Congress, and the U.S. business community needed to become better acquainted with sub-Saharan Africa in order to grasp the real problems in this region.

On Wednesday, March 12, a letter addressed to President Karl Offmann arrived from President Bush extending greetings from the American people as Mauritius celebrated the thirty-fifth anniversary of its independence. The timing of this letter was good, since I needed to visit with Offmann during this chaotic period.

Two days later, on Friday afternoon, Eric Kneedler showed me another cable announcing that the USS *Austin*'s visit to Seychelles had been cancelled. Most likely that meant the other ship visits would be cancelled as well. Not a good sign—it indicated that they were being put on alert.

At the UN Security Council, a bitter split was developing, with Russia, China, France, Germany, Pakistan, and Syria on one side and the United States, the United

Kingdom, Spain, and Bulgaria on the other. Caught in the middle were the non-aligned members: Chile, Mexico, Angola, Cameroon, and Guinea. The debate was over Iraq's fulfillment of its obligations under Resolution 1441 and whether there needed to be a second resolution. France and Russia were Iraq's largest trading partners, supplying food, technology, military supplies, and equipment worth billions of dollars. They both also had oil concessions worth billions of dollars.

On Sunday, March 16, Charlie and Lizzie arrived at our residence carrying a demarche entitled "Seeking Host Government Support on a Vision for Iraq and the Iraqi People." I had to deliver its contents immediately to Foreign Minister Gayan. At this point, Mauritius had already rotated off the Security Council, but the United States believed that its influence in support of the U.S. position was still important. I was to let the Mauritian government know that a joint statement would be issued at the Atlantic Summit by the United States, the United Kingdom, and Spain, who were taking the lead on the current resolution before the Security Council. And I was to urge the host country government to review the text, issue positive public statements to welcome it, and possibly to associate itself with it. No text was attached, however—so we were asking for support without knowing the content of the statement.

Fully understanding Foreign Minister Gayan's feelings, I knew he would not support the war or the ousting of Saddam Hussein. He was in favor of disarming Saddam, but not through military action, at least not until he thought we had exhausted all other avenues, including inspection and diplomacy.

At 10:30 p.m., CNN carried live coverage of the Atlantic Summit speeches by President Bush, British Prime Minister Tony Blair, and Spanish President José Maria Aznar, who were in agreement that Saddam must disarm or face serious consequences. President Bush noted that the moment of truth for the UN Security Council would be Monday. If Saddam continued to refuse to cooperate, the leaders' statement went on to say, "in these circumstances, we would undertake a solemn obligation to help the Iraqi people build a new Iraq at peace with itself and its neighbors."

On Monday, March 17, Secretary Powell explained on CNN that the United States and its allies had abandoned efforts to win UN backing for military action against Iraq and were prepared to deliver a final ultimatum to Saddam Hussein: go into exile immediately or face annihilation. CNN showed UN weapons inspectors and foreigners hastily evacuating Baghdad. In conclusion, Secretary Powell said, "The time for diplomacy has passed. I can think of nothing that Saddam Hussein could do diplomatically. That time is now over. He has had his chance. He's had many chances over the last twelve years and he's blown every one of those chances."

That night at 8:00 p.m. EST (5:00 a.m., Tuesday, March 18, in Mauritius), President Bush delivered a speech to the nation. The look on the President's face showed great sincerity and concern for our country as he said that Saddam Hussein and his sons had forty-eight hours to leave Iraq, and that to refuse would result in military conflict. Because the UN Security Council had not lived up to its responsibilities, the United States would use force to ensure its national security.

When President Bush finished his speech, for a moment my mind was without any other thoughts beyond his penetrating words: "We are now acting because the risks of inaction would be far greater." *We are at war,* I told myself over and over again.

I wondered what this meant for us in Mauritius. Even though Mauritius was stable, the embassy had received negative and threatening letters and two bomb threats. ZamZam and Hizbullah had radical followers who could become dangerous. It would take only one unstable radical Islamist to create chaos. And I could not forget that one of the most notorious al-Qaeda terrorists, Fazul Abdullah Mohammed, came from nearby Comoros.

In our country team meeting later that day, we focused on the upcoming war, security in general, and the need for speed in releasing a message of caution to all American citizens living in the three host countries.

We then reviewed issues specific to the American trade fair. Shariff Jathoonia, the embassy's economic and commercial specialist, spoke on sponsor and vendor participation, and their resistance to the government's decision to limit sales to only one day. The government of Mauritius also did not want to waive the 15 percent valued-added tax (VAT) on the goods sold—not even on sales of laptops meant for schoolchildren—since local merchants opposed the idea.

While I continued to ask for everyone's input on the trade fair, I felt a lack of enthusiasm and attributed it to the upcoming staff changes. Bisa Williams and Charlie and Lizzie Slater would be taking their annual leave before the trade fair began. Dan Claffey would be going to Cape Town, South Africa, as the consul general there, and Eric Kneedler would be reporting to the Secretary of State's seventh-floor Operations Center—both leaving before the end of May.

With the turnover of Foreign Service officers moving on to new assignments, the lack of continuity and follow-through became problematic. I have long been convinced without permanent Foreign Service national local-hire staff, embassies around the world would not function. Adding to the concern was the preoccupation of Foreign Service officers spending considerable time preparing their annual employee evaluation reviews, due on April 10. Their future of choice post assignments and promotions depended upon these written evaluations. Unlike in the private sector, in government there is no financial bottom line that can be used to gauge people's performance. A Foreign Service officer's performance is assessed based on the words written.

Because of all these factors, I wondered whether we could even hold the trade fair at all. Any planning that had already been done would be hamstrung by their absence, and I would have to depend on the already overloaded Foreign Service national staff. In addition, during this time the embassy would have to function with only four Foreign Service officers, assigned temporary duty officers, and the Foreign Service nationals—a recipe for major burnout.

In the end, we cancelled the 2003 trade fair. In deference to the government of Mauritius, which had invested considerable time in the planning, I quickly met with Jayen Cuttaree and Deelchand Jeeha before a news release was sent out announcing the cancellation. I was grateful that the two ministers understood.

The next day I met with Foreign Minister Gayan to deliver a demarche and talking points on a possible UN General Assembly emergency session on Iraq proposed by France, Germany, and Russia. The message was to urge the government of Mauritius to oppose such a session. The United States felt that holding an emergency session of the General Assembly would send the message that the international community was divided and that Iraq was under no obligation to comply with UN Security Council resolutions 678, 687 (from 1990 and 1991, respectively), and 1441.

The Foreign Minister understood but did not agree with our position. His advice was to allow a meeting of the General Assembly, and he added that nothing would change the decisions made by the United States or its allies. It might even reveal more support for the U.S. position, he suggested.

On Wednesday, March 19, 2003, at 10:15 p.m. EST (7:15 a.m. on Thursday, March 20 in Mauritius), President Bush made another address to the nation. As he spoke, the war had just begun and strikes were already taking place.

In the early hours, forty cruise missiles had been sent in from the USS *Donald Cook*, a destroyer sitting in the Persian Gulf. Missiles from the USS *Constellation* hit military and communications facilities, while two Stealth fighters dropped bunker-buster bombs and an F-14 Tomcat squadron had taken off from the aircraft carrier USS *Abraham Lincoln*. This attack phase was an attempt to take out Saddam and his leadership up front. Operation Iraqi Freedom was under way.

Leaving for work that morning, I noticed a number of personnel from Mauritius's Special Mobile Forces, dressed in combat gear and heavily armed, stationed at the embassy residence gates. At the embassy itself, I was told that a demonstration by the Mouvement Republicain had passed by, with fifty people carrying lighted candles and signs saying "Shame for Bush." Another demonstration was being planned for the afternoon. Police were stationed everywhere around the embassy.

Two days later, I received a cable from Secretary Powell emphasizing that more than thirty countries had joined the United States to free the Iraqi people and defend the world from the grave danger posed by Iraq and the weapons of mass destruction it was believed to have. He went on to thank and commend the State Department family in serving the country with pride, courage, and sacrifice during these trying times. Finally, he acknowledged those who had been called up to serve with the military, and he wished them well, saying he was praying for their safe return home. A second cable from Powell stressed the need for chiefs of mission to take immediate action to protect U.S. interests, the safety of American citizens, and our facilities.

I read in that morning's *L'Express* an interview with Foreign Minister Gayan in which he said that the government of Mauritius was one of the countries that had joined in support of the United States. He also noted that the Americans were not seeking any support from the island, and that the war against Iraq was in conformity with international law.

On Saturday, CNN and other media sources noted that a number of B-2 Spirit bombers would leave their base in Missouri and head to Diego Garcia, 3,200 miles south of Baghdad. I knew that there had been an effort to convince Turkey, which bordered Iraq, to allow the United States to stage troops and equipment on its soil. But Turkey had been looking for about $15–20 billion in exchange for this, and there had been a debate in their parliament on whether to even allow this to take place. Turkey's government ultimately voted against allowing United States to use the country as a staging area, and so Diego Garcia had become an even more important base in the Indian Ocean region.

Clearly, danger extended to the Horn of Africa and East Africa region. In addition to the 1998 U.S. embassy bombings, the 2000 attack on the USS *Cole*, and the Mombasa hotel bombing in 2002, Sudan and Somalia, with their large Muslim populations, were unstable, and al-Qaeda, a significant presence in Africa already, was establishing a stronger base of operations in the Horn. A new American military task force assigned to oversee antiterrorism operations in the Horn of Africa region was temporarily headquartered on the USS *Mount Whitney*, stationed off the coast of Djibouti with several hundred military personnel on board. This task force would have responsibility for providing counterterrorism training and sharing security equipment with armies in the region—and ultimately would become the nucleus of the expanded Combined Joint Task Force–Horn of Africa, based in Djibouti.

The USS *Mount Whitney* was one of the ships that recently had been in the Seychelles for shore leave and cleared by Susanne Rose, our local hire consular agent. I, the U.S. ambassador, had not been told of its purpose in the region, nor of the mission of the special military task force on board. I had delivered numerous demarches to the host country government in support of UNSC Resolution 1441, and other issues important to the United States at the United Nations. But to get information about what was transpiring, on a number of occasions I had to spend hours, often staying up late into the night, gathering news from CNN, the BBC, and other reporting services. And, of course, I believed the U.S. Embassy in Port Louis had not always been included in the information loop about U.S. activities in the region, which included Diego Garcia.

Once the war with Iraq was imminent, I shut off all conversation concerning Diego Garcia. But press reports of activities supposedly taking place on Diego

Garcia were having a negative impact on our bilateral relations with the government of Mauritius. Claims went back to 2001, when rumor had it that CIA "rendition flights" were landing in Diego Garcia. And on February 16, 2003, referring to a report by David Vine of the City University of New York, the local *Weekend* newspaper wrote about allegations that the United States had tortured captured Al-Qaeda and Taliban fighters on Diego Garcia, far from the view of the American public and the rest of the world.

After each such newspaper article appeared, I received numerous phone calls from business and community leaders whom I previously had considered friends of the United States. Now vocal about their opposition to the war with Iraq, they were developing what I considered anti-U.S. rhetoric. This concerned me. Even within the mostly passive Muslim community in Mauritius, strong feeling was developing that Islam as a religion was under attack by the United States.

The antiwar demonstrations at the embassy continued. On March 24, a local group delivered a letter denouncing the war and President Bush. Two days later, the ZamZam Islamic Movement held its third demonstration, with up to five hundred participants, including schoolchildren.

Also on March 24, the UK High Commissioner, David Snoxell, and I met with Deputy Prime Minister Bérenger, in the absence of Foreign Minister Gayan. In a complete reversal of the comments Gayan had made to *L'Express*, Bérenger explained that the position of the government of Mauritius had always been to pass a second UN resolution and give the inspectors more time. The Mauritian government did not support the war, but would not condemn it publicly nor say the war was in violation of international law.

From all the conversations I had had with Foreign Minister Gayan, I had thought the government of Mauritius supported our position at the UN Security Council. I now felt the Foreign Minister must not have had all the Mauritian leadership on board.

Meanwhile, security concerns at the embassy continued to grow. On April 3, Charlie Slater and I met with the Prime Minister's security advisor, Ramesh Shanmugham, for an update on security matters in Mauritius. He said they were prepared for the many demonstrations planned and did not believe any terrorist cells existed in their country. Hoping to reassure us that we should feel secure, he said they also had a number of people under constant surveillance, including some radical clerics. Airport security had been beefed up, and they were increasing the number of random searches of individuals and their belongings. Shanmugham had a long history in the Indian military and intelligence service and did not knuckle under to local politics, and I liked his approach to the seriousness of our concerns.

Later that night at the embassy residence, Tigar the calico cat was waiting, as he did most nights since my arrival. We had become good friends and often dined together, although I wasn't sure how much English he knew. Cassam had cared for him for many years, and I was convinced Tigar understood only Creole. Anyway,

18.1. Tigar wanting attention.

Tigar hung out with me while watching CNN, and had me fetch him at least three midnight snacks before retiring.

Early on, a UNESCO mission that had visited Mauritius and traveled to several places on the island, listed three possible World Heritage sites for submission to the nominating committee. Among them was the Ile aux Phare lighthouse, located five miles off the coast of the Old Grand Port harbor near the town of Mahebourg in the south of the island.

On April 5, the embassy took part in an ongoing community project to help clean up the precious outer islands, including Ile aux Phare. Organized by Dan Claffey, sixteen embassy staff and family members met up with a dozen Curepipe Junior Chamber of Commerce (Jaycees) members at the Old Grand Port harbor for the volunteer cleanup of the lighthouse area. We headed out to the rocky island in rubber pontoon boats provided by the Coast Guard.

By one o'clock that afternoon, we had filled and hauled out more than fifty sacks containing plastic bottles, cups, picnic papers, and other debris. It was a lot of work, but the sight of the beautiful, clean landscape made it well worth the effort. Afterward, we held a dedication and placed a permanent sign depicting the history of the lighthouse. Then, as a treat, I took the embassy staff and family members to lunch at the new Chez Nous beachfront restaurant in Mahebourg, which had a view of the picturesque and newly decluttered island.

18.2. Ile aux Phare lighthouse cleanup project, April 5, 2003.

18.3. Embassy staff and family member cleanup volunteers at Ile aux Phare, April 5, 2003.

Since the war began, we kept to the business at hand, but received many threat notices. Most led nowhere, but all were taken seriously. One such threat came in on April 7, when our regional security officer received a message regarding an email sent to the Rewards for Justice website. The anonymous source claimed three individuals in Mauritius were involved in terrorist actions and listed the suspects with their Arabic names but no addresses. The source wrote the individuals were residing in the Port Louis area, and added that something needed to be done before it was too late. I had always worried about the strangers passing through Mauritius with phony visas and passports. Questioning whether this message was a real lead, we passed the information on to Police Commissioner Gopalsingh and Security Advisor Shanmugham.

The next morning—day twenty-one of the war with Iraq—I awoke to Sky News showing a relatively quiet Baghdad. Although ground engagement in the south was taking place as daylight broke, no overnight bombing seemed to have taken place. Coalition forces were moving around Baghdad almost at will. The capital city had been isolated, though there were pockets of resistance. Reports indicated that only eighteen enemy tanks, out of eight hundred before the start of the war, were said to be usable. A new problem, however, had erupted: mass looting was taking place. With newly found freedom and no police controls, Iraqis entered hotels, government buildings, and museums and stripped them, taking ceiling fans, air conditioners, furniture, artifacts—anything worth removing was dragged away. Food storage buildings were robbed of their wares and chaos was everywhere. These unexpected events overshadowed the purposeful endeavor of achieving freedom for the enslaved Iraqi society. I wondered how the news of this chaos would affect how the citizens of Mauritius viewed the war.

At the embassy, we held an Emergency Action Committee meeting centered on reports of al-Qaeda's presence in Comoros. It appears the reporting party claimed that a training camp was being built in the outlying village of Mohoro. We were also given an update on the three strangers under surveillance as well as reports of threats that followed. I still believed these added concerns were a result of the Iraq war, and more so now that Iraqis were starting to perceive the coalition forces as conquerors and occupiers rather than liberators.

On April 10, a surveillance detection team arrived from Washington to make recommendations about residence security, travel, embassy protection, and countersurveillance. I had met with our regional security officer to discuss his concerns about certain people watching the embassy. On occasion, a large truck had been observed arriving at Rogers House at different times, practicing maneuvering functions, and parking at different locations near the building. It was our opinion the driver might be conducting test runs for a future event, and the Washington team was highly concerned, since this pattern replicated other situations that had taken place before the 1998 embassy bombing in Nairobi. We checked the driver's record and learned that this person needed to be watched, and so we continued to work with the local authorities to monitor the situation.

Mauritius has a very small Jewish community. On April 16, I was invited to attend a Passover Seder at Janet Regar's house. From the United Kingdom, Janet was a legend in Mauritius's textile sector having developed an upscale line of ladies' undergarments, sold in her stores in Britain. At Janet's house I was introduced to thirty people who had brought their children to attend the seder. The guests had different backgrounds—representing Mauritius, Morocco, Iraq, Israel, Australia, France, Germany, Canada, South Africa, England, and the United States—and traditions. What they had in common was Judaism and the Hebrew language. It was great to see this mixture of cultures enjoying a common bond of religion on this festive event.

Our embassy's extensive reporting activities continued. I reviewed one such cable being prepared by Shariff Jathoonia. The information included was needed for President Bush's report on AGOA regarding Mauritius. Mainly it covered investment, trade, trade capacity building, AGOA outreach efforts, and government and private sector meetings after the Forum. Included in this detailed report were updates on anti-corruption, anti-money laundering, anti-terrorism, human rights issues, and labor and protection laws. It also discussed some of the challenges that lay ahead.

Addressing our security concerns, Tim Taylor, whose company owned Rogers House, agreed to let us install a magnetometer at the lobby entrance. We supplied the guards with undervehicle mirrors and explosive detection swipes for guest cars and delivery trucks. Because of the wide variety of tenants occupying offices in the building, implementing these precautionary measures caused some inconvenience. The agreed-upon plan included parking visitor cars and trucks away from the building and reserving close-up parking for known tenants only.

In the meantime, the book donation program was well under way and enthusiastically received. The Seeneevassen Primary School, located in a modest neighborhood near downtown Port Louis, was chosen as one of the schools to be part of this program. Arriving at the school on May 12, I was greeted by the principal. During the ceremony, Minister of Education Steve Obeegadoo stressed the importance of reading as part of the school curriculum. Minister of Culture Motee Ramdass emphasized the support parents could provide to their children by reading to them. And the director of the National Library, Yves Chan Kam Lon, expressed his appreciation for the books destined for the library's permanent collection. Finally, Vice President Raouf Bundhun gave a passionate speech to the students about the use and value of books and why the children should not take them for granted or allow them to become damaged.

18.4. Schoolchildren at the book donation cermony, Seeneevassen Government School, May 12, 2003.

The speakers spoke both in French and Creole to the hushed students, who understood the importance of this gift. Afterward, a number of charming children from six to twelve years old, dressed in bright costumes, performed the popular Creole *sega* dance for us.

While we were at the Seeneevassen Primary School, it was reported that three Western residential complexes located in eastern Riyadh, Saudi Arabia, had been attacked by al-Qaeda terrorists. According to CNN and diplomatic security sources, there had been many warnings of this attack, and a nearby "safe house" filled with munitions was uncovered in a raid. Even after that, no additional precautions reportedly were taken. As a result, thirty-six people, including eight to ten Americans, were killed in the attack, and more than 160 people were wounded. Secretary Colin Powell, who was traveling in the Middle East and Europe, visited the devastated area a day after the bombing and was noticeably shaken. I too was stunned after seeing pictures of the damage.

In my continued engagement of the Muslim community, I accepted an invitation to attend Eid e-Milad un-Nabi, a national celebration in honor of the 1,477th birthday of the Prophet Muhammad. It was to be held at the Aleemiah College campus in the town of Phoenix. Although I had a prior commitment, I was warmly welcomed to come for the morning opening ceremony and remarks by the guest speaker. I sat off to the side so that when leaving I would not disturb the others at the event.

When President Offmann, Vice President Bundhun, Deputy Prime Minister Bérenger, and Foreign Minister Gayan arrived, we shook hands before they headed for the stage seating area. We stood in silence as the honored guest, Maulana Shah Ahmad Noorani Siddiqui of Pakistan, entered the room and sat down at center stage. Opposition party leader Navin Ramgoolam and former President Cassam Uteem also joined him.

After some introductory remarks and a number of chants by visiting mullahs, Yousuf Joonus, the chairman of the organizing committee, introduced Cassam Uteem, who was to make some brief remarks. After that Bérenger would speak to the audience of 25,000–30,000 Muslim faithful, and I was particularly interested in what he would say. That fall Bérenger would become Prime Minister, and he did not have the total support of the Muslim community, representing 16 percent of the population, so I wanted to see the audience's reaction to his remarks.

I had heard enough speeches in French and Creole and, with a diplomatic corps member helping, picked up on what Cassam Uteem said. But I was surprised to hear that, instead of celebrating the birth of Muhammad, peace, and tolerance, he talked about Iraq, launching into inflammatory remarks about the coalition forces and their terrorist acts against the people of Iraq. He said we had slaughtered more than five hundred women and children in Baghdad, he used the phrase "double standard" over and over again, and several times he made reference to not finding any weapons of mass destruction since "they don't exist." Uteem raised his voice, pointed his finger at the audience, and pounded on the lectern.

My time had run out and I had to leave immediately. Unfortunately, I was visible to the diplomatic corps sitting nearby and the guests seated on the stage, and I could feel everyone's eyes on me. Driving to the embassy, Ahmed Boodhooa, my driver, noticing I was upset, asked if I was all right. In reply I merely smiled slightly.

I thought Uteem's speech had missed mention of the 15,000–20,000 Shiite Muslims whose bodies had just been discovered in a mass grave, the 8,000–10,000 Kurds who had been killed by chemical weapons, and the thousands more Muslims who would have been killed by Saddam Hussein over the next twenty years. Cassam Uteem spoke to inflame the Muslim community and unite them against the United States and England, the key coalition partners who were there to free the country from Saddam's tyranny. If he had been concerned about human rights abuses, he could have talked about the killings going on in the Congo, Burundi, and Ivory Coast, or the civil unrest still affecting Sudan and Somalia, or even the renewed conflict in Ethiopia and Eritrea. Yet he focused only on Iraq.

This was a holy day, the celebration of Muhammad's birth, and Uteem chose to turn the event into a political platform to promote his own agenda. Uteem was also an obstructionist regarding the global war on terror, which Mauritius finally had joined, but not without the embarrassment Uteem had created by resigning in protest rather than sign the antiterrorism bill passed by the parliament.

Arriving at the embassy, I was told the press was all over Dan Claffey for information about why the ambassador had walked out on Cassam Uteem's speech. This event was a lead story in the afternoon's *Le Mauricien* newspaper. A report in *Le Socialiste* noted that the audience applauded his speech, which bothered me.

Several days later Marcia and I went to the Sugar Beach Resort to celebrate the fifty-fifth anniversary of Israel's independence. The hosts were the Israeli ambassador to Kenya, Yaacov Amitai, and his wife. The gathering was sparsely attended, since Mauritius has many Palestinian sympathizers, including government officials. I was glad to see Foreign Minister Gayan in attendance, as he and I had had some tense discussions in the past over U.S. support of Israel. In explaining the reason for my departure from the Aleemiah College event, he smiled, saying my timing had been good and that Uteem had been out of line in politicizing the event. I learned also that Bérenger too had been red-faced and angry with Uteem. High Commissioner David Snoxell said he had been disturbed by Uteem's speech, and believing it terribly inflammatory, left shortly after I did. President Offmann also commented on how out of place the speech had been.

The antiwar rhetoric had concerned me for weeks, as did the continual veiled and actual threats, and I believed that the Mauritian press played a part in stirring up the Muslim community. On Sunday I saw mention of an article in the May 14 edition of the *International Herald Tribune* that delved into the implications of the war with Iraq for the African continent. Co-authored by well-known diplomats John Prendergast and Princeton Lyman, the article noted that "the Iraq war has stirred up a great deal of resentment. Combined with a dearth of economic opportunities, this could create a growing recruitment base for extremist and terrorist groups such as Al Qaeda, whose appeal in Africa has so far been limited." They further noted that while the postwar reconstruction efforts would consume much of the Western powers' resources, the United States could not afford to turn its back on Africa. While President Bush had proposed major increases in foreign assistance to Congress, they were concerned that aid assets would be diverted to Iraq and Afghanistan.

Indeed, it was my opinion that many of the promises the U.S. government had made might be taken off the table—a dramatic reversal for the African continent. I feared that poverty-stricken, susceptible inhabitants of small Muslim countries such as Comoros and larger ones such as Somalia and Sudan would not receive the economic attention necessary to keep radical Islamic influences at bay. Instead, activities and influence of such extremist organizations as al-Qaeda were gaining ground. Worse, I thought, driving these insurgents from Iraq and elsewhere could take our full attention for years to come. The growing instability in the Horn of Africa could readily spill over into the small, nascent Indian Ocean island nations and destabilize these fragile democracies.

On Wednesday, we had yet another worldwide threat advisory against American interests. The Department of Homeland Security had raised the national threat level to orange. We quickly set up meetings with American companies doing business in the host countries, and informed all the American citizen wardens in the three countries. Later we received a telephone call back from our warden in Comoros, who believed he had credible information about a pending attack in Kenya, as related to him by a reliable Comorian source. The source wanted to relay the information directly to the embassy. The data concerned the U.S. embassy in Nairobi, and we immediately forwarded the message to the Bureau of Diplomatic Security at the State Department.

At 1:30 p.m., an FBI agent from Washington who had come to the embassy for a security briefing alerted me about telephone surveillance of a person of interest who had made suspicious phone calls to Mauritius. This person was part of a cell and possibly was involved in plotting an event. I suggested the agent immediately meet with Police Commissioner Gopalsingh to track down the phone number and user. Adding to the angst, the previous evening I had received eight hang-up calls that I hoped could be traced.

On my computer, a message popped up about a taped message from Osama bin Laden's lieutenant Ayman al-Zawahiri to Muslims around the world. It was disturbing:

> O Muslims, take matters firmly against the embassies of America, England, Australia, and Norway and their interests and companies. Burn the ground under their feet, as they should not enjoy your protection, safety, or security. Expel those criminals out of your countries.

In mid-May, President Azali of Comoros visited Mauritius, as he did periodically, and stayed at the Trou aux Biches Resort. Since he felt more comfortable speaking French, I asked Bisa to go along with me to the meeting. The President and I talked about the Iraq War, he complimenting the United States on the manner in which we were dealing with a difficult situation. Azali said Saddam was a problem and had to go.

Knowing the Comorian concerns, I wanted to clarify that the United States intended to be liberators, not occupiers; our intent was to stay only for a short time to help establish a democratic system. I referred to World Wars I and II, where we helped in the reconstruction process and the establishment of democratic governments in Germany and Japan.

Azali mentioned the need for help from U.S. aid programs, particularly in regard to military training and border control. I explained I was pressing to have the Section 508 sanctions against Comoros lifted so this could happen. We discussed the upcoming assembly elections and the resolution on the constitutional issues. He assured me the elections would take place before year's end. This was important in building my case for lifting the sanctions.

I decided to broach the subject of possible terrorist cells located on the island of Grande Comore, in the village of Mohoro. Azali was aware that strangers from several Muslim countries were entering Comoros, but he did not think they were terrorists. I ventured they might possibly be linked to Fazul and planning new attacks in Nairobi. We then talked again about airport security and the ramp and baggage handlers that might be associated with al-Qaeda or sympathizers. Since only a few airlines still operated in Comoros, any that pulled out could severely hurt their economy. Azali said that the main airport in Moroni was not well equipped; the French had operated the airport for twenty years before pulling out three years previously, taking everything with them. He expressed concern that neighboring Mayotte, a French collectivity, could be a passageway for suspect individuals.

In parting I said I would do everything possible to get programs restarted to help overcome the potential for radical or terrorist influence in his country. Azali said he would monitor the mosque activity and radical teachings, mentioning that two radical leaders had already been asked not to teach or preach anymore because of their inflammatory messages. We agreed to stay in close touch.

I then met with Mauritius's Minister of Labor, Showkutally Soodhun, at his office. He was a strikingly good-looking person with well-groomed dark hair and matching goatee; his well-tailored dark suit made a powerful first impression. He offered a warm handshake and an engaging smile. After a cup of coffee, he immediately commended the United States for defending freedom, and supported our actions in Iraq. He said he was a very devout Muslim and a leader in the Muslim community, and he wanted to apologize for former President Uteem's attack on the United States at the recent Eid e-Milad un-Nabi event, adding that Uteem would not be invited to speak again the following year. He said President Offmann had been so upset at the event that he had handed a note to Maulana Siddiqui asking him to speak of tolerance and peace, which he did. When it was his turn, Bérenger had revised his prepared remarks to emphasize tolerance and understanding and to defuse Uteem's attempt to stir up the audience. I thanked Soodhun for sharing this with me and was relieved by the openness of his comments.

With so much activity going on, Marcia and I looked forward to a weekend away, and on May 23 we flew over to Antananarivo, Madagascar. We were greeted by Ambassador Wanda Nesbitt, who was kind enough to take us to the Colbert Hotel, in the center of the capital. Along the way, we saw many people standing around, which I thought was unusual, but we were told that unemployment was at 40 percent.

The ambassador was on her way to visit a Habitat project, so I made arrangements to meet with Phil Carter, her deputy chief of mission. The embassy complex, although centrally located, was highly vulnerable, with tall buildings all around it and relatively easy surface access. At the entrance, local guards checked under the vehicles and inside as a precaution. But only a weighted pipe cross arm separated the embassy driveway from the adjacent public street.

Phil Carter was planning to leave shortly to take Zachary Teich's position as deputy director for East African affairs, and Teich was coming to Antananarivo to replace Carter. Although we talked about a number of security issues and the fishing village of Mahajanga, located on the northwest coast of Madagascar, where a large number of Comorians live, there was no mention of moving the Comoros portfolio from Mauritius. He knew, however, of the active engagement our embassy had pursued with the Union of the Comoros since my arrival.

Marcia and I were soon off with an English-speaking tour guide to explore some of the outlying villages and rain forests and learn more about the Malagasy people. Those from the highlands were mainly of Indonesian and Malaysian descent; those from the lowlands had more African ancestry.

When we finally arrived at Vakona Forest Lodge, in the rain forest near the village of Andasibe, our guide took us in a canoe to a small island where we saw a number of the rare Indri Lemurs indigenous to Madagascar. We lucked out, spotting the black-and-white, brown, and gray varieties. Curious about our presence, they came quite close to us. Several jumped on our shoulders, wanting to play and to eat the bananas we had brought along. Although they appeared friendly, we were told to be careful because some would bite. These furry creatures resembled a cross between a cat, squirrel, and dog. Some made melodic singing sounds that echoed through the forest.

During our nature walk through the Analamazaotra rain forest, we spotted a small hedgehog tenrec (like a small porcupine), geckos, chameleons, and giraffe-neck beetles clinging to wet leaves and branches. We even caught a glimpse of a large Madagascar boa curled up by the side of the road—that was exciting. Of the 115 varieties of birds found on the island, we saw at least fifteen types, including the Madagascar blue vangas, paradise flycatcher, and magpie robin.

Traveling from Antananarivo through the villages on our four-hour journey, we noticed that the roads were narrow and poorly maintained, yet heavily traveled by caravans of trucks. Older people and even young children seemed to walk everywhere, carrying massive loads on their heads and backs: pots, sacks, firewood. A lucky few had ox carts. Although I saw stretches of rice fields, I was told food shortages were widespread. Indoor plumbing was rare, and people bathed and washed clothes in the streams. There were many small family fruit and vegetable stands and other business kiosks in the villages. Although many families were poor, the Malagasy children all wore clean school uniforms; some walked great distances to their school each day.

It was sad to see Madagascar—a country so rich in natural resources—struggling with poverty and more than twenty-three years of corruption under former President Didier Ratsiraka. He left the country impoverished, with only minimal infrastructure in place. Yet the people remained resilient, pleasant, and hopeful for a better future under President Marc Ravalomanana.

After I returned to U.S. Embassy Port Louis, I read in a memo that President Bush had signed the U.S. Leadership Act of 2003, providing $15 billion for the fight against HIV/AIDS, tuberculosis, and malaria in at least twelve sub-Saharan African countries dramatically affected by these diseases. I was optimistic that other programs badly needed in countries such as Comoros would follow.

During an appreciation dinner at the six-star Oberoi Hotel Resort in honor of Maurice de la Tour, who had helped put together the successful private sector component of the AGOA Forum, Bisa Williams pulled me aside. Information had just reached her that a Boeing 727-200 aircraft had been stolen from Angola with more than 200,000 gallons of fuel on board. In Rwanda, another plane, a Russian one, was also missing, although the details were sketchy. Hamada Madi Bolero, an advisor to President Azali, had called her from Comoros about the Boeing 727. His sources indicated it might be heading there. I told Bisa to send an alert immediately to every department in Washington.

Early the next morning, Bisa called but had no new information on the whereabouts of either plane. I mentioned a Tom Clancy–style scenario about possible missions of a plane full of fuel, which put fear in both of us.

Later we learned that there were two sister planes—one tail number apart—owned by a London company. The planes had been outfitted to haul fuel to mining camps in Angola. It seemed that the British company was in financial trouble, owing more than $40,000 in landing fees and other costs, and had sold one plane and left at night from Angola with the other one without filing a flight plan, so no one knew which way they were headed.

Next we heard that the plane had made a request to land in Seychelles. This seemed to have the mark of some nefarious activity. Was al-Qaeda involved? Since President Bush would be in Qatar on June 5, visiting the troops, was this a security concern? And what about the USS *Tarawa*, which would be in Seychelles at the same time, returning from Iraq? There were many questions and no answers. Nor did we know how the missing Russian aircraft fit into this scenario.

Eventually we heard from the Naval Criminal Investigative Service in Bahrain regarding the missing Boeing 727. Apparently the request to land had been withdrawn, though the plane's location still remained a mystery. Meanwhile, the new owner of the sister plane had grounded it for the time being so that it would not become mixed up with the missing one and perhaps shot down.

We never did receive any further information on the missing Boeing jet, or on the Russian airplane, for that matter. Eventually we considered the case closed and of no security concern.

In late May I headed to the island of Rodrigues, where I rendezvoused with Dan Claffey and Lise Pun Sin from the embassy. Meeting with Joseph Chenlye Lamvohee of the Rodrigues Regional Assembly, we talked about capacity building for the island to improve people's living conditions. Afterward, I met with the island's chief executive, Claude Wong So, who had returned from abroad out of loyalty to help oversee infrastructure projects, such as the new airport terminal and runway expansion. In addition to an ambitious program for capacity building, he had major concerns about health care, education, the IT sector, and the expansion of the public library. He sincerely wanted to improve many aspects of the island's society.

Chief Commissioner Serge Clair, Commissioner for Women and Children Arlette Perrine-Bégué, and Commissioner of Health Soopramanien Sooprayen came to see me. We discussed trade-related issues such as AGOA and other programs to aid with establishing commercial ventures on the island. The AGOA program was a natural for them, and I wondered why this island had been overlooked by the government of Mauritius. I decided to take up the issue with Minister of Trade Cuttaree.

Rodrigues has long been a stepchild of Mauritius. Had it been a larger piece of real estate with a strong population base, the island could have bargained for semi-independence. Instead, they had a semi-autonomous governing structure but were fiscally beholden to the government of Mauritius. In theory, they have home rule, but in reality it is smoke and mirrors. Yet even with the limited amount of arable land on this rocky, mountainous island, there was potential for economic successes. USAID and agencies such as the Peace Corps need to allocate time and resources directly to the local government on behalf of the populace.

On Saturday morning, May 31, we met at the Passenger Terminal building in the port area for the Ambassador's Girls Education Program. Marcia had spent the past hour talking with many of the young girls eager to speak English with her. In contrast, most of the parents spoke only Creole and French.

This program was one of two Education for Development and Democracy Initiatives in Mauritius, funded by USAID and administered by the U.S. Embassy and a local church program called Restore Another Child's Hope (ReACH). This event was to celebrate the establishment of a $52,500 fund for the program, which was geared to young girls at risk. I welcomed the opportunity to speak about the importance of girls receiving an education.

Next we flew to Seychelles and landed in Mahé, where our consular agent, Susanne Rose, was waiting to give me a briefing before we went to the remodeled

18.5. Marcia at the local Saturday market in Port Mathurin, Rodrigues, May 31, 2003.

18.6. Ambassador's Girls Education Program, in conjunction with the Education for Development and Democracy Initiative and Restore Another Child's Hope, Rodrigues, May 31, 2003.

18.7. The USS *Tarawa* visits Seychelles, June 2003.

Sunset Beach Hotel in Beau Vallon on the northwest side of the island. I spent several hours walking along the beach with Marcia and practicing my remarks for Tuesday's ship visit. The USS *Tarawa* was a general-purpose amphibious warship, resembling a small aircraft carrier, designed to put troops, vehicles, and equipment on hostile shores. On board were a number of landing crafts; Harrier aircraft; Cobra, Sea Stallion, Huey, and Sea Knight helicopters; and enough equipment and supplies to stay at sea for long engagements. The ship, over eight hundred feet long, had fifteen levels and was capable of speeds of 24 knots, or 28 miles per hour. One of the thirty-two ships in Task Force 51, the *Tarawa* served as the flagship for Admiral Clyde Marsh in the Iraqi deployment.

That evening, Marcia and I, as well as Charlie Slater, were invited to have dinner with Sir James Mancham, the founding President of Seychelles, at the Mancham residence. The residence, originally owned by Mancham's father, was taken away from the family after the 1977 coup, when Mancham went into exile. It was returned to him in 1992, when he came back after fifteen years living abroad. By that time, Mancham sported a white beard and was nicknamed "Papa la Barbe," which has stuck with him ever since—as has the beard. He lived in this lovely house with his Australian wife, Kate. Also invited were several other friends and business owners, which led to a lively conversation on the island's economic concerns and current political issues.

Early Tuesday morning, a helicopter picked us up for the short flight to the anchored *Tarawa*. Upon landing, we were greeted by Captain Jay Bowling, commanding officer; Captain Ron Thomas, commander of Amphibious Squadron 7; Colonel Thomas Waldhauser, commanding officer of the 15th Marine Expeditionary Unit; and Command Master Chief Thomas Shields. After a red carpet welcome, we had breakfast in the captain's private dining room, after which Captain Bowling gave us a tour of the massive vessel. During our tour, we learned that Colonel Waldhauser was in the first landing party at the port of Umm Qasr and stayed with the troops all the way to Nasiriyah. He was also involved in the rescue of Private First Class Jessica Lynch on April 1, 2003. He noted keeping the peace was difficult with so much unrest. The lack of power, water, food, medical resources, and safety were major problems, although he thought the media overstated the looting issue. He said many of the artifacts were taken for safekeeping and returned, while others were locked up and hidden away. He was more concerned about the rampant stripping of building materials and equipment from government buildings. He used the example of people who illegally removed bricks from buildings one day and reused them by the next morning to build a house for their family in another part of town.

We went on deck for the awards ceremony for performance and end of tour of military personnel who would be leaving when the ship reached port in the United

18.8. Addressing the troops onboard the USS *Tarawa*, June 3, 2003.

States. It was a privilege to pin medals on their shirts while their names were read over the loudspeaker system. I had the honor to praise the troops on behalf of their commander in chief, President Bush. Several fun awards went to personnel who had beaten Captain Ron Thomas in racquetball.

Shortly before noon, the helicopter transported us back to Mahé to meet with Vice President James Michel and discuss the outcome of Mukesh Valabhji's meeting in Washington with the International Monetary Fund and the World Bank looking for a solution to their hard currency crisis. They were also to review the macro-economic reform plan and repayment of massive overdue debt.

Director General for Presidential Affairs and Chief of Protocol Derick Ally, who had recently returned from a stay in the United States sponsored by the International Visitor Leadership Program, had escorted me to Michel's office. I also commended the Vice President on the country's environmental projects—particularly in Aldabra, which is home to more than a hundred thousand giant tortoises. I told him our embassy would continue to financially support some of their environmentally oriented NGO operations, for which he was thankful.

As the U.S. embassy was twelve hundred miles from Seychelles, I often worked on U.S. government matters within a "Virtual Embassy" environment, although I was able to make friends with the ministry's principal secretary, Alain Butler-Payette, and work closely with him. Previously, in late February, I had placed a telephone call to Seychelles and spoken with Alain about the Article 98 agreement. I was glad that the government of Seychelles had agreed to sign; without that, naval ship visits might have been curtailed after July 2003, which would have been a great loss to their economy. I thought it also would have been a huge loss for our troops serving in critical areas, who need the stopover for rest and recuperation.

Now finishing my meeting with Michel, Derick and I then went to a private area to conclude the Article 98 signing with Charlie Slater present as a witness. This long awaited inking of the document was a historic moment.

While in Seychelles, I wanted to visit one or two commercial enterprises that could qualify under the AGOA program to expand employment and help with the foreign exchange shortage. Charlie and I met with David Curtis-Bennett, the managing director of Chelle Medical Limited, which also owned the Laryngeal Mask Company. We saw female workers, clothed from head to foot in sanitized attire inside a clean room, assembling a flexible airway tube and shield used in surgical procedures. These components were extruded in Italy to precise specifications and assembled in Seychelles.

In an adjacent operation, Bennett contracted with Orthofix International, a Texas-based NASDAQ-listed company, to make finely engineered orthopedic external and internal fixation products designed to align and secure broken bones during healing. This was an amazing operation for a small Seychelles company and

18.9. Signing the Article 98 agreement, June 4, 2003. From left to right: Director General for Presidential Affairs and Chief of Protocol Derick Ally, Ambassador Price, and Mrs. Jeannette D'Offay.

offered great potential for AGOA participation. Of particular interest was that his workers were quite well paid at 2,050 rupees (SCR) per month, or about $400–500 depending on the exchange rate at the time. We figured they could save up to 20 percent on duties—possibly $2–3 million, based on their sales projection—under the AGOA program. This surprised Bennett.

After the Article 98 nonsurrender agreement was signed, on July 8, 2003, it was ratified by the National Assembly. This helped bring the total number of countries in support of the Article 98 agreement to ninety-four. This made clear the importance of every country supporting U.S. interests around the world.

{XIX}

FINDING RESOLUTION

I was encouraged to read that at the June 2003 G-8 Summit, regarding Africa, President Bush had said he was committing $1.3 billion to the Millennium Challenge Account in 2004 and an increase in famine relief to $5 billion annually by 2006 to assist thirty-eight million people at risk of starving in sub-Saharan Africa. This was in addition to the $15 billion he had pledged to combat HIV/AIDS. The President went on to call for increased trade as a way of increasing prosperity, asking all nations to open their markets through free trade measures. He emphasized that the United States had substantially increased its share of imports from sub-Saharan Africa between 1996 and 2001.

More good news came when Dan Claffey announced that the LDS Church had a second shipment of books—two containers containing 37,537 books—plus 12,600 school kits on their way to Mauritius for Vice President Bundhun's school book program. Subsequently, in the embassy's library, we held the midyear All Hands Awards ceremony singling out exceptional performances by Foreign Service officers and Foreign Service national staff, from working on the AGOA Forum to fulfilling the constant demands from Washington for reports.

On Friday, June 13, I reviewed the briefing paper regarding my upcoming meeting with President Bush. The following morning, Marcia and I headed to the airport for our trip to South Africa, where we would meet up with our children. While waiting in the VIP room at the airport, I ran into a diplomat friend who related an interesting story about an Indian minister who was claimed to be a close ally of Uday Hussein, Saddam's son. India had participated in the "oil for food" program sanctioned by the UN, and my friend indicated that under cover of this program, offshore accounts had been set up for Uday in a number of countries, including Mauritius. There could be millions of dollars in different Indian shell companies and names. My source thought our government should try to locate and freeze these accounts. This was one of those complex scenarios that I knew I needed to report to Washington—but which I also knew American officials might not believe. But what if it was true?

19.1. All-Hands Awards ceremony, June 11, 2003. Dan Claffey, soon to depart, received a Superior Honor Award and is presented with an American flag that flew over the embassy.

19.2. All-Hands Awards ceremony, June 11, 2003. Foreign Service national GSO staff receives a Group Meritorious Honor Award.

Soon Marcia and I were in the air and on our way to the Ngala Safari Camp, nestled in its own private reserve adjacent to the Kruger Park Game Reserve. It would be great to see our children, their spouses, and our grandchildren for a few days of incredible game tracking and photo opportunities. We also intended to meet the Conservation Corporation Africa (CC Africa) public affairs officer and other senior safari camp staff for a tour of nearby village projects they supported. We visited Welverdiend Primary School, where class sizes were quite large, with only eleven teachers for eight

19.3. All-Hands Awards ceremony, June 11, 2003. Foreign Service national staff receives a Group Superior Honor Award.

19.4. Marcia greeting Welverdiend Primary School students with school kits, June 17, 2003.

hundred students and little chance of an education beyond the seventh grade. We brought along school kits to be presented to the best students in each class, and the CC Africa staff brought two new computers to be installed for student use. It was a delightful visit: students practiced their English by singing American songs for us, lovely dances and gymnastics were performed, and one girl read a charming poem.

19.5. Grandchildren Alexandra and Hannah getting to know some of the students at Welverdiend Primary School, June 17, 2003.

We lodged at Ngala until June 20 and then went to Zambia for a two-day stay at the Royal Livingston Hotel, next to the magnificent Victoria Falls. From there, we traveled to Cape Town and stayed at the quaint Cape Grace Hotel until I had to leave for Washington a few days later. The family would catch up with me in Seychelles on my return.

Early on the morning of June 22, we heard the news that a ship carrying 750 tons of explosives had been seized in Greece after an anonymous tip. Registered in the Marshall Islands as the *Baltic Sky*, the ship was traveling with a crew of eight under a Comorian flag. Apparently the cargo was headed for Sudan; the recipient had only a post office box for an address, making the entire scenario all the more suspicious. I wondered how this incident would be perceived in Washington and what the effect would be on my efforts to get the Section 508 sanctions on Comoros lifted.

We also learned that on June 24, U.S. Embassy Nairobi had been closed—the result of an intelligence report of an imminent terrorist attack against U.S. interests in Kenya. Worried about Mauritius, I believed U.S. interests in sub-Saharan Africa could be at risk because of the active presence of radical Islamic factions in the region.

The morning after checking in at the Ritz-Carlton in Washington, D.C., to attend the U.S.–Africa Business Summit, I received a message to be at the State Department for a security briefing. Having some time before I had to be at State, I went over to the Washington Hilton, where the Corporate Council on Africa was hosting a conference based on the theme "Building Partners." While there, I met with the Millicom International Cellular S.A. attorney Ed Doyle to review the company's long-standing claims in Mauritius. Millicom operated in fifteen countries, and in Mauritius they had partnered with the Currimjee family's Emtel operation. Doyle reviewed the issues in their claim against the government of Mauritius, which Millicom argued gave its own telecom preference and hence increased Emtel's operating costs.

This case had already been working its way through the courts for some time with no resolution. I suggested using arbitration to find an equitable resolution as a better alternative than going to court. Millicom could readily discount the amount of money and time it would cost to collect the claim amount and instead seek a practical settlement. Doyle agreed, and I offered the embassy's help in at least getting the government to the bargaining table.

Later in Mauritius, I would meet with Bashir Currimjee to review the status of the case, which was scheduled to go to trial in September 2004. I believed that our pushing for more transparency and the closing of loopholes on intellectual property rights abuses might have helped to dislodge this case from the shelves where it had gathered dust for years. Bashir thanked me for pressing his case with the Prime Minister. (As of June 17, 2005, when I left, the case had not yet been resolved.)

At the State Department, Blossom Perry, my desk officer, and I met with Lauren Moriarty and former ambassador Richard (Dick) Bogosian, who was filling in as temporary duty officer at the bureau, to discuss sending an assessment team to Comoros to investigate whether individuals traveling from certain suspect countries were using Comoros as a staging area. Since my arrival in Port Louis, I had been reporting the issue of strangers coming and going, and as I have noted, had we not closed the embassy in Comoros, we would have had in-country information as to the movement of these strangers at a lesser ongoing cost than with the constant start-and-stop approach of periodically sending embassy staff and other government agency personnel to Comoros.

At Assistant Secretary Kansteiner's office, we met with the Mauritius delegation, which included Foreign Minister Anil Gayan, Trade and Industry Minister Jayen Cuttaree, Information Technology and Telecommunications Minister Deelchand Jeeha, and Ambassador Usha Jeetah. Blossom Perry and Sadie Tucker, an intern in the Africa Bureau, were also present. Our main purpose for meeting was to sign the U.S. Article 98 nonsurrender agreement, culminating a six-month negotiation to bring the government of Mauritius to the table.

The ceremony was held in the seventh-floor Treaty Room. In this regal space ornamented with both the American and Mauritius flags, Walter Kansteiner sat on the right at a long table and Anil Gayan sat on the left. As one of the witnesses, I stood behind Kansteiner, while Usha Jeetah stood behind Gayan as the documents were signed.

19.6. Article 98 agreement signing ceremony in the Treaty Room at the State Department, June 25, 2003. Seated, left to right: Foreign Minister Gayan, Assistant Secretary Kansteiner. Looking on, left to right: Ambassador Jeetah, Ambassador Price.

I then went to the Eisenhower Executive Office Building (formerly known as the Old Executive Office Building), adjacent to the White House, to meet Jendayi Frazer and review the bullet points for the briefing I would conduct with President Bush the next day in preparation for his meeting with Prime Minister Jugnauth.

The following morning, I attended the conference breakfast session, "The Future of AGOA," and sat near the head table, which gave me a chance to speak with Prime Minister Jugnauth and his wife. The guest speaker, Richard Lugar, was then chairman of the Senate Foreign Relations Committee. One of the authors of the 2000 AGOA Act, he would work toward extending the AGOA program past 2008.

The Prime Minister spoke, expressing concern over the competition and the need for preferences for small island nations, as well as continued AGOA benefits for the sub-Saharan African countries. Ambassador Zoellick spoke on free trade, liberalizing access, and eventually doing away with preferences. He said Africa must be part of the global economy, and added that the current negotiations in the WTO's Doha Round were important and that lowering tariffs and implementing free trade agreements (FTAs) were necessary. The current preferences under AGOA were beneficial to the sub-Saharan African countries for access to the U.S. markets, Zoellick noted, but the negotiations with the Southern African Customs Union were important in the context of the FTA. I could see Jugnauth stiffen as Zoellick spoke about ending the small island nation preferences.

Following that session, Dick Bogosian, and I went to the International Monetary Fund to learn more about their meeting with Mukesh Valabhji on the Seychelles refinancing issues. The country's need for more transparency was at the top of their list, followed by their concern that the Seychelles Marketing Board (SMB) was the controlling factor for goods coming into the country. Although some positive remarks about Valabhji's basic plan were voiced, the bottom line remained where Seychelles was going to get the $140 million needed to close the gap in his financial plan. He had asked for sovereign loans, which the United States didn't make. At most, the IMF would loan $5 million, but first the Seychelles government would have to go to the Paris Club—a lender group comprising nineteen of the world's richest countries. An overriding factor was the outstanding $50 million of loans that were in arrears. The good news was that a review team would arrive in Seychelles on July 7 to negotiate terms in an attempt to come closer to a workable program. I told the group I had scheduled a meeting with Valabhji in Seychelles several days before the team was to arrive, and would broach these issues with him as well.

At the conference, President Bush delivered the main address, on the future of U.S.-Africa relations. The President wanted to assure everyone that U.S. government policy included both aid and trade for Africa. He was also upfront about calling out African leaders who were harming their countries, insisting that Charles Taylor of Liberia step down and urging the African nations to solve the problem of Robert Mugabe of Zimbabwe so that democracy could be restored in that country.

At three o'clock, Walter Kansteiner and I went to the seventh floor to meet Secretary Powell and ride with him to the White House. We quickly went down a secure elevator and were whisked away in a heavily armor-plated Cadillac limousine for the five-minute ride to the West Wing of the White House. Waiting outside the Oval Office, I could hear the President talking; as we walked in with Ari Fleischer, the press secretary, Stephen Hadley, the deputy national security advisor, and Jendayi Frazer, I saw the President standing near the window talking to Bob Zoellick.

President Bush got right to the point and wanted to know what he should tell the Mauritian leaders when they met. After a brief moment of being speechless, with everyone's eyes on me, I described Mauritius as a small island country that was democratic and a model for all of Africa. I mentioned its support of the global war on terror, signing of Article 98, concerns about the AGOA extension, and fiber sourcing issues. When I spoke of the Mauritians' desire that preferences be granted to small island nations, President Bush jumped in, saying that preferences would eventually have to go away.

Turning to Bob Zoellick, the President asked about the fiber sourcing issue. Bob summarized the issue and concluded by noting that Mauritius wanted to be included as a least-developed-country (LDC) beneficiary under AGOA but also wanted to keep tariffs high on larger countries. The President said the tariffs would have to go as well.

19.7. Oval Office briefing, June 26, 2003. Ambassador Price briefing President Bush, Secretary Colin Powell, Assistant Secretary Walter Kansteiner, Deputy National Security Advisor Stephen Hadley, Ambassador Bob Zoellick, Treasury Secretary John W. Snow, Special Assistant to the President Dr. Jendayi Frazer, and Press Secretary Ari Fleischer.

Then President Bush asked if there were any other issues. I said that Mauritians feared that in ten years there would be only four to five large countries in the textile business. He responded that Mauritius would have to diversify. With that, the briefing was over.

At 3:25 p.m. the door from the Oval Office leading to the reception area opened, and Chief of Protocol Donald "Enzo" Ensenat introduced the Mauritian delegation to President Bush. Prime Minister Jugnauth was first, followed by Anil Gayan, Jayen Cuttaree, Deelchand Jeeha, and Usha Jeetah.

President Bush commended Ambassador Jeetah for well representing her country and thanked the Prime Minister for hosting the successful AGOA Forum. The President repeated that he would push for the AGOA extension. He commiserated about plant closings and loss of business in Mauritius, and said we too were having problems with our own manufacturers. However, he endorsed free trade and said the people of Mauritius were better off than most of the LDCs. Suggesting diversification, he said it was cheap labor that wins in textiles. President Bush also stated he did not feel there should be preferential treatments, and again referred to conversion of their talents away from cheap labor, stressing that education was an avenue for higher-paying jobs.

Returning to the "small island" concept, the President said that while some preferences and special rules were a possibility, tariffs must go down. He stated he believed in trade liberalization globally, and added that we could not miss the Doha round of negotiations. They offered a major opportunity to conclude the WTO and FTA agreements, which would include reduction or elimination of tariffs.

Bob Zoellick said he was concerned about a Mauritian minister who had spoken at a recent conference in Egypt about not losing preferences as well as not lowering tariffs. He said that none of us could go back to protectionism. Jayen Cuttaree jumped in, explaining that the Mauritian government feared that its economy would disappear. Zoellick countered that no one could stop the world, so they would have to strengthen their economy.

Prime Minister Jugnauth talked about Mauritius's new directions in the information technology and communications sector, and asked the President to help bring U.S. investments to Mauritius. The President replied that Mauritius was good at business and attracting investors and would do fine. As the meeting ended, the President thanked everyone and extended a warm handshake to each.

19.8. President Bush greeting Prime Minister Sir Anerood Jugnauth of Mauritius in the Oval Office, June 26, 2003.

That evening at a dinner held in honor of Mauritius at the Mayflower Hotel, I sat with the Prime Minister and his wife. In the speeches that followed, both Jayen Cuttaree and Deelchand Jeeha made mention of the role our embassy had played in making the AGOA Forum a great success. Jeeha even said that I had converted him into a believer in Wi-Fi access. To my delight and surprise, Ambassador Jeetah presented me with an exquisite handcrafted nineteenth-century replica sailing ship model made by one of the great artisans in Mauritius.

On Saturday, June 28, I arrived in Seychelles and was greeted by Alain Butler-Payette and Mukesh Valabhji, who were concerned about the outcome of the IMF meeting in Washington and hoped for some positive feedback from me. I suggested we continue the conversation at our upcoming meeting scheduled for July 3. Mukesh also wanted to reconfirm our trip for Monday to the outer island of Coëtivy to tour the SMB prawn farm. Then I took a small commuter plane to Praslin Island, where I met my family at the five-star Lémuria Resort.

On the following Monday morning, the SMB pilot picked me up for the forty-five-minute flight to Coëtivy, the most southeasterly island in the archipelago. We circled the island, which is six miles long and one mile wide, so I could get a better look at the prawn farm. The new four-thousand-foot paved runway had night lighting for twenty-four-hour emergency access. Adjacent to an apron area was a new metal hangar to house the aircraft. Waiting with Mukesh was Eshantha Peiris, the general manager of the prawn farm. Started ten years previously, the farm was producing 1,000 to 1,500 tons annually of black tiger prawns, 95 percent of which were shipped to Europe and Japan. Excavated and banked, the plastic-lined holding ponds covered 250 acres of land and were fed by a constant stream of seawater. Harvesting was done at night to avoid UV light, which damages the prawns.

The breeding operation used large "mother" prawns from Madagascar and Mozambique, since they were not easily cultivated in captivity. Two separate hatcheries were used to avoid contamination problems. The spawning cycle involved a hundred females and fifty males in ten separate vats and took three days. The entire hatchery cycle was thirty days, after which the young prawns were large enough to be transferred to outdoor open ponds, where they grew to full size in six to seven months. The feed consisted of a mix of algae and brine shrimp sent in from the Great Salt Lake in Utah.

All the buildings were very clean and sanitary. On entering, people had to walk through a shoe wash and wash their hands with potassium permanganate. Adjacent to the sorting and processing area, where the prawns were cleaned and packaged, were large freezers that held the prawns until shipment. Four large generators supplied continuous power. When the orders were ready to leave, they were loaded on landing crafts equipped with a refrigerated container carrier.

Most Seychellois did not want to work in such an isolated area, so the workforce came mostly from Thailand, Indonesia, and the Philippines. This affected the hard currency issue, since foreign workers were not paid in the local currency, the rupee. When I visited, the operation had 340 employees, 20 percent of whom were women.

Mukesh's wife, Laura, had prepared a nice Creole-style lunch for us at a refurbished coral stone house dating from the copra plantation days. Joining us were their two-and-a-half-year-old daughter, Larrisa, and a young college student named Hussein Karimji, who was visiting from London. I was told the Mauritian Currimjee clans are cousins of the European and East African Karimji clans. Furthermore, Mukesh's grandfather and Bashir Currimjee's father were business associates and friends. Reportedly, these families had extensive dealings in the Seychelles.

Over lunch Mukesh told me how proud he was of this first-class prawn operation, and rightly so, I thought. Mukesh said he hoped sales would approach $10 million in 2003. At full capacity, the facility could reach $15 million in sales. From what I saw, I thought this operation could well become one of the world leaders in the prawn farming industry.

(Less than two years later, on December 8, 2006, *Le Nouveau Seychelles Weekly* reported that the government of Seychelles had decided to sell the Coëtivy prawn operation to a company from the United Arab Emirates. The article stated that a

19.9. Lunch at the Coëtivy prawn farm with Mukesh Valabhji, Eshantha Peiris (manager), Hussein Karimji (visiting from London), Mukesh's wife, Laura, and their daughter, Larrisa, June 30, 2003.

secret memorandum of understanding was signed with the government; and that the breeding ponds might have been owned not by the Seychelles Marketing Board but rather by companies registered in the Cayman Islands. Hence the prawns were sold to the SMB by an offshore entity, and then exported to customers to earn foreign exchange. This certainly was a surprise to me, since I had been told by Mukesh that the prawn farm operation was totally owned by the SMB.)

During lunch I tried to avoid getting into the IMF issues, preferring to wait until our scheduled meeting, but Mukesh was so anxious that I gave him a brief overview, especially since the country's macroeconomic reform plan was to go into effect on July 1, 2003. I found out that Laura worked at the attorney general's office and had helped write the plan, and that Mukesh had authored it. We discussed the loans that were in arrears with the African Development Bank and others, which needed to be rescheduled before the IMF would consider underwriting new loan requests. He asked if we could follow through with the Treasury to get a read on whether they would help to reschedule these loans. I told him that he and I would discuss this further when we met again, and on my return to Mauritius, I would also discuss this issue with several people at the embassy for their input.

As we left, a hard rain started falling, making the flight back to Praslin very bumpy. Mukesh and his family and their guest, who were also on board, continued on to Mahé, while I spent the next few days relaxing with my family before the bilateral meetings began.

On Thursday, July 3, I began the day by paying a courtesy call on Minister of Land Use and Habitat Joseph Belmont at Independence House in Victoria. I wanted some clarification of their continued land reclamation expansion, which added usable real estate at the expense of continued degradation of the coral reefs and the associated ecosystem. He understood that this also added to their extreme hard currency shortage, as they had to find some way to pay for the work without having offsetting income. I also brought up the need for a new dedicated port facility for larger U.S. ships so that they wouldn't have to anchor offshore.

I then met with President René at the State House to discuss my meeting with the IMF and the importance of implementing the economic reform plan as proposed. It was obvious Mukesh had briefed René before our meeting. Payette also had briefed him about the need to sign an additional document on Article 98 and to have it ratified by the assembly.

Afterward when I met with Mukesh, we continued our conversation regarding Seychelles's economic imbalance and the implementation of the economic reform plan to help Seychelles begin its move to a more stable financial environment. I knew that if the country was to achieve this, Mukesh would have to let go of the stranglehold he had on the SMB. Additionally, we discussed that during their upcoming visit, the IMF team would expect to see a timetable for solving the current loan arrears issue, know the source of new loans needed under the plan, and be assured that the liberalization of Seychelles's economy would be achieved by going to an open market format with privatization of SMB operations. I impressed upon Mukesh the need to seriously consider major changes: the hard currency shortages were draining the lifeblood from the local business community. Though he seemed to understand what was required, I was not sure he would be willing to give up control of his power base. He did agree to let me know the results of his discussions with the IMF and the timetable for implementation of the macroeconomic reform plan.

I next had a conversation with Supreme Court Chief Justice Vivekanand Alleear, who reluctantly agreed that the country was in trouble and also that the human rights atmosphere could be improved. He did insist that the trafficking and exploitation of children was not a real problem. On financial crimes, he stated his belief that there was enough transparency in the system.

Since a number of American citizens lived in the area, we decided to hold a Fourth of July celebration at the Plantation Club on Mahé Island. Rain was expected, so we moved the event into the conference center, which was decorated with red, white, and blue streamers, balloons, and flags. On the morning of the Fourth, the club was a beehive of activity as the staff set up buffet tables with hot dogs, hamburgers, french fries, pickles, beans, and relish. In addition to apple pie and three flavors of ice cream for dessert, the chef made a two-by-three-foot cake resembling an American flag. I wanted this to be a great American experience, since it was the first for Seychelles in almost ten years. Fortunately, the rain was no deterrent.

When I returned to Macarty House, the embassy staff was already preparing the grounds for the Independence Day celebration for American citizens in Mauritius. As before, we picked a Sunday, since more people would be able to attend, and we were expecting close to one thousand guests. As they had the previous year, the red, white, and blue decorations made the house and its surroundings look very American. The vendors went all out decorating their booths, and the chefs were busy preparing the American-style menu. Once Prime Minister Jugnauth, Deputy Prime Minister Bérenger, and President Offmann arrived, we had the official toast to our country's 227th birthday. The adults enjoyed the gardens, while the children enjoyed the games.

On Monday, July 7, Charlie introduced us to the military advance team that arrived in Mauritius who would brief us on the President's trip to Africa. His first stop would be Dakar, Senegal, followed by stops in South Africa, Botswana, Uganda, and Nigeria.

I was amazed at the logistics required for the trip. The standby support team arrived on a giant C-5 transport loaded with equipment. By midweek, two large midair-refueling tankers would arrive, followed by a Boeing 747 that looked similar to Air Force One from the outside, except for its large dome on top for satellite systems. This 747 was part of the National Airborne Operations Center, based at Offutt

Air Force Base near Omaha, Nebraska. As we were concluding our meeting, the leader invited our embassy to tour the aircraft on Thursday morning. Charlie and I agreed it would be a once-in-a-lifetime opportunity for the embassy staff.

On Thursday, accompanied by Colonel Sam Seager and his staff, we climbed up two long stairways into the belly of the enormous 747 aircraft and headed toward a briefing room for a PowerPoint presentation. The personnel stationed on board represented all branches of the military except the Coast Guard. We learned that four identical planes served as a survivable mobile communications center, in case of an emergency situation. Constantly in the air with fuel nearby, they were in contact with the President, the Secretary of Defense, the U.S. Strategic Command center, and other military commanders around the world. The operation was well organized, and everyone barely looked away from their screens to acknowledge us. Seager noted they would stay in Mauritius until shortly before the President wound up his trip on July 12. It was quite an experience.

For some time I had wanted to become more familiar with the fishing town of Mahajanga, located on Madagascar's northwest coast. More than half of the population of 135,000 was predominantly Comorian, and the area also had important links to the terrorist Fazul Abdullah Mohammed, as I have noted. When Marcia and I were invited to visit some new paleontological excavations in Madagascar in which several species of dinosaurs had been uncovered by groups from Stony Brook University and the University of Utah, I decided this was a good chance to get in a visit to Mahajanga. I also wanted to visit several new village classroom and medical clinic projects.

On the morning of July 11, Marcia and I headed first for Antananarivo, where we were met by Benjamin Andriamihaja, a representative of the Institute for the Conservation of Tropical Environments. By midafternoon we were on a flight to Mahajanga, where we met Dr. David Krause of Stony Brook University and Luke Dollar from Duke University. Luke also worked part-time as the Ambassador's Special Self-Help Program coordinator at the U.S. Embassy in Antananarivo.

We would be staying at the waterfront La Piscine Hotel, but I wanted to find a small local restaurant for dinner. As we drove around town, we could see the Comorian influence in everything from the manner of dress and the preservative facemask made from vegetable paste worn by women to the wares sold by the shops. The restaurant we settled on was Chez Mme. Chabaud, a small French restaurant in a side alley of a residential area. It definitely was a local's restaurant—we were the only foreigners and drew some stares. The restaurant displayed several pieces of art depicting Comorian scenes, and I had an opportunity to meet the artist and purchase one of the paintings for $20.

The next morning, we left early to visit the excavations, stopping along the way in some of the small towns and villages. On the road we saw oxcarts carrying fresh vegetables and fruits. It was market day, so we had a chance to see how people bartered and bargained for produce and staples.

We were told this area had a high incidence of malaria, cholera, and leprosy; in some cases, even bubonic plague had shown up. I knew that most of these diseases could be eradicated at minimal cost.

For two hours, we drove south from Mahajanga on a road that paralleled the Mozambique Channel, heading for the village of Berivotra. The road cut through the Berivotra sandstone formation and into the white sandy Maevarano formation underneath. This late upper Cretaceous sandstone formation, rich in fossiliferous outcrops, is where many of the great finds have taken place. Such discoveries included the skeletal remains of *Rapetosaurus*, an elephant-sized plant eater; *Rahonavis*, a primitive bird; and the pug-nosed crocodyliform.

The current dig in the Berivotra area had been initiated in 1993 by David Krause. He had come back every year since, uncovering more skeletal parts and additional species. Others who worked with David include Scott Sampson, curator of the Museum of Natural History at the University of Utah, and student assistants Mark Loewen and Mike Getty, among others. The skeletal fossils were being removed almost surgically and placed in plaster casts for shipment to Utah.

The excavation project was operating with limited funding, and shipping the heavy plaster casts to Utah was an expensive endeavor. I discussed the issue with Randy Buday, an American expatriate and one of Mauritius's business leaders. He

19.10. Berivotra dig area in northwestern Madagascar, July 12, 2003.

was the managing director of DHL Express, covering a number of sub-Saharan African countries including Madagascar. David Krause was able to strike a deal with Randy to deliver these precious gems safely to Utah at a fraction of normal costs. Randy understood the importance of this preservation project, championed the cause, and became the transportation catalyst in their excavation efforts.

From the dig, we drove five miles to a school on a windy hilltop in the village of Berivotra, which means "big wind." We drove through a metal arch etched with the name Sekoly Riambato, meaning "Stony Brook School." David had raised $10,000 for the construction of two classrooms and bathrooms for about one hundred students. We were told Canadians had contributed to the construction as well. David also helped fund school supplies and teacher salaries, and planned to add a medical clinic.

We were greeted by teachers and students, and after a short tour, the children were positioned in two rows facing two flagpoles for a flag-raising ceremony. On one flagpole, they placed the American and Canadian flags; on the other, the Malagasy flag. Songs were sung in French, Malagasy, and English. The program culminated with native dances by the women of the village; Marcia was asked to join in, and eventually we all did. You could see on parents' faces how proud they were of their children and how thankful they were that their children had this opportunity for an education.

19.11. Parents, children, and teachers welcoming American visitors with a flag-raising ceremony, Sekoly Riambato School, Berivotra, Madagascar, July 12, 2003.

19.12. Sekoly Riambato School welcoming event with parents and children looking on, July 12, 2003.

We had visited a number of schools in other African countries and could see that these students were lucky by comparison. Each child had his or her own desk, as did the teachers; there were full-size blackboards with adequate chalk, a bulletin board for information, and travel posters mounted on painted walls.

Afterward, David hosted a picnic lunch on another hilltop so that we could spend time with the dig staff, which was quite an educational experience for us. For a moment this geologic encounter took me back almost fifty years to when I had spent considerable time on the Colorado Plateau.

Resuming our journey with Luke, we traveled further south into the forest area to visit Duke University's Nicholas School of the Environment project. Luke, who was working on his Ph.D., shared with us a report about conservation, research, and development in the Ankarafantsika protected area. There was also an ongoing carnivore research project about the endangered fossa (which is similar to a bobcat but with a larger rear leg muscle structure, since it spends a lot of time in trees) and other ecological projects monitoring plants and fauna throughout the protected area. They had helped set up a tented ecotourism camp in Ambodimanga village; though it meant giving up a village soccer field, the tourist camp was a worthwhile project that could help out a community with limited economic opportunities.

We had a chance to visit with Madame Ravolaharivelo, the head of the women's group that operated the camp. Luke also introduced us to students from Duke,

Harvard, Ohio State, and the University of Antananarivo, who were all part of the conservation program. Marcia and I were proud of these young American and Malagasy students and the professors who spent their time here making a difference. These types of projects are what made USAID and the Peace Corps such great organizations. If only members of Congress would take the time to visit the areas helped by these projects throughout sub-Saharan Africa and see the wonderful things that can be accomplished with a little funding, maybe it would be a more peaceful continent. A utopian thought, I admit, but worth our engagement.

Returning to Mauritius on July 16, I met with representatives of Sotravic Ltée., a local engineering firm representing Reinke Inc., the U.S. manufacturer of pivot irrigation systems. Told that the company had been awarded a $3 million project by the Irrigation Authority, they wanted to thank us for our support during the bidding process the year before. They also mentioned the possibility of a $4.7 million project in another part of the island. I was pleased: advocating for this American company paid off and opened the door to a more transparent bidding process by the government.

The following week, Bisa Williams handed me a cable regarding the July 10 meeting of the Paris Club in reference to the current plight of Seychelles. Its debt was $65 million, higher than I had been told, with arrears amounting to $50 million. The total debt was 200 percent of the GDP and was expected to rise to 275 percent by 2008. The cable noted that the country's macroeconomic reform plan had been presented to the IMF staff for review; now it would be up to the IMF to determine if support was warranted. I hoped Mukesh could convince the IMF to give the plan its blessing so that the Paris Club would make new loans and help reschedule the old ones; the Seychellois government had few other options for getting out of this mess.

Watching CNN later that day, I saw that a house in Mosul, Iraq, had been attacked and destroyed and that Saddam's sons Qusay and Uday had been inside. For a moment I thought back to the information I had heard about laundered money from the food-for-oil program that was supposedly sitting in a Mauritian bank.

On July 24, the embassy held another book distribution program. This time we went to the Pointe aux Sables school, located in a low-income district near downtown Port Louis. Vice President Bundhun had selected the school because its students had never owned their own books. Since the two containers that had arrived on June 6 contained more than thirty-seven thousand books, we would have enough for each child, with the balance going to other low-income area schools and libraries around the island. After the inspiring ceremony, I walked through several classrooms to personally say hello. This was another proud day for the U.S. Embassy.

Around this time I met an interesting group of young people who had come from the United States with Learning Enterprises Inc., which was under the leadership of its organizer, Adam Tolnay. Their plan was to stay in the villages of Chamarel,

Sainte Croix, Cascavelle, Bambou, and Albion to teach English and Internet use to students. Tolnay had emigrated to the United States from Hungary, ended up at Harvard, and currently was at Georgetown working on his Ph.D. When he formed this volunteer teaching program in 1992, his original goal was to help some of the less fortunate children in Eastern Europe, such as Slovakia, Uzbekistan, and Kyrgyzstan. Since then, he and other volunteers had expanded the program into first China and Mexico and then Mauritius, taking the two-and-a-half-week curriculum into outlying villages. It was wonderful to see these ten young college and graduate students spend their summers in such a worthy endeavor; they had even paid their own way to get here. Their local coordinator, Gerard Noël, was from the Chamarel area and would shepherd them around the island. It again reminded me of what the Peace Corps should be doing in every country around the world, yet here were volunteers doing it on their own, for which they should be commended.

On July 28, during lunch at the Labourdonnais, Ambassador Jagdish Koonjul, the Mauritian permanent representative to the UN, and I discussed the issue of preferences in the textile sector. Mauritius was serving as the chair that year of the United Nations' Alliance of Small Island States, and Koonjul said the main agenda topic would be preferences and related trade issues. He also told me that a meeting was planned in Mauritius for September 2004. I recounted the meeting that Prime Minister Jugnauth had had at the White House with President Bush and Bob Zoellick, both of whom had suggested Mauritius not disrupt the Doha round of WTO negotiations and not push for high tariffs for competing countries while expecting preferences for small island states. However, Koonjul responded that Mauritius had no choice if it was to survive.

At the embassy on July 30, Bisa handed me a cable regarding the UN General Assembly Position Paper on Comoros Islands referencing the combining of Mayotte with the three islands of the Union of the Comoros. The State Department wanted our opinion of whether it would be a good idea and one which we would support. In our reply, we emphasized that Comorians living in Mayotte were much better off as a collectivity of France—why would they want to trade the life they had for one of only subsistence? They were also far better off because of their access to social services and other French benefits—all of which were unavailable to the citizens of Comoros. Hence, the embassy recommended no change.

In my interactions with the State Department, I developed great respect for a number of career members of the Foreign Service and noncareer political appointees who I felt wanted to make a difference and would not let considerations of personal gain become key in their decision making. Walter Kansteiner, who was a noncareer diplomat, was among this small group. After serving in previous administrations at the State Department and the National Security Council, he had left for a period of time to make his mark in the private sector. In 2001 Secretary Powell called upon him to once again serve his country, this time as Assistant Secretary of State for African Affairs. In doing so he followed in our country's proud history of citizen public servants who put aside their business interests and family obligations to take on such important roles. Walter was an effective leader and inspired others to excel, and I was sorry to learn that he would be leaving his post in November 2003, though I understood the toll that his schedule and constant travel took.

At the embassy on August 7, we held a strategy meeting on AGOA III inclusion issues. The State Department wanted our input by August 12, and so we invited several Mauritian textile manufacturers, Mauritius Export Processing Zone Authority representatives, and Raj Makoond of the Joint Economic Council to help guide us. They were concerned about business closures, loss of jobs, and, ultimately, the takeover of the textile manufacturing industry by China. I told them we needed to put a compelling plan before Congress. The issues turned out to be threefold: (1) Africa continued to need help in capacity building, even in light of the global trade liberalization that the U.S. trade representative was pushing for; (2) the sunset date for the LDC preferences should be extended beyond 2004 and Mauritius included to use third-country-sourced yarns and fabrics to stay competitive; and (3) if tariffs were lowered for the larger country producers such as China and India, some extended term preferences needed to be in place for the small island states to survive. The Mauritians expressed appreciation for our embassy weighing in on the AGOA issue.

On this, the fifth anniversary of the bombing of the U.S. embassies in Nairobi and Dar es Salaam, our discussion was followed with a moment of silence and reflection.

(XX)

ISLAND BUSINESS AND POLITICS

Fazul Abdullah Mohammed had been in and out of the Comoros islands recently to visit family members, we learned. On the island of Grande Comore lived his wife, three children, three sisters, and one brother; on Anjouan, Mayotte, and Madagascar were uncles, cousins, and another sister. Since he was very close to one sister, shortly before our recent visit to Mahajanga in Madagascar, I was told he had been spotted there as well. I suspected surveillance would be a good option, and had been pushing for more in-country surveillance for some time.

The brewing danger of terrorist infiltration in the Comoros islands continued to be high on my agenda. While in Washington during June, I had met with the State Department and the Department of Defense's Pacific Command (PACOM) team, urging them to consider doing an assessment on the islands. Such an assessment would need high-level approval, but finally word reached me at the end of August that the Comoros Assessment Survey had been approved for September 11 through September 16, 2003. Prior to that date, the survey team would meet with me at the embassy to review the details of the assignment.

In the midst of these serious matters, Marcia planned a birthday party for a milestone event—my seventieth-birthday celebration. At first it was to be a surprise, but she figured that since I don't take kindly to surprises, she'd let me in on her plans—though she offered no details. One condition I insisted on was the nondisclosure of my age: I was still sensitive to the number seven before the zero. The party was to be held at the new La Ravin Restaurant in Moka. A secluded spot adjacent to a flowing stream and surrounded by dense vegetation, it was a favorite of ours.

Arriving at six o'clock on the appointed evening, I was happy to see several of the government leaders, including Prime Minister Anerood Jugnauth and his wife, Sarojini, Vice President Raouf Bundhun and his wife, Asma, and Trade Minister Jayen Cuttaree and his wife, Swatee. Marcia had arranged for Allan Marimootoo and his ten-musician Le Boucaniers to play popular American songs. Restaurateur

Jacqueline Dalais had outdone herself with floral displays and an array of global foods, including salads, sushi, duck, pasta, beef, ham, curried dishes, and large selection of sumptuous desserts. After dinner, Allan had arranged for a talented dance team to showcase tango, mambo, and other Latin dance routines. Then came the highlight: accompanied by a drumroll, a large birthday cake with one giant sparkler blazing was rolled out. Marcia made pleasant remarks about our posting in Mauritius and the many new friends we had made, and then, with everyone singing "Happy Birthday" *sega* style, we formed a conga line with lots of hand clapping and singing. Two hours later, everyone was still dancing, including the Prime Minister and his wife, which amazed everyone present, as no one had ever seen them dancing before.

The following Monday, Foreign Minister Anil Gayan gave me a signed copy of the tentative national reconciliation agreement reached by the three Comorian island presidents and Union President Azali. The seven-page document reaffirmed the framework agreement, including the setting up of operational structures (in particular, distribution of revenues and internal security), the constitution, and the basic laws governing the island authorities as the way out of the political crisis that had evolved. The three island presidents had met in Pretoria accompanied by South African President Thabo Mbeki's special envoy, Louis Mnguni (a good friend who until recently had been South Africa's high commissioner to Mauritius), and other African Union representatives. The embassy followed up by sending an English version to Washington to further support lifting of the Section 508 sanctions.

On September 3, I was back in Washington to confer with the IMF about the findings from the July visit to Seychelles and to see if any progress had been made in resolving the foreign exchange and debt crisis issues. I was disappointed to hear about the lack of direction and unproductiveness of their visit; I did not hear a coherent plan for guiding the Seychelles out of this crisis. Any good consultant could put together a source-and-application statement with targeted suggestions for achievement, I told them, but they responded that this was not the role of the IMF. Since no one could tell me what had been accomplished up to now, I ended the meeting and went on to the State Department to tackle some administrative issues regarding the embassy.

I wanted to make the case for Charlie Slater, my administrative officer, being given the post of deputy chief of mission when Bisa Williams rotated out in 2004. Meeting with Charlie Snyder at the State Department to review the candidates, I explained that I wanted Slater to be given the opportunity to switch over to the generalist category from his current specialist category, which represented a dead end in his career path. Slater was a natural leader with great people skills, I explained. Snyder agreed with my assessment of Slater and said he would look into the situation, but he also admitted that with the current State Department culture, change would be a challenge. I went on to speak with Ruth Whiteside, the acting deputy director general for human resources for the Foreign Service, and lobby for Charlie Slater. I was promised his situation would be reviewed.

At the U.S. Trade Representative's office I met with Chris Moore and Connie Hamilton to present the Mauritian point of view on trade preferences and becoming an LDC beneficiary under the AGOA III third-country fabric provision. Told that the office was pushing to eliminate preferences for the small island states, I said it would be a mistake to lose the economic gains we had helped these nations achieve— at least not until they had had time for capacity building. It was especially important for me to weigh in on these issues before the WTO's upcoming Cancun Round, scheduled to begin in September 2003.

My next stop was at the Peace Corps office, where in a meeting with Director Gaddi Vasquez and Henry McCoy, the regional director for Africa, I once again brought up the embassy's ongoing request for an on-site assessment. I was happy to hear they intended to visit both Mauritius and Comoros, and with any luck Rodrigues, before year's end.

Returning to Mauritius, I met with the six-member Pacific Command team that would be heading to Comoros, accompanied by Bisa Williams. On their arrival they would talk with Minister of Defense and National Security Hamada Madi Bolero, whom I trusted and who was supportive of the global war on terror.

On September 11, services commemorating the 2001 terrorist attacks on America were held at the Caudan waterfront area, with government dignitaries speaking followed by a moment of silence for the lives lost at the World Trade Center, at the Pentagon, and in the field near Shanksville, Pennsylvania, where the last plane crashed. Joining us for the event were the Prime Minister, Deputy Prime Minister, several other ministers, and members of the diplomatic corps. The students from the St. Nicholas Grammar School performed our national anthem and sang "Amazing Grace." At the exact time that the attacks had begun, we had a minute of silence and reflection. Afterward, I spoke of the human tragedy of more than three thousand lives—representing eighty-seven different countries—lost, and of how we all stand united to safeguard our freedom, with respect for tolerance and diversity.

As the deadline approached for selection of a new deputy chief of mission, I sent six names to Phil Carter at the Office for East African Affairs, including Charlie Slater's. I added that I was very familiar with Charlie, having worked with him since arriving in Mauritius, and that I believed his great management and business skills had saved the United States thousands of dollars. I pointed out that the Foreign Service national employees who constituted the bulk of our staff were very comfortable with his leadership. Ambassador Cameron Hume sent a glowing letter on behalf of Stephen Schwartz, another top candidate who currently was deputy political counselor in Pretoria.

On the morning of September 16, I was working on the computer when Tigar leaped across the room and landed on my lap. He had practiced this airborne assault many times—it was his signal for me to head for the kitchen and find him something to eat.

Just then, I received a message indicating that there was a potential security concern with the previously announced midmorning pro-Chagossian demonstration in front of the embassy. I quickly got ready and arrived at the embassy moments before I would be face-to-face with the leaders.

As U.S. ambassador, I fully understood our stated policy regarding the continued use of the Chagos Archipelago, and more particularly the island of Diego Garcia, which housed our military base. Without Diego Garcia, I believed, our country's security would be at risk. However, I also understood the Chagossians' plight and the desire to go back to their ancestral home. They had never been fully integrated into the Mauritian culture; they had no roots there, and even after thirty years, most still lived in abject poverty.

On several occasions on my way to or from the embassy in Port Louis I had taken a circuitous route through the Cassis district at the foot of Signal Mountain, about a mile from the U.S. embassy, where a Chagossian community was located. Every time I drove through there I had a flashback to my own family's forced departure from our home in Germany during the Holocaust. Even years later, my parents still missed their homeland. Because of this, I had empathy for the Ilois. They lived in crowded shacks made of rusted corrugated metal, with skinny chickens picking through the garbage. With high unemployment, poor health conditions, and limited education opportunities, little would change in the lives of these Chagossians. I could see why many believed their only option was to ultimately return to the Chagos Archipelago. At least it would feel like home, and eking out a living there would be better than struggling to exist in the rat-infested environment of Cassis.

When the Pacific Command team reviewed their Comoros Assessment Survey of the areas visited, there was no justification, at this point, to go back or expand the program. The weakest areas of concern were the airport and the seaports, which could present a problem caused by the continuous stream of transiting strangers. Having met with Bolero and other government leaders, the team was comfortable with the mission. I was somewhat relieved. Yet from reports on the ground from people living in Comoros, the number of strangers coming and going spelled out a different story. Time would tell.

I had scheduled a trip to Comoros for September 18–21, just as President Azali and his delegation would be leaving for the UN General Assembly meeting in New York. Given the size of the delegation, their passports had arrived late to the embassy, so as it turned out, I became their personal courier, delivering to them the passports with the necessary visas affixed. Azali and I managed to talk at the airport and go over his schedule in Washington after the General Assembly session. Because the Mount Karthala volcano had been acting up lately, I was pleased to tell him that disaster relief funds of up to $50,000 would be made available through USAID in the event that the volcano erupted.

Later that day, I met with several ministers, including Foreign Minister Souef Mohamed El-Amine. Although they asked when the United States would help them, we all knew the answer: in order for us to move forward with aid programs, they needed first to resolve the reconciliation issues and get the assembly elections back on track. Unable to come up with a firm timetable, El-Amine blamed the island presidents for their lack of cooperation.

We also discussed the strangers residing in Comoros at the mosques. He said he was looking into the situation and that, if necessary, they would turn the newly built mosques and learning centers into general education centers. He added that President Azali supported this concept.

On an internal security matter, El-Amine pointed out the new identity badge he and others in the room were wearing. All government employees having high-level access were now required to wear one. This had come about as a result of seeing us wear badges at the embassy and noting that our guards checked them and also issued visitor badges as guests came into the embassy. He thought it was a good precaution to implement.

The next morning, we visited several of the projects that had received funds from the Ambassador's Special Self-Help Program, including *Le Matin*, an opposition newspaper that was barely able to continue its operation, even with our grant. We then toured El Marouf Hospital's physical therapy unit, run by Rod Kraybill, a member of an American faith-based organization who had committed to move to the island with his wife and two young children to help the Comorian community. I was proud of the work he and his fellow team members performed despite their limited equipment and supplies. The services were free and the rooms were very clean, however, I noticed the examination table fabric was worn through and the inner material exposed, the stretching and testing equipment was antiquated, and although they had a shop to make prosthetic limbs, it lacked tools and materials. Yet even under such conditions, Rod had a smile on his face and a positive attitude. The Ambassador's Special Self-Help Program grant he received was well deserved.

At our grant signing ceremony, we awarded a total of $32,000 to several worthwhile organizations. We also visited two village projects: one in which young girls were taught to make gowns and robes, and another where they were taught to cook. These programs were intended to help young girls learn a trade and gain the experience they would need to make a living.

On Saturday morning, Taoufik Housseine came by the Itsandra Hotel to take us around to see the sites where several new mosques, madrassas, and residences were being built. The signs on each site named the Al-Haramain Islamic Foundation, a Saudi-based nongovernmental organization, as the sponsor.

That afternoon, I boarded an Air Austral plane headed back to Mauritius with an intermediate stop in Réunion Island to change planes. I sat with Souef El-Amine,

20.1. Young Comorian women at a textile craft center where they make gowns and robes; Ambassador Price in a ceremonial robe, September 19, 2003.

who was on his way to New York, and we spoke frankly about the strangers coming into Comoros unchecked while his authorities were turning their backs. Were payoffs the issue? Surprisingly, he noted it was a possibility and said he would review the procedures used for such access into Comoros. He also felt that goods and equipment were coming in unchecked at the airport and seaport, possibly indicating a problem with the customs people. I suggested that NGOs should be required to register before being allowed to operate freely there, a suggestion with which he agreed.

I mentioned that while checking out of the hotel, I had noticed four Saudis checking in, paying with U.S. dollars from an attaché case filled with cash. I questioned what kind of business transactions they were involved with in Comoros, since only a few small cottage industries existed there and it was not a robust tourist destination. It was clear from his expression that he understood my message.

Finally, El-Amine expressed concern about Bacar, the island president of Anjouan, having direct bilateral relations with France, which had undermined the Union's efforts in reconciliation. He worried about how that would affect Comoros's relations with the United States. He also stressed the need to establish a university-level school program. We agreed to meet again in three months or sooner as new developments occurred affecting the reconciliation process.

On September 23, I flew to the island of Rodrigues for two days to visit with non-governmental organizations, attend an embassy book donation ceremony, and award Ambassador's Special Self-Help Program funds to several deserving local entities.

Shoal Rodrigues was a deserving NGO that worked on preserving the coral reefs and ocean biodiversity. One of their educational programs involved brightly colored wooden treasure chests prepared for distribution to thirteen grade schools and filled with reading material and interactive learning items to help children better understand the ocean habitat. Tom Hooper, who ran this NGO, was a dedicated environmentalist.

Paul Draper, who ran the Craft Aid NGO, was another good soul. He had devoted his life's work to help employ handicapped people and guide them toward becoming self-sufficient. He did this by creating a cottage industry for disadvantaged individuals who otherwise might be cast aside in their community. He had helped handicapped children and adults become independent beekeepers who sold their raw honey to Craft Aid at the market rate. Craft Aid then processed, packaged, and sold the honey in their gift shop. Other individuals were trained to turn out craft products from coconut shells; these too were sold in their gift shop. In a new operation that had received assistance from the embassy, chain link fencing was woven from steel wire stock.

In adjacent classrooms, several teachers were working with visually and hearing impaired youngsters so that they could learn to communicate and move toward self-sufficiency. I was sad to hear that, after many years of building up this NGO, Paul was retiring at the end of the year, but he assured us that his legacy of helping people with special needs would continue.

From there we went to visit the Main Library. Although it was small and located on the third floor of a government building, it was well stocked—the librarian told us they had twenty-eight thousand books—and very impressive. The librarian also mentioned there were six other, smaller libraries around the island. During a planned book donation ceremony that day, we would be promoting English reading.

Meeting up with Vice President Bundhun, we joined his motorcade to visit a school in the village of Malabar, in the mountainous center of the island. As we arrived, two rows of children dressed in blue and white lined the steps leading to the

20.2. The Ambassador's Special Self-Help Program signing ceremony and tour with Paul Draper, Craft Aid, September 23, 2003.

schoolyard. Under a tent set up for the ceremony were National Library Director Yves Chan Kam Lon, Commissioner of Education A. L. Roussety, Chief Island Commissioner Serge Clair, Island Chief Executive Claude Wong So, Commissioner of Arts and Culture Arlette Perrine-Bégué, and David Harmon, representing the LDS Church, which had donated the many fine books. The audience was filled with students and teachers, library staff, and their families and friends.

After the dignitaries spoke, each school principal was given a sampling of the books, and a number of school kits were given to several honor students. As poor as the families were in Rodrigues, the students were clean, well dressed, and very friendly, and their parents were proud, humble, and thankful for any help we gave to their families.

On September 30, 2003, I met with Phil Carter from the Office for East African Affairs, who was visiting for a regional briefing. In a discussion of embassy staff issues, I carefully reviewed my goals and expectations. I explained that my management style leaned more toward a business model, with loyalty to the leader and respect for the embassy staff; teamwork was essential. I especially appreciated the officers who exhibited a can-do attitude and did some creative thinking outside the box. I recognized, however, that some individuals might not be especially comfortable with that model, and I was willing to bend and work closely with them, even though their guide was the Foreign Affairs manual and not the ambassador. By the end of our conversation, I think he understood me better, though he was reserved and never looked me in the eye as we spoke. We arranged meetings with government leaders, which I felt was his opportunity to test how they perceived me.

At the embassy, one aspiring Foreign Service officer who wanted to spend time with Carter changed the agenda, which threw off several planned events. But I decided to take it in stride; after all, my time serving would be limited, whereas for someone on a career path in the Foreign Service, "face time" was important.

Tuesday, September 30 was a monumental day in the history of Mauritius: Paul Bérenger, a Franco-Mauritian, would be sworn in as the next Prime Minister of the Republic and Sir Aneerood Jugnauth would become the President. Bérenger had worked for years to reach this pinnacle in a country where the Hindu culture had been predominant since independence. His compromise with Jugnauth to unite the MMM and MSM political parties in a power-sharing agreement had brought about this moment. The diversity was good for the country, I thought, and I had faith in Bérenger. He would be a good leader and move the country to the next level.

On Tuesday, October 7, the U.S. ambassadors serving in sub-Saharan Africa convened at the Grand Palm Hotel in Gaborone, Botswana, for the annual Chiefs of Mission Conference. Located on the edge of the vast Kalahari Desert, Botswana had a population of 1.2 million, of which 200,000 resided in Gaborone. Although wealthy by African standards, with a per capita income of $4,000 per year in an economy that had multiple bases, from diamonds and semiprecious stones to textiles and tourism, the country was plagued with an HIV/AIDS pandemic that affected 39 percent of the adult population.

Running into Ambassador Bob Royall and his wife, Edith, we decided to dine at the Beef Baron Grill. We both came from the private sector and had similar opinions of the State Department culture. We reflected on the difficulty we had with staff issues and our lack of control over the selection process. We discussed embassies' need for officers with better management and operating experience, particularly at the more senior level. We agreed that while most senior officers had good reporting skills and could handle other taskings, their experience with supervising people was limited. The constant distractions of people rotating in and out were also very disruptive, especially to the hardworking Foreign Service nationals who kept the embassy flame alive. Adding to the dilemma was a shift at the State Department to assigning very junior and inexperienced Foreign Service officers to our posts.

Ambassador Joe Huggins hosted a cocktail reception at his residence on Wednesday evening, attended by thirty-seven ambassadors, Undersecretary Grant Green, Assistant Secretary Walter Kansteiner, and several other Washington officials. I took the opportunity to discuss the Special Embassy Program post staffing issue,

20.3. Touring the town with Ambassador Robert Royall and his wife, Edith, in Gaborone, Botswana, between sessions at the Chiefs of Mission Conference, October 7, 2003.

training of junior officers, and my desire to see Charlie Slater switch over to the generalist category from the specialist category, so he could enhance his career opportunities.

Several of the career ambassadors I spoke with indicated that because they had risen through the ranks on the political side, they lacked experience on business issues, which limited them in a number of ways. They suggested additional training in such areas, which would also be helpful to them when their Foreign Service career ended. Most went into retirement, academia, or think tanks, with the private sector losing the benefit of their knowledge and experience.

At the opening session of the conference, Walter Kansteiner announced he would be leaving and Charlie Snyder would become the acting assistant secretary of state. Grant Green talked about post operations, indicating there would be an increase in staff positions of 2,200 by 2004. Jamie Agnew brought up the Special Embassy Program post issue, wanting feedback about whether the program should be modified or done away with; I had spoken to her about this on an earlier occasion. Then Joe Morton, the director of diplomatic security, asked that we make certain our embassy regional security officers were proactive and watchful in these dangerous times. He also asked us to meet with U.S. companies operating in our host countries, and to include that information in our reporting.

Ambassador Robert Pearson, the newly confirmed director general, emphasized "diplomatic service readiness," which was clarified during the Q&A session as "right-sizing"—something I had been advocating in the staffing of SEP posts. I took the liberty of bringing up the issue of establishing American presence posts in countries such as Comoros. Both Pearson and Green concurred, and I felt that sooner or later the State Department would get the message about the need for proper representation in the host countries to better serve U.S. security interests.

That afternoon there were several panel discussions on such topics as promoting democracy and human rights, environmental concerns, and food aid.

In the session on Friday, General Jeff Kohler of the U.S. European Command discussed the bases that were being set up in strategic regions of Africa to store material, equipment, and a small core of military personnel for future mobilization, as part of an alert and readiness program. He mentioned the Department of Defense humanitarian program intended to build and equip schools and hospitals. Later, I talked with General Kohler and his attaché Lieutenant Colonel Bill Wheelchan about Comoros and Rodrigues as possible candidates for help. Both Central Command and Pacific Command were operating in sub-Saharan Africa, also making it more difficult to ascertain who should take the lead on these assistance projects in my host countries. I mentioned I had been pushing the other two commands, but would like a unified effort if possible. I was told they would look into what could be accomplished.

U.S. Global AIDS Coordinator Randall Tobias spoke about the President's new initiative for HIV/AIDS relief and assistance, focusing on Botswana and eleven other African countries at risk.

In closing, Walter Kansteiner gave his farewell remarks, asking us to support and work with Charlie Snyder. To a standing ovation, he ended by advising us to keep the spirit and enjoy the experience.

To show U.S. support for diversity in the host country, I continued to attend many cultural and religious events. I held my second annual Iftaar dinner on October 14 at Macarty House, ending the holy month of Ramadan. Thirty guests attended the Maghrib prayers, stayed for dinner, and watched a short video of President Bush speaking in recognition of this important event to Muslims worldwide. The honored guests included Vice President Bundhun, Ambassador Magda Hosni Nasr of Egypt and High Commissioner Syed Hasan Javed of Pakistan.

On October 19, I went to Hindu House in Cassis, near Port Louis, for the Hindu festival of lights, Divali. Attending dignitaries included the President, the Prime Minister, and other ministers, most of whom were of Indian descent. The thousands of strung lights, chanting, and colorfully dressed dancers and musicians added to the festivities. When the Hindu House leader wished us all a happy Divali, the Festival of Lights was under way: homes and businesses around the island would illuminate the sky for a week.

To keep our own American traditions alive for expatriates, Marcia and I also planned the annual Thanksgiving dinner at Macarty House, to which we would invite one hundred people. Luc planned to cook a dozen turkeys and make stuffing, mashed potatoes, yams, cranberry sauce, and pumpkin and pecan pies, which would be served with plenty of whipped cream. The Thanksgiving event would give us the opportunity to discuss the Pilgrims' arrival in America in 1620, and what that still means to American families today.

Earlier, at the embassy on October 15, I received a troubling cable about another attempted coup in Comoros. It seemed that Morad Ait-Habbouche, an independent French journalist, had been arrested and charged as an accomplice in the proposed overthrow of President Azali. The leader of the coup plot was said to be Saïd Larifou, a Franco-Comorian attorney whom I had met at a recent Ambassador's Special Self-Help Program award ceremony. Philippe Verdon, a close associate of the infamous French mercenary Bob Denard, and Pascal Luppart, a French reactionary activist, were also named. As the account went, on September 20, Major Ayouba Combo met with Verdon and, while wearing a wire, recorded Verdon discussing the details for the operation, saying it had the consent of the Quai d'Orsay (the French Foreign Ministry) and the Directorate of Territorial Surveillance. This failed coup came during the time Azali was in the United States. I was glad Major Combo had remained loyal to Azali. On October 15, Larifou was released from jail, although he would go on trial October 18; the others charged remained in jail, awaiting their hearings.

Concerns about security in the host countries were always foremost on my mind. When a cable crossed my desk about a person of interest, Abdul al-Ubaydia (among his other aliases), traveling to Comoros, I knew there was no way the Comorians could track him—after the French ceased running the airport and removed their computer equipment, Comoros was left with limited ways of checking the background of people entering the country. But another cable that day raised our hopes. The new Personal Identification Secure Comparison and Evaluation System (PISCES) immigration control system to be implemented worldwide would help enhance border security and provide critical information needed in the global war on terror.

An interesting footnote in the cable was that the State Department, FBI, Pacific Command, and NCIS, some of the U.S. government agencies concerned about the threat of terrorism, had identified the Union of the Comoros as a "prime concern" in the region.

In Mauritius, my level of concern rose twofold when it was announced the Hizbullah leader Cehl Meeah was being released from La Bastille prison after three years. He had been awaiting trial for the murders of three opposition party members and a death threat and attempted assassination of the former Prime Minister in 1996. For whatever reason, Magistrate Raj Seebaluck ordered his unconditional release from prison and dropped all charges against him.

Unabated negative press about U.S. use of Diego Garcia, constant discussions of the sovereignty issue, and the issue of compensation for the Chagossians and their return to the Chagos Archipelago dominated October. I still believed it was important to make another attempt to visit Diego Garcia, and Bisa Williams emailed Charles Gurney at the U.S. Embassy in London about my desire to visit the island and inviting Ambassador William Farish to join me. We noted that the NCIS team out of Bahrain had said it would facilitate the visit. In addition, we refreshed Gurney's memory about the trip we had planned to make to Diego Garcia the year before, though we had had to change the itinerary right before departure. If the ambassador might be interested, we listed mid-October through November as well as January and February as good options for such a planned visit.

Charles Gurney responded on October 14, saying that he had consulted with his political-military people, who did not think Ambassador Farish should travel to Diego Garcia at this time, feeling it could undermine the U.S. position that Diego Garcia is 100 percent U.K. territory. I of course disagreed with that interpretation, but decided not to make another request to Washington for clearance at that time.

I subsequently met with Prime Minister Bérenger on October 16 and with President Jugnauth the next day on several issues, among which was Diego Garcia. Jugnauth was adamant about wanting sovereignty immediately, and added that the country should have been receiving rent for the base from the U.S. government since 1966. Bérenger was not as direct; he said that while his government would continue to press for sovereignty of Diego Garcia, they recognized U.S. government sensitivities at the present time, given the global war on terror and the war with Iraq.

Aside from Diego Garcia issues, I continued to be involved in furthering U.S. interests in Mauritius. The sale by Boeing of two aircraft to Air Mauritius would be an important accomplishment. I had worked closely with Boeing executives Miguel Santos, director of international sales, and William Shaproski, executive director of the Africa region, and in an October 3 meeting they had brought with them Douglas

Groseclose, senior vice president of international sales. Miguel wanted to set up a meeting for both of us with the airline executives later that month. On October 27 he and two other sales team members came to the embassy to give us a briefing on the new 777-300 ER aircraft, which would be arriving on Thursday.

When the plane landed on Thursday, October 30, I went out to see it with the Boeing team. Standing on the tarmac alongside this enormous plane, with engines larger in diameter than a 737 fuselage, I was astounded. The plane had a nineteen-hour range and could seat 365 people. The red, white, and blue striped paint job and a world map showing where the 777 had already been sold made for an incredible billboard. The cockpit had a very compact avionics package, with digital computer screens and surprisingly few buttons. This aircraft and the PowerPoint presentation the Boeing executives had prepared would show well, I thought.

While touring the aircraft, I was patched into a call with Stephen Schwartz and offered him the position of deputy chief of mission beginning in July 2004, when Bisa Williams rotated out. He was elated, since Port Louis was his first choice. Although I had highly recommended Charlie Slater to fill the position of deputy chief of mission, the Africa Bureau's final list of candidates did not include him. Stephen, who was currently serving at the U.S. Embassy in Pretoria, seemed to have the most experience and familiarity with sub-Saharan Africa. I knew Stephen would be an ideal deputy chief of mission, but the treatment of Charlie Slater weighed heavily on me. He was a man of great ethics who understood what had to be done and was motivated always to do so.

On December 2, I was back in Washington for consultations and met with Deputy Assistant Secretary Don Yamamoto in the Bureau of African Affairs. I had first met Don when he was ambassador to Djibouti. Much of the discussion was the same issues covered with his predecessors. Meeting later with Jamie Agnew and John Sheely, we also covered similar ground, including new staffing requirements at the embassy. I had had an unsatisfactory experience with a recent office management specialist, and asked I be allowed to choose a replacement: Vianna Fieser, a temporary duty officer who had been an incredible resource for the embassy during an earlier stay with us. This did not sit well with the State Department staff, who preferred to select from their own approved pool, but I remained firm. Even though Vianna would only be available from January 2 to the end of April 2004, I gladly agreed to the arrangement, since her presence would raise the bar, and afterward I could bring in someone else with similar skills.

As it turned out, Vianna had an emergency issue and returned home on February 13, 2004, which again left me without an OMS. She felt bad, however, and put me in contact with Kelly Hopkins, whose credentials were strong. She was currently working for the Deputy Assistant Secretary for European Affairs. I subsequently offered her the position, which she gladly accepted.

Later in the day, I met with Undersecretary for Arms Control and International Security John Bolton at the State Department. Bolton was a high energy individual sporting a generous white walrus mustache. He thanked me for getting Mauritius and Seychelles to sign Article 98, but pressed for getting Comoros to sign as well. He wanted as many African countries as possible signed on, no matter how small. I promised I would get it done, probably during the first quarter of 2004.

The important intelligence meeting that Helen Reed-Rowe, my desk officer, had set up turned into one more encounter that led nowhere. We had gone to the Pentagon to meet with the Defense Intelligence Agency. In attendance were fifteen participants from the military, intelligence, counterintelligence, counterterrorism, and other sections. I said that I was pleasantly surprised to hear of their interest in Comoros; it seemed all the recent cables had finally gotten everyone's attention. None of the experts in the room had ever been to Comoros, and few had any knowledge of its background. I spent the better part of thirty minutes discussing the time from independence to the current political situation. I carefully detailed the evolution of the radical influences from individuals coming from Arab and other states, and more specifically the mosques, madrassas, and living areas that were being built in rapid numbers by the Saudi foundation Al-Haramain. In parting, all that they promised was that we would work closely together on intelligence issues, and possibly have people on the ground going forward.

On December 4, I met with Jendayi Frazer and Bobby Pittman at the National Security Council office, where the focus was again Comoros now that the Section 508 sanctions had been lifted. Jendayi knew the potential for terrorist influence in Comoros could be an issue and that the country needed financial aid and help with military training, economic development, education, and health care. I lobbied again for some permanent presence for information gathering.

On Monday, December 8, as part of the U.S. delegation, I went to the Marriott Hotel to attend the opening private sector session of the AGOA Forum, which our embassy had helped orchestrate and which was sponsored by the Corporate Council on Africa. I was pleased the participants included ministers from more than thirty sub-Saharan African countries. The American business community needed to embrace the African countries, and such conferences with the African leaders were important in attracting new investments and trade to their countries.

That evening, Mauritian Trade Minister Cuttaree and I attended a working dinner hosted by Boeing executives, including Laurette Koellner and Phillip de St. Aubin. The decision on the purchase of two 777 aircraft for Air Mauritius would be made sometime in 2004, they said. I felt this would be a great commerce capstone for my term of service.

The next day I attended the ministerial portion of the AGOA Forum at the State Department. Secretary Powell gave the opening remarks, in which he thanked Trade Minister Cuttaree for the success of the AGOA Forum held the previous January in Mauritius. At the luncheon that followed, Secretary of Commerce Donald Evans also referenced the great success of the Mauritius-hosted AGOA Forum, which pleased the Mauritian delegation.

Later, in the Eisenhower Building Theater, Condoleezza Rice expressed U.S. support for Africa and then introduced President Bush, who received a standing ovation from the African delegations. His remarks were supportive of Africa and mentioned specifically the HIV/AIDS program and the Millennium Challenge Grant program. He too touched on the successful AGOA Forum in Mauritius.

On the morning of December 10, I met with Acting Assistant Secretary Charlie Snyder and once more expressed my support for Charlie Slater, who had been informed he would not be able to transfer to the generalist category. Snyder was sympathetic but not hopeful. I also went through the argument for doing away with the SEP nomenclature so we could right-size the embassy. Having heard about the establishment of a new American Presence Post in Malabo, Equatorial Guinea, I again proposed the same for Seychelles and Comoros. Snyder agreed with my assessment of the need for such a presence but said that getting the Malabo post had taken over two years and much lobbying, with final approval required from the White House. Well, I had been at it for over eighteen months without anyone at the State Department listening. He suggested I confer with George Staples, a career diplomat and U.S. ambassador to Cameroon, who was overseeing the Malabo post. In the waiting area, coincidently, was that very gentleman, waiting to see Snyder. I took the opportunity to discuss with George the process he had gone through to get approval for the new post. He offered to help further if I followed up with him. That was a nice gesture on his part, I thought.

{ XXI }

Comoros and the Three Island Governments

The December ministerial meeting included several African heads of state and paved the way for the April 2004 elections to establish a National Assembly in Comoros—the first ever for this island nation. The Union Assembly comprised thirty-three representatives; eighteen were elected in single-seat constituencies and fifteen were representatives of the regional assemblies. This arrangement subsequently resolved monetary and budget-sharing issues and other long-standing disputes. However, executive power remained with President Azali Assoumani. Since Azali was from Grande Comore, after he finished his four-year term as President, the presidency would rotate to Anjouan in 2006 and to Mohéli in 2010.

In the 2004 election, the candidates who supported the island governments won a majority of the seats in the National Assembly. Thus, the political rivalry between the three island governments and the Union government continued. Receiving only six of the seats, President Azali suffered a major setback. To his credit, he accepted the outcome of the elections, although his government, now in the minority, might not be able to govern as effectively as he had desired.

After a long struggle, the three island governments accepted the constitution, which gave the Union government the responsibility for national defense. This had been one of the stumbling blocks before the elections, and Azali was determined to keep the Union together.

Azali and I developed a good working relationship and became friends, visiting one another when he would come to Mauritius for meetings with government leaders and sometimes getting together during his vacations. He always referred to me as his "brother," a member of the family.

For more than a year, I pressed every button in Washington to get the Section 508 sanctions against Comoros lifted. Finally in December 2003 they were lifted—a belated victory for Comoros. Azali was happy when I called him with the news; however, I could not tell him that the IMET funding that had been allocated in the 1999 budget, almost $150,000, had since been reallocated elsewhere. Not until June 2004 would IMET program funding become available again for Comoros.

I felt let down by the State Department. We had pressed Comoros to support us at the United Nations on every issue of interest to the United States, including the signing of the Article 98 nonsurrender agreement and support of the global war on terror. Yet IMET funding, which was advantageous to U.S. security interests in the region, was withheld for five years.

For more than ten years, we had expected Comoros to deal with the influx of radical Islamists without having the necessary resources to resolve this critical issue. It bothered me to see the billions of dollars wasted over the years in sub-Saharan Africa supporting corrupt rulers and governments, yet we could not jump-start Comoros with minuscule funding for security-related matters, health care, education, or capacity-building programs to fight poverty. We couldn't even provide them with six Peace Corps volunteers.

Education was sorely lacking in the Comoros. The government's aim was to raise the percentage of literate Comorians from the low fifties to the high eighties, similar to Mauritius and Seychelles. Hence, any economic stimulus program in Comoros had to include both secular education and basic health care services. Technical, vocational, and professional training programs were needed for those students who otherwise would drop out of school and choose not to pursue academic studies. Such skills would be useful in any expanded commercial and industrial sectors developed in Comoros.

Bilateral relations between the U.S. Embassy in Port Louis and the Union of the Comoros had increased significantly since 2002, when I had arrived, and Azali was elected President of the Union. The embassy staff had embraced my vision for the engagement of Comoros—but Washington was not on board.

Our need to engage Comoros was carefully delineated in a cable our embassy sent on October 6, 2003, to the State Department and other U.S. agencies having responsibility in the sub-Saharan Africa region. The on-site security analysis reported on in the message had been created by the embassy's new regional security officer. He spent the week of September 14–21, 2003, meeting with local law enforcement officials to conduct a general orientation and make a security assessment of the three islands of Comoros.

The regional security officer found that, lacking basic law enforcement assets and training, Comoros was not considered capable of assisting in the fight against terrorism or protecting its own borders. As an example, he met with a senior officer of the gendarmerie on Anjouan, who told him their island government did not cooperate with their counterparts on Grande Comore regarding law enforcement matters. When asked what measures would be taken if they were concerned about a suspected terrorist entering Anjouan, the senior officer replied they would contact only the French Embassy for assistance.

This, of course, was part of the security concerns we had regarding Comoros: without cooperation on border control issues, there was no unified policy for all three islands. The regional security officer also noted the immigration authorities on Grande Comore maintained only one working computer, and the data were entered and processed by officials who had little training. On entry into the country, visitors were not screened via a database; in fact, some records were handwritten.

The regional security officer noted that Middle Eastern and North African educational institutions and nongovernmental organizations had a major influence in Comoros, which made the dearth of law enforcement capabilities all the more poignant. He said that despite the external influences, there was an overwhelming sense of cooperation from the government of Comoros, which desired U.S. assistance in order to improve internal security. The embassy felt strongly that the United States needed to immediately engage in assisting the Comorian government to improve its security structure before adverse interests were allowed to proliferate.

At all levels and departments, Comorian government officials showed a desire to cooperate with the United States on antiterrorism and law enforcement issues. Its officials were very aware of their lack of training and equipment and expressed interest in receiving any assistance they could get to improve their law enforcement and security capabilities.

The regional security officer told us that he had received a favorable response to his report from his desk officer at the Office of Intelligence and Threat Analysis. It was nice to hear that someone had actually read the Comoros survey. But the report had been widely distributed, and the lack of response from other quarters did not surprise me. The report should have been a wake-up call to the State Department and Department of Defense that they needed to more fully support the embassy's engagement of Comoros. I continued having difficulty putting the Union of the Comoros on the radar screen in Washington.

Although Comoros was more democratically structured, its law enforcement and military forces were ill prepared for any challenges. My concerns were not about possible future coups but about today's real enemy—the al-Qaeda network in the region. Al-Qaeda had no standing army, but its sympathizers could subvert and undermine the government through their radical fundamentalist teachings in mosques and madrassas.

In 2003 Comorian immigration officials began refusing entry to certain travelers because of their suspicious behavior. In one particular circumstance, fifteen people listed their intended address in Comoros at one particular mosque, which officials knew did not have the facilities to house them. I wondered how many others had

managed to slip through unnoticed the same way over the years. Immigration officials were well aware they lacked resources and training and had asked for U.S. help
to stop the strangers from transiting through the country.

Besides the Saudi-based al-Haramain Islamic Foundation, which I have mentioned
before, other foreign nongovernmental organizations reportedly operated in Comoros,
including the International Islamic Relief Organization, a Saudi-based charity associated with Osama bin Laden's brother-in-law, which was responsible for building
mosques, madrassas, and hostels. Their teachings were quite radical, and they appeared to be well funded—their imams drove new vehicles. Comoros potentially could
become a terrorist breeding ground, with many young people who could easily be
influenced.

It was reported that a Tanzanian Islamic NGO was recruiting young men from
Comoros to fight alongside the Iraqis. A meeting was planned for these recruits in
late March somewhere in Nairobi. They would then travel via Sudan to Iraq. Recruiting activities also targeted Zanzibari male refugees who were living in Somalia.

As the home of one of the most notorious terrorists in the al-Qaeda network,
Comoros could be groomed as a safe haven for al-Qaeda and possibly indoctrinate
another Fazul Abdullah Mohammed—while we continue to stand back and do
nothing.

There have been many lessons. After the Siad Barre government collapsed in
Somalia, the U.S. embassy in Mogadishu was closed in 1991. One year later we
returned on a humanitarian mission. Then, in 1993, in what became known as the
Battle of Mogadishu, we tried to apprehend a Muslim warlord (backed by al-Qaeda
operatives) who had killed several UN troops serving on the humanitarian assignment. In the ensuing battle, we lost eighteen of our troops. Subsequently, President
Clinton pulled out all our troops from Somalia, which gave Osama bin Laden the
confidence that he could defeat the United States. The U.S. Embassy in Comoros
was closed in 1993, followed by the U.S. Embassy in Sudan, closed in 1996. By 1999
Comoros was subject to Section 508 sanctions and was unable to protect itself against
any insurgency, nor did it have the ability to support the global war on terror.

On at least two occasions in 2003 and 2004, I personally gave an interagency
briefing on Comoros in Washington. For my first briefing I began with the history
of the country from independence through a series of coups and then the free and
fair elections in 2002 and 2004. I explained how Comorians were a passive, close-
knit, and trusting society with simple goals of achieving economic advancement to
take them out of their poverty and finding ways to minimize the influence of the
Middle East and East African Islamic charities—and we needed to help.

In the second interagency meeting, which included several new members—
many of the previous ones had rotated out without leaving a paper trail from previous briefings—I began again with a history lesson on Comoros. Even the people

who had been present at the last briefing had little recall of Comoros and its issues, and no action had been taken by their respective agencies. After having several more meetings in Washington, I decided the history lessons were not being absorbed. I thought all the agencies were giving me the courtesy that the rank of ambassador deserved, but because I was a political appointee, they knew I would be serving for a limited period—and time was on their side.

Still, I persisted. I had numerous discussions with the military commanders at Pacific Command (PACOM) and Central Command (CENTCOM). Since both operated in the region, there was some question about which one would actively interface with Comoros. I took a parallel course with each, hoping one would respond to the issues.

In the Indian Ocean region, PACOM's area of responsibility included Mauritius, Madagascar, and Comoros, which were handled out of the Honolulu, Hawaii, headquarters thousands of miles away. CENTCOM's area of responsibility covered Seychelles, with oversight by the Kenya U.S. Liaison Office, which interfaced with the Combined Joint Task Force–Horn of Africa (CJTF-HOA), located in Djibouti. On two occasions PACOM sent security assessment teams to Comoros, and CENTCOM as a result of my request, sent an aid assessment team twice. Neither had promised any action until after the Section 508 sanctions were lifted in December 2003.

On January 13, President Azali arrived in Mauritius for meetings with the Prime Minister. Later in the afternoon we met at the Trou aux Biches Resort, where the government kept a guest bungalow. Since Azali was more comfortable speaking French, I asked James Liddle to join us as note taker. Dressed impeccably in a European-style dark suit, red shirt, and red-and-black tie, Azali greeted me warmly, and I thanked him for his unsolicited letter of support sent to President Bush on the capture of Saddam Hussein in December 2003. Azali was amenable to discussion of a prepared list of issues I had brought. Some of them we had discussed before, including the upcoming elections, the constitutional reconciliation, terrorist concerns, the Saudi-based charity al-Haramain, and the signing of the Article 98 agreement.

On the agreement, Azali requested a copy written in French for his government to review, and reported that he had been getting pressure from the Europeans not to sign it.

He then informed us the planned National Assembly elections would take place in April, with the island assembly elections one month earlier. He asked for financial assistance for the election process, and added that the reconciliation process was moving forward.

We had a long discussion on terrorism, in which he welcomed our security assessment teams to come to the islands if it would help root out bad elements. He would fully cooperate with the Rewards for Justice Program if it would help to find Fazul. He told me that Comorian officials recently had arrested and expelled two individuals who carried false Pakistani passports and claimed to have been working for an NGO, a situation I had not been aware of. Azali said U.S. authorities had come to Comoros requesting that his government make these arrests. I noted that they had not asked for country clearance, nor had they put the embassy in the loop.

Other new issues Azali and I discussed included the registration of NGOs operating in the country, a system for tracking money coming into the country, his University of the Comoros program, and help building up their library with English-language books. One last item Azali brought up was the possibility of an American bank opening in Comoros. Such an institution could be a good security measure insofar as it could help track funds flowing between countries. Currently there was only one French bank, and not all transactions were done through the bank. He thought another financial institution would help build more transparency regarding transactions.

In parting, Azali mentioned he appreciated my continued efforts on behalf of his people, with special acknowledgment of the recent lifting of the Section 508 sanctions against Comoros.

On January 20 I was pleased to learn that, in response to one of my requests for aid, Commander Dan Lafferty, the defense attaché stationed in Madagascar, was planning to visit Comoros. Lafferty was willing to assess the country's needs for military training, hospitals, schools, security, and commerce-related assistance. Lafferty would be accompanied by a Defense Intelligence Agency reporting officer and a PACOM intelligence analyst, and he agreed to report back to me on his return.

Increased insurgent attacks in Iraq and escalating instability and expansion of terrorist cells in the Horn of Africa and East Africa region prompted a Chiefs of Mission Conference in Djibouti for two days of briefings with top military leaders, including General John Abizaid. I met up with seven other ambassadors in Nairobi, and on Monday, February 16, we boarded a chartered Beechcraft 200 for the four-hour flight to Djibouti. We landed on the ten-thousand-foot runway at Camp Lemonier—formerly a French Foreign Legion post and now home to the CJTF-HOA.

We were greeted at the plane by seven heavily armored SUVs, one for each of us, and armed security guards. As we headed for the Sheraton Hotel, I wondered what lay ahead. Fifteen months earlier, the Joint Task Force had been stationed offshore; now they were housed in recently constructed buildings, some temporary, others permanent.

The evening's agenda included discussions on Sudan and Somalia, other concerns in the Horn of Africa, and issues regarding Liberia, Congo, and the Great Rift Valley lakes region. An interesting discussion concerned khat, a popular cash crop in East Africa and the Horn. Khat contains a stimulant and is widely used in the region, where the leaves are chewed. It was sold openly on the streets in Kenya, Somalia, Djibouti, and elsewhere. Purchases of the drug take away from the scarce money available to already destitute families.

When we returned to Camp Lemonier on Tuesday, Brigadier General Mastin Robeson, U.S. Marines, commander of the Combined Joint Task Force, explained the task force's operation and its mission there and gave a regional threat briefing. In his letter of welcome to the ambassadors, he quite succinctly characterized our service to the country in these perilous times by quoting Thomas Paine: "If there must be trouble, let it be in my day that my children may have peace."

Security concerns in the region were the overriding topic of all the speakers. Discussing the dangers of radical imams teaching in the madrassas, General John Abizaid noted this was a global issue and not isolated to any one region. Furthermore, he referenced for us (and later would testify the same at a March 2004 Congressional hearing) that terrorists are Jihad Salafists and that eliminating the senior leadership of al-Qaeda and other terrorist groups and networks would not eliminate terrorism. What was needed, he said, was support for host nations in education, health, and infrastructure to enhance stability. I thought he was right on target—but I wondered if members of Congress would understand this message.

On March 4 at Macarty House, I hosted a dinner for the Boeing sales team in honor of Air Mauritius and government leaders. I wanted a congenial atmosphere for everyone to get better acquainted. My ultimate goal on behalf of the United States was for the Boeing to receive a multimillion-dollar order for two new 777 aircraft from Air Mauritius. Cassam had set the table for sixteen guests, using our best blue and gold embossed china. Danie had prepared some beautiful floral arrangements. Luc outdid himself preparing a Franco-Mauritian dinner. Representing Boeing were Laurette Koellner and her husband, Victor, Phillip de St. Aubin, Miguel Santos, and Bill Shaproski. Representing the government were Minister of Finance Pravind Jugnauth and his wife, Kobita, and Minister of Foreign Affairs and International Trade Jayen Cuttaree and his wife, Swatee. I also invited our embassy's economic and commercial officer, DeWitt Conklin, and his wife, Emma, and from the business community, Maurice and Diana de Latour. Prime Minister Bérenger was unable to attend, but I had arranged to have him meet with the Boeing team privately at his office, where he reassured them the bidding process was "wide open." Although the Prime Minister had visited their plant and held private meetings with French President Jacques Chirac, no commitments had been made to the European Airbus manufacturer.

Boeing also hosted a luncheon for the business community on the following day. Koellner discussed Boeing's mission to come to Mauritius and become involved in a number of business ventures, including accounting and backroom call centers, whether or not they received the aircraft contract.

On January 9, 2004, *Le Mauricien* ran an article headlined "Chagos Islanders Seek to Defy Banned Entry into Waters of U.S. Base." It seemed the Chagos Refugee Group (CRG) and the Mauritius political left party, Lalit, were going to lobby the

World Social Forum in Mumbai, India, for a seagoing vessel that would enable them to go to the Chagos Archipelago. Now the pressure from the government of Mauritius was mounting, as was the Chagossians' insistence on making a visit to Diego Garcia. Hence, on March 10, I decided to make another request to visit Diego Garcia on a fact-finding mission.

Among the various people who received my email was Charles Gurney of the U.S. Embassy in London, who responded the following day. Reiterating the political sensitivity surrounding the island, Gurney suggested support for my visit should first come from Washington; then they could take the request to Her Majesty's Government to explain the rationale for such a visit.

In my reply to Gurney, I said I knew there were sensitivities about anybody going to Diego Garcia, but I wanted to have a better understanding of what exactly the Chagossians kept alluding to, and to see if their claim that they could sustain themselves on the islands was valid. The embassy had seen all kinds of media stories on the Chagos Archipelago, and the government of Mauritius raised this issue with me at nearly every meeting.

On March 15, we received an email from Helen Reed-Rowe, my desk officer, saying that the Bureau of East African Affairs would not encourage my visit to Diego Garcia at this time. The message went on to say that Diego Garcia was used only as a military base and that "Ambassador Price is not engaging any officials regarding the Chagos Archipelago." Of course, the embassy had had countless bilateral discussions with the government of Mauritius on the matter, and Jane Gaffney and Phil Carter, who had been copied on the email, knew that. I was surprised at the inaccuracy and would discuss it with the Bureau on my next trip to Washington.

During my posting, I often heard State Department travel alerts that were not only inconsistent but also sometimes misleading. I wondered where they got the information, or if the person issuing them ever stepped outside Washington. On March 16, 2004, for example, we received a major alert from the State Department about the threat of future terrorist attacks in East Africa, into which they lumped Mauritius, Comoros, and Seychelles along with Djibouti, Eritrea, Ethiopia, Kenya, Madagascar, Réunion, Somalia, Sudan, and Tanzania. Mauritius itself lies 1,200 miles off the coast of Africa in the Indian Ocean. How insensitive, I thought. How could they justify including these small Indian Ocean countries, far from the mainland, with Somalia and Sudan, two failed states with extensive al-Qaeda operations? This was especially problematic because of the role tourism played in the economies of Mauritius, Comoros, and Seychelles; people consulting the Internet would think these islands were not safe to visit. Tourism was a major economic pillar of these three countries, yet the State Department sent out a generic alert with no basis, and conflated their risk with those of Somalia and Sudan. The government of Mauritius was furious and called the embassy. I immediately requested that the State Department provide information on a country-by-country basis, but State felt the potential threats warranted the report on a combined basis. We had to notify the Mauritian government of the State Department's response, to their dismay.

On Thursday, March 18, Foreign Minister Bonnelame visited from Seychelles. He confirmed that France-Albert René would be stepping aside as President on April 14, 2004, two years before the end of his term, and turning over the presidency to his handpicked successor, James Alix Michel, his Vice President since 1996. Before becoming Vice President, Michel had been secretary general of the ruling party since 1978 and Finance Minister since the early 1990s. He was also the only politically active surviving member of the 1977 René-led coup that had deposed Mancham. (René would continue, however, as the leader of the ruling Seychelles People's Progressive Front [SPPF] political party.)

Bonnelame hoped Mukesh Valabhji would resign from the Seychelles Marketing Board, which controlled much of their economy. Saying that Mukesh respected me and valued my input, Bonnelame suggested I might be able to convince him to do so. Mainly, Bonnelame wanted to see economic stabilization come to Seychelles.

A week later, I returned to Washington to support Mauritius in the Senate hearings chaired by Senator Lugar regarding the AGOA Acceleration Act of 2004 (known as AGOA III), which would extend preferential access through September 30, 2015, and extend the third-country fabric provision. The draft version that had been circulated earlier included Mauritius but limited its exports to no more than 25 percent of the global AGOA tariff rate quotas for third-country garments—apparel using fabric or yarn produced elsewhere other than in Africa or the United States. The Mauritian government could live with that provision, but we needed to sell it to Congressman Bill Thomas, then chairman of the House Ways and Means Committee.

During the hearings, Undersecretary of State Alan Larson, USAID's Connie Newman (who had been nominated to be assistant secretary of state for African Affairs), and Florizelle Liser, assistant U.S. trade representative for Africa, all spoke in favor of extending the third-country fabric provisions beyond 2004, and expressed the importance of the AGOA program for the African countries. Afterward, I thanked them for testifying in support of the extension, and I also talked with Senator Lugar and reinforced the importance of continuing the benefits under AGOA.

Later that day, I met with Charlie Snyder, since he would soon be departing. Snyder had been acting assistant secretary for African affairs since late 2003. I had first met Snyder in 2002, when he was the deputy assistant secretary and then principal deputy assistant secretary under Walter Kansteiner. Snyder, who had retired from the U.S. Army after twenty-two years of service and worked at the CIA before coming to his present post, had spent most of his career on Africa-related issues and was considered by some as a career Africanist. I had great respect for Snyder. At times he was outspoken, but he broadened the bureau's sometimes narrow view, and he was one of the few people who supported my efforts to institute programs and advocate for the underprivileged people in my host countries. I wished him well and told him I would miss our frank talks and practical advice.

On the last day of March, I went to Johannesburg for a planned regional business conference. Our embassy had orchestrated this networking opportunity, hoping to connect businesses from both countries and beyond in the region. John Dacruz was the high commissioner in South Africa representing the government of Mauritius.

The U.S.-Mauritian Trade and Investment Mission program formally opened at the Ron Brown Conference Center and was chaired by Johnny Brown of the U.S. Commercial Service. DeWitt Conklin, our embassy coordinator, introduced the speakers. Shariff Jathoonia, also from our embassy, set up the networking and one-on-one meetings with the South Africans. I was pleased to highlight Mauritius's success transitioning from a monocrop economy thirty-six years earlier to a multifaceted economy that now also included textiles, tourism, and financial services and was quickly expanding into the information and communication technology sector.

Before noon, Johnny Brown and I drove the thirty-five miles to Pretoria to meet with Ambassador Cameron Hume at the U.S. Embassy. Nearly five hundred people representing numerous U.S. government agencies worked at the embassy there, many as support for other embassies in the region. Cameron, who would be leaving this post to become the new inspector general, would be replaced by Jendayi Frazer from the NSC, a good friend.

In the early part of April, I made my fourth visit to Seychelles to meet with government and community leaders, and, hopefully, have a discussion with Mukesh Valabhji to learn more about his future position within the government. I spoke first with Minister of Foreign Affairs Jérémie Bonnelame, who reiterated that he hoped Mukesh would retire and that my influence could be the catalyst in helping convince him to step down.

I then met up with Susanne Rose, our consular agent, and headed for the dock, where a Navy dinghy took us out to the destroyer USS *Fletcher*, where I was welcomed by Commander John Nolan. We then visited Commander Philip McLaughlin on the anchored nuclear-powered attack submarine USS *Connecticut*. I was delighted to greet the troops and tour both the destroyer and the submarine. Of interest was the compact submarine environment since I was claustrophobic.

Several hours later, Seychelles Police Commissioner André Kilindo, his deputy, and I talked about the recent dismissal of ten to twelve officers, some of whom were highly regarded and had received training in the United States. Kilindo implied they needed to cut back at the upper levels and offered no other explanation.

21.1. Visit to Seychelles of the nuclear submarine USS *Connecticut* and the destroyer USS *Fletcher*, Commanders Phil McLaughlin and John Nolan, April 11, 2004.

I wondered if it was some sort of a purge. All of them were younger, up-and-coming officers, and I silently conjectured that in the future these young officers could have become loyal to Michel, while René wanted to protect his power base as chairman of the SPPF.

Kilindo was also nonchalant about the issue of thirty-nine North Africans who had tried to enter Seychelles illegally and were deported. One who did slip in was later captured and also deported. Kilindo suggested these people were not terrorists but looking for work. I disagreed. Seychelles was not a booming country and work was scarce. I didn't think I was getting the whole story, especially with evidence of phony documentation showing work permits for a nonexistent hotel project. Luckily, we had names and copies of the passports they had used, which we would pass on to NCIS and other agencies in Washington.

On the morning of April 13, I met with President René for the last time. More press than usual were waiting in his office to take pictures to memorialize this event. The President was warm, openly charming, and relaxed. He looked forward to spending time fishing and traveling before taking over the leadership of his political party, the Seychelles People's Progressive Front. He said Michel would do an excellent job. Reminded of the importance of solving the economic crisis his country was facing, he agreed it was a priority for Michel.

I made the calculated decision not to talk about Mukesh's departure. Instead, I wished him well and we embraced on the way out.

I met next with Vice President James Michel, and congratulated him on becoming president. In our discussion, my questions about the economy had him leaning forward in his chair, especially when I asked if his plans going forward included Mukesh. Carefully choosing his words, and without emotion, he said there would be some changes in his cabinet. He did not specify if Mukesh would still be an advisor. I got the impression Mukesh would stay on for a while. Michel added that as President, he aspired to formulate the changes necessary to put Seychelles on a solid economic footing and solve the foreign exchange crisis. We agreed to stay in close contact.

Next I went to the office of the *Regar* newspaper to meet with the opposition leader Wavel Ramkalawan, who saw the turnover of the presidency to Michel as illegal. Ramkalawan said that if he was successful in the 2006 election, he would go after René and Mukesh and repatriate the billions of dollars he said had been taken offshore. He reinforced my belief that the police officers had been purged for not being more loyal to René. On the economy, he declared it was definitely getting worse as a result of Mukesh's bad policies. In parting I asked him to keep me posted on his insights.

When DeWitt Conklin and I met with twelve members of the Chamber of Commerce that afternoon, we learned they were very upset with the René regime, and especially Mukesh. Since we last met, most of their businesses had deteriorated further. Some felt there was no hope. Their hopes centered on a free market economy and the privatization of the Seychelles Marketing Board operations. Learning that they had a meeting scheduled with Michel, I suggested that they be open and mention our meeting; after all, Michel had told me he would welcome input from the business community.

As for a meeting with Mukesh, we were unsuccessful. His office said he was not available, and I wasn't certain that his elusiveness wasn't orchestrated.

When I checked out of the hotel, the foreign exchange issue again came into focus—this time personally. The cashier would not take any of my unspent Seychelles rupees for partial payment or my American Express card: only Visa or MasterCard were accepted. Then they converted my bill from rupees to dollars, based on an artificial rate of 5.16 rupees to the dollar (the black market rate exceeded 10 rupees). On top of that, they added a 4 percent fee to offset the fee Visa would charge them.

Two years after this visit, Michel would run for and win the 2006 presidency with 54 percent of the vote. And to this day, René still controls the SPPF, rebranded in 2009 the People's Party, which dominates the government of Seychelles. René will need to continue to control the party until the day he dies, since the opposition has threatened to bring him to trial for corruption if it wins an election. Community leaders and the opposition party candidate say Seychelles suffers from a lack of freedom of the press, stifled investigative reporting, unfair elections, and a lack of transparency in parastatal transactions.

After months of planning, a meeting had been set up in Washington for Prime Minister Bérenger with Secretary Powell and President Bush on May 12, 2004. I had also strategized with Boeing's Miguel Santos that while Bérenger was in the United States we should have him tour the Boeing plants in the Seattle area. Boeing arranged to have an aircraft take him there the day following his meetings in Washington, and offered me a ride, for which I would have reimbursed them at a normal commercial rate. Before accepting I had to ask for clearance, however, and for weeks a debate raged between our post, the State Department, and the White House about whether I could join the Prime Minister on the private Boeing flight. It went from no to yes to maybe, then back to yes, and finally to hold. All I wanted was to facilitate a sale to Air Mauritius of two Boeing 777s.

On May 5, a few days before my flight to Washington, I received the final word from a legal advisor in the White House: I could not travel with the Prime Minister on Boeing's private jet to their Seattle plant. Since the U.S. government was not going to pay for my commercial airfare either, I now had to call my personal travel agent to rearrange my bookings—and because it was at the last minute, the changes were costly. I felt dejected and hurt by the State Department's indecision and lack of support for my efforts to foster U.S. commercial interests. After this demeaning experience, among others I had dealt with in the past, I wondered if it wasn't time for me to come home.

On Tuesday, May 11, Jeff Eubank from the State Department Protocol Office and I went with a police escort to Dulles Airport to meet Prime Minister Bérenger. The Prime Minister was traveling with Ambassador Vijay Makhan, the secretary for foreign affairs and a close advisor, and V. L. Ramsamy, permanent secretary in the Prime Minister's office. As they went off to the Watergate Hotel to freshen up, I headed back for another meeting.

At four-thirty, Secretary Powell and I met in the lobby of the State Department and went out on the red carpet to the curb as Prime Minister Bérenger arrived. After a few press photos, we went to Secretary Powell's office suite on the seventh floor. The scheduled fifteen-minute meeting turned into thirty minutes, as there was a good rapport between the two of them. The Prime Minister discussed Diego Garcia, as expected, as well as their desire to be included as a candidate for funding from the Millennium Challenge Account. He pressed on the passage of AGOA III, which would extend preferential access for imports from the beneficiary sub-Saharan African countries. This was a commitment President Bush had made in a video shown during the January 2003 AGOA Forum. Powell understood Mauritius's position on these issues. Afterward, the entourage was escorted back to their waiting car, and I chatted briefly with Secretary Powell.

The following morning, Boeing orchestrated a meeting with the Export-Import Bank chairman Philip Merrill and Prime Minister Bérenger at the Watergate Hotel, accompanied by other bank executives and the Prime Minister's delegation. The discussion centered on financing for the new aircraft for Air Mauritius if they chose Boeing over Airbus. Bérenger felt comfortable with the offer for financing should they proceed with Boeing.

Since this was the day of the Prime Minister's meeting with the President, I invited Bérenger to first have lunch with me at the Capitol Grille, one of Washington's hot spots, where politicians, lobbyists, and consultants wine and dine. We had a nice corner table under the watchful eye of the Secret Service. It was a fine way to spend two hours alone with Bérenger, which we had not been able to do in Mauritius.

At 4:15 p.m., my driver, Keith Minor, dropped me off at the west gate and I was escorted into the White House. As soon as Prime Minister Bérenger arrived with his entourage, we met with National Security Advisor Condoleezza Rice and Jendayi Frazer, special assistant to the President and senior director of African affairs at the National Security Council. When Bérenger brought up Diego Garcia, Rice carefully explained the importance of the island as a military base for our national security. Bérenger of course agreed, having heard this same answer before on countless occasions. She also mentioned our planned visit to the Boeing plant, stating how dependable these planes would be—a nice hint.

Soon after, we walked to the Oval Office, where Enzo Ensenat was waiting at the door to introduce the Prime Minister to President Bush. Along with Bérenger, Rice, and Frazer, in this meeting with the President were Vijay Makhan, Ambassador Usha Jeetah, and V. L. Ramsamy. The President sat in his usual chair in front of the fireplace; the Prime Minister sat adjacent in the guest of honor's chair. The Mauritian delegation sat on a couch directly opposite the U.S. delegation.

Still fresh in everyone's mind was the recent beheading of an American contractor in Iraq, shown the day before on CNN and other networks. This had sparked outrage around the world, except for those who felt this was a justified act in revenge

21.2. Prime Minister Paul Bérenger meets with President Bush in the Oval Office, May 12, 2004.

for abuses suffered by Iraqis at the Abu Ghraib prison, near Baghdad, at the hands of U.S. soldiers. President Bush, visibly upset by the incident, remarked that his resolve was to continue our efforts to free Iraq from these insurgents.

The President then shifted to the subject of the meeting. First he mentioned Bérenger's background, touching on Bérenger's radical days as a young man marching in the streets, which brought a smile from the Prime Minister. Then they launched into a discussion about terrorism concerns and security issues in the region.

Bérenger briefly brought up the issue of Diego Garcia, to which President Bush replied that the United States needed the base. Bérenger then dropped the matter.

When AGOA III was brought up, the Prime Minister made a plea to include Mauritius, since multifiber sourcing was a big issue for them. The President said he would check into the situation, though he did state that the matter was ultimately up to Congress. (Fortunately, on July 12, 2004, the President did sign AGOA III.)

After the meeting, Bérenger and his team boarded the private jet for their trip to Seattle. I headed to Reagan National Airport to catch my commercial flight first to Chicago, where bad weather had us sitting on the ramp for more than two hours, and then to Seattle, arriving after midnight.

The following morning, we met with Alan Mulally, president and CEO of the Boeing Commercial Division. We were taken to a warehouse that was converted to show mock-ups of interior cabin space with different seating configurations and amenities for the 777 and 7E7 (787) models. Our group was then chauffeured an hour north to the Everett plant for a tour of its huge assembly lines, which had several airplane frames in differing stages of production. We explored a partially completed 777 and a completed version ready to be delivered to Air France.

Afterward, we headed back to Seattle to meet Governor Gary Locke, who expressed an interest in doing what he could to encourage Mauritius to place the order for the 777s. He said the sale would ensure important employment for the State of Washington.

Soon we were all off to the airport, where we were departing on different flights. Bérenger thanked me for helping with the arrangements in Washington, and mentioned that he was very impressed with the Boeing aircraft and the professionalism of their management.

Arriving back in Mauritius I reviewed my cables, noting one regarding Diego Garcia. In it, the *Sunday Express* (London) on May 16, 2004, carried a story with the headline "Do Al Qaeda Prisoners Face CIA Torture on British Isle?" The article stated that "[s]uspected top figures from the terror organization are being flown to Diego Garcia by the Americans, who lease the tiny Indian Ocean island from Britain." They alluded to human rights groups fearing there are "physical abuses at Diego Garcia similar to those revealed in Baghdad's now notorious Abu Ghraib jail" and, further, that "Al Qaeda suspects and key Taliban commanders held on Diego Garcia are known to British and U.S. intelligence as 'ghost detainees' because no one will officially acknowledge that they exist."

Similar stories appeared in local newspapers and around the world. These accusations inflamed the Mauritian populace, which in turn made for strained relations with the host government. The more I denied the claims, the more they believed them to be true. I wanted to know for myself. But I had made three attempts to go to Diego Garcia on a fact-finding mission—to no avail. My requests were rejected by the State Department.

Still, I was anguished by the constant claims that the United States was detaining al-Qaeda terrorists on Diego Garcia, and using the military base as a torture chamber. I flat out did not believe it—but I could not prove otherwise. If no such activity was taking place, why had my request to go there on a fact-finding mission been turned down?

In the first part of June, President Azali and I spoke and, getting right to the point, I asked if he had seen the recent media reports of a news conference held by Adel al-Jubeir, spokesman for the Saudi royal family, and Juan Carlos Zarate, of the U.S. Treasury Department, announcing that they were going to freeze the assets of the Saudi charity al-Haramain. I also told him that the Saudis were going to group together all nongovernmental organizations under one leadership and establish a commission of high-level individuals to oversee their charitable activities. All aspects of their operations, including funding sources, education programs, orphanages, infrastructure projects, and other programs, would need approval by the commission.

This was designed to make certain that no funding was used for terrorist activities. Singled out for particular scrutiny were operations in Kenya, Tanzania, Bosnia, Indonesia, Pakistan, and Somalia.

Although Azali had been unaware of the news reports, he fully understood where I was coming from when I said that the projects funded by al-Haramain in Comoros were suspect. He mentioned the many projects the Saudi foundation was involved in around the country and how people welcomed its support, but he agreed it needed to be watched carefully. He remarked that he hated to shut it down without having other sources of financial support.

In turn, I spoke of evidence connecting al-Haramain's Comoros branch with al-Qaeda. But when I added that the United States had received a list of seven suspected al-Qaeda members in Comoros, two of whom were associated with al-Haramain, and that training or staging had taken place there, he bristled. It was our contention that Comoros had been used as an exfiltration route for the perpetrators of the 1998 bombings of the U.S. embassies in Kenya and Tanzania, with al-Haramain supplying financial and other operational support for these terrorist attacks. I encouraged Azali to raise this matter with the government of Saudi Arabia for his own edification, and to take steps to prevent misuse of funds by al-Haramain in Comoros.

I suggested several preventive measures, some previously discussed, that he might find useful, including effective registration of nongovernmental organizations and requirements for full disclosure of their operations and funding, declaration and approval of projects by the government of Comoros, and monitoring of their activities. I also recommended that the government communicate with village elders on a regular basis to determine what activities al-Haramain and other NGOs were undertaking in their area, monitor education programs and curricula, limit the number of foreign workers and the length of their stay, require declaration of funds entering the country and implement occasional luggage checks, register and monitor offshore entities, and regulate the financial sector to keep the country from becoming a haven for moving money to terrorists.

President Azali responded that his government had already created a security department dedicated to law enforcement, and to monitor the activities of al-Haramain and other operations. He requested I meet with his chief of staff to review these matters. He also proposed sending a government representative to Port Louis the following week to pursue in detail our recommendations.

I asked him about the status of the Article 98 agreement, reminding him that we needed to conclude the signing of it. He said he was supportive but that some changes were needed, and suggested I come to Comoros to review the issues with him. I told him I would, but wanted the wording of the changes beforehand, so we could conclude the document signing at that time. He promised to send us the wording immediately.

I used this opportunity to again bring up the issue of ship interdiction. As part of the global war on terror, we wanted to enter into an agreement allowing our ships to board Comorian-flagged vessels to check their cargo. Azali acquiesced, and said he would schedule a visit to enter into such an agreement.

In concluding, I thanked him for the way he had handled the recent elections, in light of losing control of the assembly seats. Overall, I thought the long discussion had gone well and that Azali had seemed very cooperative.

The following week, at the behest of President Azali, I met with the Foreign Minister's brother, Abdou Souef, who with Captain Fakridine Mahamoud, chief of staff and head of the army, had been given the task of leading the new antiterrorism department. We reviewed issues on unregistered NGOs, and Souef understood my concerns. We then moved on to discussing Azali's preferences for wording of the Article 98 agreement, and I stressed the importance of getting it signed on my upcoming trip at the end of the month. Overall, I found Souef cooperative and fully supportive of the war on terror.

On June 10, President Anerood Jugnauth made a personal visit to the embassy to sign the book of condolences on the death of former President Ronald Reagan, who had passed away on June 5. David Snoxell, representing the United Kingdom, did as well. While Snoxell was at the embassy he brought up the Diego Garcia issue and two orders in council just signed by Her Majesty The Queen that would restore full immigration control over all the islands of the British Indian Ocean Territory, the Chagos Archipelago. Snoxell was concerned about the local fallout with possible sit-ins and antigovernment rallies. It was felt that the Prime Minister would be upset since he had been waiting for several months to have a meeting with Prime Minister Tony Blair to discuss Diego Garcia.

One of the saddest moments of my term as U.S. ambassador was when I was notified that twenty-five-year-old U.S. Marine Corporal Dominique Nicolas had been killed in Iraq.

Dominique, who was born in Mauritius but had moved to the United States when he was fifteen years old, was killed on May 26 by an explosive device while on patrol in Al-Anbar Province. Dominique was the patrol leader, and as they approached a crater made in the road by a previous explosive device, a second one detonated. It was surmised the terrorists had planted this second one to draw in patrols checking the area out. Dominique took the entire blast, saving his other patrol members from instant death.

Charlie Slater, who had received the news, said a Marine was being sent over from Dar es Salaam with the details and would arrive on Monday, May 31. We would keep the information confidential until we met with his parents, who still lived in Mauritius. At five-thirty that Monday afternoon, Charlie, the Marine, Bisa, and I left the embassy in separate cars to visit with Dominique's family. We had a general idea where they lived but had to stop several times to ask for directions, and after two hours ended up on the Beau Plan Sugar Estates, near Pamplemousses, and found their house. No one was home, so we waited for almost an hour in the driveway. I was concerned that our caravan of cars would draw attention from the neighbors, with word possibly getting out before we met with the family. At nine o'clock I suggested Charlie and the Marine stay behind for another hour and then depart. On the chance they came home during that time, the family would be given the details. I would return the next morning; I wanted to personally spend time with them.

Later that night, Charlie called to say that they had met with Dominique's parents and broken the news to them. He said they were stunned but had taken the sad news as well as could be expected. He also had told them I would go to their home at noon the next day for a visit.

When I arrived, Mr. Nicolas was waiting at the front door, while Mrs. Nicolas was seated on a couch in front of a framed picture of a handsome Marine, her son Dominique. Both parents were truly brave. They wanted to know the details and wished to talk to some of the Marines who had been with him that day. They also wanted to know when his body would be brought home for a family funeral.

Dominique's great-grandfather was American, and Dominique had always wanted to be a Marine. For his bravery, he was awarded the Purple Heart and several other commendations. On behalf of the United States and President Bush, I expressed how proud we were of his courage and leadership.

As I left their house, I felt low and sad. I told Charlie to find out about all the benefits available to them, which was the least we could do. In addition, I asked him to schedule the Marine detachment to arrive for a formal military funeral.

On Friday, June 11, I went to the airport at four-thirty in the morning to meet the Air France flight bringing back the casket with the body of Corporal Dominique Nicolas. Before the plane arrived, we spent time with his parents, his estranged wife, Jennifer, and her parents, and about twenty members of the Nicolas family. Four Marines in full dress uniforms escorted the flag-draped casket to the waiting hearse. Charlie Slater and I went in the procession to the Nicolas house, where again the Marines carried the casket into their living room. We waited for a few minutes, extending our condolences before leaving.

On Saturday morning, I went to Pamplemousses to attend Dominique's funeral at St. François d'Assise Church. Built in 1756, it had been recently restored, and was peaceful. The Marines carried the casket up the aisle to the altar, where three priests were waiting. The service was in French, as were the remarks by the speakers, which included a Marine sergeant who had served with Dominique in Iraq. His eulogy, which highlighted Dominique's leadership, brought tears to many eyes. Afterward, the casket was taken to a gravesite next to the church, where a service was held, and two American flags were folded and presented to Dominique's parents and Jennifer.

On Tuesday morning, Charlie came to my office with Ghislain Nicolas, Dominique's father, and his other son, Christian, who had come to the embassy to sign some paperwork. I again expressed my condolences, and presented them each with a set of cufflinks with the Great Seal of the United States etched in gold, a small token of our appreciation for Dominique's service to the country.

Bisa, Charlie, and Lizzie would soon be departing, and I wanted to honor them by hosting a dinner party at Macarty House and inviting government and business leaders with whom they had worked over the years. They had earned great respect from many, and sixty guests came to extend their best wishes. To the threesome's surprise, I asked each to address the group. They had nice words to say about their experiences here, and how sad they were to be leaving—especially Charlie and Lizzie, whose son, Forbes, did not want to leave behind his many friends. For that matter, neither did Charlie, an avid fisherman who was always looking for the next eight-hundred-pound marlin.

Each month, Lizzie Slater would bake an array of cakes, pies, and cookies from her own recipes for our staff birthday celebrations and never accepted reimbursement. With Lizzie leaving soon, we all lamented the thought of someone's prepackaged product. On one occasion Lizzie had been sick for two days but still came to the birthday event with her car full of baked specialties. This month was also her birthday, and the last time we would celebrate together, since they were leaving on July 9—making this day's event very special. We all said how we would miss the team of Lizzie and Charlie.

On Wednesday, June 16, we held one last country team meeting with the three departing officers in attendance. We spent the entire time reviewing a complete list of unresolved issues, creating a trail for their successors to follow. This was important to our embassy operation so that we would be able to complete projects, continue programs, and resolve problems. From the beginning, we made certain that our files had copies of what was sent to Washington. We were too far away—and with the constant rotation of people in and out of the Bureau of African Affairs, follow-up sometimes became problematic.

Under the Rewards for Justice program in Comoros, initiated to find Fazul, we received an anonymous email from a Comorian source saying that a particular person, a Pakistani, was departing Comoros on the following Sunday en route to Pakistan to make contact with Fazul. We were told that this individual sold cell phones, tapes, cassettes, watches, and so on and traveled to Comoros every three weeks, possibly carrying correspondence between Fazul and family members. The source also commented that various people from Madagascar frequently met with the Pakistani in Comoros. On one occasion, the source reported, the Pakistani had said Fazul was in Pakistan, in an area where he wouldn't have any problems. We passed this information along to Washington, but never heard back from anyone there.

Another issue involved twenty-two Chinese nationals detained at Guantanamo Bay. The Department of Defense made the determination that fifteen of these individuals, members of the Uighur ethnic group held for questioning and possible terrorist activities, were no longer of value for intelligence information or needed to be incarcerated. Since they were not considered a threat to the United States or its allies, they were approved for release. However, their fate would be unknown if they were returned to China, and they all wanted asylum, fearing torture or death if they returned. Five posts were asked to seek assistance from the host governments for resettlement of these individuals: the embassies in Port Louis, Dar es Salaam, Windhoek, Luanda, and Colombo. All of these countries had an active Chinese and Muslim presence in which to integrate these detainees. On receiving the directive on June 22, I asked DeWitt Conklin, the acting deputy chief of mission at the embassy, to confer with government leaders about this matter.

Two days later, DeWitt reported that the Mauritian government's response had been "Under no circumstances." They had a sensitive situation with the Muslim community and didn't need this additional distraction. I of course had expected that response, which was only natural under the circumstances—what if the detainees really were terrorists?

I had always believed the Guantanamo Bay detention facility was a good choice for holding enemy combatants off our shores until they were put on trial for their alleged terrorist activities. To me, a terrorist was not a foot soldier, but rather someone who sneaked around lurking in dark corners waiting to attack anyone, including blood relatives. No mercy, no style, no compassion, no conscience. I was never sure that they really understood the Koran or were just indoctrinated by some radical imam in a madrassa or mosque. But once they were indoctrinated by radical Islamists, I believed there was no bringing them back into a normal life in society or rehabilitating them to live side by side with nonbelievers whom they consider infidels.

On June 28, James Liddle, Sadie Tucker as note taker, and I traveled to Comoros. Kim Gueho, who represented the Loita Bank Group, was also on the flight. She was joining us to look at the possibility of opening a branch operation there. Another commercial bank was needed, which would allow for better control of the suspected flow of monies to and from terrorist groups and other money-laundering schemes. Currently, bank operations in Comoros were handled by the Central Bank of the Comoros, the Bank for Industry and Commerce, and the Development Bank of Comoros. Two microfinance institutions—the Sanduk network and the Meck group—had branch operations on all three islands to make small loans and serve as savings banks. (Later, in 2008, Exim Bank Tanzania would announce the opening of a subsidiary operation in Comoros.)

Wanting to stay in the capital city of Moroni this time, we chose the centrally located Hotel Le Moroni. After a quick change I went over to meet with Foreign Minister Souef Mohamed El-Amine. As always, this engaging, burly man gave me a bear hug and smiled from ear to ear. I congratulated him on the country's strides toward stability with the recent elections. He was one of those who had been elected to the National Assembly, and I encouraged him to make every effort to keep the Union together. Even though water separated the three islands, they were related through culture, language, family ties, and history. He agreed the three island presidents needed to work together in conjunction with the Union President.

This was my first trip back since the lifting of the Section 508 sanctions, and I told him we wanted to restart some assistance programs. In fact, James had packed several suitcases of books we were going to distribute. For El-Amine we brought some books for the parliament and the university library as examples of the type of books that would follow. When I mentioned that Loita Bank was here to do a commercial survey, he asked if we could put together a mentoring program with visiting business leaders and offer how-to seminars for their business community. I talked about setting up a cooperative for vanilla farmers so they would have more control of their pricing as they sell into the world markets. These co-ops would be similar to what food bean farmers did in Kenya. He liked the idea.

Now that we were able to restart the IMET program, the embassy had an allocation of $125,000 for FY 2004, about half of which we budgeted for the English Training Lab and teacher training. In PACOM's military civil action program, monies were approved for the purchase of much-needed equipment for the El-Marouf Hospital, and possibly some funding for their orphanages. I was pleased to mention the Ambassador's Special Self-Help Program had $15,000 available to award during this trip to several smaller nongovernmental organizations.

In discussing the Millennium Challenge Grant funding, I told the Foreign Minister that Comoros was being considered, but not in the first tranche. He hoped this could be done in the next phase. However, the formal application still needed to be prepared by their government; the embassy could help them prepare it.

We talked about the Saudi-funded al-Haramain Islamic Foundation at length. From previous conversations with Azali and Hamadi, I knew they were on board with the need for oversight, and El-Amine agreed as well. He said a ministry was being formed for oversight of such nongovernmental organizations.

As I was getting up to leave, El-Amine mentioned that the French ambassador had visited that morning and conveyed a three-page demarche from the European Union—on not signing our Article 98 agreement. He noted that regardless of the problems at Abu Ghraib prison in Iraq, Comoros would sign the agreement.

Early the next day, we met with the president of the National Assembly, Said Dhoifir Bounou. We were joined by Anjouan's Mohamed Djaanfari, one of the three vice presidents selected from each island. Since the two smaller islands often felt forgotten, we talked about budget concerns and problems facing the islands in working together. Bounou wanted the National Assembly to reinforce everyone's inclusion in working closely with the island assemblies. He wanted me to meet regularly with the island presidents, and asked for U.S. help for items such as audio and video equipment, training programs, and computers. Bounou viewed the United States as a country of laws and wanted to learn from us how governing bodies work; he hoped to send some assembly members to the United States to see Congress in action. We left with him several books printed in French on globalization, the American system of government, citizen involvement in government, operation of NGOs in society, media and open press, and federalism in general.

Afterward, I paid a courtesy call on the president of the island of Grande Comore, Abdou Soule El Bak, at his residence/office in Moroni. He and I had met previously, and so my encouragement on the importance of peace, stability, and keeping the Union together did not come as a surprise.

El Bak was concerned about malaria, a major health issue that was a significant cause of death among young children. He also expressed concern about education, saying that more than fifteen thousand students had few choices in pursuing higher-level studies. France had stopped accepting them, and some were finding their way to Arab countries instead. El Bak hoped the U.S. government would help with their new university program. When I asked about the curriculum taught in the islands' madrassas, his response was tempered: he told me that the madrassas in Comoros were no different from those elsewhere, and taught standard school subjects in addition to the Arabic language and religion.

El Bak added: "Look at me. I was educated in Saudi Arabia." Pointing to the two ministers in the room, he said that they too had been trained there, "and we are not radicals." He made a very important point: we shouldn't assume every Muslim being educated in a suspect country is a radical.

Next in line was a visit to the University of the Comoros, which was President Azali's answer to the problem of educating his country's growing student population. The school's scholastic programs finally offered parents the choice of having their children stay at home to be educated in a curriculum focused on a secular education with academic and technical programs of study rather than go abroad to study in a program based on religious indoctrination.

I was anxious to revisit the university. Among the greeting committee of professors at the University of the Comoros was Said Omar Said Hassane, the secretary general of the university. We went into a nicely remodeled, spacious, air-conditioned conference room donated by the World Bank; other donors to the school included the European Union, France, China, and Libya.

That day I met with professors in health care, science, technology, arts and culture, physics, chemistry, economics, communications, law, teacher training, and Arabic and civilization studies. Since most of the professors did not speak English, James Liddle served as our interpreter. During classroom visits, we met students who, having studied in South Africa, spoke fluent English.

The university offered a three-year undergraduate degree, a two-year master's degree, and a two-year Ph.D. program. We were told there were 125 teachers for the current 1,700-student enrollment, and that they were hoping in the near future to be able to offer job placement counselors. They also wanted some English-speaking teachers, English books to globalize their academic programs, and much-needed equipment such as microscopes and computers.

In each class we visited, I noticed the women outnumbered the men. Hassane mentioned that in some classes there were only two or three males. Some male students wore Western attire, while others wore Muslim garb. The female students wore traditional *shiromani* dresses and scarves. In the botany class we visited, students were drawing details of plants and writing a report on each. In another class, they were discussing health care and medical issues. On leaving the school, we gave them a sampling of books on various subjects for their main library and promised more to follow. Seeing such dedication to learning, and the lack of equipment in their classrooms, I could see their need for assistance.

As U.S. ambassador, I was determined to make President Azali's dream of the University of the Comoros come true with the help of the U.S. government. On several occasions, President Azali and I had also discussed the need to have madrassas become part of the Comoros formal education system, as a way to gain control over the curriculum. Every time I met with the State Department and other agencies for consultations, I asked for any available resources for education programs in order to help this poor Muslim country struggling to move forward as a fledgling democracy. However, I was always told by Washington that there were limited resources available—and then only for more pressing areas.

21.3. Meeting with professors and students at the University of the Comoros, June 29, 2004.

The few countries in sub-Saharan Africa that are more economically successful tend to be more democratic, with respect for human rights and rule of law, while the people in destitute countries face a more hopeless future. If we don't spend more time engaging the people in these sub-Saharan African countries and in particular those with significant Muslim populations such as Comoros, building a friendship, and helping lift them out of the poverty trap, well-funded Islamic extremist organizations such as al-Qaeda will.

Perversely, the stigma of Comoros being linked to al-Qaeda terrorists would continue even after Azali closed down the Comoros branch of the Saudi-based al-Haramain Islamic Foundation in August 2004, just weeks after our visit, and turned several al-Haramain buildings into what had become the University of the Comoros campus. For Azali's cooperation in shuttering this charity, the United States would offer no alternatives for the millions of dollars that the foundation had been providing annually for education, orphanages, and village infrastructure projects.

During the time I served as ambassador, the U.S. Embassy in Port Louis spent countless hours working with the State Department, USAID, CENTCOM, PACOM, the Department of Defense, and other agencies for help to acquire badly needed books, school supplies, materials, and equipment. As I had previously done for schools in Mauritius, I contacted the humanitarian aid program of an American faith-based organization, seeking several containers of schoolbooks. Some of my U.S. agency contacts also made promises to help; fortunately, several came through on their commitments.

After the enlightening visit with university professors and students, we headed back to Moroni to meet with military sources. Among the subjects we discussed were the possible terrorist camps on the island. Our information indicated one located near the village of Mohoro, but their information indicated that it had moved around the island to the Chomoni Beach area. They estimated that some two hundred Comorians who had lived in Sudan and Ethiopia were now back and integrating themselves among the townspeople, who housed, fed, and accepted them as their own. It was said that while their intentions were unknown, they needed to be carefully watched, but the fact that it was difficult to differentiate them from the local populace was becoming a problem.

Later in the afternoon at Grande Comore's main hospital, El Marouf, I met Captain Naoufal Boina Adam, a military doctor and chief of staff at the hospital. We discussed PACOM's upcoming gift of surplus equipment and supplies, the Ambassador's Special Self-Help Program grant for equipping the physical therapy department, and the help we contemplated giving to the university for training of medical and nursing students.

During this time, James Liddle had gone on a tour with Abdou Souef, the military officer assigned to the new intelligence section within the ministry, to review all the new structures built by the al-Haramain Islamic Foundation in the past two years. He was gone for several hours, so I surmised there were many. On his return, we went out again, so he could show me some of the larger structures nearing completion. What a major influence this rogue Saudi NGO had over the life of civil society in Comoros. I was disturbed by their influence. Yet they had operated openly for years without interference.

The following morning we met with President Azali. As the hour approached eleven, the agreed-upon time for signing of the Article 98 agreement, Azali hesitated, wanting to review the document again. I reminded him of our phone conversation in which he had promised to sign if I came to Comoros. Azali still wanted to make certain refinements to the French version but said he was fine with the English version, which for us was key, since the document stated that the English version was the final version. He also wanted the Vice President to sign the document, but would provide an affidavit from him authorizing the Vice President to sign, which was acceptable to me. Countering his offer to sign the next morning, I quickly suggested that afternoon. We agreed to three-thirty at the Foreign Minister's office.

That afternoon, after a twenty-minute wait that felt like hours, we were ushered into the office, where Secretary General Ismail Chanfi, who was to be a witness, was waiting with Vice President Ben Massoundi Rachidi. We spread out the Article 98

21.4. Meeting with President Azali Assoumani, June 30, 2004.

21.5. Article 98 agreement signing with Vice President Ben Massoundi Rachidi and Secretary General Ismail Chanfi serving as witness, June 30, 2004.

agreement on a coffee table. Upon signing, they affixed an official government stamp to Rachidi's signature. After a few photos and handshakes we were off, relieved, I left John Bolton a brief phone message to let him know that it had finally been accomplished.

Before leaving Comoros on Thursday, I had breakfast with President Azali and his teenage son, Nour el Fathou, at their family home. "Welcome, my brother and friend," Azali said, and we walked arm in arm up a flight of stairs to a veranda where a large table was set with a nice array of fruits, freshly baked croissants, and coffee that had a great Arabic flavor. Nour, who attended school in Morocco, was home on a break from school, and since he was fluent in English, he helped his father and me communicate.

I learned that Azali's family came from the village of Mitsoudje, and we talked about other villages. I raised the possibility that terrorist training might be going on in some of them, but Azali did not believe that was an issue. In talking about the new anti-terrorism department, Azali was interested in sending his chief of staff Captain Fakridine to a U.S. conference to learn more about such matters.

Given the anti-American rhetoric flourishing throughout much of the world, I was eager to support any program that highlighted what our country has stood for since independence. So on July 2, 2004, I was happy to visit the St. Nicholas School's "America Day" program. As Marcia and I pulled up to the main entrance of the school, waiting to greet us was the headmistress, Marie-Claire Heerah, and about two hundred students ages four to twelve—several saluting me. The event began with a flag-raising ceremony, the Pledge of Allegiance, which most of the students knew, and the singing of "The Star-Spangled Banner" followed by the Mauritian national anthem. Carrying small American flags, the children led us into the building. Its long hallway was filled with children's art depicting American history and culture, including scenes of the White House, the Capitol, the Statue of Liberty, Mount Rushmore, space exploration, and the World Trade Center before its destruction. Several students were dressed to represent American themes. We heard some perform selections of America's favorite songs.

On Saturday afternoon Marcia and I went to the Champ de Mars, the Thoroughbred racetrack, to present the America Challenge Cup trophy to the winner of the seventh race. Linda Henry, the embassy's education advisor, and her husband, Serge, were avid horse owners and had arranged for this trophy presentation. Many of the embassy staff were there among the thirty thousand fans.

And on Sunday, Marcia and I hosted our third annual Independence Day celebration at Macarty House. As usual, it was well attended. By noon, Marcia and I had been joined by Lucy Hall, the temporary-duty deputy chief of mission, and the soon-to-depart Charlie and Lizzie Slater, and were ready to greet our distinguished guests. After the government dignitaries arrived, Vice President Raouf Bundhun and I made a toast to our respective countries and anthems were played. We honored

21.6. St. Nicholas schoolchildren carrying American flags and greeting us for the Fourth of July school program, Port Louis, Mauritius, July 2004.

Corporal Dominique Nicolas and his parents and observed a moment of silence to reflect on this young man's service to our country.

There was no doubt we would miss Lizzie. She had just completed her last project, working long hours to install a computer lab, donated by the embassy under the Ambassador's Special Self-Help Program, at the Alexandra House School, which catered to English-speaking students. During the dedication ceremony at the school, the room was overflowing with eager students wanting their chance to browse online. It was a lovely legacy for Lizzie.

Speeding across the island, we attended Linda Henry's orientation seminar for students selected to go to U.S. schools for advanced studies. The students came with their proud parents. This year, we would be sending more than thirty students to American universities on scholarships totaling over $2 million. Linda, the education advisor since 1975, had helped hundreds of students obtain an education in the United States. Warming to my favorite subject, I said the opportunity for education is the beginning of the rest of one's life path, whether entering the job market, staying in academia, or choosing family structure options. It becomes part of you, and no one can take it away.

"Education opens doors," I said. "And you were chosen because you represent the best in Mauritius."

Marcia and I felt it was important to expose our children, their spouses, and our grandchildren to the cultures of many countries in sub-Saharan Africa. That year we would be getting together again to visit safari camps, villages, towns, and conservation projects for two weeks. Meeting in Johannesburg, South Africa, on July 8, we flew to the isolated Sandibe Lodge, located on the southern edge of the Moremi Game Reserve, on a tributary of the Okavango Delta in northern Botswana. Five days later, we headed to the next camp, Ongava Lodge, on a privately owned ranch adjacent to Etosha National Park in northern Namibia. On July 16, we took yet another small aircraft charter south to Walvis Bay, also in Namibia, where we went out on a small watercraft to Pelican Point to observe the large sea lion population there. Our son-in-law Tony Wallin was almost knocked overboard by a three-hundred-pound "friend of the skipper," Robbie the sea lion, who jumped into the boat and onto Tony's lap.

Once on land again, we traveled north by road to Swakopmund, a small German-style town dating back to 1912, with a population of twenty-eight thousand people. We took a charter flight down the coast, seeing only drifting sand and magnificent giant sand dunes along the way, as we headed for the Sossusvlei Desert area, where we stayed at the Little Kulala Lodge, sitting on a private preserve adjacent to Namib-Naukluft Park, where we saw "Big Daddy," an extraordinary sand dune that stood more than a thousand feet high.

The wildlife in each safari camp location was different, ranging from massive herds to smaller groups of animals in sparsely vegetated areas. The scenery was spectacular everywhere and the people, although poor, were very friendly. Many of the villages, though, lacked clean water, health care, and educational facilities, and they had minimal opportunity for employment.

On July 19, we headed back to Windhoek and then on to Johannesburg. This chapter of our annual family sub-Saharan Africa experience had come to an end.

Ten days later, word reached me late at night that Ahmed Ghailani, an accomplice of Fazul in the Nairobi and Dar es Salaam embassy bombings, had been caught in a Pakistan safe house raid. Now it was Fazul's turn.

{ XXII }

HOST COUNTRY AND REGIONAL ISSUES

On Sunday, August 2, 2004, I went to Seychelles to meet General Sam Helland, commander of the Combined Joint Task Force–Horn of Africa, and to attend meetings with government and military leaders as well as several separate bilateral meetings. James Liddle, who had arrived a few days earlier to set up the logistics for my visit, met me at the airport. During dinner at the small boutique Wharf Hotel, which is close to the airport and Victoria, the capital of Mahé, we noticed two Americans who appeared to be part of the general's advance team. James went over to introduce himself and then brought them to our table. They told us word had just reached them that General Helland would not be coming from Djibouti. We quickly called Susanne Rose and asked her to let everyone know we would keep our scheduled meetings without him.

Having some spare time on Monday morning, I traveled around the island to visit galleries, shops, and cultural centers. I purchased several pieces of art directly from the artists to display at Macarty House as part of a collage of art from the other Indian Ocean countries. I wanted guests to become more familiar with these countries through the eyes of their artists.

In an afternoon meeting with several members of the Chamber of Commerce board, they said little had improved since our last meeting. In fact, businesses were worse off, goods were less available, money was tighter, and there was still no loosening of import controls—the Seychelles Marketing Board monopoly pricing was choking everyone. Even the new National Tender Board, intended to establish a competitive and transparent process for privatization of SMB-controlled operations, was stacked with insiders. Only a few people benefited from this process, which seemed less than transparent, did little to decrease the foreign exchange shortage, and was ineffective in producing any significant reduction in the national debt.

The next morning, I went to the Coast Guard headquarters to meet with Lieutenant Colonel André Ciseau, the commanding officer, who again was waiting with a full color guard of about a dozen men. Over tea, we talked about increasing naval training programs, upcoming U.S. Navy ship visits, and the issue of providing better

22.1. Downtown Victoria, the capital of Mahé Island, Seychelles, August 3, 2004.

access to docking for the U.S. ships. Having to anchor offshore, as sometimes was necessary, required the Navy to provide around-the-clock surveillance by small water-craft with armed military personnel on board, circling the blocked-off areas to ensure that no other craft approached the line of demarcation. Sending tenders to transport hundreds of military personnel ashore and back was also costly and time-consuming, and raised the chance of accidents. We did not want to bypass Seychelles, I told him, but we needed more attention given to sharing security with the government of Seychelles.

I then met with Foreign Minister Jérémie Bonnelame, who was accompanied by Principal Secretary Sylvestre Radegonde. We talked about economic concerns, and I relayed the observations of the Chamber members. This did not surprise Bonnelame, who believed Mukesh Valabhji was still firmly entrenched in controlling the Seychelles Marketing Board.

Ongoing financial woes plagued this small country. I was told that considerable amounts of hard currency were going into questionable offshore accounts rather than remaining in the country. Recently British Airways had stopped air service to Seychelles because it could not get paid in hard currency. The government required all Seychellois to purchase their airline tickets in Seychelles, which made a trip an expensive venture. Tickets bought abroad could not be used for flights originating in Seychelles—again, another move to tighten hard currency restrictions. And I had already heard many Seychellois express frustration about being allowed to take only $400 in hard currency when traveling outside the country. "Where could you go with $400?" one high-ranking official had remarked during a meeting.

To save money, the government of Seychelles closed some of its embassies overseas, including those in important cities such as London. Seychelles reportedly saved €1.5 million by suspending their operation of diplomatic missions in the United Kingdom, South Africa, and Malaysia. And, stating they could not afford the annual $500,000 dues, they also withdrew from the Southern African Development Community (SADC), whose mission was to further socioeconomic, political, security, and peacekeeping cooperation among the fourteen country members. The SADC members set up guidelines in their countries for enhancing transparency and credibility in elections and democratic governance. Seychelles had been an SADC member from 1997 until withdrawing in 2003. When I emphasized that the benefits to Seychelles outweighed the cost of the dues, President Michel was emphatic: they could not afford to be a member. I suggested selling a parcel of land if they had to, in order to pay the dues; withdrawing would be perceived as a sign of financial weakness and would further injure the country's reputation in the rest of the world. I talked with several other Seychelles government leaders about this issue; they just shrugged.

I always thought Seychelles's absence from the SADC not only hurt the country's image but also slowed down its economic growth. Prime Minister Paul Bérenger of Mauritius, who would become the chairman of the SADC on August 17, 2004, wanted Seychelles to resume its membership. Mauritius, which remained very active in SADC, focused much of its foreign policy toward the other African members and continued expanding its market share in the region.

(During the 2008 annual summit of the SADC heads of state and government, President Michel would announce that Seychelles, after a four-year hiatus, would rejoin the organization as a member.)

The government of Seychelles was constantly in arrears on its payments, including important fuel purchases from Malaysia's Petronas and others. Though cash from the sale of the gasoline and oil products should have been more than enough to offset these wholesale purchases from the offshore oil companies, the arrearage reached an estimated $30 million in 2002, and pressure was put on the governor of the Central Bank of Seychelles to cover these shortfalls on behalf of the Seychelles Petroleum Company. I was told Mukesh Valabhji oversaw these transactions.

As the economic advisor to President René, Mukesh was also the architect for the macroeconomic reform plan that had been prepared for the World Bank and International Monetary Fund, and which called for privatization of the SMB operations. At the time, believing that the government was serious about instituting the reform plan, I interceded on behalf of Seychelles with senior-level staff at the World Bank and IMF, asking for their full support to work with the government of

Seychelles on the plan. Over time, however, I had gone from being a believer to a doubter, and soon concluded René and Mukesh had a different agenda in mind—one that would not allow the reform plan to succeed.

I understood that Mukesh had grown up with René's two sons, David and Glenny Savy, and showed an aptitude for finance and business. In the early 1980s René became a master at the expropriation of hotel properties, so the concept of a monopoly was not strange to him. Along the way, Mukesh also developed expertise in dealing in the offshore world. Soon after becoming an advisor to René, Mukesh began his strategy to monopolize industries and consolidate operations under the Seychelles Marketing Board.

Media and community leaders claimed that millions of dollars had gone to René, Mukesh, their family members, close friends, and other insiders. According to sources, the value of offshore entities and disguised accounts was estimated to exceed $300 million. It had also been said that one reason René wanted to stay in control of his party, the SPPF, was to protect his offshore investments.

Nepotism appeared to be the hallmark of René's administration. His son David Savy was in charge of Air Seychelles, the national airline, and deputy chief of staff of the armed forces. His other son, Glenny Savy, was head of the Island Development Company, which controlled all real estate development, fisheries, and agriculture uses on twelve outer islands and one inner island, and reportedly drained Seychelles's treasury of U.S. $3 million. Glenny Savy also was connected with the state-controlled Seychelles Broadcasting Corporation.

Later that morning in a meeting with President Michel at State House, we discussed the issue of privatization, and I reported that I had been told the new National Tender Board was stacked with insiders. The President noted that a broadening of the board was being considered, and mentioned only one individual from the private sector was on the board: the manager of the local branch of Barclays Bank. He said it was his intention to privatize most of the SMB operations, except a few that produced essential goods and basic staples. He assured me that henceforth the process of privatization would be transparent and open to outsiders. He felt that by privatizing, the cost of goods could come down significantly on a broad cross section of products. This would allow a devaluation of the Seychelles rupee to a point closer to its real value. The goal was to have a free market economy with open hard currency exchange within five to ten years.

Michel also told me he was working hard to keep the fishing fleet based in Seychelles, although Mauritius and others were trying to entice them away. Lastly, he was concerned about the bad press surrounding accusations that the Children's Fund tax on beer sales was not being properly spent. He reviewed with me a computer printout showing where the funds had gone. He shared with me more than I had expected, and I believed he was sincere.

When I met Mukesh at the SMB office later, it was clear that he took a different view of matters. He said, rather defensively, that if he stayed in charge of the SMB he wouldn't privatize many of the operations; those that did get sold wouldn't be put on the open market but rather would be sold selectively, and represent only 20 to 30 percent of the SMB operations. He claimed that costs had been reduced in many areas and that more goods were presently available—although earlier others had told me that this was not so. He also said, in direct contrast to what I had heard from the Chamber, that many import licenses had been issued.

I thought often about the complexity of Seychelles politics. When I had met with President René I would usually have a fixed agenda of bilateral issues to discuss with him. He did more listening than responding. A charming individual, he seemed comfortable talking with me, but limited the dialogue. It was hard for me to imagine that this gentle-appearing, gray-haired grandfather type had undertaken the 1977 coup and later reportedly had been implicated in the 1985 killing of Gérard Hoareau, an exiled opposition leader. It also was hard to reconcile my experience of René with the notion of him as a dictator who not only turned his country into a one-party Marxist state but also brought it to economic disaster. In all my meetings with René, though, I never brought up Mukesh Valabhji's name. I knew René considered him family, and I am a firm believer that one should not speak negatively about someone's child.

One subject bothered me from day one: the purported sale of passports by the government of Seychelles to anyone who had the wherewithal to pay for one. I brought up this issue in my first meeting with René. Seychelles had signed on in support of the global war on terror after 9/11, and I thought the government should do everything in its power to prevent terrorists from buying these passports, which gave them access to the world. The government's policy had been that non-Seychellois could travel to Seychelles and stay for a short period of time while a passport, purchased for $25,000, was being prepared. After 9/11, information reached the embassy that the price had now gone up to $65,000. Anyone who could pay this much for a passport from this small island state could have an ulterior motive. Although promises were made that this practice had ceased, it was rumored to be continuing as late as June 2005, when I departed. Furthermore, it was always questionable who really received the proceeds from the passport sales.

President Michel and I often discussed the lack of progress in implementing a sound and workable economic reform plan. When I suggested that Mukesh was just going through the motions and had possible conflicts of interest that the government of Seychelles needed to review, Michel obviously realized that I was also referring to René. I believed Michel feared René, since his former boss still controlled the SPPF.

I also thought it likely that Mukesh would continue to wield some power because of his connections with René. I wondered if Michel's government would be able to get a handle on the voluminous offshore transactions and entities reportedly controlled by René and Mukesh. (I was told that after Michel was elected President in 2006, he seemed to slowly draw away from René's control. And in 2007 *Le Nouveau Seychelles Weekly* reported that Michel had gotten rid of Mukesh Valabhji at SMB and Glenny Savy at the Seychelles Fishing Authority.)

France-Albert René's dealings in real estate went back to 1981 and 1982, a few years after the 1977 coup. The stated goal for his party, the SPPF, was that Seychelles's tourist industry resources should be for the benefit of all the Seychellois, and in 1980 René formed the Compagnie Seychelloise de Promotion Hotelière (COSPROH) as a government-owned entity. The next year, René directed the government to nationalize three hotels on the island of Mahé; later, other properties were added.

During the next twenty-six years, reportedly, problems with transparency and accountability would arise in connection with the sale of COSPROH resources. Mukesh Valabhji, who joined the board in 1985, controlled its activities until its dissolution in June 2006. According to a September 15, 2006, *Le Nouveau Seychelles Weekly* article, "The Rape of Our Country Revealed in Stark Detail," the liquidation of COSPROH did not conform to current law: its financial transactions were not audited or recorded with the Registrar of Companies at Kingsgate House. During the last four years of COSPROH's existence, several questionable transactions took place without proper disclosure. In a transaction uncovered by investigators for the Italian government, the Côte d'Or Lodge on Praslin supposedly was leased for ninety-nine years to Parmalat, the Italian multinational food giant, in 1997 for $7.5 million. However, on Parmalat's books, checks and bank transfers reflected that the sum actually spent was $12.3 million—$4.8 million more than was reported. COSPROH's books were not made available to shed light on where the difference went.

Another transaction involved the Fisherman's Cove Hotel, which was expropriated by the government from the original owners during 1981–82 and had a book value of approximately $1.2 million on December 31, 2002. COSPROH reportedly declared its real value to be approximately $40 million; so why was it disposed of for only $11 million, even when $6 million was spent on refurbishment only a short time before the sale? The Le Meridien hotel group disclosed it had signed a twenty-year, noncancelable lease in 2004 for Fisherman's Cove for payments of $2.262 million per year, giving the new owners a 20.5 percent net return per year on their $11 million investment, or almost two times the industry standard for a quality property. The owners were also given a favorable tax exemption for twenty years. The total rent generated over the lease term would be $45 million, without considering the added tax benefits. Qualified bidders, from my experience, would have paid $30–35 million or even more for this property. It should be noted that this transaction, because it involved a parastatal, had to be blessed at the highest level of government.

The government promoted Seychelles as a confidential offshore destination to register business operations in the Indian Ocean region. In fact, many companies registered there but did business outside the region as well. If Seychelles was a good place to register a business, why then was there a need for real estate transactions to involve additional layers of ownership entities registered as far away as the British Virgin Islands, the Cayman Islands, or Switzerland—unless someone wanted to further mask the true ownership? The transactions involving COSPROH should have been open to public scrutiny. That these deals, conducted under a shroud of secrecy, were layered with offshore ownership entities should have been of concern.

Hotel Properties Limited was a registered entity in Seychelles owned by another entity of the same name registered in the British Virgin Islands. Under the Seychelles Companies Act of 1972, all companies registered with the Registrar of Companies in Seychelles must disclose their directors, but they do not have to specify if they are the owners. The hotel entity registered in Seychelles listed as directors Raza Bilgrami and Hussein Karimji, whose business address was identical to that of Airtel, a cellular telephone company located in Providence on Mahé. Raza Bilgrami was also involved in the sale of shares of Seychelles Breweries to the Seychelles Pension Scheme for approximately $12 million. In this transaction, a Swiss company (whose ownership was not disclosed) was represented in the sale by Bilgrami. The governor of the Central Bank, Francis Chang-Leng, who was also chairman of the Board of Trustees of the Seychelles Pension Scheme, "recommended the purchase." I was told no one ever saw an independent fairness opinion on the valuation of this transaction.

Raza Bilgrami again reappeared as a director in another company called Belombre Hotel Development Ltd., registered in Seychelles. The *Seychelles Weekly* article noted that it too was owned by the British Virgin Islands entity Hotel Properties Limited, which owned the Fisherman's Cove Hotel. Without a competitive bidding process, the government of Seychelles gave Belombre a long-term lease on prime beachfront property adjacent to the Fisherman's Cove Hotel.

On a number of occasions, I stayed at the Fisherman's Cove Hotel and held many meetings there. During one meeting, I was told that every month a courier would deliver a brown envelope filled with 30,000 rupees for rent payments to an owner's representative at a specified spot on the beach near the Berjaya Beau Vallon Beach Hotel.

Businesses had to figure out how to deal with the problems caused by having millions of dollars' worth of Seychelles rupees. British Airways chose to resolve the problem by temporarily suspending operations in the country. In 2004, Airtel, the cell phone operator, had bought from COSPROH the Barbarons Beach Hotel for 65 million rupees or approximately $13 million, and that this had come about at least in part because Airtel had huge amounts of rupees that could not be converted to hard currency. The Seychelles thought the government should not be trading marketable property to anyone just to unlock value when many other local businesses had the same problem with an excess of rupees but were not offered a similar opportunity.

Even on the islands, the Seychelles rupee could not always be used for purchases. Many vendors (including hotels and resorts) would only take dollars or euros, since they had to pay for their product purchases with hard currency, and the lucky ones— those with global operations or accounts abroad—kept much of their hard currency offshore. I was told a number of businesses had negotiated special deals with the government for importing goods and supplies, bypassing the Seychelles Marketing Board, and that percentage splits for foreign exchange had been separately negotiated by resort hotel owners and other foreign investors—the average was between 50 and 85 percent, while a few claimed to receive 100 percent. By consistently taking away hard currency from the local business community, the government left these businesses with mostly rupees for their payroll, and allowed only a 15 percent exchange of their rupees into hard currency to import goods for their business operations. As a result, choice and quantity were limiting factors.

Even when they could use rupees, Seychellois and visitors in some cases paid more than double the true value of an item, in part because the SMB controlled more than 90 percent of all imported goods. Consequently, the Seychellois had little left to save or invest.

As I have noted previously, Seychelles was heavily indebted and had been in arrears on a number of its loans with the Paris Club, African Development Bank, World Bank, and International Monetary Fund. And the government didn't seem to be in a hurry to repay anyone. The artificially high value of the Seychelles rupee had served to underpin their loans with overvalued collateral that under a free market economy, with a floating rupee, would probably be worth only about half the claimed value. Neither the World Bank nor the International Monetary Fund wanted to force the devaluation of the rupee on Seychelles for fear of the crushing effect it would have on the collateral value of the country's outstanding debt, not to mention the repercussions for the economy. (The outstanding debt, which in 2005 exceeded $220 million, would reportedly escalate to more $1.2 billion by 2009.)

In meetings I held with the World Bank and International Monetary Fund officials, it became clear to me that they turned a blind eye on the situation; their pronouncements on the situation sounded like policy double talk. I thought it was distinctly possible that Seychelles would collapse under the weight of the overvalued rupees.

Given this overvaluation, one had to take GDP figures with a grain of salt. The GDP of Seychelles had increased from $1,000 per capita at the time of their independence to approximately $7,800 per capita in 2002, according to the *CIA World Factbook*. In 2006, the World Bank indicated the GDP was $8,600 per capita, while the International Monetary Fund listed it at $11,800 per capita that year. (From my arrival in 2002 through 2005, the exchange rate stayed nearly static, with just above 5 Seychelles rupees [SCR] to the dollar, even though we were offered anywhere from SCR 10 to SCR 14 on the local black market. Then the official government rate started rising, reaching SCR 16 to the dollar in March 2009; it has even floated around SCR 18.) Hence, the figures supplied by the World Bank and International Monetary Fund, respectively, could be around $4,900 or $6,725 per capita, based on the real SCR value.

For years the Seychellois depended upon a traditional plantation economy of cinnamon bark, copra, vanilla, and some coconut. But today agriculture is all but nonexistent. There has been talk for several years of helping farmers establish new agricultural schemes on the outer islands for farming and rearing livestock, and there is considerable interest in implementing hydroponic farming. Such programs would not endanger the environment yet could help ameliorate shortages of fresh fruits and vegetables, currently imported by the Seychelles Marketing Board.

On a more positive note, the government of Seychelles did invest to some extent in social services, education, health care, and housing. Much effort was also made to protect the environment on the outer islands and a few inner islands, including setting aside reserves and sanctuaries, restoring island habitats, and reintroducing many threatened species. I found this remarkable considering the existing political structure. The restoration programs taking place on these islands could not have succeeded without the help and devotion of organizations such as the Island Conservation Society, Seychelles Islands Foundation, Seychelles National Parks, and Marine Parks Reserves, all supported to some degree by the government of Seychelles in conjunction with nongovernmental organizations.

After returning to Mauritius, I met with Claude How, the embassy's general services officer, and several other members of the country team to plan for the upcoming 9/11 commemoration. I wanted to create a large permanent monument: a heroic effort visible to everyone. What better place for it, I thought, than Macarty House? I shared my idea of finding the largest movable boulder on the island and transporting it to a prominent place in the garden of the ambassador's residence. Everyone liked the idea, although I could see Claude cringe—after all, the responsibility to find one and get it moved would fall on his shoulders. He reminded me that the size would determine the cost (which I agreed to pay), and listed the logistics involved: lifting it over the ten-foot-high wall and the garden area, which was surrounded by many hundred-year-old trees. The easy part was to find an artisan to cast a large bronze plaque and shape the face of the boulder for its resting place. Within a week, Claude found a perfect boulder six feet high. Now all we needed was a very large truck to transport it to the residence and a crane with an extended boom arm to lift it in place. I gave him the go-ahead.

We held another signing ceremony for the twelve recipients of funds from the Ambassador's Special Self-Help Program and two recipients who received grants under the Democracy and Human Rights program, worth about $45,000 in total. I always felt good about this program, which helped NGOs that engaged in community-based activities to benefit the less fortunate.

I met with my new deputy chief of mission, Stephen Schwartz, at the embassy. He arrived in Mauritius with his wife, Kristy Cook, and their two children. We spent more than an hour getting acquainted and discussing current issues involving the host countries. I also reviewed with him the embassy staff and how I wanted to continue to interface with them. He had no problem with my style of management, and felt we would get along well—which we did until my departure in June 2005.

During this time I also met with Bert Cunningham, a Canadian expert hired by the government to oversee the country's customs operation, which was plagued with corruption. Bert had run into great opposition in his effort to implement reforms, to the point of being stonewalled in his attempts to penetrate all the suspected areas. Several times, it was reported, he was physically threatened. On more than one occasion Bert told me he had considered resigning and returning to Canada, as he didn't believe he had the government's full backing to rout out the bad elements.

In a meeting with Bert, he wanted to discuss some security matters and other local concerns. He said that to effectively secure the ports, the area would need to be entirely fenced, with only three controlled-access gates, and that more shore and sea patrols would be required. He wanted U.S. Customs to undertake a port assessment for further input on security matters, an action that I fully supported. He added that a new Chinese X-ray unit would soon be installed, which he felt was a high priority given that this port was becoming a major transshipment center.

He then mentioned a problem the government did not want to acknowledge: a drug called Dame Blanche ("white lady") that appeared to be a mixture of a small amount of heroin with other adulterants. Many Mauritians were hooked, and at a cost of $7 a dose, it was a great burden on them and their families. Bert wanted the U.S. Drug Enforcement Administration to come in and help with seminars. He also wanted laboratory experts to help test for the drug, because current procedures were faulty. I told him I would immediately get into these issues and forward the request to Washington.

On August 20, another new officer joined our embassy staff. Kelly Hopkins, my new office management specialist, came from Iraq, where she had spent five months helping set up the U.S. embassy. I was happy to finally have a permanent team in place.

In the meantime, Claude How and his crew were diligently working on placing the eight-ton boulder on the Macarty House grounds for the 9/11 commemoration

22.2. Placing the eight-ton boulder at Macarty House for the 9/11 commemoration ceremony, August 23, 2004.

project. Claude decided to use a ten-wheel dump truck to carry the boulder through the narrow gate, and then the crane would lower it into place.

In mid-August President Azali asked the al-Haramain Islamic Foundation to cease operations in Comoros, and withdrew visas from all their staff, who then had to leave the country. Although I felt relieved, I also knew that the loss of the foundation's money was a big blow. He mentioned that he would be going to the meeting of the United Nations General Assembly in September, and wanted me to set up a meeting for him with Secretary Powell while he was in the United States. He also wanted to meet with the World Bank, IMF, USAID, Department of Defense, and others to ask for assistance. President Azali's actions were commendable, and I wanted to reward him by providing assistance. We sent cables to Washington and placed several phone calls on his behalf.

On September 2 I had a meeting, set up by Stephen Schwartz and our embassy regional security officer, with Colonel Sam Jones and Chris Jackson, both with the 351st Civil Affairs Command, located in Mountain View, California. They were part of an assessment team sent to Comoros to review disaster preparedness and other needs. We agreed on many areas where we could make a difference, including the main hospital and outlying clinics that were in desperate need of virtually everything.

During my sixth visit to Seychelles, I was fortunate to have the opportunity to meet on September 6 with General John Abizaid, commander of CENTCOM, to discuss security issues. We met in Seychelles. He was accompanied by Admiral Bob Moeller, Colonel Don Zimmer, Ambassador John Holzman (the State Department senior political advisor), and several other military staff. Jeannette D'Offay, in the ministry of foreign affairs, representing the government of Seychelles, greeted them, and soon we were on our way to the Berjaya Hotel at Beau Vallon Bay.

That evening over dinner, our discussion centered on the origins of today's Islamic fundamentalist thinking. We believed that the United States needed to spend more money, time, and energy on secular education—basic reading, writing, math, sciences, and economic opportunity training and mentoring. We agreed it would take a long time to rid the world of terrorists, as we were fighting not an army or a nation but

22.3. Seychelles government representatives greeting the Combined Joint Task Force–Horn of Africa team, September 6, 2004. From left to right: Admiral Robert Moeller, Lieutenant Colonel André Ciseau, Mrs. Jeannette D'Offay, General John Abizaid, Ambassador John Price, Ambassador John Holzman, Colonel Don Zimmer, Selby Pillay.

erratic individuals who could cause a lot of damage by acting alone. We also agreed that catching Osama bin Laden would not change any of the problems we were facing. Rather, young people in these very poor countries needed hope and a desire to live for some tangible reason, rather than being coerced to die in the name of Islam.

I spoke to Abizaid about how the United States had withheld funding on programs such as IMET in Comoros from 1999 to 2004. I also mentioned having talked with General Sam Helland, who was expected on a later flight, about assistance for drilling water wells, repairing some badly needed roads, and supplying desperately needed hospital supplies and medical equipment. General Abizaid said that when he got back to Djibouti he would personally look into what could be done.

When the general and I paid a courtesy call on President Michel at State House the following morning, Abizaid emphasized how concerned he was by reports of suspicious individuals transiting through the country and by money-laundering issues. Michel quickly interjected that the selling of passports had stopped and was no longer an issue, and I mentioned that the government of Seychelles had cooperated on several occasions in turning away suspect individuals. Michel asked for assistance with Coast Guard boats and a fixed-wing aircraft for better surveillance. The discussion then led to emergency landing rights for aircraft headed for Diego Garcia, to which Michel agreed.

For Abizaid's benefit, I brought up the nagging economic problems Seychelles was facing, including the hard currency shortage, SMB's stranglehold over the economy, and the lack of transparency in the privatization process. As I spoke, I could see by the expression on Michel's face that these were sore areas, but my only purpose in repeatedly bringing up such issues was to urge the country toward transparency and a free market economy so that the IMF would be inclined to act favorably on their behalf. I also spoke of Seychelles's commendable stand on environmental matters.

At the military headquarters for our next meeting, the commander of the Defense Forces, Colonel Leopold Payet, immediately jumped in with a request for help with the latest equipment for airport security. He also needed spare parts for the older Coast Guard boats we had donated to them, and wanted to explore the possibility of students going to the U.S. Coast Guard Academy. General Helland suggested that some training programs were available in Djibouti. Payet reiterated President Michel's request for a fixed-wing aircraft, explaining that he was concerned about commercial overfishing and wanted to use the airplane for surveillance.

At the Foreign Minister's office, Jérémie Bonnelame thanked Abizaid for the naval ship visits and stressed the safety of Seychelles for our military personnel. On the issue of young radical Muslims returning from overseas, the Foreign Minister said the government was very watchful of their movements. I brought up a lingering extradition issue, which he agreed to check into immediately.

Shortly before noon, we arrived at the Coast Guard headquarters, where an honor guard was waiting, looking smart in their crisp white uniforms. Lieutenant Colonel André Ciseau was at his best as he escorted General Abizaid to the conference room. His presentation was impressive, professional, and to the point. Ciseau was prepared to assist U.S. forces during ship visits. He also wanted to have direct contact with Bahrain, Djibouti, and Diego Garcia, and offer assistance with major disasters such as oil spills and search-and-rescue missions. He expressed concern about drug trafficking in the region, which might be linked to terrorists. He emphasized the need for more training programs in counterterrorism, intelligence gathering, drug enforcement, and dock security as well as for screening equipment. One of his major requests was for an eighty-two-foot patrol boat equipped with computers, search planning software and digital maps, long-range radios, a GPS system, and portable floatation devices. Then we visited the dock area, where a short ship interdiction exercise was performed by two of the Coast Guard vessels. Afterward, General Abizaid commented favorably on Ciseau's straightforward thinking.

Our last meeting was with Vice President Joseph Belmont at a lunch he hosted at the Fisherman's Cove Hotel in honor of General Abizaid's visit. It was a casual lunch and a nice way to end a hectic twenty-four hours in Seychelles. I hoped their visit had given Abizaid and his delegation a better understanding of what was needed for Seychelles to survive and move forward on the global stage.

In the car, Abizaid commented on my being so direct with President Michel and said we needed more ambassadors who were willing to speak up. I appreciated hearing that from a seasoned career military officer. We agreed to stay in touch regarding

22.4. Ambassador Price and General Abizaid overlooking the capital, Victoria, and the harbor on Mahé, Seychelles, September 7, 2004.

the assistance programs we discussed for Comoros, and General Abizaid and his staff were soon on their way back to Djibouti.

At the embassy on September 9, I was elated to learn the Treasury Department had designated the Comoros branch of the al-Haramain Islamic Foundation as a rogue NGO with links to al-Qaeda. Now President Azali had a way to counter criticism by his government and the Comorian people for asking al-Haramain to leave the country. But I still had no response from my numerous requests to Washington for financial assistance to fill the funding gap left when the Saudi organization departed. The programs in need of support included orphanages, schools, village infrastructure, and water projects.

Claude How and his crew had accomplished their difficult task: the commemorative boulder was in place, with the bronze plaque fixed to the face. It was September 11, and we were hosting a ceremony in remembrance for the victims and their families. While sitting on the veranda with a cup of tea, I heard the lovely violin trio practicing "Amazing Grace" and "America the Beautiful." The delicious aromas of Luc's cooking filled the air. Claude was setting a ficus tree in a hole that had been dug nearby.

22.5. Commemoration of September 11, 2001, at Macarty House, 2004.

Late in the afternoon the invited guests began arriving, including American citizens living on the island and our embassy staff. In the on-and-off drizzle, we congregated under a tent that had been erected near the boulder and unveiled the bronze plaque, which read:

> In Commemoration of September 11, 2001, Ambassador John Price and the U.S. Embassy Port Louis wish to dedicate this memorial to honor and remember those who died in the tragic terrorist attacks on the United States and to those heroes who lost their lives saving others. May future generations never doubt that freedom will always prevail and, as Americans, WE STAND UNITED.
> September 11, 2004—Patriot Day

When the time came for the planting of the "tree of life," set near a stone reflection bench, each of us placed a shovelful of soil around the tree's base while the violin trio played. At exactly 4:45 p.m. (8:45 a.m. EST), with our flag at half-mast, we

22.6. Children viewing the September 11, 2001, commemoration plaque on the boulder.

observed a minute of silence. Suddenly, a chilling wind engulfed us and the sky became dark and overcast. While everyone else returned to the tent, I remained for a moment and felt an eerie, unexplainable presence in our midst.

On Thursday, September 16, Minister of Culture Motee Ramdass and I had breakfast at Macarty House and enjoyed the crisp morning air on the veranda in view of the tree of life. Motee's private sector background allowed us to discuss a number of regional and community business-related issues. We also talked about how some cultural programs were being used as political platforms, such as during the Third International Writers' Conference organized by the Mauritian Writers' Association at the end of August, when the keynote speaker, Mohamed Vayid, used the occasion to insult the United States and United Kingdom; his comments had been so offensive that our embassy's public affairs officer, Marjorie Harrison, and British High Commissioner David Snoxell walked out. Motee Ramdass too had been offended, and the cabinet was taking a closer look at participants in any program with government association to avoid such occurrences in the future.

Because so few U.S. resources were being made available to Comoros, despite all the time and energy our embassy staff had spent on the matter, I asked my political officer, James Liddle, to draft a cable to be widely distributed to all the U.S. agencies having oversight in this region. I wanted to reach anyone who might have ideas for solutions—and, I hoped, the authority to green-light funding. James drafted an excellent outline defining the important issues that our country team had discussed. With input from Stephen Schwartz, we critiqued the cable in great detail, in order to present a compelling case that no one in Washington could turn down, or so I thought.

The embassy team was reluctant to send such a strong and direct cable, saying it was not the norm at the State Department. I said it would go out under my signature and I would take full responsibility for this action. I believed it was important for the agencies in Washington and their regional field offices to have a better understanding of the Union of the Comoros and the reasons I recommended full engagement.

As part of the September 27, 2004, cable, we included a recap of the total time the embassy staff had spent in Comoros since my arrival in April 2002. For comparison's sake, I contrasted this with data going back to 2000; we could not find any records for visits before that date. The time spent working in Comoros had gone from six days in 2000 and three days in 2001 to thirteen days in 2002, forty days in 2003, seventy-seven days in 2004. With an estimated sixty-eight days to May 2005, these figures, totaling 198-people resource days, did not include the time spent in Comoros by people from other U.S. agencies at our request, which was significant. Nor did it include a number of meetings we had held with President Azali while he was visiting Mauritius or the bilateral meetings I attended with Azali and his delegation in Washington in late February 2005.

In meetings and conversations with Comorian government leaders since my departure in June 2005, I learned there have been minimal results from the State Department and other agencies that said they would help, and little time spent engaging Comoros by U.S. representatives. In fact, it was not until eight months after my departure that the Comoros portfolio was officially moved over to the already overburdened U.S. Embassy in Antananarivo, on March 5, 2006. After the portfolio was passed on, there was limited engagement of Comoros, I was told by government sources.

Several months after returning home, on March 27, 2006, I wrote a letter to the Undersecretary for Public Diplomacy expressing my views on the importance of engaging Muslim countries at risk such as Comoros in sub-Saharan Africa. I laid out the case of Comoros, which had been supporting U.S. foreign policy and, as such, deserved our help in return. The well-publicized role of the department was to engage Muslims, among others, around the world and get out our message of friendship. I believed the United States was misunderstood by Muslims around the world and that we needed to bridge the gap of our cultural differences. If we were going to make any headway in the global war on terror, we needed to engage the more tolerant Muslims and win them over by showing them respect. Comoros was not a radical Muslim country. Its leadership believed that Islam promotes democracy and cooperation, that a Muslim world can be a democratic world, and that Islam has nothing to do with fundamentalism.

As a former U.S. ambassador who had been the United States' representative to Comoros, I would have expected to hear some response to my input. It never happened. In checking with Comoros officials, I discovered that the new Public Diplomacy initiative did not make any difference in their relations with the State Department.

The issue surrounding Diego Garcia continued, with the Ilois leader Olivier Bancoult pressing forward on legal action through the British courts. There was much sympathy in Mauritius for the Chagossians' case, and consequently pressure on government leaders.

On Wednesday, October 6, 2004, I received a disturbing phone call from a reporter for the Mauritius-based Radio One, who blurted out his suspicion that the United States was storing radioactive material at Diego Garcia. He pressured unrelentingly for my response even when I told him I knew nothing about such claims. Finally I excused myself with no further discussion. Reaching the embassy, I told them to expect a nasty story; I was sure my denial would be fodder for an active and vicious reporter.

On October 7, Radio One ran with the story of Diego Garcia being a dumping ground for radioactive waste. It featured an interview with John Pilger, a London-based

Australian reporter who had recently been in Mauritius making a documentary on the Chagos Archipelago.

Later that month, Stephen Schwartz received an email from Mark Zimmer (the third country desk officer since 2002) noting that he had recently attended a meeting in Africa about Diego Garcia at which he had learned that the United Kingdom would allow the Chagossian group to visit the Chagos Archipelago. Since all parties had agreed on the matter, Zimmer wrote, he had cleared the visit from his end. Zimmer made it clear that he was the person in charge for the informal working group on Diego Garcia issues. We had previously been told that Mauritius had plans to present the Diego Garcia case to the International Court of Justice for a ruling, and I had been given demarches to convince them otherwise. Zimmer's message stated that the United Kingdom expressed its thanks for our role in Mauritius's decision not to seek a ruling regarding sovereignty that year. What was not referred to in the message from Zimmer was that when I had delivered the demarche on the Diego Garcia issue to Prime Minister Bérenger, we had had a lively debate, wherein he agreed to make sure that his UN permanent representative would not present this issue at the General Assembly in 2004, but he reserved the right to keep the option open for further review in 2005.

On the issue of the visit by the Chagossians to Diego Garcia, I strongly disagreed with Zimmer's characterization that all parties involved seemed to be on board with the decision. Zimmer was new to the job and needed guidance, or at least input, from U.S. Embassy Port Louis. I was also surprised that Phil Carter, the deputy director in the Office of East African Affairs, who was in the loop, had allowed this action without calling the embassy for the ambassador's input. Almost daily we had to explain the U.S. position that outsider access to the Chagos Archipelago must remain restricted. If the British wanted to allow the Ilois to visit two of the outer islands, that would be their decision to make, but the United States would not readily support that action. That had been the U.S. stand since my first London meetings in April 2002.

I had Stephen Schwartz send a response directly to Zimmer's boss, Phil Carter. In it, I expressed the consistent U.S. position opposing any such visits, as I felt it might open the door to many such visits. I proffered instead that what was needed was to do more to make the Ilois community viable and better integrated into the communities in which they resided. We got no response, which did not surprise me.

However, I was surprised that Zimmer had communicated directly with my deputy chief of mission, without including me in the email. And Zimmer had attended a high-level meeting in Africa on Diego Garcia even though the island was part of the embassy's portfolio and responsibility. It was the ambassador, after all, who was tasked with delivering demarches that at times were not pleasant. To top it all off, the meeting Zimmer had attended had taken place on October 6, 2004, more than three weeks before he sent us a message about it. And according to the email,

22.7. Lalit and Chagossians demonstrate at the U.S. Embassy in Port Louis, Mauritius, March 20, 2004.

forty-five people had received copies of the minutes of the meeting—but no one at U.S. Embassy Port Louis was included.

We had a hectic work schedule during October, with the AGOA legislation and the pending Chiefs of Mission Conference accounting for much of it. Early on Friday, October 8, Jayen Cuttaree called with great urgency. Apparently Congressman Charles Rangel had sent a bill to Congressman Bill Thomas regarding the third-country fabric issue under the proposed AGOA III that did not include Mauritius as an LDC beneficiary. Cuttaree thought this was possibly an oversight. But my concern was that Thomas had always perceived Mauritius as too prosperous to be considered for such a status, even though I had tried to persuade him that it would be shortsighted to do anything to jeopardize the economic success that had underpinned the evolution of Mauritius into a successful democracy over the past thirty years.

I told Cuttaree I would get on it immediately, and made a call to Thomas. When Thomas did not return my call, I reached his administrative assistant and explained the issue at length, since it was critical that he know about it before the vote on the bill. I then left a message at Rangel's office in the hope he would be supportive. I knew from my previous discussions that the Office of the U.S. Trade Representative was supportive of these benefits for Mauritius.

Four days later I was in Washington for another Chiefs of Mission Conference. The agenda included several new State Department leadership speakers reviewing embassy issues, panel discussions (with only career ambassadors participating) on challenges and expectations in present-day Africa, and discussions on counterterrorism, HIV/AIDS, conflicts, and post management issues.

In a morning session held at the Operations Center Briefing Room, Secretary Powell again stressed doing more outreach with young people in the community and greater engagement of the host country governments. During the question-and-answer period, I brought up the need to have a better interface between the military commands—in my case, PACOM and CENTCOM. I explained that it would be better to work with one unified command, as it meant fewer people had to be kept in the loop. My input was noted, and I presumed I would hear more on the subject in the coming days.

The next morning included a discussion on consular matters and a review of the effectiveness of the new fingerprint program, which many found was not yet a user-friendly process.

Meeting with the Millennium Challenge Corporation staff, I hoped the discussion would include Comoros. MCC Vice presidents Clay Lowery (market and sector analysis) and John Hewko (country relations) orchestrated the discussion. They talked about the funding proposed for 2005: $1.2 billion for the sixteen nominated countries in Africa. Comoros was not on the list, but certainly in my opinion it was as qualified as Mali or Madagascar. Clay suggested we work with our country desk officer to make the application, and I immediately called Mark Zimmer to alert him as to what was needed.

John Dinger and William Pope followed with an update on counterterrorism initiatives in the Horn of Africa region. So far the Rewards for Justice Program had seen few successes, but leads kept pouring in. They mentioned that the program was now in force in Comoros to find Fazul.

At another meeting, Deputy U.S. Trade Representative Josette Shiner spoke about the AGOA III third-country fabric sourcing issue. We learned that the program had been extended for one year and would include benefits for Mauritius. This was good news. Even though we had hoped for at least a three-year extension, inclusion of Mauritius was a start. Currently, China had a 65 percent share of the U.S. market, and retailers wanted to keep other sources viable, she told us. I thanked her for weighing in on the issue, and I stated that in ten years China would end up with the bulk of the textile business if we didn't create more checks and balances. I added that we needed more congressional delegations, especially including the Ways and Means leadership, to visit Africa to better understand the need for job creation. She agreed and said the Office of the U.S. Trade Representative would continue to support more engagement in trade with Africa.

In another session, I learned that USAID funding was very limited, although development assistance in Africa was up 60 percent since the year 2000. In

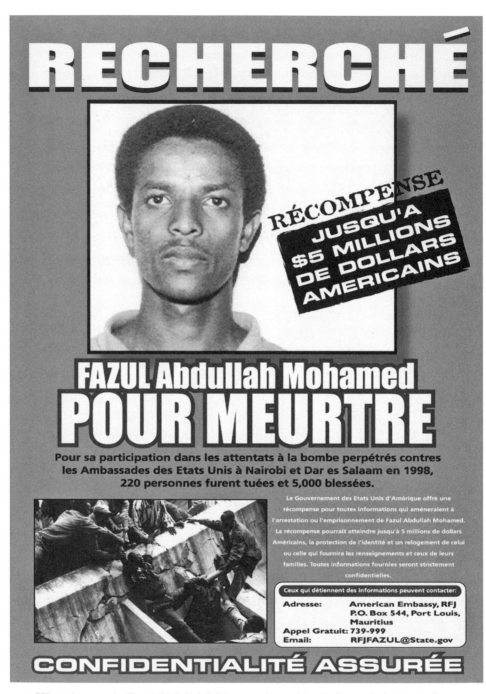

22.8. Wanted poster for Fazul Abdullah Mohammed issued by the Rewards for Justice Program.

my three host countries, however, I had not seen any appreciable funding for programs.

On Wednesday, October 20, I made my seventh visit to Seychelles for government meetings and ship visits. The next morning, in meeting with the Chamber of Commerce, I reviewed the sixteen points of economic change needed in Seychelles. They shared a letter that had been presented to President Michel requesting that the President institute these changes immediately, starting with devaluation of the rupee. In general, the economy was continuing to decline, with no sign of recovery. Michel, having a difficult time with his old boss René still casting a long shadow over the presidency, had implemented few changes. Apparently René and Mukesh were working against Michel, making implementation of economic improvements difficult.

On Friday, President Michel and I discussed the state of the economy and the Chamber's observations. While agreeing that the economy was struggling, Michel saw it as a timing issue only, though he admitted it would be difficult to remove Mukesh. René, as the head of the Seychelles People's Progress Front (SPPF), still had considerable control.

We had learned recently that Lieutenant Colonel Ciseau of the Coast Guard had been reassigned, which concerned us because of his importance to our naval ship visits. He was well trained on security matters, and his absence could change our thinking on recommending ship visits. Michel recognized my concerns but said that he needed Ciseau's talents elsewhere and had moved him to the Ports Authority, since there were many issues with the fishing fleet and problems with corruption in the operation. He emphasized it was a promotion, but I didn't feel comfortable: his temporary successor spoke almost no English, which made communicating about the current ship visits and the Coast Guard's responsibilities for port security problematic. I reminded Michel that they had the obligation to provide security twelve hours a day while ships were in port and to secure the dock and offshore areas. Since the Coast Guard had not shown up for the current two ship visits, U.S. Navy personnel had ended up undertaking the duty of twenty-four-hour security. The United States had spent considerable time and money on training programs in preparation for these ship visits, I said, and if security was inadequate, I would recommend that ships not stop in Seychelles. Visibly shaken by my remarks, Michel assured me he would personally look into the problem.

From there we drove to the dock where the U.S.S. *Hopper* was anchored. On boarding the ship, we were greeted by Commander Michael Selby and several other officers and taken on a tour. The seven-year-old, five-hundred-foot-long destroyer carried long- and short-range missiles and other attack hardware. After a conversation about the ship's recent deployment, I walked around and expressed my thanks to the enlisted personnel for their service.

Our next tour took place on the USS *Seattle*, which was anchored offshore, so we traveled there by helicopter and landed on the deck of the eight-hundred-foot supply ship. Captain Patrick Hall explained that the ship was more than forty years old and would be decommissioned in March 2005. The *Seattle* carried fuel, ammunition, food, and all sorts of sundry items, and its numerous forklifts and giant cranes made it look like a floating warehouse. We had lunch and toured the ship, allowing me to mingle with the enlisted personnel and thank them for their service.

Later that day, in talking with the manager at the hotel, I discovered we had a mutual friend in André Ciseau. I asked if he would contact him and see if he would have coffee with me at six-thirty the following morning. André and I met for breakfast on the veranda and he reassured me he had not been forced out. In fact, he said, the move was a positive one. The ports were in trouble, the fishing fleet owners were ready to move, and he needed to work with them to keep the fleet in Seychelles.

Ciseau did mention receiving a message from Michel suggesting we meet and discuss Coast Guard security for ship visits. He too was concerned about his replacement. He and Michel had agreed to promote several young officers, one of whom could do a good job as head of the Coast Guard and also spoke English. In any event, he did not want ten years of hard work building up the Coast Guard to have been for nothing.

On Sunday, October 24, President Azali arrived in Mauritius and asked to meet with me at his bungalow at the Trou aux Biches Resort. As usual, he greeted me warmly with outstretched arms: "My brother, how are you?"

Azali was pleased to say the National Assembly was working well in resolving the power- and revenue-sharing issues. He thanked me for setting up a meeting with Assistant Secretary Connie Newman, who seemed to be well informed about Comoros. He did want our help on the upcoming IMF meeting scheduled for 2005, at which the IMF planned to work with Comoros in preparing their budget, their goal being to try to get debt relief. In conjunction with an upcoming donors conference scheduled to be held in Mauritius in late 2005, he asked for U.S. participation. Comoros desperately needed debt relief, new loans, gifts, and new civil affairs projects, and he somehow believed I could help facilitate this.

Saying Comoros was committed to the fight against terrorism, he told me he had met with religious leaders, who had agreed to preach tolerance. All were against terrorism, he said. I thanked him for the update.

On October 28, I received a report indicating that, based on reports that Fazul might show up for a family wedding in Diego Suarez, near the tip of Cap d'Ambre in northern Madagascar, they had had a person under surveillance, but he turned out not to be Fazul. Although the man's identity was never confirmed, I believed the

22.9. Iftaar dinner at Macarty House, October 28, 2004. Vice President Raouf Bundhun in foreground at right; Ambassador Magda Hosni Nasr (fourth back on right).

look-alike might have been a plant to throw off the authorities, while the real Fazul, a master of disguise, went undercover to attend the wedding.

I hosted another annual Iftaar dinner at Macarty House with twenty-five Muslim community leaders and friends in attendance. The dignitaries included Vice President Bundhun; High Commissioner Sayed Hasan Javed from Pakistan, and Ambassador Magda Hosni Nasr from Egypt. I made some short remarks, including some quotes from President Bush's speech at the White House Iftaar dinner. Following this, several of the esteemed Muslim leaders emphasized that rededication to faith and charity to the needy were pillars of the holy time of Ramadan. Having many good Muslim friends with open hearts, I had great hope for broadening understanding within the Muslim community.

I believed it was important to share the U.S. national election experience with our host country friends—and with those who questioned the American way of life.

Hence, we held an Election Day breakfast at Macarty House and invited an eclectic mix of people. We had set up a giant-screen TV for CNN coverage of the presidential election, in which President George W. Bush was facing Senator John Kerry; there was also a smaller screen for BBC information via the Internet, and we set up a third for local coverage. Our staff decorated the veranda with colorful red, white, and blue decor, and James Liddle devised a large map of the United States on which he could color in red and blue as each state reported its electoral votes. To further involve our guests, we prepared mock ballots on which each could pick the winner and guess the number of electoral votes that candidate would receive.

At six o'clock in the morning on Wednesday, November 3 (nine o'clock Tuesday evening on the East Coast of the United States), I was glad to see President Jugnauth, several ministers, business leaders, community activists, members of the diplomatic corps, and other guests arrive. James was soon busily coloring in the map, and as it filled up, we could see it was coming down to Florida, Ohio, Iowa, New Mexico, and one or two other states. By eleven it was clear Ohio would be the deciding factor. We were all anxious, but the Ohio secretary of state came on television to say that there were still many provisional ballots and mail-in ballots to be counted. Without a decision, however, people started to leave, assuming President Bush would be reelected. It wouldn't be until later that day that Kerry conceded the election.

One small ray of hope emerged from our discussions with USAID when on November 4, Flynn Fuller and Yolande Miller-Grandvaux came to the embassy to discuss a planned assessment in Comoros. There was approval for an "American Corner" to be installed at the University of the Comoros, along with a funding allotment of $300,000 for specific projects that would be part of their assessment. Now we would just wait for the books, furniture, and equipment to arrive to launch this educational installation.

The American Corner was intended to serve as an information and resource center and as a space for conducting programs, including lectures, student advising, art exhibits, and professional development training. In September 2005, the American Corner was set up with the support of the State Department's Africa Regional Services, located in Paris, France, the primary source of French-language program material. The installation included computer access and a library for information about American culture and values.

Sunday, November 14, was the end of Ramadan, and a celebration of Eid ul-Fitr would be held that morning at Sunni Razvi Eid Gah, a mosque located in Vallée Pitot. I arrived at nine-fifteen for the service and was greeted by Vice President Bundhun and the Maulana. On Monday, a picture and story appeared in several newspapers showing our warm embrace at the event.

Later that day, we received information that Secretary Powell was resigning. Considered a moderate, he had been a key figure in the Bush administration and certainly would be missed by everyone at the State Department, including myself, an admirer of his many accomplishments and service to the country. It soon became apparent that, subject to Senate confirmation, Condoleezza Rice would replace him.

On November 16, the USAID team returned from their eleven-day assessment trip to Comoros and came to give us their readout. They had visited all three islands, met with their leadership and NGOs, and toured schools and hospitals. Whatever programs USAID undertook, they said, would be in conjunction with UNICEF. One area that was identified included tackling the malnutrition problem and involving the World Food Programme for help; others related to health services, education, and language training. For public awareness, Fuller wanted to involve the local radio stations to get out messages to the public. He also wanted to help with capacity-building methods for the NGOs. He suggested we keep pushing to get the Peace Corps back and seek Connie Newman's support, since she was the former assistant administrator at USAID for Africa and now was assistant secretary for African affairs at the State Department. After spending two years pressing for USAID involvement, I was encouraged by their observations.

Stephen brought me an article that had appeared in the opposition newspaper in Seychelles, indicating that the IMF mission had left Seychelles not pleased with the progress Michel had made on the rupee devaluation issue and access to open-market purchases. The article also said that the United States was considering handing Seychelles a diplomatic note threatening to withdraw all economic assistance unless there were concrete and verifiable economic reforms, not merely more promises.

On Wednesday, November 24, Minister Cuttaree and I held a joint press conference to discuss the AGOA III bill's final passage the previous weekend. With twenty members of the press present, I praised everyone's efforts toward its passage, especially those of Cuttaree, the Mauritian government's representatives in Washington, and the U.S. congressional leadership. Cuttaree also thanked everyone involved in the long process. In the question period that followed, I made sure to mention the benefit to Mauritius: an additional 60 percent of the goods produced would have access to the United States without a 17 percent duty. This included goods made from yarn sourced from outside Africa. Although the bill covered only a one-year period, from October 1, 2004, to September 30, 2005, it was a meaningful start, and would reverse the devastating downtrend in the textile sector, including a massive loss of jobs. (The Africa Investment Incentive Act of 2006—AGOA IV—did not continue to grant Mauritius least-developed-country beneficiary status. However, in 2008, HR 7222 did reinstate the benefits to Mauritius by extending the third-country fabric provisions.)

The next day was Thursday, November 25, and we again held our annual Thanksgiving luncheon at Macarty House for eighty American citizens living in Mauritius. That night I received a phone call from my son Steven to say that he was adopting a newborn African American boy whose father was Kenyan. This young lad had just won the lottery of life and would grow up in a loving family with the best of what life offers, as did our other grandchildren. What a Thanksgiving blessing Jackson was for our family.

Marcia and I flew to Washington, D.C., and on Monday morning, December 6, I met with Assistant Secretary Connie Newman at the State Department to give an update on post operations. I told her I wanted to see USAID resources and Peace Corps volunteers in Comoros, and said I thought the country would be best served by keeping it in the Mauritius portfolio, since I believed that by now she knew of the decision by the Bureau of East African Affairs to move it to Madagascar. On another matter, I suggested that we showcase Africa under the AGOA program by having the fourth AGOA Forum in one of the qualifying sub-Saharan African countries. Lastly, we talked about a White House message that had asked political appointees to stay at their posts until further notice. We both agreed that this meant until a new replacement had been selected and confirmed by the Senate, which could be as late as mid-June 2005. I agreed to stay since I had no other plans, and also wanted to finish several important projects the embassy had been working on for a long time. My concern was for the ongoing engagement of host country issues, and I was reinforced by the belief that some people in the Bureau of East African Affairs didn't share my vision of the needs in these countries, especially Comoros. I thought Connie understood where I was coming from.

On Sunday, December 26, Marcia and I were on vacation with our children and grandchildren when an undersea earthquake measuring 9.1 to 9.3 on the Richter scale created a huge tsunami. It affected Indonesia, Thailand, Malaysia, India, Sri Lanka, and the Maldives, and even reached areas of Mauritius and Seychelles as it roared across the Indian Ocean to the Somali coast, more than three thousand miles from the epicenter. The loss of life and damage was incalculable.

I quickly contacted Stephen Schwartz, my deputy chief of mission, who reported minor property damage in Mauritius and, from what reports indicated, two deaths and seven people missing in Seychelles. Property damage in Seychelles included one bridge and a stretch of road that had been washed away and damage to a port docking facility, building structures, and shoreline vegetation. I was ready to return to post, but it was determined that the worst was over. I asked Stephen to check with the respective government leaders to verify the exact extent of the damage. We would then apply for disaster relief. Since I would be in Washington in mid-January, I thought I could hasten the process, if necessary, while I was there.

From January 8 through 13, 2005, the guided-missile cruiser USS *Hué City* made a port visit in Seychelles. While there, the crew contributed more than three hundred hours of labor to help with the cleanup from the tsunami, removing tree branches and debris from the beach and roadways and clearing a youth soccer field. For this, the sailors should be commended—especially since they had just returned from active duty and were on the island for two or three days of rest and recuperation.

{XXIII}

Island Business in Washington, D.C.

Back in 2002 President Azali had requested I arrange some high-level meetings for him in Washington. After years of pressing the Bureau of African Affairs, others at the State Department, and the director for African Affairs at the National Security Council, I arrived in Washington on February 21, 2005, pleased to attend the meetings that had been set up for Azali. Though it was short of an official state visit, Azali would receive diplomatic security and VIP treatment the entire time he spent in Washington.

The long flights from Mauritius to Washington consumed more than twenty-four hours and after several trips could take a toll. As usual, my trusted limousine driver, Keith Minor, was prompt at the airport and dropped me off at the Ritz-Carlton Hotel, where I got a few hours' sleep.

Early Tuesday morning, I went over to the State Department to meet with Mark Zimmer, my country desk officer. We were to meet with Ismail Chanfi, the secretary general in the Ministry of Foreign Affairs, to review President Azali's two-day schedule.

I then met with Phil Carter, deputy director in the Office of East African Affairs, to get a better handle on how they viewed Comoros and its future. I had initially become acquainted with Carter when he was deputy chief of mission at the U.S. Embassy in Antananarivo and again when he visited Mauritius. At that time he spoke positively about our embassy's engagement of Comoros and commended the staff. Now he summarily announced that the Comoros portfolio was being moved to Antananarivo. The only rationale I could think of for moving the portfolio was that Antananarivo was closer to Comoros than Port Louis was; clearly they had not taken into account the embassy's three years of hard work engaging Comoros, any of the programs we initiated, or our opinion. And my question about the future of the programs currently under way in Comoros was greeted with silence.

Furthermore, the budget for Mauritius for 2006 would be cut back, eliminating three positions at U.S. Embassy Port Louis: the embassy's only economic officer as well as its information management specialist and the deputy chief of mission's office management specialist. In essence, the country team would be reduced to six Foreign Service officers—the same number that were there when I first arrived. Without a doubt, this would be a step backward. It would place an undue burden on the embassy staff and would affect proper representation of U.S. interests in this strategic region of sub-Saharan Africa.

I believe that in sub-Saharan Africa, the United States needs to be represented by a greater number of experienced citizen public servants from the private sector. This has been the history of service to our country, as was said by Thomas Jefferson in 1796: "There is a debt of service due from every man to his country, proportioned to the bounties which nature and fortune have measured to him."

Practical decision makers would help advance U.S. interests, oversee a meaningful and sustainable economic development agenda for poor countries, especially those at risk, and institute poverty eradication programs. In Muslim-dominated countries, a strong U.S. presence that helps give people hope for the future would also lessen the influence of al-Qaeda and other radical Islamic groups. Call it good business or humanitarian assistance, but we need to make friends in these countries. China's policy of noninterference in the internal affairs of other countries has won praise from corrupt leaders who welcome their foreign direct investment. U.S. businesses need to be given an opportunity to compete with tenacious Chinese enterprises that have entrenched themselves throughout sub-Saharan Africa to extract natural resources.

U.S. foreign policy may have served us well in the past, but in our competition with China, we will be trumped by our long list of conditions for democracy and transparency, and by the sanctions we impose when countries fail to meet them all. We need to engage sub-Saharan African countries while keeping in mind an understanding of our cultural differences. If we want to gain influence, we need to lower the bar on all the conditions we impose or we will lose out in sub-Saharan Africa.

The State Department has its share of bureaucrats who are neither practical nor proficient in business and lack management skills. I found many dwell more on their annual job critique and on turning in an over-the-top employee evaluation review, considered their ticket for advancement and a better choice of new assignments. I believe performance is affected since this process stifles creativity, thinking outside the box, and the willingness to take some risks in their jobs. I also learned that once bureaucrats move on from a post, most never check on the status of any unresolved issues. That simply becomes the next person's task to clean up. Of course, there were exceptions.

While at the U.S. Embassy in Port Louis, I found that the Foreign Service national staff consists of knowledgeable people who keep the embassy functioning. Generally members of the host country's local ethnic groups, they have a great empathy for the less privileged who live in poverty and lack education and health care. They also have firsthand knowledge of where we should invest our aid programs and which NGOs to support. The Foreign Service national staff is loyal to the United States and its principles. Since they are familiar with American culture and values, offering more scholarships in the United States for their children might lead to them becoming our best "ambassadors at-large" when they return home. Some may become leaders in their country; others may even be encouraged to become a second-generation Foreign Service national staff member at the embassy.

On Wednesday afternoon, February 23, I went to Dulles International Airport to wait for President Azali's arrival from Paris. As soon as he appeared, Azali embraced me warmly, asking, "My brother, how are you?"

While their passports were being processed, Azali told me that Mauritius had agreed to host the Comoros Donors' Conference in December 2005, per his discussion with Prime Minister Bérenger. I was happy for him, and said I hoped it would be well attended and backed by generous financial commitments by the wealthier Western nations, including France and the United States. When he was in Paris, Azali told me, he had met with President Chirac, who did promise some financial aid and would be represented at the conference. On his return trip to Comoros, Azali planned to stop in Libya to meet with Colonel Muammar Qaddafi to ask for some financial assistance as well.

Having been advised that certain issues would be brought up, we quickly reviewed the Treasury Department's stand on money laundering and the shell banks. This was a problem that mainly involved the island of Anjouan, and one that Azali hoped the Treasury Department could help resolve. Our conversation went smoothly, some of it in English, but mostly through his capable interpreter, Nailane Nakchamy, who had sat in on many previous meetings. Soon our motorcade was off, escorted by two policemen on motorcycles in front, followed by two Secret Service SUVs and two police cars in the rear. The usual one-hour trip into Washington took only twenty-two minutes. When we arrived at the front door of the Treasury Building, Stuart Levey, the undersecretary for Enforcement and head of the Office of Terrorism and Financial Intelligence, met us.

In the meeting that followed, Azali introduced his four advisors and spoke about his efforts to improve the financial situation of Comoros, with an emphasis on improving relations with the World Bank and International Monetary Fund. He was working on the Poverty Reduction and Growth Strategy Paper needed for the Donors' Conference to be held on December 7–8, 2005, as well as for the World Bank and IMF, and sought Treasury Department help with both agencies. Azali knew his mission in this document would be to set out development priorities for Comoros over the next several years. Moreover, Azali wanted guidance with economic development programs so that Comoros could move forward on the global stage.

The undersecretary explained the need to eliminate the shell banks before the Treasury Department would take a serious look at helping Comoros with any programs, and Azali asked the Treasury for technical assistance to help eliminate them. One of Levey's staff suggested Azali close down shell bank operations by revoking their licenses. Since most of these banks operated on Anjouan, whose president was not on the best terms with Azali, the situation would become more difficult; Anjouan badly needed this source of income for the island and would resist any change. (Later I would be given a list of more than two hundred shell banks that operated in Comoros, which I turned over to Azali. I wondered how many of those banks were linked to al-Qaeda and other Islamic extremist groups.)

Levey brought up the question of the Saudi-based al-Haramain Islamic Foundation and was surprised to learn Azali had already asked it to leave the country. At the meeting's end, Levey said he would try to schedule a visit to Comoros to review areas in which Treasury could be helpful.

The following day, I met Azali and his advisors at the Africare offices, located in a refurbished school building in downtown Washington. Africare's president, Julius Coles, chaired the meeting and briefed us on the organization's history. Developed by a small group of former Peace Corps volunteers in the 1970s, and now with USAID, the Gates Foundation, the Hilton Foundation, and the World Bank among its primary funding sources, Africare has grown into a worldwide organization. Africare focuses on agriculture-related matters and health care issues such as HIV/AIDS. Azali said the Comorian farmers needed help to diversify their products; on health care, he noted that in Comoros malaria was a larger problem than AIDS.

When asked how Africare could help Comoros, Coles explained the government of Comoros would have to invite Africare for a visit as the first step. I was encouraged by the prospect.

At a hotel conference center in Pentagon City, Deputy Assistant Secretary of Defense Theresa Whelan explained that the Department of Defense's interest in Comoros primarily centered on law enforcement on the three islands, and praised the Comorian security forces for maintaining law and order during the 2002 presidential elections. Stressing the importance of maritime security and cooperation, Whelan suggested that Defense would consider setting up a regional meeting in Comoros, wherein the United States and East African countries could discuss maritime security issues. Azali's face lit up at this suggestion.

While President Azali held a private meeting with World Bank and International Monetary Fund officials, it gave me a chance to break away to meet with Cindy Courville, the senior director for African affairs at the National Security Council, to discuss terrorist concerns in the region. When Azali joined us, Courville thanked him for his stand against terrorism. She felt strongly that the international community needed to have a better understanding of the plight of the Comorians. She reiterated that the fight against poverty was a key element in the war against terror.

Azali was proud of the new University of the Comoros, which provided a secular education that was an important step in counteracting radical Islamic teachings coming from outside the country. He wanted help for the University of the Comoros to train students who would make an economic difference. Courville was generally very supportive and suggested that partnering with an American university would help meet some of their needs, and she noted that the upcoming G-8 meeting agenda would include discussion on matters such as debt relief, poverty reduction, health care, and education, which might prove helpful to Comoros.

Afterward, Azali and I went to the Department of Homeland Security to meet with Assistant Secretary David Stone, who headed the Transportation Security Administration and reviewed the structure and function of his department for our benefit. Azali noted that transportation security was vital, going beyond borders and affecting economic development. He added that Comoros faced many challenges as a small island state and while he had set up a security department, it still needed more resources. He wanted to see security as a focus of the international transportation systems. In that regard, Stone explained TSA conducted visits to countries, shared information, and created vulnerability assessments and threat level analyses. Based on such assessments, TSA was then able to allocate resources as needed. Azali welcomed the idea of such a visit by Stone and his staff.

In the next meeting with the director of the Peace Corps, Gaddi Vasquez, and Henry McCoy, the regional director for Africa, terrorism was also a key issue. There were areas in which the Peace Corps could not operate for safety reasons, and if the Peace Corps was ever to return to Comoros, the first step would be an assessment visit. Vasquez said such a trip could happen when he and McCoy visited the region at midyear. (As of June 17, 2005, when I departed, an assessment team visit had not been scheduled.)

Just before Azali and I were to meet with Lloyd Pierson, USAID's assistant administrator of the Bureau for Africa, I was informed by the Secret Service that I would be excluded from joining Azali in the motorcade back to the airport, even though we were both on the same flight to Paris. I now had to leave before such an important meeting—just to beat traffic to get to the airport in time for the flight. I later found out from the State Department that USAID would send an assessment team to Comoros, with a focus on social services, particularly health care and education issues. Reportedly Pierson said he would ask his staff in Nairobi to explore whether it would be possible to fund courses at the University of the Comoros that would provide students with the necessary economic skills for job creation in areas such as agribusiness, fishing, and cattle farming.

When we met before boarding the Air France flight to Paris, Azali embraced me and said he was thankful for the meetings that had been arranged. He was optimistic about some of the commitments made going forward, and I really hoped the United States would not let him down.

After more than three years of working closely with their government leaders, I believed that Comoros had become a good candidate for U.S. aid and support. They had cooperated on every bilateral issue we presented to them. Several were critical issues for U.S. interests at the UN. I continued to press for Comoros's inclusion into the AGOA program until I left in June 2005, but to no avail. When after my departure the Comoros portfolio was moved to Antananarivo, engagement of Comoros all but ceased for a period of time, and the numerous country programs once actively pursued lay dormant. From reports and various interviews with Comoros government officials, I learned that the U.S. Embassy in Antananarivo could have pressed for Comoros's entry into the AGOA program sooner. Comoros lost precious years in which it could have benefited from developing its cottage industries. (I was pleased to learn that on July 1, 2008, Comoros got the recognition it deserved by obtaining eligibility status as an AGOA beneficiary. I hoped the United States would provide the mentoring necessary for them to quickly set up shop and gain access to American markets.)

On Friday morning, March 11, I quickly stopped at the embassy to pick up James Liddle as note taker and then went to the Royal Palm Resort to meet with President Michel, who was visiting from Seychelles as the Prime Minister's guest for the Mauritius National Day events. We discussed the December tsunami and noted that U.S. aid relief of $50,000 was coming to the Seychelles Red Cross, with another $100,000 tagged to help local fishermen, many of whom had seen their boats badly damaged.

We reviewed the progress of Seychelles's economic reforms, including the lifting of import controls and the privatization process, then spent considerable time talking about Mukesh's current status in the government. I was surprised when Michel said Mukesh was on his way out.

Michel was excited by a major oil company's new venture in exploration and offshore drilling. Since the geologic structures that underlie the islands consist of solid granite plates, I didn't think there were sedimentary formations where large amounts of oil deposits might be found, but I wished him well and hoped the country received a good exploration payment up front. As he was preparing to leave, I touched on two more issues: the injunction imposed on the *Seychelles Weekly* because of an article the SMB had claimed to be libelous, and reports of police brutality. Michel responded to the latter by saying he had appointed a trusted military leader to oversee the police force.

Back in my office, I was elated to receive a cable noting that out of forty-four posts surveyed, the U.S. Embassy in Port Louis ranked fifth overall in customer satisfaction, and our management section was given a commendation for outstanding performance. I shared the good news with the country team and Foreign Service national staff. This was a great honor for a Special Embassy Program post that was understaffed, had incurred many rotations and one curtailment, and had gone through several temporary duty officers.

One day I had the opportunity to visit the Industrial and Vocational Training Board Center in the town of Mahébourg, where the embassy had provided funds to build an air-conditioned room in which we installed twenty-four computers, one printer, and numerous desks and chairs. This center had been training people since 1989 for productive employment in commercial, technical, and vocational fields. Waiting for us at the center were one hundred young students participating in this alternative educational program and eager to access the Internet.

At the beginning of April I went to Johannesburg, South Africa, to attend a conference and several meetings, including an interagency meeting with representatives from Immigration and Customs Enforcement, the Drug Enforcement Administration, the Federal Bureau of Investigation, the Bureau of International Narcotics and Law Enforcement Affairs, and the U.S. Commercial Service. My request was for them to engage the host countries more by offering their expertise in needed training programs. All wanted to help, but funding in each department had been cut, as was the amount of travel. They agreed to consider visiting Mauritius to participate in a June 2005 conference on substance abuse prevention as well as the Indian Ocean Ports, Logistics and Shipping Conference that same month, and to focus on upgrading seaport and container security measures. I also thanked the FBI representative for his recent trip to Comoros, since counterterrorism was at the top of the list.

Following on the heels of this meeting was the two-day African Presidential Roundtable 2005, held at the University of the Witwatersrand in Johannesburg, honoring twelve former sub-Saharan African country presidents who were democratically elected. The roundtable also included invited guests from the diplomatic corps, government ministers, and public and private sector leaders. The program would continue for two more days of meetings in Massachusetts at Boston University's African Presidential Archives and Research Center. The theme of the round table discussions included: economic development, the need to open market access, democratic governance, freedom of the press, poverty eradication, and health care issues in sub-Saharan Africa.

Each president had a turn to speak. Former President Karl Offmann of Mauritius hit the nail on the head by saying he wanted Africa "to do for itself" and not look for charity. His advice to others was to start small, take one step at a time, and build the country's economy, as Mauritius had done, relying on its people as their country's resource. Emphasizing that many small projects would together build into bigger ones, he counseled Africa's nations not to look to others to solve the continent's

23.1. Former African presidents attending the African Presidential Archives and Research Center Roundtable 2005 Conference held in Johannesburg, South Africa, April 9, 2005.

problems. I thought his statements were very profound and brave, and I was not alone in that: a huge ovation followed from everyone present. Former President Daniel arap Moi of Kenya noted that when Africans fought colonialism, they had been fighting against a country, but the problem in Africa today was an internal one, that of tribalism.

The African leaders stressed that more attention should be given to the good aspects of Africa; also that the perception needs to change wherein people think of Africa as one country and combine all the problems together rather than individually. Each country wants to be judged for its own actions.

Continuing the discussion at the Boston University roundtable, Professor Adil Najam from the Fletcher School of Law and Diplomacy at Tufts University talked about the Millennium Development Goals for Africa. At a UN summit in 2000, 147 countries had agreed upon eight basic goals to be achieved by 2015: eradication of extreme poverty and hunger; achievement of universal primary education; promotion of gender equality and empowerment of women; reduction in childhood mortality; improvement in maternal health; progress in combating HIV/AIDS, malaria, and other diseases; environmental sustainability; and the implementation of a global partnership for development.

There had been insufficient progress in achieving these goals, Najam commented, and even if the goals were met, more than 500 million people would still be

23.2. Visiting with President Offmann at the African Presidential Archives and Research Center Roundtable 2005 Conference, April 9, 2005.

23.3. Former President Ketumile Masire of Botswana, Ambassador Price, former President Jerry Rawlings of Ghana, and Ambassador Charles Stith, April 9, 2005.

living on less than a dollar a day, without safe drinking water, and at risk of HIV infection.

Najam emphasized Africa was a global concern and needed more attention from the G-8 powers. When asked what the world could do to help, he responded that trade was the equalizer; aid was not a solution. He pointed out that the removal of European and U.S. subsidies on products and access to those markets by Africans was worth five times the amount of aid given to the continent.

Joseph Diatta, ambassador from Niger to the United States, detailed the New Partnership for Africa's Development (NEPAD) as a vision for Africa's renewal. NEPAD's framework document, formally adopted in July 2001, addressed issues such as escalating poverty, underdevelopment, and continued marginalization of Africa. Although it did not explicitly address the current issue of debt cancellation, Diatta said he believed Africa was on the right track, and concluded by saying Africa needed to work on its image and highlight some of its accomplishments in conflict resolution, democracy, transparency, and free and fair elections.

With few exceptions, the discussions by the former African country presidents were interesting—after all, during their years of rule, most had been part of the problem we were now trying to solve together. Speaking from a new position and moving beyond the past, they were able to offer new, meaningful solutions to help Africa move forward. It would require educating new young leaders who had integrity and a vision for the people of Africa beyond their own greed.

In Mauritius on April 22, the Muslim community celebrated Eid e-Milad un-Nabi, the 1,479th anniversary of the birth of the Prophet Muhammad. Maulana Shah Ahmad Noorani Siddiqui of Pakistan, who had presided over the previous year's celebration, had died, and the guest of honor at this year's festivities at Aleemiah College was his forty-year-old son, who would carry on the tradition.

There was an enthusiastic crowd of more than thirty thousand people. Men crowded into the tent, and women sat in the sun-drenched adjacent field. The diplomatic corps sat in the second row, behind the government ministers. The entire ceremony was conducted in Arabic, Creole, and French, but when it was the younger Siddiqui's turn, he spoke in English as well, for which I was grateful. His words were of peace, family, and brotherly love, and emphasized that terrorism is not a part of Muslim life.

Later that day, I was pleased to learn that Colonel John Strudwick, from the Combined Joint Task Force–Horn of Africa in Djibouti, would be assigned to our embassy until mid-June to help in a mission for our three host countries referred to as "Winning the Hearts and Minds of the Local Population." A month earlier, he had mentioned that CENTCOM wanted to help in consolidating Comoros into its portfolio. We had discussed disaster response, relief, and preparedness, and how to engage in port assessment activities. An interesting idea he put forth for Comoros was sending in a C-130 aircraft with drilling rigs to find sources of potable water. Such an effort would have long-lasting effects since many of the open storage areas used to hold runoff water had been contaminated by the ash fall from the recent eruption of Mount Karthala. He suggested I call General Sam Helland and ask for this humanitarian assistance as well as any surplus defense supplies that could be given to Comoros. USAID would be involved as the recipient of the surplus supplies, and they in turn could ask to have them shipped on the same aircraft. It was a great idea—if it worked, I said. And since we would soon be going to Seychelles, we could bring up this issue in one of our meetings with General Abizaid.

Arriving in Mahé as planned on Tuesday evening, April 26, I immediately went to the Fisherman's Cove Hotel, ready to retire after a long day. At nine-thirty the next morning, James Liddle and I met with the military advance team to review the schedule for General Abizaid's visit. James and I then went to meet with the Chamber of Commerce Board. It was great to hear that there was generally more transparency and that import license restrictions for most items had been lifted, so more goods were available, though hard currency shortages meant they were often very expensive. Concerns still centered on how privatization would take place and how transparent the process would be, and several board members expressed doubt as to the sincerity of the people involved. They believed privatization and other economic advances had been proposed only to obtain support from the World Bank.

The board brought up the January 2005 oil exploration deal signed by the government with an offshore company. They voiced concern about control of the country's mineral rights being moved from a direct government agency to what they referred to as a "free-wheeling entity," the Seychelles Petroleum Company, that was not subject to public scrutiny. The concern was that if this entity was privatized, it could give away ownership of all of Seychelles's mineral rights. The conjecture was that Mukesh and René somehow had their hands in this action.

That night, Commander Catherine Ripley, the defense attaché, and I greeted General Abizaid, his wife, Kathy, and several officers traveling with him, including British Commander A. V. M. Heath and Ambassador John Holzman. We resumed our frank conversation about the global dangers the al-Qaeda network presented. The general looked stressed, but asked if his senior staff had given me any indications of assistance in Comoros. My mention of Helland's assessment visit pleased him.

During an early breakfast strategy meeting the next day, I again brought up the need for more engagement of sub-Saharan Africa by the United States, and issues in my host countries. General Abizaid was supportive of the idea to send a C-130 with water drilling rigs, and we also discussed obtaining desperately needed military

23.4. Attending the Seychelles Chamber of Commerce board meeting, April 26, 2005.

surplus items, which could be shipped on the same flight. I thanked him for the $300,000 in tsunami preparedness funding that CENTCOM had committed to Seychelles.

We then met with Colonel Léopold Payet. In an open exchange, we covered diverse subjects such as the proposed tsunami preparedness funding, spare parts for Coast Guard vessels and equipment, IMET programs, disaster management training, transiting of potential suspect individuals, money laundering, fishing violations, ship interdiction, maritime security, and radical elements in the area.

In a meeting with the new Minister of Foreign Affairs, Patrick Pillay, and his principal secretary, Claude Morel, we added other issues for discussion, including the continued control on the sale of passports to foreigners, concerns over drug flow from Kenya, Tanzania, India, and Pakistan, and the economy.

At State House for a meeting with President Michel, General Abizaid presented the $300,000 funding for the tsunami preparedness program. Thanking him, Michel stressed his continued support of the United States. He talked about the economy: reforms were under way, and the privatization process would be transparent. Currently the government was working closely with visiting World Bank and IMF representatives to implement their suggestions regarding these issues. I commented that Seychelles had signed the Article 98 agreement, and early on had signed on to the global war on terror, at which Abizaid nodded and smiled in approval. Abizaid discussed our mutual cooperation in military training, invited members of the Seychellois

23.5. General Abizaid, Colonel Payet, and Ambassador Price, April 28, 2005.

23.6. Ambassador Price, General Abizaid, Minister of Foreign Affairs Patrick Pillay, and Ambassador Claude Morel, April 28, 2005.

23.7. Meeting with General Abizaid and President Michel, April 28, 2005.

military to attend training seminars in Djibouti, and spoke of security concerns with our ship visits.

Michel asked me to set up a meeting in Washington with President Bush. When I explained I might be leaving by early summer, he was taken aback for a moment, and expressed some concern about my leaving at this juncture. I agreed to pass on his request to Washington and keep him posted on my departure date.

Vice President Joseph Belmont hosted a luncheon for General Abizaid and his entourage. Joining us also were Foreign Minister Pillay, Mrs. Belmont, Kathy Abizaid, and Commander Ripley. In his toast, Abizaid thanked Seychelles for its cooperation on matters in the region. Belmont made a toast to Abizaid in which he expressed appreciation for the interest the United States had shown in Seychelles.

On Thursday evening, I arranged for us to have dinner at La Scala, the best Italian-style seafood restaurant on Mahé. During our dinner conversation, I spoke of my concern about the areas of responsibility between CENTCOM, PACOM, and the European Command (EUCOM) operations within the sub-Saharan Africa region. At times I believed we were not on the same page with the rotation of senior officers and liaison personnel. I explained that PACOM and CENTCOM were like neighbors who cut their grass to what each thought was the boundary of the yard, with the result that a strip of overgrown grass was left to grow in between. In our

23.8. At the La Scala Restaurant on Mahé, April 28, 2005. From left to right: Kate Mancham, Sir James Mancham, Ambassador Price, and General Abizaid.

region, I believed the enemy knew that a gap existed and used it to its advantage in operating throughout the area. I thought sub-Saharan Africa was important enough to be covered by one unified command. From Abizaid's reaction, I got the impression this issue had already been discussed. I hoped I hadn't touched upon a sore spot.

As the evening was winding down, Abizaid asked his staff to gather around as he made a presentation. To my surprise, the general complimented me on my work and presented me with a CENTCOM hat, an ornamental knife, an engraved pen, and the special commander's coin.

Before General Abizaid left, he told me he didn't mind my frank conversation covering a wide range of issues, and offered to look into ways in which CENTCOM could help Comoros with surplus hospital supplies and equipment, and possibly with some infrastructure projects.

On Friday morning, I had breakfast with Lieutenant Colonel André Ciseau, one of the smartest military leaders in Seychelles, who headed up the Ports Authority. Describing current needs, Ciseau listed container scanners, metal detectors, a K-9 training program, and drug interdiction training. Construction-related items were also mentioned, including a new long pier for both large naval and commercial cruise ship visits. I mentioned the tsunami preparedness program, which would include him. He was on top of the security issues and gave me great confidence that the ports were well protected within the limitations of the resources available to him.

Later that morning, I had a private meeting with Foreign Minister Pillay. Sitting opposite from me and looking very stern, he came right to the point. He wanted me to arrange for President Michel to meet with the highest-ranking people at the State Department, Treasury Department, and the Department of Defense to determine how the U.S. government could help to stabilize Seychelles's situation, as Michel couldn't do it alone. Pillay then shifted to a discussion of the visiting World Bank and IMF representatives who were supposed to be helping Seychelles find a way out of its severe financial problems. The IMF, he noted, was ready to wash its hands of Seychelles. I agreed to alert Washington and get back to him. Once back at the hotel, I asked James Liddle to work up a cable to Washington regarding the potential situation unfolding in Seychelles and the requested meetings for Michel.

On Saturday at the airport, I was introduced to James Bond—don't laugh—of the World Bank, who with other members of his organization and some IMF representatives had been here for a week. Bond said they had reviewed outstanding debt restructuring, privatization, and monetary revaluation and candidly told the government representatives he had doubts they would undertake the steps needed to resolve their problems. I told him my feelings were the same and expressed my concern that René would not let Michel put the necessary measures into effect.

On May 2, I spoke again with Assistant Secretary Connie Newman about submitting my resignation to President Bush. Generally after a president's first term ends, political appointees are asked to resign so other candidates can be nominated. I mentioned mid-June, which would give the White House personnel office enough time to have another ambassador nominated. I told her it was a hard decision for me to make. I felt that in my three-plus years in this position, I had accomplished many of my objectives—though many others remained to be completed. Whether I stayed another two or three months was not the issue, since the real goal was to carry out the promises we had made about helping the people in the host countries. She agreed to check with the White House and get back to me.

In the meantime, I was disheartened to hear from Boeing's Miguel Santos on May 3 that though his team had worked diligently for well over a year to sell two airplanes to Air Mauritius, he had been told the contract had been given to Airbus. I commended him for the work he had done and told him that the presentation and factory visit Boeing had put together were first-class and not a reflection on him. I also told him that I believed the decision had been made weeks before, when Barclays Bank had been approached for financing.

Following through on my discussion with General John Abizaid, I sent an email to General Sam Helland regarding humanitarian assistance for Comoros. I knew the Combined Joint Task Force's responsibility was primarily Seychelles, but I also believed Comoros must be given the highest level of attention in consideration of the broader region. Bringing in the drilling equipment we had talked about would both provide safe drinking water to people in need and demonstrate in a very public way that the United States was interested in helping. This would also serve as a reward to President Azali for having closed the Comorian branch of al-Haramain Islamic Foundation, which had funded, among other things, drinking water projects. While Comoros was technically in PACOM's area of responsibility, I hoped that a goodwill exception could be made. It would go a long way in the eyes of the Comorian people.

In early May, I tendered my resignation to President Bush and scheduled my departure for June 17, 2005. I was finally relieved, but also sad and concerned about the fate of all the programs that the embassy had worked so hard on. Before leaving, I would have a complete road map put together regarding continued engagement of the host country issues.

I was very pleased to hear that after two years, our request to add a local-hire employee for Comoros had been approved. On May 11, it was with great pleasure that I welcomed Bacar Hamadi and reviewed his role representing U.S. Embassy Port Louis in Comoros. In addition to consular matters, Bacar would also spend two days a week at the American Corner at the University of the Comoros. Our purpose in having him in Comoros was to serve as a local interface and to help with visa and passport issues—otherwise, Comorians would be stranded unless they came to Mauritius. Having Bacar there would also cut down the processing time for Comorians wanting to enter the United States, and he could answer questions that an automated telephone recording in English could not do. Further, any visiting American citizen would have someone local to communicate with in the event of an emergency.

I received word from General Sam Helland that he was leaving and turning over his command to Major General Tim Ghormley. I was thankful that General Helland had asked General Ghormley to visit with me soon after the Commander's Conference with General Abizaid. General Helland did not see PACOM objecting to CENTCOM's engagement of Comoros with aid assistance. He felt confident they would be able to find the right approach to engage Comoros and assist in capacity building and core competencies, helping Comoros become a partner in the struggle against terrorist activity.

In mid-May, Major General Ghormley introduced himself to me as the new commander of the Combined Joint Task Force–Horn of Africa and offered his assistance in obtaining aid for Comoros. PACOM had no problem with their engagement, he said, and asked only to be kept informed. It was reassuring when Ghormley offered to send one of his engineers and civil affairs representatives in order to expedite any assistance they might be able to provide by coordinating on the spot. Invited to Comoros to partake in their July 6 Independence Day celebration, Ghormley wanted to spend some time touring the islands to gather information.

Near month's end, I again corresponded with General Ghormley reviewing my travel plans to Comoros, but had not yet divulged it would be my final visit to the islands; I knew that the Comoros portfolio would soon be moved, but I didn't want that to affect the task force's efforts. Given the lack of response from the other agencies I had spent time with in Washington, CENTCOM was one of the more promising prospects for Comoros, but only time would tell if they would actually come through with any resources or programs.

I would be going to Comoros May 29–31 primarily to let President Azali know that I would be leaving permanently as the U.S. ambassador effective June 17, 2005. The embassy staff was well aware of all the contacts made and initiatives under way in Comoros and knew what needed to be done in terms of follow-up—at least until the portfolio was moved over to Antananarivo.

Holding what would be my last All-Hands Awards ceremony for our embassy staff gave me the chance to thank them for their efforts and achievements during my posting there. The loyal Foreign Service nationals were the backbone of the embassy—without them, the embassy could not function. None of the nine Foreign Service officers there that day had been present at the embassy when I arrived; yet I had worked closely with all the staff, considered them friends, and was proud there were so many award certificates to hand out.

In a scheduled meeting with Prime Minister Bérenger, he wanted me to know I would be missed, and I appreciated his comments. When he asked about my plans after leaving Mauritius, I said I would be meeting up with my family in Arusha, Tanzania. We had plans to visit the island of Zanzibar as well as several other countries. Bérenger advised against going to Zanzibar, as during the run-up to the October elections numerous street demonstrations would take place. I thanked him, adding that the State Department had given me a similar message.

In saying goodbye, I reassured Bérenger that the embassy would continue to follow through with programs instituted through the State Department and other agencies, and brought up congressional support of the AGOA III third-country fabric provision extension needed beyond September 2005.

On Monday, May 23, Kelly Hopkins, my office management specialist, sent out diplomatic notes to each host country and personal letters to government leaders informing them of my impending departure; letters also went to members of the diplomatic corps. Stephen and I then reviewed my departing archival cable.

During my time in Mauritius, I had become fond of Soopaya "Baby" Curpen, a Mauritian who was the honorary consul general for Israel. Curpen had spent many

23.9. Passover dinner in Mauritius with Stephen Denton of Adamas Diamonds and David Harris of Answer Plus, among other participants, April 23, 2005.

years acquiring a site and raising money for Amicale Maurice-Israel to build a synagogue and meeting center. He was the leader of an amazing group of Mauritians, some of whom had studied in Israel but were not Jews. These individuals celebrated the high holy days and other festivals throughout the year along with Jewish transplants from around the globe who had settled in Mauritius. Many could even cook kosher-style foods. And they all displayed great loyalty to a country and a faith that they had adopted in their hearts.

The event celebrating the fifty-seventh anniversary of the independence of Israel coincided with the official opening of the synagogue facility, which was attended by almost fifty people. The event had great community support, including the Mayor of Curepipe, where the synagogue was located. Ambassador Yoram Elron, director general for Africa, came from Jerusalem. The attending diplomatic corps members included Magda Hosni Nasr, Tony Godson, Ian McConville, and Dominique Renaux. The Jewish community business leaders present, who were also donors, included Owen Griffiths, Steve Denton, Andrew Slome, and David Harris. The music provided by the Mauritius Police Band added a nice touch to the event. I had purchased some prayer books and also contributed to acquiring a Torah for their small dedicated prayer room.

Having escaped with my family from Germany during the Holocaust, I was determined to make a difference in the United States, the great land of opportunity. My Jewish faith became subordinate to my patriotic devotion to the United States.

23.10. At the Amicale Maurice-Israel dedication with Soopaya "Baby" Curpen, May 23, 2005.

Living in Utah, where Jews were in the minority, was similar in many respects to living in Mauritius, and so I understood the importance of this small house of worship. The few Jewish families in this island nation had come from many different countries with different cultures, but their common bond of Judaism had created a close-knit support group. And to some degree, it helped me rediscover my roots.

On Wednesday, May 25, I received a cable reporting voter registration violence in Stone Town, the capital of Zanzibar, and news that gangs associated with the political party Chama Cha Mapinduzi had engaged in random beatings in and around the capital. Since I was planning to go there with my family in the near future, I immediately started asking around among my contacts to determine what risks we might be facing.

I continued to meet with business and community leaders in Mauritius and members of the diplomatic corps to discuss my departure. And on Sunday, May 29, 2005, I went to Comoros for the last time before my scheduled departure.

⟨ XXIV ⟩

A Time for Goodbyes

Moniza Gopaul, the bilateral assistant at the embassy who oversaw the Ambassador's Special Self-Help Program funds, accompanied me on this last trip to Comoros on May 29, 2005. Ismail Chanfi from the Foreign Ministry, whom by now I knew well, met us on our arrival. After a short while I learned that my bag had not followed me to Comoros, so I would have to wear the same clothes—slacks and a sport shirt—to all my upcoming meetings on this hot and humid day. While the search for my luggage got started, we were off to the Galawa Beach Hotel, which had been remodeled and reopened by a new South African operator.

As we had on many other occasions, we drove to our hotel at speeds exceeding 80 mph on narrow and rough roads through several small villages. It was a dangerous and dizzying ride, and Moniza kept her eyes tightly shut until we got to the hotel. I realized that once back home I was going to miss these wild drives.

In the hotel's small gift shop, I found a toothbrush, soap and shampoo, deodorant, and a T-shirt for sleeping. Happy with my good fortune, I fell asleep shortly after reaching my room and on the following morning slipped back into the previous day's clothes, hoping no one would notice.

When Bacar Hamadi joined us, our driver took us inland to the town of Mohoro. Again at excessive speeds, the car climbed up the volcanic mountainside along barely passable roads toward the other side of the island. Several times, heavily loaded trucks passed by so close they almost forced us into the rocky outcrops along the side of the road.

Mohoro is a small village hidden away in the hills. Reportedly it was used as a training area for the terrorist Fazul and other al-Qaeda members, but as we drove in, we were greeted by a group of women and young girls singing. Overhead was a sign: "Mohoro and the Population Welcome You, Mr. Ambassador." It was inspiring, everyone dressed up and singing with such joy.

Behind this lovely chorus, village elders stood looking somber but curious. I wondered how I would interact with them, but soon enough we were engaged in long, friendly handshakes and shared smiles. I was invited to sit on a makeshift

24.1. Comorians waiting for taxis in Grande Comore, May 29, 2005.

24.2. Warm welcome at Mohoro village, May 30, 2005.

24.3. Mohoro village women and young girls greeting Ambassador Price with singing as curious villagers look on, May 30, 2005.

stage with rows of well-worn plastic chairs set up in front of the stage area for the men to sit. Separated from the men, the beautifully dressed women stood on the side singing cheerfully while shaking handmade tambourines and drumming on empty cans. The senior village elder, the mayor, and visiting Finance Ministry official welcomed me in French. From the sound of the applause, their remarks showed an appreciation of my visit.

As for me, I was delighted to inaugurate a domestic science classroom project that had used some of our Ambassador's Special Self-Help Program funding and was intended to help young women to develop skills that would allow them to find work. We contributed cooking equipment, dishware, other kitchen items, several sewing machines, a television set, and audio and video equipment, which had been set up in the nearby school building. Several girls were already demonstrating their sewing skills. As poor as the villagers were, after the tour they shared with us fruit drinks and baked goods. We then spent an hour driving around Mohoro so I could become familiar with the area before heading back.

At the hotel, I was told the airline would not ship unaccompanied luggage. So before heading over for my official meeting with President Azali, I quickly showered and put on the same clothes I had been wearing since my arrival. When we arrived at the Presidential Palace compound, Ismail Chanfi smiled at the sight of me in my

24.4. Mohoro village reception program, with village elders sitting in the front row, May 30, 2005.

24.5. Mohoro village school sewing class program, funded by the Ambassador's Special Self-Help Program, May 30, 2005.

travel clothes. We were ushered through the archway lined with soldiers to the President's office.

President Azali and I went into his inner office accompanied only by Nailane Nakchamy, his personal assistant and interpreter. Azali expressed disappointment that I would be leaving my post, and mentioned his appreciation of an article published in the *Ambassador's Review* that to him proved again my commitment to promote the image of Comoros abroad. He then told me actions had been taken with the aim of putting an end to the presence of shell banks in Comoros.

My main goal for over three years had been to help Comoros become a democratic state—to witness the country move through a transitional period of setting up institutions and holding elections that would lead to stability. I had hoped that I would be able to help get Comoros on to the road of prosperity. Certainly it would happen soon—I was only sorry I wouldn't be there to witness it. Still, I told Azali that I would depart with good memories of him and the Comorian people. We embraced, and I reassured him I had prepared a cable for the State Department to follow up where we had left off.

As we walked together to a waiting audience of more than one hundred invited guests in the garden area, I suddenly realized how underdressed I was for this occasion. I tried to conceal my embarrassment as Azali complimented my service as ambassador. He went on to say this ceremony was the opportunity for all of us—Comorians and friends—to pay tribute to my work.

24.6. The ambassador's farewell event, with Comorian government leaders, dignitaries, community leaders, and other guests, at the Presidential Palace, May 30, 2005.

24.7. President Azali, as Grand Master of the Order of the Star of Anjouan, promoting Ambassador Price to Commander of the Order, May 30, 2005.

To my surprise, Azali presented me with a medal and promoted me to the grade of Commander of the Order of the Star of Anjouan, the highest honor bestowed by the President and the third ever presented. I was moved as Azali placed the medal around my neck. I then mingled with the audience, greeting many of the government and business leaders I had worked with for over three years, along with several members of the diplomatic corps.

Azali introduced me to the Grand Mufti of Comoros, Said Toihir Ben Said, the highest-ranking religious leader in the country. He was an educated, soft-spoken man, and his English was quite good, so we were able to communicate without an interpreter. He told me that he liked America; that he had read books about Roosevelt, Eisenhower, Kennedy, and Reagan; and that he stood for peace and democracy. I was pleased by his remarks of friendship, especially given the country's history of radicals in their madrassas and mosques and the large presence that al-Haramain had had in the country. I believed the Grand Mufti had been a balancing factor in the country.

My next visit took me to the military headquarters to see the new English Language Lab, with equipment provided under the IMET program. The $65,000 funding was for state-of-the-art equipment, soundproof partitions, workstations,

24.8. Ambassador Price with Said Toihir Ben Said, Grand Mufti of Comoros, May 30, 2005.

high-quality lighting, and finishes for the laboratory. This facility would help many Comorians, including members of the military, as they learned English.

On leaving I asked my driver to find an open clothing store. The shop we located in Moroni was about to close, but I rummaged through the few barren racks and found a pale blue short-sleeved shirt (made in China) and a pair of socks. I would never have imagined feeling such joy over a purchase like that.

In another visit to the University of the Comoros, we were greeted by the vice president and guided into a freshly painted room set up for their IT education program. The Ambassador's Special Self-Help Program had funded two computers, a printer, and a video projector to kick off the program. In a formal presentation ceremony attended by dignitaries and members of the diplomatic corps, I announced a personal contribution of three additional Dell desktop monitors and keyboards and one more printer, which would be delivered to the university in late June. In addition, for the biology lab, I personally contributed five microscopes. Both donations were farewell gifts to the university and the Comorian students. (I would eventually learn that by 2006, the university's student population had grown to 2,450 students; as of 2010, more than 4,000 students attended the University of the Comoros.)

24.9. Last visit to the University of the Comoros to meet with administrators and professors and to donate computers, printers, and microscopes, May 31, 2005.

On my last morning in Comoros, I had a meeting set with Foreign Minister Souef El Amine. On the way as we drove along the route, people came out of their homes and shops and saluted the American flag. They had become familiar with my presence, and I began to believe they appreciated what we were trying to do to help their country. Since my previous visit, I also saw that a Chinese contractor, financially supported by his government, had completed a new building and donated it to the Foreign Ministry.

On arriving, Souef was glad to see me, but expressed concern that with my departure the good work that was under way might not get completed. I assured him the embassy was committed to continuing what we had started. He wanted a representative from the United States to attend their July 6 National Day event, and I told him that the new CENTCOM commander in Djibouti would be coming over for the event and to get acquainted.

Deep down, I was of course concerned that with the State Department's shifting the Comoros portfolio to the U.S. Embassy in Madagascar, Comoros might not get the attention our embassy had been giving them. Souef and Azali had both become friends, so I hesitated to share my feelings.

On the way to the airport, I asked the driver to slow down. I wanted to enjoy this island for the last time. The old lava flows, the glorious vegetation, the colorful half-finished houses, and the stretches of sandy beach along the rocky coastline had grown on me. The young women in brightly colored *shiromani* dresses and the men in pure white gowns and embroidered caps made a picture that a thousand words cannot describe.

Off in the distance, I could see a vague outline of hand-hewed fishing boats balanced by their outriggers heading back with their catch. Yes, I would miss Comoros—and yet as appealing as it appeared to me, it was also appealing to Fazul and other terrorists as a potential safe haven.

On June 3, I sent a cable to the State Department, copying the other pertinent agencies, entitled "Departing Remarks by Ambassador Price." I hoped it would serve as a wake-up call to those agencies as I concluded my appointment as United States Ambassador to the Republic of Mauritius, the Union of the Comoros, and the Republic of Seychelles.

On Monday, June 6, I paid my last courtesy call on Deputy Prime Minister (and Minister of Finance) Pravind Jugnauth. The son of the former Prime Minister and one of the founders of the country, Sir Anerood Jugnauth, Pravind had risen through the political system to be his party's leader. He thanked me for embracing Mauritius and for helping them on a number of issues. I remarked that their success was also our success and that Mauritius had created a good democratic model to be followed by other sub-Saharan African countries.

Saying goodbye to Foreign Minister (and Trade Minister) Jayen Cuttaree was bittersweet. Marcia and I had become good friends with him and his wife, Swatee. In fact, Jayen and I had been connected at the hip for almost three years on AGOA issues, which had worked out well for Mauritius and saved their textile industry.

When I met with Vice President Raouf Bundhun, he thanked me for helping him with his literacy program. His chief of staff took me aside as I was leaving and told me that Bundhun enjoyed my friendship. Bundhun was a moderate Muslim who lived his faith and believed in fairness and tolerance for other people's beliefs. He constantly advocated for the betterment of Mauritian society, focusing on its future—the children who would be the leaders of tomorrow.

I wanted to avoid the normal protocol of government leaders, members of the diplomatic corps, and business owners hosting farewell events. Although I succumbed to a few such gatherings, I preempted most by inviting all these people to a farewell party at Macarty House.

The wonderful Mauritius Police Band played American songs and included Marcia's favorite, "Blueberry Hill." As was the custom, each member of the diplomatic corps chipped in to buy a piece of original art as a lasting memory. I chose a local fishing boat scene that we unveiled for everyone to see.

We were happy to see Prime Minister Paul Bérenger, Vice President Raouf Bundhun and his wife, Asma, and Foreign Minister Jayen Cuttaree and his wife,

24.10. Members of the diplomatic corps at the farewell event at Macarty House, June 11, 2005.

Swatee. They spoke of our friendship, the embassy's involvement with the AGOA legislation, the highly successful AGOA Forum in 2003, and the great honor of meeting President Bush.

I commended the country for the democratic road it had taken since independence, the quality of its people, and its high level of education and rich cultural mix. Turning to Mauritius's four major economic pillars, sugar, textiles, tourism, and financial services, I said they would continue to serve the country well. I was delighted the country was moving ahead nicely with its cyber city and information and communication technology sector, and now delving into the duty-free island concept.

On the lighter side, I said we would miss the afternoon rains, the winding roads where everyone drove down the middle, and how on this small island it took an hour to go anywhere. Most of all, I said, we would miss the warm and hospitable people. "I came here as a businessman," I said. "You have taught me the art of diplomacy, and for that I thank you. I promise I will be back."

On Monday, June 13, I went to State House in Réduit to pay a final courtesy call on President Anerood Jugnauth and deliver my letter of resignation to him. I then met with the leader of the opposition, Navin Ramgoolam, at his residence in Vacoas. In the middle of an election campaign at the time, Ramgoolam, who had been Prime Minister from 1995 to 2000, would be elected Prime Minister again on July 5, 2005.

In keeping with my open-door policy of meeting with government leaders, community leaders, religious leaders, and business leaders, I had also felt it was important to engage with the political opposition leaders in each of the three host countries, and so my first meeting with Ramgoolam had taken place on February 3, 2003. He was accompanied by Chitmansing Jesseramsing, a former Mauritian ambassador to the United States and United Nations. I had found Ramgoolam interesting and pleasant, and his goal was quite clear—to regain power. Although our conversation was testy at times, we got along well. We again met during the 2004 African Presidential Roundtable held in London, at the Boston University Kensington campus, and had a lively discussion on political issues in Mauritius.

At what would be our last meeting while I was ambassador, Ramgoolam introduced me to David Ginsberg, from Washington. A former strategist in Senator John Kerry's 2004 campaign, Ginsberg was advising Ramgoolam on his campaign. Then Ramgoolam launched into stories about when his father, Seewoosagur Ramgoolam, was the first democratically elected leader of Mauritius. One involved a state visit by his father to meet with President Nixon and Secretary of State Henry Kissinger. At the time of their meeting Nixon was distracted by the ongoing impeachment proceedings. As Prime Minister Ramgoolam thanked Nixon for the U.S. tracking station in Mauritius, Nixon suddenly looked concerned, then scribbled a note on a piece of paper and handed it to Kissinger. Later Ramgoolam discovered that the note had said, "What the hell are we doing having a tracking station in enemy territory?"—evidently Nixon had thought Ramgoolam was the leader of Mauritania.

Another story involved the ouster of James Mancham as President of Seychelles. As the number two man and head of the military, René visited Mauritius and mentioned to then Prime Minister Ramgoolam that a coup was a possibility. Ramgoolam called Mancham and warned him, but Mancham dismissed the possibility. Of course, on June 5, 1977, while Mancham was attending a Commonwealth meeting in London, he was deposed and did not return to Seychelles until the early 1990s.

Navin Ramgoolam also told me that his father had wanted the U.S. presence in Diego Garcia because it served as a deterrent to Communist ambitions in the region.

Before I left, Ramgoolam pulled out a brochure from the 1970s that had on its cover a picture of a young Bérenger and René flanked by military officers with AK-47 assault rifles. One of those officers was James Michel, current President of Seychelles. What a treasure this document was, I told Ramgoolam, as part of the history of the early independence era of both island nations.

I really enjoyed this meeting, and wished I had spent more time with Ramgoolam during my posting in Mauritius.

Back at the embassy, the Foreign Service national staff hosted a farewell luncheon for Marcia and me and again showed their hospitality with delicious home-cooked

James Michel armed with an AK47 on June 5ᵗʰ 1977, largely responsible for the current gun culture existing in Seychelles today

24.11. Photo taken at a local radio station in Mahé, Seychelles, on June 5, 1977. From left to right: James Michel, Guy Sinon, Paul Bérenger, Jacques Houdoul, France Albert Réné, and Ber[l] Louis. (Courtesy Cerean Newspaper)

specialties. It was nice to spend some social time with them and highlight their many accomplishments, their strong work ethic, and their high level of professionalism. Despite working in such a small post, they were dedicated to the goals of the embassy and community involvement. At every level, they were eager to participate—from helping with outer-island cleanups and charity events to setting up and participating in American cultural programs. I expressed my gratitude to them for making my job easier with their can-do attitude.

At my last country team meeting, I expressed my appreciation to all for their efforts on behalf of U.S. Embassy Port Louis. Stephen Schwartz, my deputy chief of mission, had a wide smile on his face as he handed me a cable stating that the Department of Defense, working through the State Department, was going to provide foreign military financing for maritime security to Comoros in the amount of $480,000 and for Seychelles in the amount of $250,000. What a great surprise this would be for both countries—and what a nice going-away present for me.

Leaving the embassy to drive home, I saw a triple rainbow—a good omen, especially given that day's news about funding for Comoros and Seychelles.

That evening, our good friends Sunil Hassamal and his wife, Kiran, hosted a dinner for Marcia and me at La Ravin in Moka. Sunil owned Shibani Textiles with partner Earle Saks, who came with his wife, Gillien. They had also invited Linda Mamet, an American expatriate active in community affairs who had been living in Mauritius for more than twenty years, and her friend Ilan Asbet, who had emigrated

24.12. Farewell luncheon given by the Foreign Service national staff at the embassy, June 13, 2005.

24.13. The country team, May 11, 2005. From left to right: Ambassador Price, David Walsh, Hava Hegenbarth, James Liddle, Kelly Hopkins, Kevin Lee, Marjorie Harrison, Ellen Brooks, DeWitt Conklin, Judith Semilota, Stephen Schwartz.

from Israel and was in the diamond-cutting business. Several members of the diplomatic corps, including High Commissioners Pripuran Singh Haer, Ian McConville, and Tony Godson, also joined us. Again, there were many toasts with good wine and fond memories.

Early on the morning of Thursday, June 16, 2005, as the packers were busy emptying out Macarty House, Marcia and I sat on some wood crates with Cassam, Luc, Danie, and Fifi, who all had made living there very enjoyable for us. The four of them were a good team, always on top of our every need. Even as we sat there, Cassam had a cup of tea for us. We couldn't thank them enough for caring about us. We gave each a letter to use as a reference for the incoming ambassador.

At ten o'clock that morning I held my last press conference, at Le Suffren Hotel. As I gave my farewell remarks praising Mauritius and its people, the sadness of leaving overwhelmed me. During the question period, the press couldn't help but ask again if Diego Garcia housed prisoners from the al-Qaeda terrorist group, to which I responded with my standard line: "We use Diego Garcia only for ship and aircraft missions." They also asked about the Kyoto Protocol, which the United States had refused to sign. I responded that our President was very conscious of the environment and that we were working on an accord that was agreeable to all. On the multifiber renewal issue, which was a concern, I said I believed there would be an extension; however, I suggested the government have its diplomats go to work on meeting with the U.S. Congress and Trade Representative. Finally, one brave writer asked whether the outcome of the elections here would change the relationship with the United States. I assured him it would not as long as the vote was free, fair, and transparent. At times over the previous three-plus years my relationship with the press had been strained, with some reporters stretching the facts, though others tried to be fair. I did thank all the members of the press that day for attending my departure briefing. Afterward, during coffee and dessert, I spent time shaking hands and wishing each of them well.

Back at the embassy, I met with Judi Semilota, our management officer, and Shirley Fok-Man, our financial assistant, concerning ongoing care for Tigar. I decided to leave a year's worth of rupees for the cat's food, medical, and dental care. Since I did not know when the next ambassador would arrive or if the cat could continue to stay at Macarty House, Cassam agreed to care for him, since he too was fond of Tigar.

On my departure, Stephen Schwartz would serve as chargé d'affaires until the next ambassador came to Mauritius. Stephen had grown as my deputy chief of mission and showed some good leadership qualities. I knew he would take care of the people at the embassy. He promised to follow through on the programs we had started in the host countries, which were important to these countries. Above all, I wanted him to continue our engagement of Comoros, even though the portfolio was in limbo.

At the last meeting with most of the staff present, the room fell silent, some people were teary-eyed, and I had to stop to regain my composure for a moment.

24.14. Presentation of the American flag by Stephen Schwartz, June 16, 2005. The retired flag was one that had flown over the embassy.

They were the best team an ambassador could have, and I knew I would sorely miss them.

Stephen presented me with a retired American flag, which had hung over the embassy, and a large picture taken by Neddy Chan Pin of the downtown area, which included the embassy building, with everyone's signature around the edges.

Then, with the American flag flying from the mast on the ambassador's vehicle, we arrived at Prime Minister Paul Bérenger's office in the Treasury Building. Inside, MBC television and photographers were waiting for our arrival. Bérenger and I had become good friends, so we were able to talk freely about many subjects. He expressed great satisfaction with the embassy's involvement in Mauritius and how we had dealt with numerous issues in Comoros and Seychelles. He emphasized that the AGOA multifiber extension would have a long-lasting benefit for Mauritius.

I briefly mentioned having seen the 1970s brochure with the picture of him on the cover. He said he had had to live with the fallout of that for a long time.

In closing, Bérenger said he was sorry to see us go, embraced us, and welcomed our return anytime.

Once my desk was cleared at the embassy, I sat quietly looking out the window at the harbor below, watching the ships coming and going. On the way out I saluted

Suresh Hurdowarsing and Karl Rouxelin, our embassy local hire security guards, and the two Mauritian police officers assigned to the embassy, and said goodbye before disappearing into the elevator for the last time.

On the morning of June 17 I was up early checking the computer for any last-minute messages. Ahmed and Cassam loaded up the car with our overweight luggage, and I went out to the garden looking for Tigar. Spotting me, he came running and jumped into my arms, wanting to be rubbed in his favorite spot under his chin. When I stopped, he started meowing loudly and followed me around, sensing we were leaving.

When I got back to the car, Cassam was waiting with a cup of tea in hand. With the flag flying on the fender mast for the last time, we passed through the front gate. I saluted the two waiting security guards and glanced back at Macarty House and the beautiful gardens. And Tigar was nowhere in sight.

On arriving at the airport, Marcia and I lingered to say goodbye to Ahmed Boodhooa, who had been our loyal and trusted driver since we arrived in Mauritius. He had always been there when we needed him and had made certain we were safe at all times. He had become part of our extended family.

Inside the airport Stephen Schwartz, Magda Hosni Nasr, Ian McConville, and Tony Godson were waiting to give us a diplomatic corps send-off. We enjoyed some

24.15. Bird's-eye view of downtown Port Louis from Signal Mountain.

coffee, light conversation, and a last group photo. Soon our Air Mauritius flight was called, and we embraced our good friends one more time.

When the doors of the airplane closed behind us, reality set in—my time serving as U.S. ambassador had come to an end. As we took off, our eyes were glued to the landscape—the sculptured volcanic peaks, the fields of sugarcane, the white sandy beaches, the azure water, and the coral reefs that ringed the island. Within minutes the plane ascended into the clouds, and Mauritius was gone.

⟨XXV⟩

Keeping in Touch with the Host Countries

Mauritius

After my return to Utah, I realized how much I really missed Mauritius and knew I would return again as a visitor regularly. As it turned out, over the years I have been back to Mauritius four times to visit friends and conduct interviews for this book with current and former government leaders from all three host countries.

During my return visits I made it a point to stop by the U.S. embassy to say hello and host lunches for the staff. I even carried packages back to the United States to mail to the Foreign Service national staff's children attending colleges and universities in North America.

On my last trip, in June 2008, I spent time with my successor, Ambassador Cesar Cabrera, who was nominated as U.S. ambassador to Mauritius and accredited to Seychelles on June 6, 2006, and arrived at the U.S. Embassy in Port Louis on October 20, 2006. We had met in early 2006, and I spent time mentoring him on embassy and host country issues during the confirmation process. The ambassador was from Puerto Rico, and as it turned out, we had many mutual friends from the time I jointly owned a major television station and production studio in San Juan, from 1974 to 1980. We also shared many friends through our political support of President Bush. We soon became good friends and corresponded regularly.

The embassy had an excellent Foreign Service national economic and commercial specialist who kept current on business-related issues in the host countries and in the surrounding region. On my visit in April 2007, I was told that many sizable economic development projects were under way in Mauritius in partnership with China and India. The United States had also made some modest program cooperation available in the commercial sector with the signing of the U.S.-Mauritius Trade and Investment Framework Agreement in 2006.

25.1. With Prime Minister Navin Ramgoolam, 2007.

I also continued to stay in touch with government, business, and community leaders in Mauritius, Seychelles, and Comoros. As part of this book project, I was interested in their continued success and stability in this important region of sub-Saharan Africa. I remained concerned about the possible influx and transiting of potential suspect individuals since the Indian Ocean islands were considered soft targets and potentially safe havens for terrorists.

On Monday, December 8, 2008, during a conversation with a person having knowledge of the region, I mentioned Jeffrey Gettleman's article on Somalia that had appeared in the previous day's *New York Times*. Gettleman quoted Rashid Abdi, a Somali analyst at the International Crisis Group, as saying that "hard-core fighters from the Comoros, Zanzibar, Kenya and other neighboring Islamic areas . . . will eventually go home, spreading the killer ethos. . . . 'The whole region is in for more chaos.'"

This individual then shared with me a recent occurrence at the airport in Mauritius, when four suspicious-looking men with Danish passports were detained on their way to Australia. It was eventually determined that these individuals had gone to Syria, where they had obtained fake Danish passports. From there they traveled to Denmark. Then they went to Paris, where they boarded a plane to Mauritius. On arriving, each went to a different immigration and customs counter, so they would not create any suspicion. They then converged and went to a small hotel in the north of the island, where they stayed for two weeks. When they went back to the airport to continue on to Australia, they made the mistake of going to the Air Mauritius ticket counter together. When none of them could communicate in English, the agent became suspicious, and they were held for questioning. It was an alert ticket agent who had stopped them—not the immigration authorities, who in fact had allowed them to slip into the country. Similar situations had occurred on several occasions while I was posted there. What these men's real purpose had been in traveling to Australia on fake passports, one can only surmise at this point, but it is possible that a rogue operation was their intent. Such incidents are likely to become more frequent with the tension mounting in Somalia and other parts of the Horn of Africa and East Africa.

SEYCHELLES

After completing my service as U.S. ambassador, I stayed in touch with Sir James Mancham, the former president of Seychelles. He kept me informed on the islands' happenings and the highlights of his speaking events around the globe.

On May 13, 2007, I visited with Mancham, who was in Washington to speak at a May 16 conference. His presentation was entitled "American Leadership at a Time of Global Crisis with Particular Emphasis to China's Rise Within the Asia Pacific Rim." He was kind enough to share his prepared remarks with me, and several pertinent sections in his speech caught my attention:

> I cannot allow the opportunity to pass without saying a few words about the U.S. decision to close down her embassy in Seychelles after the Cold War ended and about my continued protests at this "penny wise–pound foolish" decision which projected the view that the U.S. was not seriously interested in international diplomacy and the well-being and sensitivities of small-state nations.
>
> It is ironic that today the most prominent embassy in Seychelles is that of the People's Republic of China. At the time of our independence, a visionary China chose not to lease premises like the United States did but to buy and build something which would impress. Today on [Mount] St. Louis overlooking the Port of Victoria . . . the red Chinese flag proudly floats for all to see. There is not one single American flag, which once provided that certain feeling of pride and comfort to American citizens

who came as tourists, . . . to be seen in the whole vicinity. And as if to demonstrate that China agrees with me that no country is small if it is surrounded by the sea, the President of the Republic of China, President Hu Jintao, leader of over 1.3 billion people, made it a point on the 9th February 2007 to pay an official visit of 48 hours to Seychelles, a nation with 80,000 people, with the message that China will never be "a fair-weather friend" and with a cheque for 20 million dollars.

The American people are understandably conflicted and in an introspective mood, engaged in a national debate on the next step forward—but this is no time for the U.S. to withdraw from a policy of global engagement.

With the power at its disposition the United States has a profound influence on the international system and many of its component parts. Yet, in protecting U.S. national security, idealist claims are not substitutes for realistic and honest analysis or for courage on the part of policy makers to act upon it in the national interest, partisan pressures notwithstanding.

Earlier, on February 6, 2007, Mancham had made similar remarks to United Press International in Mahé, just before President Hu Jintao of the Republic of China made his official visit to Seychelles. China had a growing interest, both economically and militarily, in sub-Saharan Africa and the Indian Ocean region, as reflected in Mancham's remarks:

> President Hu Jintao of the People's Republic of China will pay an official state visit to the islands after a tour of eight African countries.
>
> For China, each country Hu visits will be to reaffirm negotiations for raw materials, energy supplies, aid assistance, debts forgiveness, and negotiations, which is aimed to secure China's quest for global positioning.
>
> China needs a military base in the Indian Ocean. It is considered that the Seychelles has the best global position for her need in Africa and the Indian Ocean region.

Strategically located in the Indian Ocean, Seychelles had become a member of the Small Island Developing States (SIDS), a group of nations that was gaining influence and becoming a dominant force. Mancham mentioned that many of the world leaders he had talked with had similar feelings regarding U.S. foreign policy in dealing with these small island nations around the world.

Currently fifty-two SIDS exist, of which six are located in sub-Saharan Africa, including Seychelles, Mauritius, and Comoros. These small island states are remote and subject to natural disasters, have small populations, are dependent on imports, and struggle to implement sustainable economic development. Even with trade preferences, some of these states lack the resources to take advantage of manufacturing opportunities. China, however, has taken an active interest in engaging these small island states on a political, economic, and military level.

In the case of Seychelles, the country had focused mainly on destination tourism and the fisheries sector. Even without a manufacturing base, under a free market economy Seychelles could rank among the top SIDS. The potential is there for a successful template if President Michel and his government decide to run the country under democratic principles of transparency and free themselves from the heavy weight of the René administration.

For President Michel, 2007 proved to be a banner year for breaking the political chains of the past, which had hampered his performance. In early February, it was reported that he had parted with Mukesh Valabhji, whose lack of transparency had reportedly led to corruption in dealing with state assets.

During President Hu Jintao's official visit to Mahé in February, he established some far-reaching economic agreements and left $20 million to show his good faith. Hu also promised follow-up meetings with some of his top ministers and military leaders to further solidify their agreements.

In June 2007, it was reported that Emirates Hotels and Resorts had agreed to invest $253 million on a 22-acre site to build a 416-unit beachfront complex. At the signing ceremony, Sheikh Ahmed bin Saeed Al Maktoum stated, "Seychelles is truly a paradise and one of the world's most beautiful locations." Reportedly, they and other Middle East Arab countries have had investments in the outer islands for a number of years.

In September 2007, I invited Mancham to be the featured speaker at the John and Marcia Price Lecture Series in American Foreign Policy at the University of Utah and the Ambassador John Price and Marcia Price World Affairs Lecture Series at Westminster College in Salt Lake City. His timely message was entitled "American Leadership at a Time of Global Crisis." The event was covered in the September 25, 2007, *Deseret News* article entitled "U.S. Warned Not to Neglect Africa." On his return home, Mancham forwarded to me an email he received from a colleague responding to the newspaper article:

> I just read the *Deseret News*, Utah, paper, which handled your speech and discussion on Communist China's long arms in the Indian Ocean and intention to increase greater military presence in the region. Congratulations on delivering the message to the United States in no uncertain terms. I believe the message has been heard clearly and without fuss.
>
> I personally believe you have done our country, Seychelles, a great service of immeasurable value. Ironically, while you arrived in Utah to deliver this message to Ambassador Price and other Americans, Colonel Leopold Payet of the Seychelles People's Defense Forces had just arrived

in Beijing, negotiating and coming to agreement on behalf of the Seychelles government for more China-Seychelles military cooperation in the Indian Ocean region.

The press in Seychelles was silent on this meeting of the colonel in China, because the SPPF knows that the people of Seychelles cherish their liberty.

Seychelles are entering a new day on the global stage, which hopefully after a long chapter under René's autocratic rule, since the 1977 Marxist coup d'état, will not now put Michel under the domination of China.

Reportedly, there was continued concern that René would not let go of the power he holds over the ruling SPPF political party, for if he did so, he, Mukesh, and other insiders could be pressured to return the money and assets they amassed in schemes over the years. Most Seychellois are hopeful that eventually Seychelles can repatriate what they consider to be illegitimately appropriated assets for the benefit of the future generations of these beautiful Indian Ocean islands.

Comoros

On August 31, 2005, shortly after my departure as U.S. ambassador, I received a letter from President Azali, who wanted to meet with me while he was attending the meeting of the United Nations General Assembly that September. He wanted to discuss the upcoming Donors' Conference in Mauritius, planned for the coming December. I had spent time with President Azali on some poverty reduction and growth strategy issues, and was disappointed that my recovery from a recent hip operation kept me from that meeting. However, Azali's representative at the UN, my friend Mahmoud Aboud, and I kept in contact and discussed issues of concern. I was especially concerned that moving the Comoros portfolio out of the U.S. Embassy in Port Louis would not be beneficial for Comoros; I feared that programs initiated during my posting could be curtailed.

Today, Comoros remains at a crossroads. In desperate need of sustainable development programs to eradicate poverty, the country's hardships allow for continued influence by outside fundamentalist preachers who are integrating themselves into the villages. Although some classroom construction and clinic rehabilitation have taken place by the CJTF-HOA Civil Affairs team, much-needed hospital equipment, supplies, books, and lab items are still desperately needed. And while some military interface and training programs, as well as educational programs, have been helpful, they have not adequately prepared Comoros to become a meaningful partner in the global war on terror or to deal with the infiltration of terrorist factions in the region.

25.2. With Comorian President Ahmed Abdallah Mohamed Sambi, September 2009.

As noted throughout the book, with a permanent American presence in Comoros, we will better understand the importance of these islands that lie in the Mozambique Channel, a main passageway for oil tankers and other cargo container ship traffic to and from the Middle East. Our limited engagement of this fragile democracy is not the answer—it is merely a Band-Aid on a puncture wound.

❨XXVI❩

The Engagement of Comoros

When U.S. Embassy Port Louis started to take an active interest in Comoros, after my arrival in April 2002, the influx of some of the radical imams and certain activities of the al-Haramain Foundation had somewhat lessened, from what I was told by government leaders. Our embassy officers visited Comoros on a consistent basis, which I believed had a dampening effect on the foreigners' activities there. My engagement of President Azali developed into a close friendship and trust between us. We further built trust with his ministers and two of the island presidents by meeting with them on our visits there.

I had often worried about the loss of goodwill between our countries since the closure of the U.S. embassy in Comoros. In late October 2002, the United States showed no interest in participating in the reconciliation process between the Union and island authorities. Because we did not send a legal expert at that time to help craft meaningful language into the constitution under which the Union would function as a democratic state, the Comorian government relied on legal advice from France, and we lost a chance to develop a closer relationship with Comoros.

I recall reading a March 2002 State Department report called "Comoros Human Rights Practices: 2001." This report was problematic because of its timing: information that might have had some bearing on the situation in 2001 was stale by 2002. In developing countries, one year can make a big difference in their governance and human rights practices. So much had changed in a short period, with the elections and reconciliation between the islands and the government, that all the work I had started for new aid and programs for Comoros was affected. I asked my deputy chief of mission to review the report and have the embassy file a current status report; otherwise, no U.S. agency—such as USAID or the Peace Corps—would consider providing the much-needed help we were seeking for the country.

I wondered what effect the belated State Department report on Comoros's human rights practices had on World Bank officials, as when I met with them in late January 2003 they said Comoros lacked democracy and transparency in spite of the country's recent elections. In addition, it was reported that President El Bak of

485

Grande Comore received most of his financial support from Sudan, which raised concerns about the islands' stability. The World Bank officials concluded there was no real way they could help Comoros at that point. I disagreed, although I wondered if they might possibly have more credible information than we at the embassy had. (After I left in mid-2005, the World Bank finally gave consideration to Comoros for its efforts toward democratization.)

I continued to think the State Department should have been more supportive in championing such a small Muslim country struggling on the road to democracy as we envision it. It was bewildering to hear everyone's take on what democratic steps Comoros had to achieve as a precondition for the United States and international agencies to financially engage with it. All I could say was that the country was trying to overcome more than a quarter century of instability, and Comoros needed help from the United States if it was going to move forward and survive as a democracy. At the time, sanctions were in place, and there were many conditions Comoros would have to meet before it would even be eligible to compete for the limited funding that was available.

Other countries did not impose such pre-condition barriers. On January 6–7, 2004, Chinese Foreign Minister Li Zhaoxing, who was on an African tour, visited Comoros and signed a financial agreement for €1.8 million—and this was in addition to a previous disbursement of €4.6 million. On April 29, 2004, Saudi Prince Al-Waheed gave $1 million to assist the energy sector in Comoros. On October 8, 2005, the Libyan government made a donation of 115 million Comorian francs ($250,000) to assist the University of the Comoros.

The Donors' Conference was held in Mauritius on December 8, 2005, as scheduled, with Prime Minister Navin Ramgoolam serving as the co-chairman of the event. My former deputy chief of mission, Stephen Schwartz, attended the conference, and wrote on December 11, 2005:

> I met with President Azali on Saturday for over an hour. He was in Mauritius for the Comoros Donors' Conference, which went as well as could be expected. . . . Azali very much wanted me to give you his regards. He said he and the bilateral relationship miss you. He was very genuine; you should be quite flattered.

During my posting as U.S. ambassador, I had befriended Mahmoud Aboud, who under President Azali's administration was the chargé d'affaires of the Permanent Mission to the United Nations. Subsequent to the Donors' Conference, Mahmoud sent me a detailed recap of the commitments made there. Twenty-one countries and twenty-nine organizations participated. The government of Comoros presented their Poverty Reduction and Growth Strategy Paper outlining a four-year plan comprised of thirty-five priority programs, beginning in 2006 and running through 2009. The total budget envisaged for the realization of these priority programs was U.S. $500 million.

According to Mahmoud, some of the donors specified in-kind aid programs, while a larger percentage of the donors pledged cash. Of the $200 million pledged, $140 million was in cash. Among the donations:

1. South Africa pledged $1.7 million.
2. France pledged $100 million, with assistance being directed specifically for rural development, health care, and multiple sector economic development.
3. The World Bank indicated that Comoros was eligible for additional International Development Association resources of $10 million in grants over two years.
4. The European Union pledged $55 million in subsidies over four years.
5. China would complete the expansion of the Moroni International Airport, supply of equipment for civil protection, offer tariff preferences for certain Comorian goods, and forgive the total amount of its loans to Comoros.
6. India pledged aid of $1 million for the creation of a professional training center.
7. The Arab League pledged $4 million for an electrification program and $1 million for the projects listed in the Action Plan of 2006–9.
8. The Arab Authority pledged $1 million for agricultural investment and development.
9. Algeria pledged money for teacher training, scholarly programs, textbooks, and training in the fields of jurisprudence and law enforcement.
10. Egypt pledged $24 million for construction of a medical clinic, the salaries of medical doctors, equipment, and student scholarships, and additional funding for training and deploying experts necessary to help with the implementation of the Action Plan.
11. Qatar pledged $1.5 million and forgiveness of Comoros's debt.
12. The African Development Bank pledged a contribution of $7 million and a reduction of Comoros's debt obligation by 69 percent ($24 million).
13. Mauritius pledged an interest-free line of credit of $1 million for importing goods and services from Mauritius and would provide technical help in the agricultural and health care sectors.
14. The United States pledged $2.6 million for training professionals in the community development and national security sectors.

On August 19, 2006, Iran—with a long history in the region going back to Persian traders of the fifteenth and sixteenth centuries—signed a financial cooperation agreement with the Comorian government covering various fields, especially defense and agriculture.

The Chinese government was the most proactive foreign country in Comoros and was rewarded on October 27, 2006, when the Chinese oil company Sinopec was given the exclusive rights to conduct oil exploration in the Comoros archipelago. Then, on May 17, 2008, Chinese Deputy Minister for Trade Gao Hucheng came to Comoros to inaugurate the Moroni-Hahaya airport, built by a Chinese contractor, and to boost economic cooperation between the two countries.

When I learned the Comoros portfolio was slated to be moved to the U.S. Embassy in Antananarivo, I wondered about its future. Madagascar is the fourth-largest island in the world, more than one thousand miles long and four hundred miles wide, with a 2003 population of seventeen million people living below the poverty level. By comparison, the largest island in the much smaller Comoros Archipelago is twenty-five miles long by twenty miles wide, and at the time the country had six hundred thousand people across the three islands living below the poverty level.

On October 24, 2004, James McGee officially became the U.S. ambassador to Madagascar. I first met the ambassador, a career member of the Foreign Service, during the Senate confirmation hearings in November 2001, when he was nominated for Swaziland. When I saw him again during the October 2004 Chiefs of Mission Conference held in Washington, he had become the ambassador to Madagascar—and later would also become ambassador to Comoros.

I remember talking with McGee on the margins of this conference, suggesting we get together to discuss some common issues. Since more than eighty thousand Comorians were living in Mahajanga on the northwest coast of Madagascar, considerable traffic took place between the nearby Comoros Islands, which I believed could become a security problem. Adding to my concern were reports of Fazul visiting there on a number of occasions.

Though McGee said he was agreeable to a meeting, Stephen Schwartz, my deputy chief of mission, tried unsuccessfully to reach him to arrange a time either at his embassy or at ours. Since we were the only two ambassadors covering the Indian Ocean region, a critical area in the global war on terror, I was disappointed. Mutual dialogue on in-country security issues would enhance our intelligence in these countries and add to our knowledge base.

I had assurances from the Office of East African Affairs that a complete file on Comoros would be made available to Ambassador McGee. The Bureau had received all the reporting cables relating to our engagement of Comoros beginning in 2002, so continuity and follow-up should not have been an issue, but I worried that it would. There were those in the Bureau who considered Comoros a distraction. Radical imams came and went in Comoros, and they would certainly know when the United States is taking an interest in their presence or had the will to challenge them—as was done with the expulsion of the rogue Saudi-based al-Haramain Foundation. Yes, moving the Comoros portfolio to Madagascar gave me concern.

One could ask why the United States should be interested in such a small, poor Muslim island nation in the Indian Ocean. How could it make a difference? The answer lies in the example of Fazul Abdullah Mohammed, who received radical Islamic indoctrination and training in madrassas in his hometown of Moroni from extremist imams, some of whom reportedly came from foreign countries. After the United States closed the embassy in Comoros in 1993, we had no viable way to gather intelligence information, including about the large influx of imams from Pakistan, East Africa, and the Middle East.

Radical Islamists seek safe havens in low-key areas where they can blend in, such as the Somali fishing village Ras Kamboni, Lamu in Kenya, and the small islands off the coast of Africa: Zanzibar, Pemba, Pate, Mafia, Socotra, and the easily accessible Comoros, where security is lax. Our need to maintain an American presence in all the countries was paramount then, and still is now.

Mahmoud Aboud and I met on several occasions whenever I went to New York or Washington for meetings and consultations, and after my departure from Mauritius on June 17, 2005, he became my ongoing link to Comoros. In 2006, under the administration of Ahmed Abdallah Mohamed Sambi, Mahmoud continued on as chargé d'affaires and later, in 2009, became the ambassador at large of the Comoros to China, Japan, South Korea, and Thailand. We had often discussed the possibility of setting up an economic development project in one or two Comorian villages, funded by the Price Family Foundation, in conjunction with CHOICE Humanitarian, a Utah-based NGO that had village projects in Kenya.

During one of our meetings in New York, on November 8, 2006, I asked for his observations on the 1993 U.S. embassy closing there, and how it had directly affected Comoros.

Mahmoud's response to these questions reinforced my belief that the United States was shortsighted and did not understand the dangers of the Islamic extremist movement. He said that he had reported the strange movements of people in and out of Comoros to the State Department more than once in the mid-1990s, but we did not heed his warnings.

Frank and open in responding to my inquiries, he clearly expressed his friendship for the United States. He also voiced disappointment that his small country didn't have the available resources needed to eradicate poverty and address needs in health care, education, and sustainable economic development.

J.P.: What were the consequences of the U.S. embassy closure in Comoros?

M.A.: If the U.S. Embassy were there, they would have seen all the activities going on. I knew something was wrong since I saw a movement of many foreigners coming and going.

J.P.: Who were these foreigners and how did they get to Comoros?

M.A.: Most of them came through Mauritius from parts of Pakistan and East Africa. At the time, there were no direct flights between Comoros, Tanzania, and Kenya, but they could easily travel from Mauritius by plane, and many came. The strange part was they weren't living in the cities, but out in the villages. They had their own agenda, and hid from city life so they wouldn't be seen. But you could see them coming and going out of the country.

Several months before the bombings of the Nairobi and Dar es Salaam embassies in 1998, Mahmoud went to the United States, where he called the State Department and talked with Charles Gurney, a desk officer in the Bureau of African Affairs who covered Tanzania, Kenya, and Comoros.

J.P.: What happened?

M.A.: I told him about these strange activities in the region and said that the U.S. should look into Comoros. If it were not taken care of now, it could be bad for the region or the whole world. He didn't take my advice into consideration because, he said, this was not part of the present foreign policy of the State Department. He didn't seem too interested in what I had to say, because he told me he was being transferred anyway. I thought he said to South Africa, but I am not sure. As far as I know he never followed up, nor asked me to put any of this in writing to him, which I would have done.

Mahmoud's remarks were reinforced by an August 4, 2002, BBC News article recap, "Kenya Hunts for al-Qaeda Fugitive," which noted that the man who had led the investigation into the Kenya bombing, Major Marsden Madoka, said that "Kenyan intelligence passed on information to the U.S. embassy ahead of the attack in 1998, but it was not acted on." Madoka went on to say, "The failure may have been due to a lack of communication between the embassy and U.S. intelligence agencies."

J.P.: How did foreign imams live once they were in Comoros?

M.A.: They spoke English [Comorians understand French, some Swahili, and even some Arabic], slept in mosques, and had their own agenda. I wondered how they could sustain themselves, or who is supporting them. Had there been a U.S. presence at least we could have some notion of what is going on around Comoros, but no one was there to see or to look at the situation.

J.P.: What is your opinion about the departure of al-Haramain, the Saudi Islamic foundation, from Comoros?

M.A.: The U.S. came and put pressure on us to pull out al-Haramain. Well, al-Haramain was doing something that not any other country in the world has done in Comoros. They built mosques, madrassas, orphanages, other buildings, water systems in the villages, and other infrastructure projects. Al-Haramain graciously did this work without being paid back, since it was a donation. They would still be building now if we had not asked them to pull out, without any conditions attached. But when the U.S. government asked us to pull al-Haramain out, we moved them out because we saw that it could be a threat for the country and for the region. We respected your wishes and waited to see what would happen. The U.S. didn't replace anything that al-Haramain did for us. We accepted it without [having] anything and without regret—but the Comorian people haven't. They saw that al-Haramain built schools and other projects that the U.S. never did. Coincidently, one of the main buildings of the new University of the Comoros was originally a mosque and madrassa built by al-Haramain.

J.P.: What did Comoros feel about the U.S. pressure to sign the Article 98 nonsurrender agreement?

M.A.: They knew of negotiations with the U.S. by some countries who got special agreements for aid, by signing the Article 98 agreement. We accepted that as a friend. I don't know if we were naive, or just accepted it because we were told to do so. It created confusion because we already were signatory to the Rome Statute of the International Criminal Court, which only needed ratification by the members of our parliament. Some of these members refused to ratify the bilateral agreement with the United States under Article 98, which granted immunity to any U.S. troops from potential prosecution by the ICC. They wanted instead for us to be a member of the ICC. Finally we ratified the Article 98 agreement because we were told if we didn't sign the agreement we would not receive any U.S. military assistance. As it was, with the Section 508 sanctions in place, we did not get any military assistance after signing on, or any other aid.

J.P.: What are the consequences of the State Department's decision to move the Comoros portfolio to the U.S. embassy in Madagascar?

M.A.: Even though we have a good relationship with Madagascar, I think Mauritius was the perfect place and could devote more time to our needs. The issues in Mauritius are much less than in Madagascar, which is a huge, poor country with lots of its own activity demands. Most likely the U.S. programs and activities will be absorbed by Madagascar with little left for Comoros. With project needs in both Madagascar and Comoros, I think Comoros will be forgotten. But it has only been six months, so I will see what will happen going forward.

J.P.: What can the United States do to improve the lot of the people, and make some positive inroads to help the country progress, since aid alone is not the answer?

M.A.: Ecotourism and resort projects using U.S. ingenuity would help the people in the villages find work. The return of the Peace Corps to work in the villages would help—[as would] English education courses, school equipment and textbooks for the university, more computers for Internet access, aid in business formation and investing, help to diversify our economy, poverty alleviation programs, and a social habitat program to build housing for the poor. In the late 1980s, the Peace Corps was one of the most successful programs and admired by many Comorians. On several occasions, both President Azali and later President Sambi requested the U.S. government to reestablish this program in the Comoros. Promises were given and several observation missions by U.S. authorities visited the Comoros but until now Comorians are waiting for the Peace Corps [to return.]

J.P.: What did you think when the Millennium Challenge Account review committee determined Comoros did not meet the required sixteen indicators used to assess national performance relative to governing justly, investing in people, encouraging freedom, transparency, and rule of law?

M.A.: It is ironic that Madagascar qualifies to get funds from the MCA program and Comoros does not, when you consider recent events. While preparing for the presidential elections the government there refused a candidate from the opposition to come back into the country to be a candidate and campaign. While the law calls for free and fair elections, President Ravalomanana stated if the candidate comes back into the country he would be arrested. At the same time, the U.S. supported Madagascar—which doesn't say much for [your] concerns over democracy in Madagascar.

It is difficult to understand your U.S. policy and how you deal with countries that are inconsistently democratic. It is even more difficult to understand, since countries like Comoros who have a democratically elected government and follow the rules are not eligible for an MCA grant. Who makes the decisions, and when does something come back our way from the U.S. government? It is the same issue looking at countries in Africa and Asia who get help and who are not democratic. Again, I say it is difficult to understand the foreign policy and what the Americans are expecting. For us it appears the policy is a wait-and-see policy. In other words, "Do this for us now, and we will wait to see if you continue to be democratic or support other U.S. issues before we give you something back."

I understood Mahmoud's frustration. For example, the December 16, 2001, presidential elections in Madagascar were marred by a political crisis, large demonstrations, and fighting between the two opposing factions. There were also political killings and other human rights abuses. There were major road blockades, and destruction of the bridges leading to Antananarivo, the capital city. Marc Ravalomanana claimed victory unilaterally, and swore himself in as President on February 22, 2002. Eventually a number of countries recognized the election's outcome, and Ravalomanana was sworn in again on May 6, 2002. As President, he promised to clean up the rampant government corruption.

Ravalomanana was a successful dairy business owner, and so one would think he was above corruption himself. However, people claimed that not much had changed in his new government. To add to the mistrust were claims that he made it more difficult for his business competitors, by instituting new regulations and taxing measures that dramatically affected their businesses.

Stories abound revealing self-serving acts by Ravalomanana. This man ran on a platform that stressed fairness and how he would clean up the government, but he was no different from other sub-Saharan African leaders who had succumbed to greed once elected to office.

The December 2006 reelection cycle once again comes to mind. Ravalomanana, concerned about any opposition, made certain he would be the only candidate running. His main competitor for the presidency was exiled former Deputy Prime Minister Pierrot Rajaonarivelo of the AREMA party. Ravalomanana barred him from participation in the election by not allowing him to enter the country—once he closed the small airport in the eastern city of Toamasina, where Rajaonarivelo would land, and another time, he did not allow his opponent to even board a Madagascar-bound plane in nearby Mauritius. As a result, Rajaonarivelo could not personally sign the required registration papers and was rejected as a candidate. Three other presidential candidates were rejected for claimed infractions, such as not paying the required deposits. To ensure his election, Ravalomanana moved the election dates ahead by several weeks to reduce the amount of campaigning time that would be available to the opposition candidates.

Madagascar was widely heralded as a "model of democracy" in sub-Saharan Africa. On March 31, 2005, the U.S. government named the country as its first Millennium Challenge Account grant winner, to receive $110 million over the next four years. Back in March 2002, President Bush announced that the Millennium Challenge Account "will reward nations that have more open markets and sustainable budget policies, nations where people can start and operate a small business without running the gauntlets of bureaucracy and bribery." Yet, given Ravalomanana's corrupt behavior, I wondered how the Millennium Challenge Corporation, with the support of U.S. Embassy Antananarivo, decided that Madagascar qualified for this award, when nearby Comoros, with a better track record, did not.

On April 1, 2005, at a press conference held at the Hotel Colbert in Antananarivo, Ambassador McGee praised Madagascar for being the "first country in the world" to achieve a compact with the Millennium Challenge Corporation. This surprised many people who knew of the actions and lack of transparency by Ravalomanana and his administration.

On April 19, 2007, a U.S. delegation led by Eunice Reddick, the director of the Office of East African Affairs, and Ambassador James McGee met with Comoros government leaders. In a memo reportedly sent to Washington on April 24, 2007, Ambassador McGee stated that a meeting was held with President Sambi. The meeting was deemed to be "the first ever bilateral discussions" with the Comorian government. Further, the talks were reported to consist of mainly the government of Comoros presenting its "wish list" to the United States, a vision for their future economy, energy needs, education, health care, and security matters.

Emphasizing that this was the "first ever" bilateral meeting since the establishment of the relationship between the United States of America and the Union of the Comoros overlooked the fact that for more than three years, U.S. Embassy Port Louis held extensive meetings and had ongoing bilateral relations with the government of Comoros. It seemed that neither the Bureau nor the embassy had access to the vast files of cables and reports listing the many bilateral discussions that embassy personnel held with Comoros government leaders; nor the quality time spent by our staff engaging the Comorian people; nor the September 27, 2004, cable sent to Washington that laid out a clear road map to follow up on the programs started, and requested U.S. government agencies to press for performance on promises made to the country; nor my departure cable I sent as ambassador, on June 3, 2005, which reemphasized the road map on continuing our engagement of Comoros.

The United States would have been better served by thanking Comoros for working hard to build a democratic environment, which allowed us to lift the Section 508 sanctions and reinstate the long-overdue IMET funding to train their military in support of the global war on terror. U.S. acknowledgment would have gone a long way in recognizing President Azali, who ousted the rogue Saudi-based al-Haramain Islamic Foundation in early August 2004—a month before the U.S. Treasury Department designated al-Haramain as a corrupt charity that underwrote terror and provided financing to al-Qaeda. And it was President Azali who pushed through the signing of the Article 98 agreement, which Undersecretary of State for Arms Control John Bolton had pressed for incessantly.

In an email to Mahmoud Aboud on September 4, 2007, I asked if Comoros had received any program funding or financial support through U.S. Embassy Antananarivo after I left on June 17, 2005, and if any follow-up information could be obtained from the extensive meetings President Azali and I had in Washington on February 23–25, 2005, with the State Department, USAID, Peace Corps, DOD, and the CIA. I also asked if they had heard from CENTCOM or PACOM.

On September 11, 2007, Mahmoud responded by email:

> This is what I found from Moroni, Secretary General of the University. They have not received anything since 2005. . . . they're only working with the American Corner in Moroni. The American Corner received books and some equipment from the U.S. Embassy in Mauritius in 2005 and never since . . . and they haven't received any container. The Secretary General of the Ministry of Health confirmed that the Comorian hospitals have never received anything from CENTCOM since 2005.

The mention of a container referred to a faith-based organization's offer of containers of schoolbooks and materials. This same group had graciously provided more than forty thousand books for schoolchildren in Mauritius. It would have required only an embassy follow-up for the gift of books to be sent.

In addition, in subsequent years, the United States provided some IMET funding for English-language training, a Foreign Service national local consular agent, officer training seminars, and a long-distance education program.

In 2007, U.S. Navy Seabees began the construction of a six-room building in Hamramba that would accommodate 250 students, with two more buildings scheduled for completion in 2009. However, I was told the first small classroom structure had to be partially torn down and rebuilt because the civil affairs unit had not obtained input from the local people as to their needs. And it wasn't completed until early 2010, in part because the Seabees units rotated every three to six months. The locals claimed that the Seabees were dragging their feet because time in Comoros was being treated as a vacation perk. They compared this project with another in the town of Nioumamilima, where the villagers were given the materials and with their own labor completed a similar school project in less than nine months. Had we a permanent mission in the country, such humanitarian assistance could be better coordinated with the civil affairs units and other agency-funded programs.

As it happened, many Comorians perceived the building of schools by the United States as a calculated threat to their culture. A more charitable move would have been to build medical clinics, provide medical supplies, provide school building materials, and help with sustainable development projects, such as for the fishing industry and agriculture diversification.

Still, there were the occasional positive steps. I was delighted to read in the August 8, 2010, *Military News Virginia Beach* that Petty Officer First Class Dennis Harris and four of his Maritime Civil Affairs colleagues had pitched in to help rehabilitate a school building and a village's water system. When they learned that local fishermen risked their lives working with small wooden outrigger canoes—some were swept out to sea, while others lost their bearings—they set about teaching them navigation and safety skills. Focusing on helping the country, by the end of their deployment they had trained six ministry officials so they could pass on the skills to other fishermen.

President Azali spent the better part of his four-year term in office working his way through complex issues: each island wanted to fly its own flag, have its own revenue sources, and provide separate health care, education, and police and military forces—in general, they wanted total autonomy. This opened the door for each island president to seek separate bilateral relations with France and other countries.

I counseled with Azali on a number of occasions about this unwieldy structure. Based on my corporate governance experience in the private sector, I told him that once a title was given, it would be difficult to remove or change it. But for peace in the country he went along with this structure in the reconciliation process. My discussions with the different island authorities revealed that each island president believed he was equal to Azali. Even worse was that in case of security issues or emergencies, the island authorities would separately contact the French first, instead of working through the Union government.

Although there were several coup attempts in 2003–4, none succeeded. To his credit, Azali did not attempt to extend his term of office beyond the mandated four years, which set a good democratic example for rotation of the Union presidency, as provided in the constitution, between the islands every four years.

In 2006, President Azali stepped down peacefully, allowing a new election to take place. On May 26, 2006, Ahmed Abdallah Mohamed Sambi was installed as President of the Union of the Comoros. The inauguration of President Sambi was a milestone for this young democratic country, since it was the second nonmilitary transition of power. Sambi was a well-respected, moderate Sunni cleric and businessman who had studied in Sudan, Iran, and Saudi Arabia. His friends and allies referred to him as the "Ayatollah."

A U.S. presidential delegation attending the swearing-in ceremony reportedly met with Sambi and lectured him on tolerance and nonviolence. Another Foreign Service officer from the U.S. Embassy in Madagascar separately met with religious leaders from Grande Comore and Anjouan to discuss religious tolerance, as part of an overall policy to promote human rights. They would have been better served to praise Comoros for their second consecutive free and fair election process.

Following Sambi's election as President of the Union, the islands of Grande Comore, Anjouan, and Mohéli were to hold their presidential elections on June 10, 2007. The Grande Comore and Mohéli elections were held on schedule and deemed to be free and fair. When violence and intimidation threatened the election on Anjouan, it was rescheduled for a week later.

Two months prior, on April 28, 2007, President Sambi, with the support of the African Union, had appointed Dhoihirou Halidi as interim president of Anjouan until elections could be held. However, Anjouan's president, Mohamed Bacar, who served from April 2002 to April 2007, refused to step down after his term ended and would not let Halidi take office. Independently, Bacar organized a presidential election, printed his own ballots, and went ahead with the election on June 10, claiming victory with 90 percent of the vote. Although the election was declared illegal, Bacar held an inauguration ceremony on June 14 and was sworn in. The other four candidates in the campaign boycotted the election, which was not recognized by the Union government as legitimate. Under the federal constitution, Bacar, after serving out a single five-year term as island president, could not have been a candidate.

The African Union was called in to help resolve this political crisis, which included sanctions and a naval blockade of Anjouan. Bacar continued to defy the Union government and the African Union by not stepping down.

Hopes for a peaceful solution dimmed, and a planned military invasion of Anjouan by African Union-supported troops was set for sometime in March 2008. On March 19, a French police helicopter coming from Mayotte crashed near the town of Sima on Anjouan. The French admitted it was owned by their air and border police force. Since the French had interfered and taken part in the destabilization of Comoros's internal affairs over the years, one can only suspect that they came to help Bacar escape to Mayotte, to nearby Réunion Island, or directly to France.

Six days later, on March 25, an invasion force comprising Comorian troops and African Union troops landed on Anjouan with the mission to depose Bacar. They met little resistance in their pursuit; however, Bacar and his entourage had escaped by boat to Mayotte, reportedly seeking asylum.

When I met with Mahmoud Aboud on February 28, 2008, the final chapter of Bacar's presidency had not yet unfolded. I probed about the president of Anjouan staying in office ten more months after his term ended and whether he had the support of the French. According to Mahmoud, people believe the French want to continue to destabilize Comoros so they can move forward in making Mayotte an overseas department of France—especially since the present status of Mayotte as an overseas collectivity ended in 2010. (On March 29, 2009, Mayotte had overwhelmingly voted to change its status to become France's 101st overseas department, effective in 2011.) Comoros, supported by the African Union, continues to oppose France's "occupation" of what it considers part of its island archipelago.

I also asked Mahmoud's views on China's strong interest in sub-Saharan Africa, since I believed that oil and mineral extraction and political influence had become the primary focus in China's bilateral relations with the countries there. "In Comoros, the Chinese government has forgiven all of the loans outstanding since independence in 1975 through the end of 2005," he said. "The existing Chinese embassy is being taken down and a new, larger one is being built."

I said the existing Chinese embassy had been fairly new, and conjectured the Chinese might be expanding their intelligence gathering in the Indian Ocean by increasing their tracking or listening capabilities in the new embassy. With the Middle East to the north, the Horn of Africa to the west (with CJTF-HOA operations in Djibouti), and the U.S. military base on Diego Garcia to the east, China certainly had a good reason to install a tracking station in Comoros.

Mahmoud recalled a Chinese contractor who had built the Union's parliament building in Comoros twenty years earlier and stayed on to construct many other projects, including a television broadcasting facility, a number of government buildings, a new airport terminal, an extension of the airport runways, and roads around Grande Comore. Currently, this contractor was building the new Chinese Embassy.

While the Chinese government donated some of these projects, others were contracted directly with the Comorian government. These projects kept more than one hundred Chinese workers continually employed. Rarely did the Chinese company use local labor, but when they did, they didn't teach the Comorians any construction skills.

Mahmoud and I then discussed the whereabouts of Fazul, the fugitive terrorist. It was reported he had spent considerable time in Lamu, Kenya, and in an al-Qaeda training camp near Ras Kamboni in southern Somalia, where U.S. aircraft attacked some Islamist militia and al-Qaeda fighters on January 7–9, 2007. According to reports, Fazul's wife, Halima, and their three children were captured on January 9, 2007, in the town of Kiunga, near Lamu in Kenya, only a few miles from the Somalia border. They were held for questioning and spent four months incarcerated in Kenya and Ethiopia. Released on May 4, 2007, they returned to Comoros. Apparently they had spent considerable time in Pakistan, probably with Fazul, since their children spoke English fluently with a Pakistani accent.

Fazul had escaped capture in Comoros, leaving on August 22, 1998, and reports indicated he went to Pakistan. His wife claimed she divorced him and went to Mahajanga on the northwest coast of Madagascar, where she supposedly married a Pakistani, giving her a way of escaping as well. She reappeared in Kenya in January 2007. In reality, she never divorced Fazul.

It was also rumored that Fazul may have taken a second wife, from either the town of Mahajanga or the island of Pate off the coast of Kenya near Lamu, which he reportedly had used as a safe haven for a period of time.

Meeting with Mahmoud in May 2007, he related a story about a trip he had taken back to Comoros five months earlier. Arriving at the airport, he saw twenty teenage students dressed in Western-style clothing, which he thought unusual. In questioning them, it became apparent they were students heading to somewhere in Tanzania as part of a scholarship education program. When asked which school they would be attending, they replied their instructions were to meet a person waiting for them at the airport in Dar es Salaam. When Mahmoud asked about their school in Comoros, they mentioned a small classroom located in a two-story building near the French Embassy, but could not recall the name.

Mahmoud then asked for the name of the teacher and the phone number, which they gave him. When Mahmoud called that cell phone number, a male answered but would not give him any information about the school or what subjects they taught. Since parents might inquire, Mahmoud said, he asked for contact and lodging information at the school in Tanzania, but no information was offered. Mahmoud discreetly tried to obtain more information without raising suspicion. Later, he even visited the so-called school only to discover it was an apartment house, not a real school operation. He said he would try to find out more information and call me.

Not having heard from Mahmoud, on July 14, 2007, I sent an email inquiring about the students. A few days later, he responded, saying the twenty students supposedly were at a boarding school some twenty-five miles from Dar es Salaam. He told me that he had spoken with one of the parents who said that their daughter had called and wanted to come home, but then for some unknown reason she changed her mind. None of the other students had been heard from since leaving Comoros. Mahmoud was worried about their safety.

In Comoros, several people told me radical Islam is a big danger, since young imams, both foreign and homegrown, are cropping up everywhere. They are more dangerous than the older ones of the 1990s. The Comorian government is not controlling their activities or their teachings. Nobody knows what will happen in five years. What is known is that they are preaching that the West is bad and Islam is the real religion and culture. In schools now, the students are required to wear caps and long gowns, while in past years they wore anything they wanted.

My concerns for these young students were echoed in a July 14, 2007, *Economist* article, "An Unusual Haunt for al-Qaeda," in which it was reported that some Comorians "resent the arrival of conservative Pakistanis intent on 'teaching the Koran' in villages. 'They're hiding something,' says Soihili Ahmed, editor of *Al Watwan*, the local newspaper. A group of them has set up in a historic mosque in N'tsaoueni, in the north of Grand Comore. The bearded Pakistanis deliver a stern but polite message. Sitting cross-legged on a dusty carpet, brewing tea and eating nuts and sweets brought with them from Karachi, they say the Comorians should 'return' to Taliban-style rule. A few of the listeners are Comorian boys. Wild-eyed, speaking alternately with gentleness and religious certitude, could they resemble Mr. Fazul at the start of his journey?"

On another matter, Mahmoud noted that the CJTF-HOA had sent a civil affairs team consisting of eighteen army soldiers, headed by General Sanford Holman, the deputy commander, to paint and repair several hospitals and schools, which the Comorian government appreciated. But the needed medical supplies and educational material were not included in the mission. However, they arrived dressed in their military fatigues, resembling a military occupation force to the Muslim villagers, who didn't understand their real purpose and thus were suspicious. "When soldiers go to the villages, the imams are telling the people U.S. soldiers are killing Muslims in Iraq, Gaza, Afghanistan, and so on," Mahmoud said.

The U.S. military uniforms are sending the wrong signal that imams use against our good deeds. We should operate these missions as would Peace Corps volunteers in a more civilian appearance or through an NGO. The Chinese workers have been there for twenty years and are not resented. They are low-key and wear normal construction workers' clothing.

The local Comorian press agency, HZK-Presse, interviewed General Holman and wrote on December 24, 2007: "For Holman's part, the U.S. general underlined that the strengthening of relations between Washington and Moroni depends on the political will of both parties, while the importance of the programs to be put in action are the results of discussions led by the two sides. 'We are soldiers,' said Mr. Holman, 'we just do what we are asked to do.'"

On April 14, 2008, I read a Center for Strategic and International Studies article, "Comoros: Big Troubles on Some Small Islands," written by Matthew B. Dwyer, a former Peace Corps volunteer who served in Comoros in the 1990s and now teaches at the International School of Luxembourg.

"The United States has a clear interest in preventing the Comoros from becoming an attractive place of refuge for wanted terrorists such as Fazul," Dwyer wrote. "The Comorian government is on record as being eager to cooperate with U.S. and UN anti-terrorist efforts. Unfortunately, this cooperative attitude has gone unappreciated." He added, "There is an International Military Education and Training (IMET) program in Comoros, budgeted at just $95,000 in 2008, but this is the only U.S. assistance the country receives."

Dwyer did not embellish the situation that exists in this destitute Muslim country. I could not understand why the State Department had not taken more of an interest there. In fact, no State Department personnel had engaged Comoros more actively than the Peace Corps volunteers who worked there in the 1990s.

Dwyer did summarize the concerns I had expressed to Washington in a number of consultations about our need to have a permanent U.S. presence there. "In the Comoros," he wrote, "the United States has committed only sins of omission. This must change, and the first step should be the reinstatement of the U.S. Embassy to the Union of the Comoros. It is no coincidence that the most peaceful period of Comorian independence coincides with the presence of a full U.S. diplomatic mission in the islands. It is time for Comorian[s] to once again be able to count the United States as a friend." Indeed, it is time the United States become a reliable and true friend of Comoros.

In the hunt for terrorist leaders, Fazul Abdullah Mohammed—born in Comoros, weaned on radical Islamic indoctrination, and once considered a man of no consequence by our government—has risen in the ranks of violence and inhumanity. As the new leader of the growing al-Shabaab terrorist organization in Somalia, he can no longer be ignored.

In December 2009, Mahmoud recounted a chance meeting with a former class-mate of Fazul's who recalled how he had been considered a very crafty teenager. This person said that when Fazul was thirteen or fourteen years old, he constructed a homemade bomb and detonated it in front of his friends. No one stopped him.

After the U.S. embassy bombings in 1998, a violent act of terrorism in which Fazul was involved, he returned to Comoros and visited the school in Moroni where his brother was a teacher. His former classmate ran into him but at first did not rec-ognize him. Shortly thereafter Fazul left the country. At the time, no one in Moroni knew he had had anything to do with the bombings. A few days later the FBI came to the island, and even then no one knew who or what they were pursuing until sometime later.

The FBI missed by just a few days their opportunity to catch Fazul while he was there. If the United States had had an active presence on the island, we might have been better able to glean the clues Fazul left behind. We could have been the conduit between the FBI and the Comorians to capture him before he did any more damage.

During our conversation, Mahmoud also shared recent information about Fazul's wife, Halima. In 2009, Halima received a new electronic-type passport (an e-passport) from the Comorian Department of National Security. The government of Comoros had not stopped the issuance of the passport. The United States took no action. It did not advise the Comorian government to watch her movements or prevent her from getting such a passport, which would open the world to her.

Subsequently, Halima flew to Anjouan and then sailed to Mahajanga, Mada-gascar, and on to Antananarivo. There she boarded a plane to Nairobi, Kenya. Crossing the porous border, she went into Somalia. Her purpose was to be present at the installation ceremony of her husband, Fazul Abdullah Mohammed—reportedly the head of al-Qaeda in East Africa—as the new leader of Somalia's al-Shabaab, a youth terrorist organization.

Nobody followed her. No one checked the sources of money affording her the opportunity to make this trip. And no one knows her part in Fazul's future activities.

Al-Shabaab is the outgrowth of the Islamic Courts Union after they lost power in their fight with Ethiopian forces in 2006. This jihadist group is intent on starting a holy war against Christians in Ethiopia, the Somali transitional federal govern-ment, African Union peacekeepers, the United Nations, and Western NGOs on hu-manitarian missions. Fazul's terrorist activities would include the use of car bombs, suicide attacks, road mines, and other disruptive bomb attacks in densely populated areas. Daily we are aware of the destruction al-Shabaab is causing in Somalia and, recently, in Uganda and other countries. They are actively recruiting young Somalis, many from the United States and elsewhere. We can only expect more attacks, pos-sibly reaching our soil in the near future.

⟨XXVII⟩

OUR FOREIGN POLICY

Can One Size Fit All?

When I arrived in Port Louis on April 24, 2002, Mauritius was considered a Special Embassy Program (SEP) post, with oversight and reporting responsibilities for two additional sovereign states, Seychelles and Comoros. In an SEP post, the embassy staff is supposed to have a reduced workload and be exempted from certain reporting requirements. In reality, we had the same reporting responsibilities as other larger embassies.

My country team in 2002 consisted of six Foreign Service officers and thirty-eight Foreign Service nationals who worked long hours with reduced benefits; to categorize this embassy as an SEP post was unjustified. It didn't take long to realize that this designation was a way of circumventing budget constraints imposed by Congress and masking the real extent of this embassy's operations. I brought up this very issue at several consultation meetings in Washington and at the Chiefs of Mission Conferences. Finally, in May 2005, the State Department abandoned this nomenclature for a number of smaller embassies, including Mauritius. I was glad to weigh in on this issue before departing as U.S. ambassador on June 17, 2005.

From my very first day at the embassy, I could see that Bisa Williams, my deputy chief of mission, was overworked. Her workspace resembled a newspaper reporter's office, with newspapers, magazines, books, and papers stacked on her desk, the nearby coffee table, the couch, and the floor. The time she spent on reporting requirements and oversight of the embassy operation was daunting. Perceiving that the embassy staff needed more mentoring, since personnel morale issues came up immediately, I decided it was important for me to be more involved with the staff. Subsequently, I changed the structure to have more interaction with both the Foreign Service officers and the Foreign Service national staff. I also changed the Foreign Service officer weekly one-on-one meetings with the deputy chief of mission

27.1. Ambassador Price in his office at U.S. Embassy Port Louis.

to two-on-one meetings, which included me. On a number of occasions, when the deputy chief of mission had a conflict in her schedule, I held the meetings anyway, to maintain a consistent schedule with the Foreign Service officers. There were also times when I didn't want any delay in receiving information that might require action.

I made sure we held our country team meetings with the Foreign Service officers on a regular basis and even moved travel schedules around to accommodate these meetings. In addition, any government agency visitors that interfaced with our embassy were invited to participate in our meetings to discuss host country and regional issues. Additionally, I asked to be copied on all internal memos and outgoing correspondence from the Foreign Service officers, which was not usual practice. It was important to know what was happening in the host countries and in the region, since I was responsible for U.S. Embassy Port Louis and did not want to have any failures on my watch.

Becoming a chief executive officer in a business enterprise involves years of learning the different aspects of the company. This training is like climbing a tree with many limbs to navigate, and each one is a learning experience. A good executive candidate will climb several trees for a different learning experience. When such an executive is selected to take charge, that person will know most every facet of the operation, from manufacturing to warehousing, logistics, sales, marketing, accounting, financial reporting, and possibly public governance. The executive also will have developed some sound people skills along the way.

It seemed to me that in the State Department, people easily became compartmentalized, with little cross-pollination of knowledge. As such, a management officer with a vast background in finance and management rarely would reach the ambassador level. So when you climb that tree, you are climbing the one that will not bloom for you.

There needs to be more cross-pollination between the political, management, public affairs, economic, consular, and security sections to better prepare a deputy chief of mission for the wide range of challenges and business decisions involved in operating an embassy, which I view as a quasi-business enterprise. Often, business and management skills are alien to deputy chiefs of mission who come up through the political ranks. Management officers, on the other hand, have a better grasp of business and management issues and the ability to lead an embassy staff of fifty or more people in addition to the various regional support agencies assigned to the embassy.

Political officers are incredibly talented, and their efforts are best served to focus more on foreign policy issues than on embassy operations. Most chiefs of mission I met came from the political ranks, which seem to get more exposure at the State Department. The State Department needs to change its advancement requirements, as well as develop leadership with more business and management training programs for all career Foreign Service officers.

Most of those who make it to the top, the chosen few, are very capable in reporting and have great writing skills. They eventually become a deputy chief of mission and, in the State Department structure, also have operational control of the embassy. In other words, the deputy chief of mission acts as the chief operating officer, with the other Foreign Service officers reporting to the deputy chief of mission, and only indirectly to the ambassador. As I've noted, most have little in the way of management or fiscal training, and most have never been in the private sector. Nor have many of the people training them at the Foreign Service Institute and the other agencies of government.

I later brought up this issue with the State Department leadership, as I advocated on behalf of an excellent administrative officer. I believe he had the potential to become a deputy chief of mission and eventually an ambassador. But the State Department's narrow guidelines would not allow this highly capable, multifaceted executive to move from one tree to another that had the branches that led to the top. As an example, his excellent reporting ability, people skills, and good business practices, which had saved the U.S. government well over $1 million while he was working at the embassy in Port Louis, weren't enough to give him a chance to advance and have the government benefit from his innate leadership qualities.

I was determined to be an effective chief of mission, and equally determined to work within the State Department culture. Although the letter from the President outlined my duties and responsibilities regarding executive branch employees in the host countries, it also instructed me to report to the President through the Secretary of State, which meant the State Department. Hence, though I was a politically appointed ambassador, for the most part I would be dealing with career government personnel, some of whom I thought did not appreciate ambassadors who had not come up through the ranks. In essence, we were seen as taking away jobs from some of the career members of the Foreign Service. They did not understand the vast business and management background, experience, and diversity many political appointees brought to the Foreign Service mix.

Even though our closeness to the President could allow for better relations in dealing with the host countries on issues important to U.S. interests, there were intimations we were a distraction to the State Department because of the extra time and effort they believed was needed to bring politically appointed ambassadors up to speed on foreign policy matters. It was as if we were not informed about or conversant with matters affecting America's interests around the world.

The country desk officer turned out to be the most important link I had within the State Department. This person provides support and assistance for most briefing and consultation meetings and can also make life easier for you when you need to interface with the other agencies in Washington. All requests generally move through this person, who in some instances handles several other countries in the region at the same time. Unfortunately, the State Department Foreign Service officers generally spend only one to three years in a post before they are rotated to new assignments. As an example, I had three desk officers during my three and a half years of service. There were also numerous other rotations throughout the State Department and the other agencies we worked with regularly. Each person also had a different level of experience, so for the embassy it meant lost time reviewing issues that had been previously covered. The time spent reviewing the current status of all the outstanding issues in the host countries detracted from our timely performance.

Often I thought the Foreign Service officer rotation process is anything but a relay race, where the baton is passed on seamlessly to the next team member. It was interesting to meet with contacts in Washington who would let me know that they would be leaving shortly after our meeting for another position. Eventually, before discussing any details, I would ask everyone I met with if they were going to be around for a while so I wasn't wasting my time. The revolving door was sometimes frustrating, and trying to recall where we had left off with someone's predecessor was almost impossible. Therefore, taking good notes became very important, so as not to cover the same ground again.

In the end, however, I made some lasting friendships at the State Department and with career members of the Foreign Service who understood and appreciated the diversity that a business background could bring to the otherwise structured culture. To attract top-caliber Foreign Service officers, we need to be competitive with the private sector, including additional compensation for the measured risk conditions at difficult posts. At the same time, we need to weed out Foreign Service officers who add little to the bottom line and are protected by the State Department tenure system. We cannot just run lean at our overseas missions; we need to be right-sized. With the knowledge Foreign Service officers gain in their positions, they need to continue in a post for a longer period to complete programs that are under way. The constant rotation also needs to be reviewed for effectiveness in terms of getting the job done.

The Foreign Service Institute programs need to include private sector experts to give management and business courses to enhance embassy operations. Any career member of the Foreign Service considered for promotion to the deputy chief of mission level should be evaluated by an independent panel, including members outside their bureau. In addition, there should be interviews with Foreign Service officers and Foreign Service national staff at the embassy of the candidate's prior assignment. The current peer culture within the Bureau ranks, with the massaging of each other's employee evaluation reviews (sometimes to an over-the-top level), has to be overhauled completely. In reality, much of the work that make a Foreign Service officer look good might actually be generated by Foreign Service national employees who receive little credit and are grossly underpaid for what is expected of them. It is important that all embassy Foreign Service officers be fairly considered for promotion to the position of deputy chief of mission so that we do not leave out any talented people who either come from different backgrounds or have made a midcareer change. In my three-plus years of service as U.S. ambassador, I met several such Foreign Service officers who had limited experience in the government but had excellent management skills, better than several in line for promotion. The State Department culture of basically grooming the select few does not allow for a diversity of experience, nor do those candidates gain the broad management and business skills needed to operate an embassy.

I also learned that U.S. foreign policy does not always take into account the impact on the host countries. The ambassador's input and recommendations on many issues were often merely taken under advisement. Programs or ideas to advance the image of the United States or to make a difference in the host country were limited.

At times, I felt my efforts to serve my country were marginalized by people in Washington. A citizen public servant, as I considered myself to be, who is fired up and wants to help change the world for the better can find it challenging to deal with the regimented government culture. I took actions that were within my area of responsibility and in the best interests of the United States to develop good bilateral relations, establish friendships, and spread some goodwill with the people in the host countries. At times this raised eyebrows in Washington. Thinking outside the box was discouraged, I found out.

The State Department is not right-sized in the overseas missions. I believe many of the job roles in Washington overlap, and there is the potential for substantial redundancy. But it is almost impossible to dislodge anyone from this ingrained and protected structure. Hence, I will focus on the issue that affects American citizens the most: our foreign relations and security around the world.

During my posting, I came to understand that many members of Congress had little understanding of sub-Saharan Africa or the real issues in the Indian Ocean region. I believe that members of the Senate Foreign Relations Committee, especially the African Affairs Subcommittee, need to visit sub-Saharan Africa on a more regular basis. After all, the continent is three times bigger than the United States, with more than three times the population. Newspaper reporters are often better informed on issues in sub-Saharan Africa than most members of Congress or their staffers. With terrorism a high priority for the United States, I would have thought that more senators would have visited the continent at least once since 9/11. This holds true for members of the House of Representatives with oversight for Africa.

Going back to 1970, I was fortunate to have visited twenty-two African countries. I revisited some a number of times, stayed longer in others, and was often joined by members of my family. My earlier visits were as part of an observation team for humanitarian organizations, such as CARE and UNICEF. I also met many other Americans who were giving their time to help the underprivileged African Diaspora. I always felt that if private citizens can take an active interest in sub-Saharan Africa's poor and devastated countries, so could Congress.

During my confirmation hearings, I expected a lively exchange on important current issues facing the three sub-Saharan African countries to which I would be accredited. I fully expected to discuss foreign affairs during the Senate Foreign Relations Subcommittee hearings or afterward, but never did. I anticipated more questions on aspects of security and terrorism concerns in the region where I would be serving; I thought we would talk about Fazul Abdullah Mohammed, the most-wanted terrorist from Comoros. There was no such discussion. There was nothing said or asked about the rogue Saudi al-Haramain Islamic Foundation in Comoros, or the spread of radical Islam in the region, or how we should plan to build friendships in places where we are considered fair-weather friends.

I expected more discussion on trade-related issues and also how we could qualify more countries under the AGOA program to help reduce poverty in the sub-Saharan African countries—the very conditions that al-Qaeda and radical Islamists feed on. These were some of the issues and questions that could have been addressed by the Senate subcommittee. But again, this did not happen.

Sub-Saharan Africa currently has the greatest number of weak, failing, and failed states in the world. More than three hundred million people live in a belt of poverty that stretches across most of the continent. The majority of the population lives on less than $1 a day. If we want to keep these countries from becoming failed states that eventually open the door to radical Islamic domination, I think the State Department needs to focus more on maintaining a consistent diplomatic engagement and presence there. Neither lip service nor maintenance of the status quo is going to make a difference. Only meaningful action will help prevent a poverty-stricken country from becoming another failed state.

We can surely afford to help bring impoverished Africans to the next level in their lifetime. We need to do this, if for no other reason than our security. I recognize that Africa is about as far away from the United States as one can travel, but for al-Qaeda the United States is only a doorstep away.

Members of Congress should take part in at least one congressional delegation visit during their term of office, and again if reelected. Ranking committee members should be required to go more often and make more than cameo appearances. Granted, these trips are tiring and time-consuming, but not any more so than campaigning or raising money. The knowledge that members of Congress would personally gain from such information-gathering trips could possibly help make their constituents' lives much safer and protect the United States against potential acts of terrorism at home.

Most Americans lack a real understanding of the plight of the many Africans who are no better off today than when I first visited in 1970. At the time, I observed U.S.-supported food distribution and other critical aid programs in poverty-stricken countries that had only recently gained independence from their colonialist rulers. In addition to the poverty issues, today we also have to deal with terrorists and other radical Islamic extremist groups who prey on these poorest of the poor. Adding to their struggle, autocratic and corrupt rulers have stolen millions of aid dollars. That should have been a real concern to all members of Congress and been on their radar screens long ago.

In an opinion survey that was taken between February 2007 and March 2008 by the Fund for Peace, when asked, "What is the most critical cause of state failure?" Some 42.3 percent of respondents answered "corruption." A 2008 Brookings Institution report, "Index of State Weakness in the Developing World," noted that two-thirds of the weakest states are located in sub-Saharan Africa (Comoros was number thirty-one on the list). Twelve of the poorest countries in the world are in sub-Saharan Africa.

If I were making such an index, I would add a few criteria. I would indicate, for example, those states where democratically elected rulers come from the country's dominant ethnic group, to the exclusion of other groups from the governing process. I would also highlight states where non-transparent elections keep a ruler in power indefinitely, as with Robert Mugabe in Zimbabwe. I would list rulers who come to power poor and leave rich while their country remains poor. I would list all the secret bank accounts around the world maintained by these rulers and to which aid money is undoubtedly transferred. Finally, I would measure the effectiveness of governments in helping to spread their country's wealth among all the people—but I wouldn't base a country's success on the number of Mercedes and BMWs driven by rulers, their families, their ministers, and their supporters.

The United States has pumped well over $500 billion in aid into sub-Saharan Africa in the past fifty years. Yet nearly 50 percent of its population continues to live on less than $1 a day—the highest rate of extreme poverty in the world. The basic criteria for a "Success Index of Sub-Saharan African Countries" would be more meaningful with everyone eating regularly. I would begin by counting these people.

The number of poverty-stricken people in sub-Saharan Africa doubled from 1981 to 2001, to more than 300 million. The number is expected to reach 340 million by 2015, with most of the population still living in weak, failing, and failed states. Without the ingredients of good governance, education, health care, sustainable development, and job creation, it will be difficult for sub-Saharan Africans to survive without massive infusions of humanitarian assistance.

It is when people have a way to feed themselves and have a little extra money in their pockets that life acquires new meaning. It is only then that violence and strife tend to become secondary. It is important that the United State develop a meaningful and consistent foreign policy and cultivate diplomats who want to make a difference. We must have a diplomatic mission in every sub-Saharan African country, with adequate security as needed.

The members of Congress are consumed by "constituency satisfaction polls," rather than focusing on issues such as the danger that the United States' lack of engagement in sub-Saharan Africa might create for their constituents' security. The increased presence of Islamic extremists and al-Qaeda terrorists in the region since the early 1990s is alarming. These rogue groups are gaining support in populous, poverty-stricken Muslim countries. The U.S. embassy closures in the early 1990s increased our exposure to global terrorism, with al-Qaeda recruiting and training young people in the Horn of Africa and East Africa, and spreading to West Africa.

I believe Osama bin Laden and his radical Islamic followers will continue in their fanatical quest to take the world back to the time in the twelfth century when Sultan Saladin controlled vast regions of northern Africa and the Middle East. Osama bin Laden has consistently stated that he considers all non-Muslims infidels and invaders of Muslim soil; he has called for a global jihad against all the Western powers, with the United States being foremost on the list.

For this reason alone, the United States needs to more actively engage all the Muslim countries in sub-Saharan Africa. We need to reach out to the imams who preach hatred. We need to support the more moderate imams and Muslim leaders who preach peace. Hopefully, our message of friendship will resonate with the young people—the next generation.

Today, we are living in the most crucial time in modern history since the Cold War. At least then we could see our enemy, which is no longer the case. Today's enemy has no name, no face, no uniform, and not even a standing army. It's a theological movement that has been around for over a thousand years. Its mission is to control the world under shari'a law, which would take us back to the twelfth century, when Islam ruled much of the world.

So how is the United States' foreign policy dealing with these issues? First of all, we beefed up our military budget, so in 2009, 21.4 cents of every taxpayer dollar spent went for military operations and technology. We only spent 1.25 cents on international affairs, which included diplomacy and foreign aid programs. Congress spends more on wasteful earmarks every time it passes a lengthy bill than the State Department spends on operating and staffing all the embassies around the world. The total international affairs budget was $39.5 billion for fiscal year 2009, of which amount the State Department appropriation was $26.1 billion to fund the programs, operations, and infrastructure essential to conduct U.S. diplomatic and consular affairs in more than 180 countries. The Defense Department's base budget for that same period, $513 billion, was substantially higher when emergency discretionary spending and other supplemental spending totaling over $140 billion are included.

Embassy operations are the front line for the security and well-being of our country, serving as eyes and ears so that we know what is going on outside our borders. Congress's never-ending earmarks are put in place to enhance their chances for re-election, while these funds could better be used for embassy operations, which serve as a line of defense around the world so that Americans can sleep safer at night.

State Department funding is needed to establish U.S. embassies or American Presence Post representation in all 192 countries that have voting rights at the UN. Some of these countries are in strategic locations, while others are in more dangerous areas with ongoing conflict.

In addition, we need to operate our overseas missions in a more businesslike fashion, with the necessary support agencies located at the embassy. As noted earlier, we also need to bring in more private sector management and financial experts to help train Foreign Service officers at the Foreign Service Institute. All embassies must also operate in a more secure environment, which should have been part of a master plan once expansion started around the world after World War II.

We waste money on building extravagantly designed embassy campuses in a few places, while we skimp on numerous others. Our Overseas Buildings Operations program should have three or four basic building designs that are shelf-ready, depending upon the size, the location, and the risks involved. Architectural indulgence should not be the overriding criterion; rather, we need to focus on a more practical, secure, yet visitor-friendly environment.

As I mentioned earlier, in 1996 Ambassador Prudence Bushnell sent cables to the State Department regarding the lack of proper security at the U.S. Embassy in Nairobi. These went unheeded. An official at the department felt the ambassador was overreacting on these security concerns. A security team was sent to inspect the embassy and reported that it met their standards for a medium-threat facility.

General Anthony Zinni visited the embassy in early 1998 and reported there were significant risks and that the embassy would be an easy target for terrorists. Again, the State Department felt no security upgrades were necessary. The U.S. Embassy in Dar es Salaam was no better protected from any potential attacks.

The world knows what happened on August 7, 1998, with the terrorist bombings of both embassies and the tragic loss of 224 lives. Why didn't the State Department take these warnings more seriously? Why was Congress so shortsighted that it did not protect our overseas operations by providing adequate funding? Why were U.S. intelligence sources so naive in their belief that sub-Saharan Africa did not have a well-organized al-Qaeda network? I believe the attacks could have been avoided with a more consistent engagement of the countries in the Horn of Africa and East Africa as far back as the early 1990s. These countries didn't want the legacy of terrorists who infiltrated their countries, carried out their ill-intentioned deeds, and exercised control over segments of their populations.

The disastrous effects of these embassy bombings cost the United States at least several billion dollars, while a properly conceived new embassy compound, at the time of the warnings, would have cost a fraction of that amount.

New embassy construction was stepped up in 2001 by the Bureau of Overseas Buildings Operations. Reportedly, forty-two projects had been completed by 2007, and another thirty-nine were under construction, out of the almost two hundred facilities needed. But looking at many of these complexes, I find it is not difficult to determine where function and cost considerations were less important than the notion of an architectural statement.

After the end of the Cold War in the 1980s, we focused our attention on the Eastern Bloc countries and very rapidly built more than a dozen new embassies, although the real threat to U.S. security lies in Africa. We continued to build up our military might for future ground-style campaigns, but we did not see the brewing danger of terrorism that would erupt into a new, different kind of warfare.

We could have learned a lesson from the terrorist style of fighting in the early 1980s, when there were thirty-six suicide attacks against Americans and others inside Lebanon, including Hezbollah's bombing of the U.S. Embassy in Beirut on April 18, 1983, which killed sixty-three people. In 1982, the Lebanese government requested that the United States establish a peacekeeping force to control conflict between Muslims and Christians. The Muslim military forces viewed our soldiers as their enemies and attacked them regularly. On October 23, 1983, two truck bombs struck two buildings housing U.S. and French troops, part of the multinational force. In the attack on the American barracks, 241 American servicemen were killed; France lost fifty-eight of their military personnel. Islamic Jihad took responsibility for the bombings on this occasion. Then, on December 12, 1983, a truck filled with gas cylinders and explosives rammed into a three-story administrative wing of the U.S. Embassy in Kuwait City, killing five people, none American. Reportedly the attack was undertaken by a radical Shi'ite Islamic group with ties to Iran.

We need to remember the words of Osama bin Laden when he referred to the American troops coming to Saudi Arabia in 1990 as infidels occupying Muslim soil and declared a jihad against us. He didn't want any foreign troops on their sacred soil in the "land of the two mosques," Mecca and Medina.

In a March 1997 CNN interview, Osama bin Laden said, "In our religion, it is not permissible for any non-Muslim to stay in our country." A similar message had come several years earlier from radical Muslims in Beirut who did not want American troops on their soil and attacked our soldiers.

During the most trying times in recent history for the State Department, from 2001 to 2005, more than one thousand new positions were absorbed by assignments to Afghanistan and Iraq; at the same time, there was a shortage of more than one thousand positions elsewhere around the world. The budget cuts mandated by Congress in the 1990s for overseas embassy operations and the subsequent terrorist attacks and threat of attacks against U.S. embassies gave rise to an increased budget for the Bureau of Diplomatic Security and almost eight hundred new positions related to security, yet no real increase for our foreign affairs programs.

The establishment since 2007 of the new House Appropriations Subcommittee on State Foreign Operations, and a similar Senate committee, directly places more emphasis on State Department foreign operations and programs such as USAID, the Peace Corps, and the Millennium Challenge Account. Hence, budgeting for our foreign affairs should no longer take a backseat to other agencies. It is crucial that the structures that carry out U.S. foreign affairs programs be funded adequately so that we are not perceived around the world as isolationists.

In my meetings with sub-Saharan African leaders while I was U.S. ambassador and subsequent interviews with African leaders for this book, I heard repeatedly that the United States is considered a "fair-weather friend." The U.S. government needs to have a consistent, dependable foreign policy, including foreign assistance programs for sub-Saharan Africa, that aims to rebuild trust and friendships.

We should not forget that "foreign assistance is a real bargain for American taxpayers," as Secretary of State Warren Christopher noted in 1995. He went on to add, "Recent polls suggest that the American people think that up to 25 percent of federal spending goes to foreign assistance, and that 8 percent should be the maximum. In fact, we spend less than 1 percent of the total federal budget on foreign assistance—about 12 cents a day for each American citizen—in contrast to about 18 percent still spent on defense."

Asserting that our "diplomatic 'field offices' abroad also constitute an invaluable early-warning intelligence system," the secretary added "their rapid-fire political, military, and economic reporting is essential to the crisis-prevention work of Washington national security decision-makers."

Responding to questions about whether our foreign assistance made any real difference in developing countries and what would happen if we just stopped giving it, Secretary Christopher responded by saying, "Both we and they would suffer. Our foreign assistance programs are intended to promote the kind of economic growth and political stability that are critical to U.S. national security and economic well-being. Failing to provide aid to developing countries would therefore jeopardize our national security."

The Secretary pointed out that "it costs a hundred times as much to deal with humanitarian crises as it does to prevent them." For example, it cost the United States more than $2 billion to deal with Somalia, and $1 billion to address Rwanda's problems.

Secretary Christopher, under pressure from Congress, recommended that USAID close down twenty-eight missions abroad, shutter ten U.S. Information Agency (USIA) offices, and cut more than three thousand job positions; USIA's activities and programs merged with the State Department programs.

Secretary Christopher and former Secretary of State Henry Kissinger asserted that the United States could still maintain a strong diplomatic presence overseas. Secretary Christopher talked about "the principle of universality," wherein the United States must maintain an official diplomatic presence in every country where it is welcome. I would have gone further and said that we should maintain a presence in every country that is a voting member at the United Nations.

Operating leaner in carrying out our foreign affairs was the goal of Congress and State Department. Cutting resources for such basic programs as books, libraries, research tools, and an American Corner filled with reading and educational material about our country gave radical imams the edge by allowing them to take over as the main source of education in many Muslim countries. Only where a vestige of colonialism still existed were some books and educational material still available for secular studies.

The United States has pushed the "electronic highway" as the new paradigm to replace the physical experience of touching, feeling, and reading a book or even the social experience of visiting a library. But in the less developed countries of sub-Saharan Africa, where computers and dependable power are not readily available, such an approach to learning is limited, if not impossible. Without books, students in these countries wouldn't have a chance.

The total savings in eliminating the USIA libraries, reference centers, and associated cultural activities were estimated to be $9.1 million annually—a minuscule amount to keep open the main highway of knowledge.

While the State Department allowed the budget cuts to reduce or eliminate the U.S. diplomatic presence in a number of countries, the Diplomatic Security Service suddenly saw a dramatic increase in funding to strengthen security at the remaining embassies. This money would have been better spent on prevention in the first place, by having an American presence on the ground providing good intelligence and reporting. A continued presence in Sudan and Somalia, for example, would have allowed us to engage directly with the leaders in one country and the warlords in the other, rather than having to do so peripherally. Part of the problem with our foreign policy is that we will not engage people we consider our enemy, and in a number of cases have used our military might to resolve political and ideological differences. Fighting doesn't always provide for a long-lasting, peaceful outcome. I truly believe that having embassy representation in every country to engage the leaders is better than having CIA operatives or military troops on the ground, as they are often perceived as destabilizers, invaders, occupiers, or infidels.

Al-Qaeda has been working hard to gain a foothold in every country that has a significant Muslim population, and to destabilize the region and its Western interests. China has been diligently working for more than fifty years to make friends and gain advantages in sub-Saharan Africa in order to lock up all the natural resources there. Currently, China is purchasing almost 60 percent of the oil produced by Sudan, which has the third-largest reserves in sub-Saharan Africa. China is also actively involved in oil and other trade deals with over forty sub-Saharan African countries. But China has turned a blind eye to genocide and war in Sudan. China's economic investment in sub-Saharan Africa has brought it many new friends thanks to its policy of not interfering with the internal affairs of these countries or questioning their stand on democracy, human rights, and the rule of law.

Even the presence of rogue and corrupt governments or Islamic extremists in some of these countries has not deterred China's quest for those countries' oil, gas, mineral resources, commodities, and agricultural land.

The United States, on the other hand, has withdrawn from countries in sub-Saharan Africa because those countries lack democratic institutions or have perceived security concerns; because of congressionally mandated budgetary cutbacks; or because a country had been labeled as a supporter of terrorism, and had economic sanctions placed on them.

We cannot give up our long-established democratic principles and tenets of freedom, but we need to stay and work within the framework of understanding other cultures—not necessarily to enhance access for our own economic gain, but rather to address people's need to escape the trap of poverty.

I believe that when we closed our embassy in Comoros, replacing it with a smaller American Presence Post (APP) comprising one political-economic officer, one regional security officer, and one consular officer would have given the United States a diplomatic presence and a way to obtain credible information. The APP in turn would interface with the nearest U.S. Embassy where an accredited ambassador is located. The ambassador and other embassy staff would also make regular visits in furtherance of bilateral relations with the host country.

The State Department has had experience with several consular APPs in Europe. In 2003, an APP was approved for Malabo, Equatorial Guinea (located off the coast of West Africa), to interface with the U.S. Embassy in Cameroon. In October 2006, the U.S. Embassy in Malabo was established with a fully accredited ambassador living on-site.

In a September 2006 interview I had with Congressman Jim Kolbe, then chairman of the Subcommittee on Foreign Operations, we discussed the importance of having a U.S. presence in every country. He explained that in areas such as the Lesser Antilles in the West Indies, one U.S. ambassador could cover several of the smaller islands, and he supports a similar system in parts of Africa. "We don't have an unlimited budget," he told me. "The ultimate decision on which countries we cover has to be based on strategic interests. If a country is small but has very significant interests, I think we would have to do it."

The roots of power and corruption in sub-Saharan Africa first took hold in a generation of young, politically motivated rebels, reformers, and nationalists in the 1950s, whose socialist and Marxist ideals became part of their independence movement. In the 1960s, many succumbed to the euphoria of power rather than struggle with democracy in a multiethnic society. Sitting on the throne offered these fledgling dictators a way to satisfy their thirst for personal wealth. While free elections and power-sharing opportunities sounded good on paper, they were difficult to achieve. Not only did each leader want to put members of his ethnic group in control of the country, but the presidency was often enmeshed with the personal enrichment of family, friends, and confidants. This is why billions of dollars in financial aid and loans never reached the very people who needed help.

Greed soon became intoxicating, and social and economic reforms for the people were long forgotten. This vicious cycle has continued with coups and counter-coups; in some cases, power is handed down from father to son. Today, we find a new generation of leaders interspersed with the clique in the African Union that has controlled their countries for decades, creating weak, failing, and failed states with dictators hanging on until death so they won't be prosecuted for their unjust personal enrichment.

Over time, some sub-Saharan African leaders have developed altruistic goals of sustaining social change and building democratic institutions, but they are in the minority. In the postcolonial era the United States and other donor countries have supported more than fifty corrupt dictators with billions of dollars of financial aid and loans, creating dozens of billionaires and countless millionaires. They and many others reportedly have plundered and killed to reach the top and stay there as long as they could. Independence from colonialism has been rewarding for these dictators but has not changed for the better the lives of most people in sub-Saharan Africa. For many dictators, personal greed also has become more important than the concerns of international security; the global war on terror remains a cliché to many.

It will be difficult for respect for human rights, rule of law, transparency, and democracy based on the American model to gain traction in the destitute conditions in many of these countries. Poverty's companions are hopelessness and a susceptibility to reach out to anyone who is willing to help. Islamic extremists and al-Qaeda are well funded and will fill a void of hope for them.

We need to ask ourselves whether we have done enough to reduce poverty by offering job creation solutions, health care, and secular education for Africans hoping to have a better and independent future. Have the aid and debt relief we supplied helped to reduce the potential for terrorism?

We need to understand the thousands of years of African history, with its many different ethnic groups and cultures, and the impact of European traders, missionaries, and colonialists. We need to be sensitive to the inequities created by power struggles, interethnic conflicts, and thoughtless partitions of historical ancestral lands. And we need to understand that even though it has been over fifty years since independence began to take hold in sub-Saharan Africa, it may be another fifty years before the American model of democracy takes hold.

If the United States insists on placing too many democracy-related conditions on economic assistance after years of either ignoring or interfering with the internal affairs of these countries, we will lose sub-Saharan Africa. To gain respect and effect change, our form of democratization—alien in this part of the world—must become a secondary issue. But as the United States fully engages the sub-Saharan African countries, we will have a greater chance to leave a positive footprint and guide these countries onto the path of freedom and prosperity, eradicating poverty, reducing the impact of disease, and diminishing the influence of the jihadist movement in its quest to create a worldwide caliphate.

APPENDIX A

LETTER OF CREDENCE
FROM PRESIDENT GEORGE W. BUSH

THE WHITE HOUSE
WASHINGTON

January 30, 2002

The Honorable
John Price
American Ambassador
Port Louis

Dear Mr. Ambassador:

Thank you for your willingness to serve the American people
and the cause of freedom and peace around the world. I
extend my warmest congratulations and wish to say how proud
I am of you for agreeing to serve as my personal representative to the Republic of Mauritius, the Federal Islamic
Republic of the Comoros and to the Republic of Seychelles.
This is a moment in history of wide possibility and
enormous opportunity, and I have no doubt you share my own
sense of excitement about what together we can achieve.

In addition to conveying my personal thanks and congratulations, this will also serve as a letter of instruction to
you as United States Chief of Mission. In the widest
sense, your mission is to protect America's vital
interests, promote the growth of freedom and democratic
institutions, and help set loose the creative energies of
millions of people through the spread of the free-market
system. The underlying principle here is a belief that the
talents and dreams of average people -- their human hopes
and loves -- should be rewarded by freedom and protected by
peace. You have the opportunity to engage in a distinctly
American internationalism: idealism without illusion,
confidence without conceit or arrogance, realism in the
service of American ideals.

In carrying out these objectives I ask that you fully
understand the authority extended to you in this letter and
closely consider the duties listed here which, though of
necessity described sometimes in technical or legal terms,
are of vital importance to the successful completion of

2

your mission. Furthermore, you should know that these
instructions have been shared with all Departments and
agencies, and I have directed that they give you their full
cooperation. You are to carry out these instructions and
your mission to the best of your ability and consistent
with applicable law.

As Chief of Mission, you have full responsibility for the
direction, coordination, and supervision of all United
States Government Executive Branch employees in the
Republic of Mauritius, in the Federal Islamic Republic of
the Comoros and in the Republic of Seychelles (except for
elements and personnel under the command of a U.S. area
military commander [i.e., a geographic combatant commander]
or employees on the staff of an international
organization). This also means that, except for the
personnel exempted above, you are in charge of all United
States Government Executive Branch activities and
operations and their conduct in accordance with the
International Affairs Strategic Plan in your Missions. It
is my hope you will take good care of all those under your
supervision, seeing to it that each individual has every
opportunity for professional advancement and career
fulfillment, as well as the best possible chance to serve
our country and its mission abroad.

Please report to me through the Secretary of State. Under
my direction the Secretary of State is, to the fullest
extent provided by the law, responsible for the overall
coordination and supervision of all United States
Government activities and operations abroad. The only
authorized channel for instruction to you is through the
Secretary or from me. To this, there are only two
exceptions: (1) if I personally instruct you to use a
private channel; or (2) if the Secretary instructs you to
use a non-State channel.

In charging you to exercise full responsibility for all
Executive Branch personnel in the Republic of Mauritius, in
the Federal Islamic Republic of the Comoros and in the
Republic of Seychelles except elements and personnel under
the command of a U.S. area military commander or on the
staff of an international organization, I wish to make
clear that this encompasses all American and foreign
national personnel, in all employment categories, whether
direct hire or personal services contract, full- or part-
time, permanent or temporary [regardless of where located

3

in your country of assignment]. All Executive Branch
agencies under your authority, and every element of your
Mission, must keep you fully informed at all times of their
current and planned activities so that you can effectively
carry out your responsibility for United States Government
programs and operations in the Republic of Mauritius, in
the Federal Islamic Republic of the Comoros and in the
Republic of Seychelles. You have the right to see all
communications to or from Mission elements, however
transmitted, except those specifically exempted by law or
Executive decision.

You should provide the necessary support, both political
and material, for consular operations at your missions.
You should be diligent in minimizing the threat of
terrorism and advocating for its victims. You should
constructively address uncompensated and wrongful
expropriations of Americans' property including their
intellectual property rights.

As Commander in Chief, I retain authority over the U.S.
Armed Forces. On my behalf, you have full responsibility
for the direction, coordination, and supervision of all
Department of Defense personnel on official duty in the
Republic of Mauritius, in the Federal Islamic Republic of
the comoros and in the Republic of Seychelles except those
elements and personnel under the command of a U.S. area
military commander. You and the area military commander
must keep each other currently and fully informed and
cooperate on all matters of mutual interest. Should you
and an area military commander disagree, any differences
that cannot be resolved in the field will be reported by
you to the Secretary of State; area military commanders
will report, through the Chairman of the Joint Chiefs of
Staff, to the Secretary of Defense.

I expect you to take direct and full responsibility for the
security of your Missions. Unless an interagency agreement
provides otherwise, the Secretary of State and, by
extension, you as Chief of Mission must protect all United
States Government personnel on official duty abroad (other
than those elements and personnel under the security
protection of a U.S. area military commander or on the
staff of an international organization) and their
accompanying dependents.

4

This includes their physical security within and outside
the chancery gate. The proper handling of sensitive
information and material is also imperative. You and the
U.S. area military commander should develop appropriate
security procedures, arrangements, and documentation for
all Department of Defense elements and personnel, assigning
them to either your authority and security responsibility
or to that of the area military commander. You and the
U.S. area military commander should also consult and
coordinate responses to common threats. I will also expect
your sustained personal attention and energy to combat the
proliferation of harmful technologies or weapons of mass
destruction.

Every Executive Branch agency under your authority must
obtain your approval before changing the size, composition,
or mandate of its staff regardless of the employment
category [or where located in your country of assignment].
I ask that you review programs, personnel, and funding
levels regularly, and ensure that all agencies attached to
your Mission do likewise. Functions that can be performed
by personnel based in the United States or at regional
offices overseas should not be performed at post. In your
reviews, should you find staffing to be either excessive or
inadequate to the performance of priority Mission goals and
objectives, I urge you to initiate staffing changes in
accordance with established procedures.

If a Department head disagrees with you on staffing
matters, he or she may appeal your decision to the
Secretary of State, to whom I have delegated my
responsibility for resolving such matters. In the event
the Secretary is unable to resolve the dispute, the
Secretary and the respective Department head will present
their differing views to me for decision.

All United States Government personnel (other than those
elements and personnel in country under the command of a
U.S. area military commander or on the staff of an international organization) must obtain country clearance before
entering the Republic of Mauritius, the Islamic Republic of
the Comoros and the Republic of Seychelles on official
business. You may refuse country clearance or may place
conditions or restrictions on visiting personnel as you
determine necessary.

5

As Chief of Mission you are not only my personal representative in the Republic of Mauritius, in the Islambic
Republic of the Comoros and the Republic of Seychelles but
that of our country. I expect you to discharge this trust
with professional excellence, the highest standards of
ethical conduct, and diplomatic discretion, and use your
personal diplomacy to press issues of importance to
American citizens when that is useful and appropriate. I
urge you to see that there is no discrimination or
harassment of any kind at your Missions. I ask you to
ensure that your staff similarly adheres to the same strict
standards and maintains our shared commitment to equal
opportunity. In that regard, I instruct you to visit the
Department of State's Office of the Inspector General prior
to your posting for useful instructions on issues relevant
to proper operation of your missions.

America remains engaged in the world by history and by
choice, shaping a balance of power that favors freedom.
Besides United States Government activities, this means
assistance to American citizens, institutions, and
businesses as they pursue a multitude of charitable and
commercial interests ranging from the promotion of American
products and services exported overseas to people-to-people
assistance in foreign lands. All this means not just sound
management but inspired leadership from U.S.
representatives abroad.

I know how anxious you are to render such service to our
country and the principles and ideals for which the United
States has always stood. For all of the instructions and
duties outlined above, I know your own sense of patriotism,
selflessness, and desire for excellence is America's
greatest hope for the success of your Mission.

As you begin your work, please be assured of my warmest
regards and the best wishes of a grateful Nation.

Sincerely,

George W. Bush

APPENDIX B

THE HORN OF AFRICA

The New Epicenter

When the missionaries came, the Africans had the land and the Christians had the Bible.
They taught us to pray with our eyes closed. When we opened them,
they had the land and we had the Bible.

JOMO KENYATTA, FOUNDING FATHER AND
FIRST PRESIDENT OF KENYA, 1964–1978

The battle against al-Qaeda will not be primarily military. It will be political, economic,
and ideological. It will require the international community to fight, too. We must not let
al-Qaeda get hold of any country. It will result in our worst nightmare. Picture life in
Afghanistan under the Taliban, that is what al-Qaeda's ideology has as a goal.

GENERAL JOHN ABIZAID, COMMANDER OF CENTCOM,
IN HIS SPEECH AT THE NAVAL WAR COLLEGE, NOVEMBER 10, 2005

For some time now, the Horn of Africa and East Africa have been considered by the United States among the most dangerous places in the world as a major source of terrorism—and are under intense scrutiny in the war on terror. With their considerable presence in the region, al-Qaeda and other terrorist groups not only challenge a country's stability but also threaten U.S. interests and human life. While radical Islamic sects spread their influence, the Horn of Africa and East Africa remain at a high level of risk—all the more reason for CODEL visits to see firsthand the extensive and growing presence of these extremists and their history in these regions.

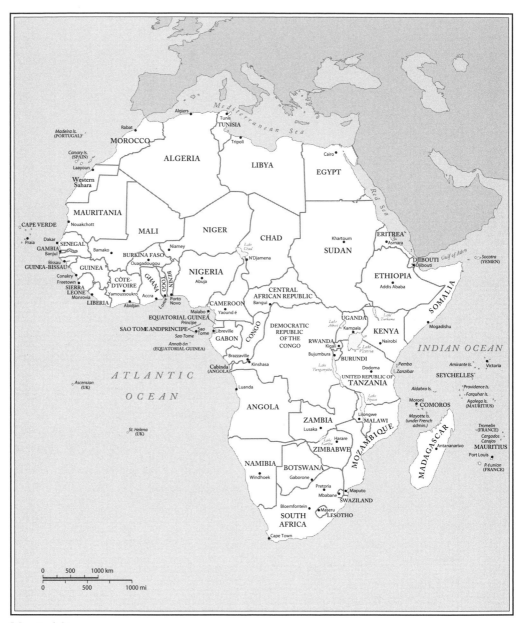

Map 6. Africa

During the Cold War, the United States installed tracking stations in several countries in the Horn of Africa, East Africa, and the Indian Ocean. Used for surveillance of Soviet and Chinese military movements in the region, these tracking stations provided U.S. "boots on the ground," which today's space satellites do not. During this intense era, we had a number of scares and avoided major incidences. We also averted potential military standoffs because we were security conscious. As we entered the 1990s, we lowered our guard, and other than our installation on Diego Garcia gave up tracking stations in the region. Sophisticated technology in cyberspace does not ensure better world safety. Yet, when dealing with an enemy today that operates from multiple cell phones, wears no uniform, and has its military office in a tent, having a presence becomes all the more necessary for gathering sound intelligence.

In the late 1990s, when we shuttered thirty-six embassies and consulates and cut more than 1,600 positions, we combined in some missions the separate, important economic and political functions; relinquished reliable intelligence reporting; did away with some consular oversight affecting control of suspicious travel; eliminated direct bilateral relations with some countries that impact our interests at the United Nations; and eroded our ability to guarantee protection of our U.S. interests and American citizens in the very countries where our presence was needed.

As noted, the positions cut by the State Department involved experienced multilingual officers and affected agencies such as USAID, the U.S. Information Agency, and the Peace Corps that had initiated successful programs in sub-Saharan Africa—with countries like Comoros feeling the sting.

After the Cold War, Congress did approve a budget for the State Department to open thirty-one new overseas missions primarily in the former Soviet Union bloc countries and the divided regions of Yugoslavia. These actions were worthwhile and extensive, but I believe the United States should have kept the other missions in critical areas abroad. In part, these missions would help us maintain crucial intelligence gathering in areas where the threat of terrorism continues to grow and our challenges become more complex—specifically with the Islamic extremists allied with Osama bin Laden and his al-Qaeda terrorist network.

During the nine-year Soviet invasion of Afghanistan (1979–1988), the United States supported the mujahideen (Muslim guerilla fighters) in their fight against the Soviet Union. When the war ended, the United States abandoned them, and in the chaos that followed, mujahideen warlords fought among themselves while thousands of Afghans fled to refugee camps in Pakistan. In these refugee camps, Islamic students distrustful of the United States banded together as the Students of the Jamiat Ulema-e-Islam. They withdrew from society and evolved into the fundamentalist Taliban (students) organization. The Taliban, a radical Sunni Islamist political movement, came to the forefront with the help of Saudi money that established an extensive network of radical madrassas (religious schools). Pakistan assisted in developing militia training schools where recruiting took place.

In Afghanistan, the Taliban defeated the corrupt warlords and ruled much of the country as an "alternative government" enforcing strict Sharia (Islamic law based on the Koran). Under their regime, modern-day radical Islam was born. Many former liberties were denied and activities banned. Television, movies, music, dancing, alcohol, and kite flying were banned. Women were required to wear head-to-foot burqas and were no longer allowed to receive an education. Men were required to wear their hair short and grow their beards long.

Since the war in Afghanistan, numbers of radical-teaching madrassas have sprung up and taken hold around the world, pulling away students from the study of Islamic theology, the Koran, and the humanitarian lessons on ethics, morals, virtues, and justice and cordoning them within a growing society of extremism and violence.

All of this has fueled the theocratic zeal of Osama bin Laden, who, having helped fund Afghanistan's fight against the Soviet Union, said he wants to unite all Muslims, overthrow Muslim governments he views as corrupt, establish a government that follows the rule of the caliphs, abolish state boundaries, drive away Western influence, export terrorism, and use martyrdom operations inside and outside the United States to defeat the "infidels."

Most Muslims are strict adherents to the edifying tenets of Islam. They honor education and have religious and cultural ties to their community. They are peaceful, family-oriented people concerned about their children's welfare and the potential for economic sustainability. Yet in regions such as the Horn of Africa and East Africa, where poverty, poor health care, and a paucity of educational opportunities exist, individuals could be easily subverted to adopt a more fundamentalist view of Islam—and many have done so.

To understand bin Laden's far-reaching fervor to destroy us as a country, it is imperative to have an actual presence in these countries to acquire valid intelligence information—rather than relying on paying in-country "con artists" who will tell us anything we want to hear. We need to keep the vital links of information open in al-Qaeda's backyard—so they don't reach our backyard. Lacking reliable information on all fronts will make it more difficult to root out the extremists associated with Osama bin Laden, his al-Qaeda movement, and their allies.

The second largest continent, Africa covers over 11.7 million square miles and is more than three times as large as the United States. The Horn of Africa consists of a series of mountain ranges in the western part and expansive arid and semiarid lowlands in the eastern part extending to the Indian Ocean. In the lowlands, one of the poorest areas of Africa for agriculture, rainfall is scant even during the monsoon season, and the ground is often parched. On the windward side of the mountain ranges in the western region, monsoon rains can be heavy and in many areas are the sole source of water. Depending on how much rainfall occurs during the monsoon season, life becomes one of feast or famine for its inhabitants.

Africa's population, according to the July 2006 CIA *World Factbook*, was estimated to be 910 million (increasing 10 percent by 2009), of which 410 million (45 percent) were Muslim. The forty-eight countries located below the vast Sahara Desert, known as sub-Saharan Africa, had a population of 748 million, of which 258 million (35 percent) were Muslim. The population of the six countries that make up the Horn of Africa was 165 million, of which 80 million (49 percent) were Muslim, including Ethiopia at 48 percent; Sudan, 70 percent; Somalia, 100 percent; Kenya, 10 percent; Eritrea, 50 percent; and Djibouti, 94 percent. Ethnic Muslim Somalis make up 25 million of the population, most of whom live in Somalia and the contiguous border regions in Ethiopia, Kenya, Djibouti, and neighboring Eritrea. The Comoros Islands, with a Muslim population of 98 percent, are considered part of East Africa. Population trends indicate that by 2050, Africa will be home to almost two billion people, of whom 900 million (45 percent) will be Muslim.

Islam arrived in the Horn of Africa and East Africa as seventh-century Arab traders sailed into the various ports along the coastline for refueling, gathering supplies, and selling wares. Gradual colonization of sub-Saharan Africa followed with early European traders who secured coastal enclaves as a base of operations for their trade activities. Ultimately, the British, French, German, Portuguese, Spanish, Belgian, and Italian colonizers established port settlements ringing the entire African continent and nearby offshore islands.

It was not until the late 1880s that these colonizers journeyed farther into the vast interior of the African continent, grabbed land, and created settlements, dislocating local tribes along the way. This rapacious land rush led to the 1885 Berlin Conference that established guidelines for the acquisition of African territory. Within a thirty-year period, by 1914, the African continent was carved up by these European powers. In the 1950s, fighting for independence from the colonialists became endemic, and by the 1970s, most African countries had gained their independence.

Islamist influence continued to proliferate in the Horn of Africa and East Africa, areas that were readily accessible from North Africa and the Middle East. Unknown in sub-Saharan Africa as late as the 1950s, Wahhabism, the strictest interpretation of Islam's tenets, was soon exported into the region by Saudi Arabia and followed by numbers of mosques, Islamic centers, and madrassas. While several nongovernmental organizations (NGOs), such as the Saudi-based charity al-Haramain Islamic Foundation, offered education, humanitarian aid, and other charitable programs, they clearly introduced their version of Wahhabism.

In the Center for Security Policy's January 2005, No. 4 Occasional Paper, "An African Vortex: Islamism in Sub-Saharan Africa," David McCormack noted, "Saudi money often ends up in hands of militants. Saudi-sponsored NGOs operating in sub-Saharan Africa have been unmistakably linked to global terrorist groups. [T]he Somalia office of the Saudi-sponsored charity al-Haramain has been connected to al-Qaeda and the group Al-Itihaad Al-Islamiya (AIAI) that has terrorized the Horn of Africa."

Reportedly, Fazul Abdullah Mohammed received his primary education at one of these radical-linked madrassas in Comoros, the small island nation off the coast of Africa. He went on to become one of the lieutenants of Osama bin Laden—who was from Saudi Arabia—and his al-Qaeda network.

Terrorist activities associated with al-Qaeda go back to the 1993 attacks on U.S. and UN soldiers in Somalia, while Osama bin Laden was living in nearby Sudan. Twelve of the twenty-two terrorists included on the "Most Wanted Terrorist" list after the disastrous attacks on the United States on September 11, 2001, were listed as coming from African countries. According to an "allAfrica.com" October 10, 2001, news release, seven of the terrorists were from Egypt; two were from Kenya; and one each were from Libya, Zanzibar, and Comoros. Noting most of the Africans listed were involved in the 1998 U.S. embassy bombings in Kenya and Tanzania, journalist Charles Cobb Jr., wrote, "The large number of Africans reflects the continent's fertility as a recruiting ground for the radical Islamist movements that, some believe, have emerged due to the failures of post-colonial African governments to provide adequate education systems and healthy economies."

I believe Africa's colonial legacy opened the door to Wahhabism and the influence of organizations like al-Haramain, which directly benefit terrorist organizations such as al-Qaeda. The United States was never a colonial ruler in Africa. As the most powerful country in the world, though, it needs to help find a solution for the blunders created by the European colonial powers. They not only extracted the riches of these countries for over two hundred years, they left behind a destitute continent.

As it is today, Africa has fifty-three independent and sovereign countries, of which forty-eight are located in sub-Saharan Africa. Most have to contend with not only the irrational borders drawn during the colonial era but also conflicts across those borders and internal civil wars and strife that continue unabated.

One need only look at the Horn of Africa countries of Sudan and Somalia, where genocide and terrorism run rampant, and in Kenya, Ethiopia, and Djibouti, where Somali Islamic extremist factions are attempting to take control and annex the regions that have a dominant Somali population. Rampant fighting for control of disputed land between Ethiopia and Eritrea continues while radical Islamic factions back Eritrea. This regional dysfunction has opened the door to the jihadist movement and ultimate Islamic caliphate that could spread throughout sub-Saharan Africa.

In reviewing Sudan's history since the 1950s and the succession of governmental regimes dominated by Arab extremists in the north exercising Muslim control of the entire country, you can see the progression and consequences of Sudan's relationship with bin Laden and organizations fostering terrorism.

Sudan is the largest country in Africa, and shares a border with Egypt and Libya to the north; Eritrea, Ethiopia, and the Red Sea to the east; Kenya, Uganda, and the Democratic Republic of the Congo to the south; and the Central African Republic and Chad to the west.

For more than fifty years, while this region was under British and Egyptian rule, little thought or understanding was given to Sudan's vast tribal, ethnic, and religious distinctions; cultural and social differences; historical boundaries; or regional separation. Defined by the colonialists, Sudan's boundaries were geographically based. Muslim Arabs lived in the northern areas and Christian Africans and animist tribes occupied the southern areas. In the western Darfur region, more than eighty tribes composed of farmers who were predominantly black Africans with Muslim beliefs and nomads who were of primarily Arabic descent eked out their livelihood.

In February 1953, Sudan signed an agreement with both Britain and Egypt providing its own government and self-determination that led to its independence on January 1, 1956. But the country's inherent problems were deep-rooted and many. The contentious geographic boundaries had scarred the country, its government was splintered, and its people were left with a legacy of tribal and ethnic conflicts.

Moreover, no sooner was the ink dry than the Sudanese government broke its many promises to the south, inciting much bloodshed, genocide, and instability. Civil war and military uprisings took over the country and raged on for nearly twenty years—a ruthless bloodbath in which more than two million people were killed.

In 1972, peaceful coexistence seemed possible when the Arab-speaking Muslims in the north made a commitment to the predominantly English-speaking African Christians in the south that they would create a federal system allowing for autonomy in the southern region. The Addis Ababa Agreement (or Accord) was brokered offering compromises and a degree of self-rule in the south that led to a status quo for a period of ten years.

But civil war and strife had caused a debilitating agricultural and economic catastrophe that further eroded the country's stability. Outside investments dwindled. Food shortages caused by agricultural neglect, the lack of education, limited health care, and unemployment affected both the north and south. In Sudan's south alone, almost four million people were forced to flee to neighboring countries.

In 1982, civil war was again ignited, exacerbated by the Sudanese government's Islamic policies toward the south, and seven years later the National Islamic Front came to power with the intention of building an Islamic state. Radical Islamists from around the world were given free rein and safe haven—a lead that would soon be taken by Osama bin Laden, who, having left Afghanistan, had worn out his welcome in his home country of Saudi Arabia in 1991.

When Saddam Hussein invaded Kuwait, bin Laden offered to organize a group of Arab Afghan fighters to defend the Saudi kingdom against threats from Iraq. The royal family instead invited U.S. troops onto Saudi soil, which led to a protest by the zealot leader. After calling them "infidel forces," Osama bin Laden was put under house arrest and asked to leave the country.

Sudan was the only country to offer refuge to bin Laden, his more than one hundred Afghan fighters, and some of the most dangerous terrorists in the world. Included were Ayman Zawahiri, the chief planner of the September 11, 2001, attacks;

Mamdouh Mahmud Salim, an electronics expert; Wadih El-Hage, bin Laden's personal secretary; Saif al-Adel, a senior al-Qaeda member; and the young man from Comoros, Fazul Abdullah Mohammed, implicated in the 1998 U.S. Embassy Nairobi and Dar es Salaam bombings.

The Khartoum government welcomed other Islamist movements into the country such as the Egyptian Islamic Jihad, Palestinian Hamas and Islamic Jihad, and Lebanese Hezbollah—all of whom had been involved in terrorist attacks against the United States.

Although he was a guest comfortable among the Islamic extremists running the government, reportedly bin Laden was not asked to support the conflict with the south and in fact appeared immersed in daily business and construction activities. He even helped the economy by interesting some Saudi businessmen to make investments in the Khartoum economy. Coincidentally, it was said bin Laden established thirty training camps called farms to export his terrorist activities within the Horn of Africa and East Africa and abroad. Apparent in his speeches were references to the 1993 attacks on U.S. and UN soldiers in Somalia and the first World Trade Center garage attack in New York, as well as the 1996 bombing of the Khobar Towers in Saudi Arabia.

Most of the terrorist plots against America began while Osama bin Laden was in Sudan. Today, Sudan continues to be a sponsor and supporter of terrorism, with an open-door policy to insurgents. Like a growing cancer, al-Qaeda has spread its network worldwide into more than fifty countries. And, it turns out, the Islamic Jihad group, given safe haven in Sudan, claimed responsibility for the U.S. embassy bombing in Beirut and was reportedly involved in the August 7, 1998, U.S. embassy bombings that killed 224 people.

In the early 1990s, when CIA intelligence information of possible terrorist attacks was released, the State Department placed Sudan on its list of states sponsoring terrorism and the U.S. embassy in Khartoum was closed for short periods of time. Increased threats against the U.S. presence reportedly caused the withdrawal of U.S. business interests and some of our diplomatic presence. Then, in 1996, the United States pulled out all our diplomatic presence including our intelligence resources, and the U.S. embassy in Khartoum was shuttered on February 7, 1996. Thus, we lost access to all opportunities to secure further ongoing, credible in-country intelligence and had to rely instead on exiles, political factions, and sources in neighboring countries as well as questionable CIA contacts. (In one of my discussions with a Foreign Service officer associated with the U.S. embassy at the time, I learned the staff was reluctant to leave, believing that by doing so we would lose all our credible intelligence-gathering sources.) Without U.S. embassy representation, we had a vacuous picture of what was happening inside Sudan. The United States then became more dependent upon paid information.

The full withdrawal of the embassy personnel was based on CIA intelligence reports. Only later did we learn that before the withdrawal, the CIA in 1995 had realized it had faulty intelligence reports based on claims revealed to have been fabricated.

All operations at that point were transferred to the U.S. embassy in Nairobi, and it wasn't until seven years later in 2003 that the U.S. embassy in Khartoum reopened with limited resources for bilateral relations. Even now, the United States does not have an accredited ambassador in Khartoum.

If we had kept a diplomatic presence in all the sub-Saharan African countries, we might have been able to learn where al-Qaeda was training, recruiting, and funding destabilization with the help of rogue Saudi Arabian Islamic charities and other groups. We might also have been able to secure valuable intelligence in critical Muslim countries to avoid the terrorist bombings that followed.

We should have been forewarned even earlier with the bombings of the U.S. embassy in West Beirut in April 1983 and the U.S. embassy annex in Beirut in 1984. All these attacks took place well before the August 7, 1998, terrorist attacks on the U.S. embassies in Kenya and Tanzania, which killed hundreds of people, and put Osama bin Laden on the U.S. Federal Bureau of Investigation's "Ten Most Wanted" list.

For that matter, since there were many signs of al-Qaeda's presence in the Horn of Africa and East Africa, the State Department could have made extensive embassy assessments to determine which facilities were adequately protected and had appropriate setbacks and perimeter separation and the ability to withstand the shock of a high-level earthquake. The United States had enough warning and knowledge from the prior U.S. embassy bombings to upgrade and protect or replace every embassy in sub-Saharan Africa. A minimum fifty- to one-hundred-foot separation from adjacent buildings, with security fencing and barricades, could have sufficed to secure an embassy from bomb attacks while new secure compounds were built. In areas where this was not possible, the embassy should have been relocated temporarily for safety. No embassy should have been located in multi-tenant buildings.

In a September 28, 1997, *New York Times* article, "Slowly, U.S. is Returning Some Envoys to the Sudan," by Clifford Krauss, Ambassador Timothy Carney, a proponent of continued engagement with Sudan, said, "With a permanent American diplomatic presence in the Sudan, we [would] press Khartoum to make good on its continual public statements that it opposes terrorism." Two years later, in a December 5, 1999, *New York Times* article, "The World: Friendly Fire; In a War, Even Food Aid Can Kill," by Jane Perlez, Undersecretary of State Thomas Pickering also recommended that the U.S. reopen its embassy in Khartoum, suggesting "staffing an embassy did not confer approval but did provide a listening post," but his recommendation went unheeded. Nor have we lifted the economic sanctions. Since 1997, U.S. firms have been barred from doing business with Sudan, and today the country is identified as a "State Sponsor of Terrorism."

In May 1996, Osama bin Laden and most of his al-Qaeda operatives were expelled from Sudan and returned to Afghanistan where the Taliban had taken control. He built a strong network to raise money and arms for the Taliban and became a close associate of its leader, Mullah Mohammed Omar, Afghanistan's unofficial head of state from 1996 to 2001. Enforcing the narrow Islamic Sharia, the Taliban continued to destroy Afghanistan's civil rights, modern-day lifestyle, and rich culture. Banding together with al-Qaeda factions, it also infiltrated Pakistan, creating instability in its regions, and persisted with ongoing terrorist attacks against government leaders.

On October 12, 2000, suicide bombers attacked the Navy's guided missile destroyer USS *Cole* at the Port of Aden in Yemen. Reportedly, Sudan helped with the logistical support, weapons, passports, and explosives for the terrorists. Evidently, the Lebanese Hezbollah bomb experts in Sudan prepared the explosives for this mission. An Osama bin Laden business provided cover for the purchases that the government shipped in diplomatic pouches—which were not searched—and delivered them to the waiting terrorists in Yemen. Without an active in-country presence in Sudan, we had to depend on intelligence from third parties, reports from State Department country-watchers, and CIA operatives. Obviously, our information-gathering sources were not adequate and did not stop the bombing of the USS *Cole*.

In writing about Sudan, I am concerned with the western Darfur region, which has become a humanitarian disaster with a rootless society of more than five million people. Since 2004, the United States had given to Sudan over $4 billion in humanitarian assistance. Today, Sudan is one of the richest oil-producing countries in Africa, with over six billion barrels of oil reserves. Reportedly, the income from the rich Abyei region is more than $2 billion per year, equating to almost $50 a person, based on the country's current population.

In 2003, as peace talks were underway between the Sudanese government and the southern rebels, fighting resumed and a new rebellion took place in western Darfur. This revolt involved two main groups: the Justice and Equality Movement, which was supported by Sudanese Islamists, allegedly former friends of Osama bin Laden; and the Sudan Liberation Army. Among the current ongoing tribal disputes and power struggles, more than twenty-eight rebel armies are competing.

Both the Sudanese government forces and the rebels have been accused of violating human rights and committing atrocities throughout Darfur. But much of the blame has been placed on the rogue Arab militia group known as the Janjaweed. Reportedly, they have been trained and armed by the Sudanese government and al-Qaeda members, and have continuously attacked the non-Arab tribes in Darfur.

Since then, more than four hundred thousand people have been killed—annihilated—and over two million more driven from their homes. Many fled Sudan to neighboring Chad, on the west, and to the northern regions of Uganda, which lies to the south. Even though numerous ceasefire agreements have been reached with the Sudanese government, the destruction of the Darfur villages in the west persists today.

The United Nations and the United States have provided most of the humanitarian assistance in Sudan, but on many occasions, the Sudanese government has obstructed the distribution process. In 2004, African Union (AU) peacekeepers were stationed in Darfur with a force of 150 troops. In 2005, that number increased to 7,000. Ill-equipped and poorly trained, these intermediaries struggled to stand up to the more organized factions. They could not stop the Sudanese government forces and the Janjaweed militias from destroying the villages.

The AU mandate for the peacekeepers in Sudan was extended twice, through mid-2007. In July of that year, a UN resolution was finally approved for the takeover of the peacekeeping operations by merging AU forces with UN forces. On September 30, 2007, rebel forces attacked and killed twelve soldiers at an AU base.

By the United Nations' committing 26,000 peacekeepers, the international operation would have a stronger presence in the Darfur region. By 2008, the United Nations had deployed 9,200 peacekeepers. In 2009, according to *afrol News*, a "joint-UN-African Union force in Darfur [totaled] 11,500 troops," with the promise of the rest of the troops to arrive by the year-end.

All along, the Sudanese government had been resisting the larger presence of non-Africans inside Sudan. However, they welcomed 150 Chinese noncombat troops and engineers to be deployed with the UN troops in Darfur. For China, this was a first—one that, many thought, was economically motivated by China's vast oil interests in Sudan. U.S. sanctions against Sudan as a supporter of terrorism forced American oil companies to leave the country—Marathon was the biggest.

During this current peacekeeping mission, by October 2009, 26,000 UN troops were deployed in Sudan. The peace negotiations have been persistent, but progress can be measured only by optimism rather than substantive gains. It is my opinion that in the final analysis the partitioning of Sudan may be the only viable solution to resolving ethnic differences between the Muslim and Christian regions: each of those religious groups would be given its own homeland with full independence as sovereign states. An alternative but not necessarily a lasting solution would be to split the Muslim north from the Christian south with defined boundaries: each region would become an autonomous state under a federal system with equal power sharing. Since the oil resources are located in the Christian south, this economic obstacle would need to be overcome in a fair revenue sharing arrangement between both states. Darfur needs to be addressed at the same time, as ethnically or culturally the tribes do not fit into either the north or south region.

On October 23, 2007, Osama bin Laden added fuel to the fire in Sudan with his call for a jihad in Darfur against the UN peacekeeping forces to drive them out of Sudan.

I believe the mayhem that ensued in the semiautonomous south and Darfur region in the west might have been avoided had we stayed actively engaged with a diplomatic presence in 1996. As for the killing fields of Darfur, if solutions are not found and implemented, genocide in Darfur will continue.

Today, the U.S. embassy in Sudan is headed by a chargé d'affaires and not by an accredited ambassador. Although the United States has had a number of special envoys in Sudan, the effect has been nominal since they were there for only short periods of time. It was erratic diplomacy at best. To successfully engage Sudan and be effective, we needed to have been there with a full-time, top-level diplomat—an accredited U.S. ambassador.

Now our inconsistent diplomatic solution is to remove Sudan's president Omar Hassan Ahmed al-Bashir, have him arrested, and send him to the International Criminal Court in The Hague to face charges of genocide, crimes against humanity, and war crimes.

According to Stephanie McCrummen and Colum Lynch's December 8, 2008, *New York Times* article, "Sudan's Leaders Brace for U.S. Shift," political science professor in Khartoum and ruling party lawmaker Saswat Fanous warned, "Any destabilization of this government and all these Islamist elements will certainly turn into a dangerous force. They will be driven underground, and they will invite in a flood of radical Islamists coming from the region into Sudan."

Instead of pressing the UNSC indictment of al-Bashir, in the upcoming 2010 presidential elections we should encourage the political process to replace him with a moderate candidate who supports democratic governance.

In the April 11–15, 2010, election, President al-Bashir was reelected with almost 70 percent of the vote. The opposition candidate, Yasir Arman, a member of the southern-based Sudanese People's Liberation Movement, withdrew from the race due to claimed irregularities.

In early January, 2011, a self determination referendum vote was held in Southern Sudan, as provided for in the 2005 peace agreement between the Khartoum government and the Sudan People's Liberation Army/Movement. On February 7, the results were announced with the majority of the people voting in favor of independence. As planned, Southern Sudan will officially become an independent state on July 9, 2011. A further referendum vote on the oil rich Abyei region's annexation will need to be held once its borders are established and residency issues are resolved.

SOMALIA

Referred to as Somalia—the result of a July 1, 1960, merger between Italian Somaliland and British Somaliland—the Somali Republic has had a long, turbulent history. The country is considered a failed state, and terrorist groups operate freely and transit regularly through its surrounding porous borders.

The easternmost country in the Horn of Africa, Somalia shares a border with Djibouti to the northwest, Ethiopia to the west, and Kenya to the southwest and juts out into the Gulf of Aden to the north and the Indian Ocean to the east several hundred miles. Its shoreline is two thousand miles in length. In its early history, sailing ships along the spice route used many of the ports on this coastline for refueling points.

From 1969 to 1991, Somalia was controlled by Mohamed Siad Barre, the country's military dictator and president. Indoctrinating the country with a form of "scientific socialism," Barre nationalized industry, business, and banking; created cooperative farming; and attempted but eventually failed to rid the country of tribal rather than governmental alliances.

In 1977, Siad Barre wanted to incorporate the Somali-inhabited Ogaden region of Ethiopia into Somalia. A conflict began in which troops from Somalia invaded the Ogaden region with the help of separatist groups to whom the Somali government had supplied military arms. As the war with Ethiopia escalated, the Soviets, who backed Ethiopia, prevailed on Cuba for help. In November 1977, seventeen thousand Cuban troops from Angola arrived and fought alongside the Ethiopian troops. Prior to Somalia's attack on Ethiopia, the Soviet Union and Cuba were allies of the Somali government. Ethiopia also received military assistance from Yemen and some military training from North Korea.

Somalia's troops advanced deep into the Ogaden territory, but ultimately they became battle weary and were driven back. Siad Barre ordered his remaining troops to the border of Somalia in March 1978, and the rebels, backed by the Somali government, continued a guerilla-type war in the Ogaden region until 1981 when they were finally defeated.

At the beginning of the war, as noted, when the Soviet Union was supplying both Somalia and Ethiopia, the Soviets were attempting to broker a ceasefire, which failed. The Soviets, deciding to abandon arming Somalia, then gave their sole support to Ethiopia. The Chinese then stepped in to fill the void and emerged as the major arms supplier for Somalia.

China continued to provide Somalia military assistance until the downfall of the Siad Barre government on January 26, 1991, and then withdrew by closing its embassy in Somalia. The United States had developed a relationship with the Siad Barre government in 1979. The following year, Washington signed agreements for the use of the ports and airfields in Somalia in exchange for defensive military equipment and over the next few years increased military assistance to Somalia by more than $100 million a year. In 1989, the United States supplied arms reportedly used for attacks against the autonomous northern state of Somaliland.

A year earlier, in 1988, a second conflict had erupted with neighboring Ethiopia. This too ended in a stalemate, with both sides withdrawing their troops from the borders. Yet, later that same year, civil war broke out in Somalia and was fraught with many human rights abuses by the Siad Barre government. Shortly thereafter, the United States withdrew most of its financial and military support and maintained only a security assistance program in order to keep access to the air bases and port facilities. Siad Barre and his close allies reportedly had benefited from widespread corruption and siphoned off millions of dollars from foreign assistance funds which the United States and others had supplied.

As the civil war raged on, several rival tribal clan factions made substantial regional gains. Some formed an alliance with the common goal of ousting the Siad Barre government. By 1991, Mogadishu, the capital of Somalia, was under pressure from these well-armed factions. The powerful clan led by the warlord Mohamed Farrah Aidid, together with a coalition of clans, fought against government forces and overthrew Siad Barre on January 26, 1991.

With his supporters, Siad Barre fled Mogadishu in late January 1991 and temporarily remained in the southwest region of the country where his Marechan clan had its power base. He continued to battle to regain control of Mogadishu but was overwhelmed by Aidid's forces in May, at which point he went into exile in Nigeria. For Aidid, this was a personal victory. He had served in Siad Barre's military and rose to the rank of general. Suspected earlier of plotting a coup d'état against Barre, he had been imprisoned for six years.

Ali Madhi Muhammad, a rival warlord from one of the coalition clans, was chosen to take over as the president, but managed to stay in office only until November 1991. He was never able to unite the country, which fell into chaos.

The Ali Madhi and Aidid clan militias started fighting each other for control of Somalia. During this period of instability, a dominant faction in northwestern Somalia, the Somali National Movement (SNM), declared independence and on May 18, 1991, renamed the territory the Republic of Somaliland with their leader Abdirahman Ahmed Ali Tuur becoming the first president.

It was from the late 1970s until Siad Barre lost his power, the United States had given financial and military assistance to Somalia. The country had also received assistance from Italy, West Germany, and Libya. At the time of Siad Barre's downfall, though, U.S. military assistance consisted only of some limited training and technical assistance. And shortly after the corrupt leader whom we supported for years was overthrown in January 1991, the U.S. embassy in Mogadishu was closed. After that, we had no further in-country diplomatic representation there to deal directly with the different warlords and their clans, who began fighting with each other for control of the country.

While these warlords and their clans fought for power, a radical Islamic faction known as al-Ittihad al-Islamiya associated with the newly formed Islamic Courts Union (ICU) also were fighting for control and, gaining parts of Mogadishu and some nearby southern villages, instituting their version of Sharia. Eventually, the interclan-faction fighting in Mogadishu spread to other areas of the country and more than twenty thousand people were killed. This conflict brought about the destruction of agricultural production throughout Somalia, which led to mass starvation.

On December 3, 1992, the United Nations approved Resolution 794, supporting a major coalition of UN peacekeepers led by the United States to go into Somalia to aid in a humanitarian food and supply distribution program and to see if peace could be established. The UN humanitarian aid support troops arrived in January 1993 to start their "two-year mandated effort" to alleviate the serious famine conditions in Somalia.

However, the corrupt warlords and their clans who controlled Mogadishu and the surrounding areas interfered with the food and supply distribution program. They hijacked the humanitarian-sent quantities headed for the needy people in the outlying villages and distributed them instead among their own families and friends. They even sold them to neighboring countries in return for weapons. With less than 20 percent of the supplies remaining to feed the people, an estimated three hundred thousand died of starvation.

The famine relief assistance program suffered dramatically. Extortion, corruption, theft, and infighting had become a common hallmark among the rival warlord clans. Clashes between warlord clans and Islamic extremist militias added to the instability in Mogadishu and the surrounding areas. By the summer of 1993, there were at least twenty competing warlord clans and just as many Islamic extremist factions—including Osama bin Laden's al-Qaeda—with the numbers growing.

Aidid formed the Somali National Alliance (SNA) in June 1992, a political alliance of several clan factions, whose militias were subsequently involved in the 1993 battle with U.S. and UN forces in Mogadishu.

On March 3, 1993, the United Nations Operation in Somalia II (UNOSOM II), a second phase, was authorized to establish a secure environment for humanitarian operations and help rebuild the country by achieving national reconciliation to establish a democratic state. At the March 15, 1993, Conference on Reconciliation in Somalia held in Addis Ababa and represented by fifteen Somali clan factions, an agreement was reached in principle on terms to restore peace and democracy there. But by May 1993, Mohamed Farrah Aidid, the dominant warlord, would not cooperate on the implementation of the agreement.

On July 12, 1993, in a U.S.-led operation, troops went to what was thought to be a safe house in Mogadishu looking for the warlord Aidid and key leaders of his Habar Gedir clan. They had been involved in an attack on UN peacekeepers on June 5, 1993, wherein twenty-four Pakistani troops were killed in an area of Mogadishu controlled by Aidid.

A short attack followed, and U.S. Cobra helicopters fired missiles into a building by mistake, killing more than seventy clan elders who had been meeting to discuss possible peace solutions. This was believed to be the turning point of unifying the Somalis and turning them against the U.S. and UN humanitarian aid efforts in Somalia.

In early October 1993, another military operation struck out to apprehend the warlord Aidid and his lieutenants in the Mogadishu stronghold of his Habar Gedir clan. The U.S. and UNOSOM II forces consisted of 19 aircraft, 12 vehicles, and 160 soldiers. Forewarned of the impending attack that morning, Aidid's clan combined with the Somali National Alliance (SNA) militias totaling two thousand to four thousand fighters who, well armed with grenade launchers and automatic weapons, were ready and waiting. In the battle that ensued, rocket-propelled grenades shot down two Black Hawk helicopters and damaged three others. Some of the wounded troops were evacuated, some were trapped and cut off, and the battle continued throughout the night. Because of some confusion, aid did not arrive immediately. The next morning, a task force was sent in to rescue the trapped soldiers. However, one of the crash sites had been overrun by the clan militias—when the battle was over, eighteen U.S. soldiers had died and another seventy-three were wounded. Among the UN forces, one Malaysian soldier died, two Pakistani soldiers died, and seven others were wounded. Reportedly, more than five hundred clan and SNA militias died in the battle, and a number of civilians were caught in the crossfire. Angry Somalis, SNA militia, and clan members dragged several of the dead U.S. soldiers through the streets of Mogadishu. This failed operation, known as the Battle of Mogadishu, shook up our administration.

On October 7, 1993, President Clinton ordered the withdrawal of all U.S. troops from Somalia. By March 31, 1994, the U.S. troops had left, leaving behind only the UN forces that stayed until 1995, with no peace in sight for Somalia.

In a 1997 interview with CNN reporter Peter Bergen (who later wrote the book *Holy War, Inc.*), Osama bin Laden credited al-Qaeda for training, supporting, and funding the Muslim warlord Aidid and his clan and asserted his fighters were involved in killing the American troops in Somalia in October 1993.

Since the downfall of the Siad Barre government in 1991, the United States and United Nations had struggled to put in place a new secular government in Somalia. Although warlords and Islamic extremists continued to create instability with inter-clan fighting for control, attempts for reconciliation between all the parties failed. After a new Transitional National Government (TNG) was formed in April 2000, the country's instability continued. The TNG also faced internal problems, changing prime ministers four times in less than three years; in December 2003, it failed. In November 2004, a new Transitional Federal Government (TFG) was established in Nairobi, Kenya, because it was too unstable to function in Mogadishu. In early 2006, the new government set up an interim base of operations 150 miles from Mogadishu in the town of Baidoa.

During this period, the United States accused the Islamic Courts Union (ICU) in Mogadishu of harboring al-Qaeda terrorists involved in the U.S. embassy bombings in 1998 including the mastermind Fazul Abdullah Mohammed. In an attempt to capture the al-Qaeda terrorists, the CIA covertly funded the Alliance for the Restoration of Peace and Counter Terrorism (ARPCT), a coalition of secular Somali warlords who ruled different sections of Mogadishu.

The secular warlords were opposed to the Sharia and Taliban-style rule that the ICU wanted to establish, which led to heavy fighting between these factions in February 2006 in what became known as the Second Battle of Mogadishu.

By June 2006, Sheikh Aweys led the stronger ICU militias and ended up taking control over most of Mogadishu from the U.S-supported ARPCT warlord clan coalition. President Abdullahi Yusuf Ahmed was disturbed about the United States financially working through warlords instead of directly working with the two-year-old fledgling TFG, which lacked the strength and financial resources to challenge the warlord clan factions and ICU militias who had controlled different areas of the capital Mogadishu.

Our U.S. sources for in-country information were limited, with Somalia covered out of the embassy in Nairobi. Reportedly, one State Department Foreign Service political officer (FSO), covering Somalia from Nairobi, was reassigned to the U.S. embassy in Chad after sending a cable to Washington in which the FSO criticized the U.S. policy of paying Somali warlords. The FSO should have been promoted instead of being sidelined. Through 1996, the United States had spent over $2 billion on this failed state for humanitarian assistance and in trying to get our arms around the crisis.

In July 2006, Osama bin Laden urged the mujahideen in Somalia to fight anyone who might weaken their grip on power. By then, the ICU factions had strengthened their grip on Mogadishu and the surrounding villages as far south as Kismayo and were pressing for their Sharia to be instituted throughout the country.

Ethiopia supported the Transitional Federal Government (TFG) and moved some of their troops into Baidoa. Meanwhile, the Islamic Court Union (ICU) militias received help from Eritrea. In the ensuing Baidoa battle, the TFG and Ethiopian troops defeated ICU militia units who retreated to Mogadishu. Aided by the Ethiopians, the TFG continued to fight the ICU militias for five days and finally took control of the capital on December 28, 2006.

U.S. intelligence sources indicated that ICU extremists were harboring the senior al-Qaeda leaders—Abu Talha al-Sudani, Fazul Abdullah Mohammed, and Saleh Ali Saleh Nabhan—all reportedly responsible for the 1998 bombings of the U.S. embassies in Nairobi and Dar es Salaam. Reports further indicated the ICU and al-Qaeda leaders fled south toward Kismayo, where some of the ICU Islamist fighters had split off and were headed toward the towns of Afmadow and Dhobley, and others farther on to Ras Kamboni, an isolated fishing village near the Kenyan border which had served as a training camp for the Islamic extremists and al-Qaeda operatives.

Pursued by TFG and Ethiopian troops, the Battle of Ras Kamboni against the insurgents began on January 5, 2007. That same morning, a jihadist website sent out a message from al-Qaeda's second-in-command Ayaman al-Zawahiri urging Muslim brothers to "rise up and support your brothers in Somalia."

The following day, two U.S. AC-130 gunships originating from the CJTF-HOA base in Djibouti flew to a small airport in eastern Ethiopia serving as a U.S.-led staging area. The U.S. Special Ops Forces and Kenyan troops had positioned themselves on the Kenyan border preparing to capture any fleeing ICU fighters and al-Qaeda leaders.

Early in the morning on January 7, the U.S. AC-130 gunships proceeded down to Ras Kamboni and carried out air strikes against the ICU militia, Islamist fighters, and suspected al-Qaeda leaders embedded with them. The next day, AC-130 gunships attacked a suspected al-Qaeda camp on Badmadow Island near Ras Kamboni. Ethiopian helicopters struck ICU and Islamist fighters in the Afmadow and Dhobley areas. Another AC-130 strike aimed at Islamist fighters was reported near the Hayo area.

Three days later, conflicting reports were aired regarding the success of these air attacks. News reports indicated Fazul Abdullah Mohammed, one of the most wanted al-Qaeda terrorists, had been killed. But when I heard this, I strongly felt Fazul would *not* be among the eight insurgents killed. Numerous people called me. My response to all of them was *They didn't get him.*

Reports claimed at least thirty-one civilians died in an assault. These air strikes against civilians caused an international outcry aimed mostly against the United States. Although witnesses described the helicopters as being American, they turned out to be Ethiopian. These were the first such air strike operations within Somalia since October 3–4, 1993, when U.S. and UN troops attempted to capture the rogue warlord Aidid—and we lost eighteen U.S. and several UN troops.

In a January 10 interview, the *Washington Post* reported that Abdirizak Hassan, the chief of staff for Prime Minister Ali Mohamed Gedi, stated he heard from American officials that Fazul Abdullah Mohammed had been killed. On the same day, without confirming the status of Fazul, U.S. Department of Defense spokesman Bryan Whitman alluded to the incident in Somalia, saying, "As we pursue the War on Terror, we will seek out . . . locate, capture and if necessary kill terrorists."

During my posting as U.S. ambassador accredited to Comoros, Fazul was careful and constantly moving around. Fazul was a wily, smart individual—I didn't believe he would let himself be caught in such a war zone. I had come to think of him not as the typical radical Islamic foot soldier but as an astute planner and strategist capable of plotting specific terrorist events. I also didn't think he would involve himself in hand-to-hand combat. People have argued otherwise. I believe Fazul probably had been in Somalia as an instructor helping train young recruits.

Based on my discussions with the Comoros government regarding the elusive Fazul Abdullah Mohammed, it seems that Fazul moved around the Horn of Africa and East Africa regularly and has been known to visit the smaller islands off the coast of Somalia, Kenya, and Tanzania. He had family farther east in the Indian Ocean in the Comoros Islands, where he was born, and possibly on the larger nearby island of Madagascar. Consensus was that when he did spend time in the Horn of Africa, it was mostly in the quiet coastal village of Lamu, Kenya, but not in the conflicted countries. Fazul, I believed, preferred being in quiet, safe havens, such as the small islands off the coast of Africa, where he could go unnoticed.

On January 11, the U.S. ambassador to Kenya came out publicly to say Fazul Abdullah Mohammed was still alive, and that "none of the al-Qaeda members were killed in the air attack[s]." The TFG and Ethiopian forces won the battle of Ras Kamboni. As it turned out, with outside support, the remaining Islamic extremists regrouped and fighting continues today between the different factions. The fledgling TFG continues to be at great risk with the Ethiopian troops leaving Somalia in 2009.

Since January 2007, fighting has continued in Mogadishu. There have been several car bombings and other terrorist-type disruptions—all signs of al-Qaeda's presence—but no sign of Fazul. On June 2, 2007, the destroyer USS *Chafee* fired its heavy guns into a remote northern coastline area of Somalia where reportedly several Islamist fighters were embedded. It was later disclosed one of the targets was again Fazul Abdullah Mohammed, thought to be hiding in this isolated area.

Since the closing of the U.S. embassy in Mogadishu in 1991, there has been a major void in diplomatic relations. Any credible information bought from the warlord network is suspect and the State Department's "Virtual Embassy" website problematic.

With no American "boots on the ground" for direct in-country relations, the State Department's website greeting from the U.S. ambassador to Kenya (who has responsibility for U.S. relations with Somalia) to Somali people seeking information about U.S. citizen services, visas, passports, and other embassy communication is vacuous. Missing is a robotic voice and a list of African languages—since the site I visited was in English:

> Welcome to Somalia's Virtual Presence Post (VPP). Thank you for pay-ing a visit to our new website. The VPP is a new tool of the U.S. diplo-macy that enables us to have a presence in regions where there is no U.S. Consulate or Embassy physically located. Through a regular program of activities supported by the VPP website we aim to enhance interaction and understanding between Somalis and Americans.

For most of Somalia's nine million Muslims with limited education, this virtual presence actually meant "no access" to U.S. information. Somali Internet users in 2007 were approximately ninety thousand, or 1 percent of the population, and for Somalis living in remote regions, there was no Internet access. For that matter, in Sudan, Internet users were only 8 percent of the population; Kenya, 6 percent; Ethio-pia, 0.4 percent; Eritrea, 0.2 percent; Djibouti, 0.02 percent; and Comoros, 3 per-cent. Hence, a VPP program for people living in the Horn of Africa and East Africa would provide little if any direct access to U.S. information.

Somalia is on the threshold of being totally dominated by the most fundamen-talist form of Islam. The growing influence of the al-Shabaab (the youth) faction, an outgrowth of the Islamic Courts Union (ICU), began its rise to power after the ICU militia was defeated in 2006. This movement now controls much of the outlying southern region and considerable parts of the capital of Mogadishu. Al-Shabaab seeks to unseat the TFG and drive out the African Union Mission to Somalia (AMISOM) troops, who are there as peacekeepers also supporting the TFG. Al-Shabaab has publicly waged war against the "enemies of Islam." They are pushing to institute Sharia in its strictest form similar to the Taliban structure in Afghanistan—a battle the United States would not want to repeat in the Horn of Africa.

Kenya

Kenya shares a border with Ethiopia to the north, Somalia to the east, Tanzania to the south, Uganda to the west, and Sudan to the northwest, and the Indian Ocean lies to its southeast. In 2006, Kenya's population was 35 million people, of whom 3.5 million, or 10 percent, were Muslim (although some claim more than 15 percent).

Unlike nearby Tanzania, which adhered to a socialist doctrine, Kenya strived to be pro-Western and anti-communist. Until his death in 1978, Jomo Kenyatta, head of the powerful Kikuyu tribe, remained in power as Kenya's autocratic ruler. When Vice President Daniel Moi became Kenya's next president, the autocrat controlled the country for the next twenty-five years. In 1992, under international pressure, the country held its first multiparty elections in which Moi won. He was reelected again in 1997, serving until 2002. In both elections, reports were heard of irregularities and charges of Moi stealing the elections, which led to considerable civil unrest.

Although Fazul Abdullah Mohammed had reportedly lived in Kenya (in Lamu) for some time and was considered to be the head of al-Qaeda in East Africa, the Kenyan government continued to deny any existence of al-Qaeda cells in its country. It took the 1998 bombing of the U.S. embassy in Nairobi, the 2002 bombing of the Paradise Hotel Resort in Mombasa, and, in the same year, the missile attack on an Israeli-owned airliner to prove otherwise. The al-Qaeda cells in Kenya reportedly received support from radical Islamic groups in neighboring Sudan and Somalia, the Middle East, and Pakistan.

Kenya had its first taste of terrorism during the Moi administration, when the Norfolk Hotel in Nairobi was bombed in 1981 by a radical Palestinian group. Kenya had long been suspected of housing al-Qaeda cells—beginning with Osama bin Laden's confidant Wadi el-Hage in 1994. Although the Kenyan government denied the allegations, al-Qaeda cells and training activities were set up in Nairobi, in Mombasa, and near Lamu in the Kenya border area and Ras Kamboni in the nearby Somalia border area. The porous 400-mile border between Kenya and Somalia reportedly served as the crossing points for Fazul and other al-Qaeda terrorists operating in the Horn of Africa and East Africa. Sudan's border area was also a major crossing point for terrorists who were training inside that country.

I believe had we acted quickly, al-Qaeda might not have succeeded in its disastrous attacks on the U.S. embassies in August 1998 and the resort hotel in November 2002. But even with the terrorist attacks against the United States and Western interests in Kenya, the country was mostly stable and not considered a failed state where Islamic extremists could easily gain control.

That thought, however, changed on December 27, 2007, with the election fiasco between President Kibaki and the opposition leader Raila Odinga. Claims of massive fraud by the opposition, as witnessed by international and local observers, encouraged Odinga to demand a new election, which Kibaki refused. This led to violent protests by opposition supporters. Rival tribes armed with machetes and bows and arrows clashed with each other and destroyed many tribal villages. On both sides, hundreds of people were killed, thousands were wounded, and many were left homeless.

As the mass destruction of tribal villages continued, between January and February 2008, both the State Department and the former UN secretary general Kofi Annan acted as mediators to bring the two leaders together for a quick and equitable resolution. Kibaki stayed stubbornly entrenched and Odinga refused any resolution other than a new election.

This bloody tribal clan feud for control of the country shows how fragile democratization still is in sub-Saharan Africa. Kenya had been held up as the model of how democratic institutions had evolved since its independence in 1964. Yet in 2008, in a country of thirty-five million people, opposing leaders vying for presidency were encouraging a barbarous feud to resolve an election dispute.

Kenya could become another failed state in sub-Saharan Africa. The reconciliation between Kibaki and Odinga agreed to on February 29, 2008, may prove to be a difficult unity, since their power struggle is more tribal clan related than it is about the democratic process of fair elections, rule of law, or regard for human rights.

The U.S. government reportedly gives aid of over $500 million a year to Kenya. Such funding is based on the democratic principles such as the rule of law, protection of human rights, transparency, and of course the free and fair election process. The United States has also contributed millions of dollars to other autocratically ruled states, failing states, and failed states in sub-Saharan Africa over a number of years and continues to do so.

For this very reason, aid tied to democratic principles in a tribal society may prove to be futile. And we've learned such financial aid rarely reaches its intended people at the village level. It's no wonder that most of these sub-Saharan African people, not sharing any of the financial benefits, may not see us as a friend.

As part of the U.S. engagement of the sub-Saharan African countries, instead of giving financial support directly to the rulers or their governments in these countries, we should give more financial support to qualified low-overhead humanitarian organizations that work directly at the village level, but we should not forget the need for adequate oversight.

Maintaining stability in Kenya is important since the United States and Kenya entered into a border patrol program with neighboring Somalia in 2006. This joint effort was in conjunction with the Somali TFG and Ethiopian troops replaced by the AMISOM troops in 2009, in tracking down and capturing al-Qaeda terrorists and other extremist Islamist fighters attempting to cross over from Somalia to Kenya. Any further instability in Kenya could put this military program in jeopardy, allowing al-Qaeda terrorists to transit freely through the Horn of Africa and East Africa.

ETHIOPIA

The only landlocked country in the Horn of Africa, Ethiopia shares a border with Eritrea to the north, Sudan to the west, Somalia to the east, Djibouti to the northeast, and Kenya to the south. Ethiopia has the largest population, with seventy-five million in 2006—nearly half the population in the Horn of Africa, of which thirty-six million are Muslim.

Emperor Haile Selassie came to power in 1930 and continued until 1936 when Italian forces occupied Ethiopia, forcing Selassie into exile. In 1941, British and Ethiopian forces pushed the Italians out, returning Selassie to the throne. He continued to rule through a period of civil unrest until September 12, 1974, when he was deposed.

As mentioned, it was in 1977 that Somalia, claiming the ethnic Somali region of Ethiopia belonged to it, took advantage of the civil unrest in Ethiopia and sent troops in to take control of the Ogaden border region. With Soviet military supplies and Cuban reinforcements, the Ethiopians drove the Somali forces out of the Ogaden region and back to Somalia in March 1978.

Lieutenant Colonel Mengistu Haile Mariam, who ran a totalitarian, communist-style government backed by the Soviet Union, had increased his hold over Ethiopia and purged his opposition. In May 1991, though, the Ethiopian People's Revolutionary Democratic Front (EPRDF) forces took control of Ethiopia's capital, Addis Ababa, and Mengistu fled to safety in Zimbabwe.

In July 1991, several factions formed a transitional government in Ethiopia, although splinter groups withdrew from the coalition in early 1993. Thereafter, the country did not have a stable government in place. During this dysfunctional period in Ethiopia, the province Eritrea in the north established a provisional government in Asmara in May 1991. On April 27, 1993, the Eritreans by a unanimous vote, under UN supervision, gained their independence from Ethiopia. Then Ethiopia made an effort to become more stable by holding multiparty elections for the national parliament and regional legislatures in May and June 1995, respectively. In August 1995, the government of the Federal Democratic Republic of Ethiopia was born.

In May 1998, Eritrean forces seized the border area of Badme, a territory Eritrea claimed should have been ceded to it at independence. The border dispute between Ethiopian and Eritrean forces raged on for two years. More than one hundred thousand people lost their lives. It was a futile battle that ended in the signing of a peace agreement on December 12, 2000. Afterward, a UN peacekeeping force was sent in to monitor the fifteen-mile-wide security zone along the border.

In April 2002, the Ethiopia-Eritrea Boundary Commission (EEBC) did not clearly designate to which country the Badme territory belonged. In March 2003, the Commission declared the Badme Plains area was largely in Ethiopia, while the Badme village itself was in Eritrea. In a 2005 UN Security Council resolution, Ethiopia was to demarcate its borders in compliance with the earlier commission finding, which did not take place.

Today, the border dispute persists with neither side giving in. This dispute is an issue that won't go away until Ethiopia cedes the region to Eritrea, which insists the entire Badme territory belongs to it.

Ethiopia's fledgling democracy slipped backward when the 2005 elections were not deemed to be free or fair. The government was undaunted by these accusations and proceeded to make arrests of opposition leaders, journalists, and civilian protesters with charges and convictions continuing into mid-2007. There have been ongoing discussions with the ruling party and opposition parties on the issue of democratic governance, as a result of the problems that arose in the 2005 elections, in hope of establishing parliamentary rules for a future free and fair election process.

In June 2006, the ICU militias took control of Mogadishu and strengthened their hold in parts of southern Somalia. Ethiopia, seeing the ICU militias as a threat to the security of Somalia and the surrounding region, sent troops to support the weak TFG in Baidoa, where the interim government headquarters were located.

Today, Ethiopian troops have withdrawn, and only a small UN peacekeeping force remains in Somalia in an effort to bolster the TFG, as the TFG struggles to be accepted as the official government in Somalia. With the instability created in Somalia by the different factions, and the political wrangling going on in Ethiopia, both countries continue to be susceptible to more influence by the Islamic extremist factions. It seems like after each battle, the Islamist fighters disperse but soon blend back in with their tribal clans and regroup. This leaves al-Qaeda operatives sitting on the sidelines planning their next move to take over Somalia.

In April 2007, the Ogaden region of Ethiopia was again the scene of violence when separatist rebels attacked a Chinese-run oil field operation, killing over sixty Ethiopian soldiers and nine Chinese workers. As China continues to seek more of the natural resources in sub-Saharan Africa, there will be more such occurrences, but I don't believe China will ever pull out or fight back.

In Ethiopia, the Muslim population does not seem to support a radical Islamic ideology at this point. However, if Ethiopia's political process falters or doesn't fairly include Muslims, radical Islamic factions could gain influence and destabilize the country. The radical ICU factions and al-Qaeda operatives in Somalia continue to try to erode the fragile political stability there, and are just waiting for the right opportunity to create chaos and destabilize Ethiopia.

It doesn't help matters when food shortages become endemic and seventy-five million people need to eat. The differing climatic conditions and political instability at times in this large country have affected the availability of agricultural products. Ethiopian farmers have gone through boom-and-bust cycles, wherein their bumper crops lie fallow when prices are too low and their harvests are reduced during droughts. Crop sales by farmers in the world market also depend on prices from traders who are not consistent, fair, or transparent with everyone, and the farmers never know at what prices the traders have sold their products to the buyers.

In Roger Thurow's February 27, 2008, *Wall Street Journal* article, "Ethiopia Taps Grain Exchange In Its Battle On Hunger," Ms. Eleni Gabre-Madhin, who served at the World Bank and the International Food Policy Research Institute, advocated modernizing Ethiopia's farm markets. According to the article, the country had made great strides in boosting production, but Gabre-Mahdin's concern was that the effort also needed markets to take harvests to during abundant times without depressing the prices.

In sub-Saharan Africa, only South Africa with its modern agriculture system had established a flourishing commodities exchange to solve market fluctuations. It was fortunate Ms. Gabre-Madhin had agreed to return to her native Ethiopia to study its agricultural market. The Ethiopian government agreed to make it a priority to set up a commodities exchange, and provided over $2 million for the project. The World Bank, UN agencies, and donors such as the United States provided the balance of the initial $21 million budget needed.

Ms. Gabre-Madhin was asked to head up the project to help establish a commodities exchange based on the U.S. Board of Trade model with "uniform quality standards, fair price discovery, and futures contracts." The UN World Food Program saw the commodities exchange as a solution for helping to also reduce food and distribution costs by buying more products from places in Africa such as Ethiopia.

The Ethiopia Commodity Exchange that opened in Addis Ababa in 2008 gave farmers more choices on how and when to market their products, long-term planning, and balancing production and sales to market conditions. Damage from periodic drought can be more readily bridged as a result. The Ethiopian commodities exchange model, if successful, could then be replicated throughout other sub-Saharan African countries. Further, if poverty can be reduced successfully in Ethiopia by improving agricultural production, that success could serve as the best countermeasure to the increased influence of Islamic extremists in highly populated Muslim countries, such as al-Qaeda and others who prey on the impoverished people.

Other agricultural models of success have been established by USAID, which, among its programs, supports economic growth and trade in numerous sub-Saharan African countries. In addition, the "Farmer-to-Farmer" program for international agricultural development is active in a dozen sub-Saharan African countries, providing technical assistance, with the aim of reducing poverty and stimulating sustainable economic growth.

Eritrea

Eritrea shares a border to the south with Ethiopia, to the southeast with Djibouti, and to the west with Sudan, and to the east lies the Red Sea. Its population is predominantly Muslim with 4.5 million people of a Somali tribal heritage. Christians, in the minority, have been persecuted.

Until 1944, Eritrea was under Italian rule, which was then replaced by the British, who in the early 1950s suggested partitioning Eritrea between Sudan and Ethiopia to separate the Muslim and Christian factions. Although the United States favored Eritrea's becoming part of Ethiopia, our ally at the time, Eritrea opposed the partitioning. In late 1950, the United Nations voted to have Eritrea become part of Ethiopia but self-administered with its own parliament and representation in the Ethiopian Federal Parliament, which was incorporated as part of Ethiopia in 1952.

Ethiopia became repressive and vicious in its attempts to restrict Eritrea's autonomy. This led to the dissolution of the federation in 1961 and, shortly after, the parliament. Eritrea thus became a northern province of Ethiopia, without the autonomy it had enjoyed since the early 1950s.

Eritrea's thirty-year struggle for total independence from Ethiopia began in 1961. Originally, a conservative group of Muslims led this rebellion; eventually, Marxist rebel factions had a conflict with them, which led to an internal power struggle over the region in the late 1970s.

The U.S. government supported Ethiopia to protect our security interests in a military tracking station at the Kagnew base near Asmara in the north. The United States needed to protect this important military base—but because the powerful rebel group was Marxist dominated, the United States was not willing to support Eritrea in its struggle against the Ethiopian military regime backed by the Soviets. Ultimately, the United States lost its presence there and closed the tracking station in the process.

Without U.S. support, Eritrea in its struggle against Ethiopia looked instead toward its neighbors Sudan and Somalia. In the civil war between Eritrea and Ethiopia, more than five hundred thousand people fled to Sudan for safety. The tenacious Eritreans, however, continued to strike at Ethiopian targets. Over time, the Eritreans undermined the Ethiopians' military strength. By 1989 as the Cold War was winding down, the Soviets withdrew their military support from Ethiopia, which allowed the Eritrean fighters to make some major offensive inroads.

In 1991, most of the northern territory was under the control of the Eritreans, while Asmara, the capital city, was held under siege by Eritrean rebels and Ethiopian troops. Fearing potential defeat, the cruel and corrupt Ethiopian communist dictator, Mengistu Haile Mariam, fled the country and took refuge in Zimbabwe, where he was protected by another cruel and corrupt dictator, Robert Mugabe.

By the end of May 1991, the Ethiopian forces capitulated to the Eritrean rebels in Asmara; the rebels then helped Ethiopian dissidents take over the government of

Ethiopia. The newly formed government allowed Eritrea to undertake a UN-supported referendum in April 1993, leading to Eritrean independence on May 24, 1993.

Isaias Afewerki became Eritrea's first president on May 25, 1993, and still remains in power today. His political party, the Eritrean People's Liberation Front, was renamed the People's Front for Democracy and Justice (PFDJ), which established the country's new government. At first, Afewerki began to rebuild the institutions of governance from the bottom up, including a locally elected judicial system, and expanded people's access to the educational system.

As with most post-independence presidents in sub-Saharan Africa, he eventually became an autocratic ruler overlooking respect for human rights, rule of law, and transparency. Afewerki's interpretation of democracy was a single-party system, with his PFDJ the only party allowed to operate in the country. Afewerki purportedly supported the Global War on Terror (GWOT), but in name only. He used the GWOT as an excuse to arrest and put in prison several hundred political opposition and pro-democracy leaders. This has also divided the factions in the country between more moderate and radical Muslims.

In 1994, a dispute arose between Eritrea and neighboring Sudan that lasted for ten years. Each one accused the other of supporting rebel and terrorist factions trying to destabilize each other's country. In addition, Eritrea's long-running border dispute with Ethiopia regarding the Badme region has not been resolved. To this day, the "saber rattling" continues over this property.

After the events of September 11, 2001, the State Department placed Eritrea on the list of countries harboring terrorists since the Eritrean Islamic Jihad movement had alleged links to al-Qaeda. Eritrea has also taken part in the destabilization of the region with its military support of the ICU militias in Somalia against the TFG. In power since 1993, Afewerki has been listed as the thirteenth worst dictator in the world.

Djibouti

Djibouti shares a border to the northwest with Eritrea, to the southeast with Somalia, and to the west with Ethiopia, and to the east lie the Gulf of Aden and Red Sea. Djibouti was formerly French Somaliland, which gained independence from France on June 27, 1977. Djibouti is a small country of five hundred thousand people, with 94 percent of the population being Muslim. It is located strategically on the African coast, a key terrorist transit point from Perim Island in Mayyum, Yemen, just seventeen miles off the coast of Djibouti.

Djibouti is controlled by a one-party system, the People's Rally for Progress party, headed by its current president Ismail Omar Guelleh. There is a power-sharing arrangement between two ethnic Muslim political factions, with the president, prime minister, and cabinet posts divided among the competing tribal clans. Prior to 1999, for a period of twenty years, Djibouti was autocratically ruled by Hassan Gouled Aptidon. Djibouti's population ethnically consists of 60 percent Somali Issas, 30 percent Afars, and approximately 10 percent of Arab and French ancestry. The ten-year civil war, which ended in 2001 with a peace agreement, left Djibouti weak.

After the September 11, 2001, attacks against the United States, there was a critical need to establish a U.S. military presence in the Horn of Africa in the event al-Qaeda operatives returned there from Afghanistan. In mid-2001, the United States signed a lease with the Djibouti government for the use of Camp Lemonier, a former French Foreign Legion base. In December 2002, the U.S. Central Command established the Combined Joint Task Force–Horn of Africa (CJTF-HOA) to cover the geographic region of Djibouti, Ethiopia, Eritrea, Kenya, Sudan, Somalia, Tanzania, Uganda, Seychelles, and Yemen. Its primary functions beyond peacekeeping, border security training, infrastructure construction, school and medical assistance, and emergency humanitarian assistance were to conduct security operations and military-to-military training, help combat terrorism, and prevent extremist Islamic groups from utilizing the vast territories in the Horn of Africa and East Africa as a safe haven. At the time of my visit in 2004, highly trained military personnel were stationed at the Djibouti CJTF-HOA base. Among the wider Muslim population in the region, there was a mistrust of the real purpose of the CJTF-HOA.

The economy in Djibouti is service oriented and includes the rail line that connects Ethiopia with the Gulf of Aden ports. The lease of the military base at Camp Lemonier provides substantial income to the Djibouti government. Low rainfall in this arid region limits crop production to growing fruits and vegetables for local consumption—most other food needs are imported. Drought conditions in the region, which affect over thirty thousand people, prompted the United Nations to establish an ongoing food distribution program.

With its porous borders and close proximity to the Gulf Arab States, Djibouti is suspected of being a transit point for al-Qaeda and other Islamic terrorist groups. The U.S. military presence increases the risk of terrorist attacks against our interests and a possible disruption to the rail and port activities, which would affect landlocked, highly populated Ethiopia. Added to the list of concerns, since 1998, the Saudi-backed NGOs have built structures that house almost seventy new mosques and madrassas staffed with imams reportedly teaching radical Islamic doctrine. The Saudi al-Haramain Islamic Foundation was one of these organizations, and was active throughout the Horn of Africa and East Africa before being closed down at the request of the United States.

Al-Qaeda terrorists have been active in nearby Yemen since the October 2000 attack on the USS *Cole* in which seventeen U.S. sailors were killed. In October 2002, a similar attack took place on the French tanker *Limburg*: one Bulgarian crewman was killed and twelve others were injured. There were further attacks against oil facilities that hired foreign workers; in March 2003, a Canadian worker was killed. In September 2006, four terrorist bombers and a security guard were killed in a foiled suicide attack against two western oil refineries, and on July 2, 2007, tourists were attacked at the historical site of the Queen of Sheba Temple in Marib when a suicide bomber drove his vehicle into several tourist cars, killing eight Spanish tourists and two Yemeni guides. Subsequently, Yemeni security killed four of the al-Qaeda members involved in that attack.

With a population of twenty-one million Muslims, Yemen has become more politically and economically unstable and its youth radicalized by imams in mosques and madrassas. Numerous Islamic militant fighters returning from Iraq also added to the instability of the Yemeni government. Consequently, Yemen has been fighting radical Islamic militant groups in recent years with the help of U.S. Special Ops Forces based in Djibouti.

President Ali Abdullah Saleh reportedly has developed ties with Islamic clerics and politicos such as the popular Sheik Abdul Majid al-Zindani, a mentor to Osama bin Laden. With readily available weapons flowing into Yemen and a cadre of young radical Islamists, Yemen's weak government could make it another failed state. This should be a concern to the United States—having well-trained and armed radical Islamic militants in Yemen only seventeen miles from Djibouti, the closest country to the Gateway of Africa.

A bridge proposed by Tarek bin Laden, the half-brother of Osama bin Laden, to link the countries could also create major security risks for the CJTF-HOA operation in Djibouti. The Horn of Africa and East Africa will be more at risk with the potential increase in al-Qaeda operatives and other radical Islamic groups coming across the bridge from Yemen, Saudi Arabia, and elsewhere in the Middle East.

On April 25, 2007, Middle East Development (MED) gave the go-ahead to Noor City Development Corp., located in Napa, California, to design a proposed seventeen-mile bridge crossing the Red Sea at its shortest point, connecting Yemen to Djibouti at a cost exceeding $10 billion. MED was controlled by Tarek bin Laden. In the 1990s, Tarek was the general supervisor of the International Islamic Relief Organization. This was a Saudi-backed NGO that was also designated by the United States as financially aiding al-Qaeda and other terrorist groups.

We recognize that al-Qaeda operatives know how to operate under the radar. They also know how the Areas of Responsibility function between the different military commands of EUCOM, CENTCOM, and PACOM with their "fuzzy seamless borders" in the Horn of Africa and East Africa.

In my meeting on April 28, 2005, with General John Abizaid, I discussed this issue and the need to consider unifying the USCOM structure in sub-Saharan Africa and the Indian Ocean region under one command, which would provide for a seamless operation.

On February 6, 2007, President George W. Bush announced the creation of a unified U.S. Africa Command (AFRICOM) to be headquartered in sub-Saharan Africa. Under this command, all military operations would be placed in one or multiple locations in Africa. According to the February 6, 2007, press release from the Office of the Press Secretary, this new command would "strengthen our security cooperation with Africa, and create new opportunities to bolster the capabilities of our partners in Africa. [The] Africa Command will enhance our efforts to bring peace and security to the people of Africa, and promote our common goals of development, health, education, democracy, and economic growth in Africa."

On October 1, 2007, AFRICOM officially unified the fifty-two African countries under one command (with Egypt remaining under CENTCOM), temporarily headquartered in Stuttgart, Germany. AFRICOM was to be fully operational by September 30, 2008. Some sub-Saharan African countries have already expressed that they do not want U.S. troops stationed on their soil. Locating AFRICOM in Djibouti would make sense logistically since we already have an established presence. Blending the resources of EUCOM, CENTCOM, and PACOM into the U.S. AFRICOM would make for an easy transition. There are risks, however, with this concentration in Djibouti and our ability to move quickly to the vast reaches of North Africa and sub-Saharan Africa from there.

With China's insatiable interest for Africa's oil reserves and mineral deposits, we can expect to see a SINO-AFRICOM not only to protect China's vested interests but also to stand toe-to-toe with the U.S. AFRICOM. Since the 1950s, China has had an economic and military presence in Africa and could become a distraction to the United States in the future. It will also become a challenge as we seek to establish security against al-Qaeda insurgents and push our pro-democracy agenda in the sub-Saharan African countries. China will do whatever it takes to protect its multibillion-dollar deals with the African countries. In October 2000, China launched its First Ministerial Meeting in Beijing with a number of invited African leaders. A Second Ministerial Meeting held in Addis Ababa followed in December 2003. Since these successful ministerial events, China plans to hold a Sino-African Summit every three years, alternating with Beijing and an African destination, to advance its (China's) economic interests in these countries. Leaders from forty-eight African countries attended the Third Sino-African Summit on trade and investment on November 4–5, 2006, in Beijing. Then the recent Fourth Sino-African Summit was held in Sharm el-Sheikh, Egypt, on November 8, 2009, with leaders from fifty African countries attending. China has pledged more than $15 billion in new loans for capacity building in these African countries and promised to cancel the debt of some of the poorest African nations.

ETHIOPIA

Ethiopia, which partnered with the Transitional Federal Government in Somalia against the Islamic Courts Union militia factions, has proven to be a friend of the United States once again, and although it is a land-locked country, locating a military presence there might be more central to the troubled Horn of Africa and East Africa region. The African Union (AU) is also headquartered there, and AFRICOM could readily plan strategies to interface with the AU forces for emergencies as they arise. Camp Lemonier would continue to be important for security in the Horn of Africa, with the potential increase of insurgent traffic and risk of attacks coming from Yemen and the Middle East.

Currently, there is a perception concern about the "real role" of the CJTF-HOA operations beyond the periodic humanitarian assistance, training, infrastructure, and facility construction activities. This was the case in Comoros when soldiers wearing uniforms arrived to make improvements to schools and hospitals and to carry out cleanup and painting projects. Even though our military is very professional and does a great job, its uniforms are a source of concern to the villagers since they represent authority or perceived occupation status. A more civilian approach for nonmilitary humanitarian assistance, infrastructure work, and building projects would help solve these problems.

Since my early visits to the Horn of Africa and East Africa, and later as U.S. ambassador attending meetings and Chiefs of Mission (COM) conferences in the region, I believe our U.S. foreign policy needs to include more engagement with both democratically and autocratically run states—that is, if we are going to stop the civil wars, boundary disputes, ethnic tribal cleansing, endemic corruption of rulers, and infiltration of Islamic extremists—all of which lead to a "failed state" status.

In the poverty-stricken countries of the Horn of Africa and East Africa, we cannot continue to allow the deterioration of Sudan with its instability, its civil war, and the devastating killing fields of Darfur; the failed state of Somalia with its long, turbulent history and potential takeover by al-Shabaab insurgents; the at-risk state of Kenya, which had been enmeshed in bloody tribal clan-related feuds for control; Ethiopia's fledgling democracy and ongoing border wrangling; Eritrea, with its long-standing connection with harbored terrorists in Somalia; and Djibouti, important to U.S. interests, to become at risk again of civil war with Afar rebels and the Issa-controlled government, or allow the expansion of the al-Qaeda network or other terrorist organizations in the region.

The only way to be effective is to understand the countries at risk with solid in-country intelligence information. As part of a consistent foreign policy, along with a U.S. presence in every country, we need to engage the people to show the United States really cares. We need to carefully consider the veracity of our intelligence sources before we take any military action within a sovereign state and consider how such actions affect our long-term relations with these countries. We need to understand that democratization will not take hold everywhere, so we must listen to what these countries want to achieve and work with them, rather than exclude them from our aid programs for not complying with our standards. It is necessary to consider having a focused public diplomacy message to reach the people more directly, including those at the village level, so they can participate in programs the United

States is funding for their governments. In that way, there will be expectations from these governments to perform on such programs, which will hopefully reduce the siphoning off of aid funds intended for the people.

Most importantly, we need to be "onsite" to institute and oversee our funded programs—not just write a check—which should include the new MCA and PEPFAR programs. This is crucial if we hope to overcome poverty, improve health care conditions, develop secular education programs, and help mentor people in sustainable development programs to increase their ability to find work and ultimately participate in the global economy.

APPENDIX C

SOMALILAND

A Case for Sovereignty

Somaliland lies in the northwest region of Somalia. It shares a border with Ethiopia to the south and west and Djibouti to the northwest, and the Gulf of Aden lies to the north. It was a British protectorate from 1884 to 1960 known as British Somaliland. It was occupied for a short period of time by Italy in 1940 and recaptured by the British in 1941. On June 26, 1960, less than a week after independence, Somaliland, by a referendum vote, supported unification with Italian Somaliland. Together, they formed the Somali Republic on July 1, 1960.

The borders, which were set by colonists dividing up the land in the late 1800s, left many Somali tribes scattered in several countries including Kenya, Ethiopia, Eritrea, and Djibouti. Much of the bloodshed over the years in this region has resulted from this arbitrary partitioning done without consideration of the tribal cultures of ethnic Somalis.

Somaliland has a 3.5 million Muslim population, and functions today as an autonomous state since independence in 1960—although there was a coup attempt in the early 1960s. In January 1991, Siad Barre was ousted as president of Somalia by several warlord clans, and in May 1991, Somaliland reaffirmed its independence.

The country has overcome the interclan differences by instituting a multiparty political system. With a president elected as head of state, Somaliland's legislature is composed of two chambers of parliament, which are regularly elected. Somaliland has established bilateral relations with several countries but has not formally been recognized as a "sovereign nation" by the African Union or at the United Nations.

Somaliland is more populated than fifteen other countries in sub-Saharan Africa, which include Mauritius, Comoros, Seychelles, Djibouti, Gabon, Swaziland, Cape Verde, Botswana, Equatorial Guinea, Gambia, Guinea-Bissau, Lesotho, Mauritania, Namibia, and Sao Tome & Principe. In landmass, Somaliland is bigger than seventeen of the countries in sub-Saharan Africa also.

As Somaliland continues to strive to seek self-determination and sovereignty, it continues to be controlled by chaotic Somalia, a country that has never seen peace or a functioning democratic government. This remains the case today.

On May 16, 1993, Muhammad Haji Ibrahim Egal became president of the new Somaliland. Reappointed in 1997, he remained Somaliland's president until his death on May 3, 2002. Egal was a popular politician. Selected to serve as prime minister of the self-declared Independent State of Somaliland in June 1960, over the years he also served in Somalia's government as defense minister, education minister, prime minister, and ambassador to India. Under the dictator Siad Barre, Egal was imprisoned two times.

After Egal's death, Vice President Dahir Riyale Kahin became the interim president and was elected president on April 14, 2003, in Somaliland's first free and fair election.

Somaliland has continued to improve its commercial interests. Its main trading partner is Ethiopia, which depends on Somaliland for port access to the Indian Ocean. There is an emphasis on education and health care in Somaliland with access to two quality universities and the modern Edna Adan Hospital in the capital Hargeisa.

From April 15 to April 24, 2007, I was in Nigeria serving on the International Republican Institute (IRI) election observation team. I had the honor of meeting and spending time with Mrs. Edna Adan Ismail, the former foreign minister of Somaliland from May 2003 to 2006 and wife of Muhammad Haji Ibrahim Egal, Somaliland's former president.

In meeting with Mrs. Ismail, I wanted to get some insights on Somalia and her homeland of Somaliland. We also discussed the concerns about al-Qaeda's presence in the HOA and the terrorist threats. We further discussed the possibility of peace being achievable in the region. I then asked Mrs. Ismail what the United States needed to do to more fully engage the region as part of our foreign policy.

Mrs. Ismail was kind enough to respond to these broad and complicated questions in a very thoughtful and straightforward manner. I felt her emotion concerning the plight of Somaliland's future, and the necessity of achieving recognition by the international community as an independent sovereign state with full rights to UN membership. The following edited excerpts were taken from her interview.

A Long History

The Horn of Africa is certainly a most interesting and strategic part of the world that has a long, very old history. It was the trading route as far back as the Pharaohs. It was also on the spice route to the Far East and India and the Arabian trade links with Africa. Long ago there was also an important pearl diving industry there.

We would like to think that one of the three wise men that brought gifts to baby Jesus brought frankincense and myrrh, the best in the world, from the hills of Somaliland, formerly known as the Land of Punt. So Somaliland is an old part of the world that deserves attention, deserves to be studied, and [needs] to look for a solution.

The Horn of Africa was divided up by the colonial powers, [in which] many areas were inhabited by ethnic Somalis. This is a dominant Islamic part of the world, and the Somalis are people who are a mixture of Bantu, Arab, Hermitic, and Semitic races. They have a very distinct culture, and a similar language with some variations.

We [Somalis] had been divided up into the small French Somaliland, now Djibouti, inhabited by ethnic Somalis and a few Afars. The Afars live mainly in Eritrea and Ethiopia. Then there was the former British Somaliland, a protectorate, which became Somaliland; and Italian Somaliland, an Italian colony, which became Somalia, one of three in Africa which also included Eritrea and Libya. Part of the Somali-inhabited Horn of Africa lies within Ethiopia, an area known as the Ethiopian Fifth Region, and a Somali-inhabited territory in the northern part of Kenya known as the Northern Frontier Districts of Kenya. Now these were regions, each with a different colonial power, different administration, but all inhabited by ethnic Somalis.

Back during the time of the British, because Somaliland was a protectorate rather than a British colony, it was the only one that had its own administration, [and] its traditional values and culture [were] left intact. We shared a Treaty of Protection with Britain, had their British penal code and British criminal law, but our own culture and way of settling disputes and differences. This gave the people of Somaliland the ability to solve their own internal conflicts, differences, and disputes. The others, because they were colonies, were discouraged from practicing their own traditional ways of conflict resolution, and only had the colonial power way of settling disputes and running their country.

After the Second World War there was the desire of nations to become independent—and the proverbial winds of change. We remember Kwame Nkrumah, who became president of Ghana and one of the most influential Pan-African movement leaders working to free Africa of colonial rule, bringing all of Africa together. That was what inspired the people of Somaliland to bring all Somali-speaking people together under one yoke, under one administration.

The Price of Freedom

Somaliland had leaders who believed in unity—in bringing all the Somali people back under one administration. Our politicians advocated and campaigned for Somali unity. Many of them went to jail because of this idea. My former husband, our late president Mohammed Ibrahim Egal, was one of the first Somalis who thought of bringing all Somali people together.

He had been a young student at the London School of Economics, 1953–1954. He was a forward-looking person and well-respected, dynamic young man. That was the time when Kwame Nkrumah was campaigning for Pan-Africanism. When my former husband came back in 1955, he continued to campaign and made contact with former Italian Somaliland leaders and other Somalis. By 1959, the British and the leaders of Somaliland agreed on a date for Somaliland to become independent, at which time Mohammed Ibrahim Egal was elected leader of the government.

He was the person to whom the British handed over the reins of power on June 26, 1960, when Somaliland became independent. He thereafter became the first prime minister of the independent state of Somaliland. We are very proud of Somaliland's seniority as being the first Somali state to attain independence.

Immediately, we campaigned for the independence of neighboring Italian Somaliland, which gained independence on July 1, 1960. We held seniority of independence by one week. Somaliland and Italian Somaliland, both now independent and sovereign, voluntarily united to form the Republic of Somalia.

I want to emphasize it was a voluntary union because it was not a conquest of one nation taking over another. We were looking to the future, trying to make our union work. We went into it with a lot of goodwill, and with a lot of good intentions.

But then with all good intentions, some marriages work and some do not. Unfortunately, the union we had with Somalia did not work for the benefit of the people of Somaliland. Having been the first born, it did not work for us. Having been the ones who had conceived this union, campaigned for it and spent a lot of resources and energy, it did not work for us. That is why on December 10, 1961, just one year and a few months after the union, the army staged an attempted coup to separate Somaliland and Somalia because of the injustice that was taking place in Somaliland. Unfortunately, it did not work.

Once the coup was crushed, Somalia became very forceful to prevent such things from happening again. Anybody who was educated from Somaliland would not be employed and others were dismissed from service. We were encouraged to flee the country or be incarcerated. Businesses were taken over. Banks were told not to give credit to people from Somaliland. All institutions were moved to Mogadishu including embassies, consulates, banks, and the reins of government. Somalilanders were the senior partners but suddenly lost their importance and became second-class citizens. This continued until 1967, when Mohammed Egal, our first head of state, who had been in the opposition, was elected prime minister of Somalia.

A PROCESS OF RENEWAL

A revival of law and order, a revival of democracy, and a revival of contacts with our neighboring countries Kenya and Ethiopia took place. We developed a close friendship with the United States and Great Britain. Our late president and prime minister

C.1. Somali Prime Minister Muhammad Haji Ibrahim Egal and First Lady Edna Adan at a White House reception given in their honor by President Lyndon Johnson and Vice President Hubert Humphrey, March 1968. (Official White House photo)

Mohammed Egal became a guest of President Johnson at the White House. We met with Secretary of State Dean Rusk and Vice President Hubert Humphrey. We even flew on Air Force One and were received with a lot of dignity. We had similar state visits in West Germany, Britain, and Italy. These were the years when a young democratic, dynamic government was born in Somalia.

But what pleased one group of our friends displeased others. That was also the time when Russia, the Soviet Union, and the Cold War were at their peak. Russia took steps to try to put us out of business, if I may use that expression. It went into partnership with certain military elements in Somalia—and Siad Barre. They encouraged, armed, prepared, and plotted with him to overthrow the civilian government on October 21, 1969. The then President Abdirashid Ali Shermarke was assassinated and that was the last time Somalia had a democratically elected civilian government.

Prime Minister Egal was thrown in jail and all his property was confiscated. As his wife, I was put under house arrest and everything I had was taken. I survived that revolution with eighty-three dollars to my name. You know, that's life in Africa. Luckily, because of popular pressure, we were not executed. People respected us, and they would have had a revolution on their hands if they had executed the prime minister or any members of his government.

Dictatorship

In 1969, Siad Barre became president of Somalia. There was an epidemic of greedy, ruthless, heartless dictators in Africa. Idi Amin was in Uganda, Mengistu Haile Mariam in Ethiopia, and for over twenty-one years, we endured Siad Barre as a dictator.

By 1980, Somalilanders started an open revolt to free themselves from the oppression of Siad Barre. They started the Somali National Movement (SNM), which was operating from inside Ethiopia. Then came Siad Barre's troops, an aerial bombardment, killings, executions, and mass graves. A week before I left Hargeisa to go to Nigeria to become an election observer, a new mass grave was discovered in Somaliland.

Of course the UN came and made an inventory. They agreed this is a mass grave, and a human rights abuse, but that's as far as it goes. The survivors and relatives of those who were put into these mass graves are still waiting for justice. They know who did it, the Somali troops and the Somali government, but [they have] no retribution, no closure.

In January 1991, after a long civil war, Somaliland managed to [help] oust Siad Barre, who fled to Zimbabwe, which is ruled by another dictator. At that time, Somaliland closed its border according to the original British borders and declared independence from Somalia. The UN and AU both have stated that African borders must be as they were at the time of independence from a colonial power, and this is what Somaliland had done. Somaliland is not a secessionist or breakaway state as it was accused of being. Instead, it was separating from a voluntary union.

When Senegal and Gambia united as two sovereign states, [the union] lasted only six months so they separated. Neither one was accused of being a breakaway region. It was a union and a separation, which has also happened between Somaliland and Somalia.

Part of the problem is the world thinks it is all one country, since Somalia and Somaliland are confusing, which was not the case between Senegal and Gambia. We can't change our name: it has a proud heritage dating back to 1884 when the British came to our country.

Rebuilding Our Country

In 1991, we closed our borders and started to rebuild our country, which was leveled by aerial bombardment and every other known military method of destruction.

Somalilanders put their roof back on their little hut. Then we brought back over one million people from refugee camps in Ethiopia.

Meanwhile, Somalia still sends people into exile today, while Somaliland is bringing people back into the country. Today, people are voluntarily returning from Canada, America, the United Kingdom, and other parts of Europe. The climate is conducive for people and families to come with their kids. Schools are opening up, hospitals are being built, roads are being built, land mines have been removed, and administration is in place. We have a parliament, an elected president, courts, and a vibrant and energetic civil society. We have in Somaliland what many African countries do not have nor have been able to achieve. We are proud of the fact that we have been able to put all of that in place without international recognition.

That international recognition has been denied to the people of Somaliland. So instead of encouraging law and order, democracy, human rights, and justice, the world has chosen to encourage, support, and recognize lawlessness [in Somalia].

Warlords

The world has encouraged warlords. When you call a bandit a warlord, you give him the title of lord, and he believes at the end of the day he is a lord. And so other bandits also wish to become lords, and that is exactly what has happened in Somalia. Every single one of the fourteen governments they've had in Somalia was headed by one or another warlord. And every single reconciliation conference held for the people of Somalia in one of the world capitals was funded by international taxpayers' money, only to fund another warlord—a bandit, killer, and mass executioner—to head a government.

This is where the Americans, the British, and the international community have gone wrong. You backed the wrong horse. By backing Somaliland you would have backed a democracy. By encouraging and supporting what Somaliland has been doing, you would have given value to what you have been preaching. You would have been practicing what you have been teaching us in your universities. Instead, millions of dollars of your money and everybody's money has gone into Somalia—and into [the pockets] of the warlords.

When you started in 1992, when you had the American troops there, when twenty-eight international nations landed on the beaches of Mogadishu with CNN and the floodlights recording the landing, there were just two warlords. There were Aidid and Ali Mahdi. Because there was so much publicity given there, a third and a fourth said, "Hey, wait a minute, why do you call him a lord? I was a bandit just like him. You're calling him a lord—why can't I be a lord, too! Just because he's got 250 militia—I can bring 300 militia together, and I can become a bigger warlord than he is." And it became a competition between bandits to see who was going to be the biggest warlord.

That's when all the arms flew in and traders became rich. Anybody who had hardware to dispose of there [found] a ready market. By the time they had their fifth reconciliation conference in Mogadishu they had eight warlords, having started with two in 1991. By the time they had the thirteenth reconciliation conference in Arta, Djibouti in May 2000, they had 25 warlords. Later when they convened again in Kenya there were 53 warlords. Two years later there were 100-plus. It has become like the stock market: "You need to look to see what the number of warlords is today. Is it 205? Has it gone up; has it gone down?" It's a joke, but it's a joke that is causing a lot of hardship to the people on the ground.

THROUGH IT ALL

Yet, sixteen years after independence, today Somaliland after separation from Somalia is a peaceful country. Of course, we have some disagreements, and things we would like to see working better.

On May 3, 2002, we lost our founding father, first prime minister, and president of Somaliland. Four hours later, the vice president was sworn in according to our constitution. There were no squabbles and no scratching his eyes out. The parliament endorsed it and that was it. He had eight months as a mandate of the presidency; thereafter elections took place. Three candidates competed against the incumbent, who won by eighty-seven votes. It was taken to court. The courts endorsed it and that was it. The candidates who lost conceded and congratulated the winner. That's Somaliland! That's what Somaliland is all about, a country that exists in spite of [the absence of] recognition.

CONCERNS ABOUT TERRORISM

We are Islamic. We have always been Islamic. Being Muslim is not synonymous [with being a terrorist]. In fact, it is to the contrary. If you are a good Muslim, you are anything but a terrorist. Islam is a very sobering, very pacifist religion that forbids violence.

We are one of the first nations that became Muslim in Africa after Islam arrived here over 1,500 years ago. Islam does not prevent one nation that is Islamic [from being] law abiding. It does not cause another nation to become a terrorist. Whether a person is Muslim, Catholic, Buddhist, atheist, or whoever, it is not the religion that makes one become a terrorist. It is the behavior of that individual or that group of people that has become violent and has become terrorist.

So what has caused terrorism? It is not the religion, but dollars, money that has gone into these countries that has encouraged lawlessness and greed, a certain behavior of taking what you can, whichever way you can. That has caused the terrorism.

The Western world, and I am particularly singling out Britain, knew Somaliland well. They were the previous partners during the time when we were a British protectorate. The British before anybody else should have come out to say that we attest to the fact that Somaliland is a free, independent state because we signed the treaty of independence with them. They should not have had such a short memory. They should have come to our side. By watching what we are doing, the track record of sixteen years of stability should have encouraged the western world to support what Somaliland is doing. And that would have become a lesson to Somalia, and it would have given value to democracy instead of giving value to terrorism.

The Way Forward

Everybody is giving money to Somalia only to buy more guns, only to create more terrorists. It's the Western money, the money of the international community that is creating the terrorists because it is giving value to terrorism. It is encouraging and giving power to terrorists. The Arabs have given money to Somalia. I don't know how much money Libya has given, or Kuwait has given, or Saudi Arabia has given. Yemen is giving now. The Emirates are giving. Every Arab country is giving money to Somalia. The European Union is giving money, the Americans are giving money, and the British are giving money. Only by closing the tap, stopping the money flow, and saying we will not support you unless you put the guns down, unless you stop killing your own people, unless you stop shooting in the streets of your capital, can we effect a change.

There must be a ceasefire in Mogadishu because what is happening in our neighboring country Somalia is affecting the entire region. We have tens of thousands of refugees that are flowing into Somaliland. We have limited resources, which are being depleted. We don't have enough water, food, or jobs for our own people, and there is no way we can accommodate that many people coming in from Somalia.

We are concerned that many will probably bring in guns. When they come, they also bring their behavior with them. I mean there is one baggage that doesn't weigh much: it is the behavior that is inside of you, the behavior in your mind, the attitude that you have. So we can search your pockets for weapons, and [your] shoulders for the gun that you are carrying, but then we cannot search your mind. We do not want them to bring into Somaliland the kind of attitude they have had in Somalia that has caused the destruction of Somalia.

So the sooner we are able to close our borders, with support from the international community, to the borders at independence, the sooner we can stop being infiltrated by whomever. We don't want to allow people to come in to destroy our country.

The world must know there are Somali terrorists and then there are also Somali humanitarians who value human rights, human dignity, and human life. We must not all be put into the same basket. By putting us in the same basket, the international community will be destroying a very valuable friend in Somaliland, the people of Somaliland.

Do you know that Somaliland is the only African country where we have apprehended al-Qaeda terrorists in our country who shot at international health workers and aid workers? It was not the government, but it was people: the villagers who caught the terrorists, the killers, and handed them over to the government. We had them tried and we sentenced them. They are now in prison being fed by our own taxpayers' money.

Now which other African country has done that? Somaliland, which is preventing terrorists from taking root in the Horn of Africa, is keeping watch while your children sleep. Djibouti sleeps because Somaliland is keeping watch, and you have got a friend in Somaliland. They are extending a hand of friendship to the international community, and the only thing that the international community does to that hand of friendship being extended by Somaliland is to slap it: "You are a fragment of Somalia, you are a breakaway region, you are a secessionist region." I think that is most unfair and will have very bad repercussions for what happens in the Horn of Africa in the future.

ADVICE

You have a friend, an ally, and a partner. Make use of it! Don't turn that friend into an opponent. Don't turn him into an enemy. Don't turn him through desperation against you! Because if we're not able to give our people the one commodity that they value most—their dignity and their identity—they will become hostile. They will become opponents, and they will only fill the ranks with those who have behavior that is not favorable to the rest of the world.

U.S. POLICY TOWARD SOMALILAND

[As to U.S. policy toward Somaliland,] it has been far less than desirable. I have been to the State Department time and again. I spoke with Jendayi Frazier three months before I left the office of the foreign ministry. I said to her exactly what I am saying to you: Somaliland is extending a hand of friendship. Please take that hand of friendship.

Send a fact-finding mission to Somaliland. Become acquainted with what we are doing right and what we are doing wrong. Base your decision on the facts that you find. Don't base your judgment on what Somalia tells you about Somaliland. Somalia, who put airplanes in the air to bomb Somaliland, is not going to say good things about Somaliland. This is one occasion when the victim is being defended by the assassin! I don't think there is another case like that.

There is no way Somaliland will ever go back to Somalia again, however much pressure the world puts on us. And to tell us that our situation would be settled only after Somalia is settled means we are being linked to people who do not wish to settle problems. Why should we suffer the penalty of crimes that are being committed elsewhere? During all of our struggles, we have survived without food aid. We receive no grants from the World Bank, and we receive no loans from the International Monetary Fund. We have survived because of our good governance.

Ethiopia, with seventy-five million people, receives massive food aid, and one quarter of the food aid destined for there comes through the Port of Berera in Somaliland, without military escort, without any of it being looted, without any bag being diverted. It travels through Somaliland intact all the way to Ethiopia. That's something the world doesn't know about Somaliland.

Life after the Foreign Ministry

I made my decision, when I retired from the foreign ministry, to build a hospital. I put everything I had including all my personal assets, government service benefits, grants, repatriation money, and my personal jewelry into building a hospital for my people.

Our interview concluded; the time I spent with Mrs. Ismail was a most enlightening, interesting, and informative experience. The case she built for sovereignty of her native Somaliland was very compelling. I felt the United States needed to seriously review Somaliland's desire for self-determination, and give support at the United Nations, as we have done for other smaller countries in sub-Saharan Africa that previously became sovereign states.

The United States needs to support Somaliland's sovereignty in lieu of being left under the control of Somalia. The United States needs to take a stand in support of Somaliland's desire for sovereignty as an independent democratic nation, rather than being left under the control of a failed state, with constant infighting between corrupt warlord clans, Islamic extremist factions, and a weak Transitional Federal Government caught in the middle of infiltrated Islamic extremists and al-Qaeda terrorists.

U.S. foreign policy needs to be consistent in sub-Saharan Africa and help such democratically formed states as Somaliland desiring self-determination. We need to stop the civil wars over boundary disputes left as a legacy of colonialism, the constant ethnic tribal cleansing by corrupt dictators, and the instability created by Islamic extremists. Ultimately, these factors lead to failed states, which become fertile breeding ground for al-Qaeda terrorist networks.

On February 18, 2008, the *New York Times* article, "Kosovo Declares Its Independence from Serbia," by Dan Bilefsky, reported the United States, Britain, France and Germany had agreed to recognize Kosovo after it declared its independence from Serbia. They urged the rest of Europe to follow suit—good news for Somaliland's similar request at the United Nations. If our U.S. foreign policy truly supports democracy and freedom of choice, we cannot allow Somaliland to (potentially) become another failed state in sub-Saharan Africa.

A good start was when Somaliland's president Dahir Riyale Kahin was invited to the United States on April 17, 2008, which was described as a state visit to meet with officials in Washington. Reports indicate a number of aid projects were "inked" while he was there. In addition, reports indicated Somaliland was being considered as a candidate for a new AFRICOM base in the HOA.

Another milestone took place on June 26, 2010, in the election for president, when Ahmed Mohamed Silanyo was elected with almost 50 percent of the vote. Although the election date had been moved forward by two years due to political differences and power struggles, the election process was generally peaceful, fair, and transparent. According to a July 2, 2010, *CNN World* article, "Opposition leader wins election in Somaliland," by Mohamed Amiin Adow, the national electoral commission chairman, Ise Yusuf Mohamed, stated, "This is an important election for the people of Somaliland; it is also a major step toward the democratization of the country."

The next step is for the United States to take the lead at the United Nations to support Somaliland as an independent sovereign state with full voting rights and privileges.

INTERVIEWS WITH COUNTRY LEADERS

ANIL GAYAN, MAURITIUS, OCTOBER 3, 2006

Anil Gayan was the former minister of foreign affairs and regional cooperation under the administration of Sir Anerood Jugnauth, and then under Paul Bérenger's administration was the minister of tourism. The following excerpts were edited from our interview.

J.P.: What are some of your thoughts on such issues as sustainable development in sub-Saharan Africa?

A.G.: My first comment on the sustainable development in sub-Saharan Africa would be with regard to the leadership. I think Africa had very good leaders at the time of independence. But over time, especially when the coups d'état started in Africa, I think we had problems with leadership. If we can rid Africa of all coups, and all coups are condemned, we might have the chance of having a leadership that is acceptable to the whole of the sub-Saharan Africa countries. But I must also say that sub-Saharan Africa is poor except for South Africa and a few other countries. So poverty has, I believe, been caused essentially by this lack of leadership. When you look at the economies of the colonies in Africa at the time of independence, they were in much better shape than they are today.

So whatever one might say about colonialism, we have to recognize that colonialism at times did work better than the current leadership in Africa. I'm not saying that all of sub-Saharan Africa is like this, but there are quite a number of countries where trade has fallen. Also in the colonial days, there were some of best medical facilities in sub-Saharan Africa. Today that has changed because of the leadership and corruption. In order to solve this problem and to have sustainable development, we need responsible leadership.

We need to combat corruption—corruption is a big disaster in Africa. We need to raise the level of education—which means making an investment. Unfortunately, the investment is not there. Although we can know what the diagnosis is, we don't have the tools to remedy whatever problems we have in sub-Saharan Africa. Still, one should not despair. There are a lot of positive signs in sub-Saharan Africa that must be commended. If you look at the number of countries that hold elections, they may not be the perfect elections but they are their elections and they involve multiple parties.

The other problem we must attribute to the leadership was the need at one stage to have single parties, and not a multiplicity of political parties. The fear of hearing the other side saying, "We don't agree," was also a problem. Dictatorship, lack of leadership, and the lack of democracy caused a lot of problems in sub-Saharan Africa, but things are changing, as I said. If you look at southern Africa today we just had the elections in Zambia. Botswana has elections. The Lesotho has elections, the Namibia, South Africa, Mozambique, Tanzania; Madagascar also has elections, [as well as] the Comoros, Kenya, [and] Uganda. So things are moving in the right direction. Not that everything is bright. Of course, after every election, people will challenge the results, but the process is there, and I think this is a major step toward ensuring the sustainable development in sub-Saharan Africa. There's the possibility of holding leaders to account, of holding them to their promises made in the election campaign as something worthwhile.

So let me move on to the factors we need in motion to ensure the continued economic success. I believe in spite of economic success we have a major problem today in Mauritius. It is cronyism. We have this problem under all governments. I'm not blaming this political government or previous governments, but I believe Mauritius is too small. That it is inevitable that there will be a degree of cronyism. But when cronyism becomes *the* major trigger for all decisions, that becomes a problem.

I believe that the smallness of the country is a big handicap. We also have an ethnic dimension in elections. So if we want to do something to ensure the economic success of Mauritius, we have to be like Singapore and go for meritocracy wherever it happens. If we don't have that, whatever we can say, whatever rhetoric we utilize, it is not going to work because the country is not going to be able to sustain the progress that it has achieved in the past years. We are aware of the challenges of globalization, et cetera, but I believe that we need to also ensure that we can meet those challenges. We need the right people, people who are totally dedicated not to one political party, or one political leadership, but to the country. Unfortunately we don't have it today. I think for the sustainable development in sub-Saharan Africa to succeed, we [also] need to have the freedom of the press. I mean, the press plays a major part, and this has been one of the gross absences in sub-Saharan Africa.

When you ask why Mauritius has succeeded when other sub-Saharan African countries failed, I believe that Mauritius has been lucky in the sense that we have had the [Franco-Mauritians] who have been in business, who have been the entrepreneurs, who have been the professionals. They have ensured the continuity in Mauritius with regard to the business climate. In the sub-Saharan African countries, once the colonialists departed, it was all left to the Africans who did not have the expertise and the professionals to take care and to handle matters. I believe that that has been a *major* impediment in the development of sub-Saharan African countries.

Also, we had *la chasse aux sorciéres,* the witch-hunt, in many sub-Saharan African countries. If you take a country like Guinea, under Sékou Touré—with whom I had the pleasure of meeting in 1983 when he was the president of Guinea and I was then minister of foreign affairs— Touré was one of the intellectual giants of Africa, and yet, he was such a dictator that all the intelligentsia from his country left. So that was also one of the problems: persecution of the intellectual class, the hounding of those who might oppose the people in power.

This intolerance toward the opposition was not present in Mauritius. Mauritius has been a democracy. We had a short spell when elections were postponed but generally, I think, Mauritius has survived because of the Francos and because of a free press. I think we are one of the countries in this region to have had a free press for much longer than anybody else. We have had a fairly high level of education. And we are also lucky in the sense that we have countries that have been our friends: countries like India, France, the UK, and, to some lesser degree, the United States was also there. We have been lucky in that sense. So I believe that all of these things have helped Mauritius when the other countries didn't have them. It is only now that India is moving into Africa, but we have had an Indian high commission since just after the Second World War. The involvement of other countries in the welfare of the country has also helped Mauritius, much more than other countries in sub-Saharan Africa.

I believe democracy is something that has to be promoted in sub-Saharan Africa. It has been said, and can be repeated, that there is no better system than democracy. Naturally, in the countries that have not known democracy for years, it is going to take time before it takes root. But the concept of democracy must be the same. You cannot have one democracy for Africa and another democracy for western European countries or the United States. Democracy must be one. We have to work toward having a single concept of democracy, and I personally do not believe that you can have different shades of democracy depending on which countries or which regions you're talking about. So the ultimate objective has to be free and transparent elections. The rule of law has to be there. We have to weed out corruption, we need to promote human rights, and all these things are happening.

J.P.: What do you think about NEPAD's (New Partnership for Africa's Development) goals?

A.G.: NEPAD was constructed at a time when there was a lot of ambition in Africa. Africa failed; NEPAD failed—not because of Africa. There was a time when we were very, very enthusiastic about NEPAD. We all believed that NEPAD was going to be the savior in Africa, that we could tell the world that we had moved on, and that the Africa that they used to know was no longer there. But then 9/11 happened, and Africa moved off the radar screen from the western countries and the United States. After 9/11 we had Afghanistan. Then we had Iraq. Then we had the terrorist attacks in Madrid, in London; then we had Lebanon. So each time we are trying to make an effort, something happens. When that something happens, Africa simply disappears. Africa is not a priority for the United States or for the rest of the international community that matters. So Africa suffers, not because it had to suffer, but it suffers as a result of what happens in the Middle East, what happens in the Bali bombings. So the focus shifts. And it is unfortunate that it has happened, but I am sure that if 9/11 had not happened, NEPAD would be the great symbol of progress and democracy in Africa. I believe that this is the way I look at it; and when you look at it historically, it makes a lot of sense.

J.P.: The U.S. has put together the program called Millennium Challenge Act, and I was thinking that the best thing might be to combine the Millennium Challenge Act goals with NEPAD [goals] and reduce the amount of requirements [for funding]. What is your opinion?

A.G.: I think you are right, John, about the conditionalities that are attached by any program or project that the United States or the European Union or other donor countries have. These conditionalities sometimes are so heavy it is virtually impossible for any African country to meet them. Sometimes, it begs the question: "Is it done deliberately?" Because at the time these projects are conceived for these countries, the United States knows full well the constraints of those countries that might become the beneficiaries of such programs. I believe that there must be more generosity in the way of working out the architecture of these programs, rather than just imposing a program knowing full well that these conditions will not be met.

But anyway, let me move on. I think we have touched on the ethnic aspect of African society. Inevitably, when the Treaty of Versailles was signed and the European countries decided to carve up Africa, they didn't take into account the ethnic dimension in Africa and the tribes. A lot of the problems today in sub-Saharan Africa go back to the signing of that treaty.

The other problem in this respect has also been the Charter of the Organization of African Unity that said that the boundaries of African countries at the time of independence should be respected. It could have been possible with hindsight to say, "No, let us see what would be the best geographical boundaries for each African country," because, if we say that we are the Organization of African Unity, then it would be possible at the level of Africa to look at these issues and to solve them. But we did not. So we perpetuated this crisis. Did we do that deliberately? Were we influenced into that? Were we just the playthings for the major powers when the charter was being drafted? What role do the major powers have in all the crises in Africa?

But tribes, ethnic dimension, must be taken into account. I believe if you have democracy, and if Africa will also look at meritocracy as something important, we can transcend these ethnic barriers. In Mauritius, we have ethnic barriers—lobbies, communities, races, cultures—we have the big problem also. If we can get to them through meritocracy, then we can say that we have achieved something. You see, Africa is a big continent, while India is a big country with lots of tribes, lots of regions, each region clamoring for its own identity, but it has been able to work as a viable democracy. So if India has done it, I suppose it to be possible for us in Africa also to do it.

J.P.: What about the rise and influence of Islamic fundamentalism?

A.G.: The democratic process is being threatened because of the rise of Islamic fundamentalism. Islam is very prevalent in Africa. If you look at the map of Africa, the whole of northern Africa is Islamic. This move is being pushed downward, so many of the countries in sub-Saharan Africa have a heavy contingent of Muslims. Not that Muslims are all fundamentalists, but the presence of Muslims in a country might affect the way we look at problems in Africa. So I am just flagging this issue. It is something that might become a major problem. While we're trying to solve the economics problem we may be faced with another kind of problem that we don't know how to handle. So this is something that is happening in eastern Africa. You have the problems in Mombasa with the bombings. Somalia now. You have Muslims in Ethiopia, in Tanzania, in Mozambique; so this is something that has to be looked at. I believe that it is such a sensitive issue that everything has to be done to bring in the African Muslims to think not as Muslims first but as Africans first. I don't know whether you'll be able to write this, but the influence of countries like Libya, in many of the countries that do not have any Muslim population, is also to be watched, I believe, because with money today and poverty in Africa, it makes a fertile ground to implant this kind of situation which might be the source of great problems in the future.

I also believe what I said about Africa with regard to this established doctrine applies also to Mauritius. Terrorism is definitely a major problem for development. Terrorism frightens everybody. The only source of terrorism will come from Islamic fundamentalists in Africa. I don't see any other group or tribe or religion that is going to embark on this kind of activity. So this is something that has to be handled with care. Definitely, if terrorism were to strike in Africa in the way that it has struck in other countries, economic development in our part of the world would be seriously handicapped.

With regard to the U.S. involvement in Africa, I believe there is a lack of awareness in the United States about what Africa is. It is my hope and my wish that policymakers in the U.S. look to Africa more, get to know Africa, and not only a few countries. Right now what is happening [is], the United States is interested in Nigeria because it's an oil producer; in South Africa because of Mandela and for the economic potential that South Africa is; in the northern African countries; in Sudan because of the oil; but not so much in the other countries. Although I can understand the United States is very keenly promoting its own interests—that's fine—the United States is a major power, and as a major power it has major responsibilities.

Africa can become a breeding ground for terrorists because of the poverty and because of the rise of Islam in the continent, so the United States has an interest in ensuring that these things do not happen. The United States has been very present in Southeast Asia, but that was in the past. I think this decade should be the decade of U.S. involvement in Africa. I believe that if we can get the United States' leaders to think more about Africa, not only in terms of what Africa can do for them, but what they can do for Africa, it is going to help.

J.P.: Are U.S. political leaders visiting Mauritius?

A.G.: I think they just come for a holiday, and there isn't that interest. Maybe Mauritius is so small that it doesn't count; it doesn't have any weight in all the thinking that goes on about strategy and so on. But I believe U.S. political leaders must also help Mauritius on the Diego Garcia issue on the Chagos Archipelago. In Mauritius now, we have said we have no problem with the American base staying on Diego Garcia. For the other islands and for the economic potential that the outer islands of the Chagos represent, the United States must show some understanding about the need of Mauritius for the use to which we can put these islands for tourism and other purposes, because we do not have resources. Our two resources are the sea and tourism, so I believe that if political leaders in the U.S. could look at it positively, it is going to help.

J.P.: What do you think the United States can do to create more of a balance in trade with Mauritius?

A.G.: We in Mauritius have always relied on preferential regimes for our trade. The dismantling of the multi-fiber agreement has affected Mauritius. AGOA came along, but AGOA also has many conditionalities. Mauritius is a middle-income country. As we are middle income, we are penalized on all sides because we cannot benefit from concessional aid. We have to go to the open banking system. The United States needs to look at all the developing countries in the same manner, not having artificial barriers, and have a broader picture of the way aid and trade develop. As I said, although we may be middle income, we are a resource-deficit country.

J.P.: What would be your recommendation of what the United States could do to help a country such as the Union of the Comoros?

A.G.: The Comoros is a country that is in a special situation. They are a group of islands without their resources, with a lot of poverty. I believe it is this kind of country that the United States can look into and help financially. The economy of the Comoros is so dependent on foreign aid that the United States can supplant the help given by the Arab countries. You know, very often the paymaster calls the tune. The Indian Ocean is a strategic area for the United States. The Comoros is in the Indian Ocean. So if only from a military and strategic point of view, the United States has a lot to gain by investing.

These countries don't need a lot of money, but having some presence and helping not only in terms of the economy globally but also by having teachers, doctors, nurses, architects—who can improve the lot of the people—will create a lot of goodwill for the United States. I think you need a lot of goodwill right now.

J.P.: How has the U.S. embassy closing affected Comoros and terrorist activity?

A.G.: The presence of the United States in the form of an embassy in the Comoros certainly had helped in not having the kind of potential that the terrorists could have. The United States by itself is a deterrent.

Very often whenever there is a problem, the United States and some countries in Europe try to move out instead of staying put and putting up a fight. Very often it amounts to a sort of withdrawal syndrome that might not be in the long-term interest of the United States. I think countries may be small, but their strategic importance might be different. I'm sure that you'd never pull out of Singapore, whatever happens. You have embassies in all the countries in Europe, however small. That also creates a pressure in the minds of the people that the United States doesn't care. I believe that you must show that you care.

J.P.: Before we conclude this interview, do you have any other input to add?

A.G.: I'd like to thank you, John, for coming to me to find out what I think about some of these issues. I think I've been very honest in my views, and I hope that they help you in the preparation of the book. I think I did say I'm also very concerned about the risks of Africa becoming radicalized in the ways that you have described. The risk is there. Poverty is there, so the best way to avoid this radicalization is to improve the quality of life of all the people in sub-Saharan Africa so that they realize it's better to live than to die.

JAYEN CUTTAREE, MAURITIUS, OCTOBER 3, 2006

Jayen Cuttaree served as minister of trade, industry, and international trade in Sir Anerood Jugnauth's administration. In the administration of Paul Bérenger, Cuttaree served as minister of foreign affairs, international trade and regional cooperation. The following excerpts are edited from our interview.

J.P.: What are the necessary ingredients for sustainable development in Africa?

J.C.: It is a truism that in Africa some resources are needed. To me the most important thing is education. You can't have development without people, and you can't have development—or understand the problems of development—on a continent where you've got a large proportion of the people who either cannot read or write, or have only limited education.

Everyone talks about the development of the agricultural sector in Africa that is mainly based on peasant farming. If you really want to trade in agricultural products, you need to have commercial farms. So how do you transform peasant farmers into commercial farmers?

Infrastructure in Africa is also a big problem. The economy is not prosperous enough to feed the people properly, so how can [Africa] generate the level of funds to create the infrastructure—the roads, railways, telephone system, cold storage, and port facilities—necessary for exportation? Developing a region involves entrepreneurship, leadership, and also resources. I think the United States can play a very important role.

Unfortunately, if you look at my experience of Africa and the United States, I find the U.S. focus is on oil. How [will] Congress and the private sector of the United States go into Africa to do something in addition to the exploitation of natural resources? This is where the real development is going to take place. This is where the gains of oil and exploration are going to trickle down to the poor people. People realize today that you cannot have a continent with so many resources where people are so poor. This is where the first challenge is.

[Concerning health issues], I think that the United States should focus, obviously, on the poorest countries because resources are not infinite. AIDS, malaria, and all these big pandemics in Africa today are threatening the livelihood, the actual existence, of various areas of the [continent]. A massive investment is needed in order to bring health care to the people.

But at the same time, I think the type of aid [needed] in countries like Mauritius isn't the same as [that needed by] other poor countries in Africa. For example, we need help with certain parts of our infrastructure, and in health for those people who are suffering from AIDS. We have had some projections about how many resources we will need in the future to prevent the little problem we have here from becoming a pandemic. But we find that no one gives us any support for that. I think this is bad, because something like AIDS is a problem of the whole world community, and no one should be looking at your income per capita to decide whether you need help to fight AIDS.

Of course, we have the Millennium Development goals aimed on reducing poverty, and bringing water and other essentials to poor people. But this is a reactive thing, and only one part of the development. If you look at the development, you should look at it from a holistic point of view in terms of education, health, resources, and investment funds. We need to have a more modern education system that trickles down to every part of our population. We need to have social mobility in our country.

You also need to understand the sociology of the population, the cultural aspects of the various parts of Africa. If you don't understand all the sociological problems or the cultural problems of the people, it is very difficult to bring development, even if you are very well meaning and you want to do things.

J.P.: In regard to Mauritius, what is needed for the country's continued economic success?

J.C.: If you look at the factor endowments of Mauritius, we don't have any natural resources. We have people with a certain level of education who are hard working. These people could have worked in the textile sector or in the agricultural sugar sector. But our young generation does not want to work the land. They don't want to go and work in factories. In addition to that, the cost of labor is high. The cost of imports is high because with development all costs such as electricity, water, and wages have gone up.

We cannot [continue to] use the same things that have been produced before and try to sell them to the outside world. I don't think that will succeed. I think we need to go into the services sector, such as tourism and ICT.

We are in the middle of nowhere with nothing around us—the nearest place to us is mainland Africa, where, if you want to have development, you need to have economic activities going on around you. At the present time, as we all know, such activities are hardly the thing to talk about in that part of our continent, and will take time to pick up. But we do have advantages. Very often I think of Mauritius a bit like the United States. It's a country that has been populated by people of different origins, where people have worked very hard, have succeeded, and have been an example to others. In other words, if I work very hard, if I have the chance, even if I am very poor today, within one generation I can change my status.

In Mauritius, this is what people want to do, but we've got a very big problem because we lean on globalization. We don't have protected markets. We are not competitive enough to sell on the world market. Even if you look at AGOA as it is now, a protected market, with the WTO and the fall of tariffs our competitive margin is going to diminish. We are in for a difficult period until we actually develop a services sector to serve the region. This is why, when I was minister for Regional Cooperation, I pushed very strongly for more regional integration because you'll have the resources, the trained people, and the people who want to be trained. Together, you'll have the critical mass to be able to develop and to bring prosperity to the region. It's a difficult task, but I think it's possible.

To me this is essential: You can't develop unless you have good governance and democracy. [A] dictatorship in which one or two people decide what is good for a country and impose it on the country cannot lead anywhere today. The people have to have the ownership of the development process, and they can only do that within a democracy.

J.P.: What recommendations would you make to the U.S. to improve the understanding of sub-Saharan Africa to better assist the economic development for the people?

J.C.: I think the problem is the continent is so far away from the United States and there are people who are not interested. For example, if Africa had a geopolitical importance, then the people in Congress would have been more interested in Mauritius. I know this problem of world security is at the top of the agenda, not of the administration but of every American. Everyone is concerned especially after September 11 about the need to have a global fight. President Bush has been talking about global fighting against terrorism and all that. But as I said before, the global fight against terrorism also includes the global fight against poverty. I think that when this bombing happened in East Africa, it may have been far away, but people realized that American interests are not safe even on a continent like Africa. It is extremely important for Americans to focus much more on Africa, and to understand the intricacies of African societies—that there is not one society. To help, put special resources at the disposal of Africa, because Africa is unique. It's a continent with boundless resources, but with the poorest people. And it's a continent that is hardly getting any investment apart from the investment in oil.

J.P.: What do you think about NEPAD and the U.S.-sponsored Millennium Challenge Account program?

J.C.: NEPAD raised lots of hope in terms of new areas for development, in terms of cooperation among the various countries. There was going to be lots of financing coming in to meet the NEPAD goals. But, if you look at it from the past three or four years, people have almost stopped talking about NEPAD rather than talk more about it. Yet, I think that NEPAD with the Millennium Challenge Account could be beneficial.

If you want to integrate a continent, the first point to make is that all sub-Saharan countries should benefit, whether [they are] Mauritius or South Africa. They shouldn't be punished for having done better than the others. I think in many ways we all agree to the conditions [set] in the U.S. program.

This peer review of MCA candidates was actually to push the countries to aim at these things. This is what is happening in Africa. At the time we are talking, elections are taking place in Zambia, and I think that everyone who is there—the Commonwealth, the SADC [Southern African Development Community] people, the European Union people—are all saying they are satisfied with the way the elections are going. I think things are moving in Africa, but I don't think we should wait until *all* the conditions are satisfied to go forward. Once people are on the right track, they should be helped.

J.P.: Is everyone on the right track?

J.C.: You can have a multicultural society where what you want out of life and how you want to live are the same. In any society there are also certain things that are important. For example, like in Mauritius: respect for authority, solidarity with those who don't have the same beliefs, and the fight against corruption and poverty. These are things that are common to all civilized societies.

In Mauritius, all these various groups—the atheists, the Christians, the Hindus or the Muslims—generally realize that they have to live together. The Islam we've got here is a soft Islam, which tries to live in peace with the others. [The Muslims have] good religious leaders, which I think is the key thing that lends to the bearing [demeanor] of the community. So therefore I'm not so much worried about this.

The problem in Africa is different. You've got large areas of the continent where the Muslim religion is very ingrained, and where you have poverty and ignorance. The possibilities of extremism catching up are high. And I am worried. Unless you have a fast development where people realize they have to work together and at the end of the day [believe] economic development is more important than jihad, I think you have problems.

J.P.: Is there a link between terrorism and economic development?

J.C.: Very much so. I know some economists who say [terrorism] has nothing to do with [economic development]. But if you have poverty, poor people are generally much more religious and desperate than people who are well off. They tend to hold on to hope in whatever way it is projected to them. This is where I think religious militancy can be a very important factor in terrorism.

J.P.: What is the U.S. role in Africa?

J.C.: No doubt there is this desire for the United States to get closer to Africa. Obviously, economic reasons—oil exploration and minerals—have pushed the U.S. closer to Africa. But, I haven't seen much political commitment to [otherwise] develop Africa. I've seen it in individuals but I haven't seen it collectively. [In fact,] it is very difficult to get the American investor to be interested in anything but oil exploration in Africa.

The last time I was in Washington, I tried to get people interested in looking at the Indian Ocean region from a tourism point of view. South Africa has its wildlife, Mauritius is there with its beaches, and Madagascar has its ecological paradise. But I haven't been able to convince anybody to come and look at Mauritius to invest in tourism. Most Americans living in Mauritius will say Americans don't like to travel so far away, and there is the problem of security on the airlines, and all that. They like to go places where they know what to see, and all that, you know.

J.P.: When U.S. political leaders come, do you think they help you?

J.C.: I think the more you get political leaders coming to a place like Mauritius, [the more] they understand the problems, although this hasn't served us in certain instances. When Bill Thomas [the chairman of the

U.S. House Ways and Means Committee (2001–2006)], came here, he said, "Oh, Mauritius, you don't need any of this help that we are giving in AGOA. You've got a booming economy, and you are doing very well." Whereas Bob Zoellick [former U.S. trade representative and deputy secretary of state] was [so] impressed by Mauritius he thought that we could set an example to the rest of the region in terms of good governance and democracy and success in developing the country. So you have a different reaction from people.

From that point of view, it is necessary that people come here and see how well we have been doing. That serves us. You know the feeling of going and helping people who are poor is a great feeling. But when people come to Mauritius and think we are not poor and/or should be able to fend for ourselves—then this doesn't serve us. For example, on a very simple matter like exporting our textile products to the [United States], what we wanted to do is maybe use for a certain period of time fabric coming from outside Mauritius or outside Africa to be able sell our products during which period we are building up the yarn industry here. But still, Bill Thomas, the chairman of the Ways & Means, had expected to have a demonstration to give this benefit to all the African countries except South Africa; he was adamant that Mauritius doesn't need this.

Very often, you know, in Mauritius, we've suffered from the rivalry between the United States and Europe. For example, when I was in the United States and went to Congress to make a case for Mauritius, I was asked questions about our relationship with the European Union and how we've been selling our products at subsidized prices in Europe, and how the policy in Europe on agriculture is going against the American farmers. Can you imagine a small country like Mauritius having to answer questions not about how we are planning our development but why we have this close relationship with Europe? I think this is ridiculous.

J.P.: You were one of the prime candidates and runner up for the WTO position, and, of course, you were beaten out. What second thoughts do you have now about the direction that the WTO is going in under the new leadership versus what you would have done?

J.C.: I think the developed countries didn't want that organization to go into the hands of a developing country like ours. I was very much involved in Africa with the poorer countries that needed the WTO: they needed the rule-based trading system, better organization, and better market access. My philosophy was that the big countries don't need the WTO. Well, it has been a failure as it is now. Three big groups—the Europeans, the United States, and the G20, namely, the large developing countries, Brazil, India, China, and even Thailand—are wrapped up in the WTO. But those who are left behind are in fact the countries that in the [World Trade Organization's] Doha Round supposedly were going to be helped. The agreement that had been reached on the cotton farmers is now on the back burner. The agreement reached on the elimination of agricultural export subsidies of developed countries by 2013, which should have been of help to these poor countries, is also on the back burner. Now everyone is talking about what should the United States and the Europeans do to move forward. The whole debate is centered on the interests of the big and the rich countries. And I think this is very bad, especially if we are talking about a globalized world, if we are talking about how trade is important for the poorer countries and all that, and I think this round has gone in a very bad direction.

J.P.: Two conferences have followed the 2003 AGOA forum. What are your observations of the AGOA forum held in Mauritius and those that followed?

J.C.: First of all, we considered it a very great honor that the United States proposed the first AGOA forum outside the Untied States should be held in Mauritius. I mean, we are so far from the continent, and to get all these people to come over from the U.S., the private sector, and various members of the administration was by itself a feat. We were expecting the president and the secretary of state, but for the reasons we all understand, they couldn't make it.

Now, the message that I've been sending since AGOA was voted on and came into existence is the expression of the political will of the United States to get closer to Africa and develop Africa. This is the message we tried to send during the whole forum. We also had discussion on issues, not necessarily trade issues. We were talking about development; we were talking about politics. And I think this is what makes it unique. I don't know whether those who decided to write AGOA in the United States in fact had in their mind that this piece of legislation could be the springboard for cooperation that goes beyond economic cooperation between Africa and the United States.

I thought when we finished the forum this [sentiment] was shared by everybody. Unfortunately since then, I think the AGOA meetings have been concentrated too much on market access, and that the political dimension of AGOA has been put on the back burner. This is what I think is unfortunate.

KARL OFFMANN, MAURITIUS, OCTOBER 4, 2006

Former president Karl Auguste Offmann and I met when I first arrived in Mauritius and presented my credentials in April 2002. President Offmann has been in the political structure of the country for many years, and was one of the founding individuals of the MSM Party. He served in Parliament, and as a minister under several administrations. He is now a member of the African Presidential Archives and Research Center (APARC), a new organization of former presidents in Africa. The following excerpts are edited from our interview.

J.P.: What were your expectations about an independent Africa, and what are they now?

K.O.: In the early 1960s when we were to take our destiny in our hands, to take out all the colonial powers so that we can make our effort by ourselves, so many people accepted to die to achieve this. There was, I would say, a great movement toward that spirit of independence and of self-reliance. And we thought we had obtained independence. When I look at Africa today I am disappointed.

I've been reflecting a long time about this and I think we made a mistake because at a certain time we thought our only goal was attaining political independence. We did not forecast that it was [actually] two things: political independence and economical independence. Once we attained the political independence, some of us sat on our glory and waited. Our aim was good, but our forefathers had erred: they should have said gaining political independence was only halfway to having complete freedom. It was our duty to do the things by ourselves: to create jobs; to build roads, factories, and hospitals; to create schools; to give health and security to our people; to divvy up agricultural resources. It was up to *us* to do that! We didn't. So today instead of achieving progress, we have gone backward.

Mauritius, a small country, which is part of the fifty-three countries of Africa, is without any resources. It was written [in] black-on-white [that] during the time of independence there was no economic future for Mauritius. Hence, many people left Mauritius. Some went to Australia, some went to Canada or the UK, and some even went to the States. We even created a Ministry of Immigration to help people go abroad. And we made the economy called Mauritius with what was left.

I think if Africa is going to survive and to progress we must re-create that spirit of the early 1960s. Beyond freedom, we must go that other half way to [achieve] total political and economical independence. If we do that then we'll succeed, and Mauritius has done that, and we have succeeded.

A while back, I heard [future French president] Nicolas Sarkozy say if we don't solve the problem of Africa, Europe will have big problems. He said, "We must do a lot of micro-projects in Africa." This is the same point I've been pushing forward for some time.

If we want Africa to progress, to be on development, to reach the Millennium goal in 2015, there is only one thing: we must make a multiplicity of small projects. But don't ask us to make big projects. You see, in the 1950s many countries survived economically. They grew their maize, their sugar, or their coffee. They had it. But now why don't they cause it to grow again? Do they have problems? Is it a question of transport? Is it a question of water? Is it a question of the possibility of energy? Why don't we help them? You will tell me, yes, we are doing that. But I'm questioning people, the World Bank, and other international organizations that are only doing big projects.

Look at the Chinese people. They can feed 1.3 billion people. The Indians are doing the same thing. I don't say there is no poverty in India. I don't say there is big democracy in China. But they have succeeded in a way. In Africa, also, it is possible, but we need many small projects to benefit the people.

J.P.: What are your thoughts on Aid for Trade?

K.O.: Let's take the Ivory Coast, for example. The Ivory Coast produces the best cacao in the world. If we practice the "Aid for Trade" and let the Ivory Coast trade the cacao at a given price, you will not need to help them anymore. That's all. For the cotton in Africa, it's the same thing.

So if I do better in cacao, help me to do my cacao. Give me for some years a good price to sell my cacao. That's what I mean by "Aid for Trade." [Doing] what I know to do best, help me to sell my cacao. Do that favor to me. Do that in cotton. Do that in any kind of raw material that I know how to do the best. And for a certain time only, and then I can change from there to other things.

What I would propose first is a state of mind. Those who want to help us must clear their minds. What do we really want? Do we really want to help Africa? Are we sincere in what we are saying? If we really want [to help], it's easy, and I assure you it's not going to cost a lot of money. Why are people leaving Africa every day, risking their lives taking boats on the open seas to go to Europe? It is because they don't have the work. So if we want to create work, we have to create work in the village. Let us send our experts into the different villages. What was the product of this village? Was it maize? Was it rice? Was it good? Whatever it was, why can't you produce it again? Ask them. Let them try to restart what they know how to do. Don't ask them not to plant sugarcane, because the price of sugar is down. Don't ask them to remove all the sugarcane to produce rice. They don't know how to produce rice. Help them see to progressively make a mixture of rice and sugarcane. You see?

Now, let's take the case of Mauritius: a country that has succeeded. You want democracy? We have had democracy for I don't know how many generations. You want good governance? We have it. You want a country that makes efforts? We have it. You want a country that takes advantage of the possibilities that you put at its disposal—and uses the money properly—we do it!

Now, we are telling the world today one [other] thing. In the 1970s, sugar represented 90 percent of foreign currency earnings. Today, sugar represents 19 percent. Why? It's not because the price of sugar has gone down. No, because we have created textiles, tourism, offshore banking, services, and IT—and next year, the seafood [hub], and after that education technology.

But the problem we currently face with sugar is pricing, and also because of the opening of the markets for textiles we are having some problems. Help us for only a few years in order to get out of it, [and we will become sufficient again].

Yet, people say, "No, no, no. We can't help you any more because you have reached such a level you can do your own business. We can't help you. We are not going to help you." But this is not right. If you [use] Mauritius as a showcase to tell others that we are a multiracial society living in peace and harmony, a country without any resources that has succeeded, [what] happens if this country collapses? Where is your showcase then?

J.P.: How do religious groups get along in Mauritius?

K.O.: Now that's another point we are facing worldwide[:] about religion. Mauritius is unique where the big religions of the world—Islam, Christianity, Hinduism, Buddhism—we live in peace together. We are one of the rare countries of the world to have this. Tell me another country where you have it. We can kill one another here, but we are not doing it. [World leaders] can use Mauritius to show Africa and the people who are fighting between different or religious communities that peace can happen. Leaders don't see that you can exploit what is good to the benefit of the majority of the people. Use Mauritius to show Africa that its people resources can survive. Use Mauritius, as a small country visited by cyclones [that] stays alive. We must exploit the best we have.

If we can make people understand that the world of tomorrow is going to be a world of moderation or we'll have a world that is not going to be black or white—it's going to be gray. We are going to mingle with one another. It's going to happen. I don't know in how many years. It's going to be thousands or millions, but it's going to happen. Why don't we help it to happen? You see. In this world of today, we have everything that is supposed to make us happy.

J.P.: You said you could do a lot without a lot of money. We've spent over $300 billion in aid for Africa and show very little for it, so how do you see this going forward? What kind of aid are you talking about?

K.O.: There are two things that come first. We must double up on agriculture. We must give water. Let's link the two things. I believe that there is enough water available in Africa to irrigate for water consumption, for everything for the whole of Africa. But I'm not talking of big towns. I'm talking what was done in America during the time of the early pioneers. You had pumps and windmills to pump the water. Instead of creating big things to bring the water there, let the people do it for them in the villages. This is what the Chinese have done.

Now, we have biogas. You can have energy. With solar energy you can have, so a small village in the middle of the jungle can have its own infrastructure—solar, wind, and biogas—and the people would be happy. This is what we should do. With only these two aspects—agriculture and water—you change everything. You even change the problem of HIV/AIDS, because if you give better living conditions, there will be fewer problems in other areas.

J.P.: Can you link that also to terrorism?

K.O.: Yes! Because when the villages have got food, what's the body of this people to do? The people will say, no. We have got food. We can sell our cows. We have the money. We can send our people to school, so what's the problem? No problem. Why do people go for terrorism? When they are starving. When they don't have resources. But if you give them the possibility of food, staples, [they] will not ask for anything. Still, let the village have the autonomy like you did in America. You succeeded by small, medium, and big. Now you are looking at the problem as a big huge problem of all Africa. But subdivide it into small units, [and] you will spend less money and have better results.

J.P.: How do we help this village concept?

K.O.: If you want to give education to the people, do you think we need a big building? No, don't put this idea first. Start it by helping them under the verandah, under the tree, and develop it afterward. Why do *you* say, "No, it must be like this: it must be to scale." You always compare Africa and Asia: "Look, Asia has done it." The criterion is not the same there. You know that. Here it is different. When you want to give a school to the children of the country, you want it to have the same criteria like in your own country. No, don't do that! But help them to grow. You can't run before you know how to walk. I may disappoint you when I'm saying that. I'm telling you, you want them to run, but let them learn to walk first. Then they will understand what it means.

J.P.: What are your impressions of NEPAD?

K.O.: In the beginning NEPAD was a very good idea. But first there were some people who thought NEPAD was going to be a structure. Now they have accepted that it's an idea, an idea that is at the service of all the people. But the idea is good. There is a slowdown about [achieving] the [projected figures] that NEPAD created in the beginning, because I think people wanted to do it quickly.

In the beginning of that concept, I would not do a structure like they have done. I would take all the ideas [and see] what works and does not work. Like we discussed earlier—corruption, for instance. Some people will say in Mauritius there is a lot of corruption. You have been here; you know. Yes, there is some corruption—not to the level people mean what *real* corruption is. But if you listen to some people, or read some article, or read some newspaper, you consider this country is corrupt from the top to the bottom. This is not right.

Whether it is good governance, whether it is corruption, whether it is liberty, whether it is agenda, [whatever] it is, you must let the people—the country—do their own system. Don't force it. But make it a point that you talk about it every time. You can encourage people to have it. You see? It's good. You can see democracies having free elections taking place, and it's more common now these days. We are going to have one in Madagascar in December. We had one just recently in Zambia. In the newspaper there is a small problem in Seychelles. There has been fighting about freedom of press. There has been firing on the opposition. Yes, it is sad, but it is nothing compared to other countries.

You know, these are the results when you have put in democracy. I think NEPAD is a good thing in the concept of ideas. We must not [designate] NEPAD as a rigid structure. We must not put NEPAD as a structure itself. NEPAD must be the idea between all Africa Union, all the countries. How else are we going to deal with these particular things: good governance, freedom of press, freedom from oppression, gender things, corruption, and liberty—yes.

J.P.: Are there any time frames?

K.O.: No! No, because you'll be disappointed. Don't forget you're dealing with human beings. You have different people, you see?

J.P.: Do you believe in the Western concept of democracy?

K.O.: You know this is one thing that I always tell them, our western people. Look at how many years it took you to [rise to] the level [where] you are today—sometimes, thousands of years. Now you want Africa to reach that level in less than fifty years, when you have taken thousands of years. Please, please. Give us a chance. You see?

J.P.: Do you believe the Western concept can eventually work?

K.O.: It is one of the ideas. It is not the only idea. It is one of the ideas that can help to improve the situation. Democracy is good. Good governance is good. Liberty is good. But when you are living in a different society where there is a multiplicity of opinions, you have to take care because [with] your freedom you can do something against another's freedom. How far do you go? How far are you prepared to let them go? So on that aspect of liberty, I don't go 100 percent with the Western side.

J.P.: But there's concern about the radical Islamic doctrines that are spreading.

K.O.: Yes. I have not seen any Western leaders tell the Islamic people or asking Muslim leaders—when every day in Baghdad sixty to seventy people are killed by their brothers during Ramadan time—what are you saying to that when your own Muslim brothers are killing their own Muslims during Ramadan time? You don't say anything. You should start saying that. I have not seen even the Pope, or even your president, ask that. What are you saying? You don't like me, okay. But I ask you one question. Every day in Baghdad or Afghanistan or any place, Muslims are killing Muslims in the name of Allah, and during Ramadan. What are you saying to that? You don't like me, okay, but I want you to say something there. I don't hear you. That's why I said there must be a dialogue, a real dialogue, and we can talk. There must be a point that a real dialogue must [be reached] where as Christian and non-Christian we can say truths to one another.

J.P.: There's a radical element of Islamic faith you can't communicate with, and they are growing rapidly in Africa.

K.O.: Yes, because we are only looking at that aspect. Look at the other aspect. The radicals are minorities. You know as a former politician, you can have a room of 2,000 people. Out of these 2,000 militants coming to meet you, 50 of them are radical, and they start shouting in the room against you. All the others stay silent. If the others start telling them "Stop it!" they will stop it. What we should do is use the majority against the minority. We are not using that. We are not using our mind to exploit every possibility that we have. We have much more opportunity in front of us. Why don't we use them? We can stop that, you see, because they are minorities. There are a lot more Muslims who are moderate. Let's work with them. Let's ask them to say the things there.

We can't do anything about these extremists because they have something you can't beat. When you tell them "Stop the violence," for them they kill to get to heaven. So how can you stop that? It's the pride to be killed in the name of Allah because they go to heaven. So how can you stop that? By saying to them "Don't do that," they interpret it as: you don't want me to go to heaven. You must understand that. So I don't fight them on that aspect because I can't win. I fight them on the other aspect.

One of the things we should start saying to Saudi Arabia, to Mubarak [of Egypt], even the president of Syria and Iran: Yes, you don't like me. You're telling me a lot of things, but I'm asking you one plain question: Every day in Baghdad, Sunnis kill Sunnis. What do you say about that? That's all. Let them answer.

Now why are they killing in Darfur? Muslim Arabs are killing Muslim Africans in Darfur. That's all. It's not Christian or Muslim, it's Arabs and Africans. So ask them: Why are you killing your brother? Look at what is happening in Nigeria. You remember during Ramadan some years ago: they go into a village and kill—fifty family, everyone. I ask that. You have got the media in your power. Use them. Use the right tools. Sometimes I don't know. [He sighs.] Your advisers don't know. They don't know what is going to happen, really.

J.P.: How do you see the role of the United States in Africa? Obviously we should do more, but how do you see our role?

K.O.: I think you have a leading role. You are the leader of the world today. You are number one. Use your position. AGOA is a very good tool. "Aid for Trade" is a very good tool, but you [must be] prepared to do what the Chinese and the Indians do. Don't impose a lot of conditions. Do it. Help. You will have the merit of it. If you don't do it, somebody else will do it, and will take the merit from you. You know what I am afraid will happen if you don't realize that the focus of the economy of the world today will be between Asia and Africa? Europe and America will be marginalized, and be even taken out; you will lose, because Asia and Africa are going to work together. It's going to happen. To keep the influence and economic power you have, you must invest today, and not only in oil. Invest everywhere, but go for small things. Make a multiplicity of small projects in the fields of agriculture and of water. If you do only these two, this will solve many, many, many problems.

J.P.: What about education?

K.O.: Education will come by itself. Don't go into many things. Give food first. Give water first—because with food and water, you give health. Then from there let them create the question of education. Don't impose on them very big buildings with all the sophisticated equipment—no, no, no. Yes, it is good, but don't do that. You had it in the past in a room where there was somebody to teach children. Sometimes there were about twenty in a room. One is six, one must be sixteen, and they are teaching. You have done it this way. Yes, we have [tried] to reach a level in 2006 that can't be, so don't impose it. You are trying to be good to them, but at the same time you are imposing a situation that has not been there.

Another issue is gender and child labor. What have you done in the States? The family has got six, seven children, and the mother is [working] in the fields. Yes, a child needs to go to school. This is the rule. But there is the law and there is the spirit of the law. You must see the difference between the two. So don't impose. Now if you say to me, "In your country where you have child labor, I'm not going to help you because you have twenty percent of your children doing child labor," you are imposing on me a constraint. Please, change your mind. Help me to change it, but don't impose on me these things. I will change it, but help me to change it. We need to solve the basics for survival.

J.P.: If you were to speak to the American people who don't understand Africa, what would you say to them?

K.O.: I say don't mix the issues. America has fifty states. Many of you think that Africa can be one state. It's not the same thing because the fifty-three different countries have fifty-three different realities, and even within one country sometimes you have ten, fifteen, or more different situations, different cultures, different religions, and different tribes. In a country like Zaire I think they have about three hundred languages. Can you imagine that? So, please, please, don't try to put it simply. Yes, there might be a time when we will perhaps have a federation of Africa, but this is not now.

J.P.: What are your thoughts on Diego Garcia and the United States?

K.O.: One day I had a meeting with some people at the university level in California or Atlanta[, Georgia]. I asked, "Do you know that Mauritius [has a bone of] contention with the USA?" They said, "No." I said, "Yes. Diego Garcia." I think our prime minister used a platform during his visit with President George W. Bush to put forward a message, and the message is simple. Look, when we had independence in 1968 the British government excised, bought our territory for a purpose. And we have said every time we are not against the purport of security. But we want people to recognize that Diego Garcia is our territory. If tomorrow the British and the Americans recognize that Diego Garcia comes from parts of the territory of Mauritius, and deal with Mauritius, you will be surprised the base, Diego Garcia, will still be there. So [the prime minister] has used every opportunity to put forward this issue.

J.P.: How does the World Trade Organization affect your economy?

K.O.: You know the WTO has been a flop. Why? It's because people think that everything is possible. Look, if you have the potential or the capability of producing things at a given price, and I have to open my market to kill my producers, and I can't face it, how do I survive? How can I produce? I can't produce! So people must know that in that open world market we have to make differences. We have to take into account there are countries that are landlocked, or small countries that are far from every resource, and have difficulties to survive in normal competition. So we must make [these] differences. If we don't make that difference, there will be no possibility, and we will die. Everyone will say, no, we don't want you to die. We want you to progress. But how can I progress if I can't sell my goods? How can I be in competition with you if your goods are less than mine? Like what you're facing with China. So this is one concept. There must be some specialties. If we try to understand this, and devise new ways, a new approach to things, perhaps we can do it.

J.P.: How can the United States of America and Africa work together?

K.O.: I think we can work together. As I have told you, we have created a group called the African Presidential Roundtable (APARC). President Chissano is the president for the time being. We have meetings, for example, in Brussels, to talk about the vision of Africa. If the need be, if you find the opportunity to invite our group in the States, we are prepared to do that. Use us! Use us so that we can explain and give us the opportunity to make the maximum contact with people, and please feel free whenever you have a question, whenever you want to deal with a problem, you want to have our counsel, you want to have our advice, please don't hesitate. Call me, as you have done. Send me an email. I will be very happy to help you.

J.P.: Can the success of Mauritius be exported to Africa?

K.O.: Yes, I think we can do that. We can do that in two ways, because Mauritius can [do] what Singapore has done with Asia. We want to be the Singapore of Africa, and we even want to be the bridge between Asia and Africa. Mauritius has the potential. We are bilingual. We are developed to such a level, and we are linked to the continent of Africa. We are a poor country without any resources. We have survived. And we have succeeded. So it is possible to show them how to do it. I think Mauritius is well situated for that.

Paul Bérenger, Mauritius, October 9, 2006

Paul Bérenger, the former minister of finance, former prime minister and currently leader of the opposition in Mauritius, has a long history and strong background in the political system. The following excerpts edited from his interview address some of the issues important to sub-Saharan Africa and to the future of the Indian Ocean countries.

J.P.: What are the ingredients necessary for sustainable development in sub-Saharan Africa?

P.B.: I do hesitate to speak on behalf of sub-Saharan Africa; it is true that Mauritius belongs to Africa. We belong to the African Union. We belong to SADC, the Southern African Development Community, but Mauritius is certainly *not* a typical African country if only because

70 percent of our population is of Asian origin. Therefore, I do hesitate to speak on behalf of sub-Saharan Africa.

But I would tend to say that the ingredients necessary for sustainable development of sub-Saharan Africa are no different from elsewhere, and there is no single ingredient. Too often people believe that "Aid for Trade" or this for that is sufficient as an ingredient for sustainable development. I believe that this is not so; there must be a number of ingredients, a number of conditions fulfilled for sustainable development. That includes aid and trade, but also includes institution building, a strong solid constitution, the rule of law, education, and so on. I'm mentioning what comes to my mind. For success for sustainable development there must be an addition of those different ingredients.

J.P.: What factors are needed for the continued economic success of Mauritius?

P.B.: Relatively speaking, since independence in March 1968 Mauritius has been an economic success. But as for the continued economic success I am concerned. We have to realize that we've been hit very badly in some of the vital sectors of the economy: textiles, with what's been happening in China and elsewhere; and sugar even more, with what's been happening with the sugar regime in Europe and the World Trade Organization. So, there is no choice but diversification.

When I was prime minister I said we could not afford to let any opportunity pass by—including the seafood hub that we started, and the integrated resorts schemes. As prime minister I made it a duty to jump on *every* opportunity. Diversification. Diversification. Diversification. We started going in that direction, and Mauritius has no choice [but to continue]. We must keep on doing the best to keep in the textile industry and in the sugar sector.

J.P.: Since independence, why has Mauritius succeeded while other sub-Saharan countries failed?

P.B.: Well, there are other sub-Saharan countries not far from us that have known relative success: Botswana, for example. As I said, Mauritius is not a typical African country. It is not a typical sub-Saharan African country. All our people came from the outside here—the French, and then the people brought in from Madagascar, Mozambique, China, and India. We have had down the ages a strong private sector in Mauritius, and that's part of the success also.

I think we owe a lot to the very strong constitution that Sir Seewoosagur Ramgoolam left to us. Our educational base and the fact that we are bilingual, English and French, has helped also. There are other reasons, but I would mention these as the most important.

J.P.: Do you believe that the Western concept of democracy can ever completely take hold in sub-Saharan Africa—free and fair elections, freedom of the press?

P.B.: Yes, yes, and in spite of us moving backward in certain parts of sub-Saharan Africa, generally we are progressing. We are progressing as far as democracy is concerned, and we must keep on pushing in that direction. Yes, democracy is taking hold in sub-Saharan Africa, and even in the worst places these days—places where there is conflict, and where there is not the required amount of democracy or respect for human rights and so forth. No, I'm confident that we are moving, with great difficulty sometimes, but in the right direction.

J.P.: Do you feel the goals of NEPAD can be achieved in sub-Saharan Africa?

P.B.: I was against this whole idea of NEPAD. The OAU, the Organization of African Unity, had just become the African Union, and it was my point of view that we should have been consolidating the African Union and not duplicating or setting up all sorts of schemes of organizations of secretariats and parallel with the Africa Union. I have been proven right. I think NEPAD is on its way out. The African Union's decisions, among others, are to the effect that NEPAD must be completely integrated in the African Union. It is not taking place, mainly because NEPAD has taken a life of its own. But it's not going to last long, if you ask me, and then we will have to concentrate on the African Union, which is doing a lot of good work.

J.P.: In talking about the tribal aspects of African society, do you think that affects democratic governance, that is, tribal leadership versus the free election process?

P.B.: Why, I don't think there is any country in the world not divided by tribes, by communities, and so on—but some are more divided than others. The history of colonization in Africa is that there are a lot of problems left behind as a consequence. You had kingdoms; you had tribes; and the colonial powers just drew on the map countries that were not meant to be in that shape. But even in a small place like Mauritius, you don't have tribes, but you have what we call communities, and there are ways of surviving and consolidating unity in diversity. Certainly, it has been an additional problem for sub-Saharan Africa.

J.P.: What about the radical Islamic movement that may or may not affect you in Mauritius, but certainly affects East Africa and the Horn of Africa?

P.B.: Fortunately for us, a few years back there was a strong radical Islamic group coming up in Mauritius, but it's a thing of the past. Today that problem is nonexistent in Mauritius, and I don't see any way that it will become a problem again like it was a few years back.

J.P.: Terrorism is a big problem.

P.B.: Fortunately, again for us, it's been no problem at all locally. But it is a world problem. I tend to side with those who say we must look very carefully at the causes that feed extremism and not just at its expressions. There is no doubt that the Palestine issue is at the heart of the whole problem. There is no doubt about that. There are other causes, other reasons. So we don't have that problem at all in Mauritius; but, nevertheless, I personally have done my best in the region for that problem not to crop up in Comoros or elsewhere. But certainly, yes, we have to be careful in that part of the world.

J.P.: Do you think the fact that we've closed embassies is a big issue?

P.B.: Well it's not linked to terrorism, but generally when a great country these days closes down an embassy in a small country like Comoros, it doesn't help at all. Not at all. But I must say that during these last months and years, Washington has been moving in the other direction. Rather than closing down more diplomatic missions in small countries, I think other countries should be present in all countries, and that there should not be this discrimination against very small countries.

J.P.: In Seychelles we did the very same thing.

P.B.: It's not helpful at all locally; it's not helpful regionally; and it's not helpful internationally.

J.P.: What is the U.S. role in Africa and our U.S. policy toward sub-Saharan Africa—what can we do to improve our standing and image in Africa?

P.B.: Well, things like AGOA have been helpful, very helpful. I believe in spite of the principles that were adopted at the World Trade Organization that there needs to be positive discrimination in favor of the small countries, the regions, the countries small or not that have been left behind. This idea of having a completely level playing field won't work. It certainly won't work. It will make the poor countries poorer. So there is need, I believe, at the World Trade Organization and in economic matters, financial matters, at the IMF, at the World Bank, to *act* so that countries, the regions that have been left behind, *do* catch up; and for that to happen, there needs to be what I would call "positive discrimination."

J.P.: What do you think about the Millennium Challenge Account that we talked about, and the sixteen indicators—the difficulty in achieving them? Madagascar was one of the first countries to qualify.

P.B.: Conditionalities have a limit, and if you have them they must be applied in fair play and not in a discriminatory manner. Let's say there is room for improvement as far as your country is concerned in applying the rules. The rules themselves are sometimes too tough, but then when they are applied in a discriminatory way, that doesn't work. That backfires completely. Madagascar is one of the five countries where the people of Mauritius came from in the past, so we are very close to Madagascar. When the new regime, the new president came into power, there was a lot of hope generated. Good for them that they qualify. Maybe at that point in time it was hoped also that Madagascar qualifying would help them along. Madagascar is going through a very delicate period with elections at the end of the year, in December. I wish Madagascar every success.

J.P.: You have a great and exciting and interesting background. Will you elaborate on your early days in Paris, coming back here? You have been a Marxist follower, and then became conservative. Will you share your thoughts about this?

P.B.: I don't think I'm conservative, not at all. But it's true that I started as a revolutionary, or rather I didn't start, because when I left Mauritius as a student—for family and sociological reasons—I had a completely Western view of the world. Two things changed me completely: the Vietnam War and what happened in your own country; and the events in Europe, especially in Paris in 1968. So when I came back after my studies I was a complete idealist. I was not at all what you usually describe as a Communist, no. We were idealists. We were real revolutionaries. We wanted to reinvent the world. We wanted an ideal democracy, the whole thing. I came back in that frame of mind.

Here something happened. The two parties that had fought in 1967 for or against independence joined together and postponed the elections to come in a number of years, which created a complete vacuum. Young kids that we were, without any experience, we were just pushed into that vacuum. If there had been general elections two years after we created our party in 1969, we would have run and who knows what we would have done. But anyway, we started trade unions in 1970–1971. I was at the head of all the trade unions in the harbor, the transport sector, and the sugar industry.

Then I suppose nature has its own laws. The result was a complete clash in 1971. In those days, Mauritius was like the Far West. There were political thugs that tried to kill me a number of times. They killed other people in our cause. It developed into a general strike in 1971, and we spent a year in political detention: the whole year of 1972. Then the two parties I mentioned earlier split, and the situation returned to normal. We went through general elections in 1976. That is nine years after the independence elections of 1967.

The first time we went to elections, we got thirty-four seats. The old Labour Party got twenty-eight, and the Right Wing Party, eight. They joined together, thirty-six to thirty-four, and formed government, and we agreed. We played by the rules. We could have gone out in the streets and so on, but we didn't. Sir Anerood Jugnauth was becoming the leader of the party in the meantime, and was a legalist a generation before us. It helped, so we became Her Majesty's opposition. We learned, and we won all the seats in the 1982 elections. After I had been the main trade unionist ten years, I became minister of finance at a time when we were on our knees in front of the IMF and World Bank. So tough decisions had to be taken. They were taken, and I am proud to say that in 1982 the budget I presented put Mauritius back on track. It was not easy then; we mellowed; today we are a left-wing, center left, democratic party. But no, I'm certainly not conservative, and not just in politics, but generally, no. It's not my style, but yes, I've changed a lot when it was inevitable. It has happened in a number of cases.

J.P.: What about terrorist threats in Comoros, and would you speak about the future of Comoros?

P.B.: I don't see any terrorist threat in Comoros or emanating from Comoros. But this being said, they need all the help they can get; but they must help themselves, and I must say they have been helping themselves lately. They used to call me "The Comorian" here because I took so much interest in Comorian affairs. But it's the same in the case of the Seychelles, and the same in the case of Madagascar. I feel very, very close to these neighboring countries.

It won't be easy for Comorians to consolidate democracy. The last elections were very free and fair, very good. But they are very poor people with a lot of problems. Down in history, the different islands were used to fighting each other, so they need every bit of help that they can get, and the first help is not to close an embassy in a small place like that. That should be corrected. For the United States and South Africa, its neighbor to the south, to close their embassies hurt them terribly. We must help them. We are now helping them—we, I mean the United States, Mauritius, the region, South Africa. I don't see any threat emanating from there. I remain an optimist also in the case of Comoros.

I hope they join SADC in the time to come. There was a point when I proposed that Madagascar should join SADC, and no one was for that in Madagascar, and no one was for it in SADC because we had just admitted Congo as a member and with all the problems that came with it. Now Congo is pulling through, and I hope that it does so successfully. Seychelles had a desire to leave. I tried desperately to keep them in SADC. Now they are back, and I hope that little Comoros also will find its place in the region, in SADC, in the days to come. It will help consolidate democracy and development in Comoros.

J.P.: How do you think Seychelles is doing?

P.B.: Ah, Seychelles, she's doing nicely. I was there for the last presidential elections, and it went beautifully for Seychelles. I don't mind who wins in Seychelles, Comoros, Madagascar—in all those places I have friends on both sides. I don't interfere in their local politics, and it's helpful to people to have friends on both sides. Seychelles is going the right way. They are now a democracy. There can be improvements. Everywhere there can be improvements. In Florida, the way elections are carried out there can be improvements. But Seychelles, she's doing nicely. There's been a little clash recently. Unfortunately, the leader of the opposition and some of his friends got beaten up by the riot police. They'll have legislative elections next year. I hope everything goes nicely, and the economic policy of the new president recently elected is on course. So I am very optimistic as far as the Seychelles are concerned. Seychelles in fact is my second home. After Mauritius, Seychelles is really my second home. I feel very close to them. I love that country, and I wish them also every success.

Sir Anerood Jugnauth, Mauritius, October 10, 2006

The following edited interview was done at the State House in Réduit, the residence and principal office of the president of Mauritius, with Sir Anerood Jugnauth.

J.P.: What were your plans for Mauritius?

A.J.: When I became prime minister, the first thing I had most on my mind was to preserve our democratic system, and we have managed to do it. I think Mauritius is today recognized as a real democratic country. The second thing that was always paramount in my mind, especially given my background as a lawyer, is to give independence to institutions so that they can function properly, and particularly to the judiciary, which should be completely independent.

In so far as [the] economy is concerned, when I took over we depended more or less on sugar alone. That was very dangerous for the country, so I wanted to diversify the economy. But in order to be able to diversify the economy, we had to create the trust and confidence in the country and have the necessary infrastructures. We should attract investors from abroad. We managed to put up the necessary infrastructures, modernize our telephone communication system, build roads, modernize the airport and harbor, and then create other sectors of the economy, such as textiles, tourism, offshore [banking], as well as a modern financial center. We have also now coming up the ICT sector, and [the Mauritius] Freeport that is also flourishing.

So, I think the future vision must be now on bringing other sectors in the country. I've always believed the private sector should be given the opportunities to function and operate. Of course, they have to make profit, but we want them to make sure that all the profit doesn't go into the pockets of those who have invested, and that the workers also would get their fair share. I've always believed that if the country is prosperous, that prosperity will filter among the population. That was what people called the "Mauritian Miracle." In fact, the country became prosperous.

We had the big headache when we took over the unemployment problem in 1982. People were really very poor. They could not afford to have two meals a day, so we made sure that the situation was reversed, and we succeeded in doing that. I used to say that people in the towns were much better off than people in the villages. There was a lack of infrastructures and the standard in the villages was very low. One of my ambitions was to fill in the gap. Today, if you drive around the country you will see the villages prosperous with all the amenities, big shops, and everything that is required and you need in your own village. In the early years of the 1970s, if you wanted to build a house in the village you had to go to the town to purchase your materials and bring them to the countryside. So, that is one of the things that I achieved and of which I am very proud. I think we have done a tremendous job. I hope this present government will continue along the same line, and make the country become more prosperous.

J.P.: Weren't you also the person who said that our country's resources are our people, and you started an education plan?

A.J.: Exactly. Well, to come back to the present budget, the budget of the IMF and World Bank, because this is exactly what IMF [International Money Fund] and World Bank wanted to do with us in 1982. In all, they wanted us to remove free education, close down schools, colleges, and remove all the subsidies, and make people pay for health and all that. Well, I resisted all this. I said it can't be done because already people were suffering so much. If we were to do that, all of a sudden that population would suffocate. I resisted, and then I said, "The only resource that we have is the human resource, and I can't afford to have an uneducated population." Ultimately IMF and World Bank made lots of concessions, and we proved to them that we were right; otherwise, Mauritius would have been doomed, in so far as I'm concerned.

J.P.: Because your country started to do so well, the agencies like the World Bank and the IMF and others didn't want to deal with you. Would you elaborate on that?

A.J.: Yes, that I have always said is wrong. Even some friendly countries, because they believe that we are doing well, cut off everything. Instead of it being an incentive that you were doing well and to boost up that incentive, they are doing the contrary, you see? They remove all that, especially at this juncture when we are going through so many changes with globalization. I think this is a time when countries like ours, small island states, need to be helped especially and particularly for them to survive. But unfortunately, today people are thinking very differently. It seems that you must stay in poverty to be helped by others and so it's a negative approach in so far as I am concerned.

Vijay Makhan, Mauritius, October 12, 2006, First Session

Vijay Makhan served as the Organization of African Unity (OAU) deputy secretary general, and when it became the African Union (AU), as commissioner for trade, industry, and economic affairs. Together, that was an eight-year term in Addis Ababa, where the OAU/AU was housed. Being Mauritian, he returned and became the foreign secretary, 2004–2005 in the Bérenger government. He currently serves on many special missions, and is the chief negotiator for resolving problems in Mauritania to find its way into democracy. In the following edited interview, Mr. Makhan offers his insights on some of the sub-Saharan African issues that are facing us today as well as on Mauritius.

J.P.: What is the U.S. role in Africa today?

V.M.: I find the question quite pertinent and relevant to what's happening in the world today. One of the things that seemed to interest you, John, is the kind of U.S. policy in Africa on matters such as trade, aid, terrorism, et cetera. You see, there's one thing that has always struck me during my time at the OAU from 1995 down to 2003. I always thought there was an absence of the major powers in Africa. Let me explain: an absence in the sense of concern. They were there, but mainly for their own commercial interests. They were there for economic interests, but there was no sort of genuine concern for a continent of that magnitude: complex yet easygoing; complicated yet understandable. There was this lack for direct concern, you know, from countries, which had taken the mantle of superpowers or developed countries, or countries that knew all the answers or had all the answers to all the problems of the world, and yet there was this absence of direct concern.

While they were handling, talking to governments, they seemed to have cast aside the interests of the people, which I believe is the basic tenet of democracy: for the people. Regimes—they come and go, but the people are there to stay. These are the people who make up nations. These are the people who as a sum total create the wealth of the country to which they belong. We think in this world, which we call globalization now, there is a total absence of commitment on the part of those governments, the Western powers we say, toward the people of the continent. And yet this continent makes up eight hundred million people!

For everything that we tried to do in Africa, there was always a counteraction as well—be it at the level of the institutions like the World Bank and the IMF, or be it at the level of the capitals: Washington, London, and Paris. Everybody seemed to believe that they had the answers to the problems of Africa, yet they turned out to be all wind, all talk.

J.P.: Hot air?

V.M.: Yeah, hot air, there you are. In terms of concrete action there is nothing much to show on the ground. We talk of democracy. Now, you have referred to the Western concept of democracy. Now I believe that democracy is democracy. There cannot be an Eastern concept or a Western concept, although there is a tendency of trying to sort of dissect the precepts, the fundamentals, of democracy—"we set the rules of the game, and that's it; you follow them" kind of thing. But democracy has to be adaptable according to the situation on the ground.

In terms of Africa, there have been moments of democracy that go back to even before democracy was born elsewhere, or for what we call democracy in its modern terminology. Even in the choice of the chieftains of the tribe there was a form of democracy. There was a form of choice. How do you choose? The fact that you have elements that guide you to choose a leader, a chieftain, means there is an election; means there is a selection process; means there are procedures. Even if it meant to fight for that title or to run courses for that title, or confront a lion or tiger you had to do it to prove yourself worthy of a chieftain. You had to go through that process. And that for me was a choice. It was a question of, okay, I throw my hat in prepared to take up all these challenges, and that's a form of democracy so far as I am concerned, because the tribesmen then acclaim this guy. They say, "Oh, this guy was able to cross that river full of crocodiles, was able to tackle a lion; he was able to climb this mountain, and he was able to fight the other chieftain there, and he was about to win the heart of this woman, or whatever it was (I don't know the procedures), so, okay, we shall acclaim him. He's our chief." That's a form of choice.

Okay, it's not as familiar as the democracy—where you go and vote, you go and cast your ballot in the ballot box (and that's it), or the freedom of press, the freedom of expression, or freedom of choice, et cetera, but Africans have freedoms in their own way. Now when you come here and talk about democracy: "Okay, you guys. If you don't have democracy we won't help you." Not helping those people means that those people will still be living under the poverty line. It's a chicken-and-egg situation here. That is why I personally have always favored a policy whereby one would tackle the politics as well as the economics of a given society at the same time. While looking after the economic development, you look also after the political development. When there are conflicts, you address the conflict's situation, but at the same time try to help those people who are in conflict to come up from the economic rut that they find themselves in. And that's the best guarantee.

If you look at politics only, look at Darfur. If you try to help people only from the political angle, they will slide. All you're trying to do is settle the political situation, trying to settle a political difference without addressing the core of the wound. What is it that gets people involved in picking up small arms and fighting if it's not the belly? If you have enough to eat then they will look for the next best, which is [taking care] of your children, trying to educate your children so they grow up and graduate. But first, you've got to fill that belly, and that would relieve you from trying to take the easy course, which is very easy for leaders who will just come and exploit people who are famished. It's very easy. "I give you a dollar; pick up that gun and shoot that fellow." Like I said, "Okay, I'm going to get a dollar. With that one dollar I can feed my people say for one day, give them a couple of meals, or whatever it is, so let's do it," and I shoot.

That's the way it is. So when we come to policy, the U.S., for example, there was a total absence of homogenous policy toward Africa. Before, of course, it was dictated by the geopolitical situation of the continent, because you had this: The U.S. saw the Soviet bloc, okay, fair enough. There was a Cold War; it went on. There was a total disinterest toward Africa. If you look at what people got from taking sides during the Cold War, there's nothing much to show. It was regimes that were being supported— not the people, not the countries. This regime was being supported by the U.S.; this regime was being supported by the Soviets. Let's face it; it's history. It's there. You know I'm not inventing anything; everybody knows this.

Now, John, you see, the crux of the matter, therefore, becomes this: was there a genuine U.S. policy in Africa? I say no. The only policy that came up for Africa was with AGOA, and that was a calculated one, and that was bipartisan, which was why I was the first one to welcome that as the participation of the OAU. I was in Washington, and I remember Congressman Charles Rangel, as well as Congressman Bill Thomas. There was Congressman Jim McDermott, who came to Mauritius. I met them.

I went to them. I talked to them, and they talked to me about the AGOA. I said, "Fantastic! This is good, but please send it to us. We shall try to give you our own input on that so that you can better the thing." It was the House of Representatives' bill, I remember. I had taken a closer look at the first draft and said, "Okay, the principle is good." So I made a statement. They recorded that statement, and then when they went to talk to the press about it, the administration was unkind.

These people were against this, so at one time they asked a question. I wasn't there. I couldn't attend the press conference launching this AGOA because I had my other appointments in Washington. Then one guy from the Department of Commerce said, "Why, Congressman, are you talking about this for Africa, but does Africa want it? Does Africa welcome this kind of thing?" So these guys then took out my statement and said, "Look, we have in town the deputy secretary of the OAU and this is what he had to say about AGOA, welcoming the principle."

To tell you, because that was the first time the U.S. had churned out a common policy for Africa, of course, based on conditions, but these conditions were what? This is where I fought with my own people back in the various member states. I told them, "Look, this is something to do with trade, and this is a U.S. bill. It is not an Africa-America bill; it is not a U.S.-Africa coordinated action. No, it is not. It is the U.S. bill; they are going to pass the bill whether you like it or not. It's *their* parliament. So please, do understand. Let us see what benefits, what advantages one can derive from that, and let us see how we can strengthen the relations at another level other than politics, how we can strengthen relations between the U.S. and Africa." I had a lot of convincing to do.

I explained to them, "Look, you say that AGOA has these conditions, but these are the conditions that we ourselves have decided to do, which we passed in 1995 during talks about good governance, and this is what they are saying. So they are saying something that we have already decided ourselves to do, so where is the harm? Where is the problem? Why do you only look at the conditions?"

They talked about freedom of press. Well, what we've said is, we have our charter. So I tried to explain. I *labored* through that. I sent the bill to all the capitals, fifty-three member-states, to all of them over there, and letters to all the ministers. I wrote to them; I said, "Look, this is what the U.S. is going to pass. Please get your people to study this, and send me back your input or any amendments that you may have so that I can forward them to the people who are proposing all this."

John, I did not receive a single reply from anywhere. So what I did was to put my own people to work. I got them to dissect the bill, the provisions of that, and bring out the things we thought would be objectionable, and things that would be offensive as reading, to try to redo it, recast it. So we did that. I sent it back. I can tell you, 95 percent of all the amendments that I sent to Jim McDermott and Charles Rangel got included in the final version of the bill.

Then I met the first assistant U.S. trade representative for Africa at USTR: Rosa Whitaker. Rosa came into a meeting of the Council of Ministers of the OAU. This was a first! And unheard of for a high echelon of the U.S. government to come and address a council of ministers, a technical one (the ministers of trade [meeting] in Harare). But I cautioned her. I said, "Rosa, please, this is Africa. There's a need to understand the African psyche. You need to understand the African character. Don't come here and try to patronize. Don't do that because they will eat you up."

Well, of course, Rosa is Rosa, very human, very good, good fighter, stands up for things, very good. In fact, she was very good for Africa. Not everyone was pleased, but this is politics. And I have to tell you, that was the first time the U.S. really had a policy for Africa.

Now, in terms of trade, one gets the impression the U.S. is always trying to sell its products, whereas one requires a two-way traffic. But what is it that Africa has to be able to export to the U.S.? South Africa, of course—if you take South Africa out, you take Nigeria out, you take oil out, diamonds out, gold out, what is there? Textiles? So on this textile issue, which was part of the AGOA, not all countries benefited, and, John, you were ambassador to Mauritius. You know how Mauritius suffered because in fact Mauritius and Kenya were the two countries that suffered because there was a quota that was slapped on them, if you recall. We fought very hard to get Mauritius and Kenya out of this quota system, to say that it's not fair that countries that are trying to come up, that are following very good governance principles, but are being penalized because they are doing well. And because you are supposed to have reached this standard, therefore you can't, you know?

I've always kept saying to the World Bank and the IMF, especially when they came up with this Heavily Indebted Poor Countries [HIPC] Initiative, which was backed by all these Western countries within the World Bank to fight against poverty, what they were saying is: you've got to be able to do this, this, and this, six steps, to qualify, and it takes about six years for you to get to that level. I equate it to a sick man in bed who requires the medical treatment right now, and the doctor is at the door. He says, "Okay, get up from your bed, walk these six steps to the door, and I'll give it to you." You know, that kind of thing, by which time, of course, the guy is already dead. So these are some of the things that upset probably the good intentions of the guys who churn out these policies.

The other problem has always been that people on Capitol Hill do not pay sufficient attention to the determination of a people. Take the issue of cotton. There are four West African countries that produce cotton, apart from many others that do it, but these four countries are penalized because of the heavy subsidies the U.S. grants its own farmers. You make the equation; you'll find that it doesn't cost much. There are certain things that the U.S. could easily do to ease up the situation.

For the past four or five years that we've been negotiating on the WTO, this has been a sore point, and it still is a sore point with these guys. But this is so easy. You could find other ways of doing. Do you know of the billions of dollars of subsidy that goes to them? I'm not saying you should not help your farmer. You should, but not to the detriment of the others. These are people who need it, who need it more than your own farmers. I'm not saying, please take off the shirt from your farmer's back and give it to the farmer in Africa. No, I'm not saying that. I'm saying, keep his shirt on, but let the other one also wear a shirt. Give him a chance to wear a shirt.

These are fundamental things that seem to escape the policymakers in Washington. Certainly, from that point of view, it cuts across politics in the states; whether you are a Republican or a Democrat, you have the same approach to the issue. The language changes, but the objective is the same. Guys will come and make the most beautiful of speeches, get applauded for it and believed by people, but then when you look at the action that follows, it's not there.

We had our own Abuja Treaty—our own policy for development that was kind of a blueprint. And then the British came. They decided to have something else. Then we had NEPAD. We had a commission. Then they [the British] came up with a commission for Africa, and taking Africans themselves in that, but coming out with the same kind of thing. You know, it's the same article but packaged differently. When you open the package, it's the same stuff. You're talking about development of infrastructure. You're talking about development of agriculture. You're talking of valorizing your national resources. You're talking good governance. You're talking of democracy. You're talking of giving a choice to the people, and all these are talked about in this. You're talking about centralizing some of these policies, harmonizing policies, rationalizing policies—and all these exist in blueprints that are not by Africa.

That's the wrong approach. Sit down at the table. Let us be true partners: you as the developed partner that has; and we as the partner that does not have. Let us both become accountable to each other. We are accountable for the commitments that we've taken. For those that we're not doing, you can tell us. You become accountable to do things that you have promised to do but you are not doing, despite the fact that we are trying to satisfy that part of the contract that we've entered into with you.

If you look at the WTO, it's the same thing. We are fifty-three countries, and we have strength in the international forum. When we created the group of ninety in Cancun I was asked, "You're a group of ninety, but you represent hardly a minimal percentage on the world economic scene."

I said, "Well, it is not the percentage of world trade that we deal in that matters here. It's the billions of people that we represent here. We're talking about people. We don't come here to talk about policies to enrich the regimes. We're talking about the people, because whatever we are doing here, it's supposed to affect the livelihood of the people, and we are deciding on their behalf. We are talking about these ninety countries representing more than half of the humanity that you are talking about here. If you add to that the Brazilians, the Indians, the Chinese, and all these guys who also claim to be developing countries, then we represent more than three quarters of humanity here. So, please, let us understand this. Of course these are not always acceptable to people who are there, you know. But there needs to be constant dialogue. People need to come.

Here are the kinds of things we need the Congress people, whether in Washington or in London, to understand. Get them to understand the basics. Talk to them about these kinds of things. You go to a government in a government system—of course, it will be very formal. You put your card on the table; they put their card on the table. You turn yours this way; they turn theirs that way, and that's it. This is a half hour and you have gone through: what is it that bites? What is it that makes people tick? This is the kind of thing that they need to understand. What is the psychology of this country or this continent? That is what they need to understand, because these people are also dignified in their way. They may be poor, but they have dignity. They may be poor, but they would like to be taken care of in a way that doesn't wound their sensibilities. This is what they need to do.

J.P.: The Western powers have put over $300 billion in the last thirty-plus years into the African continent. There's very little to show for it. What is your observation?

V.M.: When you say that $300 billion have been pumped into Africa and there's nothing much to show for it, I think it is an unfair comment. On the face of it, it may appear correct; but if you dig deep down you will find that it is incorrect to say so, because there is more money that goes out of Africa than comes in, at the end of the day.

If you look at the number of Africans who are providing services in all the other countries, at whatever level, you'll find that it is extremely important to look at. You'll find that it is phenomenal. This is one thing that has come up recently in terms of the amount of money that national governments have been providing for the training of their people, and once these people are trained, they stay abroad there—doctors, nurses— the UK, for example. Today you go to the UK and you'll find most of the well-qualified doctors all come from Africa, including Mauritius, South Africa.

J.P.: How do you see us going forward at this point to develop sustainable growth while overcoming issues of enigmatic regimes?

V.M.: This in itself can be a subject of another book, John. But, when you discuss again with regimes, it's bound to be when the regime does something or if the regime is not one that is accountable to its people. Therefore, it can get away with murder. But if it is someone in the regime that has been put up by the people, they have to be accountable to the people. And if there is aid money, if there are transparent procedures that are put in place, which may not be there—I mean, look at Chad. Why the sudden interest in Chad—just because oil was struck? Before oil was struck in Chad, where were all these governments? The only Western power that was around in Chad active on a very political level was France. But when oil was struck, everybody moved in. Even the World Bank moved in.

Look at Equatorial Guinea. One or two people in the process may be making a quick buck, but the country itself is not because the country is already, after having struck oil and signed the contracts, indebted for the next twenty-five years. In other words, the income you're deriving from oil doesn't come to you. It goes to the people who are exporting it because they have decided, the contract being what it is. That is why I say in terms of government development, aid, or whatever it is, there is a new way of handling aid. You need to make sure that it really is going to the people.

So how do you do that? Take a country like Mauritius. Because we have very basics, we have fundamentals, we've only known democracy here, and we are not always satisfied with the kind of democracy we have. Every now and again we think we are making progress, but there is not enough of it sometimes, as you know. You've been in this country for four years, and this has been the song of all political parties whether they are in power or in opposition.

So what do we do? We need to set down procedures and agree upon them. Of course the fundamentals may be different, but at least the objective is there. It is the same principle; it's the same parameter. It's the approach that is different, and that is when you talk about the Western concept of democracy, you should give some elbow room to these regimes to maneuver within that parameter. You can't have a rule to fit all. There is a question of one size fits all. It doesn't work that way. It has to be adapted to the circumstances, to the environment of the people of the country that you are targeting, and let the people emerge out of their own. You tell them, okay, this democracy means that you have to choose a government. How do you choose that government? How do you do your elections? It need not be the American way, or the British way, or the French way. You decide your own way, provided you exercise your freedom of choice, freedom of expression the same way.

So what do you do with Africa? What do you do with this sustainable development that you are talking about? There are certain basic things that you need to do. You need to get to the people again. How do you get to the people? There are so many ways that you can get to the people. The regimes are interstate relationships and adaptable. Whichever be the government in Washington, whichever be the government say in Germany, they sit down and talk. But it's the people that we need to reach. You need to establish a contract with the government, because the government represents the people first.

You have so many people on the ground. The people require, let's say, assistance in education, or seeds for their farm. They require all sorts of things, you know. There are so many ways that one can sit down and do. There are regional organizations, and this is the beauty of it all, because our own blueprint in Africa at the continent level does make room for regional organizations, harmonizing policies at all levels. For example, with SADC now you also have all sorts of protocol.

J.P.: What about SADC?

V.M.: There are certain things you can't do if they don't meet with the objectives or the parameters set down by SADC as a group. So these are the things that you can work through. It is not necessary to work directly with a country on a bilateral level, but you can work more laterally. You can do that. Sit down and say, okay. We want to be able to assist. We think that the way we have been handling aid hasn't been useful or provided [what was needed]. People are still poor. Let us sit down and see how best we can do it now and decide on the parameters that need fixing.

Once you have agreed, SADC goes back to its own principals, that is, the Council of Ministers, and says, "Look, these are the things that we have agreed with our partners would be the criteria, that would trigger the kind of aid that we are looking for. Let us see whether we agree with them." At the end of the day they say, "Okay, we'll agree with this. See with the partners whether these are acceptable." Yes, acceptable. Once this is done, this is it. Country X that is a member state of SADC is not doing what needs to be done. Very sorry; our money will not be going there because we are responsible, accountable to our taxpayers as well. This is what Washington would say or the EU would say, or anybody else would say. That's the way I think we can do it. Reach the people.

J.P.: What have the Americans done in Mauritius?

V.M.: I've been foreign secretary and, without divulging any secret, I can tell you very little. There's very little to show for the kind of friendship that we have always shown to the U.S., and we don't do it because it's only politics. We do it because we believe in certain parameters. We believe in certain fundamentals of democracy, and we are not going to change that unless, God forbid, something else happens in this country. As long as we people are here, we love our freedom too much to allow any other form of government to come by here. It's just going to be a democratic country; even if that means changing our method every four years, so be it. We want to choose our leaders, we want to choose our government, and these are things that are very dear and near to the Americas, I would like to believe. Freedom of choice. Freedom of expression. We have so many newspapers in this country. We have free radios, et cetera.

But then, on the other hand, when we come to the States, we say, look, why don't you give us a little help for something that we are trying to push for at the WTO? We don't find it. We look around for our friends; we don't find them. It hurts, you see? We say, "What is it that we get in return?" Look at when Mauritius was at the Security Council, you know?

J.P.: They were constantly asking for your support.

V.M.: Absolutely. And we were always there answering "yes" on matters of great principle. We have taken a stance in Africa that had been unheard of against Saddam on the issues of human rights, against Nigeria and the question of human rights, but, on the other hand, when we look to our friends—it's not that we're doing it so that we can get help from you. No, no. We are doing it because we believe this is the right course to take. See, these are near and dear to you, and you find that this country is struggling economically; there's something that we need to do. Give us a hand.

Look at the situation of Mauritius today. All the preferences on which we based ourselves for our economic development are being eroded as a result of the WTO's rules and regulations, including a 36 percent reduction in sugar. The Textile Multifiber Arrangement had been dismantled in 2005, and we have tough competition from the Chinese. You may have tough competition from the Chinese, but we suffer from it more. Therefore, we need the kind of assistance that we're looking for. We need investors, but how do the American investors come this way? It's too far for them? I don't know what it is. We just don't seem to be able to attract that, and yet we are trying our best to sell our wares, so there is something somewhere, some disconnect between what the Americans stand for, what they publicly sort of clamor, and what actions do they take for those who are trying to do it.

If we [Mauritians] are not too careful because of the economic conjecture right now, we may slide. Once you start sliding, it means that you are affecting the middle-class society that keeps the country going. You are a big country; you will have the clout, and therefore you have the voice. We are smaller countries, so many of us, so please try to understand. Ask, what is it that we can do to open markets for you? How do we help? Let's sit down and talk.

J.P.: In Mauritius, you have a multiethnic, multicultural, multilingual society. You have some tribal aspects here, but Africa has had thousands of years of tribal aspects, so when a tribal leader gets democratically elected, he surrounds himself with his own tribe, and when he receives money, or loans, or aid, much of the improvements for schools and hospitals goes into his village, not to the other villages. How does one get away from that tribal concept to a more democratic concept?

V.M.: I can't pretend to have the answer, but what I can say is that all these issues with tribes have been the curse of Africa. This has been the curse of most of the countries of Africa: tribalism and chieftainship here and there. But there is a way of getting around that, and that's through education—the people. Getting them to understand that everybody has the same equal rights as the other.

What do you do when you provide assistance, or monies coming in, and you find that the leader first tries to help himself or herself, or his own people or his own tribe? It doesn't go to the people, per se. It goes to the people, but people belonging to a certain category. Again, this is what I was saying earlier. There is need to sit down and discuss the ways that this can be dished out. There is a new way of giving development aid. You don't have to provide money for that.

As a basic example, let's say there is a school that needs to be built in an area where there is no school, assuming there are many tribes. You build a school there. You don't provide the money for the school to be built because then you run the risk of that school being elsewhere, or something else taking place. So it has to be directed. That's what I'm saying. Directed aid.

There are many aspects because these are things that we need help to right Africa: health, education, and of course infrastructure, which is for the national benefit. But most countries do not want to invest in the infrastructure because it is not something that gives them a return for their investment. It's as simple as that. They do not want to build, but they want to go into the mining area, because for every dollar that you put into Africa, you get back twenty-seven dollars.

And this too is what was happening: corruption. There is corruption in Africa. Incidentally, if you look up the word "corruption" in the African language you will not find it. For every corrupted official, though, there must be a corrupter somewhere. So corruption should be tackled at both ends, from source to the end. That is the end receiver, the guy who gets corrupted to do a certain thing, who takes money and does something else with it, or who wants a kickback, or who wants to give a concession because he's got a kickback. We need to tackle it at both ends at the same time.

We have our convention against corruption in Africa, but there is not much help we are getting from our partners to try to empower that convention. At the end of the day, it depends on the regime and the current government and their priorities. And this can differ as much as the time differs from region, you know, areas of the world to other areas of the world, the same way their priorities differ. Some governments have got their priorities right. It's their people, the intents of their people. But others have got their priorities upside down. They think it's their interests first, and then the interests of the people. If our partners find their own interests, then they'll be more than happy, because that will provide them the twenty-seven dollars for every dollar that they put in. If they think, okay, let me work with this guy even though we know he's corrupt, but we shall turn a blind eye to it because our companies are getting a return for their money. You see, this is the thing that we need to fight— the quick return.

J.P.: In the African society, terrorism didn't exist many years ago. I mean, tribal fighting did, but terrorism now is something that's taking place in Africa. How do you see, in your opinion, a solution to the issues of terrorism?

V.M.: Let me tell you something that maybe many Americans don't know. Africa tackled the issue of terrorism much before the September 11 regrettable incident that triggered all this huge concern for terrorism in the developed world. When we are attacking terrorism, again, our partners did not come to assist. It was not important. We've been told to go and sign the International Convention Against Terrorism, but we had our own convention against terrorism, the Algiers Convention. If you look at the Algiers Convention, it captures *more* than the International Convention. These are things that people, the Americans, need to know, that the Africans were there, concerned about terrorism right from the beginning, and they decided to sit together and decide collectively, how do we fight this?

Again, one of the basic things that triggers terrorism is what? The guy who doesn't have his belly full—he's prepared to do any act to get a quick buck somewhere, whether it is right or wrong. He just doesn't care. He's been brainwashed, you know. Terrorism is a despicable act, and we need to fight it collectively. Many of my colleagues in Africa and I said, "Look, we are prepared." There is no problem signing the International Convention on terrorism. We can go and sign any piece of paper, but we have our own African Convention on terrorism, and we needed help to put it into activity, because there are certain positive actions in that convention that need to be required, that need to be done. But for these to be done, to be translated more quickly, we need the funds that we don't have. You know that we are cash strapped. Look at Darfur. The AU forces are there, but if the AU is not making a dent there it's because we are cash strapped, and we depend on the assistance of the international community, of the Western world, or the EU or the U.S.

The African citizen, the African guy or girl, is a discreet, docile person. They are not belligerent. It is not in their way of life to be aggressive. No, no, no. They may look aggressive, but they are basically a very tender, soft person. They have been exploited by others who have scores to settle, or whatever; therefore, they use people. They themselves won't come forward because they are the cowards. They will send other people. They'll take other people, you know, give them promises, give them all sorts of help for their immediate family, and then get these guys to be sort of enslaved to their ideas, enslaved to their objectives, whatever they are.

These guys know that if they go and blow themselves up their family will be okay for the next so many years. These are the kinds of things that motivate these people. Of course, there are many also who think they are doing it for the just cause. They are convinced about it, and we have failed somewhere. We have failed to educate them. We have simply failed as an international society to reach all segments of society, to give them an equal opportunity. We have not been able to do that, and that is what creates poverty, and when a poor person becomes weak.

J.P.: In Seychelles we don't have an embassy—in Sudan, Somalia, and other countries. Do you think that our being there is important in fostering and moving the policies forward that would be beneficial to Africa?

V.M.: I think especially now it is very important for the U.S. to have a physical presence. I'll tell you why. It is now known, rightly or wrongly, that the U.S. is *the* superpower. It's a question of dignity. It's a question of sensitivity also. A country that is a neighbor to another country that has a U.S. embassy, but doesn't have one for his country, cannot help but question: "Am I less important? Are we less deserving? Are we not worthy of any concern, of any interest?" And this is when things start going wrong.

You have the means. You have the capacity, and you have the role. Therefore, there are certain responsibilities and obligations that go with that role: to be where you are required and needed to be. You need to make sure that on these parameters you have established on the context of developing your concept of democracy, you are there to monitor this. You cannot be absent. You cannot close down. It's bad for the country. It's a reflection that there is something basically wrong.

On the other hand, also when you are there, you should not be seen to be patronizing, but rather use constructive engagement.

VIJAY MAKHAN, MAURITIUS, OCTOBER 19, 2006, FOLLOW-UP SESSION

J.P.: How can we help the African continent?

V.M.: Let's start with this issue of village. To get the people out of the rut, you need to approach them directly. It's not the regime that is going to change it. You need to approach the people.

So one of the ways of doing it is through the lowest rung of an organized society; in this case, let's say it's the village. Within the village also you have different groups. So let's take the pilot project that was started in Mauritius in the 1970s and evolved into the NDU, the National Development Unit. This is what has now changed in Mauritius. The genesis is precisely this village concept, which was trying to bring the village closer to the town [amenities]. It was basic and I often wondered why the World Bank, which was behind this project and funded the project, did not create others on the continent elsewhere, because it had worked here.

It was a good concept: "Work for everybody." First you give them employment, and then you change their quality of life. That is, you bring them up. You try to lift them from where they are, bring them up higher, and try to make them understand they are no different than those living in the urban areas, in the towns. You do a kind of survey. What is it that they have? Do they have trees? Do they have chickens; are they rearing rabbits? Do they have a kitchen garden? What is it? How do they send their children to school? Is there a school? Do they like the school?

You do a survey, and then you do a report, but basically it boils down to a five-point concept, beginning with water. You need to bring water to them so that they don't have to wake up early in the morning at four and go walk for kilometers to try to get to the water point. Bring water to them. Give them a couple of water points in the village. Bring them a village center to be able to express their wishes, and give them a place where they could meet, which we call the community life that they didn't have. Then give them a health center in the event they require one. Give them the school. Give them the roads. Give them the sanitation facilities, and then inculcate in them the notion of self-help. You don't have the money? We give you the material, but you do your own roads. You do your own drains. You do [it on] your own, and it worked! It worked!

The village of Tamarin, on the west coast, was started under my responsibility. The village center is still there, as is the health center. The water has gone down to them. It started with a couple of pumps, and then it developed. People started having their own water. The drains that people built are still there. Low-cost housing remains. Hotels have come up, and people have just emerged. They don't need to come and live in Quatre Bornes, or in Port Louis, or in Curepipe, which are the known sort of urban areas in Mauritius, but stay there. It worked—and there are other similar villages.

So if we can do it here in Mauritius on a small scale, you can imagine the same concept implemented in the continent. People would enjoy that. You see, because the guy in Africa, busy doing whatever chore he has, is happy. The guy doesn't need more than enough to eat, a hut, to feed his family; and let him be. All these huge concepts of, you know, free trade, this-and-that—he couldn't be bothered about it because he hasn't yet reached that level there.

So what we need to do is to take development to the village. You can't ask the villages to come to development. Development has to go to them. We discussed earlier that the resources belong to the people, but unfortunately we have regimes who believe or who have been made to believe that because they are at the helm of affairs in the country, they hold sway over the resources of the country. Well, that's not true. They never created that wealth to start with. They never invented the resources. Those resources are there, and the people should be the beneficiaries.

You see, I always say that whenever any regime, any government, be it democratically elected, or autocratic, or tyrannical, or whatever you want, wants to do something, they talk about development. Development is meant to satisfy the needs, the aspirations of the people. Development is supposed to benefit the individual. If development has to benefit mankind, man has to be at the center of development and the vehicle of that development. You cannot come and impose development on the people. You have to bring them along, make them understand what that development is, whether it is the kind of development they require. Do they want a cinema hall in the village where there is no electricity? No, that is not development, because that would be just concrete, money being pumped, and somebody getting rich somewhere.

What is it that the village requires? Putting a cinema hall or market or whatever it is, is not going to develop them. What they need first is you address their basic needs, and from there they will start emerging. There is no point in bringing in a big, huge super factory in the middle of nowhere, and yet we know that past colonizers have done that. Africa is replete with such examples: a factory that was idle or deemed unusable because there was no material or trained personnel for maintenance. Boilers have been set up for nothing. So this is not the kind of development that we are talking [about]. It's good for those who have found the money, because for their own electorate, for their own people back at home, they can say, "Oh yes, development aid, this is how much we've spent in so-and-so country." But the people do not know whether this money has been a benefit to the people that they were meant to benefit.

I told you once about all these blueprints being churned out from the World Bank and Washington. People who come here, sit in the comfort of our hotels, look into the ocean and say what they think needs to be done for Mauritius. They don't know the reality. And presently, this is what we are suffering from—these people who have come and prescribe without knowing what is needed. Then if we don't carry out that prescription, we won't be given the funds. So the prescription is taken because our hands are tied, we need that kind of funds, and we do all these things, while in the process, you are doing a reverse trend of development.

You get my point. So the village concept is something very good. You cannot bring in something which is foreign to them, and suddenly say, "Okay, this is the way to development." No. They know what is needed for development. You need to talk to them, to the village elders, to the villagers, and ask what is required. Do you want to be New York or do you want your village to emerge respectful of your culture, your religion, and your traditions at the same time you are developing in life?

On the same issue, we talk about poverty reduction, which in my mind means one can live with some poverty. I say no. Nobody should live with *some* poverty. Your end, your objective, should be the *eradication* of poverty. People should be brought out of this level of poverty. Everybody has some pride in himself. He's on this earth. That is what makes us different from animals. We have senses; we have sensibilities. Everybody is born dignified. We should continue to aim at whatever we do to ensure that the people retain their dignity, to live and to die in dignity. That's what we need to do—and poverty is the scourge of this century, an indictment on the international community. We need to eradicate it without making all these speeches about poverty reduction or eradication. Everything that needs to be done has been said, except that nobody is doing it—or if they are, very little has been done. What we need to do is eradicate poverty like a bad disease, like a bad epidemic. It might take longer than we think, but we need to take aim at poverty eradication, just like the other scourges that affect the world today.

Terrorism is another scourge that you cannot reduce, but must eradicate. And if you have to be ruthless you have to be ruthless. To eradicate terrorism you must eradicate poverty. Bring in development. Let me stop here and tell you that we need to go back to the Chinese proverb that tells you: you give man a fish, he will be able to feed himself just for that one meal. But you teach him how to fish, he will be able to live for [his] entire life. This is what you need to adapt, and get people to understand. Give them the means to have their own livelihood, bring them up, without their losing their dignity. That's very fundamental. It's very, very fundamental.

Once, the UN invited me in the context, again, of capacity building to lift people from Africa, improve their lives, et cetera. I talked about preventive, just like you have preventive diplomacy. I said that development has to be used as a preventive measure to prevent people from sliding into poverty. It's very, very important that when Congress sits and talks about what kind of aid, what kind of development should be given to Africa, it's not enough to say, "Okay, four billion U.S. dollars are being spent to get people to bring their textiles in." They need also to see whether it is reaching the people who are supposed to benefit from that kind of policy. To accomplish that, they really need to know the aspirations of the people.

J.P.: Where would you start to help, what village, and what country? Would you start in a country that is totally corrupt, partially corrupt, one that is democratic?

V.M.: Where does one start? The concept of corrupt societies differs from area to area depending upon who is passing judgment on which society is more or less corrupt. It's a question of relativity, and it depends on who is involved, how, and where. So this concept of the village, where do we start? I agree with you, there are millions of villages in the continent, strewn across the massive plains that constitute Africa, so where does one start?

J.P.: With different cultures.

V.M.: Yes, with different cultures, so there you are. I think it's not difficult to do that once you know what you want to get, where you want to go. You have to take some of the societies that have shown some progress, but which are still a long way away. And this is where you start. The others, next door, whom you classify as corrupt, you may not want to help believing that there is a risk that whatever you pump in might be siphoned away. So what you need to do is to try to get a country that is according to your own definitions, according to your own terms and terminology, you think is a society which is viable, which would like help, and which you can claim later on as a success story. This is important.

Congress should do well to flag these success stories, such as Mauritius, and make sure that these countries do not pay the ransom of their success by penalizing them. You start doing it in a few countries, but you flag it. Wherever you go in the international community, every now and then you make a progress report. Okay, this is what was started— a school was started in 2006; in 2010 we had the first batch out, and this is what these people are doing today in their own village. You take development, the idea being to take development back there, and therefore you do not start in all the millions of villages, because you will not be able to. Choose a couple of countries which you think have the right potential or the right goal, who have the right parameters, and then you flag these as success stories. The other partners will follow.

J.P.: Which countries do you think?

V.M.: If I say so it might be a bit subjective. As an example, take Botswana, where you have a good level of development, but a problem with AIDS. The life expectancy in Botswana has dropped down to about forty-five, or even forty. This is one kind of problem that affects a development society, and something has to be done.

Each society has its own specificity, which you need to know about to make the right decisions. Things should not be imposed. It has to be homegrown, it has to be demand driven, and not supplied. Okay? Let's see how best we can organize that, how best we can do it; leapfrog into development things that you have known.

This is where I wanted to just underline something about AGOA, and the use of the word "obsolete." In the AGOA bill is mentioned it was the intention of the U.S. administration to send to Africa what they call "obsolete equipment." And it's wrong. It's still there. If you go to the [bill] you'll find it there. Please do not do that because it means that whatever it is no longer of use to you now, you're passing it on.

Let me give you an example. During a huge conference on the depletion of the ozone layer, they decided that the culprit was CFCs [chlorofluorocarbons]. So they decided they would no longer make refrigerators or other equipment, air conditioners, that produce CFC. They have to be CFC free. In the process, after having given this technology to developing countries, they banned these things, so that the developing countries now were left with the very refrigeration system and technology that if they put in practice would create CFC, and therefore contravene the convention.

J.P.: How can the U.S. help make NEPAD a success?

V.M.: I think NEPAD has been used by some of our partners in a divisive way rather than a constructive way. As I said the last time, NEPAD's objectives are the same as those of the Abuja Treaty, which came into being in 1995. It's the same objective, except that it has been dressed up with more frills and more cosmetics than anything else, but basically the objectives are the same, so why do we keep churning this kind of thing, you know? It's like the new wine in old bottles situation.

J.P.: How can the U.S. help with the program?

V.M.: Bring the synergy about NEPAD, what is pushing NEPAD, into the objectives of the African Union. NEPAD has to be consumed into the program of the African Union. You can't have two programs or three programs running in parallel because there is a diversion of funds.

J.P.: Then the U.S. really can't get involved with that.

V.M.: Well, like I said, the premier institution of Africa is the African Union. That's the premier institution. Therefore, if you want to develop a policy of development, or aid, for Africa, the people you need to talk to are the African Union people because in them rests the entire policy, them and the subregional organizations.

Rama Sithanen, Mauritius, October 12, 2006

In the following edited interview, the vice prime minister and minister of finance and economic empowerment, Minister Rama Sithanen of Mauritius, offers insight on the overall specter of Mauritius and the Indian Ocean region.

J.P.: What are the contemporary image and future goals of Mauritius?

R.S.: We've reached the end of an economic model based on trade preferences for sugar and for textiles and clothing. Unfortunately, with preference erosion fast catching up with us, we need to find a new economic paradigm that will sustain the current development of Mauritius.

Mauritius has been late and slow in adapting to the challenges of globalization affecting the economy. That's why we have to move quickly if we want to address the structural problems we see in the economy. The price of sugar is coming down by 36 percent over the next four years, and we have been adversely affected by the phasing out of the Multifiber Agreement. Both have impacted negatively on the growth, which has come down. The budget deficit has gone up. Debt has increased significantly. Investment is down. Unemployment is high, and external balance also is in deficit. What we need to do now is to articulate a new strategy that will help us restructure the economy and, at the same time, lay the foundation for new growth. So we are restructuring sugar; in fact, we are shifting from sugar to cane. So instead of exclusively relying on raw sugar, we are going to manufacture white sugar. We are going to use the by-product of sugar, which is begasse, to produce energy. We are also going to manufacture ethanol to mix with gasoline to propel cars.

In textiles, we've lost our competitive advantage in the high volume, low-value end of the market because the cost of production has increased, and there are competitors, such as China and India, that are doing much better than we are. They have lots of raw materials that are available locally, their labor cost is lower than ours, and in many cases they are closer to the markets. So what we've done in the textile and clothing sector is basically to consolidate and vertically integrate, and move into the high end of the market where we can compete.

In tourism, instead of relying only on beach tourism, the resort, we would like to diversify by offering conference and exhibition space to the trade industry. We would also like to promote Mauritius as a duty-free island where people from the region will come and source their products. While we have developed the financial services sector, we now need to add depth and width to the sector so more substance and value will be added within Mauritius.

A new sector that we would like to develop, obviously, is the ICT [Information and Communication Technology] sector. We have invested in the infrastructure: a modern, state-of-the-art building. Now we have to bring down the cost of communication, and train our people.

One of the most important constraints we face is that ability of the pool of talents, which is why in the last budget we opened the country to the outside world. We've made it easy for people to come and invest in Mauritius, working as professionals or employees. You can get your work permit in three days, and you can stay in Mauritius for a usual period of three years. After that, you can apply to become a permanent resident of Mauritius. The reason why we've done that is to attract foreign talent and investment, to attract people to bring in talents, know-how, knowledge, so these people can help us to develop our economy.

We are also investing in property development. Much of the land on which we used to grow sugarcane is going to be leased for other sectors. We would like to build what we call an "Integrated Resort Scheme," which is a combination of luxurious hotels, golf courses, and expensive villas for high net worth individuals. That will give jobs to the people, and bring foreign direct investment into the country.

We are also opening up the country so that retirees can spend more time in Mauritius. They can become residents of Mauritius provided they spend about $40,000 a year in our country. Many people who don't want to stay in Mauritius for the whole year may also not be happy spending only eleven or twenty days in Mauritius. They would like to stay here for three months and then move back to the States or Europe, or wherever it is, for the rest of the year. We have now made it easy for these people to come and spend time in Mauritius.

Taxation still remains one of the most important criteria that people choose before they decide where to invest, so we've brought down corporate tax and personal tax significantly from 30 percent to 15 percent. This will happen over a three-year period. So Mauritius will be one of the few countries where there will be a single rate of taxation for companies as well as individuals.

We have also improved considerably the business climate. Very often when people came to Mauritius, it was an obstacle race to get your permit, have your licenses, and to start your business. So now, we have changed this completely: you can get your license and your permit in three days. So we have shifted from an extended detailed investigation of your plan to a shortened enforcement of rules and regulations you need to comply with in order to do business.

We are also very busy in negotiating market access. We need to attract people to come and invest in our country. But it's a small market, so most of the products will have to be exported. We need to facilitate access to the market. We are a member of SADC and COMESA [Common Market for Eastern and Southern Africa], which are two free-trade areas in Africa that comprise approximately five hundred million people. Their standard of living is bound to increase over the years, and obviously this will represent a major market for our goods and for our services.

We are in the process of finalizing a comprehensive economy partnership and cooperation agreement with India. We would like to do the same with Pakistan and China, with a view to opening up markets for goods and services. We would also like to enhance cooperation with these countries, so we are creating a more conducive environment and appropriate climate for people to come and invest in our country. I must say there are many opportunities in Mauritius for people from outside the country— not only in the traditional sectors that are being revisited and/or restructured, but also in new sectors. I mentioned the seafood hub, medical tourism, and the Freeport. We would like to make Mauritius a center for services in the region. But you can also use Mauritius as a gateway, springboard, to do business with the rest of Africa, India, and Southeast Asia. So we invite people not only to invest here but also to structure their business so as to invest in the rest of Africa.

J.P.: How does U.S. policy fit into this, and what lack of U.S. policy do you see where we can improve on any issues, such as the AGOA, third country fabric provision?

R.S.: Access to the market is extremely important for a country like Mauritius, which has always supported the Western world and is a match for democracy. We have free and fair elections regularly, respect of the rule of law, and alternation in power on a regular basis. We're going through a difficult phase, so I think for us access to markets is extremely important. We would have an advantage by having no restrictions imposed for third country fabrics, but this has also helped us to vertically integrate our sectors. Now we are importing cotton that is being spun and weaved, adding to the value.

What we need to do in order to help countries like Mauritius is to go on value addition—the value that is added by the process of transformation in Mauritius before it is exported to the U.S. The value should not be very high so as to exclude the products from Mauritius. We need to also make it easy not only for textile and clothing, but also for a range of other products while Mauritius has some competitive advantage—because in AGOA there are not only textile and clothing, there's also a whole range of other goods we can export. I think market access is extremely important.

We will need technical assistance through that process of transformation, investment, and aid. I realize that probably aid might be difficult because the GDP per capita of Mauritius is quite high. But, a country cannot be penalized also because it has done well.

The very basis why Mauritius has done well is fast disappearing. We need to work because we harness very well our resources in order to take advantage of trade preferences. Unfortunately the days of trade preferences are numbered. So, we now need support to ensure Mauritius does not suffer as a result of the erosion of these preferences.

I think, too, in terms of technical assistance and capacity building, they are doing it! I mean, some people from the United States are helping, yes, in debt management, and in other sectors of the economy where they can enhance our capacity or strengthen our institutions in order to meet our ongoing challenges. As far as I am concerned, I think the most important thing for us is probably market access, and second, to attract investment into our country. By attracting investment into our country, we are going to build the capacity of Mauritius to export goods and services.

So with technical assistance and investment from Americans not only to Mauritius but to the region, if the region does well, so will Mauritius benefit from the prosperity.

J.P.: Any final thoughts, Minister Sithanen?

R.S.: One of the sectors that we have developed over the past ten years is in the international financial services sector. But we would like to have more substance. We would like to add value. And we would like to add depth in which to grow the sector. This is what we are doing through a network of treaties with many countries. If you add substance and add value to Mauritius, you get our benefits that are contained in some of these treaties. So obviously we welcome investment in the financial services sector.

VIVEKANAND ALLEEAR, SEYCHELLES, OCTOBER 17, 2006

Vivekanand Alleear is the chief justice of Seychelles. We met at the beginning of my posting. I found him to be an astute individual. The following excerpts were edited from his interview. They reflect his viewpoints on the Indian Ocean region and sub-Saharan Africa.

J.P.: How would you describe the Seychelles society and your role?

V.A.: I went to the Seychelles as a lawyer in May 1981. I had just returned from England to Mauritius, and when I reached Seychelles I was struck by the way things were being done.

In Seychelles, I found a society that was very disciplined, and with the passing of time, I found out why there was the difference between the two people from sister islands, so to speak; why in Mauritius it was different from Seychelles. Then it dawned on me that for the people of Seychelles, it was a one-party state. The minister of defense at the time called it a one-party democracy. He told me in those days everyone who sang was singing songs for the party, for the president, for the things that they thought were good. But everything was geared to one thing. In the Seychelles, if you ask for something to be rectified, it would be done almost immediately, but this was because the people were doing what the party wanted them to do. Things were being done, but they had no initiative on their own.

These people had lived for too long on an island where there was no discipline whatsoever. There was dissatisfaction with the head of state, Mr. James Mancham. The SPUP [Seychelles People's United Party] party of Mr. France Albert René and his followers were of the opinion that they had been cheated every time in elections. They would get 48 percent of the votes. Mr. Mancham would get about 52. Mr. Mancham would then again get more than two thirds, and Mr. René would be left with a few.

So when I spoke to these people and the supporters of the government, they told me that in Seychelles there was no other way but to overthrow that regime of Mr. Mancham. Mr. René was, of course, different from Mr. Mancham. He was a man who believed in hard work. He believed in discipline. He wanted to change everything.

The first thing he did was decide to have the National Youth Service whereby every student who had attained the age of sixteen would spend about two years in an institution where they would be taught political science. I think the youth service was modeled on a similar system they had in Cuba. He had been to that country, and was inspired by these people. In the beginning, his friends were from North Korea and Algeria, where we had teachers coming in to help out. We had the Russians then. They were helping out, I think, by giving petrol at a cheap price to the government, or even donating [services] to the people. They wanted to prop up the system because Mr. René was more aligned toward being pro-Russia than pro-America. Although he had studied in Britain, I could sense that he was more pro-socialist; he was leaning in favor of socialist policies.

But after many years, I could feel that socialism, the way the Seychelles government leaders had envisioned it, did not work. Everything was being provided by the government: health, social welfare, education, and free housing—and the Seychellois people started believing that the state was like a father and they are like children. They were entitled to everything. They were entitled to a house. They were entitled to education. When I first went to Seychelles, every pregnant woman used to go to health care centers. They were given milk. They were given rice, even if they did not have money. Before the babies were born, they would go to the social services; they would be assisted. It became like that.

But that kind of system had a price. We had help from North Korea, and I think at one time Cuba used to provide us with assistance from that far away, but with the dismantling of the USSR, everything [eventually] dried up. Then the Seychellois people started feeling the pinch, and there was, of course, dissatisfaction. I could see when the people could not get as much as they used to because they had a price to pay for it. So there emerged in the mid-1980s, close to 1990, a group of people who started moving away from the idea of socialism, which they thought was not working as they would have wished.

That is how the young priest, Mr. Ramkalawan, started first of all by distributing the flags, and so on, but he and his followers were stopped by the police because this was a one-party state and you could not do it. After Mr. René had attended the Commonwealth Conference [in Harare, Zimbabwe], I think pressure was brought upon him to open up the [political] system. Otherwise, help would not come. There would be no investments. At one time, I could see that very few people were coming to Seychelles for investment purposes. Between 1985 and 1993 there were no new investments, no new hotels being built, and so on.

When Mr. René came [back], he said to the people that he thought the Seychellois people have matured, and now we could have multipartisanism. In 1993 there was a body that sat and very democratically decided on a constitution. Every party sent in their representative according to votes cast in their favor. There was a new constitution drafted that provided for multipartisanism. When multipartisanism was restored, Mr. René invited Mr. Mancham, who had remained in exile in England after the coup had taken place, so Mr. Mancham came back.

There was a lot of apprehension about what would happen to Mr. Mancham. His supporters thought that he might be harmed, and so on, but eventually it worked out. The first meeting held by him drew a large number of people. I would never have believed that in the Seychelles, where I thought 90 percent of the people supported Mr. René, at the first meeting about fifteen thousand people had come to greet Mr. Mancham.

But I would say that Mr. Mancham missed a great chance in his life. He had the support, so to speak, but was responsible for his own ruin. If not winning the election, it could have been so close that if anything could work, they would have to have a coalition with him. Soon everyone found out that he appeared more interested in getting back the properties that had been acquired by the government or he had left behind. That is the reason people started thinking: he will never work. He would like only to travel, like he used to do in the past. When Mr. Mancham's party failed, that was when Mr. Ramkalwan's party rose. So today they are a force to reckon with, and the last election they got 25,500 votes in their favor, with the SPPF winning about 30,200.

But what had happened [later] is: when Mr. René decided to step down, Mr. Michel came in. Mr. Michel, I would say, is a man who wants transparency. With Mr. René, if I had to attend a conference, I would ask what he thought of it, and his opinion. With Mr. Michel, though, he would say: "Look, in this country we have strict separation of powers. You are the head of the judiciary. If you think you must go to attend a conference abroad or locally, you need not ask me. I will never interfere with what is going on. You have the responsibility. You know that I have told my people that I will crack down on drugs, on housebreaking, on sexual abuses, assaults; and I think you know what you have to do as a responsible person." He has never *ever* phoned to say what is happening in that case or in any other case.

I have always believed the good of the judiciary in Seychelles must be made very clear for investors to come and invest in the Seychelles. If they do not have a favorable perception of the judiciary, if they think that it is a vehicle used by the government or the executive, then we are doomed. We will have nothing.

J.P.: Can you tell me how Mr. Ramkalawan is perceived by the Seychellois society?

V. A.: [Mr. Ramkalawan] has a lot of support from the people who are in business and think Mr. Michel is only an extension of—or influenced by—Mr. René. I do not think so. I think that Mr. Michel is a man of his own. He wants to open up. He's trying his best. He has been trying to attract more investments in the country. There have been a few hotels being built, and so on. But still, unless and until we resolve this problem of foreign exchange, we have a serious problem in the Seychelles with a parallel market. In fact, if you can't get money from the bank, you may be sure to get it on the black market at the double price—of course you have to pay a high premium. There are so many people doing this kind of business, I think the authorities are turning a blind eye on purpose.

Recently, Mr. Michel brought about certain economic changes, certain amendments in the law. The laws haven't been changed, but the amount of foreign exchange that the commercial bank was expected to remit to the government has been reduced drastically. Now there is only a requirement of 15 percent. The bank will collect the foreign exchange and allocate to their clients and the government. Also recently, the government got a loan of about U.S. $200 million. There is a balance of U.S. $160 million in the Central Bank. The rest has been used to repay to the arrears of debts, so there is no pressure on the government right now. So Mr. Michel in difficult circumstances is trying to do the best for the country.

If the opposition has failed to win, it is for this reason. Some people do not think Mr. Ramkalawan is fit to be a head of state. [A]lthough I do not see anyone else around who could lead. In Seychelles, Mr. René was always seen as the man who was the savior for the Seychellois people. The only person who could win the election was and is Mr. Ramkalawan, but Mr. Ramkalawan has failed four times in succession to win the election and now finds himself in a difficult situation whereby some people believe that he should step down. What he has been trying to do is to deflect attention, going on the road, and getting his people to be more vocal on the streets.

I think that if, like in Mauritius, the opposition feels the government is not doing well, then they could come to Parliament and ask for a vote of no confidence. I do not believe that it is in the interest of Seychelles that we have people on the road. We want stability. We want people to know there is stability here and an independent judiciary. If you have a disagreement with the government, the judiciary is not going to [automatically] side with the government, because we want to protect that institution, and it is for the good of the country. And everyone surely has agreed, especially Mr. Michel, who sees to it that there is no interference at all.

Mr. Ramkalawan has been involved recently with wanting a radio station license review, called Radio Freedom, for his political party. The general feeling in Seychelles, being a small country, was that perhaps if they had a [license], they would start digging up the dirt in individuals' private lives, and it would not be good. They justified their decision, and the government came with an amendment to say that political parties and religious bodies would not be given a license.

J.P.: Have democracy and transparency been achieved in Seychelles?

V.A.: Democracy has been established. The last election I personally feel was free and fair, and the people had given the verdict. I think that they must allow Mr. Michel to continue. If he fails—because he has promised many things—and he cannot deliver at the end of the day, then we will change and replace him with other people.

J.P.: Now to come back to Africa, why is it that in the colonial days relative peace and law and order were maintained?

V.A.: It is because people had one master who was not of their tribe, who was from abroad. They respected the man. They were firm in their application of the law and order. The people obeyed, as they did in the early days of Seychelles with the one-party state. Perhaps people could not openly come out and express their opinion if it was against the state. That is why perhaps during the colonial days people were frightened to express their views.

These days, what do we see? In all these African countries, belonging to a different ethnic group or a different tribe could be a real cause of strife. Those who belong to one tribe, in order to subdue the other tribe, persecute them. So, likewise, they are not using their economic power for the benefit of the country, but for their own benefit and to put down the other tribe.

Perhaps there is hope in the new generation, but I don't think that's how we can get out of this. That is why I am fully in support of the policy of Mr. Bush. I think that if in a country there is no transparency, we should not give them any economic help. Of course, if you want peace, if you want economic progress, you must forget the past, sit down, resolve your differences; donor countries would come because there are many problems in the country to resolve.

I think that to have peace in the world you cannot have an irresponsible government with weapons that are mass-destructive, and irresponsible people that appeal to emotion and not to reason. I fully support the action of America in Iraq, although we have difficulties—and the things that they are now advocating, some sort of Islamic state; but even if they have an Islamic state, that doesn't detract from the fact that they could still have democracy.

Even in Africa if we find that these people do not want democracy, we cannot support them. The only way to support and help these people is to make them and their people understand that unless they have democracy and respect for other people's rights, we are not going to invest in that country. Those who wield the power should do that, should take the lead. I see it as the only way out; otherwise, these people will always divide and rule, destroy, kill other tribes to maintain themselves in power.

The United States has a duty to safeguard its people, and I think rightly that if we have to intervene, we cannot allow groups of people in the name of religion to kill and to massacre with impunity innocent people. What they did in England, what they do elsewhere, what they did in America, can never be condoned, and these people have to be dealt with, hunted.

I think all right-minded people of the world must support the United States so that we can put some order in Africa, as well as in the Middle East and everywhere. I do not think there should be one dissenting voice, because I think America is paying a high price also to see that democracy is achieved in every part of the world. If we have a world that is democratic, it would be so much easier and nicer, for all of us that inhabit this world.

J.P.: Two things come to mind. One is the Seychelles Marketing Board which controls just about everything, and controls just about every bit of the foreign exchange, needed to be able to meet its commitments to bring goods into the country. The second is the terrorism issue that could develop with the new influx of young Muslim men who may have been schooled by radical imams. Would you mind commenting on that?

V.A.: I said many years ago to the head of state that in Seychelles we have two problems: one, drugs; the other, Islamic fundamentalists. I view that with alarm. I'm not against religion—I want to make it very clear; but these people are not content; they are not satisfied with worshipping the Lord or Allah. They want to destabilize everywhere in the world if they can. I feel that there must be a strong presence of the Americans in Seychelles to watch these people really carefully.

I think one of the greatest threats, apart from the economy problem, is that we have more than a thousand Muslims that are now in Seychelles, and these young people send me little charity flyers or "come to this-that" and so on. I've never attended any of their things because I am not interested to know. I have gone to their source, though. I read the Koran. I'm happy with that. I think the government should watch these people. Perhaps the government central intelligence is not sufficient to deal with the issue. In five or ten years, this will be a real problem.

In Seychelles we have to watch this group. One day with their subversive elements, they [might] try to have a strong grip on the government, to control the judiciary and try to control more. They deal in drugs, in arms, in everything that is illegal. Most of these people who attend this, they sound curious, but I am sure that they are dealing in drugs. Not all, but the majority of them. Where do these young Muslims get a big new jeep? I do not know, but I don't think the bank will be giving it to them.

Now with the SMB: Just in the month of June, we have a new shop called Supersave. This store gives people more choices. I think now that the bank is free to allocate foreign exchange on merits, I think SMB should not be in a privileged position. This is what Mr. Michel, I think, eventually has in mind, to do other things rather than giving more control to SMB.

I do not think now SMB is getting priority over the allocation of foreign exchange, because recently I think that has stopped. I believe that business should be left to business people. Of course, everyone would want to make a profit, but if we think we are being cheated, then we will not go. There must be choices. The more shops we have, the more variety there will be and the more choices people will have. Those who are over-pricing would have to close. And this is how things ought to be in an open market situation.

J.P.: Any other thoughts about the Indian Ocean region?

V.A.: We must have good intelligence, not only in the Seychelles but everywhere else in the Indian Ocean, *at all costs*, to be very vigilant. We cannot afford that people from Somalia export these people in Seychelles. Really these groups have to be watched closely. Most of these governments, perhaps they do not give it the priority that it deserves; and only with the assistance of the United States that can be done. We have to have the presence, your presence in the Seychelles.

J.P.: I have one more thought, and that while the U.S. naval ship visits are good for the Seychelles economy, security issues without American embassy personnel present remain a concern. Would you comment on this?

V.A.: To tell you the truth, you have been there in the Seychelles, and know that 95 percent of the population support America. But, 1 percent can spoil the whole thing. I would emphasize that we need to have a very strong presence. The Americans are always welcome. They will always be welcome, but we have the obligation to make them, their vessels, their persons, secure. When it is the interest of the state that is at stake, the United States should have a presence. Especially since Seychelles is in a strategic position.

To come back again to my point, we need the Americans to open their embassy, to have a strong presence, and that is, in itself, a deterrent to those groups. When they know the cat is not there, the rat can do whatever it wants. You see? The presence of the cat there is a great deterrent.

When America is there, they know the superpower is here. They can't do anything that they want, and you have the best intelligence in the world, and we would know. Then we feel secure and safe, you see? Thank you.

Sir James Mancham, Seychelles, May 13, 2007, First Interview

Sir James Mancham was the first president of Seychelles. It was in 1977 when he was deposed by France-Albert René in a coup. For over fifteen years, he went into exile, returning in the early 1990s.

J.P.: Tell us about the 1970s era, the coup, the U.S. tracking station, the U.S. embassy closing, and China's influence on the Seychelles.

J.M.: Before Seychelles became independent, we had the arrival of the United States in the region. About that time the British decided to pull out of the Suez Canal. It was important that the Indian Ocean, which had been a western lake for several generations, [continue] to have a Western presence. So the British and Americans decided that the American presence was necessary, and a first choice for this was the island of Aldabra, a very special island and part of the Seychelles archipelago. What happened is that conservationists in [both] Washington and London heard about the Anglo-American plan to build a big base in Aldabra, which is home to about 200,000 tortoises and thousands of sea birds—some of which are endemic. The conservationists started to protest, and as the Anglo-American scheme was being pursued quietly and rather secretly, the United States and the United Kingdom decided to drop the idea of getting this base built on Aldabra. They then decided to go to the island of Diego Garcia, which is part of the Chagos Archipelago. So what happened is, where the birds and tortoises of Aldabra won, the people of Diego Garcia lost. As we know, it was part of the Anglo-American plan to take away the islanders from Diego Garcia and get them resettled in Mauritius. At that time, Mauritius was advancing toward independence. And the British bargained with Sir Seewoosagur Ramgoolam, who became the father of the Mauritius nation, saying, "Okay, we will give you independence but we shall keep the Chagos Archipelago. We shall also give you [about] five to six million pounds sterling to resettle the Chagossians." Unfortunately around that time a huge cyclone hit Mauritius, and the Mauritius government, my understanding is, utilized that money for other priorities so that the Chagossians, after they arrived, were almost left residing in a slum situation.

This isn't the end of the story, but Seychelles became independent in 1976, and at that time the Chinese opened up an embassy in Seychelles.

The United States, with which we had enjoyed a very close relationship during our time as a British colony through the embassy in Nairobi, decided also to open up an embassy in Seychelles. It is to be noted that the opposition party in Seychelles of France-Albert René had a married situation with the Communist Party of China. Well, a year after our independence, I was overthrown in a violent coup when I was attending the jubilee of Her Majesty the Queen in London, and about to attend a summit meeting of the Commonwealth organization. So it came to pass that I lived in exile for more than fifteen years.

Now, the United States should have reacted. At least one of the reasons why I supported the buildup of the American tracking station in Seychelles and the buildup of Diego Garcia was that by having a United States presence in the vicinity, the United States would ensure that democracy prevailed and would oppose any activity of the nature of a coup d'état. Unfortunately what happened was that René was very well advised and immediately after the coup d'état he notified, I think, all nations that could be of possible interest to our strategic situation that business could proceed as normal. The strategic situation brought, I think in terms of rental, about seven or eight million dollars to Seychelles every year, which was very useful, very helpful. Besides that there was money also spent within the country, which was very useful. I know about the tracking station because it was being built when I was there. The American corporations that built the station were, namely, Philco-Ford based in Palo Alto near San Francisco, RCA based in Texas, and Pan American then based in Cape Canaveral, Florida. There was a negative reaction and René, immediately after taking over, started to turn the country into a Marxist state. One of his first meetings outside Seychelles was in Cuba, where he allowed himself the latitude of saying, "Here next to the kingdom of imperialism, I cry: Castro *si* (yes); U.S. imperialism *no!*" Again nothing was done to react to these blatant anti-American sentiments. René, however, started to modify his attitude after President Reagan took the unilateral action on the island of Grenada. After Reagan went into Grenada with the general turmoil there, René started thinking the U.S. could do something like this in Seychelles. And then he stayed quiet, less outspoken, about it.

Now for all these years, I lived in exile and René ruled the country in a one-party state with a lot of support from China. China kept on providing assistance, but not in a consistent way until the last few years, when we saw that the help was being augmented. It's interesting to note that today the most impressive embassy standing in Seychelles is the Chinese Embassy. And today Seychelles is a country that relies on international tourism and on fishing. We have a company: a tuna canning factory, of which 60 percent was owned by H. J. Heinz until last year, and then sold to Lehman Brothers, a merchant banking group from New York. This factory cans 1.5 million tins of tuna a day.

Now the point of this tutorial is that today there is not one American flag flying in Seychelles to provide comfort to American visitors to our shores. I have questioned this situation as to how the only superpower in the world could go about a situation where the Seychelles is a blank spot on its globe. I have argued and continue to argue that no country is small if it is surrounded by the sea.

After the Falkland Islands war, Admiral [Robert J.] Hanks, who used to be head of the Institute of Strategic Studies in Washington, D.C., and used to be chief of staff of U.S. naval forces based in Bahrain, wrote a very special report pointing out that if it were not for the island of Ascension, the British would never have been able to recover the Falklands, because friends of Argentina were also friends of the U.K., and nobody wanted to get involved. However, because you have such an island on which the Americans built a modern air force base, the British were able to land there and recover the Falklands. Now as a consequence of this, Hanks argues that small islands like the Seychelles should be considered as an unsinkable aircraft carrier: in other words, they could be used as a landing and launching pad on which to launch rockets, et cetera. And when you take into account the geopolitical position of Chagos, you can see why the islands of Seychelles also remain within a striking distance. Of course, it is from Chagos that B-52 bombers departed to fight the war in Afghanistan. Chagos also provided a lot of logistical support to the war efforts in Iraq. So the closing down of the tracking station in Seychelles sent a wrong signal, a wrong message, the message being that the United States was not really interested in international diplomacy and the sensitivities of small island nations.

For this reason, I wrote this book *War on America: Seen from the Indian Ocean*, which carries with it a letter from President Bush and one from Colin Powell. I had written to both of them, asking them to consider the situation which had happened under the democratic government when Madeleine Albright took the view that they needed money to open up embassies in eastern Europe and to support the United Nations: we had to pay the price in our tracking station and our [U.S.] embassy closing. Now, as I was telling you, earlier on February 11, we saw the arrival of China's president, Hu Jintao. The Chinese president was giving to Seychelles—a nation of 80,000 people—forty-eight hours of his time, paying us an official visit from a nation of 1.3 billion people. Well, Jintao was clearly not in Seychelles just for the love of the Seychelles people, although he said that his arrival in Seychelles demonstrated the Chinese would never be "fair weather" friends. It's interesting that on the week of his arrival, the United States had given Seychelles a mortuary built on the island of Praslin by the Navy, which had cost $20,000 and the British handed Seychelles a check to fight dengue for 10,000 rupees. And there were the Chinese arriving with a check for $20 million. And even before Jintao's arrival, the chairman of the Chinese import-export bank arrived by private plane. Lots of projects were discussed. They said they were interested in fishing, in new port development. One interesting aspect of this was the Chinese request of the government of Seychelles that they pass legislation to protect their investment. That's very interesting when you take into account China, where everything started with compulsory acquisition of the people's property—now that they are putting in their own money, they would like a little protection. I think this is an interesting factor, showing that markets are going along the way of wealth preservation as they go for wealth growth.

Sir James Mancham, Seychelles, September 25, 2007, Second Interview

J.P.: Could you elaborate on what the U.S. needs to do to engage Africa?

J.M.: We must first and foremost identify the weaknesses prevailing in Africa. We must recognize that we are living in a world where we have seen the richer nations getting richer and most of the poorer nations getting poorer. Nobody can argue with the extreme poverty in Africa. We must also realize that in a free world, in a free market situation, against a background of the history, the African doesn't have the streetwise mentality that one would find in China or in India. So therefore here's a role for education. Africa is also subjected to a lot of health problems including HIV/AIDS. In order for the U.S. to be more positively engaged in Africa, I believe they must treat Africa as a special case situation.

For example, we have the question of giving to Africa a good price for their local commodities. We know that Africa is rich in several areas of resources that are required. But also we know at the moment a lot of products, which are of African origin, are given added value, which does not mean very much for Africa, especially if it doesn't get down to the African farmer in the field. There is a question of opening up the U.S. market more to African products, in which case we must analyze what must be done to these products in order to meet the American criteria of satisfaction. We've got to accept the fact that if we had to leave the Africans to themselves, because they have no sense of comparison, they would not know the sort of standards which Americans expect in order for their goods—their fruits, their vegetables—to be able to be sold on the open market.

So I think American leadership must have an enlightened approach to this situation and take steps to provide assistance in this area, which would allow the Africans to be able to get more money by being able to sell more of their products. But unless they have some education in that area, some protection and some enlightened sort of advice and encouragement, I cannot see them going very far, you know. There's already a factor that you should examine: if you look in Africa today, you'll see that in most areas where there has been free immigration most of the businesses have fallen under the domination of Asians, or Asian-Indians. You go to Nairobi and all the leading entrepreneurs likely will be the Chinese. So this is an aspect. How do you train an African? Life discipline didn't really help train them to become much aware about modern business practices, et cetera. So this is an area where we've got to bend a bit backward to help them if we want them to catch up. The U.S. immigration from Africa, which should be beneficial, but is not really entirely beneficial. The question when you are in America, a lot of people who are of African origin unfortunately are not really engaged or too proud of their roots, and there is disillusionment on the part of Africans who come to the United States to study and get a better life. When they arrive they believe they are going to find it easy to befriend African-Americans. But they find out sometimes it is easier to be friends with white Americans than with African-Americans. I don't know why.

J.P.: What should U.S. policy be in Africa in light of countries like China, Russia, and others gaining influence there?

J.M.: China is gaining influence by putting up a lot of money. Africa needs money for its development. It needs outlets for its products. China needs these products. Perhaps China needs that more than the United States. So China also needs a market for cheap commodities. Sources in China go into Africa, overlooking the fact that there is no good governance in the country, making this an advantage point—especially since many leaders and their countries are now being boycotted by the United States and other European nations. Thus, China goes behind their backs and assists them to stay in power. As a result, China is able to enter into contracts that will provide them with the raw materials necessary for them. So China is in a different situation. The United States is certainly in a different situation because it doesn't really need a lot of the raw materials that Africa produces—although there are, in fact, a lot of energy products that the United States should be interested in. The United

States must rise up to take a more proactive focus on what the Chinese are doing and to counteract the Chinese situation by adopting a new approach to Africa.

Many of the nations in Africa are bankrupt and in need. The United States has done quite a lot by putting money behind all the banks, the African-influenced banks. But because of this, the United States has also been able to impose conditionality, which has made it impossible for these African nations to get any other help from the outside and, therefore, [these African nations] are really happy to jump on the Chinese bandwagon. The United States must also reconsider the policy of not giving help to African nations that have succeeded in increasing their GDP standard. This is penalizing success. We see that situation in Seychelles because the GDP has reached 7,000 U.S. dollars [per capita]. Seychelles is not able to attract any support from any American institutions. Instead, I would suggest that when you see a nation that is on its way to success, then assistance is given, encouraging the roots to deepen to consolidate a position.

I believe the United States should seriously consider a policy that sometimes the little bird in the hand is worth many birds in the bush. There are some situations where the United States has the potential of consolidating its position, so these nations cannot be treated at par with a lot of other neighboring nations where whatever help you may give would only amount to a drop in the ocean. The U.S. must find certain areas where it can have what I would call meaningful engagements to bring about positive results. Otherwise, most of these African nations with vast needs would always expect more and more, which is not possible to deliver.

I still believe if we speak about democracy we must speak about education. The United States has already educated a lot of African people. China is now opening its doors. At its recent meeting in Beijing, China said that it was going to open the doors to many more people from Africa. In my own experience, African leaders, all those who come to the United States, most of them have returned pro–United States. They've acquired the taste of freedom, the way Africa does things, and that's a great advantage. Scholarships should be given. But one condition of scholarships is that the people must return to their country and must not seek to stay in the United States. This may be difficult, but this is what has happened. We find a lot of people trained by the U.S. from different African nations are today filling jobs elsewhere, so that their countries are not really moving forward at all. This is a matter that should be addressed.

The problem with Africa is that you have a lot of governments that are only in power because they have established armies enabling them to rule by fear. In a lot of these countries, they aren't in the position to make meaningful points; the populace lives in fear; and the situation carries on. We have seen that the fact there are fears economically in an African nation doesn't mean they are changing the regime. So it must be accepted that Mugabe, for example, should have been out long ago, but somebody's helping him, and China is putting money behind him. How do we tell China not to do so, if they are not themselves prepared? The United States must realize that it's okay to play the promotion of democracy internationally if every competitive player is also agreeable to play on the same field and under the same criteria. But it looks to me that China, for example, is not going to be persuaded to play the democracy game as we see it being played in the United States and in Europe.

J.P.: Do you have any further comments on other countries, and their policies vis-à-vis China? Because there are many looking at Africa, such as Russia, Korea, and even the resurrection of the early colonialists from Europe, looking at rebuilding relationships in Africa.

J.M.: It is very obvious that this new eye-level interest that China is showing in Africa is going to bring about a lot of attention from other players with respect to Africa and where Africa is going. It is an area where United States leadership becomes very crucial and important to come to a balance with Chinese penetration with the interest of other nations in the world. The U.S., Europe, India, and Japan should meet to discuss and have a common policy [on] how to counteract the penetration of Africa by China.

Now the Japanese: in terms of building up a special trade relationship with Africa, they initiated a diplomatic conference long before the Chinese. But since then, the Chinese have had three conferences: one in Beijing, which resulted in what was the Beijing Declaration; a second conference in Ethiopia, and finally a [more recent] big bash in Beijing. [Again,] I think in view of what China represents, in terms of its ability to take raw materials and turn them into commodities at low cost because of low labor costs, the problem of counteracting China's engagement in Africa should be to do a collective approach led by the United States in association with Europe, which as you know has fundamental and very important ties.

J.P.: One last observation: could you tell us about the Chinese and Seychelles relationship that really started in 2006 and 2007?

J.M.: The intensity of the relationship, which has come to the surface in the period you mentioned, has not been a surprise to me. As a student of international political development I could see this on the horizon. Now, the Chinese have been consistent. First, the Chinese came to Seychelles at the time of our independence because the United States was there. Now what has happened is that the United States departed and the Chinese stayed behind and kept on being very actively engaged at a normal sort of bilateral level in helping Seychelles.

But now there is a very active indication that China is playing the international power game, as we have seen by the arrival of the Chinese president. And that is a job for him because for the last ten years Seychelles has been plagued with a grave forex problem. Seychelles cannot change its rupees into forex; it is a very great problem. The government is bankrupt. The Chinese themselves have accumulated, we are told, trillions. So the Seychelles situation is a sinking situation. We see a lot of gestures being done by the United States on this title or that title, ambassadors, friends, or what not. But these things were symbols of friendship and could not really solve the problem.

In my view, the Chinese have seen that we are sinking and know it's time to move in. China wants raw materials. These raw materials have got to be transported by a maritime route. China has already the second largest shipbuilding program in the world. They have the largest amount of commercial ships; ships flying the Chinese flag are the largest group in the world. That's why China has also taken an interest in Panama and even in places like Pakistan. So when the Chinese president arrived— and this is an example we can quote: we had a situation with the U.S. looking forward to making up the political capital because the Navy had gone and they had put up some money and had built this mortuary, and suddenly the environment changed. Before the Chinese president arrived, a special plane arrived with the chairman of the Export-Import Bank of China. China had been prepared and was doing fantastic public relations. The chairman of the bank had discussions and already indicated various areas they would be interested in promoting investments. Then two days later the Chinese president arrived with a big entourage to make an impression. This is when he gave Seychelles the $20 million and indicated that China could be interested in fishing, and could be interested in trans-shipping.

In my view, if the Chinese were to build a trans-shipment center in Seychelles, or a container port, it would have a clear side, one that may not have been obvious from the beginning, but they would make sure there is some sort of a military-level potential. If you look at the Indian Ocean, what do you see? You see a situation where the Americans have a presence in Diego Garcia. In the Chagos Archipelago, you are there. You've got Mauritius, and Mauritius is considered to be a small India. The Chinese are not going to try to convince the Indians in Mauritius because mother India doesn't allow this to happen. The Seychelles, home to 80,000 Creole people, is bankrupt but has under its sovereignty all these islands spanning a wide surface, which is very important [relative] to the Gulf, et cetera. The Seychelles is outside the cyclonic belt, small but strategically located. Africa is next door. Obviously, if China was going to think in terms of possible confrontation with the United States at any time, a development in Seychelles could more or less neutralize the development in the Chagos Archipelago. Let me quote something that should be of interest to you that the *Times of India* editorial said: "We Indians had for too long assumed that the Indian Ocean was India's Ocean. But the arrival of the Chinese President has manifested our delusion." Now against this background you have got to realize that the United States, too, in looking at the whole area, we see that soon the United States, against wise advice, is jumping into bed with India. I don't think the motivation is merely falling in love with the Indians, but it is taking awareness of the need to have, let's call it, the big brother on our side, if there was to be a problem with China.

Now around the same time we are seeing the development of a lot of naval exercises in the zone of the Southern Indian Ocean; over recent weeks we had America, Europe, Singapore, Japan, and Australia engage in naval exercises. The one missing is China. So it is a very clear indication that what one is watching is the absence of China. Now suddenly the Seychelles government, when they do these matters, never speaks about it until it is a fait accompli. We also hear Seychelles appointed an ambassador to Beijing. Seychelles has no money, so China gives to Seychelles an embassy in Beijing. Then Pillay, the minister of foreign affairs, goes for the opening of the embassy in Beijing, at which time the ministry of foreign affairs declared they would like to put the bilateral relationship with China at the preferred plus status level. In other words: not only friends, but very special friends. Now Pillay was gone, and then Chief of Staff Leopold Payet, in charge of the Army, was made a brigadier general, and he's a guest of the defense minister of China who said that they want to establish with Seychelles a higher degree of military collaboration. Payet responded we would welcome this. And three days later it is announced in Seychelles that China has provided Seychelles with $25 million plus for building a powerhouse for electricity in the southern part of Mahe. And meanwhile, different delegations are arriving and having discussions with the Seychelles government. Because the Seychelles government doesn't talk until it's a fait accompli, we can only speak of it, but what are they talking about? And there is a point, as you said, why is this leader of 1.3 billion people coming to Seychelles for forty-eight hours and every minute talks and has discussions?

So for your information, I know the Indians have been shocked because up until now the Indians were doing quite a bit of collaboration.

The Indians announced something in the daily media communication about $1 million, or whatever for us. I know because I have seen a lot; the Indians been coming to me to talk and all the discussions were about China and what is this government doing—that they [Indians] have been friends, traditional association, between most of the people of Seychelles. China now says they are also interested in giving training programs. And just the other day before I left Seychelles, we had a flotilla of five warships flying the flag of NATO under the leadership of Admiral Mahon of the United States Navy. The admiral and some other captains went to pay their courtesy to James Michel. I was invited to visit, I went onboard; the ambassador to Mauritius went onboard, and I looked around and there were no other government personalities of any standing. Most opposition forces were there, but the government officials that had been invited didn't turn up. This is the same day that the military statement was issued in Beijing and I took a copy that I had received and handed it to the ambassador, who had not heard about it. Michel had not told them. They had no notion from Michel that the Chinese had proposed military collaboration, et cetera. But the *Regar* paper put it in their publication afterward. In our weekly paper we singled out and made a point to say how we were surprised at this low level of representation to that reception, which in fact was a specially prepared reception by the standards of visiting warships. At the reception there was a really big turkey, a suckling pig, and everything else one could imagine. There was the normal toast: the admiral says something about Seychelles and the minister of Seychelles says something also. But there was low representation.

J.P.: And what do you think the reason was?

J.M. Well, the fact that it coincided. I don't know what message they wanted to send, whether there was a message there or whether they had become cross, or they didn't want to offend the Chinese. I don't know but this is a point of observation. I don't know if one can come to any specific conclusion in terms of the intention. But normally there is always an invited contingent of government, coast guard, and other people who turn up. This time there were practically none of them.

Ahmed Abdallah Mohamed Sambi, Comoros, September 25, 2009

The following edited interview was conducted with President Sambi of the Union of the Comoros.

J.P.: What impact have you made since taking office such as with good governance, reconciliation, and the issues with the island presidents?

A.S.: First of all, I think it is very important to tell you that one week after I took office and started reading the reports on the country, I was able to get a picture of my country. From this picture I realized that it was impossible for a sovereign country, independent country, member of the UN, member of the Arab League, member of the African Union, of the Organization of the Islamic Conference, of Indian Ocean Commission—it was impossible for a country like mine—to live with forty million euros of average annual earnings. It was not possible.

So, from this picture I realized what was the problem of the Comoros. The Comorians suffer and they are going to continue to suffer, as long as they remain poor. Therefore, from the first day I needed to think how to get money for the country. And from that point on, I conceived a plan. Since the day of our Independence in 1975 until 2006, all the projects realized in the Comoros had been sponsored by foreigners through donations or credits. These include all the projects with no exceptions. And the big projects, of course, required large amounts of money. Funds were sent from abroad, by the financial institutions, by foreign banks, but also in donations. What does it mean? It means that there is no money inside the country. And this is the reality. Our annual income does not exceed forty million euros. Imagine a sovereign country that has to be managed with forty million euros.

So I planned. I said to myself: "It is true, we have political problems in the Comoros, but it is also true that politicians have always tried to convince us that we have political problems. As for me, I think we have, first of all, economic problems rather than political ones. Therefore, we needed an economic solution, not a political one. This is why from the first day I decided to facilitate the return of financial institutions. Because, as you know, since the 1990s the International Monetary Fund, the African Development Bank, and Arabic bank left the country when they realized we were not able to pay our debts after they gave us credit. So there was a need to facilitate their return.

We planned. I told the government to start in all seriousness paying back the debts. Thank God, we made sacrifices, and after a year, we could pay the debt to the African Development Bank and they came back. In 2007, after we paid back quite a bit, they noticed that the country was changing and agreed to write off 70 percent of the debt, and asked us to pay just 30 percent. At that point we requested help from Paris Club, and they helped us to pay the 30 percent. And now we are in good shape, with the African Development Bank, which contributed to the realization of many projects in our country.

We also started paying back the IMF, the World Bank. And I can announce that now, while I am in New York, three days ago we heard good news that the IMF has approved the program that we had been requesting since the 1990s. After we achieved the status of a post-conflict country (and this was important, because we made sacrifices and paid the price), the program was approved. I hope we are going to succeed.

And this is not all. I understood that apart from the financial institutions there are also international banks, and we needed to find money to attract them to our country. I made some phone calls, particularly to the Arabic and African countries. I think that today—everyone recognizes that we made a significant breakthrough in the Arabic and African worlds. I opened the country. I asked the investors to come. And they came. I can tell you that since our Independence, we only had one bank: the Bank for Industry and Commerce. Since I came to power, we now have three more banks. This is also a good sign, I believe. All of this happened because I understood we needed to make money come to the country. There is Exim Bank of Tanzania and the Federal Arabic Bank that came. We also have our bank, the Postal Bank that is a 100 percent Comorian bank. All of that was a good sign. We made the investors come and they started to invest in our county, in the hotel business, and particularly in tourism and fishing, because fishing is a natural unexploited wealth. We made agreements with the Arab banks, the Kuwait fund, the Abu Dhabi fund, the Islamic Bank—all of whom left the country, but now they are at least back.

Therefore I can tell you that up to a certain degree, after I penciled out this plan, we took off and up until this moment we had good results. As I always say, we planted yesterday and are beginning to collect the fruit now.

Speaking of wealth politics, you probably know that I agreed (and this happens by the way everywhere in the world) to accept monetary contributions as an investment into the country in exchange for the Comorian nationality. So we had this law for nationalization that went through the National Assembly. Economic citizenship, as we call it. We are hoping to get a lot of money very soon, approximately $200 million. For a country like ours it is huge. There will be $25 million of budgetary help, and $175 million that will be targeted for the base infrastructure of the country. All this is done within the politics of finding wealth.

So I am telling this to let you know that from the first day I understood our problems were economic problems, so what we need are economic solutions. Unfortunately, politicians always want to tell us that we have political issues. The Comoros, as you know, is a country that has long traditions. Since our Independence, there were coup d'état attempts, president assassinations, and a lot of events. Recently there was also a problem of separatism. When I came to power, there was a problem with Nzwani [Anjouan]. The island was still in rebellion. And you know that with the help of the international community and particularly of the African Union, we were able to put an end to this rebellion in 2008. After we were able to regain control in Nzwani, I was willing—how should I say it?—I was willing to do a lot more for the country, being a bigger country now. Before regaining Nzwani, I had no power in Nzwani. This was the reality. Officially, I was the president, but I had no power in Nzwani; I was not even able to appoint a single person in the administration for any post. So since that time, we made a good effort, and I can confirm to you that today we are able to gradually start seeing the fruit of what we planted.

You know, I also inherited this constitution, which I don't believe really was the constitution of the Comoros. It was not really possible for a small country like ours to have four presidents, four constitutions, four parliaments, and four governments. So there was an urgent need for a change. I had to ask the Comorian people to change some—not too many, but some—items in the constitution that I thought were necessary to change. We were able to organize a referendum, which changed some things. I wanted, in particular, not to have four presidents anymore. It was so expensive for us, unfortunately, for a country with no resources. Instead of having a parliament of thirty-three deputies, we had a parliament, the parliament of the islands, with more that eighty deputies. Instead of having about ten ministers, we had almost thirty-six ministers. So, it was very costly. Fortunately we were able to organize this referendum, it went well, and today we are seeing the results of this change.

I know the two governors of the islands Ngazidja [Grande Comore] and Mwali [Mohéli] are still trying to resist that. I don't understand it. They used to be called presidents; now they are called governors—and they used to have their own flags. So they resist it, but I know that it is the will of people. We are working on creating a democratic country, of which the sovereignty belongs to the people and the people agreed upon and accepted this change.

I am not saying we resolved the problems. The Comoros still remains a fragile country. We are currently reorganizing the institutions of the country, reinforcing the country's security. At the same time, we still live with the problem of Mahore [Mayotte], which remains a political problem of our country. And it is because of this problem that we had also other problems. Maybe you know that even yesterday here at the General Assembly I made a new proposition to France, that I hope they are going to accept. In short, this is where we are: we have accomplished quite a bit in less time than the previous regime, and I hope that the Comorian people are going to recognize it.

I made a summary of what we were able to do since we are in power. As far as the economy goes, we accomplished quite a lot of things. I did a lot for the resolution of the energy problem, the electricity problem. Since long ago, for example, in Ngazidja, there was no electricity. Even in places where the network was available. But now, since recently, everyone has electricity. In Nzwani [Anjouan], we already financed the project to get the network for little villages. The funding is ready.

There is a problem with water, which remains one of the major problems in our country. Today we began looking for funds. I can confirm to you that today the picture of the Comoros is an attractive one to those abroad. A lot of people, including westerners, including the United States of America, are showing a lot more interest in our country. And this is a good sign.

Of course, among the biggest events that happened during my administration is the liberation of the island of Nzwani. We were able to put an end to the rebellion without bloodshed. It was a military operation, a delicate one. But thank God there was no bloodshed. There was not a single death. Not a single death; just two or three persons were wounded. That was a real success.

To round up, as long as the Comoros remains poor, our issues will remain the same—especially with the persistent demographic growth in the island of Nzwani. You know that in Nzwani we have almost 600 people per square kilometer. This is a lot. In Mwali there are approximately 125 people per square kilometer and in the Ngazidja, 250 people per square kilometer. So we live with this demographic issue.

I was working a lot and continued working on trying to find money for the country. You probably heard the good news that I recently invited geologists and they started to give us good results. It is the first time we invited geologists to this country to find out if we have anything in this country. Several weeks ago they started reporting back to us having apparently discovered some things. This is also part of the wealth politics, of the national wealth.

Of course, in the Comoros we don't want to go to the Moon yet, but we are attributing a lot of importance to the development of infrastructure, of education. I read your questions and among them I saw the one about the challenges of education. It is true that education is one of the challenges in our country. When our young university—the University of the Comoros—was created in 2003, we had 700 students. Now we have 4,000 students at this university, but the budget remains the same. How is this possible? Well, this is the reality of our country.

The problem of the Comoros is that we have a functional budget, but not one that allows for investment. This is it. Eighty percent of our income goes directly to the payment of salaries. This is not possible. What can you do with the remaining 20 percent? It is problematic to even manage the country, let alone the investments, the infrastructure.

So the country has unfortunately remained stagnant. We are waiting for the whole world to help us. So we need diplomatic action; this is what we are focusing on. We need the international community. Now we are beginning to see this trust, the trust of the international community is being built; this is something we were looking for. I believe that if we are able to solve our education problems, we will solve our unemployment problems. In the Comoros today we even have graduates who are unemployed. Yes, graduates are even unemployed in the Comoros. So it is one of the biggest challenges of our country.

But again, I am telling you, this is simply because we don't have money. Even if we have ideas, even if we have projects, even if we know what direction we need to take, it is not easy to achieve what we want to achieve, because we don't have money. So the politics that I led up until now is the politics of finding wealth, finding funds. We've planted the seed. I hope that very soon we will be able to harvest the fruit.

J.P.: What benefits have the Comoros derived from the December 2005 donors conference? In other words, did the donors come through on their promises?

A.S.: Unfortunately, not much. We worked a lot on this file, but because there was always this problem of rebellion in Nzwani, we couldn't really make progress on it. After we were able to get Nzwani back, we made some progress, but to tell you the truth, the promises have not yet been fulfilled. And we are behind on this. Frankly speaking, all the promises have not been fulfilled.

J.P.: What have the U.S. embassy and other U.S. agencies accomplished since you came into office to help Comorians?

A.S.: All I can tell you is that since I am in power, I noticed America was very interested in my country. You mentioned the coast guard. Personally, I also made this request and was informed that there is a ship that is being built. We are waiting for it. We were told that perhaps before the year's end, we would have the results.

I know Americans have helped a lot in the field of education, particularly, elementary schools. They are still there. They are not really building the schools, but they are renovating the schools in the villages. And this is also very interesting, I think, that they are working directly with the communities.

I was very happy to see that the United States of America really supported us, when we decided to proceed with the operation in Nzwani, a military operation. They were among these rare countries that helped us, supported us politically. I noticed that American authorities are becoming more interested in my country.

By the way, I took advantage of the meeting with President Barack Obama and the presidents of African countries. In my speech, I asked him to help the African people, and I asked him to give a chance to African kids to go study at their universities. I asked him to let the American investors come to Africa, and also to my country. It went well; he took note of it. I hope that they are going to do that.

So, I don't know all the details, but I know about American support at the moment. We requested greater assistance. Personally I also asked if they will give us a chance to send some kids to get military education. You know that our country remains still very fragile, as far as security. And as I always say, without security, we can't have stability and without stability we can't do anything. Even the big economic projects cannot be realized if the country is not stable. So I hope that America, the United States of America is going to help us in this regard.

I think that first of all we have a problem of staff. Imagine a country that is composed of three islands and we only have 1,500 people to maintain security for a population of 700,000. It is very few, very few. Again, what we need is, of course, education. We need appropriate infrastructure. So we have great hope that America, as they have always promised us, will help us.

There were exchanges of opinions, and there were visits of U.S. officials that are based in Djibouti, who came to visit us in the Comoros. There was even an American ship that came to us, and I personally met them. So apparently, we are on the right track. But up until now not everything that was said has been accomplished. We are waiting for the ship for the creation of our maritime unit. We are waiting patiently for this ship that is going to help us build our maritime unit, and of course keep our coast under surveillance, and also to help the stabilization. As far as infrastructure goes, there were not really a lot of agreements in this regard, but we are still waiting. Promises were made and we are still waiting.

J.P.: Over the years there has been an influx of imams from other countries such as Pakistan, Saudi Arabia, Yemen, and Sudan. Do you feel the continuation of imams coming from different countries pose any stability issues or goals that you have for Comoros?

A.S.: Which imams?

J.P.: Well, we've had reports of Pakistanis . . .

A.S.: There were some Saudi Arabians that came in the previous years. Now they are no longer there, by the way. There are some Pakistanis that come and spend time in the mosque for one or two weeks, but no more than that and they are not imams. They are people who come to pray in the mosque. We never had imams at the mosque, no, no, there were no Sudanese or Egyptians. In the 1980s there were Egyptians in the Arab schools, but currently there are not a lot of Arabs in the country let alone Pakistanis. At the moment, there are only Comorians who teach because there are a lot of Comorian people who came back lately from Arabic Islamic universities. So we don't really have a big need for imams. And the imams in the mosque have always been Comorians. We never had foreign imams in the Comoros.

J.P.: Sometimes they are more radical in their approach, and affect people such as Fazul Abdullah Mohammed, who was indoctrinated and left the country.

A.S.: Well, everyone knows that we are Muslims. All the Comorians are Muslims. But we have our Islam; as you said it very well, it is a "pacifist Islam." As for the example of Fazul, it's an exception. He was not educated in the Comoros.

But previously, those people who were coming: first of all, they were—how should I say it—not intellectuals. They were not big religious authorities who have any influence. I know who they are. It is a [Pakistani] organization called Jamā'at al-Tablīgh. They are not even interested in politics. They are people who only talk about belief and such.

But in the Comoros up until now we have been protected from this fundamentalism, from this ideology. And I hope that we will always be protected. So I don't think that Fazul is a good example to consider. He was not even in the Comoros. He is not known in the Comoros. And there is not a single person in the Comoros who spreads these ideas.

So, most importantly, until now and until the contrary can be proven, the Islamic leaders of our country are Comorians. And the big imams, the big Ulemas of the Comoros are Comorians, pacifists, who don't believe in this kind of Islamic politics and ideas. And thank God, we are protected.

So, from our side we try to protect our religion. We are Muslims; we have to protect our religion, and in order to do that we have to protect it from these ideals.

I think that to fight against fundamentalism in countries like ours means to fight against poverty. This is what I understand. You know that I, considered a theologian and a great Muslim scholar of the Comoros, I have always said that if we really want to protect our country from these ideas that unfortunately gave a bad picture of our religion, we need to fight against poverty; because it is poverty that helps these people to find followers and adherents. So I think that if the United States of America helps particularly Muslim countries to reinforce their potential, and improve human life, the Muslims will be protected from the ideas that really distorted the real face of Islam.

J.P.: Mr. President, Where would you like to see Comoros ten years from now?

A.S.: You know, in the Comoros, when people speak about President Sambi, they always say that he is a president-dreamer. And sometimes they say it to make fun, but I prefer to be a president-dreamer than to be a president who does not have dreams. In fact, I think that ten years from now there should be a big change in the Comoros under condition that we find a solution for our economical problems. We need wealth here in the Comoros. So if we succeed in finding this wealth, if we succeed in getting investments, the Comoros will change, simply because Comorians are great people, peaceful people trying to enjoy life, but who need help. I think that the Comoros, as you know it, is situated in a very strategic place. We can have a real breakthrough in our relationship with neighboring countries. We can make a big leap in five or ten years, and become a little country that took off. At this moment, our takeoff is delayed; we are looking for our wings necessary for our takeoff. But I think that as soon as the train is on the tracks, as soon as it leaves, we are going to succeed in having big changes in this country.

Today, the Union of the Comoros has entered a new chapter in its democratization process, with their first full rotation, between the three islands, of the Union presidency. In the election that was held on December 26, 2010, the former Vice President Ikililou Dhoinine of Moheli was elected with 61 percent of the vote. This was the country's third nonmilitary election of their head of state.

APPENDIX E

COMMUNITY AND CIVIC INVOLVEMENT

In addition to my numerous business ventures over the years, I took the time out to participate on a variety of community, state, national government, and educational, cultural, service and charitable organization boards—my payback for being so blessed with success.

In the 1960s through the early 1990s, I served as chairman of the Utah Department of Contractors, and helped develop the first contractor bonding law. I also was a member of the Salt Lake County Planning and Zoning Commission, Salt Lake County Master Plan Committee, Board of Governors of the Salt Lake Chamber of Commerce, and Advisory Board of the March of Dimes; co-chairman of the March of Dimes Telerama; chairman of a Muscular Dystrophy Telethon; member of the State of Utah Board of Business and Economic Development, Utah Symphony Board, and the Utah Opera Board. I was on the advisory board and then a member of the Utah Committee for the Sundance Institute. I served on the Junior Achievement Advisory Committee; and was a member of the Board of Trustees of the International Council of Shopping Centers (ICSC); the Planning and Construction Committee for the Utah Bicentennial Arts Complex; and construction manager for the 80,000-square-foot Symphony Hall, 28,000-square-foot Art Center, and restoration of the Capitol Theatre.

Then in the 1990s through February 2002, I served as a member of the Industry Sector Advisory Committee (ISAC 14) on Small and Minority Business for Trade Policy matters; Small Business Administration (SBA) Advisory Board; Utah State Fair Park Board; University of Utah Board of Trustees; Advisory Board of First Security Bank of Utah; Management and Audit Committees of Salt Lake Organizing Committee (SLOC) for the 2002 Winter Olympics; United States Olympic Committee (USOC) Government Relations and Planning Committee; Board of Trustees of the U.S. Ski and Snowboard Foundation; Board of the Utah Sports Commission; Board of Governors of the National Association of Real Estate Investment Trusts (NAREIT); and Print Committee Board at the Whitney Museum. I was a member of the National Finance Advisory Council of the George and Barbara Bush Endowment for Innovative Cancer Research at the

E.1. March of Dimes Telerama, 1969. From left to right: Rita Billinis, John Price, Marcia Price, Maurice Warshaw, John Billinis.

M.D. Anderson Medical Center, and member of the Hoover Board of Overseers at Stanford University.

My political involvement on a community, state, and national level led to my serving as the Utah Republican National Committeeman.

I was pleased to be a member of the American Academy of Achievement. And I was most proud to have been the co-founder of the Utah Chapter of the Young Presidents' Organization (YPO), which was inaugurated in 1982. This was the beginning of what would become one of the most successful chapters of business executives in the country. Because of the YPO strength in business mentoring and personal and family bonding, some of the local and national business success stories had their roots in the Utah YPO chapter. I was proud when my son Steven became a second-generation member of YPO.

GLOSSARY OF ACRONYMS AND TERMS

ADMIN: Administrative Section overseas.

AF: Bureau of African Affairs, State Department.

AF/E: Office of East African Affairs, State Department.

AFRICOM: U.S. Africa Command.

AGOA: African Growth and Opportunity Act.

AMCHAM: American Chamber of Commerce.

AMISOM: African Union Mission to Somalia.

AmCits: American citizens.

ANC: African National Congress (political party).

AOR: Area of responsibility.

APARC: African Presidential Archives and Research Center.

APP: American Presence Post.

ARPCT: Alliance for the Restoration of Peace and Counter-Terrorism.

ARS: Africa Regional Services.

A/S: Assistant Secretary of State.

AQSL: Al-Qaeda senior leadership.

ATA: Anti-Terrorism Assistance.

AU: African Union.

BIOT: British Indian Ocean Territory.

CCA: Corporate Council on Africa.

CC Africa: Conservation Corporation Africa.

CENTCOM: U.S. Central Command.

CEO: Chief executive officer.

CEP: Consular-economic-political officer.

CIA: Central Intelligence Agency.

CJTF-HOA: Combined Joint Task Force–Horn of Africa.

CODEL: Congressional delegation.

COM: Chief of mission.

COMESA: Common Market for Eastern and Southern Africa.

Cone: One of five specialties for Foreign Service officers (consular, economic, administrative, political, public diplomacy).

COO: Chief operating officer.

CRC: Convention for the Renewal of the Comoros (political party).

COSPROH: Compagnie Seychelloise de Promotion Hôtelière.

CT: Counterterrorism.

DAS: Deputy Assistant Secretary of State.

DATT: Defense attaché.

DCM: Deputy chief of mission.

DEA: Drug Enforcement Administration.

Demarche: A request for support of U.S. policy, or protest about a host government's policy or actions.

DIA: Defense Intelligence Agency.

DG: Director general of the Foreign Service.

DGAR: Diego Garcia (DG).

DP: Democratic Party of the Seychelles (political party).

DS: Bureau of Diplomatic Security, State Department.

DEA: Drug Enforcement Agency.

DOD: Department of Defense.

Duty officer: Assigned during non-office hours to be responsible for any emergency.

EAC: Embassy's Emergency Action Committee.

EDDI: Education for Development and Democracy Initiative.

EER: Employee evaluation review.

EU: European Union.

EUCOM: U.S. European Command.

EX: Executive.

Expatriate (expat): A person living overseas.

Ex-Im: Export-Import Bank.

FAM: Foreign Affairs Manual, the general and authoritative guide for Foreign Service procedures.

FBI: Federal Bureau of Investigation.

FDI: Foreign direct investment.

FinCEN: Financial Crimes Enforcement Network.

FMO: Financial management officer.

Forex: Foreign exchange.

FSI: Foreign Service Institute.

FSN: Foreign Service national.

FSO: Foreign Service officer.

FTA: Free trade agreement.

GDP: Gross domestic product.

GOC: Government of Comoros.

GOM: Government of Mauritius.

GOS: Government of Seychelles.

GSO: General services officer at the embassy.

GWOT: Global war on terror.

H.C.: High commissioner (a Commonwealth rank, the same as ambassador).

HOA: Horn of Africa.

HOR: U.S. House of Representatives.

IAEA: International Atomic Energy Agency.

ICC: International Criminal Court.

ICT: Information and communication technology.

ICU: Islamic Courts Union.

IG: Inspector general.

IMET: International Military Education and Training.

IMF: International Monetary Fund.

IMS: Information management specialist.

IOC: International Olympic Committee.

IPO: Information programs officer.

IRS: Internal Revenue Service.

IT: Information technology.

KPCS: Kimberly Process Certification Scheme.

KUSLO: Kenya U.S. Liaison Office.

LDC: Least developed country.

MCA: Millennium Challenge Account; Millennium Challenge Act.

MCC: Millennium Challenge Corporation.

MDG: Millennium Development Goals.

MERP: Macroeconomic reform plan.

MLP: Mauritian Labour Party.

MMM: Mauritian Militant Movement (political party).

MO: Management officer.

MOU: Memorandum of understanding.

MPP: Mission performance plan.

MOI: Memorandum of intent.

MSM: Militant Socialist Movement (political party).

MUSBA: Mauritius-U.S. Business Association.

NATO: North Atlantic Treaty Organization.

NEPAD: New Partnership for Africa's Development.

NCIS: Naval Criminal Investigative Service.

NGO: Nongovernmental organization.

NSA: National Security Agency.

NSC: National Security Council.

OAU: Organization of African Unity.

OBO: Overseas Buildings Operations.

OIG: Office of the Inspector General, State Department.

OMS: Office management specialist.

OPIC: Overseas Private Investment Corporation.

OSM: Overseas staffing model.

PACA: President's Advisory Committee on the Arts.

PACOM: U.S. Pacific Command.

PAO: Public affairs officer.

PEPFAR: President's Emergency Plan for AIDS Relief.

PERMREP: Permanent representative.

PISCES: Personal Identification Secure Comparison and Evaluation System.

POLAD: Foreign policy advisor, State Department.

PRGSP: Poverty Reduction and Growth Strategy Paper.

REIT: Real Estate Investment Trust.

ROTC: Reserve Officers Training Corps.

RSO: Regional security officer.

SADC: Southern African Development Community.

SACU: South African Customs Union.

SBA: Small Business Administration.

SD: Surveillance detection.

SECSTATE: Secretary of State.

SEP: Special Embassy Program.

SFOR: Multinational Stabilization Force.

SFRC: Senate Foreign Relations Committee.

SIDS: Small Island Developing States.

SMB: Seychelles Marketing Board.

SNA: Somali National Alliance.

SNP: Seychelles National (political) party.

SPPF: Seychelles People's Progressive Front (political party).

SPUP: Seychelles People's United (political) party.

SSH: Ambassador's Special Self-Help Program.

SSS: Selective Service System.

TDY: Temporary duty officer.

TFG: Transitional Federal Government.

TNG: Transitional National Government.

TSA: Transportation Security Administration.

UNDP: United Nations Development Programme.

UNESCO: United Nations Educational, Scientific, and Cultural Organization.

UNGA: United Nations General Assembly.

UNMIBH: United Nations Mission in Bosnia and Herzegovina.

UNOSOM: United Nations Operation in Somalia.

UNPERMREP: United Nations permanent representative.

UNSC: United Nations Security Council.

UNSCR: United Nations Security Council resolution.

U/S: Undersecretary of State.

USAID: U.S. Agency for International Development.

USG: United States government.

USIA: U.S. Information Agency.

USSTRATCOM: United States Strategic Command.

USTR: Office of the U.S. Trade Representative.

VAT: Value-added tax.

VE: Virtual Embassy.

VPP: Virtual Presence Post.

WB: World Bank.

WHO: World Health Organization.

WMD: Weapons of mass destruction.

WTO: World Trade Organization.

BIBLIOGRAPHY

BOOKS

Alden, Chris. *China in Africa*. London: Zed Books, 2007.

Ayittey, George B. N. *Africa in Chaos*. New York: St. Martin's Press, 1999.

———. *Africa Unchained: The Blueprint for Africa's Future*. New York: Palgrave Macmillan, 2005.

Bergen, Peter L. *Holy War, Inc.: Inside the Secret World of Osama bin Laden*. New York: The Free Press/Simon and Schuster, 2001.

Bowman, Larry W. *Mauritius: Democracy and Development in the Indian Ocean*. Boulder, CO: Westview Press, 1991.

Bush, George W. *A Charge to Keep*. New York: William Morrow and Company, 1999.

Calderisi, Robert. *The Trouble with Africa: Why Foreign Aid Isn't Working*. New York: Palgrave Macmillan, 2006.

Crystal, Susan R. *U.S.A. – Mauritius 200 Years Trade, History Culture*. Moka, Republic of Mauritius: Mahatma Gandhi Institute Press, 1996.

Easterly, William. *The White Man's Burden*. New York: Penguin Press, 2006.

Epley, Thomas. *The Plague of Good Intentions: We Broke Africa Here's How to Fix It*. Self-publication: Xlibris, 2008.

French, Howard W. *A Continent for the Taking: The Tragedy and Hope of Africa*. New York: Vintage Books, 2005.

Fuller, Errol. *Dodo: From Extinction to Icon*. London: HarperCollins, 2002.

Gabriel, Brigitte. *They Must Be Stopped: Why We Must Defeat Radical Islam and How We Can Do It*. New York: St. Martin's Press, 2008.

Gribbin, Robert E. *In the Aftermath of Genocide: The U.S. Role in Rwanda*. Lincoln, NE: iUniverse, 2005.

Guest, Robert. *The Shackled Continent: Power, Corruption, and African Lives*. Washington, DC: Smithsonian Books, 2004.

Harari, Oren. *The Leadership Secrets of Colin Powell*. New York: McGraw-Hill, 2002.

Heunis, Jan. *The Inner Circle: Reflections on the Last Days of White Rule*. Johannesburg, South Africa: Jonathan Ball, 2007.

Hirsch, Susan F. *In the Moment of Greatest Calamity: Terrorism, Grief, and a Victim's Quest for Justice*. Princeton, NJ: Princeton University Press, 2006.

Hoffman, Bruce. *Inside Terrorism*. New York: Columbia University Press, 2006.

Makhan, Vijay S. *Economic Recovery in Africa: The Paradox of Financial Flows*. Basingstoke: Palgrave Macmillan, 2002.

———. *Policy Consensus in a Strategy Vacuum: A Pan-African Vision for the 21st Century.* Nairobi: Macmillan Kenya, 1997.

Mancham, James R. *Paradise Raped: Life, Love, and Power in the Seychelles.* London: Methuen, 1983.

———. *War on America: Seen from the Indian Ocean.* St. Paul, MN: Paragon House, 2001.

Meredith, Martin. *The Fate of Africa: A History of Fifty Years of Independence.* New York: Public Affairs, a member of the Perseus Books Group, 2005.

Morgan, Helen. *Blue Mauritius: The Hunt for the World's Most Valuable Stamps.* UK: Atlantic Books, 2006.

Moyo, Dambisa. *Dead Aid: Why Aid Is Not Working and How There Is Another Way for Africa.* 1st American ed. New York: Farrar, Straus and Giroux, 2009.

Patman, Robert G. *The Soviet Union in the Horn of Africa: The Diplomacy of Intervention and Disengagement.* New York: Cambridge University Press, 1990.

Perkins, Edward J., with Connie Cronley. *Mr. Ambassador: Warrior for Peace.* Norman: University of Oklahoma Press, 2006.

Podhoretz, Norman. *World War IV: The Long Struggle Against Islamofascism.* New York: Doubleday, 2007.

Richburg, Keith. *Out of Africa: A Black Man Confronts Africa.* New York: Basic Books, 1997.

Sachs, Jeffrey D. *The End of Poverty.* New York: Penguin Press, 2005.

Siciliano, Rocco C. *Walking on Sand: The Story of an Immigrant Son and the Forgotten Art of Public Service.* Salt Lake City: University of Utah Press, 2004.

Sullivan, Joseph G., ed. *Embassies Under Siege: Personal Accounts by Diplomats on the Front Line.* The Institute for the Study of Diplomacy. Washington, DC: Brassey's, 1995.

Suskind, Ron. *The Price of Loyalty: George W. Bush, the White House, and the Education of Paul O'Neill.* New York: Simon and Schuster, 2004.

Twain, Mark. *Following the Equator: A Journey Around the World.* Hartford, CT: The American Publishing Co., 1897. Reprint, New York: Dover Publications, 1989.

Williams, Paul L. *The Day of Islam: The Annihilation of America and the Western World.* New York: Prometheus Books, 2007.

Woodward, Bob. *Bush at War.* New York: Simon and Schuster, 2002.

———. *Plan of Attack.* New York: Simon and Schuster, 2004.

Wright, Lawrence. *The Looming Tower: Al-Qaeda and the Road to 9/11.* New York: Alfred A. Knopf, 2007.

Zakaria, Fareed. *The Future of Freedom: Illiberal Democracy at Home and Abroad.* New York: W. W. Norton, 2003.

Reports

"African Leaders State of Africa." *Report 2003.* Boston: Boston University.

"CARE: Began Operations in Kenya in 1968." *Kenya Country Profile,* www.care.org.

Crowder, Michael. "Whose Dream Was It Anyway? Twenty-Five Years of African Independence." *African Affairs* 86, no. 342 (Jan. 1987): 7–24: Oxford University Press. JSTOR archive, May 15, 2006.

"Current Issues in the Middle East." Edited by Ahmed Kamal. Graduate class project. Teaneck, NJ: Fairleigh Dickenson University, 2009.

Davis, Hunt R. "Interpreting the Colonial Period in African History." *African Affairs* 72, no. 289 (Oct. 1973): 383–400: Oxford University Press. JSTOR archive, May 15, 2006.

Dickson, David. "Political Islam in Sub-Saharan Africa: The Need for a New Research and Diplomatic Agenda." United States Institute of Peace, *Special Report* 140, May 2005.

Diplomatic and Consular Programs. House Report 104–676. Departments of Commerce, Justice, and State, The Judiciary, and Related Agencies Appropriations Bill, Fiscal Year 1997: Library of Congress.

"The Establishment of a New House Appropriations Subcommittee for State, Foreign Operations and Related Programs, Section VIII: Congressional Relations." Foreign Affairs Council, Washington, DC, p. 18.

Evans, Alexander. "Understanding Madrasahs." *Foreign Affairs: Council on Foreign Relations, Inc.* 85, no. 11 (Jan.–Feb. 2006).

"The Failed State Index." Foreign Policy and the Fund for Peace, 2006, www.foreignpolicy .com/articles/2007/06/the_failed_states_index_2007.

Fidler, Kenneth. "Ward in Comoros: What You Say Matters to Us." U.S. AFRICOM *Public Affairs*, January 23, 2009.

Fisher-Thompson, Jim. "U.S. Official Sets Scene for 2003 AGOA Forum in Mauritius." *The Washington File*, Office of International Information Programs, U.S. Department of State, January 8, 2003.

———. "U.S., Starbucks, Rwanda Coffee Partnership Equals Success." *USINFO.STATE .GOV*, April 11, 2006.

Hoile, David. "The Darfur Crisis." European–Sudanese Public Affairs Council, 2005.

"Index of State Weakness." Brookings Institution, 2008.

Lake Heffelfinger, Chris, and Olivier Guitta. "Proposed Yemen—Djibouti Bridge Threatens AFRICOM Security." *Terrorism Monitor* 5, no. 19, October 11, 2007.

Lortan, Fiona. "Rebuilding the Somali State." Africa Security Analysis Programme, Institute for Security Studies, Pretoria. *African Security Review* 9, no. 5–6 (2000).

Lyman, Princeton N., and Patricia Dorff, eds. *Beyond Humanitarianism: What You Need to Know About Africa and Why It Matters.* New York: Council on Foreign Relations, 2007.

Lyman, Princeton N., and J. Stephen Morrison. "More Than Humanitarianism: A Strategic U.S. Approach Toward Africa." *Independent Task Force Report* 56 (2006). New York: Council on Foreign Relations.

"Managing Secretary Rice's State Department: An Independent Assessment." *Task Force Report.* Foreign Affairs Council, June 2007.

Massey, Simon, and Bruce Baker. "Comoros: External Involvement in a Small Island State." *Programme Paper* AFP 2009, no. 1. Chatham House, July 2009.

"Mauritius Historical Interest." Library of Congress Country Studies; CIA *World Factbook*: www.photius.com, 1994.

McCormack, David. "An African Vortex: Islamism in Sub-Saharan Africa." *Center for Security Policy*, no. 4 (January 2005).

"Millennium Challenge Account: Economic Perspectives." *An Electronic Journal of the U.S. Department of State* 8, no. 2 (March 2003).

Office of the United States Trade Representative. *2003 Comprehensive Report on U.S. Trade and Investment Policy Toward Sub-Saharan Africa and Implementation of the Africa Growth and Opportunity Act*, May 2003.

Perl, Raphael, and Ronald O'Rourke. *Terrorist Attack on USS* Cole: *Background and Issues for Congress.* Congressional Research Service: Library of Congress, January 30, 2001.

"Pioneer Profile: White House ForSale.org." *Texans for Public Justice*, 1998.

Prendergast, John, and Colin Thomas-Jensen. "Blowing the Horn: Washington's Failings in Africa." *Foreign Affairs* 86, no. 2 (March–April 2007): 59–74.

Quinn, Charlotte A., and Frederick Quinn. "Pride, Faith and Fear." *African Islam: A Complex Reality*. Oxford Scholarship Online: Oxford University Press, 2006.

Radelet, Steve. "Will the Millennium Challenge Account Be Different?" *Washington Quarterly* 26 (Spring 2003): 171–187. Center for Strategic and International Studies, MIT Press.

Richardson, William. "Praising Our Diplomatic Corps." *Congressional Record*, April 30, 1996.

"Seychelles: Opposition Movements and Interest Groups." Seychelles Government and Politics (text from Country Studies Program, formerly the Army Area Handbook Program). mongabay.com, N.d.

Simon, Steven, and Daniel Benjamin. "America and the New Terrorism." *Survival* 42, no. 1 (Spring 2000): 59–75. International Institute for Strategic Studies.

"A Sound Investment in Global Leadership: Questions and Answers." *The International Affairs Budget*. U.S. Department of State, 95/10/01: Bureau of Public Affairs. DOSFAN Electronic Research Collection (ERC) archive site.

"State Sponsors: Sudan: Has Sudan Harbored al-Qaeda or Other Terrorist Groups?" *Council on Foreign Relations*, December 2005.

"Terrorism in the Horn of Africa." United States Institute of Peace, Special Report 113 (Jan. 2004): 1–14.

"Terrorist Threat in Horn of Africa." *Department of Defense Background Briefing:* U.S. Department of State, March 8, 2002.

Union of the Comoros: Memorandum of Economic and Financial Policies for 2005. As submitted to Mr. Rodrigo de Rato, Managing Director, International Monetary Fund, February 2, 2005.

Volman, Daniel. *AFRICOM: The New U.S. Military Command for Africa*. African Security Research Project, June 27, 2008.

Wannenburg, Gail. *Organized Crime and Terrorism*. War and Organized Crime Research Fellow: South African Institute of International Affairs, n.d., 1–10.

Welsh, Steven C. "Saudi-Based Charitable Organization Sanctioned for Supporting Terrorist Activities." Center for Defense Information (August 7, 2006): 1–5.

Yunus, Muhammad. *Spreading Grameen Around the World*. Grameen Foundation, Washington, DC, December 2008.

Articles

Abdallah, A. "Comoros/U.S.: THE USAID grants $500,000 in the Education of the Archipelago." *Agency of Comoros Press* (HZK-press), December 4, 2008.

"Aspirations and Obligations: The Millennium Development Goals Cannot Be Met; Some Can Barely Be Measured. What, Then, Are They For?" *The Economist*, September 8, 2005.

"The Assassination of Gerard Hoareau," *Le Nouveau Seychelles Weekly*, December 1, 2006.

Bhalla, Nita. "U.S. Says Comoros No Longer Haven for Militants." Reuters, October 28, 2004.

Bilefsky, Dan. "Kosovo Declares Its Independence from Serbia." *New York Times*, February 18, 2008.

Binnendijk, Hans. "Tin Cup Diplomacy: Federal Budget as a Political Bargaining Chip in the Post Cold-War Era." *National Interest Inc.* (National Defense University, Institute for National Strategic Studies), 1997.

Borchgrave, Arnaud de. "Reconnecting al Qaeda Dots." *Washington Times*, July 14, 2006.

"Brewery's Finances Highlight the Flaws in Seychelles Financial System." *Le Nouveau Seychelles Weekly*, November 10, 2006.

Childress, Sarah. "People Power: In Africa, Democracy Gains amid Turmoil." *Wall Street Journal*, Eastern edition, June 18, 2008.

"Clinton Admits Passing Up bin Laden Capture; Lewinsky Played Role." *NewsMax.com*, September 10, 2006, 1–5.

Cobb, Jr., Charles. "Majority on 'Most Wanted Terrorists' List from Africa." *allAfrica.com*, October 10, 2001.

———. "Sudan: Did US Ignore Khartoum Offer to Help Stop Bin Laden?" *allAfrica.com*, December 7, 2001.

"The Comoro Islands: An Unusual Haunt for al-Qaeda." *The Economist*, July 12, 2007.

Cooper, Helene. "For African Nations, Trade Bill Alters Thread of Economic Fate." *Wall Street Journal*, January 3, 2002.

De Young, Karen. "U.S. Strike in Somalia Targets Al-Qaeda Figure." *Washington Post*, January 9, 2007.

Duhul, Salad. "Helicopters Strafe al-Qaida in Somalia." *Associated Press*, January 10, 2007.

Dwyer, Matthew B. "Comoros: Big Troubles on Some Small Islands." *Online Africa Policy Forum*, April 14, 2008.

Easterly, William R. "Africa's Poverty Trap." *Wall Street Journal*, March 3, 2007.

"Eid Milan Party in Vallee Pitot: Moving Tribute to Yasser Arafat." *Le Mauricien*, November 15, 2004.

"Faithful, but Not Fanatics: African Muslims Are Not as Militant as the Headlines Suggest." *The Economist*, June 26, 2003.

Garamone, Jim. "Backgrounder: U.S. Policy on Africa Seeks Stability." *American Forces Press Service*, April 2002: 1–2.

Gerson, Michael. "Losing the Fight for Darfur." *Washington Post*, November 13, 2009.

Gill, Christopher. "China About to Check-Mate USA in Africa and Indian Ocean." *Le Nouveau Seychelles Weekly*, February 2007.

———. "The Plantation Club Hotel and Casino Debacle." *STAR* (Seychelles Truth Accountability Reality), July 29, 2009.

———. "IMF Says It Is up to the People of Seychelles to Find Out About the Missing US $2.4 Billion." *STAR*, August 25, 2009.

———. "United States Back in Seychelles: Beware of Old Communists!" *STAR*, August 22, 2009.

Gordon, Michael R., and Mark Mazzetti. "U.S. Used Base in Ethiopia to Hunt Al Qaeda in Africa." *New York Times*, February 23, 2007.

"The Heart of the Matter: Africa's Biggest Problems Stem from Its Present Leaders— But They Were Created by African Society and History." *The Economist*, May 11, 2000.

Heavens, Andrew. "Sudan Soldiers Attack UN/AU Peacekeepers in Darfur." Reuters, January 8, 2008.

Holmes, Erick S. "NMCB 11 Builds Foundation for Comoros Education." Blackanthem. com, *Military News*, March 16, 2009.

Ijaz, Mansoor. "Clinton Let Bin Laden Slip Away and Metastasize." *Los Angeles Times*, December 5, 2001.

———. "Politicized Intelligence: The 9/11 Commission's Achilles Heel." *National Review Online*, April 15, 2004.

Jaffe, Greg. "A General's New Plan to Battle Radical Islam." *Wall Street Journal*, September 2, 2006.

Johnson, Bryan T., and Brett D. Schaefer. "False Alarm over Foreign Affairs Spending Cuts." *Heritage Foundation*, January 31, 1997, 1–4.

King, Jr., Neil. "Diplomatic Moves: Rice Pushes Envoys to Spend Time in Hardship Posts." *Wall Street Journal*, August 10, 2006.

Kithi, Ngumbao, and Ali Abuldsalamad. "Kenya: Five Terror Suspects Arrested." *The Nation* (Nairobi), May 28, 2007.

Krauss, Clifford. "Slowly, U.S. Is Returning Some Envoys to the Sudan." *New York Times*, September 28, 1997.

Kristof, Nicholas D. "More Schools, Not Troops." *New York Times,* Op-ed, October 29, 2009.

Lacey, Marc. "Alliance of Somali Warlords Battles Islamists in Capital." *New York Times*, May 13, 2006.

———. "Islamic Militias Take Control of Somali Capital." *International Herald Tribune*, June 7, 2006.

———. "Militant Leader Emerges in Somalia." *International Herald Tribune*, June 26, 2006.

"Launching the Jewish Community of Mauritius." *africanjewishcongress.com*, May 2005.

Linhorst, Stan. "Terrorism Expert Bruce Hoffman Tells Syracuse University Audience How to Win the War on Terrorism." *The Post-Standard*, February 23, 2008.

Lippman, Thomas W. "Embassies Can Never Be Fully Protected." *Washington Post*, August 8, 1998.

———. "U.S. Diplomacy's Presence Shrinking." *Washington Post,* June 3, 1996.

Makary, Adam. "Sudan Peace Deals in Jeopardy." *Al Jazeera*, March 5, 2009.

McCormack, David. "An African Taliban." *National Review Online*, October 4, 2006.

McNeil, Jr., Donald G. "Assets of a Bombing Suspect: Keen Wit, Religious Soul, Angry Temper." *New York Times*, October 6, 1998.

Morris, Jason. "Africa Partnership Station East Arrives in Kenya." *Africa Partnership Station East Public Affairs*. Mombasa, Kenya, January 12, 2010.

Munene, Mugumo, and Kevin Kelley. "Why Kenya Matters to the West." *Sunday Nation*, October 11, 2009.

Mutiga, Murithi. "Eyes Now Turn to Kenya's Former 'Terror Island': Fazul Planned Bomb Attacks from Island Where He Lived for More than Two Years." *Daily Nation*, October 11, 2009.

———. "Fazul Abdallah Kept Us on Tenterhooks." *Daily Nation,* December 23, 2009.

"Never Too Late to Scramble: China Is Rapidly Buying Up Africa's Oil, Metals and Farm Produce. That Fuels China's Surging Economic Growth, but How Good Is It for Africa?" *The Economist*, October 26, 2006.

Noakes, Greg. "Somalia's Last Foreign Minister Warns Somaliland on Secession." *Washington Report on Middle East Affairs,* April–May 1994.

O'Brien, Robert. "China's Africa Play: Facing the Prospect of an Africa Dominated by China." *CBSNews.com*, January 19, 2010.

O'Donnell, William P. "Fighting the Wrong Foe with the Wrong Weapons." *New York Times*, March 14, 2008.

"The Path to Ruin: Special Report—Horn of Africa." *The Economist*, August 12, 2006.

Perlez, Jane. "The World: Friendly Fire; In a War, Even Food Can Kill." *New York Times*, December 5, 1999.

Peters, Ralph. "The Other Jihad: Islamist Subversion in Africa Threatens the People of That Continent and, Indeed, the People of the World." *USA Today*, August 24, 2005.

Pham, Peter J. "Strategic Interests: Al Qaeda Moves to Africa." *World Defense Review*, July 27, 2006.

"Policing the Undergoverned Spaces: The Americans Are Intensifying Their Hunt for al-Qaeda in the Sahara and Beyond." *The Economist*, June 14, 2007.

"The Rape of Our Country Revealed in Stark Detail." *Le Nouveau Seychelles Weekly*, September 14, 2006.

Roggio, Bill. "Al Qaeda Names Fazul Mohammed East African Commander." *Long War Journal*, November 11, 2009.

———. "U.S. Naval Task Force Strikes at 1998 al Qaeda Embassy Bomber." *Long War Journal*, June 2, 2007.

Rozen, Laura. "Eight Former Secretaries of State: U.S. Needs More Foreign Diplomats." *Politico.com*, June 25, 2009.

Schanzer, Jonathan. "Pretoria Unguarded: Terrorists Take Refuge in South Africa: Jewish Policy Center, May 21, 2007." *Weekly Standard*, May 28, 2007.

"Somalia May Fall into Al-Qaeda's Hands." *Assyrian International News Agency*, October 4, 2006.

Soufan, Ali. "Somali Extremists Have al Qaeda Ties: Another Failed State Has Become a Training Ground for Terrorists." *Wall Street Journal*, April 15, 2009.

Stolberg, Sheryl Gay. "In Global Battle Against AIDS, Bush Creates Legacy and Draws Bipartisan Praise." *New York Times*, January 5, 2008.

"Sudan Ruled Guilty for the Bombing of USS *Cole* in 2000. *Muslim World News*, March 15, 2007.

Thomas, Gordon, and Yvonne Ridley. "Do Al Qaeda Prisoners Face CIA Torture on British Isle?" *Express Newspapers (Sunday Express)*, May 16, 2004.

Thome, Wolfgang H. "Rwanda Puts on Brave Face over Woes of Dubai World: African Investments Now on Hold." *eTN*, December 16, 2009.

Thurow, Roger. "Ethiopia Taps Grain Exchange In Its Battle On Hunger." *Wall Street Journal*, February 27, 2008.

Timberg, Craig. "Ethiopians Help Seize Somali Capital." *Washington Post Foreign Service*, December 29, 2006.

———. "From Competitors to Trading Partners: Africans Adjust as Business Ties with China Grow." *Washington Post*, December 3, 2006.

"An Update of Seychelles Involvement with IMF." *Le Nouveau Seychelles Weekly*, Special National Day Edition, 2009.

Verkaik, Robert. "UK Provided Base for Rendition Flights, Says European Inquiry." *The Independent*, June 9, 2007.

Vine, David. "Politique: The Importance of Diego Garcia." *WEEKEND*, February 16, 2003.

Wax, Emily, and Karen De Young. "U.S. Secretly Backing Warlords in Somalia." *Washington Post Foreign Service*, May 17, 2006.

Weiner, Tim, and James Risen. "Decision to Strike Factory in Sudan Based Partly on Surmise." *New York Times*, September 21, 1998.

COMMUNICATIONS AND LECTURES

Abdou, Faissoili. "Our Aim Is to Strengthen Stability in Countries." General William E. Ward. Press conference held at IFERE (The institute of teacher training and educational research) on Ward's first visit to Comoros, January 21, 2009.

Abizaid, John. "Naval War College" speech, November 22, 2005, www.freerepublic.com/focus/f-news/1527192/posts.

"Africa Overview: Patterns of Global Terrorism, 2000." U.S. Department of State, April 30, 2001.

"Alliance for the Restoration of Peace and Counter-Terrorism (ARPCT)." *Source Watch*, 2006.

"Behind Parmalat Chief's Rise: Ties to Italian Power Structure." notizie.parma / Rassegna Stampa: 4.

"China Pledges $10bn Africa Loans." *BBC News*, November 8, 2009.

"Current Whereabouts: (Fazul Abdullah Mohammed)." *Midi Madagasikara*, February 2007.

Hassan, Mohamed Olad. "U.S. Launches Two Airstrikes in Somalia." *Associated Press*, January 9, 2007.

Hassani, M. "The Debut of a Warming of Bilateral Relations." Press Conference of a U.S. Officer: Comorian Press Agency (HZK-Presse), December 24, 2007.

"Internet Usage Statistics for Africa." *internetworldstats.com*, December 31, 2007.

"Islam in the Later Twelfth Century." *Crusades.boisestate.edu.*

Johnson, David. "Osama bin Laden: Wealthy Saudi Exile Is a Terrorist Mastermind." *Infoplease*, 2007.

"Kenya Manhunt for al-Qaeda Wanted." *BBC News*, August 4, 2008.

"Letter to America: Osama bin Laden's Message." *BBC News,* November 12, 2002.

Mancham, James R. "American Leadership at a Time of Global Crisis with Particular Emphasis to China's Rise Within the Asia Pacific Rim." Washington, DC, Conference: May 16, 2007.

Mann, Jonathan. "Insight: Diego Garcia." *CNN.com Transcripts*, June 18, 2003.

"Message to U.S.: Osama bin Laden." *Al Jazeera*, October 18, 2003. In Special Dispatch Series No. 811(04): Osama bin Laden. *Memri.org*, November 5, 2004.

"Millennium Challenge Corporation Press Release." Secretary of State Condoleezza Rice, Malagasy President Marc Ravalomanana, and MCC CEO Paul Applegarth's remarks at the Signing Ceremony for the Millennium Challenge Corporation's Compact with the Republic of Madagascar, April 18, 2005.

Neff, Robert. "What Led Seychelles to North Korea—Assassination?" The Marmot Hole: *Feed Burner*. April 21, 2010.

Noe, Chuck. "Aide: Clinton Unleashed bin Laden." *NewsMax.com*, December 6, 2001.

"On Tape, Clinton Admits Passing Up bin Laden Capture; Lewinsky Played Role." *NewsMax.com*, September 10, 2006.

"Prawn Yields Bounce Back." *Seychelles Nation Online*, July 27, 2003.

"Regions and Territories: Somaliland." *BBC News*, July 2, 2008.

Reynolds, Paul. "Somaliland's Path to Recognition." *BBC News*, April 25, 2008.

Seychelles Chamber of Commerce & Industry. Letter to President James Michel, October 18, 2004.

"Seychelles Not Involved in Parmalat Scandal, Govt Says." *Virtual Seychelles: News*, June 17, 2004.

Shinn, David H. "China's Approach to East, North and the Horn of Africa." China's Global Influence: Objectives and Strategies. Testimony before the U.S.-China Economics and Security Review Commission, Dirksen Senate Office Building, July 21, 2005. Professor Shinn is Adjunct Professor, Elliott School of International Affairs, George Washington University.

Spingola, Deanna. "Diego Garcia, Swept Clean and Sanitized." *www.conspiracyarchive.com* (October 16, 2007): 1–5.

"Topple Somali Leader: Bin Laden." *BBC News*, March 19, 2009.

"Trade to Top China–Africa Summit." *BBC News*, November 3, 2006.

"Union of the Comoros: Summary of the Conclusions of the Meeting of the United States–Comoros Mixed Committee." Ministry of External Relations and Cooperation for the Diaspora, the Francophone World and the Arab World, April 19, 2007.

"U.S., Africa Strengthen Counter-Terrorism and Economic Ties." White House, Office of the Press Secretary, October 29, 2001.

"U.S. Strikes in Somalia Reportedly Kill 31." *CBS News*, January 9, 2007.

"USS *Cole* Update: Hezbollah Built Bomb." Wires: *NewsMax.com*, May 21, 2001.

Vance, Laurence M. "Guarding the Empire: U.S. Embassies in Foreign Countries." *LewRockwell.com*, October 4, 2004.

"Yemen Bomb Kills Spanish Tourists." *BBC News*, July 2, 2007.

INDEX

Note: Page numbers in italics refer to photos.